D1736947

THE
JEWS
OF HUNGARY

THE

JEWS
OF HUNGARY

History, Culture, Psychology

RAPHAEL PATAI

Wayne State University Press Detroit

Manufactured in the United States of America.

99 98   5 4 3 2 1

Library of Congress Cataloging-in-Publication Data

Patai, Raphael, 1910–
The Jews of Hungary : history, culture, psychology /
Raphael Patai.
p.   cm.
Includes bibliographical references and index.
ISBN 0-8143-2561-0 (alk. paper)
1. Jews—Hungary—History. 2. Hungary—Ethnic
relations.
I. Title. II. Series.
DS135.H9P33 1996
943.9′004924—dc20   95-21756

Published with the assistance of
The Louis and Minna Epstein Fund of the American
Academy for Jewish Research
The Lucius N. Littauer Foundation
The World Federation of Hungarian Jews

Dedicated
To the Memory of the Members of
My Paternal and Maternal Families
Who Were Among the Half Million Victims
of the Hungarian Holocaust
תנצב"ה

Contents

Contents

Contents

9

Contents

Illustrations and Maps

10

Preface

To begin with, a few words must be said about the shabby treatment the Jews in Hungary have received at the hands of the authors of the standard general histories of the Jewish people. A quick glance at the three global Jewish histories available to date, those of Graetz, Dubnow, and Baron, suffices to show that their presentation of Hungarian Jewish history is perfunctory at best, and at worst close to total neglect.

Heinrich Graetz (1817–91) is generally considered the father of modern Jewish historiography. The final edition of his eleven-volume *Geschichte der Juden* (first published 1890–1909) was translated into English and published in six volumes in 1956 by the Jewish Publication Society of Philadelphia. The text of this edition contains close to 3,400 pages, of which not more than two to three pages are devoted to the history of the Jews in Hungary, and which, in addition, contain about a dozen single-sentence references to events in "Hungary and Poland" or "Bohemia, Austria, and Hungary." In a word, the millennial history of Hungarian Jews is blithely overlooked.

The Russian Jewish historian Simon Dubnow (1860–1941) wrote his ten-volume history of the Jewish people in the interwar era, and it was published in German, under the title *Weltgeschichte des jüdischen Volkes*, by the Jüdischer Verlag of Berlin between 1925 and 1929. Dubnow pays a little more attention than Graetz to the Hungarian Jews but still treats them cavalierly. Of his nearly 6,000-page magnum opus, not more than a few scattered paragraphs, amounting to a total of some forty-five pages, deal with the Jews of Hungary. This stands in peculiar contrast to the extensive chapters he devotes to the Jews of Germany, Russia, and other countries.

Salo W. Baron (1895–1989), the great modern American Jewish historian, covers in the eighteen volumes of his magisterial *Social and Religious History of the Jews* (2d ed., Columbia University Press and Jewish Publication Society, 1952–93) the history of the Jews from 500 to the eighteenth century. Despite the huge number of new sources he utilizes, he disposes of the Hungarian Jews with like brevity. In Volume 3, for instance, a fifty-page chapter deals with the history of the Jews from 500

11

to 1200 in Eastern Europe, including Byzantium, the Khazar kingdom, the southern Slavic lands, Russia, and Poland. Hungary obviously belongs in this chapter, but only a scant two pages deal with the region that in 896 became Hungary. Likewise, in Volume 10, close to 300 pages cover the history of the Jews in the lands outside Germany in the years 1200 to 1650, but only eleven of them deal with Hungary.

This summary treatment of the Jews of Hungary can be explained, partly at last, by the paucity of the available data. Until about 1500, the Jews in Hungary were not a literarily productive community: they left behind no books, no responsa literature (religious inquiries addressed to rabbinical authorities and the responses to them), not even letters or any kind of notes—that is to say, no documents through which the historian could gain insight into their lives. What we know about these Jews until about 1500 is based almost entirely on a few tombstones and inscriptions and, from the eleventh century on, royal or ecclesiastical decrees relating to them, other documents and letters issued by authorities, and a few references in the Hebrew writings of other countries.

The neglect of Hungary by these three general Jewish historians is paralleled by neglect within the works dealing specifically with Hungarian Jewish history. For while there are many studies on individual Jewish communities in Hungary, as well as on specific periods in the history of the Hungarian Jews as a whole, there exists not one general work to tell the story of all the eighteen centuries since the first Jews appeared in the Carpathian Basin. The first author to make an attempt in this direction was the Moravian Jewish physician, poet, medical writer, anthropologist, and amateur historian Joseph Bergel (1802–84), whose *Geschichte der ungarischen Juden*, published in 1879 in both German and Hungarian, was judged by Samuel Kohn "a most unsuccessful attempt."

Samuel Kohn himself was a man of serious scholarship. In 1884 he published his own *A zsidók története Magyarországon a legrégibb időktől a mohácsi vészig* (The History of the Jews in Hungary from Earliest Times to the Disaster of Mohács), which ends in 1526, the date of the Disaster of Mohács, as the Hungarians' defeat by the Turks is known in Hungarian history. Kohn planned to follow this up with a second volume, which was to continue the story down to his own times, but he never wrote it. The extant volume remains valuable to this day, but it suffers from two serious shortcomings. One is that Kohn, imbued with the Magyar patriotism that peaked in his day among Hungarian Jews, tried to show that there had always been an affinity between the Hungarians and the Jews, even extending to a common origin, and that the position of the Jews had always been better in Hungary than in any of the neighboring countries. This patriotic bias gives his book a pecu-

12

liar red-white-green—Hungarian nationalist—coloring. The other short-coming is that most of the sources for such a history were not available to Kohn: they were published only from 1903 on, in the invaluable eighteen-volume *Monumenta Hungariae Judaica—Magyar Zsidó Oklevéltár* (Hungarian Jewish Archives), the main primary-source collection for the history of Jews in Hungary.

Kohn was chief rabbi of the Israelite Congregation of Pest, and the next general historian of Hungarian Jewry, Lajos Venetianer, was also a rabbi, chief rabbi of the Israelite Congregation of Ujpest, a suburb of Budapest. His *A magyar zsidóság története* (History of Hungarian Jewry) was published in 1922, almost forty years after Kohn's, but it displays the same two shortcomings. Venetianer, too, was a great Magyar patriot, and the thrust of his history is to show to what extent the Jews contributed to Hungary's economy, commerce, industry, culture, and so on—in other words, to show what an invaluable element of the population they were in promoting the material and intellectual development of the country. As for the source material, only one volume of the *Monumenta* had been published when Venetianer wrote his book, and that volume contained documents pertaining only to the pre-1526 period, which he treats most summarily. In fact, he condenses that period into a mere fifty-eight pages, and then in the remaining 410 covers only the nineteenth century and the first few years of the twentieth. Thus, by no means can his book be considered a general history of the Jews in Hungary.

For more than fifty years after Venetianer's work, no history of Hungarian Jews was written. Then, in 1976 in Jerusalem, as part of a large Hebrew volume titled *Pinqas haQ'hillot—Hungaria* (Ledger of the Communities—Hungary), Nathaniel Katzburg published his brief survey *Toldot Y'hude Hungaria meReshit haHityashvut v'ad Shnot Milhemet ha'Olam haShniyya* (History of the Jews of Hungary from the Beginning of Their Settlement to the Years of World War II). This is a fine study but so short (ninety pages) that it is merely a sketch, a barest outline of that long, fascinating, and in many respects unique history.

Finally, in 1992 in Budapest the book *A zsidóság Magyarországon 1526–1945* (Jewry in Hungary 1526–1945) was published by László Gonda, a Hungarian Jewish historian who from 1951 to his death in 1985 lived in Israel. In it, Gonda judiciously and conscientiously uses all the sources that were by that time available. Thus, his general observations and conclusions are based on a much richer factual foundation than Venetianer's book. Nor is Gonda beholden to the "patriotic imperative" under which both Kohn and Venetianer labored. It is regrettable that Gonda's book covers only the 420-year period from

1526 to 1945, and in particular that the crucial events of the post-Holocaust decades remain untold. György Litván, in his Introduction, informs us that Gonda carried on his story to 1960 but his editors deemed the last chapters incomplete and hence excluded them. Pity. On the other hand, no blame can attach to the editors for the summary treatment Gonda accords the 1526–1800 period—a mere forty-five pages—while devoting his remaining 330 pages to the nineteenth century and the first forty-five years of the twentieth. In this, Gonda follows his predecessor, Venetianer, although, of course, the nature and amount of the available sources also play a role in this concentration on modern times.

As can be seen from these comments on the few existing Hungarian Jewish histories, each of them partial, the discussion of the full eighteen centuries of the Jews in Hungary presented in this book has no precedent. However, mine is but a first attempt, and not without shortcomings of its own. I was over eighty when I began working on this book. At that age, one no longer has the patience—or the time—to follow up meticulously every lead, or to undertake all the myriad minor tasks that could go into writing such a major historical study. I am sure that in the coming years young historians will take up the subject and will produce better and more complete histories of Hungarian Jewry. I shall not be here to see them, but I want to welcome them in advance.

The history of a people or community, in the simplest terms, should be an account of its past experience, of what it and its members did, felt, thought, wanted, of how they acted among themselves, of how they related to their neighbors, and of how they reacted to what was done to them. Regrettably, owing to the scarcity and nature of the primary sources, what we know about the history of the Jews in Hungary in the first twelve or thirteen centuries of their presence there (and to some extent later as well) concerns primarily not what they did, felt, and thought but rather what was done to them by the non-Jewish majority. Only occasionally do we hear, or can we conclude by analyzing non-Jewish sources, what steps the Jews themselves took in response to the measures affecting them enacted by the kings, the nobles, the Church, and the towns. Whether those measures were inimical or favorable, the documents relating to them treat the Jews as passive objects of restrictions, impositions, persecutions, extortions, and expulsions, and at times of favors and protection, from one or another of the authorities who considered them their property. Prior to the nineteenth century, the typical documents speaking of the Jews refer to them as if they were human chattel, with whom and to whom the powers could do whatever they wanted.

It is also because of the nature of the sources that we know the name of almost no single individual Jew until the fifteenth century. What the decrees and other official documents reveal is that Jewish communities did exist in many towns and localities in Hungary, and one can learn from them about the occupations the Jews were allowed to engage in, their financial status and the taxes they paid, the rights and privileges granted to them, the inabilities and restrictions imposed upon them, the attitude of the gentiles toward them, and the like. While thus we do get some idea as to the life of the Jews of Hungary as a group, they remain throughout these centuries shadowy figures, mere types, classes, categories of anonymous, underprivileged people who acted, or rather reacted, as groups to the varying conditions under which they were forced to live. The available documents scarcely reveal the existence of a single individual by name, nor do they contain any information on such a person's life and work. In brief, what we see is a distorted, or at any rate one-sided, picture.

As for the Jewish sources, up to the fifteenth century they are extremely meager. The Hungarian Jewish communities had rabbis, of course, but we know practically nothing about them, and if they did engage in any writing, whatever they wrote did not survive. Thus, the historian faces the unusual situation of having to piece together a picture of Hungarian Jewish life in those early centuries largely on the basis of references in non-Jewish documents left behind by Hungarians and by foreigners who visited Hungary. Even the work of the Jewish prefects, who played extremely important roles in the life of the Hungarian Jews between 1475 and 1531 (see chapter 8), is known not from Jewish sources but from Hungarian royal and other official documents. No other phenomenon points more clearly to Hungarian Jewry's having remained outside the mainstream of Jewish cultural developments until the fifteenth century than this absence of Hungarian Jewish writings.

Finally, a word about the subtitle of this book: *History, Culture, Psychology.* My main interest within the overall history of the Hungarian Jews throughout has been in their culture and their psychology. In thus focusing on special aspects of Hungarian Jewish history, I followed in the footsteps of Salo Baron, who called his magnum opus *Social and Religious History of the Jews* because social and religious developments were at the center of his historiographical interest. The reader will find that I devote more attention to the cultural, and especially literary, activities of the Hungarian Jews than one might expect in a general history. The reason is my conviction that the key characteristic in the portrayal of a people, hence deserving of special attention, is the culture that constitutes its ancestral heritage, that endows its existence with a specific coloration, that holds it in its thrall, and to which it contributes the best of its talents. In the case of the Hungarian Jews, however much they gave to the economy, finance, industry, science, medicine, and politics of the country, there can be no doubt that their most significant contributions were in the cultural fields of the arts, and especially literature. My general impression is that up to World War II, Hungarian Jews had a greater share in the culture of their country than had the Jews of any other country. A tragic testimony to this record is the list of Hungarian Jewish writers and poets killed in the Holocaust (see chapter 42), whose length is unduplicated in any other country whose Jewish community was destroyed by the Nazi genocide.

As for psychology, I felt I had to interrupt the flow of historical narrative from time to time with attempts to understand the motivations behind Hungarian Jews' overt reactions to the governmental, political, economic, social, and cultural forces affecting them, as well as those behind the various initiatives they took to maintain and improve their position in the country and to combat the ever-present threat of anti-Semitism. The question to which one returns again and again is, why did they act as they did? This question is of special importance in view of the fact that Jewish communities in other countries, exposed to similar outside pressures, experiences, and events, reacted quite differently. The explanation seems to lie in the different psychological configurations characterizing the Jews of different countries. Thus, Hungarian Jewish psychology becomes an essential part of the history of the Jews in Hungary. For lack of specialized studies on the subject, all I can do is to touch upon it in a few occasional comments.

Acknowledgments

In the preparation of this book I enjoyed the help and advice of many friends and colleagues in the United States and in Hungary, as well as the courtesy of libraries, without which the book could not have been written. My indebtedness to them can be expressed here only briefly.

In the first place I owe heartfelt thanks to Michael L. Furst, Esq., who was president of the World Federation of Hungarian Jews throughout the time that I was engaged in writing this book. It was in conversations with him that the idea first emerged that I write a history of the Jews of Hungary, and, once I embarked upon it, he encouraged me in persevering in the difficult task by emphasizing again and again that it was simply my duty to write it (with this I agreed), and that I was the last living scholar of Hungarian Jewish origin able to write it (with this I could not agree). I owe him thanks also for being instrumental in the allocation by the World Federation of Hungarian Jews of a grant to Wayne State University Press to help with the considerable publication expenses of this large book.

Next I owe special thanks to János Kőbányai, editor-in-chief of the quarterly *Múlt és Jövő* (Past and Future), and Ágnes Fenyő, manager of its editorial office, both of whom acted as my hosts in Budapest in the fall of 1993, when I spent several weeks there gathering material and interviewing old and new friends in connection with the concluding chapters that deal with the most recent period in the history of Hungarian Jews. Without János and Ágnes I could not have set up the many interviews and could not have utilized my time in Hungary as intensively as I was able to do with their help. They themselves also proved valuable sources of information on contemporary Hungarian Jewish life.

Of the others who generously gave me of their time and answered my questions in interviews in Budapest that occasionally stretched over several hours, I am indebted in particular to: Károly Ákos, M.D., and his wife; Eva V. Bálint, staff member of the Budapest daily *Magyar Hirlap*; Maria Ember, author of several books on the Holocaust; Tibor Englander, president of the Hungarian Zionist Union and director of a

17

Acknowledgments

research group in psychology at the Hungarian Academy of Sciences; Péter Feldmajer, attorney, president of the Association of Hungarian Jewish Congregations; Dénes Gábor, head of the dramatic arts department at the Lauder-Yavne School; György Gadó, member of Parliament, a leader of the Union of Free Democrats; Péter Hanák, professor emeritus, University of Budapest, the author of numerous studies on Hungarian Jewish history; Kinga Hanthy, staff member of the Budapest daily *Magyar Nemzet*; György Haraszti, historian, headmaster of the American Endowment School–Mesorat Avot; László Herzog, secretary of the Budapest Orthodox Jewish Congregation; George Hoffman, a retired Hungarian-American technical photographer; László Karsai, professor of history at the University of Szeged, author of several studies on the Jews of Hungary; György Lippner, headmaster of the Lauder-Yavne School; János Quittner, managing director of the Soros Foundation in Budapest; Rabbi Tamás Raj, member of Parliament; György Szabad, historian, president of the Hungarian Parliament; Miklós Szabolcsi, professor emeritus of literature at the University of Budapest; Gábor Szántó, book designer; Mrs. Pál Vidor, née Zsuzsa Kálmán, a retired teacher, widow of my old friend and colleague Rabbi Pál Vidor; Vilmos Voigt, professor of folklore, University of Budapest; and Lajos Weber, photo-journalist on the staff of the Budapest daily *Magyar Nemzet*.

I also wish to thank David Moskovits of New York, American chairman of the American Endowment School–Mesorat Avot, whom I interviewed in New York; George Prager, Toronto, Canada, who supplied me with information on ancient Hungarian Jewish numismatical material; Rabbi Ferenc Raj of Belmont, Main, who gave me valuable suggestions in connection with the chapters on the Jews in Turkish Hungary and in the most recent period; Prof. Ivan Sanders, Stony Brook, N. Y., who let me benefit from his expertise in modern Hungarian Jewish literature; Prof. Menahem Schmelzer of the Jewish Theological Seminary of New York, who kindly lent me from his private library source books of Hungarian Jewish history not available elsewhere in this country; the library of the Jewish Theological Seminary in New York, and especially Meir Rabinowicz, Terry Schwarzbard, Marion Stein, and Annette Muffs Botnick; the Hungarian National Széchenyi Library of Budapest; the Library of Congress of Washington, D.C.; the Jewish Division of the New York Public Library, and especially Leonard S. Gold, Norman Gechlik, Claire Dienstag, Roberta Saltzman and Ruth Yarden. I am greatly indebted to Wayne State University Press, its director Arthur B. Evans and its managing editor Kathryn Wildfong, for the attention they devoted to this book, my ninth to be published by Wayne State.

Acknowledgments

My sincere thanks are due also to William Lee Frost, president of the Lucius N. Littauer Foundation, and to Norman N. Gati, president, and Dr. Ervin Farkas, executive vice-president, of the World Federation of Hungarian Jews, for their interest in this book.

Forest Hills, N.Y.   Raphael Patai

1

The Jews in Roman Pannonia and Dacia

The sources relating to the history of the Jews in the land conquered in 896 by the Hungarian tribes first appear, in dribs and drabs, some seven centuries prior to that date. The Carpathian Basin, as the area is termed geographically, enters history with the Roman period. In 8 B.C.E. Emperor Tiberius, having overcome the resistance of the Pannons, established a Roman *limes*, a fortified frontier line, along the Danube, claiming for Rome the area to the west of the great river, which became known as Pannonia. Some hundred years later, the Romans also established themselves along the lower reaches of the Tisza River as far east as the southern Carpathians, holding on to that territory, Dacia, until 271 C.E. Pannonia remained Roman for about another century.

Pannonia as a Roman province was controlled by a legate of consular rank who had at his disposal a strong garrison stationed along the Danube. Around 103 C.E. Trajan divided the province into Pannonia Superior in the west, with its capital at Carnuntum (near Vienna), on the Danube just west of the present Austrian-Hungarian border, and Pannonia Inferior in the east, with Aquincum (now part of Budapest) as its capital. Both capitals comprised bases of Roman legions and separate civilian settlements.

In the early third century C.E., Pannonia reached the height of its prosperity, attracting immigrants from as far as Syria, but soon thereafter it began its rapid decline under the impact of invasions from the north and the east. In 405, when the Ostrogoths occupied the area, Roman administration collapsed, leaving behind its legacy in a degree of romanization of the native aristocracy.

Historical documents attesting to the presence of Jews in Roman Pannonia are tantalizingly few and laconic. They consist of a few inscriptions on tombs and other monuments that show that Jews and Syrians did live in various parts of Pannonia, and especially in the neighborhood of the Danube, from the second or third century on but

21

tell little beyond this. Such monuments were found in Brigetio (later Szőny-Komárom), Solva (Esztergom), Aquincum (Budapest), Intercisa (Dunaujváros or Dunapentele), Triccinae (Sárvár), Dombovár, Siklós, Sopianae (Pécs), and Savaria (Szombathely). The Jewish provenance of these monuments is indicated by the appearance of the adjective *judeus* (Jew) in conjunction with names; by Jewish symbols such as the seven-branched menorah; by the words (usually in Greek) "God is one"; or by references to some function of the person in the Jewish community. Occasionally the name itself or the place of birth indicates that the individual was of Jewish descent. These inscriptions permit the conclusion that in Roman Pannonia there lived Jews in sufficient number to form communities with synagogues, but that they (or those who happened to leave inscribed monuments) were thoroughly assimilated into Roman culture. Thus, for example, in Intercisa a tablet was found from the times of Emperor Alexander Severus (r. 222–35) inscribed as follows: "To the Eternal God! For the salvation of our Lord; the pious, felicitous Emperor Severus Alexander; and the Empress Julia Mamea, mother of the Emperor; Cosmius, chief of the Spondilla customhouse, head of the synagogue of the Jews, gladly fulfills his vow."

Much can be learned from this single inscription: first, the Jews of Spondilla were numerous and religious enough to maintain a synagogue; second, Cosmius, the chief of the synagogue (perhaps head of the community), was sufficiently assimilated to have a Roman name and to follow the Roman custom of setting up an inscribed monument commemorating a fulfilled vow; third, he was still Jewish enough to invoke the "eternal God" in his Latin memorial table; and fourth, he had an important position as head of the local customhouse, permitting us to conclude that the position of the Jews was favorable enough that they could rise in the administrative hierarchy.

All in all, of the inscriptions left behind by Jews in Roman Pannonia, some two-thirds are those of soldiers, while the remaining one-third were executed at the behest of Jewish officials. All of them show a considerable degree of cultural and even religious assimilation to Roman civilization. Take the tombstone found in Siklós, Pannonia, erected in the early third century. It reads: "D.M. To Septimia Maria, a Jewess [*Judaea*], who lived eighteen years. Actia Subinilla, her mother." While the designation *Judaea* shows that she was Jewish, the customary pagan abbreviation D.M., which stands for *diis manibus* ("to the gods of death"), testifies to the influence of Roman paganism.

Other inscriptions point in the same direction. In some, the head of the family who serves in the army is a Roman citizen with a Latin name, with no indication that he was Jewish other than the typically

Memorial tablet found in Intercisa, Pannonia, from the third century, preserved in the Hungarian National Museum, Budapest. It reads (supplying full words for the abbreviations): Deo aeterno pro salute domini nostri Severi Alexandri pii felicis Augusti et Iuliae Mameae Augustae matris Augusti, votum reddit libens Cosmius praepositus stationis Spondilli, archisynagogus Iudeorum; which translates: To the eternal God! For the salvation of our Lord; the pious, felicitous Emperor Severus Alexander; and the Empress Julia Namea, mother of the Emperor; Cosmius, chief of the Spondilla customhouse, head of the synagogue of the Jews, gladly fulfills his vow. (Courtesy of the Műszaki Könyvkiadó [Technical Publishers], Budapest.)

Jewish names of his mother, wife, and daughter. In another type of inscriptions (such as three found in Intercisa, Siklós, and Aquincum, all from the Severian period, 193–235 C.E.) the name of the father is typically Roman, but that of his son is Jewish. One is tempted to speculate as to whether this alternating between Roman and Jewish names indicates changes in the social and civil conditions of the Jews in Roman Pannonia.

In addition to inscriptions, objects decorated with Jewish motifs also attest to the presence of Jews in Pannonia. Among them are a fourth-century ring with the seven-branched menorah found in Sopianae, an amulet with the same decoration from the vicinity of Sopianae, and a

23

lucern (clay oil lamp) decorated with the menorah and palm branches from Savaria. All in all, several dozens of inscriptions and relics prove Jewish presence in Roman Pannonia.

As to the origin of the Jewish communities in Roman Pannonia, we can only conjecture that some Jews came with or in the wake of the Roman legions that conquered the province in the early first century C.E. From 167 on, the Romans were subject to constant attacks by the Marcomans and Sarmatians, nomadic tribes of horseback riders who roamed the territory on the left bank of the Danube across from Aquincum and, riding their small and swift prairie-bred horses, were able to inflict painful losses on the Roman garrison. This bloodletting forced the Romans to replenish their Pannonian legions from other parts of the empire. Coincidentally, in 175 C.E. a rebellion broke out in the Syrian and Judean provinces of Rome, and Avidius Cassius, the governor of Syria, had himself proclaimed emperor against Marcus Aurelius (121–80). After Cassius was killed by his own troops, Marcus Aurelius decided to remove part of the unreliable Syrian army and transfer it to remote Pannonia. Two cohorts, each consisting of one thousand men, were sent to support Aquincum. One of them, organized in Antiochia, Syria, was stationed in the camp of Ulcisia Castra (later Szentendre) on the Danube, north of Aquincum, where it became designated "infantry cohort one of the Syrian archers, called Aurelia Antoniana." The other cohort, stationed south of Aquincum, in Intercisa, was called "first cohort of the Syrian Hemesian archers," because it was recruited in the Syrian city of Hemesa (later Homs). Among the soldiers of these Syrian cohorts there were Antiochian and Hemesian Jews.

The Syrian cohorts consisted of light cavalry, had a fighting style similar to that of the Sarmatians, and hence were better able to deal with them than the heavily armed, slower Roman cohorts. The Syrian legions were replenished from their homeland for many decades, and thus the Syrian soldiers in Pannonia could maintain contact with their home communities. This explains the otherwise puzzling fact that, as the inscriptions on the monuments show, among the Jewish soldiers of the Syrian contingents, even in the second half of the third century there were still some who had been born in Antiochia or Hemesa.

The ongoing contact between the Syrian soldiers in Pannonia, whether Jewish or non-Jewish, and their relatives and friends back in Antiochia and Hemesa explains yet another development. This is that, in addition to recruits, civilian Jews also moved into the Pannonian settlements inhabited by Syrians. From 226 on, the Sassanid Persians put increasing pressure on the eastern boundaries of the Roman Empire, and their incursions were catastrophic for the Jews, especially in Antiochia, Tharsus, and the cities of Cappadocia. Many Jews sought refuge in the west, and some of these opted to join their relatives in Pannonia, where under Alexander Severus the Jews had full security, were free to practice their religion, and even enjoyed privileges. The historical evidence shows that organized groups of Jews came to Pannonia around the year 230, and that later in the third century their numbers were augmented by Jewish newcomers whose names indicate that they hailed from the Hellenized parts of the Roman Empire. This immigration continued until the middle of the fourth century, when the eastern territories seceded from the Roman Empire; this, too, is shown by the last historical evidence they left behind in Pannonia before the Romans evacuated the province.

These data, meager in themselves, are supplemented by information from the writers and historians of the period, who frequently remark that the Jews were not different from the others among whom they lived, in either custom or costume, language, manner of writing, or names. It was especially difficult to differentiate between them and the Syrians, with whom in their old homelands they had lived in constant enmity, but with whom in the strange environment they lived in harmony and kept together, probably owing to their common past and common traditions. The Jews were known to be excellent soldiers and hence filled important positions in the army, and their expertise and talent also enabled them to participate effectively in the economic life of the provinces.

A modern Hungarian historian of the period, Dr. Klára Póczy, suggests that the paucity of historical monuments left by the Jews of Pannonia is due precisely to their strong assimilative proclivity. In the fourth century, when a belief in one God no longer differentiated Jews from those among whom they lived, it was easy for them to assimilate to the early monotheistic Christian sects. On the other hand, the Jews' ability to practice their religion openly led to a revival of orthodoxy. Iconoclasm set in, and (in the words of Dr. Póczy) "the tradition-abiding Jews themselves destroyed and annihilated with wild rage the earlier sepulchral monuments, architectural inscriptions, and other relics of their coreligionists, whom they branded renegades."

Despite the research done in recent years, the information unearthed so far about the Jews in Roman Pannonia is woefully slight. Here is a field of inquiry that calls for the attention of young historians and holds the promise of significant results.

If little is known of the history of the Jews in Roman Pannonia, even less is known about Dacia, the other Roman colony within the Carpathian Basin. In fact, the historical data relating to the Jews of Dacia are so scant that one must resort to legend for any indication of their presence in that Roman territory, which later became Transylvania, constituing for centuries the eastern part of the kingdom of Hungary.

One of the legends is attached to Decebal, king of Dacia, one of the strongest and most effective foes of Rome, who, after causing serious troubles for the Roman Empire, committed suicide in 106 C.E. The legend has it that when Decebal prepared to fight Rome, he called upon the Jews, expelled from their homes by the Romans, to help him. Among the Jews who responded was a rich man, a descendant of the tribe of Dan, who brought with him enormous treasures and became a close friend of Decebal. As a reward for their services, Decebal permitted Jews to work in gold washing, mining, and commerce and to build themselves a city near the Wallachian border. The city was called Thalmus (modern Talmats or Talmács), and its Jewish inhabitants prospered. The Jews multiplied not only in Transylvania but also elsewhere in the Carpathian Basin. The story of Thalmus became the subject of a Latin poem, which, though lacking a firm historical basis, possibly does contain a memory of actual events.

2

Medieval Origins and the Khazar Question

The history of the Carpathian Basin is wrapped in almost unpenetrable darkness during the half-millennium that passed between its evacuation by the Romans and its conquest by the Hungarians in the late ninth century. We therefore know almost nothing about the Jews who lived there —not even whether any Jews remained in the country after the Romans withdrew their legions in the early fifth century. It is only in the early ninth century that historical sources begin to flow again, or rather, to trickle.

In 866, some three decades before the arrival of the Hungarian tribes, the Bulgarian ruler Prince Michael Bogor, who shortly before had converted to Christianity, sent a number of questions to Pope Nicholas I (r. 858–67) concerning religious practices. One of them was whether it was permitted to work on Saturday and Sunday. The pope replied that to rest on the Sabbath was "a Jewish custom," and he who follows it "subjects himself to the infidelity of the Jews." Since Prince Bogor could have gotten the idea that it was forbidden to work on Saturday only from Jewish inhabitants of his realm, this exchange of letters is proof that in the middle of the ninth century Jews did live in the country controlled by the Bulgarians, which included parts of southern Hungary.

Another piece of information dates from the very beginning of the tenth century but refers to a situation that must have developed some decades earlier. The customs regulations adopted between 903 and 907 in Raffelstetten, Bavaria, deal with commercial relations between Bavaria and Moravia and specify that the Jews and other merchants whose ships ply the Danube between Moravia and Bavaria, selling slaves and other merchandise, whatever their country of origin, have to pay "just customs dues, as was customary in the times of the previous kings." Jewish slave traders, who purchased slaves in Poland, brought them into Hungary, and shipped them on the Danube to Bavaria to sell them there, are also referred to in ninth-century Polish historical sources.

Writing in the tenth century, the Jewish traveler Ibrahim ibn Ya'qub of Tortosa, whom al-Ḥakam II, the second Umayyad caliph of Spain, sent in 966 as envoy to the German king Otto I, reports the presence of Jews among the slave traders in Prague. It is unlikely that at a time when Jews lived in both the northern and southern border areas of Hungary, separated by only 120 miles, they should not have been settled also in the area in between, that is, in central Hungary.

With the arrival of Magyar (Hungarian) tribes in the Carpathian Basin, a second Jewish contingent was added to the one already present. Our knowledge of these Jews is also very scanty, as is the historical information on the Hungarian tribes themselves prior to their irruption into Pannonia. The search for the origins of these Jewish groups leads us into Central Asia, whence the Hungarians came, and where they had contact with the Khazar kingdom, for which historical information is somewhat more plentiful. About the Khazars it is known that their kingdom extended over the area bounded by the Crimea and the Black Sea in the west and by the Volga River in the east, that in the middle of the eighth century their king and nobles converted to Judaism, and that some two centuries later their empire disintegrated under repeated attacks by the Russians. What seems to have occurred then is that members of one of their groups, the Jewish Kabars, and then other Khazars as well, fleeing the superior power of the Russians, joined the seven Hungarian tribes who at precisely that time were about to leave the steppes north of the Black Sea and start their westward trek across the Carpathians into Hungary. Although the exact relationship between the Khazars, Kabars, and Magyars is unknown, it is clear that they were in close contact. One indication is that the runic alphabet, of Central Asian Turkic origin, was adopted by the Magyars from the Khazars. (It survived among the Székelys, the Hungarian-speaking inhabitants of Transylvania, until the eighteenth century.) Another is that the conquerors who arrived in Hungary in the late ninth century comprised not only seven Hungarian tribes but also three Kabar tribes, and probably also Khazar contingents, which included Jews. The Jewish Khazar presence among them is indicated by a rare find: a Khazar ring with Hebrew letters, unearthed at Ellend near Pécs.

Some of the available data about the Jewish Khazars and Kabars has led historians to the conclusion that their Jewishness was less than complete—in fact, rather partial and superficial, resembling that of other Judaizing groups, of which there were several in late antiquity. Nothing is known of the relationship that developed between these Jewish or half-Jewish Khazars and Kabars, on the one hand, and the older Jewish inhabitants of the Carpathian Basin, on the other. However, the general Jewish proclivity to seek out and establish relations with other Jews furnishes some basis for assuming that once the trauma of being overrun and subjugated by the invading warlike tribes subsided, the old Jewish inhabitants managed to establish contact with those of the invaders who observed some Jewish precepts, and succeeded in drawing them fully into the Jewish community. (A similar process occurred in the sixteenth century, when some Transylvanian Hungarian Christians first became Sabbath-observing "Sabbatarians" [*szombatosok*], and then many of them converted to Judaism.) It is in the fusion of autochthonous Jews with semi-Jewish Khazars and Kabars in the tenth century that we must seek the earliest demographic basis of the Jewish population of medieval Hungary.

There is one additional historical reference to Jews in tenth-century preconquest Hungary. In 953 a Croatian delegation arrived in Cordoba, and two of its members were Jews, Mar Shaul and Mar Yosef by name. They were received by the Spanish Jewish statesman and physician Ḥisdai ibn Shaprut (ca. 915–ca. 970), who for several years before that had tried in vain to establish contact with the Jewish rulers of the Khazar kingdom. Mar Shaul and Mar Yosef offered Ibn Shaprut their services. As Ibn Shaprut stated in a letter to the Khazar king: "Seeing my predicament, they comforted me saying, 'Give us your letter; we shall hand it to the king of the Croatians, who for your sake will send on your letter to the Israelites who live in the land of the *Hungrin* [Hungarians], and they, in turn, will send it on to Russia, and from there to Bulgaria, until your letter will, as you wish, reach the place to which you intend it." Here we have direct information from two Jews who lived in Croatia, the southern neighbor of Hungary, attesting not only to the presence of Jews in Hungary in the mid-tenth century but also to their commercial relations with Croatia and Russia. It stands to reason that such relations did not develop overnight, and we therefore conclude that by the 950s the Jews of Hungary could look back upon a history of at least several decades in the country.

Under King István I (r. 997–1038) and his successors, all the Magyars were converted to Christianity, often by force. This development opened the door to closer contact with the economically and culturally more advanced countries of Central and Western Europe. However, for several more centuries Hungary did not adopt the typical medieval Western anti-Jewish position, and no attempts were made to convert the Jewish (or Muslim) merchants to Christianity. The early Hungarian feudal system that developed in this period had a special feature that also determined the status of the Jews in the country: every individual was, directly or indirectly, the king's servant. This included the most exalted individuals who derived their wealth from part of the royal income assigned to them as compensation for their services as administrators (called *ispáns*) of the counties or royal domains. As we shall soon see, this system made the Jews dependent on the will of the king, but at the same time it provided them with royal protection against arbitrary exploitation by the towns, where most of them lived.

3

After the Magyar Conquest

From the eleventh century on, we have somewhat more information on the life of the Jews in Hungary. About 1050 an incident, in itself insignificant, took place in Esztergom (Gran), a city on the right bank of the Danube some thirty miles northwest of Budapest, that left its traces in the rabbinical literature of the age and throws some light on Jewish life there.

Two brothers, Jewish merchants from Regensburg, Germany, were on their way back from Russia when, not far from Esztergom, a wheel of their heavily laden wagon broke. This happened on a Friday, and by the time the damage was repaired and they could drive on, it was late in the day, so that they arrived in the city after the onset of the Sabbath—a blatant desecration of the holy day. For this, the rabbi of the community imposed a heavy punishment on the two men. A description of the incident found its way into the thirteenth-century halakhic compendium *Shibbolei haLeqet*, authored by the Roman rabbi Abraham haRofe 'Anav. The account is of such importance for the history of the Jews in Hungary in the eleventh century, a period for which almost no Jewish documents exist, that its full presentation (in my literal translation) is warranted.

And this is the sentence passed by our master Kalonymos, son of R. Shabtai the Ḥazzan [cantor] of blessed memory in the Land of Hagar [Hungary] on R. Abraham, son of R. Ḥiyya of Regensburg, and his brother R. Yaaqov, who came from Russia with laden wagons on the eve of the Sabbath while it was still day, with *goy* [non-Jewish] hirelings and with their Jewish companions, to the community, and they remained on this side of the River Danube, at a distance of a little less than a *mil* [mile], for one of the wheels of their wagon broke, and they tarried there until they repaired it. And when they reached the community, the [people of the] community were just coming out of the synagogue on the eve of the Sabbath, and the community did not give them peace [did not greet them], and did not let them enter [next] morning into the synagogue, lest others draw an inference from them, from minor to major, saying, 'This is how N. and N. [so-and-so] acted' [hence we can act likewise], lest an even greater breach be made by desecrating the Sabbath willfully. And on the first of the week [Sunday] they came to the synagogue to receive the sentence. And they were ordered to fast seven weeks, fifty consecutive days, except the Sabbaths and holidays and new moons, to fulfill fifty work days in fasting and lashing. And why fifty days? For he who desecrates the Sabbath becomes deserving of *karet* [divine punishment by premature death], and the sages taught in [the tractate] *Mo'ed Qatan* [folio 25 or 28], and it is explained in the Jerusalem Talmud in the tractate *Bikkurim* [chapter 2, halakha 1], that he who dies at the age of fifty dies a death of *karet*. And they imposed on them to fast and be whipped fifty days, as against those fifty years of death. And they also imposed on them to give from their own money a life ransom to the alms box, and then they ordered them to fast three days every month of the twelve months of the year, on Monday, Thursday, and Monday, which are thirty-six days as against the thirty-six *karet* [punishments] contained in the Torah, so as to be freed of the *karet*, as we have learned [in *B. Makkot* 23b], "All those who deserve *karet*, if they are flogged they are freed of *karet*." But had they, Heaven forfend, acted thus deliberately, they would have been punished more severely by being prohibited to shave for thirty days and being put under a ban, as it is stated [*B. Mo'ed Qatan* 16a], "an ordinary excommunication is for thirty days." And he who acts even more strictly in this matter, let blessings come upon his head.

This brief account provides rare insight into the conditions of the Hungarian Jews in a city along the banks of the Danube in the eleventh century. First of all, we learn that German Jewish merchants passed through Hungary on their way from Russia to Germany, and that it was their custom to spend the Sabbath as guests of one of the local Jewish communities. Upon their arrival, they would first go to the synagogue. The town in which these two men arrived had an organized Jewish community, with a *beth din*, a religious court, headed by a rabbi. It had a charity organization, which the members of the community supported by putting their contributions into an "alms box." The leader of the community had the authority to arrest persons guilty of a transgression and to punish them with the full severity of halakhic law. Had that not been the case, the two Regensburg Jews would have, or at any rate could have, simply left the city Sunday morning instead of appearing before the court. These two merchants were not particularly observant: they rode into town on their repaired wagon after the onset of the Sabbath, and they did not wear beards, as religious Jews did, but were shaved. On the other hand, the local Jewish community was deeply religious: they were so scandalized by the arrival of the two Regensburg Jews after the onset of the Sabbath that they refused to welcome them, and even the next morning barred them from entering the synagogue and attending the Sabbath service.

That the community of Esztergom was a sizable and probably even important one can be concluded from the fact that R. Kalonymos ben Shabtai, a well-known and highly respected Italian rabbi, served in it for a period of unknown length in the capacity of *av beth din* (head of the religious court) before returning to Rome. Sometime later (ca. 1070) he moved on to Worms in the Rhineland, where he functioned as head of the talmudic school. He was a man of great learning and reputation, as we know from a remark made by Rashi, (1040–1105), the greatest biblical and talmudic commentator of all times, who writes (in his comments to *B. Betza* 24b), "Just now came to me a letter from Worms [that informs me] that a great old man arrived there from Rome, who sits [presides] in the yeshiva, and his name is R. Kalonymos, and he is an expert in all the Talmud and the Torah." It must have been while he was back in Rome that R. Kalonymos told his colleagues of his experiences in Hungary, and it was thus that a report of the incident found its way into the *Shibbolei haLeqet*, written in Rome some two centuries later. (Incidentally, the father of R. Kalonymos, referred to by Anav as R. Shabtai the Ḥazzan, is well known in the history of Hebrew literature. He was a liturgical poet—this is what the designation *ḥazzan* seems to refer to—several of whose poems have survived.)

The report of the sentencing of the two Regensburg travelers is the earliest historical reference to the existence of a Jewish community in Esztergom. From other sources we know that in the early period of its existence, the community did not yet have a *miqveh* (ritual bath), and its members used the local hot springs for ritual purposes. By the thirteenth century the community lived in a closed Jewish quarter, under the protection of the archbishop and the royal court. Its cemetery is mentioned the first time in a rescript addressed in 1326 by King Károly I (1310–42) to the city of Esztergom. Its advantageous location, on the banks of the Danube and along a main commercial route between Central and Eastern Europe, attracted traveling merchants, who settled there. The community grew to one thousand persons before they were exiled to Turkey by Sultan Suleiman, who took the city in 1526. During the eighteenth century Jews again settled in Esztergom, and continued to live there until their destruction during the Holocaust.

We mentioned above the extreme paucity of Jewish sources referring to the Jews in Hungary in the eleventh century. Were it not for references to Jews in the Hungarian state, county, and city documents, we would know practically nothing of their history until the fifteenth century. While the Jews in the countries to the west, north, and east of Hungary excelled in halakhic and other Jewish studies, those in Hungary itself formed a Jewishly ignorant, one could even say Jewishly illiterate, community. They had few rabbis, cantors, and teachers, and their familiarity with Jewish liturgy and ritual was so poor that often they could not even perform the communal prayers because no single person among them knew the order of prayers and could recite them and function as *hazzan*, prayer leader.

That this was the situation in the twelfth century is known to us not from a Hungarian Jewish source—there are none from that period—but from a statement by R. Eliezer ben Yitzhaq, who had moved from Bohemia to Speier in Germany, and who wrote around 1190 that in most Jewish communities of Hungary there were no Jewish scholars, "but if they find somewhere a knowledgeable man, they take him on to be their cantor, rabbi, and the teacher of their children." Such a cantor-rabbi-teacher made a living only from the donations he could obtain on the occasion of marriages and certain holidays. If these proved insufficient, he was forced to leave his post, and the community "remained without knowledge of religion, prayer, and rabbi." It was for this reason that R. Eliezer ben Yitzhaq sharply attacked the Parisian rabbi Yehuda ben Yitzhaq, who had condemned the custom of giving donations, because, the rabbi of Speier argued, if the donations should cease, "a great confusion would arise" among the Jews of Hungary.

Another example of the Hungarian Jews' need to be instructed by foreign rabbinical scholars comes from 1217, when R. Yitzhaq ben Moshe, who later became rabbi in Vienna, visited Esztergom (Gran) and Buda (Ofen). In both communities the local Jews asked him whether it was permitted for the women to use the local hot springs as their prescribed ritual bath. The rabbi responded yes, it was permissible. These two communities were the oldest and best organized in the country, and if even they lacked a scholar who could make such a ritual decision, one can assume that in other communities the situation was even worse.

When the problem that arose was an urgent one, Hungarian Jews could not wait for the fortuitous visit of a foreign rabbi and applied to rabbinical authorities abroad. This happened in Nyitra about 1220, when the community turned to the same R. Yitzhaq ben Moshe in Vienna in connection with the validity of a marriage contracted in unusual circumstances. In addition to the Viennese rabbi, other rabbinical authorities also gave their opinions on the issue, but no Hungarian rabbi was among them.

Dr. Samuel Kohn, the chief rabbi of Budapest whose 1884 history of the Jews in Hungary from the earliest times to 1526 remains to this day the only comprehensive study of the subject, considered the absence of Jewish scholarship among the Hungarian Jews until the fifteenth century "an additional proof that the original Jewish inhabitants of Hungary were a population element differing from the other European Jews in that their overwhelming majority consisted not of born Jews but of pagans who converted to Judaism, so that for a long time they did not at all participate in the intellectual work of the other Jews, and also later did so only to a very small extent." One cannot help suspecting that the overriding patriotism of the Hungarian Jews in the late nineteenth century, which Kohn shared, may have colored his judgment and induced him to seek a blood relationship between the ancient Jews and Christians of Hungary.

A more likely reason for the Hungarian Jews' lack of talmudic scholarship and rabbinical authorship is simply the generally low level of education and culture that characterized not only the Jews but even more so the Christians up to the 1400s. The latter is indicated, for example, by the fact that the first Hungarian translation of the Bible was not produced until the fifteenth century, and then not by Hungarian authors but by preachers who had come from Moravia. Since in this early period the Jews were less isolated from the gentile environment in Hungary than in nearby countries, it is likely that the general absence of literary activity meant that the Jewish community, too, failed to produce a counterpart to the scholarly authors in the neighboring countries who had by that time greatly enriched Jewish literature. In any case, the Jews of Hungary were until the fifteenth century a Jewishly ignorant community, as is evident from the conspicuous absence of Jewish literary works until that time. This means that they left behind almost no documents of their own to reveal their history in the first six centuries after the occupation of the country by the Hungarian tribes.

But few historical generalizations are without exceptions. The name of one single Hungarian Jewish scholar who lived in the eleventh century is known: he is mentioned by Rashi, who writes in his *Sefer haPardes*: "And thus did a *qatzin* [person of high position], our master Yitzḥaq Yasqont of the land of Hagar [Hungary], propose a different meaning." Kohn identifies the name Yasqont with the Hungarian name Jászkont. Whether this is correct or not, it is clear that Rashi refers to a Hungarian rabbinical master whom he styles *qatzin* and *rabbenu* (our master), a designation given to only the most outstanding rabbinical scholars.

Only one other Jewish scholar with any connection to Hungary is known by name from this period. He was R. Yehuda, called Liberman, of Pressburg. He was a fifth-generation descendant of the famous R. Eliezer ben Natan of Mainz, who lived around 1150. Nothing else is known about him, but it stands to reason that he settled in Pressburg to serve as rabbi of the community.

While information concerning internal Jewish life in eleventh- to thirteenth-century Hungary is extremely meager, we know, thanks to documents preserved in Hungarian archives, a little more about the position of the Jews in relation to the country's rulers and cities. It is under the reigns of King Endre II (1205–35) and his son King Béla IV (1235–70) that we hear for the first time of individual Jews known by name, and learn at least something about the role they played in the country. It is typical that we learn of these men not from Jewish sources, which simply do not exist, but from Hungarian official documents.

One such man was the highly influential Jewish treasury count Teha, whose name appears in the contemporary documents in many forms— Teha, Techa, Teka, Techanus, Tebanus, Thebanus, and so on. Teha was probably born between 1180 and 1190 and died, again probably, after the Mongol invasion of Hungary in 1241–42. His father—name unknown—was a rich man who must have performed valuable services to the crown, for, as one source states, he "owned since antiquity, thanks to royal liberality, the Villa Besseneu," that is, Besenyő, to which belonged extensive landed properties. The same document refers to his son *Judaeus Teha comes* (the Jew Count Teha) as *hospes* (guest), possibly indicating that he was of foreign origin. After the death of his father, Teha remained in possession of the Besenyő estate until 1232. In addition, he also owned an estate near Sopron (Ödenburg) called Ruhtukeur, which may be identical with the modern Hungarian Rőjtőkőr.

We first hear of Teha in a document from 1225, when King Endre entered into an agreement with Austrian Duke Leopold, who undertook to pay the king 2000 marks. The payment of this amount in two installments was guaranteed by Teha. Nothing more is known of this transaction, but one thing is clear: Teha must have been by that time an established high financier and very rich, able to undertake the payment of what was a huge amount, and he was a man on whose financial responsibility the Hungarian king relied more than on that of the Austrian duke.

King Endre II was a spendthrift who brought ruin to Hungarian state finances, but he was provident enough to empower his energetic son Béla to investigate the status of all the estates in the country, and to recover for the royal treasury the properties that his father had given away without due cause or that were part of the inalienable property of the crown. All grandees, whether secular or ecclesiastical, had to produce their deeds of gift, and if these were found invalid or unlawful, the estates in question were confiscated.

These measures were applied to Teha as well. He had a claim to the Ruhtukeur estate, which the king then presented to a certain Knight

Simon, who had immigrated to Hungary from Aragon. The transfer of the estate from Teha to Simon was not effected without considerable difficulties. Teha, behaving as did the other grandees, disobeyed the king's ruling, and Simon had to lodge repeated complaints with the king, accusing Teha of forcefully and unjustly retaining the estate. Endre called upon Teha three times to present his documentary claim to Ruhtukeur. Finally, when these royal demands remained ineffective, he issued in 1228 a rescript in which he annulled Teha's title to the property, and presented it to Simon. Now the Aragonian knight was finally able to take possession of Ruhtukeur, which he subsequently left in inheritance to his descendants.

This incident is remarkable for two reasons. First, it shows that Teha, like the other grandees of Hungary, dared and was able to defy a royal order for something like three years. Second, despite his open defiance of the king, Teha was not punished, but quite to the contrary, within a year after having relinquished Ruhtukeur, he was given control of the revenues of the royal treasury, called *camera*, and thus obtained the title *comes camerae*, or "treasury count."

Despite his financial talents, Teha was not able to manage the royal revenues profitably. He accumulated a sizable debt to the treasury, until finally, in 1232, with the consent of the king, he sold his estate of Besenyő, which he had inherited from his father, for 500 marks. The buyer was none other than the Aragonian Count Simon.

At the same time, Teha felt he ought to leave Hungary. Those were the days when the Church increasingly pressured the king to limit the activities of the Jews in the country, and in 1233 the king actually entered into the so-called Bereg Agreement, which made it impossible for Teha to retain his high position, or even to appear in public without the degrading Jewish badge. We do not know when exactly Teha left Hungary, but by 1235 we find him in Vienna, where he continued his large-scale money business in partnership with several Viennese bankers. One of the transactions of this partnership was to loan 120 Viennese pounds to the Austrian nobleman Poppo Pecachi against a mortgage on the latter's estate.

The threat of the Mongol invasion forced Endre's son and successor, King Béla IV, to rescind that part of the Bereg Agreement that barred Jews from public office. This induced Teha to return to Hungary, where he again held a high position. What office he filled is not known, but it most likely had to do with the royal treasury. He seems to have loaned large amounts of money to the king, who was in dire need of funds for his preparations to resist the Mongols. In gratitude, King Béla presented Teha with another large estate called Csenke, on the banks of the Danube. Interestingly, at an earlier date the king had given the Csenke estate to Knight Simon, but he now took it away from him and presented it to Teha. After the Mongol invasion, however, the king again presented the same estate to Simon and proclaimed that Teha had from then on no rights whatsoever in it.

The possession of Ruhtukeur continued to be an object of litigation between the heirs of Count Simon and Count Teha. As late as 1299, Simon's heirs found it necessary to present the deed to the estate to the royal chancellery to prove that the estate in fact belonged to them.

Another high financial officer known from the times of King Béla IV is Henuk, a Jew of German or Austrian origin, who was appointed treasury count by the king and entrusted with the management of the royal revenues. He seems to have filled the same position Teha had prior to the Mongol invasion. After that invasion, as a reward for large loans or other meritorious work, the king gave Henuk the castle of Komárom with its estate of twenty-one villages, as well as a mill located next to Tata. Henuk died shortly before 1265, owing the royal treasury a large sum. Since this situation repeats his predecessor Count Teha's management of the treasury, one is inclined to conclude that it was nothing exceptional for the treasury count to collect taxes and postpone paying the agreed amount to the royal treasury until finally the king was compelled to bear down forcefully upon him. In any case, when Count Henuk died, King Béla took the Komárom estate away from his heirs and sold it to Treasury Count Walter for an amount equal to Henuk's debt. Because of this and subsequent legal entanglements, the Hungarian documents preserved the names of Henuk's heirs, his three sons, Wolflin, Nikkel, and Altmann, whose German names testify to Henuk's German origin. Some time later the sons were able to settle the debt their father left them as his legacy, and before long we find them again in possession of Komárom. More than that: Queen Maria, with the consent of Béla, let them rent the income of her own estates. But the sons, too, encountered the recurring problem of tax renters. They were unable to pay the queen the full rent and remained indebted to her to the amount of 800 marks fine silver. As a security for their debt, they mortgaged to the queen their Komárom castle, together with all the villages and incomes belonging to it, and also their mill next to Tata. The due date came and went, and even after several extensions the three sons were unable to defray the debt. In the meantime, the interest on it increased sharply. The debtors finally had no choice but to offer the queen possession of the castle and the mill. In 1268 the queen, in turn, sold the properties, which she thus owned, to Count Walter for 800 marks fine silver. The documents relating to the indebtedness of the

Henuk sons show that at the time, the prevailing rates of interest were exceedingly high. Within three years the interest (*poena*) they had to pay amounted to more than the principal of their debt.

Two of Henuk's sons, Nikkel and Wolflin, also appear in an Austrian document from 1257 as treasury counts of the "most illustrious duke of Austria," indicating that, like Teha before them, they served in that capacity not only in Hungary but also in Austria.

In the late thirteenth century, an event took place that was a harbinger of the deterioration in the position of the Jews of Hungary that set in in the fourteenth century. This was the first ritual murder libel in the country, accompanied by the killing of several Jews. The little that is known about the case is derived not from Hungarian or Hungarian Jewish sources but from the *Memorbuch* (Memorial Book) of Mainz, which states very briefly that a certain R. Jonah and his companions were killed or burned in Pressburg. The event is not dated, but it is listed between a reference to Jewish martyrs in 1243 and another to Jews killed in 1287, so it must have taken place between those two years.

This tragic incident presents a disconcerting contrast with the otherwise favorable position the Jews enjoyed in Pressburg in this period. In 1291 King Endre III (r. 1290–1301), the last monarch of the House of Árpád, issued a letter patent to the city of Pressburg, in which he stated that "the Jews resident in that city should enjoy the same freedoms as the other citizens." In the country as a whole, Jews could acquire and own landed property without any limitation. This is shown by a document dated 1300, according to which two citizens of the town of Trencsén sold their lot and the garden adjoining it to a local Jew, Daniel by name, and the city of Trencsén confirmed the sales deed.

4

The Jews in Early Hungarian Law
(Eleventh to Thirteenth Centuries)

In contrast to the scanty information suppied by Jewish sources, the Hungarian legal dispositions from the eleventh through the thirteenth centuries, which regulated the position of the Jews in the country and determined their rights and disabilities, contain many details elucidating the conditions under which the Jews lived in that period, as well as the activities they engaged in.

First, an exception. Since historical sources testify to the presence of Jews in Hungary from the mid-tenth century on (see chapter 2), and since the Hungarian laws promulgated from 1092 on invariably contain provisions pertaining to the Jews, it is remarkable that the "Two Law Books" produced under King István I (St. Stephan) in the early eleventh century have nothing to say about them. The laws in these two books aim at strengthening the position of the newly adopted Christian faith in the country. Directed against the pagans, restricting their rights and public functions, they do not even mention the Jews. How can we interpret this legal silence about a population element that was unquestionably present and was certainly more resistant to Christianization than the pagans? The most likely explanation seems that in this early period of the formation of Hungarian society, during which Christianity struggled to establish itself within an overwhelmingly pagan population, the small Jewish minority was not considered important enough to be the subject of legislation.

However, from the restrictions imposed on the Jews from 1092 on one can conclude that prior to that date, during their first two centuries in the newly established Hungarian kingdom, the Jews enjoyed all the rights of which the 1092 and later laws successively deprived them. No conclusion concerning the position of the Jews can be drawn from the law that Hungary, following the example of other Christian countries, adopted under Béla I (r. 1061–63). This decreed that the weekly market was to be held not on Sunday, as was the old custom (the Hungarian word for Sunday is *Vasárnap*, "market day"), but on Saturday. The purpose of this law was simply to enable the newly Christianized population of Hungary to attend church on Sunday instead of going to the market. While this law was not directed against the Jews, nevertheless it was incidentally very detrimental to them, because it meant that inasmuch as they were observant, they could not attend the weekly market, thus greatly impeding their ability to sell their products.

The first definitely anti-Jewish law was passed in 1092, at the very end of the reign of King (St.) László (1077–95), and from that time on successive legal provisions limited the living conditions and economic activities of the Jews more and more and increasingly restricted them to the money business. However, the historian can use these same legal restrictions for a tentative reconstruction of the activities the Jews engaged in before they were prohibited. Thus, one gets a picture of a Jewish life apparently conducted with exactly as much (or rather as little) freedom as was available to the rest of the nonnoble population of the country at the time.

Take, to begin with, the first anti-Jewish laws, issued in 1092 by the Council of Szabolcs, a religious convocation held with the participation of the grandees of the country, as well as its Christian religious leaders. With reference to the Jews, this Council resolved as follows: "If Jews live in marriage with Christian women, or if they keep Christian individuals as slaves, these should be taken away from them and returned to freedom. . . . The Jew who is found working on Sunday or on another holiday—so that Christendom should not be offended by it—should lose the implements with which he worked." The inclusion of these two laws among the decisions of the Council of Szabolcs only makes sense if up to that time the Jews in Hungary *could* marry Christian women, own Christian slaves, and work unhindered on Sunday and other Christian holidays.

Within a year after the death of King László, armed irregular contingents of the First Crusade swept through Europe and, on their way to the East, massacred Jews wherever they encountered them—in France, Germany, Austria, Bohemia. Crossing the Hungarian border, they proceeded to attack the Jews and loot their houses as well as those of Christians, but King Kálmán (1095–1116) put up armed resistance and in a pitched battle almost annihilated them.

Although King Kálmán's purpose in preventing the Crusader incursion into Hungary was to protect the population of the country as a whole, his action did save the Jews of Hungary from the fate that befell their coreligionists in the neighboring countries. As a result, the reputation of Hungary as a country where Jews could live in safety spread abroad, and the events of 1096 were followed by an influx of Jewish refugees and migrants from the lands to the north and the west, where the Crusaders had annihilated entire Jewish communities. It would seem there was a connection between this Jewish influx into Hungary and the subsequent issuing of a series of anti-Jewish laws by King Kálmán.

However, the Jews were not the only non-Christian population in Hungary to feel the weight of Kálmán's restrictive laws. There lived in Hungary—especially in its southern parts—also Muslim Bulgarians, remnants of the preconquest population of the area. These Muslims, referred to in the Hungarian documents as Saracens or Ishmaelites, suffered increasing antagonism as a consequence of the intensification of religious fervor during the Crusades. The decisions of the Diet convened by Kálmán in 1101 imposed very strict restrictions on these Muslims, while the activities of Jews were subjected to relatively mild regulations.

First of all, King Kálmán's Decree, as it became known, reiterates the 1092 law of the Council of Szabolcs prohibiting Jews from owning Christian slaves. It sets a deadline for the Jews to sell their Christian slaves by, after which the slaves would simply be taken away from them. It goes on to state that "those of [the Jews] who are engaged in agriculture should have it done by pagan slaves. The Jews who wish to purchase landed property are allowed to acquire it, but they themselves can live only in places that are seats of bishops." It seems that the last provision remained a dead letter, because in the post-Kálmán period there were no Jewish residents in the episcopal cities of Hungary, while it was precisely the nonepiscopal cities of Buda and Pozsony that the largest Jewish communities developed.

About the same time, Kálmán issued his Jewish Law, whose seven articles contain additional restrictions on the Jews. Translated from the Latin, they read as follows:

1. From now on a Jew should not dare to purchase or sell a Christian slave of any language or nationality, nor to keep him in his service.
2. If a Christian wants to give to a Jew, or a Jew to a Christian, a loan worth two or three *pensas*, the lender should take from the borrower a guarantee, for which Christians and Jews should be called in as witnesses, so that in case one should deny that he got a loan from the other, this guarantee should be proved through the witnesses of both [parties].
3. And if one of them lends the other an amount greater than three *pensas*, this guarantee with witnesses should be executed as stated above. In addition, they should write down the amount of money and the names of the witnesses on a paper, which both parties, that is, the borrower and the lender, should affirm with their seals, so that in case one should want to commit violence against the other, the truth should be revealed through the writing and the seals of both.

42

4. If a Jew wants to buy something from a Christian, or a Christian from a Jew, he should buy the merchandise being sold before suitable Christian and Jewish witnesses; the merchandise itself and the names of the witnesses should be noted in writing. This writing, furnished with the seals of the seller and the buyer, should be kept by [the buyer] himself, so that if he should be accused of stealing in connection with this purchase, he should be able to produce the owner of the [allegedly] stolen property [the seller of the merchandise] found with him and the aforementioned witnesses, and be freed of the accusation.

5. If [the buyer] cannot locate the owner of the [allegedly] stolen property found in his possession, but can produce the writing confirmed with the seals, he will be freed by the oath of the witnesses [whose names are] contained in it.

6. And if [the Jew] has no Christian witnesses but can produce suitable Jewish witnesses, and he should be declared innocent through their oath, according to the law of the Jews, he should pay the price of the stolen property fourfold.

7. If he can produce neither the owner of the property found in his possession, nor the writing confirmed by seals, he should be sentenced according to the custom of the country, and should pay the price of the stolen property twelvefold.

The decisions of the 1101 Diet and the seven brief articles of Kálmán's Jewish Law afford quite some insight into the Jewish condition in eleventh-century Hungary. We learn that Jews could and did own landed property, as well as Christian and pagan slaves who worked their lands, as was also the case on the lands of Christian landowners. The Jews also lived in the cities, where they engaged in money lending and in buying and selling merchandise. In case of litigation arising from these transactions, the testimony of Jewish witnesses was admitted, provided they rendered an oath according to the laws of the Jews. Evidently, Jewish landowners, merchants, and moneylenders played an important role in the country's economy, making it necessary to issue special rulings covering their activities. Underlying all this was, of course, the principle that the Jews constituted a special, different population element whose rights and duties, and status in general, had to be regulated by special laws applicable only to them. (As we shall see, the principle or the feeling of Jewish otherness was to remain, despite all subsequent developments, a determining factor in Jewish-Christian relations in Hungary down to the end of the twentieth century.)

A comparison between Kálmán's anti-Jewish laws and contemporary laws of other countries shows that Kálmán's were somewhat more equitable for the Jewish party in litigations. However, the first of these seven laws was a severe economic restriction for the Jews. Since it prohibited them from owning Christian slaves of any nationality, the only way Jewish landowners could work their estates was by hiring slaves from Christian owners. Before the end of Kálmán's reign, in 1114, the Council of Esztergom closed even this loophole. It decreed that "the Jews should not dare to keep Christian male slaves or female slaves, whether as property, or for the purpose of selling them, or by hiring." Since by the early 1100s there were very few pagan slaves in Hungary and the only work force available for agricultural work consisted of Christian slaves, this law effectively cancelled out Kálmán's earlier law giving Jews permission to practice agriculture. As a consequence, the position of the Jews rapidly deteriorated, and they were forced to concentrate more and more on money lending, the one major avenue of earning a living still open for them.

It appears that this general prohibition did not apply to those few Jews who had achieved exceptionally high positions. Outstanding Jewish nobles and high officials were still able to own estates, as indicated by official Hungarian documents. Two of them, Count Teha and Count Henuk, we met in the previous chapter. A third, the Jew Scechtinus, had a *castellum* in Vasvár, but in 1276 King László IV presented it to somebody else. To this castle belonged the settlement later called Zsidófölde (Jew's land), which subsequently became a part of the city of Vasvár.

The word *Zsidó* (Jew) survived from this period as the name of dozens of localities, which in the opinion of Hungarian historical linguists testify to Jewish land ownership. Documents mention the existence next to Nyitra (today Nitra, Slovakia) of a *mons Iudaeorum* (Jews' mountain) in 1113, and others refer to a *castrum Iudaeorum* (Jews' castle) in 1247. There was also a Jews' castle in the south (Jdioara, Rumania), and there was even a noble clan called Zsidó, from which descended the family of the Counts Csáky.

For a century after the death of Kálmán, the Hungarian laws have nothing to say about the Jews. Kohn and others interpret this as indicating that no new restrictions were imposed on them during that period. The Jews reappear in the Golden Bull of King Endre II (1205–35), issued in 1222. Article 24 of that important document states that "[only] the nobles of our kingdom should be *comites camerarii* [chamber counts], mint officers, salt officers, tax officers; *Hysmaelites* [Ishmaelites, i.e., Muslims] and Jews should not be able to."

That this law was not obeyed becomes evident from a letter addressed by Pope Honorius III to King Endre in 1225, in which he sharply reproaches the king, rails bitterly against the cruelties and abuses of the Saracens, and complains that despite the clear prohibition of the canons and the Golden Bull, the Jews still fill state and other public positions. The situation is referred to again in an exchange of letters between Pope Gregory IX and Robert, Archbishop of Esztergom, in 1231. A year later,

King Endre issued his so-called Second Decretum, in which he repeated the exclusion of the Jews from public office. This decree, too, remained ineffective. The primate of Esztergom, following papal orders, therefore placed the king and the officers of the treasury under an interdict (1232). However, the document mentions only the abuses of the Saracens; not a word is said about the Jews. These, as well as other similar documents, point to a situation in which the Jews did not arouse antagonism, while the Muslims were considered by the Christians the major offenders.

To absolve himself from the ban, in 1233 King Endre entered into a compact with Jacob, bishop of Praeneste, the papal nuncio, in which he swore that the Jews and Saracens would under no conditions be allowed to fill public offices, such as those of the supervisor of salt and tax collector, not even as associates or agents of Christian officials. He repeated the prohibition barring Jews and Saracens from owning or employing Christian slaves, and stated that the officials of the realm would support in every respect the bishops in whose counties there were Jews, pagans, or Saracens. He decreed that those Jews and Saracens who lived in a legal or nonlegal marriage with Christians should be punished by confiscation of all their property and by being sold into eternal slavery to Christians. In addition, this compact contains for the first time in the history of Hungary a royal instruction that "the Jews and the Saracens or Ishmaelites, in order to be recognizable, would be distinguished from the Christians by certain badges" to be worn on their clothing. These provisions constituted a pronounced success for the anti-Jewish policy of Pope Gregory IX, who also prevailed upon the king of Aragon and the prince of Toulouse to proceed harshly against the Jews, and who in an encyclical demanded of the kings and the priesthood of England, France, Aragon, Castile, and Portugal that they burn the Talmud publicly.

As mentioned above, the very fact that the same anti-Jewish provisions were repeated again and again indicates that they were not carried out. The reason for this was not any special consideration for the Jews but the hard truth that economic interests were stronger than edicts, stronger even than oaths rendered by the king to the Church. The continued activity of Jews in legally prohibited areas is attested to by historical data showing that Jews were *monetarii*, officials in charge of the royal mint, and that they worked as tax collectors, *tributarii*, for the royal and ecclesiastical courts. That Jews were in charge of the royal mint as late as the reign of István V (1270–72) is proven by coins from that period, which are marked with Hebrew letters, possibly the initials of the mint chief's name. As for the taxes, until the end of the Arpadian period (ca. 1300), they were administered by Jews.

The Jews' relatively favorable position can also be deduced from a 1236 letter sent by Pope Gregory IX to the Abbot of Pannonhegy in Hungary. Some time earlier, the abbot had prevailed upon two Jews, Nevronius and Anselmus, "to convert from Jewish error to the true faith," promising to "supply them to the end of their lives with a certain sum of money annually as well as other incomes." While offering money to Jews to induce them to convert to Christianity was nothing unusual, the fact that this was done by the abbot nevertheless indicates that the position of the Jews in Hungary was good enough for them to be unwilling to renounce their religion without considerable financial gain. The reason the case of the two renegades came to the pope's attention was that the abbot did not live up to his promise, whereupon the two men appealed to the pope. In his letter, the pope reproaches the abbot and admonishes him "to provide for the two converts so generously that they should not regret their conversion to the Catholic faith."

Some Jews, as well as Muslims, who converted—either voluntarily, under pressure, or in order to obtain or retain a public office—still remained faithful to their old religion. It seems they did not hide their adherence to their ancestral faith too carefully, because the fact that they were "false Christians" was widely known and resented. King Béla IV (1235–70), when he confirmed the oath of his father, King Endre II, promised that he would "exterminate the false Christians with all [his] might." One of these false Christians was Chamber Count Samuel, who converted in order to retain his office but was found guilty of continued practice of his old religion and was sentenced to ecclesiastical punishment. Since Samuel refused to subject himself to the Church's penalty, Archbishop Robert of Esztergom put him under the ban, accusing him of continuing "to support and protect other false Christians similar to him." (As we shall see in chapter 12, exactly this behavior was exhibited in the fifteenth century by a much more famous Hungarian Jewish convert to Christianity, Emericus Fortunatus.)

While the case of Count Samuel indicates that Marranism—a way of life in which Judaism was kept secret—was not unknown among Hungarian Jews, there is also evidence of another medieval Jewish religious feature, messianic expectation, among the Jews of thirteenth-century Hungary. A Christian chronicler notes that when the Hungarian Jews learned about the approaching Mongol hordes, "many of the Jews began to exult, believing that their Messiah was coming and that their liberation was beginning in that year which was the year 1241 of the incarnation of the Lord." What actually happened instead was that the Mongols devastated Hungary, indiscriminately slaughtering about half of its population.

Once the Mongols withdrew, King Béla IV energetically took in hand the reconstruction of the country. One of his first steps was to mint new coins to replace the coinage looted by the invaders. Among the minters he employed there were relatively many Jews, who, following the custom of their predecessors, stamped the new copper coins with Hebrew letters, the initials either of their own names or of the places the mints were located.

King Béla's policy of reconstruction included attracting immigrants from other countries, and for this purpose he tried to make conditions in Hungary attractive for Jews. (One of the immigrants was a rich German Jew by the name of Henuk, whom we have already met.) To attract such Jewish immigrants, the king promulgated his own Jewish laws, taking them, with some changes, from those of Frederick II the Bellicose, issued in 1244. Béla's laws, issued on December 5, 1251, became of such importance for the position of the Jews in Hungary for many generations that they merit full presentation here. In my translation from the Latin, they read as follows:

Béla, by the grace of God king of Hungary, etc., to all believers in Christ, who will see this document, salvation in the Savior of all of us!

Wishing that men of all conditions living in our kingdom should partake of our grace and goodness, we granted to all Jews living in our kingdom the following rights, which should be preserved for them without any impairment.

1. First of all, we decided that in all matters of money, movable or real property, or criminal proceedings that concern a Jew's person or other affairs, a Christian alone should not engage in testifying against the Jew, but only a Christian together with a Jew—except if the facts of the case are so well known and clear that no doubt can be cast upon them and they need no kind of evidence. We wish that this equitable rule should be considered valid for all points in this letter patent.

2. If a Christian brings an action against a Jew, alleging that he has given him a pledge, and the Jews denies it, and if the Christian does not want to believe the simple word of the Jew, then the Jew, by rendering an oath as to the value of the object [allegedly] left as a pledge with him, should prove his assertion and should be relieved of the accusation.

3. If a Christian gives a pledge to a Jew and asserts that he pawned it with the Jew against a smaller amount than the one stated by the Jew then the Jew should render an oath with respect to the pawn given to him, and [the Christian] should pay him the amount he confirms with his oath.

4. If a Jew, without having witnesses, alleges that he gave a pledge to a Christian, and the latter denies it, then the Christian, through rendering an oath himself, should be relieved of the accusation.

5. A Jew can accept as pledges objects called by any name, without any investigation—except church garments, unless they are pawned by the superior of that church, as well as bloody and wet clothes, which he should accept under no condition.

6. If a Christian accuses a Jew that the pledge that was in the hands of the Jew had been stolen from him, the Jew should swear concerning that pledge that when he accepted the pawn he had no knowledge that it was stolen or robbed property. This oath should also include the amount against which the object in question was pawned, and after this proof the Christian should, without any curtailment, repay the debt against which the loan was given.

7. If the Jew, as a result of fire, or theft, or robbery, loses his things, and together with them also the pledges given to him—and this is certain —and if the Christian nevertheless sues the Jew, the Jew should be relieved through his own oath alone, unless the matter was evident and public knowledge, as stated above.

8. If a disagreement or a quarrel arises between Jews, the city judge should not dare to exercise judicial power over them, but the judgment will be pronounced either by us or by our chief chancellor. And if [the Jew] is accused of a capital crime, then the sentencing will be preserved solely to our royal person.

9. If a Christian inflicts a wound on any Jew, the culprit should pay us the penalty usual in our country, while to the wounded he should pay twelve marks silver and the expenses incurred by his treatment and medicaments.

10. If a Christian kills any Jew, he should suffer just punishment, and all his moveable and immovable property should pass to our treasury.

11. If a Christian beats any Jew, but so that he sheds no blood, he should pay us a penalty according to the custom of our country, and to the attacked four marks silver. And if he cannot come up with the money, let him suffer another penalty according to our discretion.

12. A Jew, wherever he goes in our country, should not be hindered, molested, or pestered by anybody. If he carries merchandise or other property for which custom duty is due, he should pay at every customhouse only that custom money which would be paid by any citizen of the city in which the Jew sojourns at that time.

13. If the Jews, following their custom, carry a deceased of theirs from one city to another, or from one province or one land to another, the toll collectors should not extort anything from them. And if any toll collector should extort anything from them, this crime should be punished as if it were robbing a corpse.

14. If somebody recklessly disturbs the schools [synagogues] of the Jews, he should pay the Jew judge one and one-half marks.

15. If a Jew is sentenced to paying a fine to his own judge, he should never pay him more than twelve denars.

16. If a Jew, upon being summoned by his own judge, does not appear the first and the second time, he should pay four denars to the judge for each time; and if he does not appear even upon the third summons, he should pay to the mentioned judge twenty-six denars.

17. If a Jew wounds another Jew, he should pay as a punishment one and one-half marks to his own judge.

18. Furthermore, we decree that a Jew is not obliged, because of a trifle, to swear on the book of Moses, which is called *rodale* [?], except if he is summoned before our majesty.

19. If a Jew was killed on the sly, so that his relatives cannot prove through witnesses who was the murderer, but after an investigation is carried out somebody is suspected, and they adduce just and likely reasons for this suspicion, such matters we want to be decided through duels.

20. If a Christian commits violence on any Jewish woman, let him suffer for it the just punishment, which should correspond to mutilation of the hand.

21. The Jew judge [see chapter 6] should not take before his court of justice any quarrel between Jews, unless he is called upon [by the Jews] in a complaint to do so.

22. If a Christian redeems his pledge from a Jew, but so that he does not defray the interest due for it, this, if not defrayed within a month, will also grow through interest.

23. We shall not take up quarters in the houses of Jews.

24. If a Jew lent money on an estate or a letter to the grandees of the country, and proves it with a due bill provided with a seal, we shall award the pawned estate to the Jew, shall protect it for him against all violence, and shall ensure that he enjoy the proceeds as long as no Christian presents himself to redeem the estate pawned in this manner. However, the Jew can exercise no authority whatsoever over the Christians living on such an estate.

25. If somebody, man or woman, kidnaps a Jewish child, the kidnapper should be sentenced like a thief.

26. If a Jew took a pledge from a Christian and has already kept it for a year, and the value of the pledge does not exceed the amount borrowed and the interest, let the Jew show the pledge to his own judge, and then he can sell it.

27. If the pledge has remained for a year beyond the stipulated time limit, without any notification, in the hand of the Jew, he is no longer responsible for it vis-à-vis anybody.

28. Nobody should dare to force a Jew to hand out a pledge on his holiday.

29. If the Christian takes away his pledge by force of arms from the Jew or commits violence in his house, he must be punished as severely as one who has damaged our royal treasury.

30. Against Jews, in lawsuits that arise between them, their judge can dispense justice only in front of their school [synagogue].

31. We furthermore decree that the judge of a city inhabited by Jews who does not want to proceed in their affairs in accordance with our letter patent, but would harm them despite the prevailing custom and the regulations of their rights valid until now, should, after he has been reported to us, be removed, and with our consent somebody else should be appointed in his place.

So that this decree of ours should gain validity for all times, we have issued the present letter confirmed with our double seal. Dated on the fifth of December, 1251, in the sixteenth year of our reign.

This important law was to remain the basis of Jewish rights in Hungary for several centuries. Just as it became the accepted practice of every king to confirm at his coronation the rights and privileges of the nobility, so he also confirmed the provisions concerning the Jews contained in this law. At the same time, Béla's law also affords insight into the life and occupations of the Jews in the country. First, it makes it appear that the major Jewish occupation was pawnbrokering and money lending on both small and large scales, followed in importance by itinerant peddling. Next, we learn from it that criminal acts, even felonies punishable by death, were committed by Jews, although it was extremely rare that Jews should commit violent crimes (see chapter 11). We gather that some Jews lived in places where there was no Jewish cemetery, from whence they had to transport their dead to other cities, counties, or lands. They had synagogues, called Jewish "schools" in the law, and had their own religious courts of law, whose functioning was assured and supported by the royal edict. They were religiously observant and did not work on the Jewish holidays, as can be concluded from article 28.

What article 5 of the law meant in practice is illustrated by a case recorded in 1263, in which a sacred object owned by a monastery was used as a pledge for a loan from a Jew to a nobleman. "Magister Wyd filius Pethed de genere Gutkeled," patron of the monastery of Csatár, took a loan from the Jewish pawnbroker Farkas of Vasvár, and as a security deposited with him a two-volume Bible that belonged to the monastery. In circumstances not explained, the Bible got lost, evidently after Farkas returned it into the hands of Wyd, and Wyd, to compensate the monastery for the loss of what must have been an extremely valuable item, gave it two of his estates. It was article 5 of Béla's Jewish law that enabled Wyd to give, and the Jew Farkas to accept, a sacred object from the monastery as a pledge.

Of special interest for conclusions about the demeanor and character of Hungarian Jews is article 19, which specifies that if a Jew was murdered and his relatives suspect a person of having committed the crime, and if investigation shows that the suspicion is well founded but no proof can be found, the issue should be decided by a duel. This law, too, is taken from Frederick's Jewish Law, but with a significant difference. Frederick's law—and following it also Moravian, Czech, and Polish laws—stipulates that in such a case the Jewish accuser should be represented by a duelist (*Nos Iudeis contra suspectum pugilem volumus exhiberi*). That the Jewish relative of the murdered man should himself fight a duel with the suspect could not be envisaged, for the simple reason that the old German law strictly prohibited Jews from carrying arms. As against this, Béla's law says, "such matters we want to be decided by a duel." Hungarian legal historians interpret this wording as indicating that in Hungary, in contrast to the other mentioned countries, the Jewish accuser could himself engage in a duel with the suspect. If correct, this interpretation would mean that Jews, or at least some Jews, did bear arms in Hungary, and that they were skilled enough in using them to trust their fighting ability to avenge the death of a kinsman in a duel with the suspected murderer. An actual case in which such a duel was expected to settle a lawsuit between Jews and their opponents was recorded around 1300 in Kőszeg. The duel was supposed to be fought by Jews and people of the village of Körmend. However, an agreement was reached, and the duel did not take place. The ability and willingness of Hungarian Jews to fight duels may have been a heritage from the days of old, when among the tribes that conquered Hungary there were Jewish Khazars and other Jewish fighting tribes. (As we shall see in chapter 30, Hungarian Jews had a proclivity for fighting duels in modern times as well.)

This detail apart, Béla's Jewish Law firmly established in Hungary the Austrian and German concept of the Jews, as servants of the royal chamber, being the property of the crown. This is evident especially in article 29, which states that a Christian who commits violence against a Jew should be punished severely, because by hurting the Jew, he has damaged the royal treasury. The same concept underlies the provisions of articles 9 through 11, which impose heavy fines, payable to the royal treasury, on criminals who kill, wound, or even beat up a Jew. While on the one hand, being "owned" by the king meant that the Jews had no civil liberties (of which very few were enjoyed even by Christian nonnoble Hungarians), on the other, Béla's law also endowed them with certain privileges otherwise enjoyed only by the nobility and some privileged cities.

Béla's law, issued in one single copy, was far from enjoying popular approval, and in some parts of the country local authorities even refused to acknowledge its authenticity. As a result, frequent disagreements arose between the cities and the Jews, who felt compelled to bring their grievances to the king's attention. In 1256, the king therefore had the letter patent reproduced in several authenticated copies, certified them by his royal seal, and issued them to the Jews "so that the content of this letter patent should everywhere find undoubted credence."

The activities of the Hungarian Jews as agents of the crown came to the attention of Pope Urban IV and provoked his ire. In 1262 he wrote to King Béla, sharply reproaching him for "giving opportunities to Jews, whom their own sin has condemned to eternal servitude, to exercise official authority over Christians." The papal admonition notwithstanding, Béla continued to lease to Jews his own revenues, as well as those of the state, and did so without even appointing Christian controllers to supervise them.

After the death of Béla, during the reign of István V (r. 1270–72) and the early years of László IV (r. 1272–79), the Jews enjoyed a relatively favorable position in Hungary. They functioned as tax renters and rent collectors for both the secular and the ecclesiastical grandees, headed the royal mint and had the Hebrew letters aleph and shin impressed on the coins they minted, and lived together with gentiles, often within one apartment. Their situation began to change for the worse with the 1279 Council of Buda.

In the second half of the thirteenth century, the Roman Church intensified its efforts to restrict the influence and position of the Jews in Hungary. Pope Nicholas III (r. 1277–80) dispatched Bishop Philip of Fermo to Hungary, ostensibly for the purpose of tightening the slackened Church discipline, but in actuality for the equally important task (from the Church's point of view) of depriving the Jews of their rights and privileges. In 1279 the bishop convened a church council in Buda that began to pass resolutions, some of which King László considered infringements upon the rights of the crown. This intensified the king's anti-Church attitude, and he ordered the judge and citizens of Buda not to sell victuals to the assembled priests and their servants, forcing them by this simple and nonviolent method to leave the city. Consequently, the council was unable to complete its agenda, and it disbanded in the very midst of its deliberations. However, before doing so, it summarily approved the remaining articles as drafted by Bishop Philip, among them article 125, which dealt with the Jews.

This article was so lengthy that it had to be divided into two sections, which read as follows:

Section 1. About the Badges to Be Worn by Jews on Their Breast.
    Since it is very dangerous and wholly in contrast to the sacred canons if the Jews, whom Christian love shelters and tolerates, are not distinguished from the Christians by certain signs and badges, if they live or sojourn together with the Christians in one family, or are present in the latters' courtyards and houses, or if Christians live together with them, we herewith resolve: in all those countries for which we have been appointed as legate of the Holy See, every Jew, man or woman, whenever he leaves his place of lodging or enters it, or appears in public in any manner, or shows himself, should wear as a distinguishing badge a red circle made of red cloth, which should be sewn on at their breast on the left side to that upper garment which they commonly and regularly wear over their other clothing. For the application of this badge a certain time limit is set, after the expiration of which it is no longer permitted to tolerate that Jews should walk among the Christians without this badge. As for the Christians who carry on commerce with Jews who walk without this badge, remain in familial or friendly relations with Jews, or only live in one courtyard or house with them, they are prohibited from entering a church. Whatever

has been decided concerning the Jews, we order it also concerning the Saracens, Ishmaelites, and all kinds of infidels, except that where the Jews wear a red circle as a badge, the others mentioned above must wear a yellow badge.

Section 2. Jews Should Not Collect Taxes.

This section prohibits the Jews, Saracens, Ishmaelites, and schismatics from being entrusted with collecting taxes and tolls and filling all kinds of public offices. It states that "Especially the chief priests should not dare to sell or transfer the revenues of their churches to such persons." It provides that all ecclesiastical persons of any rank, including bishops, who act against this prohibition should be suspended from their priestly office for three months; and if during that time they do not expel the unbelievers, or if they again take back those who were expelled, they should be excommunicated. "As for the laity, even those of the highest rank, if they should entrust Jews with these kinds of offices or retain them in their positions, will be instantly excommunicated and will remain under this ban as long as, after the removal and expulsion of the Jews and the other unbelievers, they do not supply satisfactory assurance that they will not relapse into this sin; thereupon the ban can be lifted."

Since the council had to disband before finishing its work, however, the resolutions were not properly publicized and had little effect. The king had neither sympathy for them nor interest in restricting the financial activities of the Jews. Only about a hundred years later did the provisions begin to penetrate the life of the country, and only then did the position of the Jews begin to deteriorate, and to resemble that of their coreligionists in other countries. Still, the 1279 Council of Buda can be considered the beginning of the legal deprivation of the Hungarian Jews of the rights enjoyed by the Christian inhabitants of the country.

5

Expulsion and Recall
(Fourteenth Century)

Until the Nazi Holocaust, which brought an entirely new and formerly unimaginable dimension of horror into the history of Jewish persecution, the fourteenth century counted as the darkest time in the history of European Jewry. In that century the Jews were cruelly persecuted in Austria and Bohemia, expelled from Styria and Carinthia (in 1312), and accused of desecration of the host (alleged profanation of the wafer consecrated in the Catholic ceremony of the Eucharist) and the murder of Christian children. More than 120 Jewish communities were destroyed by the Pastoreux in France and northern Spain in 1320; 5,000 Jews accused of well poisoning were burned to death in France in 1321; in Germany the so-called Jew-killers massacred Jews during the two years of 1336–37; and the Jewish community of Deggendorf in Bavaria was exterminated in 1337. This was followed by cruel persecutions of Jews in Austria, Moravia, and Bohemia. In 1348–49 Jews, accused of having caused the Black Death, were murdered all over Europe, from Spain to the very borders of Hungary. When the Flagellants went from city to city robbing and killing Jews, they managed to penetrate the northern borders of Hungary, but, receiving no encouragement from the local population, they soon moved on to Poland, where they brought horrible destruction to the Jews.

In the midst of this sea of murder and mayhem, Hungary was a haven of tranquility and security for Jews. As Samuel Kohn puts it in his flowery late-nineteenth-century Hungarian: "In this cruel age, all other countries were a desert for the Jews; but Hungary remained a gentle oasis, where peace, respite, and security smiled at the unhappy, who outside, in the great world, were persecuted and slaughtered like wild beasts."

Hungarian historical documents, perused and interpreted by Dr. Kohn with meticulous scholarship, serve as the basis of his characterization of the Hungarian conditions. From the first half of the fourteenth century, the Hungarian documents are silent about the Jews. While the

historical sources from other countries show that there they were frequently accused of all kinds of crimes and were oppressed, robbed,
murdered, and persecuted in many ways, Kohn takes the absence of any
reference to the Jews in Hungarian historical sources as proof that no
such things occurred in Hungary, that the Hungarian Jews were not
accused of group crimes as in other countries, nor did they serve as subjects of discriminatory legislation. When this historical silence is finally
broken, however, the documentary evidence enables the historian to
draw definite conclusions about the situation of the Jews up to the time
of the new regulations it contains.

Several of the documents pertain to the Jewish community of Pressburg, at the time one of the most populous in Hungary. From one of
them we learn that the Pressburg community built itself a new synagogue in the vicinity of the chapel of the Cistercian monks. The Cistercians appealed to Pope Benedict XII (r. 1334–42), complaining that the
noise made by the Jews in their synagogue disturbed their own devo-
tions. On November 13, 1335, the pope wrote to the archbishop of Esztergom, instructing him to have the synagogue in question demolished
and to have those who dared to object, if Christian, subjected to ecclesiastical punishment or, if Jewish, barred from all contact with Christians. It is not known whether or not these papal instructions were carried out, but they throw some light on the situation of the Jews in
Pressburg in the early 1300s. The Jews evidently could practice their
religion freely; they were able to build a new synagogue; they felt secure
enough to recite their liturgy so loudly that it could be heard in the
neighboring Cistercian monastery; and the Hungarian municipal or
other authorities were unwilling to interfere by ordering the synagogue
to be closed down, so that the Cistercians had to appeal to the pope.

It was under the reign of King Lajos I (r. 1343–82) that the situation
of the Jews in Hungary took a turn for the worse. This king, the second
Angevin ruler to reign in Hungary, surrounded the country with a ring
of dependencies, also acquired the throne of Poland (in 1370), consolidated the internal order in the country, broke the power of the rebellious
oligarchs, confirmed the liberties of the minor nobles, and regulated the
obligations of the peasants. Industry and the arts flourished under him,
the towns multiplied and grew, and the population reached some three
million. He was considered a just, pious, and chivalrous monarch, was
loved as well as feared, and earned the title Lajos the Great in Hungarian history.

Unfortunately for the Jews, the inclinations and policies of Lajos the
Great led him to embrace a more and more inimical attitude toward
them. In the early days of his reign, he showed no intolerance or antipa-

thy toward the Jews; in fact, he recognized and confirmed the loans the Jews had given to the magnates against pledges, and in 1345 he decreed that the Jews of Pressburg contribute to the fortification of the city and other public burdens in equal measure with the other citizens. However, after he completed his conquest of Serbia (1359) and forced its population to convert to Catholicism, he turned his attention to the Jews and pagans inside Hungary and tried to impose conversion upon them, too. As a result, many of the non-Catholics (especially those of the Mármaros district) either emigrated or rebelled against the forced conversions.

As for the Jews, they were servants of the royal chamber, and as such were subject to the direct jurisdiction of the king. At first, the king tried to persuade them to convert. He promised that if they converted, they would enjoy all the rights and freedoms of the Christian Hungarians, as well as full tax exemption. He repeated these offers several times, had the prelates of the Church preach to the Jews and exhort them to convert (in all probability, in accordance with medieval custom the Jews were forced to attend and listen to these preachments), but all these efforts were in vain. Thereupon, around 1360, as János Túróczi reports in his Latin chronicle, "Ludovicus [Lajos], in his religious zeal, wishing to convert the Jews to the Catholic faith and to win them for Christ, since he could not carry out this intention of his because of the Jews' headstrong stubbornness, liberated all the Jews in the whole kingdom of Hungary and ordered their expulsion. [However,] he did not wish to acquire or possess any of their goods and objects accumulated through voracious usury, which he despised like dirt. In this way, all of them left the kingdom of Hungary for Austria and Bohemia, where they continued to live dispersed."

The "liberation" of the Jews mentioned by the chronicler was a necessary preliminary to their expulsion: as long as they were servants of the Hungarian royal chamber, that is, property of the king, they were not allowed to leave the country; once they were "liberated" from this condition, their expulsion could take place, and rulers of other lands could take them in, acquire rights of possession over them, and give them their protection.

Most of the expelled Jews went to Austria and Moravia; those of Pressburg went to Haimburg (Hainburg, Austria), those of Sopron to Wiener Neustadt, and those of the northern and northeastern districts of Hungary to Poland, where Casimir the Great granted them a friendly reception. (Some twenty years later, King Lajos, who by that time was king of Poland as well, proceeded against the Jews of Poland in the same manner; however, there his decree of expulsion was not carried out.) Still, despite the religious zeal that made him deal harshly with the Jews, even while expelling them he touched neither their persons nor their movable property. This contrasts with the fate the Jews suffered in the same period in other countries, where they were imprisoned or even massacred, their property was either looted or given to the murderers by the king, and then the survivors were expelled. In Hungary, too, when the Jews were expelled, their landed properties were confiscated by the royal treasury and presented by the king to his favorites, to the cities, and most often to church prelates. Thus, in 1361 Lajos bestowed the new synagogue of the Pressburg Jews, built in 1336, to his physician. But—unusually, in the European context of the times—he enabled the Jews not only to take along all their movable property but also subsequently to submit claims for the loans they had made to Hungarians prior to their expulsion, and to recover them with the help of the Hungarian authorities.

A case in point is the controversy that developed with the Jews who found refuge in Haimburg after their expulsion from Pressburg. Soon after settling in Haimburg, they began to press their demand that the citizens of Pressburg who owed them money should repay their debts. The Pressburg debtors refused the demand, arguing that the expulsion of the Jews nullified all indebtedness to them. Probably because of royal intervention, the judge of Pressburg went to Haimburg, where he reached an agreement with the council and with Jew judge Nicolas Schickerlein to the effect that the Jewish lenders should within a year present their promissory notes to the Haimburg Jew judge and the judge of Pressburg and deposit the notes with the Haimburg judge until they were repaid (for a discussion of the position of Jew judge, see chapter 6). The city of Pressburg itself owed the Jews who found refuge in Haimburg 118 pounds, which sum it repaid them in 1364.

The debtors of Sopron resorted to a more successful strategy. They maintained their financial relations with the Jews expelled from the city, who found refuge in Austria and even obtained new loans from them. But as soon as the possibility of readmitting the Jews arose, they appealed to King Lajos, requesting that he annul the debts they owed the Jews. The king, wishing to show favor to the city, granted their request. At that point a serious difficulty arose. Since the king, when he expelled the Jews, released them from the status of servants of the royal chamber, the Jews who settled in Austria became the servants and subjects of the Austrian duke Rudolf, so that only he could dispose of the debts claimed by them. The king was forced to ask the duke to annul the debts the people of Sopron owed the Jews, which request the duke granted in 1365.

This is the only case known from the reign of Lajos the Great of *Tödtbrief*, or "letter killing," which had long been the practice of sovereigns in neighboring countries, especially in Germany. The term refers to the annulment, by the simple measure of issuing a decree, of all or part of the debts an individual or an entire city owed Jewish moneylenders. Such a decree in effect "killed" the promissory notes (referred to as "letters") held by the Jews. It would seem that Lajos refrained, with the exception of the aforementioned case, from utilizing this ultimate financial weapon sovereigns had against Jewish moneylenders lest it effectively discourage the Jews from practicing their "usury," without which the financial wheels of the realm would have ground to a halt.

The banishment of the Jews from Hungary by Lajos the Great was short lived: it lasted only four years, from 1360 to 1364. The Jews utilized the years of their exclusion from Hungary to engage in financial transactions in the countries that admitted them. That they were successful in this is evident from the fact that after they were allowed to return to Hungary, many of them preferred to stay on abroad in their new places of residence. Thus, we find quite a number of Hungarian Jews living in Vienna and in Wiener Neustadt from the fourteenth century on. Documents dating from 1374 to 1386 frequently mention the Jew Isaac of Ödenburg (called Ayzel or Ayzek in the documents) and his two sons, Schmerl and Eferl (also called Schmerlein and Eferlein in the German documents and Smerel and Ewal in the Latin ones), who had been expelled from Hungary, had settled in Wiener Neustadt, and there engaged in large-scale money lending. They issued a large loan to the city of Vienna, and a loan of twelve Viennese pounds to Hungarian borrowers, for which Count Nicholas of Nagymarton undertook the guarantee. Isaac also made a large loan available to the Hungarian landowner Péter Harkai, against a mortgage of part of his estates in Harka and Egred; the loan was redeemed in 1400 by the city of Sopron. Evidently, the expulsion of the Jews from Hungary did not prevent Hungarian borrowers from doing business with them.

The return of the exiles after four years gave rise to disagreements between them and the Christians who during their absence had taken possession of their houses. The Jews demanded back their properties; the Christians refused to give them up. Litigations ensued, some of which dragged on for years. One case took place in Sopron, where the city took possession of the house of the Jew Israel. When he returned, he wanted his house back, as provided by royal decree. The city refused. For three years no resolution could be reached, so in 1368 the city sent the city judge and a councilman to plead with King Lajos. The delegation managed to gain the ear of the king and the support of the very religious Queen Elisabeth, by stating that the city planned to build a chapel for St. George, to be financed by selling the houses formerly owned by Jews. The king postponed decision (he was busy at the time fighting the Orthodox Wallachian Voivod Vlajka), and the final outcome of the case is unknown.

A similar case occurred in Pressburg. A certain Nykus, son of the Jew judge Jakus, owed the Jews of Germany and Pressburg fifty-seven florins. Queen Elisabeth granted him an extension of the repayment date, but Nykus was unable to meet even the new date. Thereupon his real estate holdings were attached for the benefit of the creditors. In 1374 King Lajos issued a decree ordering Count Temlinus, the national Jew judge, as well as the city of Pressburg to return the attached property to Nykus, and ordering Nykus to repay the principal of his debt. The Jewish creditors were ordered to deposit the notes in their possession lest the compound interest grow. The king reserved for himself and "his baronial council" the decision concerning the interest to be paid by Nykus.

The Jews of Pressburg, when issuing a loan, used to stipulate that the repayment be in gold florins, even if the loan was issued in some other currency. Lajos found that this manner of repayment was too oppressive and in 1378 ordered the judge and council of the city of Pressburg to see to it that the Jews should thenceforward receive the repayment of the principal and the interest of a loan only in the currency in which they issued the loan. He simultaneously informed the Jews of this decision.

Although in Jewish-Christian business relations it was usually the Jew who was the creditor and the Christian the debtor, reverse transactions also took place. When Jewish merchants were in need of money, Christians lenders were willing to make loans available to them at the usual high rates of interest. The Jew Eysack obtained a loan from János, Count of Bazin, but when the time for repayment came, he was unable to come up with the full amount. Between 1376 and 1378, the count concluded a new agreement with him to the effect that Eysack would pay him eighty florins and remain indebted for forty florins. Eysack seems to have been domiciled in Pressburg, and Count János duly notified the city of the arrangement.

For a Jew to have money dealings with a magnate, a member of the high nobility, was often a risky business. The Hungarian magnates, many of whom had private militia or guards, could, whenever their interests so dictated, refuse repayment of loans from a Jew and harass him in various ways. In light of this, it is interesting to note that on more than one occasion, Hungarian cities—which were usually dominated by strong anti-Jewish sentiment—nevertheless extended their protection to Jews against harassment or violence by magnates or high officials. In 1384 the city of Pressburg submitted a complaint against the Hungarian count Szentgyörgyi and the Moravian margrave, who had captured and imprisoned a wealthy Pressburg Jew. In 1394, the Christian tax collector of Pressburg was arrested following a complaint against him by the Jews of Nagyszombat. The case was brought before King Sigismund, who ordered the city to appear before him within fifteen days for his decision. In another case, in 1413, a Jew, Baruch of Kőszeg, unhappy with the decision of the local court in a lawsuit against a Christian, Nicholas Matichprack, asked for a change in venue: he applied to the Sopron court to hear the case.

By the late fourteenth century, many Hungarian Jews felt that it would be unwise to keep all their capital in Hungary and hence made investments in real estate in nearby Vienna. At the same time, probably for similar reasons, several Jews sold the landed property they owned in Hungary. Three such sales, all of them of vineyards, are known from 1379 and 1417.

These few cases, whose documentation happened to survive, indicate that after their return to Hungary the Jews enjoyed a legally protected status and were able to continue their money business, their principal source of livelihood. They were able to sue powerful adversaries, such as magnates, high officials, and municipalities, apparently without fear of violent retribution, and were sure of due process behind which stood the supreme authority of the king.

Why did King Lajos, despite his religious fervor, readmit or recall to his realm the Jews who had refused to respond to his repeated appeals to convert to the faith that he sincerely believed to be the only true one? The evidence points to the increasing need the king felt for the services of the Jews in view of the financial disarray of the country and the growing Turkish threat on the southern borders of his dominions, which to resist he needed great amounts of money not available to him from any other source.

In any case, to be able to offer the Jews a safe niche within the social and economic structure of the country, the king created a new position: that of the national Jew judge, authorized to be in control of all the Jews, to see that they fulfilled their obligations—primarily tax payments to the crown—and also to make sure that they were protected in person and in property from the Church, the cities, and all other elements inimical to them.

6

The Jew Judge and the "Perfidious Jews" (Thirteenth to Fifteenth Centuries)

The position of the Jew judge (*judex Judeorum*) in Hungary goes back to the Jewish Law promulgated by King Béla IV in 1251, closely following the example set in the Jewish Law of 1244 issued by Duke Frederick the Bellicose of Austria. In King Béla's Jewish Law, references to a "Jew judge" occur in six articles (14, 15, 16, 17, 21, and 30), which specify the authority of the Jew judge and the judiciary tasks he was empowered to fulfill. From these articles it appears that Jew judges were appointed in the cities with sizeable Jewish populations, and their primary task was to adjudicate in litigations that arose between Jews and Christians. Secondarily, they supervised legal proceedings taking place between two Jews, in which cases the actual legal decision was in the hands of the Jewish law court, the *beth din*, as a rule consisting of three rabbinical experts in traditional Jewish law. Other tasks within the jurisdiction of the Jew judges included supervising of the tax payments the Jews, as servants of the royal chamber, were obliged to render the royal treasury, and seeing that they did not fall behind in their taxes. The Jew judges were always Christian noblemen of high standing whom the king appointed from among the leading citizens of the cities.

Building on this preexisting institution, Lajos the Great created a new office, that of the *judex Judeorum totius regni*, "judge of the Jews of the whole kingdom." The task of this high office, again always filled by a Christian nobleman, was to represent the king and act in his name in all matters pertaining to the Jews of the realm. As a result of the creation of this office, all the affairs of the Jews were centralized in the hands of one man. He spent most of his time at the royal court, but if an important case arose anywhere in the country, he traveled to the spot or sent one of his deputies to settle the matter.

Although the most frequent incidents brought to the attention of this new chief Jew judge were major disputes between a Jewish and a Christian party, he regulated and was in charge of all aspects of the relationship between Christians and Jews. He protected the rights of the Jews, saw to it that their legally approved demands were met with the help of the local judiciary, and ensured their timely payments of the taxes imposed on them by the crown. He settled the ever more frequent quarrels between Jews and city authorities. Much of his work concentrated on the cities, and especially on the privileged royal cities. This was because the primary locations where the Jews could settle were the royal cities, which were the property of the king, as were the Jews; in other cities, or on estates owned by the high nobility, Jews could settle only if the king endowed the city or the lord of the estate with a special privilege or a temporary permission "to keep Jews," which otherwise was the exclusive privilege of the king.

The first national Jew judge known by name was Master Simon, appointed in 1371. He was followed in 1376 by the national judge and lord chief treasurer, Jacob. In 1378, the chief Jew judge was Temlinus, Count of St. George; in 1381, Lord Chief Treasurer Miklós Zambó; from 1416 to 1431, Palatine Miklós Gara; in 1435, the chief treasurer Mihály Ország; in 1440, Palatine Lörincz Hédervári, who was probably the last of the national Jew judges.

Not all of these Jew judges performed their duties justly and equitably. When King Lajos the Great died and his widow Elisabeth ruled in the name of their minor daughter Maria, Miklós Zambó took advantage of the unsettled conditions in the country to enrich himself at the expense of the Jews whom he was supposed to protect. In 1383 he had several Jews arrested and maltreated, and their property confiscated. When upon her return from a royal visit to the restless provinces of Croatia and Dalmatia, Queen Elisabeth learned of this, she issued an order addressed "to her faithful Jews living in Buda, Pressburg, Sopron, Nagyszombat, Fehérvár, and other cities," in which she exempted them from the overlordship of Zambó until such time as he gave them satisfaction for the injuries and damages he had inflicted upon them.

One of the prerogatives of the national chief Jew judge was to appoint the Jew judges of the cities. Even as late as 1431, shortly before the abolishment of the chief Jew judge's office, Miklós Gara removed from office the Jew judge of the city of Sopron and appointed in his stead Miklós Kolcsa as "his Jew judge," to serve as long as Gara wished. Simultaneously, he called upon the city to support Kolcsa in his office and "to obey and submit to this Miklós in every permissible and honest affair exactly as to [himself]."

Since the chief Jew judge was an appointee of the king, his prime duty was to serve his lord and master by securing the undisturbed flow of taxes paid by the Jews to the royal treasury. In this work he often clashed with the cities, which were more interested in imposing local taxes on, and extracting them from, the Jews than in what they paid or did not pay to the royal treasury. Quite apart from this issue, the cities throughout the Middle Ages were focal points of anti-Jewish sentiment and agitation. The Jews, concentrated in the royal cities, were practically the only source of loans of which the citizens, whether artisans or merchants, as well as the nobles and the grandees were constantly in need. Also, the treasuries of the cities were in most cases empty, owing to either carelessness or unscrupulousness, and were frequently forced to obtain loans from the Jews. To secure loans from a Jewish moneylender, a city occasionally had to mortgage to him items as significant as a Christian chapel located within its boundaries. This situation obviously did not contribute to Jewish popularity.

Beyond this were the ethnic differences: most of the citizens in western Hungary, economically the most developed part of the country, were German ethnics whose attitude to the Jews reflected the typical and widely prevalent medieval German intolerance and Jew-hatred. Reviewing the anti-Jewish outbreaks that occurred from time to time, Samuel Kohn concludes that "without exception," bloody attacks against the Jews *"are encountered always only in such cities,* as for example in Pressburg, Nagyszombat, Bazin, and Buda, *where the German element preponderated"* (emphasis in the original).

In the cities, which experienced a marked development under Lajos the Great, the guilds, introduced from Germany, flourished, and they used their growing power to promulgate the kind of anti-Jewish laws and regulations that were in force in Germany and Austria. Thus, local laws came into being, restricting and humiliating the Jews and imposing on them onerous tax burdens they had to bear in addition to their taxes due the royal treasury.

Not infrequently, these local laws directly defied royal edicts. The law of Béla IV had prohibited the localities from imposing special road tolls on the Jews; nevertheless, the city of Sopron made the Jews pay a special toll of two denars, and in the Sopron County one public thoroughfare was called Jew Toll, demonstrating that there, too, the Jews had to pay a special toll. In the city of Sopron, the Jews were even deprived of the use of seals, with serious detrimental effects on the Jewish money business: a document written by Jews had legal force in proceedings against them, even without a seal, merely by strength of their signature, which was not always a reliable testimony.

The city elders of Pressburg were especially hard on the Jews. In addition to the Jew tax, the priestly tithe, and participation in all kinds of municipal expenses, they imposed on the Jews a special tax payable for the wine they prepared for use in religious rituals such as the Friday evening kiddush (sanctification) and the Passover "four cups." For several years after their return to Pressburg, the Jews paid this tax, but then they demurred. The judge and council of the city thereupon appealed to King Lajos, who in 1371 issued a decree "to all the faithful Jewry living the the city of Pressburg," in which he severely admonished them to continue paying the tax due for the wine they prepared. Foreign Jews who brought wine from abroad had to pay an even higher tax.

About the same time, the city of Pressburg passed a new municipal Jewish Law, which in general followed the state law promulgated by the Hungarian kings but which introduced a stricture in connection with the Jewish oath. The Jewish Law of King Béla had ruled that a Jew had to render an oath on the Torah scroll only in major legal cases, and only before the king himself or before his representative, the chancellor. In minor cases, following the custom of some German cities, the Jew was led to the synagogue, where he had to swear "on the ring," that is, the ring fastened to the front door, which had no other knob or handle. Now the new Jewish Law of Pressburg stipulated that the Jewish litigant render the oath on the Torah scroll before the municipal court as well. It also doubled the indemnity the Jewish lender had to pay the borrower if he lost the borrower's pledge.

Another disagreement between the city of Pressburg and its Jews developed around the slaughtering of animals. It was probably at the instigation of the butchers' guild that the city prohibited the Jews from slaughtering animals in the traditional manner and then selling to Christians those parts of the carcass that, according to the Halakha, Jews could not eat. In 1376 King Lajos sent chief Jew judge Jacob to Pressburg to mediate, and he worked out an agreement between the city and the Jews. Thenceforward, the Jews were allowed to slaughter animals for their own use, "but the rest of the meat, which they do not eat and do not use, they have to sell in their own houses or in front of their houses, but cannot sell it to butchers."

Another change introduced by Pressburg at this time was the substitution of the "Jew book," called in the Pressburg documents *registrum perversorum Judaeorum* (register of the perverse Jews), for the individual bills of debt in use up to that time. The "Jew book" was a thirteenth-century French invention that by the fourteenth century had also been introduced in many German and Austrian cities. It was a ledger in which all the details of loans from Jews to Christians were inscribed, and it was held in safekeeping by a Christian councilman, usually the Jew judge of the city. When an entry was made into the "Jew book," it was in the presence of a Christian and a Jewish juryman, who had to be present whenever the book was opened again. Against the contract as recorded in the book, there was no appeal. Among the particulars entered were the description of the pledge the borrower deposited with the Jew, the amount of the loan, and the interest payable for it. The interest, according to the Pressburg law, was 86¾ percent annually on amounts less than one pound, and 43⅓ annually on larger amounts, "not more." These exorbitant rates explain, on the one hand, how Jews could make a living and even amass capital from money lending and, on the other, why this business, in which the Jews were forced to concentrate, created so much resentment against them.

An important document relating to the position of the Jews in fourteenth-century Hungary was the *Law Book of Buda*. Even though this compendium of laws was completed only in 1421, it was in major part a product of the late 1300s. It was formulated largely after the example of the laws of German cities and is characterized by a strongly anti-Jewish tendency.

To make the Jews recognizable from afar, it prescribed that they must wear a tall, conical "Jewish hat," a red cape, and at a most conspicuous spot, over the breast, a large yellow patch at least a span in size. That the basic purpose of this costume was to humiliate the Jews is indicated by the fact that the same yellow patch was prescribed for prostitutes, and the tall hat also for witches and warlocks who, in punishment, were exhibited to the throngs at the Friday fairs wearing this headdress and sitting on ladders.

The *Law Book of Buda* severely limited the Jews' ability to sell merchandise: it states they may do so only once a week, and only in the Jewish street, in which by that time the Jews were concentrated. Should they venture among Christians, their merchandise will be impounded. All foreign merchants, and Christian merchants from outside Buda, are prohibited from doing business with them. Even the last resort of Jewish livelihood, money lending, is regulated and restricted. They must not accept as pledges church vessels, jewels, or clothes. Once a year they must present the notes of debt they hold to the city judge, who then notifies the debtors. If the Jewish pawnbroker does not obey this rule, his loan is forfeit. To obtain any official document, the Jews have to pay double the fee collected from a Christian. And they have to pay, as in Pressburg, a special tax for the wine they produce.

Hatred of the Jews and contempt for them are evident throughout the *Law Book of Buda*. The adjective *perfidious* appears as a veritable Homeric epithet always accompanying the noun *Jew*. Even when the collegiate church of Buda produces a document concerning the testimony in a private affair of a Jew of high standing, it refers to him as the *perfidus Judeus.* The *Law Book of Buda* calls the Jews "evil and villainous" and speaks of them in a rude, scurrilous tone, as if calculated to incite popular sentiment against them. For instance, the article speaking of the tax on the "Jew wine" begins: "The Jews, the despicable, hardnecked, stinking betrayers of God . . ."

This being the tone of the official documents, little wonder that the populace was not satisfied with the legal oppression of the Jews but sought, and frequently found, opportunities to attack them, rob them, and despoil them. Such attacks were only unwillingly and belatedly punished by the municipal judiciary, which occasionally did not dispense justice to the Jews even when royal edicts called upon it to do so. In Nagyszombat in 1340 a respected Jew was killed in his bed, and a major outbreak seems to have occurred there in 1391, the year called in an inscription on a tombstone "the year of wailing." In Pressburg, the Jews were frequently harassed on their holidays, especially Passover. Also in Pressburg, in the 1360s, during a conflagration a Christian citizen by the name of Kudleb broke into the burning house of the Jew Honel and, with the help of his brother, mother, and son-in-law, emptied it of everything they could carry away. They took the things into the house of Kudleb, thereby appropriating them. In addition, he forcibly placed Honel's wife under arrest. The Jew Honel sought justice from the Pressburg authorities but in vain, and even King Lajos's rescript to the city remained without effect. Finally, in 1371, the king dispatched one of the barons of the realm, Master Simon, the Jew judge at the time, together with Lord Chief Treasurer János, to investigate the case on the spot. When Kudleb and his relatives confessed, the two royal emissaries found grounds for Honel's complaints, and so reported to the king. Lajos consulted with the barons and prelates of the realm and sentenced Kudleb and his accomplices to imprisonment and satisfaction. Moreover, he instructed the city to carry out his sentence in the presence of the subprefect of County Pressburg, who was the local Jew judge, and an official to be delegated by the church chapter. Nevertheless, it seems that the city was tardy in obeying the royal decree, because some time later Honel had it officially copied and deposited the original with the church chapter "since, due to the dangers of the road, he did not dare to carry it with him."

The contemptuous tone and the anti-Jewish laws contained in the *Law Book of Buda* were to some extent mitigated by certain rights it accorded to the Jews. Thus, it prescribed capital punishment for the murder of a Jew. If somebody kills a person, it states, "he cannot say, 'He was only a Jew, or a heretic, or a pagan'; he who kills him is a murderer, and should be punished by beheading" (article 258). It permits the Jews to acquire landed property (article 62) and requires them "to work together with the Christians, and not to take usury from anybody" (article 192). "Usury" was, of course, the consistently used term for money lending with interest, and its prohibition was not taken seriously even by the *Law Book* itself, for, in sharp contrast to the severe punishments it provides for various other transgressions, it leaves usury unpunished, and only says that the usurer "will be responsible for it on the Day of Judgment." Evidently, while the *Law Book of Buda* wanted to go on record condemning usury as a forbidden and immoral practice, it was fully conscious of its indispensability in economic life and did not wish to make it impossible, or even too difficult, for the Jews to engage in it.

7

From Sigismund to Matthias (1385-1490)

Upon the death of King Lajos the Great in 1382, his minor daughter Maria was elected queen, and her mother Elisabeth reigned in her name. In 1385 Maria married Sigismund of Luxembourg, son of Holy Roman Emperor Charles IV. At first Sigismund ruled as his wife's consort and then, from her death to his own demise (1395-1435), as the sole ruler. In addition to the crown of Hungary, Sigismund also wore the crown of the Holy Roman Empire from 1410, and later from 1419 also that of Bohemia. The several realms over which he reigned required a dispersion of his attention, and in Hungarian history he went down as a monarch who neglected the country and allowed its national fortunes to decline. From Sigismund's point of view, Hungary was a frontier state, whose major role within the totality of his realms was to serve as a buffer and defense against the advancing Turkish power.

To be able to withstand the Turks and indulge in his wastefulness, what Sigismund needed above all was money. This basic need remained a constant throughout his long reign, forcing him to mortgage most of his castles and estates and to pawn thirteen towns in northern Hungary that were never redeemed. It also determined his policies with regard to the Hungarian Jews, whom he neither hated nor favored, neither consistently persecuted nor protected. He related to them neither with missionary zeal nor with compassion but considered them purely valuable goods and chattels from which he tried to squeeze as much money as possible. While this attitude placed a considerable burden on the Jews, it also enabled them to purchase from him justice, rights, and even privileges. Always acting in accordance with his financial interests, at times he smote them with one hand and protected them with the other.

One of the first acts of Sigismund as coruler of Hungary in 1385 was to assemble an army and eliminate his rival Charles II (the Little). He obtained the money needed for this purpose by mortgaging the district of Hungary lying between the Danube and the Vág rivers, which included the city of Pressburg, to the Moravian princes Yoza and Procop. The two princes sent the Moravian Jew Isaac to Pressburg to conclude the deal. This Isaac, it seems, also rented from the city its revenues, and before long the citizens of Pressburg owed him considerable amounts. Under pressure of the two princes, the city attached the properties of those of its citizens who did not defray their debts, and thus the new, turreted mansion of the heirs of a certain Jacob Richter became the property of the Jew Isaac. The city subsequently purchased the house from Isaac and made it into the city hall, which capacity it continued to serve down to the nineteenth century.

Early in his reign Sigismund began to practice "letter killing." In 1392 he exempted the citizens of Pressburg from paying interest on the loans they had obtained "from his Jews." He did this in response to the citizens' argument that their vineyards, for whose cultivation they used the loans, were stricken by frost. Once "letter killing" became the practice, Jewish moneylenders insisted, when giving a loan to a Christian, that he undertake not to apply to the king for such an annulment of his debt. A case in point is the 1440 letter of indebtedness by the city of Sopron in connection with a loan of 1,238 florins and eighty pennies from the Jew Frewdmann, containing their assurances that they will not resort to this step.

"Letter killing" did not, of course, redound to the financial advantage of the king, but it served to secure him the goodwill and support of the cities. The goodwill of the grandees of the realm was served by another type of decree issued by Sigismund, endowing them with the right, otherwise reserved to the king himself, of "keeping and owning Jews." A royal decree of 1393 endowed Miklós Gara, the *bán* (warden) of Macsó, and his brother János "with the free and unlimited power to admit Jews arriving from Germany, Bohemia, or from any place abroad, into their city of Kőszeg, in the County of Vas, settle them there, keep them and own them, preserve them in their religious and legal customs, tax them, and freely dispose of them. The lord chief treasurer, the treasurer, the Jew judges, and royal officials called by any name, cannot interfere in any manner in the affairs and doings of these Jews." A similar privilege was given to the Kanizsai family over the territory of Kismarton.

The oppression they suffered as a result of these privileges, which the municipalities and barons did not hestitate to abuse, prompted the Jews to engage in common action. The major Jewish communities of the country dispatched delegates to a conference for the purpose of deciding on an agenda, and to elect representatives to present their grievances and requests to the king. Thereafter, for more than a century, delegates of the communities met from time to time, elected spokesmen, and thus laid the foundations, if not of a countrywide Jewish organization, at least of common action in the court in the name of Hungarian Jewry. These conferences decided whom to send to the king, what to request of him, what amounts to offer to pay into the royal treasury or into the treasuries of the grandees, what presents to give the king on the occasion of his crowning or wedding, how to allocate the shares of these expenses among the communities, and the like.

One of the most important activities of this first countrywide Jewish conference was to seek reaffirmation of the old, almost entirely forgotten 1251 Jew Law of King Béla IV. The memory of that law survived among the Jews; they knew that it had granted them certain rights and privileges, but they had neither the original nor official copies of it in their possession and did not even know that it was issued by King Béla IV. They found out that an original copy of the document was kept in the archives of the Székesfehérvár (Stuhlweissenburg) church chapter and entrusted a Jew named Solomon who resided in that city to request that the king provide the Jews with an authorized copy of it. One can assume that Solomon's petition was not submitted without a suitable and sizable present accompanying it. In any case, the king consented and in 1396 instructed the chapter of Székesfehérvár to "search for and find the letter in question" and issue an authorized copy of it to Solomon and the other Jews living in the kingdom, "for the purpose of acquiring their rights."

The royal instructions were carried out, and King Béla's old letter of privilege again became the basis of the Jewish condition in Hungary, and remained so until the Mohács Disaster of 1526.

Not that the letter of privilege instantly became everywhere an instrument of protection for the Jews from the arbitrary treatment accorded them by the cities. On the contrary, at the 1405 Diet of Buda the king himself, in order to counterbalance the powers of the barons and to help the cities in their constantly dire financial situation, granted the cities independent legislative and punitive powers over all their inhabitants. This meant that the Jews, most of whom lived in cities, found themselves at the mercy of the municipalities, whose anti-Jewish stance by that time was traditional. Furthermore, in places where the Jewish community could not produce an authenticated copy of the 1251 privileges, the cities blithely ignored their existence.

In this situation the Jews felt that it was vital to have several official copies of the precious document. Delegates of the communities again convened, right after the 1405 Buda Diet, and resolved to obtain additional copies. In 1406, two Jews residing in Székesfehérvár, Saul of Buda and Saul of Pest, obtained authenticated copies from the chapter of the city, "for the greater security of the two Sauls and of the other Jews living in Hungary, and for the sake of truth." It might be mentioned here that a quarter of a century later, in 1431, a Jew by the name of Farkas (Wolf) appeared as the emissary of the Sopron Jewish community before King Sigismund, who, at his request, had the document copied and authenticated with his seal. One copy was deposited in the Buda archives, the others handed to the Jews.

The significance of the wide availability of this old letter of privilege was that, in accordance with its provisions, the Jews were subject not to the jurisdiction and power of the cities but directly to the king or his appointed representative. This meant that local laws and statutes aimed at narrowing the rights of the citizens had no legal consequences as far as Jews were concerned. Concurrently, the position of the national Jew judge, which in consequence of the growing power of the cities either had ceased to exist or had lost much of its significance in the preceding decades, was resuscitated. From 1416 to 1431 Palatine Miklós Gara filled the post, and his energetic representation of the royal interests exerted considerable influence on the affairs of the Jews. He collected the taxes due the treasury from the Jews either directly, through his officials, or through the intermediary of the Jewish communities in the cities, and effectively protected the Jews against the abuses of the local authorities.

In 1416, Anna, wife of Palatine Miklós Gara, and his son, Miklós, Jr., dispatched to Sopron a representative of theirs, a Jew, to supervise the collection of taxes from the Jews. They furnished their Jewish bailiff with a letter in which they called upon the city to proceed with the collection of Christmas taxes according to his instructions. In general, Gara's attitude to the Jews was typical of those who wielded power over them: on the one hand protecting them, on the other taxing them ruthlessly. In his rescript to Sopron, Gara ordered the city not to abridge the privileges of the Jews and made the city responsible for the taxes payable by them, which of course meant that the city had to make sure that the royal taxes were duly collected from the Jews.

Typical of the manner in which the Jew judge protected the Jews is another rescript Gara sent to the city of Sopron in 1421. In it he wrote: "We beg you in a friendly and urgent manner that you should keep and preserve uncurtailed and undisturbed all the Jews living among you in their old privileges, as well as in those you can read in the letter patent the august prince King Sigismund gracefully granted them."

On more than one occasion the king himself took a hand in regulating the affairs of the Jews. In the year 1421 alone, several cases occurred in which the cities of Pressburg and Csanád denied due juridical process to foreign Jews who tried to pursue claims against local citizens. The cities' position was that, being foreigners, the Jews' demands could not be handled by the local Jew judge. The Jewish claimants found a way to appeal to the crown, and Sigismund issued separate rescripts to the two cities, instructing them to assist the Jews in the satisfaction of their demands.

The result of these developments was that the Jews living in the Hungarian cities constituted a special class, over whom not the cities but the crown had jurisdiction and who, while heavily taxed, were protected by the royal power. Comparing the position of the Jews in Hungary with that of Jews in the neighboring countries, even those over which Sigismund himself held sway, we find that in Hungary they were definitely better off. In the other countries, atrocities against the Jews occurred from time to time; they were expelled from several cities, imprisoned, forced to convert to Christianity, or burned at the stake, and the indebtedness of the Christians to Jewish moneylenders was summarily annulled. Sigismund himself found ingenious ways to rob the Jews of German cities—Znaim (Moravia), Cologne, Frankfurt—of huge sums, leaving them virtually destitute. These were the times when Jewish chronicles spoke of Austria as "the bloody country" and the "accursed country." In contrast, Hungary under Sigismund was a country in which the Jews could live, not precisely comfortably, but in satisfactory safety of their property and persons. As a result of this difference, Jews from neighboring lands, especially Bavaria and Austria, sought refuge in Hungary, where, as the Sopron and Csanád cases mentioned above show, they found legal protection.

Thanks to the chance preservation of a contemporary document, we know that even Jews from France settled in Hungary in this period. When the Jews were expelled from France in 1394, some of them went to Germany, where they were treated so cruelly that many thought they would fare better in Austria. As a consequence of the 1420 general persecution of the Jews in Austria, some of these then crossed the border into Hungary, where Bertrandon de la Broquinière, first *écuyer tranchant* (meat cutter and server) of Philip II (le Bon), duke of Burgundy, encountered them on his way back from Palestine. As he writes in the narrative of his voyage to the Holy Land, to his great surprise "he found [in Hungary] many Jews who spoke French very well, and who got here from among those expelled from France."

Toward the end of Sigismund's reign, the Jews of Hungary succeeded in obtaining from him a complete renewal, reaffirmation, and extension of their old privileges. Circumstances indicate that the Jews obtained these favors by paying huge sums into the royal treasury. In 1436 Sigismund went to Székesfehérvár to conclude a peace treaty with Bohemia, and on that occasion he distributed 60,000 gold florins among the Bohemian envoys who had come to the city. Then he proceeded to Prague, where he issued two letters patent. One was addressed to Bohemian Christian debtors and exempted them in all Bohemia from paying any interest they owed Jewish moneylenders. The other, issued to the Hungarian Jews, had the purpose of "remaining for all times valid for all Hungarian Jews and their heirs and descendants." The simultanous issuing of these two letters patent, the one causing great financial losses to Bohemian Jews, the other granting new privileges to Hungarian Jews, indicates that the latter must have paid dearly for theirs. The Hungarian document was handed to two Jewish representatives, one from Pressburg named Jacob and one from Buda named Nyúl (Hungarian for "rabbit"), who seem to have traveled to Prague for that specific purpose.

The new privileges granted by Sigismund are contained in five articles. The first instructs the Jew judges that they could transact legal proceedings arising between Jews, and pass sentence on them, only together with Jewish jurymen, that is, rabbis and aldermen. This article is a clearer formulation of article 30 in the letter patent of Béla IV presented above (chapter 4). It renders the Jews in litigations among themselves totally independent of the municipal authorities, and it restricts the role of the Jew judge to being present and witnessing the proceedings conducted by Jewish religious judges.

The second article imposes new duties upon the Jews. It obliges the Jews to pay the usual taxes to the royal treasury. Since previously the king had granted jurisdiction over the Jews to the grandees of the realm, so that the grandees had the right to extract from "their" Jews any taxes they wished, the Jews living on the estates of the grandees were now burdened by double taxation. It is likely that this decree was motivated by the king's wish to induce the Jews to live in the royal cities rather than on the estates of the quasi-independent grandees. The fact is that after this letter patent was issued, the Jews concentrated more and more in the cities, in turn bringing about an intensification of their religious life and the begininng of the production of halakhic writings by Hungarian Jews.

The third article prohibits the tax and toll collectors from exacting any payment from the Jews when they transport the body of a deceased from one locality to another. This again repeats a provision contained in the letter patent of Béla IV, which seems to have become necessary because of the increasing concentration of the Jews in a few major cities, which ruthlessly extracted exorbitant payments from those Jews who had to bring their dead there since no Jewish cemeteries existed in the small places where they lived.

The fourth article provides that "if a Christian, following a loan of money, gives a pledge to a Jew without any [specific] agreement, or if he, without such an agreement, takes from a Jew a loan with interest in some other manner, in that case the Christian has to pay the Jew an interest of two denars weekly for every hundred denars." What is significant in this article is that it raises the officially chargeable interest rate to around one hundred percent annually, double what the 1376 local laws of the city of Pressburg permitted as the highest interest rate. One can conclude from this raising of the interest rate that the economic situation in the country had deteriorated and the dearth of money worsened.

Finally, the fifth article prohibits the imposition of higher taxes upon the Jews than upon the Christian inhabitants of the city or estate where they lived. While this provision protected the Jews against discrimination by the municipalities and barons, at the same time it made the Jews better able to pay the additional taxes imposed on them by the crown.

A few concrete case histories have survived from the days of Sigismund to show his conduct in relation to the Jews. About 1424 he decided to build a church dedicated to St. Sigismund in the immediate vicinity of the royal palace in Buda, together with a residence for the provost and other appurtenant ecclesiastical buildings. The available area on the narrow Castle Hill was limited, and the most suitable location was on the Jewish street, one end of which adjoined the palace. Several houses on the street had been confiscated from their Jewish owners when they were expelled by Béla IV and still belonged to the crown or the Church. Also, the lots and houses required to be demolished could be acquired most easily from the Jews, who were not in a position to refuse any purchase offer. The church and attached ecclesiastical buildings were actually erected right outside the royal palace on the Jewish street, which was renamed St. Sigismund Street, though the designation "the old Jewish street" also remained in use.

The Jews who had to move out of their houses were given accommodation next to another Jewish street, which was located to the north of the palace. Two of the houses the king gave them he had purchased from their Christian owner, János Kapy, to whom he promised payment. This promise remained unfulfilled at the time of King Sigismund's death in 1437, whereupon Kapy instituted proceedings against the Jews demanding the return of his houses, arguing that he had received no compensation whatsoever for them. The Jews, who by that time had lived for some thirteen years in the houses in question, countered that the houses had been given to them by the king and were thus their legal property. The lawsuit dragged on for years, and the last we hear about it is in 1440, when it was under advisement by Lőrincz Héd-erváry, the national Jew judge. His decision is not known. However, the fact that such litigation was handled by the highest royal authority in the country indicates that, within the limits set by the various letters patent, the Jews did enjoy protection under the law.

With the death of Sigismund, all the rights and privileges he had granted the Jew became null and void, in accordance with the generally prevalent view in medieval Europe. Since the Jews were the property of the king, they were inherited by his successor, who, as German law put it, "on the occasion of his coronation could take away the property and the livelihood of all the Jews dwelling in the country." This view gained ground in Hungary as well, and consequently, until the Mohács Disaster, every king with the exception of László V reaffirmed the Jewish Law issued by Béla IV and renewed by Sigismund. The interval between the death of the old king and the reaffirmation by his successor of the Jewish Law was a dangerous time for Jewish communities: their temporarily unprotected status was in many cases exploited by the omnipresent anti-Jewish elements who harassed and attacked them. Nor could the Jews foretell the attitude of the new ruler toward them, or whether they would be financially strong enough to satisfy his demands and thus secure his protection.

After Sigismund, Albert II of Habsburg reigned over Hungary for the short period of two years (1437–39). Like his long-lived predecessor, Albert also accorded the Hungarian Jews much better treatment than the Jews of Austria and Germany, who were subject to him in his capacity as duke of Austria (Albert V, 1404–39), king of Bohemia (1438–39), and king of Germany (1438–39). Under his rule, the Jews of Vienna were accused in 1420 of having killed three Christian children, whereupon 300 Jews were burned to death before the bodies of the children, who had drowned in the river, were found. About the same time in Enns, Austria, the Jews were accused of having desecrated the host, whereupon Albert imprisoned all the Jews of the city and sentenced them to burning. While in prison, many Jews killed one another in order to escape the painful death of being burned alive, and others converted to Christianity. One hundred ten Jewish men and women were burned at the stake and their children placed into monasteries, where they were brought up as Christians. On that occasion Albert expelled all the Jews from Austria and confiscated their property. In Germany as a rule he approved the cruelties committed toward the Jews. As an Austrian chronicler wrote about him, "raging against the Jews, he commanded that all of them who were under his rule and did not want to accept Christ, the true and only God, should be killed." Yet this same monarch manifested no enmity toward the Jews of Hungary. More than that, on the occasion of his coronation as king of Hungary at Székesfehérvár in 1438, he reconfirmed the privileges granted them by Béla IV and Sigismund. In fact, two Jews representing the Jews of Hungary were present: they were Jacobus parvus (Little Jacob) from Buda and another Jacob from Pressburg.

It is tempting to speculate about what produced the lenient attitude of both Sigismund and Albert toward the Jews of Hungary, in such sharp contrast with the cruelty they exhibited toward their Jewish subjects in the other countries under their rule. One cannot assume that they had greater sympathy for Hungarian than for Austrian or German Jews. The difference must have hinged on some experience the monarchs had in Hungary that convinced them that there they could obtain greater financial advantages from the Jews by enabling them to live peacefully (although by no means in comfortable circumstances) without persecution by either the authorities or the people. Perhaps relative to their number the Jews contributed more to the royal treasure in Hungary than in the neighboring countries, and the kings knew that any bodily or financial harm to them would diminish their ability to maintain the flow of taxes. In this direction points the fact that within four years after he expelled them, King Béla IV had recalled the Jews: evidently this short period was sufficient to make him aware that without the Jews, the money economy of the country and the treasury revenues suffered a serious decline. (Perhaps it is in this factor that we must seek the source of the less inimical treatment also accorded the Hungarian Jews by the monarchs who succeeded him, who suffered from a chronic shortage of money.) It is known that in the mid-fifteenth century the special taxes imposed on the Jews of Hungary amounted to 4,000 gold florins annually, while at that time the total royal revenues stood at no more than 25,000 florins. That is to say, a considerable part of the budget of the crown came from the Jews, without even counting the special levies the king could, whenever he so wished, impose upon the Jews, who, in contrast to other sources of royal revenues, had no effective ways of resisting or protesting such impositions.

As far as King Albert as concerned, his unwillingness to persecute the Hungarian Jews did not extend to a protection of their monetary interests. Like his predecessors, he frequently made use of his powers to dispose of the property of the Jews. Two cases happen to be known from his short reign in which he "forgave," that is, annulled, the interest Christians owed to Jewish moneylenders. Many others probably occurred.

Albert also frustrated the efforts of Jews who tried to prevent the conversion to Christianity of individuals within their community who were inclined to do so or who actually converted. It is during his reign that we hear for the first time in the history of Hungarian Jews of cases of conversion in which royal protection was accorded to the converts. A Jewish youngster named Salman, probably a minor, wanted to convert to Christianity and, at the demand of his father, Mertlein, was arrested by the Jew judge of Pressburg, Gaspar Ventur. Mertlein made it known that he objected to his son's conversion and threatened to disinherit him if he should persist in his plan. The case was brought to the attention of Albert, who in 1438 instructed the city to protect the youth and to see to it that he receive his due share of his father's inheritance.

A similar intervention was made by Queen Elisabeth, Albert's wife, while the king was in southern Hungary engaged in fighting the Turks. A Jew living in Molk, Master Paul by name, converted to Christianity, whereupon his sister with her children escaped to Pressburg to avoid being forced to follow him into his new faith. Paul demanded of the city of Pressburg that it deliver his sister and her children to him, arguing that he was their guardian. The city seems to have been reluctant, whereupon Paul appealed to the queen, who ordered the city to hand over the woman and children to Paul.

A third case of conversion in the same period is known, not from Hungarian official sources, as the former two, but from the Hebrew responsa decisions of R. Israel Isserlein (1390–1460), the foremost rabbi of Germany in the fifteenth century, who from 1445 to his death was rabbi of Wiener Neustadt. A renegade Jew who had lived for some time in Pressburg proceeded to Buda and there, hiding the fact of his conversion, married a Jewish woman. According to witnesses who came forward subsequently, this man, without properly returning to Judaism, converted twice to Christianity, "in the manner of those good-for-nothing vagabonds who convert to Christianity, from time to time return and declare themselves Jews, and from time to time declare themselves Christians." Such conversion, as we have seen above, may have been induced by Christian churchmen's offers of monetary rewards to converts.

After the death of Albert in 1439, his widow, Queen Elisabeth, intensified his policy of squeezing as much money as possible out of the Jews and resorted to some measures that amounted to outright confiscation of property. In her struggle for succession with Polish king Vladislav (in Hungarian Ulászló), who was elected king of Hungary by the estates in Buda, she tried to gain the support of the cities. In 1440, she had her infant son László, born after the death of Albert and hence known as

Posthumus, crowned king in Székesfehérvár and then went on to Győr, where she issued a decree to the Jews of Pressburg ordering them to pay, for one full year from that date, all the taxes they owed the royal treasury not to the treasury but instead to the city of Pressburg. The reason she gave for this royal generosity was that she wished to help the city strengthen its fortifications and maintain what today we would call its infrastructure. A year later she extended this royal gift for ten more years. From that time, the municipal ledgers of Pressburg contained a recurring item called *Judengeld* (Jew money) or *Schutzgeld* (protection money). In the same year, the queen relieved the citizens of Pressburg of repaying all the loans they had borrowed from the Jews and canceled all the privileges of the local Jews, including the office of the Jew judge. This measure subjected the Jews totally to the municipal authorities.

The queen proceeded in a similar manner in Sopron, where she took the infant László when she felt that Győr did not offer sufficient security. To improve the city's fortifications, she had the houses skirting the city walls demolished and indemnified the Christian citizens who had lived in them by simply presenting them with the houses of the Jews located in the inner city. She justified this confiscation by stating that "the divine law commands that the adherents of the true Christian faith must be valued more highly than the Jews and the infidels, so that the faith should in this manner bring its generous reward." She also exempted the citizens whose houses were demolished from repaying the mortgages they owed the Jews, and restricted the right of the Jews to live in the city to four houses.

It so happened that the city was unable to enjoy all this royal bounty, for within a few months it came under the control of her late husband's cousin, Duke Frederick of Austria (Frederick IV, king of Germany, later Holy Roman emperor as Frederick III), to whom Queen Elisabeth pledged the city of Pressburg against money she needed to be able to pursue her war against Ulászló. Frederick, evidently acting upon the request of the Sopron Jews, annulled Elisabeth's decree, ordered the city of Sopron to leave in the hands of the Jews their synagogue and their sixteen houses in the Jewish street, to pay the loans plus the interest owed the Jews by the citizens, and to leave them undisturbed in the pursuit of their occupations.

Ulászló, the rival king of Elisabeth's son, treated the Jews in much the same manner. Both parties in the civil war they conducted were in dire need of money, and the Jews were fair game for royally ordered extortions from both sides. The Diet of Buda, convening in 1444, soon after the death of Elisabeth, was scandalized by what they considered irresponsible royal largess and the consequent diminution of the revenues of the royal treasury. It passed a resolution invalidating all the royal gifts and mortgages and strictly prohibited the giving away of revenues accruing to the treasury from taxes paid by the Jews. However, this resolution remained a dead letter. Soon after the Buda Diet, King Ulászló was killed in the Battle of Varna, and the throne was inherited by the child László (Ladislas) V Posthumus, who was under the guardianship of Frederick. In the absence of the young king, the Diet of 1446 elected János Hunyadi, commander of the late Ulászló's troops, as governor of the country. Hunyadi soon established himself as legitimate regent for the young king and thus the actual head of state.

The cities took advantage of the interregnum to increase financial pressure on the Jews, whose situation became almost intolerable. In Pressburg, for instance, in order to extort the exorbitant taxes imposed on the Jews, several of them were thrown in jail in chains. The Jews, invoking the letter patent of Béla IV, which was reaffirmed by several kings, applied to János Hunyadi for protection. Responding to their request, Hunyadi in 1447 instructed the city of Pressburg not to impose any kind of taxes upon the Jews in violation of their old privileges, not to inflict damage on their person or property, and to release unharmed those who had been imprisoned. Should the city have any complaint against the Jews, its representatives could appear before him in the company of two Jewish leaders, and he would justly adjudicate the disagreement.

Occasionally Hunyadi extended his protection to individual Jews as well, for example, to Myssel of Nagyszombat (Trnava) against harassment by the city of Pressburg. On the other hand, circumstances also made him dependent on the goodwill of the cities, forcing him to favor them against the interests of the Jews. Thus the city of Pressburg supported him in his unsuccessful war against the Turks in 1448 by supplying him with arms and men. In the next year, when Hunyadi needed assistance in the war he planned against the Czechs, he acted contrary to the resolutions of the Buda Diet, and not only reaffirmed Queen Elisabeth's gift of the Jewish taxes to the city of Pressburg for ten years but extended it. The language in which this document refers to the Jews is characteristic of their position as servants (almost chattels) of the crown, in this case embodied in the person of the regent. Hunyadi writes that he "donated the local Jews, together with the sundry taxes and revenues payable by them," to the city of Pressburg for two additional years, and sternly ordered the Jews to pay the city the taxes punctually and to obey it in every respect.

This decree did not in itself place a greater financial burden on the Jews, for whom it made little difference whether they paid the taxes to the royal treasury or to the city of Pressburg. However, the very next year Hunyadi went a decisive step further and concluded that since the city of Pressburg had become the owner of the Jews, its municipality and citizens did not have to repay loans or other debts they owed the Jews, and he declared all the demands of the Jews null and void. Since much of the arms and units the cities supplied to Hunyadi's army had been financed by loans from the Jews, the annulment of these loans meant that in effect it was Jewish money that had paid to assemble that armed force. For the Jews, of course, this was a near-catastrophic financial loss.

Nevertheless they managed to continue their money business, as can be concluded from events of the subsequent three years. In 1452 Hunyadi resigned as regent, and in 1453 László V proceeded from Vienna to Pressburg to take over the helm of the ship of state. Among his first acts as reigning king were two apparently contradictory decrees. First, to reward the citizens of Pressburg for their faithful support, to enable them to receive the sovereign with due pomp and circumstance when he first set foot in his realm, and to help them in their dire financial straits, on February 6, 1453, László remitted all interest the Christian debtors of Pressburg owed the Jews, on condition that the principal of the debts be paid back by the next St. John's Day. Subsequently he modified this decree to the effect that by that date they had to repay only half of the principal, while the repayment of the other half he postponed until the next St. Martin's Day. These documents show that within an astonishingly short time after the loss of all their loans the Jews of Pressburg were again in a position to grant substantial loans.

The second decree issued by László, on either February 6 or 7, also in Pressburg, seems at first glance a direct contradiction of the first. At the request of two Jews of Buda, Farkas and Mayor (or Mayer), as the representatives of all the Jews of Hungary, the king, with the knowledge and consent of the magnates of the country, reaffirmed the Jewish Law of Béla IV, together with the favorable additions of King Sigismund. The contradiction between the two decrees, however, is only apparent. Both letters patent are based on the principle that the king, as owner of the Jews, is free to dispose of their property, including their monetary demands on non-Jews. Hence, he can, as he wishes, confirm their rights and privileges, or annul them, or even present their persons and property to somebody else, if that is what his interests dictate.

In this situation it becomes increasingly clear that the Jews enjoyed peace and security only as long as that served the interests of the king. If a situation arose in which the king found harshness toward the Jews to be in his interests, he did not hesitate to act against them. Thus, for example, still in 1453, as a sign of his special grace (*ex gratia speciali*) László V forgave all the interests (*universam usuram*) owed the Jewish moneylenders by the citizens of Nagyszombat, the nuns of the local Virgin Mary nunnery, and the inhabitants of the four villages that belonged to the city.

Apart from frequent financial harassment—most common in times of war, when extraordinary expenses necessitated the tightening of the financial screws—the Jews of Hungary lived in relative peace and safety under László V; that is to say, their persons and property were secure. This situation is again remarkable in its contrast with the cruel persecutions of the Jews that not only were daily occurrences in the other countries of László but took place with his consent. And it is doubly remarkable in view of the fact that during his reign there took place the violent anti-Jewish agitation of the Franciscan friar John Capistrano, who earned the appellation "scourge of the Jews" and whose activities resulted in anti-Jewish restrictions, abrogations of Jewish privileges, introduction of the Jewish badge, cancellation of debts Christians owed Jews, and anti-Jewish violence in Poland; burning of forty-one Jews in Breslau; and other cruelties against them in Bavaria, Austria, Moravia, and Bohemia. King László himself, after the Breslau atrocity, expressed his thanks to that city and openly shared with Breslau and six other Silesian cities the properties of the murdered or expelled Jews. In addition, he banished the Jews for all time from several Silesian and Moravian cities, stating that he did it "for the glorification of God and the honor of Christianity." And yet, when John Capistrano, with the fanatical mob that followed him, passed through Hungary, where he went from town to town and village to village, preaching a crusade against the unbelievers (the Turks threatening Hungary from the south), this same King László evidently made Capistrano understand that no anti-Jewish excesses would be tolerated in this country, for the fact is that the friar's agitation in Hungary was not accompanied by any anti-Jewish act that left its traces behind.

In 1458 Matthias Corvinus (r. 1458–90) became king of Hungary. Remembered in Hungarian history as the country's great Renaissance king, he had an ambivalent attitude toward the Jews. On the one hand, he instituted the office of the Jewish prefect, which was of great importance in the life of the Hungarian Jews for more than half a century (see chapter 8); on the other, he increased their tax burden ruthlessly, and he resorted to "letter killing" more frequently than any of his predecessors. He reduced, or annulled, the cities' indebtedness to Jewish moneylenders many times (e.g., in 1462, 1467, 1475, and 1486), and furthermore in 1475 issued a decree that prohibited the citizens of Pressburg from mortgaging real estate as security for loans from Jews and prohibited the Jewish moneylenders from taking any real property in mortgage from borrowers. He gave as the reason his wish to protect the welfare of his subjects and stated that "it was the legal duty of every good Christian to avoid contact with Jews as far as possible" and that the passing of mortgaged real estate into Jewish hands was "a manifest scandal for all the Christian people." He even exempted the city of Pressburg from dispensing justice to Jews in their claims against citizens from outside Pressburg, because this would cause difficulties for a city already worn out by times of war. In 1486 he authorized the city of Nagyszombat to bar the Jews from dealing in wine, another instance of his willingness to restrict Jewish commercial activities.

Matthias showed definite favoritism toward Jews who converted to Christianity. A case in point is his magnanimity toward a renegade Jew, Michael Kremniczer, who while still Jewish had taken a loan from Blasius, suffragan bishop of Győr. After his conversion Kremniczer refused to pay the debt, whereupon he was imprisoned. Matthias, in consultation with his barons and the prelates, decided that Kremniczer "was not to be pressed to repay a debt that he incurred while he was still Jewish, since by converting to the Christian faith he left behind everything he had owned, and thus he abandoned also his debts, together with his possible claims." This argument applies to the legal-commercial arena the doctrine adopted by the church, according to which a pagan or Jew convert to Christianity is considered a neophyte, that is, a newborn person, who begins a new life to the extent of nullifying his entire past, including his rights and duties. What this meant in practice was to hold out the inducement of financial gain to Jews who considered conversion to Christianity, in addition to the direct subsidy some ecclesiastic authorities promised to pay them.

While not much is known about the conversions of Hungarian Jews for financial reasons, two very rich Jews who converted to Christianity and came to play important roles in the country did leave traces in historical documents. One of them was a German Jew by the name of Hampo who immigrated to Hungary under King Sigismund and converted some time later, probably in order to be able to rent the very lucrative copper mines. He took the name John Ernust, and was to become the ancestor of a Hungarian noble family. King Matthias had great confidence in him and in one letter calls him "his pal." In 1464 the king entrusted him with the management of the copper mines, and in 1467, when Hampo-Ernust was already a knight and a nobleman, the king appointed him chief customs supervisor and called upon the royal cities to receive him and his officials decently and to support them in every respect. In 1470, in recognition of his services, Matthias presented him with the domain of Sklabinya and appointed him the chief *ispán* (governor) of Thúrócz. Subsequently, however, Hampo-Ernust fell out of grace with the king, who in 1475 confiscated his huge properties, which according to some contemporary sources he had acquired dishonestly. By 1478 his oldest son, Sigismund Ernust, was the bishop of Pécs (Fünfkirchen) and remained a staunch adherent of Matthias, and after him of John Corvinus.

The other highly influential converted Jew was John Thuz, the godfather of King Matthias. He owned the domains of Csáktornya, Kaproncza, St. George, Krapina, and Strigo, and was the *bán* (governor) of Croatia. As such, he was among the richest and most powerful magnates of Hungary. His brother Oswald was the bishop of Zagreb. For a time Matthias had great respect for John Thuz, but at the end, when Thuz tolerated without reaction the Turkish incursions into Croatia, he, too, fell out of favor. In 1480, when Matthias summoned John Thuz together with several other truculent magnates to stand trial in Zagreb, Thuz escaped, with 60,000 gold florins, to Venice, where he was accepted into the ranks of the patricians and lived happily ever after.

Under King Matthias, Jews played important roles in diplomatic relations between Hungary and other countries. Already by the early years of his reign, when Matthias concluded a peace agreement with Sultan Mehmet II (r. 1451–81), the Sublime Porte was represented at his court by a Turkish Jewish envoy, according to Venetian sources. Some years later another Jewish envoy appeared at the court of King Matthias. He was Isaac, a Spanish Jew, the personal physician to Uzun Hassan (in the documents: Usson Cassan, Husam Chasan, and the like), the powerful ruler of Azerbaijan. In 1472, at the inception of his struggle against Mehmet, Uzun Hassan entrusted Isaac with the important diplomatic mission of persuading the European powers to join Azerbaijan in his efforts to defeat the Ottoman Turks. Isaac Beg—or *Isach hebreo medicho et ambassador*, as he is referred to in the documents—arrived at the court of Matthias in the summer of 1472, then went on to Venice and Rome with the same mission: to forge an alliance between Azerbaijan and the Christian powers against Turkey. From Italy he returned to Buda, where he had an important role in bringing about peace between Matthias and Prince (Voivod) Stephan of Moldavia, and succeeded in persuading King Matthias to agree to an all-out war against the Turks. However, at the urging of Pope Paul II, Matthias turned instead against Bohemia to suppress the heresy there.

A year or two after Isaac's mission to Matthias, a converted Spanish Jew of Toledo, an artist by the name of Martin Cotta, settled in Buda.

He seems to have been a scion of the branch of the Toledo Cottas that moved to Naples, and apparently came to Buda in 1476 when Beatrix, daughter of the king of Naples, arrived there as the bride of King Matthias. From 1486 to 1488 Queen Beatrix issued several payments of hundreds of ducats each to Cotta—it is unknown whether for artwork or as part of business transactions. In 1488 King Matthias presented Cotta with a house in Buda; in the deed of gift the king speaks with the greatest admiration of Cotta's art, without, however, specifying the art form in which he engaged. In the early sixteenth century, when, incidentally, also other Jews or ex-Jews of Spanish or Italian extraction lived in Buda, Cotta was one of the most respected merchants and bankers of Buda, and he established important business connections with Venice. By 1505, while still a cititizen of Buda, he was domiciled in Venice. After Martin Cotta's death, his nephew Franciscus (son of his brother Johannes) became the head of the Cotta firm in Buda.

Like his predecessors on the Hungarian throne, Matthias dealt much more harshly with the Jews in other countries than with the Jews in Hungary. In 1485, after conquering Lower Austria, he issued a decree expelling the Jews from Vienna and several other Austrian cities that had come under his rule. As his reason, he stated that the Jews counterfeited money and frustrated his police measures. As against this harsh proceeding, throughout his thirty-two-year rule Matthias never ordered the expulsion of Jews from any Hungarian city. He repeatedly pressed them financially—in fact, the data show that during his rule the Jews of Hungary experienced an economic decline—but the tenor of his reign was such that no breach against their security was even attempted. Matthias was primarily concerned about making sure that no civil disturbance interfered with the ability of the Jews in his realm to pay the huge taxes he imposed on them. This was the central issue around which all the activities of the Jewish prefect revolved, and it was the basis of his every action in representing the interests of the Jews in the court, and those of the court in the Jewish community.

8

The Jewish Prefects:
The Mendels (1475-1531)

When the office of the national chief Jew judge was abolished (around 1440), individual cities continued to have local Jew judges. It was usually the city that appointed one of its councilors as its Jew judge. In some places the Christians and Jews of the city jointly elected their Jew judge, and sometime later these positions were filled, on occasion at least, by Jews. The main tasks of the Jew judge consisted of adjudicating disagreements between Jews and Christians in the city, seeing to it that the ordinances pertaining to the Jews were carried out, and delivering guilty persons to the responsible authorities.

About 1477 King Matthias Corvinus created a new high office, that of the Jewish prefect. He took this step in all probability at the request of the Jews themselves, who were under the jurisdiction of the cities and had great difficulties in obtaining juridical protection and satisfaction. But at the same time, he also had in mind a tightening of the treasury's control over the vital Jewish taxes.

The powers of the Jewish prefect were greater than those of the defunct Jew judge, in that it was his responsibility to allocate the royal taxes among the Jewish communities. As a result of systematizing the collection of Jewish taxes, the revenues from this source grew to some 20,000 gold florins annually, which was a fivefold increase over the yield under Matthias's predecessor, King László V.

Despite this greatly increased tax burden, which the Jews were able to bear because their revenues also increased, they were satisfied with the functioning of the new office, because it provided them with greater personal, legal, and financial security and resulted in more settled conditions in their internal affairs as well. They did whatever they could to make sure the Jewish prefect would be a Jew. Matthias fulfilled their request for he himself was of the opinion that only a person well versed in the affairs of the Jews could determine and allocate the taxes in accordance with the Jews' ability to pay.

This arrangement resulted in the presence in the royal court, for the first time in Hungarian history, of a high Jewish official who represented the country's Jews and was responsible for them in every respect. In the fifteenth century, this is the only known example of a Jew being the royally appointed and legally recognized head and representative of a country's Jewish community at a court.

The Jewish prefect is first mentioned in an edict of Matthias dated 1482, but other historical sources show that the position must have been established several years earlier (see below). From 1482 to 1526 the Jewish prefect is referred to many times in official documents. In a Hungarian-language document dated 1511 he is called "the superior [*elöttük járó*) of the Jews." In a royal decree issued in German he is referred to as "the highest superior of the Jews," in a French ambassadorial report he is called "*prince des Juifz*," and in Latin he becomes "*princeps Judaeorum.*"

To be able to obtain direct instructions from the king and to present Jewish complaints and grievances to him directly, the Jewish prefect had to live in the capital, Buda, and had to have free access to the king. Later kings also saw to it that the Jewish prefect enjoyed due respect at the court and in the country. In periods when Jews were forced to wear special clothing or identification marks, the Jewish prefect was, as a rule, exempt, for the kings felt that only thus could he most effectively represent the interests of the treasury. The Jewish prefect participated in all the festive official occasions of the court, and he appeared on horseback in ceremonial processions, wearing arms and accompanied by a contingent of similarly armed horsemen. To all appearances, he was one of the magnates of the realm.

Over the Jews, whether individuals or communities, he had almost unlimited power. In Buda he had a jailhouse of his own where he could imprison Jews who were guilty of a criminal offence or who failed to pay the taxes he imposed upon them. The jailhouse also served as safe deposit where valuable objects left as pledges in the hands of Jewish moneylenders were kept. The Jewish prefect had armed contingents at his disposal to help him enforce his decisions. Under Lajos II (r. 1516–26) the Jewish community of Buda employed armed mercenaries as guards of its quarter, who likely were under the Jewish prefect's command. The Jew judges of the cities, as well as the city authorities, were obliged to help the Jewish prefect carry out his duties. However, since the cities were more than reluctant to acknowledge the Jewish prefect's authority, each time his work involved a visit to a city he first obtained a royal rescript cautioning the local authorities to help him execute his duties.

The position of the Jewish prefect was as difficult as it was powerful. The regular and special taxes payable by the Jews to the royal treasury were determined in a lump sum by the royal authorities, and it was up to the Jewish prefect to divide them up and allocate them among the individual communities. Then it was the task of the leaders of each community to apportion the tax imposed upon it among its members. This arrangement was apt to cause tension, disagreement, and quarrels between the Jewish prefect and the Jewish communities, as well as between the community leaders and members. At times the leaders of a community felt that the amount of taxes imposed upon it by the Jewish prefect was unduly high, and they refused to pay it. This in turn would induce the prefect to send down his armed detachment, arrest the leaders, and bring them to Buda to be imprisoned in the prefect's jailhouse until they agreed to pay.

As for internal disagreements, since each Jewish community had to pay the royal tax in a lump sum into the hands of the Jewish prefect, it was against its interest for individual Jews to leave the community and settle elsewhere; if the number of Jewish householders diminished, the taxes payable by the remaining Jews had to be increased to make up the balance. Hence it occasionally happened that the community tried to prevent its members, even by force, from moving away. The same circumstances also led every community to desire to see more Jews settle in its midst, for in that case the tax burden falling on the individuals decreased—except, of course, if the tax demanded of the community was correspondingly increased.

This situation was the background for many internal quarrels within the Jewish communities, whose settlement was the task, first of all, of the local Jew judge. The laws of Béla IV also provided that if a Jew committed a crime against another Jew, such as theft or bodily injury, the local Jew judge should supervise its adjudication by the local Jewish law court (the *beth din*, termed "Jewish school" in the Hungarian documents) and carry out its sentences. However, after the establishment of the office of the Jewish prefect, the local Jew judge could only arrest the person found guilty and deliver him into the hands of the Jewish prefect, who had him brought to his jailhouse in Buda. In cases that arose between a Jew and a Christian, the lawsuit was adjudicated by a jury consisting of Christian and Jewish jurors, and it was the task of the local Jew judge to pass sentence.

As can be seen from these details, quite a bit is known about the civic and legal status of the Jews in Hungary in the fourteenth to early sixteenth centuries. The official documents also provide some information concerning the economic life and activities, and the internal relations, of the Hungarian Jews as a group. One can see that they played an important role in the economic life of the country, that they contributed substantially to the treasury revenues, as well as to the incomes of the nobles and the cities, and that the various levels of authority, often in competition for Jewish tax money among themselves, were ready to extend a certain amount of protection to them. On the other hand, the Jewish concentration in the money business, into which they were forced by restrictive legislation, made the Jews hated by the general population, most of whom were serfs of the king or the nobles, or city-dwelling merchants and artisans, and whose rights, too, were limited. The Jews, being practically the only source of loans, were both needed and hated, and they became almost inevitably the target of occasional anti-Jewish outbreaks and excesses.

What are nearly missing from the picture one can construct from Hungarian legal material are individual life histories, which would complement the skeletal structure represented by these legal documents. I say *nearly* because, despite the absence of contemporary literary documents by the Hungarian Jews themselves, we do know, mostly from official Hungarian sources, about the lives and work of several members of an illustrious Jewish family of high officials whose influence with the crown made Jewish life less onerous in the fifteenth and sixteenth centuries. They were the members of the Mendel dynasty of Jewish prefects, to whom we now turn.

The first Jewish prefect was Judah Mendel, who seems to have officiated from 1476, or soon thereafter, to his death in 1482. Prior to his appointment, he was the head of the Jewish community of Buda. In that capacity, in 1476, when King Matthias held his festive arrival with his bride Beatrix at the Buda fortress to celebrate their wedding, Judah Mendel headed a mounted contingent of Jewish dignitaries that was among the cavalry troops riding out to receive the king. The German chronicler Johann Seybold describes the scene:

> In this [chronicle] there is a description of the splendors at the praise-worthy marriage of the most serene and mighty prince and lord, Lord Matthias, king of Hungary and Bohemia, to his spouse, the Lady Beatrice, daughter of the king of Naples. [The list of guests follows.] In the year 1476 of our Lord, as I came to Ofen [Buda], I was told at once of the great opulence and splendor that our most serene lord, King Matthias of Hungary and Bohemia, etc., is said to have shown there. [There follows a description of the luxurious clothes the burghers of Buda wore to receive the royal couple.]
>
> The Jews, too, had come out and, the King sending word to them that the Jews should make their entry, the Jew Mendel led them into the inner castle, where he made a short speech at the fountain; and he was attended by thirty-one fine horses. On the first of these rode a young boy who

played smartly on a trumpet, and from this trumpet there hung a banner. After him rode two boys, each of them holding reins made of silver with large pummels and buckles as high as a silver beaker, tall enough to hold a jug of wine, and intricately worked. At their sides they carried long silver swords with chased hilts and sheaths. After them rode the Jew Mendel, who was dressed in a gray cloak with a pointed hood trimmed with fur and lined with taffeta, and there was a spangle on his hat. At his side he carried a long silver dagger. After him rode several in ranks of two, all clad in violet garments decorated with silver threads, and each wore on his hat two white ostrich plumes and a violet one between them. And they remained in the castle for an hour.

After that came the King mounted on his horse, and Duke Christoph was with him; and they rode after the Jews out of the castle and toward Stuhlweissenburg [Székesfehérvár] for the coronation, but the Jews took a different road. [There follows a detailed description of the wedding at Székesfehérvár and the coronation of the queen.].

I forgot to mention another procession, in which the Jews rode out to greet the queen before the gates of the city of Ofen. First there arrived thirty-two, all dressed in violet garments decorated with silver ornaments, like those mentioned above when they rode out to the coronation, except that these also carried a great banner, and on it was written in golden letters, in Hebrew, *Schina israhel* [Sh'ma Yisrael], which is to say, Hear, Children of Israel; and on this flag was also an escutcheon displaying a witch's foot, the arms of King David, and three golden stars surmounted by a Jew's hat: all this in gold and surrounded by a gold border. Behind the banner went on foot young and old in ranks of two, more than a hundred and fifty of them, wearing on their heads hoods of silk and damask. And they sang a chant with loud voices and carried a canopy, and an old Jew walked under the canopy carrying a bundle wrapped in cloth to which was affixed a golden tablet. And two Jews were leading him, and they made a short speech to the queen. Then the king and the queen together approached on their mounts, and as they came to the canopy the Jews opened the bundle and offered it to the queen to kiss, but she did not wish to kiss it.

In the succeeding passage the chronicle enumerates those who gave presents to the royal couple on the occasion of the New Year, and mentions the Jews in the last place: "The Jews presented gifts of two loaves of wheat bread, a violet hat with a large bush of heron feathers on it, two live stags, two does, and eight peacocks."

The festive Jewish delegation that welcomed the royal couple before the gates of Buda is also described in a Latin chronicle, with minor differences in detail. According to it, the delegation was led by the aged chief of the Jews and his son, both on horseback, followed by twenty-four horsemen all clad in purple, and after them went two hundred Jews on foot, carrying a red flag embroidered with a five-clawed owl's foot. Seybold interpreted the same emblem as a witch's foot, that is, the footprint of a witch, whose sign was the pentagram. What both gentile observers saw was evidently the Star of David, whose six corners they mistook for the pentagram, more familiar to them. The Latin chronicler also mentions that all the Jews who marched on foot had their heads covered with the *ephod*, that is, the *tallith*, or prayer shawl, which Seybold describes as a "hood of silk and damask." The red flag embroidered with the Star of David was a *parokhet*, a curtain used to cover the Torah shrine, which they removed from their synagogue and carried in the procession. The "bundle" wrapped in cloth and hung with a golden tablet was, of course, the Torah scroll, referred to by the Latin chronicler as "the decalogue." The "old Jew" led by two other Jews, who carried the Torah scroll, must have been the rabbi of the community.

Apart from these ritual details, the reports of the Jewish delegation show that the Buda Jews were a well-to-do community, many of them owning expensive gala outfits, including imported luxury items, and that they possessed and were allowed to bear arms. Their participation in royal festivities indicates that they constituted an important community among the inhabitants of Buda.

Both chroniclers mention the sword, or long dagger, carried by Mendel, the chief of the Jews. A similar sword from that very period was preserved down to the late nineteenth century, when it was in the possession of Count Manó Andrássy, who showed it to historian Samuel Kohn. It had a finely forged blade with inlaid Hebrew sentences in silver lettering, reading "O God the Lord, the strength of my salvation" (Psalm 140:8) and "Blessed be the name of the Lord" (Psalm 113:2).

Jacob Mendel I was appointed Jewish prefect upon his father's death, and is first mentioned as holding the office in a 1482 document. He served until 1502. After him the honor was inherited by five more Mendels. All in all, therefore, seven Mendels served as Jewish prefects:

Judah Mendel (1460?–82)
Jacob Mendel I (1482–1502)
Jacob Judah Mendel (1502–12)
Jacob Mendel II (1512–23)
Israel Mendel (1523–26)
Isaac Mendel (1529–?)
Tobias Mendel (1531)

After the Mohács Disaster of 1526, the scope of authority of the last two Mendels was confined to the western and northern parts of Hungary, which remained under the reign of Ferdinand I (1526–64).

Some information is available about the position and activities of the Mendel prefects and their family. Jacob I (who together with his father led the Jews in welcoming King Matthias) was several times the recipient of royal favors. When John Elderbock de Monyorókerek failed to repay on time the sizable loan he had borrowed from Jacob Mendel, Matthias furnished Jacob's agents with a royal letter instructing all authorities of the country to arrest the serfs of Elderbock, wherever they could find them, confiscate their merchandise and other property for Mendel's benefit, and hand them over to his agents. On another occasion the king instructed the city of Pressburg to satisfy the claim "the prefect of his Jews" had against a Pressburg citizen. At the coronation of King Ulászló (Vladislav) II in Székesfehérvár (in 1490), Jacob Mendel repeated the performance of his father, appearing at the head of a troop of twenty-four Jewish horsemen and attracting much attention with his splendid arms.

An example of the kind of mediation the Jewish prefect was required to perform between the king and the Jews is the forced loan Ulászló II imposed upon the Jews of Pressburg in 1491. The king, engaged in besieging the city of Székesfehérvár, which at the time was occupied by Holy Roman Emperor Maximilian, sent an empowerment to Balázs Posa, the *dictator comitatus posoniensis* (governor of County Pressburg), to send several Pressburg Jews, "by whatever means, if necessary by force," to Buda, because he wanted to settle a matter with them "in the interest of the country." As it subsequently transpired, the matter the king had in mind was to pressure the Pressburg Jews to give him a sizable loan. This was an affair in which Jacob Mendel I, as prefect of the Jews, had to be involved, and he in fact undertook to exact a loan of 400 gulden (gold florins) from the Jews of Pressburg, and to guarantee that the money would be forthcoming. Mendel proceeded to Pressburg, but the Jews refused to let him have the money. The king thereupon sent a rescript to Pressburg, instructing the city to help Mendel raise the amount by "proceeding harshly against the Jews, and keeping them in jail until they do our will, and lend us, in our great need, the 400 florins." It can be imagined that representing the king in this manner, and actually extorting the money from the Pressburg Jewish community by threatening them with imprisonment, did not contribute to the popularity of Mendel among the Jews.

Two years later we find Jacob Mendel functioning as a true representative of Hungarian Jewish interests. At his succession, Ulászló II promised the Jews to reaffirm their old rights and privileges, but he did not follow up the promise with action until 1493, when Jacob Mendel succeeded in procuring the long sought-after letter patent. It was addressed to him and stated that the king recognized and reaffirmed the Jewish law issued by King Béla IV and reaffirmed by kings Sigismund, Albert, László V, and Matthias. The declaration was prepared by Thomas, bishop of Győr, and signed by several prelates and magnates, as well as by the king. Once the precious document was in the hands of Jacob Mendel, he had several authenticated copies made—some issued by the king himself—and sent them to the major Jewish communities, to be available in case of need. Thanks to this multiplicity of copies, several of them survived in the archives of Hungarian cities.

Similar work carried out by Jacob Judah Mendel, Jacob Mendel I's successor as Jewish prefect, is recorded in a royal rescript issued by Ulászló II to the city of Pressburg on June 10, 1502. Its impetus was, one gathers from the rescript itself, repeated attacks by the people of Pressburg, who hurled stones at Jews and physically assaulted them. The city authorities refused to intervene and even threatened the Jews with imprisonment and fines. The Jews then appealed to Jacob Judah Mendel, who brought the matter to the attention of the king. In his rescript, the king reminds the city that the Jews have been "always and since antiquity under our power, and after Our Majesty, [under that] of our master chief treasurer," and most firmly orders the city to dare no longer to impose imprisonment or fines on the Jews, but rather to protect them against "illegitimate attackers." Documents such as this make it clear that the Jewish prefect was the spokesman of the Jews, had access to the king, brought their grievances to the king's attention, and saw to it that injuries they suffered were remedied.

The Jews of Pressburg figure frequently in the fifteenth- and sixteenth-century royal rescripts in connection with their financial dealings with the city. On May 6, 1503, Pressburg obtained from King Ulászló II a decree releasing its residents from the payment of interest on loans they had taken from the Jews of Pressburg and other places in Hungary, provided they repaid the principal by the next St. Martin's Day (November 11). Moreover, impoverished burghers were given the benefit of paying only as much as they could, and the rest of their debt was declared null and void. This order was a serious financial blow for the Jews of Pressburg. They appealed to Jacob Mendel, who within five weeks was able to obtain a rescission of the decree. However, aware that the city would put up stiff resistance to this annulment of the financial advantage it had achieved, the Jewish prefect sought further help in high places. Queen Anna, who had been crowned in Fehérvár only a few months earlier, where the Jews received her with great pomp and lavish gifts, was an energetic helpmeet and advisor to the weak king, and it was to her that Jacob Mendel turned. On June 20, 1503, the queen, referring to the king's letter addressed to the Jewish prefect, warned the city of Pressburg to proceed equitably in the matter. She wrote:

> We have been informed by the prefect of the Jews that you have recently extracted a certain letter from His Majesty the King, our lord and dear spouse, against the Jews, your cohabitants, to their very great damage. However, after His Majesty now inspected more diligently the privileges of the Jews that at the time happened to escape his memory, he has recognized that issuing the letter in question resulted in an excessive oppression of the Jews. Therefore, he issued to the aforenamed prefect, as he asserts, another letter in which he orders that you should compose the disagreement that has broken out between you and the Jews in such a manner that neither you nor the Jews should suffer excessive damage

Continuing, the queen orders the city to come to an equitable agreement with the Jewish prefect, who was going to Pressburg to settle the matter in the name of the Jews. Should the city not do it, "you can be sure that we shall never tolerate that you should, contrary to justice, oppress and damage the Jews, but we shall help them and undertake to protect and maintain their privileges."

Apart from the intrinsic interest this energetic queenly intervention in favor of the Jews has for the historian, there is an important difference in terminology between it and the usual royal rescripts. Where the Hungarian kings regularly refer to the Jews as "our Jews" and to the prefect as "the prefect of our Jews," Queen Anna in her letter speaks of "the Jews" and "the prefect of the Jews." This seems to indicate that the Jews, whom, as we know, the Hungarian kings considered their personal property, were not claimed by the queen to be her property as well.

The effect of this intervention is not known, but data are available that indicate that the city of Pressburg continued to oppress and harass the Jews, forcing them to appeal frequently to the Crown for help and protection. Ulászló warned the city several times to cease and desist, but in vain. In 1511 Jacob Mendel's successor as Jewish prefect, Jacob Judah Mendel, sent his deputy, called Fekete Mendel (Black Mendel), to Pressburg to work out an agreement, and the king again warned the city to do so.

This Fekete Mendel—referred to in contemporary documents as Judeus (or *perfidus judeus*) Mandel Fekethe, or Mendellus Niger—was not merely a deputy of the Jewish prefect Jacob Judah Mendel, and possibly a relative of his, but also a large-scale moneylender in his own right, who gave sizable loans to Hungarian nobles. In 1503 he loaned one hundred gold florins to János Chethneki, on condition that if the borrower failed to repay the loan on time, he would have to pay double. As time passed, the amounts Fekete Mendel was able to lend increased markedly. He lent 800 florins to Gábor Csáky, which the debtor repaid in 1508. In 1510 Ferenc Balassa repaid him a debt of more than a thousand florins. Fekete Mendel's money business extended far beyond the

borders of Hungary. He gave several loans to Margrave George of Brandenburg, the guardian of King Lajos II, which were repaid in 1511. In
1520 Fekete Mendel undertook to pay Palatine István Báthory twelve
florins annually for certain rights the Palatine accorded him. The Latin
document covering this arrangement carries a Hebrew summary of its
content that shows that Fekete Mendel was more at home in Hebrew
than in Latin.

By 1526 Fekete Mendel had fallen out of grace, and on June 6 of that
year Lajos II sent a rescript to Pressburg ordering the city to arrest him
and deliver him into the king's hands. We do not know what happened
to him thereafter.

Fekete Mendel's daughter Melamen, referred to as Domina Melamen
Judea, married the Jew Yane, likewise a big moneylender, and after
being widowed she continued her husband's work, becoming one of
several Hungarian Jewish women who are known to have engaged in
the money business. In 1511, Gábor Csáky took a 200 florin loan from
Melamen against a mortgage of his estates in County Bihar. She also
loaned him another 400 florins, and when he failed to repay these loans
at the stipulated time, she transferred the mortgage to the church chapter of Buda for a payment of 800 florins.

Another Jewish woman engaged in the money business was Rusa, the
sister of Jacob Mendel I, who worked as pawnbroker. Of several other
Jewish women it is known that they were already lending money against
mortgages in the first half of the fifteenth century. Among them were
Henndel and Teubel of Pressburg, Yakel of Sopron, and a Jewess of
Teben (Dévény). The picture of Jewish women in the money business is
supplemented by data showing that Pressburg Jewish women were
heads of households in the fifteenth century, and as such paid taxes to
the city. All in all, Jewish women figure with surprising frequency in
documents from the 1400s and 1500s covering financial transactions,
usually loans to Christian borrowers. Even though in most of these cases
the women appear together with their husbands as lenders, in quite a
number they alone are named the moneylenders.

But to return to Jacob Judah Mendel, it is known that he acted as
purveyor of valuable merchandise for King Ulá36szló II. When the court
was not in Buda, he would ship the items he purchased to wherever the
king happened to sojourn. On several occasions he defrayed debts owed
by the king. In 1511, when Mendel's son Joseph traveled to Venice to
take care of his legal affairs there, the envoy of Venice to the court of
Matthias wrote to the doge requesting that he exempt Joseph from wearing the yellow hat that was obligatory for the Jews, to avoid embarrassment, and stated that Joseph's father "had no small influence with the

magnates of Hungary, and especially with the palatine." This brief letter is especially instructive because it shows that the Mendels had business dealings with Venice.

Incidentally, exemption from wearing the Jewish garb was granted in Hungary as well, to Jews whose work was of exceptional importance for the general community. In 1511 Mózes Buzlay de Gergelaka, the Christian royal majordomo, whom the king had entrusted with the special protection of the Jews of Pressburg, informed the city that Ulászló had exempted Zacharias, *medico et phisico* [sic] *Judeo*, from wearing the Jewish cape, so that he could visit his patients with greater security; he ordered the city to see to it that the Jewish doctor should in no way be harmed if he walked about without the Jewish garb.

Despite royal protection and the efforts of the Jewish prefect, the position of the Pressburg Jews deteriorated to such an extent that they repeatedly had to ask the Jewish prefect's intervention. For example, in March 1511, they were prohibited by the city from selling new clothes, in an abridgement of their old privileges. They appealed to Jacob Judah Mendel, who in turn brought the matter to the attention of the palatine, Imre Perényi. Perényi instructed the mayor, judge, and city council of Pressburg to protect the Jews until such time as the king returned to Hungary. As was usual in such rescripts, Perényi added the request that the city help the Jew judges in their work of collecting the royal taxes imposed upon the Jews.

Nevertheless, in 1512 the Jews of Pressburg felt constrained to notify the king through Jacob Mendel II, the new Jewish prefect, that "if they continue to be harassed, they will all leave at once and place themselves under the power of the count of Szepes." This was a serious threat for the king (or rather for his treasury), and he, as well as his chief treasurer, Nicolaus de Herend, wrote to the burghers asking them to cease harassing the Jews and come to an agreement with Jacob Mendel, who was about to visit Pressburg representing the Jews. The treasurer asked Pressburg not to cause such damage to the royal treasury, but what was of greater influence on the city's treatment of the Jews was that their exodus from Pressburg would have meant severe financial losses to the municipality as well. In any case, in the event, the Pressburg Jews did not leave.

From a document likewise dated 1512 it appears that Jacob Mendel II's lobbying efforts at the court targeted not only the king and the chief treasurer but also other high dignitaries. On May 9 of that year John Podmanin, count of Pressburg and *cubiculariorum regalium magister* (master of the servants of the royal bedchamber), and on June 16 Miklós Herendi, the royal treasurer, wrote to the city of Pressburg calling upon them to render all possible assistance to *Judeus Mendel*, prefect of the Jews, who was going to Pressburg to settle persistent disagreements and controversies among the Jews there.

The surviving documents relating to Jacob Mendel show that while he did everything he could to obtain protection for the Jews, he also could treat them harshly when it came to collecting taxes imposed by the king. An example of Mendel's severity is provided by a rescript addressed by Ulászló on July 31, 1514, to the city of Pressburg. The king was about to recruit an army against the peasant uprising that caused trouble in the land, and he needed money for paying the mercenaries. He imposed a special tax on the Pressburg Jews, who were tardy in paying it. Jacob Mendel sent his man (*hominum suum*) to Pressburg to collect the tax, and the king called upon the city to help the man in every respect and to send to Mendel in Buda those Jews whom his man would name. To send to Mendel in Buda, of course, meant to send them under armed guard to be imprisoned in Mendel's jailhouse until they rendered payment.

Another incident where Jacob Mendel had to make use of the force at the municipalities' disposal took place in 1517 in Sopron. In that year, soon after his succession, King Lajos II imposed a special tax on the Jews, and it was Jacob Mendel's task to allocate it among the individual Jewish communities and ensure its payment. The total amount of the tax is not known, but documents inform us that he collected 110 florins from the Jews of Pressburg and was unable to collect the 80 florins he imposed on the Jews of Sopron. Therefore, on April 30, 1517, Lajos instructed the Sopron city council to summon the well-to-do Jews and "compel them in all manner" to pay the amount in question to Mendel's deputy. Under Lajos II such extraordinary taxes were imposed on the Jews almost every year.

In 1515 Jacob Mendel II had been involved in international negotiations between Ulászló and Maximilian I (r. 1493–1519), the Holy Roman emperor and archduke of Austria. Maximilian, as emperor, claimed that since all Jews were descendants of the Jews of Jerusalem defeated by Rome, they were his subjects: "We, as Roman Emperor, to whom all Jews are directly subject," he wrote to the Hungarian estates and authorities on July 26, 1515. He also claimed to be the king of Hungary, as well as Dalmatia and Croatia. In the rescript mentioned he informed the Hungarian authorities that, with the consent of King Ulászló, he had "taken the Hebrew Jacob Mendl [sic], chief [*supremus*] of all other Hebrews in the kingdom of Hungary, with his family and all the Hebrews in all of Hungary, wherever they live, under our protection." He went on to instruct the magnates, prelates, and civil and military authorities in Hungary that in case of the death of Ulászló, "which God should wish to avert," they should maintain the said Jews' enjoyment of their rights and privileges and should not dare to harm them. It is remarkable that Maximilian, who in Germany, for example in Norimberg, expelled the Jews and divided up their property between himself and the cities, should appear as the protector of the Hungarian Jews. However, by doing this, he acted in conformity with the behavior of several Hungarian kings who persecuted the Jews in their other realms, while protecting them, or dealing less harshly with them, in Hungary.

Precisely what the role of Jacob Mendel was in getting this imperial decree issued is unknown, but since he is mentioned in it by name, it is likely that he conducted the negotiations with the imperial authorities in Vienna that resulted in this rescript. As it was issued four days after the conclusion of the treaty of Vienna between Ulászló and Maximilian and the double marriage treaty between the two royal houses, it is also probable that Jacob Mendel was among the Hungarian negotiators who represented Ulászló in Vienna, and that he made use of that opportunity to obtain from Maximilian a declaration of special protection for the Hungarian Jews.

The royal example of taxing the Jews more and more harshly was followed by the magnates, the prelates, and the cities and prompted the indefatigable Jacob Mendel II to lodge a series of complaints with the king. However, all the king could do was to issue rescripts in favor of the Jews that were in most cases disobeyed. A case in point is that of Thomas Bakacs, cardinal of Esztergom, in whose domains many Jews lived. After the death of Pope Julius II in 1513, Cardinal Bakacs aspired to the papal throne and went to Rome, where he lived and spent lavishly. To cover his enormous expenses, he took many illegal steps, and among others he had his tithe collectors extort huge amounts from the Jews. Jacob Mendel complained to Ulászló II, and in 1513 the king instructed Pressburg to protect the Jews of the city and other places against the extortions of the cardinal's officers.

The tension between the king and the cities is illustrated by the fate of the royal edict issued by Ulászló II exempting Jacob Mendel II and his family from wearing the Jewish garb. This privilege was recognized in Buda but not in Pressburg. In 1517, when Mendel's son-in-law, Jacob, sojourned for a time in Pressburg in connection with some private affairs, the city forced him to wear the Jewish garb. The royal treasurer, László Szalkay, protested energetically against this autocratic imposition and demanded that Pressburg give justice and satisfaction to the Jew Jacob from his debtors.

Other high dignitaries were also involved in helping the Jewish prefect perform his tasks, and he, in turn, knew how to secure their goodwill through lavish gifts. Thus, on July 24, 1520, Jacob Mendel undertook in the name of all the Jews of Hungary to pay the palatine of the kingdom, Stephan Báthory, a lifelong tribute of 400 florins annually in exchange for his protection. The document attesting to this is of considerable interest, because it shows to what extent the Jewish prefect (or rather his Latin scribe) adopted the style of the royal edicts of the time, and with what diplomatic finesse he informed the palatine of the Jews' decision to let him have what was in effect nothing but a huge bribe. He wrote:

> We, Jacob Mendel prefect, and the other chiefs and all the Jews established and living anywhere in this kingdom of Hungary, willingly and freely acknowledge and recognize by these presents that because the respectable and magnificent Lord Stephanus de Bathor, palatine of the kingdom of Hungary, . . . wishing to satisfy the decrees and orders that our most gracious lord, His Majesty the King, issued for us in a letter, has until now endeavored to protect us in our several affairs and doings that have arisen at this time, against the violence of several kinds of illegal persecutions, with the authority and in the name of His Majesty the King; and since we hope that in the requisite place and time he will take all our affairs under his protection also in the future; and since we do not want to fall into the sin of ungratefulness toward the palatine—therefore we assure him until the end of his life of an honorarium of 400 florins annually, payable in four installments, with the condition that if we do not defray this amount or each of its partial payments, we shall owe him double the amount, which, by these presents, he can exact and extort from us in any manner.

The document is signed in Hebrew by two witnesses: "David son of Abraham of blessed memory, *shammash* [beadle] of the holy community of Oven [Buda]" and "Aaron son of Gamaliel, may God avenge his blood, beadle of the holy community of Oven." The abbreviation for "may God avenge his blood" is normally used in mentioning the name of a martyr. It is therefore possible that this Gamaliel was one of the Jews burned at the stake in Nagyszombat in 1494 (see chapter 9).

Let me interject here a brief comment on the fact that this document is signed by the witnesses in Hebrew. These Hebrew signatures show that the Hebrew language was either the only language those witnesses were able to write, or that it was the language they preferred to use when it came to signing important official papers. This conclusion is strengthened by the existence of other documents from the same period which too are signed or written in Hebrew. Thus a commercial contract containing a guarantee of payment dating from about 1510 from the city of Veszprém contains this sentence in Hebrew: "I, Aharon, son of R. Gedl, testify that you have taken three barrels of wine for my brother Pessaḥ on his account. Should my brother not pay for it, I shall be obliged to pay. For this I gave my signature." It would seem that to write or sign a paper in Hebrew gave added weight to it.

But to return to the protection the palatine extended to the Jews, it took the form of several rescripts, one of which he addressed six months later to the city of Pressburg, instructing it to protect the Jews against all kinds of attacks and "not to dare force the Jews of the city to wear the Jewish garb." As was usual in these rescripts, this one, too, contains the added exhortation to the city to help Jacob Mendel in collecting the Jew tax. Similar rescripts were addressed to Pressburg also by George, bishop of Pécs, on April 4, 1521, and June 11, 1522.

Despite the general letters of protection issued by the king, the palatine, and others with reference to an entire Jewish community, individual Jews still felt the need for special protection against harassment and persecution by the cities and magnates, who had little respect for decrees emanating from Buda. Consequently, rich and influential Jews, including the Jewish prefect himself, obtained special letters of protection for their own personal safety. On September 21, 1518 László Szalkay, bishop of Vácz, issued a letter of protection in the name of King Lajos II to the Jewish prefect, Mendel; his son-in-law, Jacob; and the Jews Joseph Niger ("black"), Solomon Parvus ("small"), Zarwas (Szarvas, i.e., "deer," probably standing for the German name Hirsch), and Joseph of Tata. In it he informs all the authorities of the kingdom that these Jews were taken under the special protection of the king and himself, and he cautions them to treat the Jews in a humane manner and protect them "against all violators and oppressors." One can assume that such letters of protection were obtained by the Jews against sizable payments, as exemplified by Jacob Mendel's offer to the palatine quoted above.

Similar efforts were made by the Jews to obtain exemption from wearing the Jewish cap and cowl, or to have them abolished altogether. In fact, the degrading law was abolished prior to 1520, as we learn not only from the quoted rescript of Palatine Báthory but even more clearly from a letter from Pál Várday to the city council of Pressburg, reproaching them for still forcing Jews to wear the cowl, "whose wearing at present in the breadth and width of this country is an unheard-of thing, since His Majesty the King has liberated them in this respect." The fact that Pressburg continued to force the Jews to wear the Jewish garb while it had been abolished in Buda shows that Pressburg was more anti-Jewish than the capital. The royal rescript on this matter will be discussed below in connection with Jewish criminality in this period (chapter 11).

When Israel Mendel inherited the office of Jewish prefect, he was faced right away with the same type of problems that had taken up so much of the time and energy of his predecessors. As early as 1524, Israel Mendel was informed that an innocent Sopron Jew, at the "calumnious words of a woman," had been imprisoned and mistreated. He appealed to King Lajos II, who in response ordered the mayor and city council of Sopron to release the Jew forthwith and not to harm him either in body or in property. "If you have," the King wrote, "any complaint against him, that should be dealt with by [the king's] regular judge."

A few months later, Israel Mendel appointed one of the Pressburg Jews as his representative to take care of tax collection. To give weight to the demands of this official, King Lajos II sent a rescript on May 18, 1524, calling upon the city of Pressburg to support Israel Mendel's man in every respect and instructing the Jews to obey him as if Israel Mendel himself were there. On October 16, 1524, Lajos was forced to repeat this order.

To ensure the smooth flow of Jewish taxes into the royal treasury, the king insisted that both Jews and Christians cooperate with the Jewish prefect and his officials to enable them to fulfill their assigned tasks. Therefore, the king often ordered the local authorities to obey the Jewish prefect. As a mark of his high position, the Jewish prefect and his family were officially exempt from wearing the special garb identifying the Jews. The king also secured these privileges for the Jewish prefect and his family when they traveled abroad.

The Jewish prefect had almost limitless power over the Jews. We have heard about the jail in Buda that was at his disposal, and which doubled as a vault for the valuable objects pawned by Christian debtors as security for loans from Jewish moneylenders. The prefect also had at his command mercenary troops and deputies, whom he would dispatch to various communities to see that his instructions and decisions were obeyed. In larger communities, such as that of Pressburg, he had permanent representatives.

In effect, the Jewish prefect controlled Jewish life all over the country. The royal decrees pertaining to the Jews were addressed to him, and it was his duty to make sure they were forwarded to the communities and obeyed. On the other hand, he represented the Jews in negotiations and signed binding contracts in their name. If there were disagreements within a Jewish community, he mediated them and, if necessary, settled them by decree. If, as it often happened, a conflict arose between a Jewish community and the town authorities, it was again he who mediated. Even the appointment of a chief rabbi lay within his powers. This we learn, again, not from Jewish sources (still few and far between) but from a decree issued before 1516 by King Ulászló II ordering all the Jews of Hungary to accept any Jewish "pharisee" (i.e., rabbi) from abroad whom Jacob Mendel II appointed, because Jacob and his predecessors had been given the right to appoint rabbis by Ulászló and previous kings.

Whenever Jews suffered abridgement of their rights or privileges anywhere in the country, they turned to their prefect, and he presented their claims to the king, usually orally. In most cases he obtained satisfaction. Numerous documents preserved in city archives show how emphatically the king, after intervention by the prefect, ordered the local authorities to remedy the situation. The arguments the prefect used to convince the king of the justice of the Jews' cause varied, but typically he pointed out that the royal rights and the interests of the treasury would be harmed if the Jews were oppressed or made to suffer. This argument is reflected in many royal decrees: they state that anyone who disturbs or hurts the Jews in their business indirectly causes damage to the treasury, because if money is extorted from the Jews or they are forced to sustain losses, they will be unable to defray the various taxes or will be able to do so only with great difficulty. Since the taxation of the Jews was totally in the hands of the prefect, he could use this situation for the protection of his community. If the need arose, he even threatened, and insisted on royal protection. He could, and did, intimate that if the wrongs suffered by the Jews were not remedied, they would leave the royal cities and move to the domain of a nobleman, which would mean loss of revenues to the royal treasury.

The official Hungarian documents of this period not only provide information on the business activities and legal position of the Jews but, incidentally, also tell us about the apostasy of several Jews in high positions, as well as about the branching out of some Jews into crime. Again it was the Jewish prefect who had to deal with such cases. A Jew by the name of Briccius (perhaps a distortion of Barukh) committed unspecified crimes, described only as "excesses." He was imprisoned by Jacob Mendel II in Buda but managed to escape, and he found refuge in St. George and Bazin, from where he proceeded to cause many injuries to the Jews of Pressburg. Mendel submitted the case to King Lajos II, who instructed the city of Pressburg to have the culprit arrested and delivered into the hands of the Pressburg Jews so they could send him back to Mendel in Buda. In the same rescript Lajos instructs the Pressburg Jews to obey the Jew Oroszlán ("lion"), Mendel's deputy, who was a leader of the Pressburg Jewish community.

Two royal rescripts issued in 1521 by King Lajos II deal with a Jewish criminal called Pelcz. This man, too, had been imprisoned in the jail of the Jewish prefect, Jacob Mendel II, but he escaped with a loot of gold and silver objects pawned by debtors with the Jews of Buda and deposited in the vault within the jailhouse. It became known that Pelcz was hiding out somewhere in the vicinity of Pressburg, and therefore on February 15, 1521, Lajos II instructed the Pressburg authorities to apprehend him and deliver him to the local Jew judge. In the same document Lajos "firmly" called upon the city not to tolerate harassment or injury of the Pressburg Jews because they dressed like the Jews of Buda: determining the Jews' garb is the sole responsibility of the king and, he concludes, "we have provided that our Jews should be able to remain in peace and tranquility."

Shortly after this edict was issued, the Jew Pelcz succeeded in leaving the Pressburg area and moved to Vienna, where he made false accusations against the Jews of Pressburg. Jacob Mendel brought this development to the attention of King Lajos, whereupon on March 26, 1421, the king issued a rescript to the authorities of Pressburg instructing them "to protect those Jews of ours" who as a result of the calumnies of Pelcz had suffered damage and injury "against the mendacity of the said Jew Pelcz. . . . Presume in no way to act otherwise." No information has survived as to what ultimately happened to this Jewish criminal. However, the two cases of Briccius and Pelcz demonstrate that arresting and imprisoning Jewish criminals was among the duties (and privileges) of the Jewish prefect.

A few more royal rescripts contain information on the work of the Mendels, who held the office of Jewish prefect until just before the Mohács Disaster. From one of them we learn that Jacob Mendel II was assisted in his work by Jewish officials called *jurati Judei* (Jewish jurors). In a 1521 rescript to Pressburg, King Lajos orders the city to help the "jurors of our Buda Jews" dispatched by Jacob Mendel to Pressburg in collecting the regular taxes payable by the Jews on St. George's Day, as well as the extraordinary taxes imposed on them by the royal will. Some time after the issuance of this rescript, Israel Mendel replaced Jacob Mendel as Jewish prefect, and the next royal rescript, on July 29, 1523, refers to him as "Israel Mendel Judeorum nostrorum prefectus." In it the king tells the Pressburg authorities that Israel Mendel had informed him that a Pressburg woman, the widow of the fisherman Glebitz, had somehow obtained a royal letter exempting her from repaying all the debts she owed *Judeis nostris posoniensibus* (our Pressburg Jews). The king states that the letter in question had been issued inadvertently, it did not accord with justice, and it was therefore annulled herewith. At the same time the king instructs the city of Pressburg to protect the local Jews vigorously against harassment by a converted Jew named Leonardus, or by anybody else.

These royal rescripts afford insight into the way Hungarian kings from time to time reaffirmed the protection they accorded "their Jews." When a case arose that required their intervention in favor of a Jew or Jews, they frequently appended a paragraph to the rescript to the local authorities reminding them that the local Jews in general were under his protection and that the city should protect them against harassment, harm, and injury.

Jacob Judah Mendel was the only Jewish prefect whose family is known to have sought security against possible attacks. Beginning in the late 1400s, sessions of the Diet, held in Buda or in Rákos, were often followed by outbreaks against the Jews, perpetrated by the mob that usually assembled where these meetings took place. Hence, as a precaution, prior to the opening of a Diet, the well-to-do Jews of Buda would send their families, and probably also their valuables, to a different location. This is what Jacob Judah Mendel and his relative Israel did in 1505, two weeks before the Diet convened in Buda. They moved their wives, children, and relatives to Pressburg, after obtaining a letter of protection from Ulászló II. In that letter the king calls upon the city of Pressburg to take under its protection the Mendel family, whom Jacob Judah Mendel, "for certain and reasonable reasons," is sending to Pressburg for a period of time. Despite this edict, Israel Mendel, who remained in Pressburg for several months, was persecuted and attacked, so that three months later the king again had to order the city to take Israel Mendel under its protection. The fact that such orders had to be repeated indicates that royal edicts from Buda were not taken too seriously in the remote city of Pressburg.

The Mendel prefects were the major suppliers of money to the royal treasury and household, in the form of very substantial loans and credits. Their services were employed not only by the king but also by the magnates of the realm, in connection with their business dealings. In 1529–30, when Margrave George of Brandenburg, who was both uncle and guardian of Lajos II, planned to sell the castle and domain of Hunyad (the ancestral seat of the royal Hunyadi family), he entrusted the negotiations with the prospective buyer, Péter Perényi, the voivod (prince) of Transylvania, to the Jew Mendel of Buda, probably Isaac Mendel.

After the Mohács Disaster of 1526, the office of the Jewish prefect survived for a number of years in that part of the country which came under the rule of Ferdinand I (r. 1526–64), the Holy Roman Emperor and brother-in-law of Lajos II. In 1531 we hear of the Jewish prefect Tobias Mendel, and in the summer of 1534 a rich Jewish merchant submitted an offer to Ludovico Gritti, King John Szapolyai's governor of Hungary, to the effect that if Gritti lets him have the house of Mendel (that is, Tobias Mendel) and the street of the Jews, he would pay the regent 10,000 marks annually, for ten years. As a further inducement, the offer mentions that Italian and Greek merchants promised to build magnificent palaces in Buda to make it a city the likes of which existed nowhere else in the world. The mention of the house of Mendel indicates that his home must have been the most important building in the Jewish street of Buda.

When and why the office of the Jewish prefect was abolished are not known. But we have some information on a member or members of the Mendel family who emigrated to Germany. One of them was a certain Jacob Mendel, who moved to Norimberg in 1499, got involved in an ugly quarrel with the local Jews, and was instrumental in their expulsion from the city. This might have been the same man who in 1534 converted to Protestantism, assumed the name Christoff Mandel von Ofen, and published three books of Christological content.

Besides the Mendels, who held sway over the Jews of Hungary for some three-quarters of a century, the only influential Jewish leader known from the late fifteenth century is Akiba ben Menahem haKohen of Buda, who is referred to in Jewish sources as *nasi* (duke) and "head of the entire Diaspora." He entered into history as a leader of the Buda Jewish community, where he was greatly revered for his religious fervor, his mastery of Talmud and Halakha, his riches, and his exceptional charity. It seems he occupied a respected position in the court as well. It is reported that he signed his name with "golden letters," probably similar to those found in illuminated medieval manuscripts.

Akiba's riches and influence engendered jealousy among the Hungarian magnates, who denounced him with slanderous accusations to King Matthias. He was forced to leave Hungary (it is unknown whether he left of his own free will or was expelled) and settled, together with his large family, in Prague. There he established a talmudic school where he himself taught. However, in Prague, too, his wealth and authority aroused jealous attacks: slanders embittered his life, and no fewer than three times his very life was in danger. In memory of his triple escape, he donated three identical, richly embroidered curtains for the Holy Ark in the Prague synagogue.

Akiba had twelve sons and thirteen daughters. Twelve of his daughters he married to Kohens, descendants of the high priest Aaron, of whom he himself was a scion. In his old age he proudly mentioned that thus there were twenty-five men in his family who together recited the priestly blessing on the holidays; in this manner he truly fulfilled the biblical commandment, "Thus shall ye bless the Children of Israel"

(Num. 6:23), where the word "thus" (*koh* in Hebrew) had the numerical value of twenty-five. His daughter Jochebed married R. Shabtai, one of the greatest talmudic luminaries of the age. This couple was to become the ancestors of a great scholarly rabbinical family, among whom was R. Samuel Edels (the "Maharsha"). Akiba died in 1496, and was buried in Prague. His tombstone refers to him as "Rabbi Akiba, the Kohen and *Nasi* of Buda." His authority was so great that even 150 years after his death a decision of his was invoked in a responsum.

We must return once more to the Mendels to consider briefly what it meant psychologically to be the Jewish prefect (*princeps*), and as such responsible for the well-being, and the very life, of the Jews of a whole kingdom. To fill the position effectively the Jewish prefect had to have the capacity of identifying on the one hand with the Jewish community of which he was the representative and on the other with the interests of king and country, in particular with those of the royal treasury. Fulfilling the roles imposed by this double identity was a formidable task. It required the ability to navigate incessantly the narrow course between the Scylla of Jewish resentment and the Charybdis of royal displeasure.

The relationship between the Jews and the court was one of both mutual need and opposed interests. Each benefited from the other, but the interest of the Jews was to pay lower taxes and enjoy more protection, while that of the court was to obtain higher taxes from the Jews, in exchange according them as little protection as possible so as not to antagonize the nobles, the Church, and the cities on whose support the crown relied. In this constant tension between the two antagonistic interests it was the duty and the challenge of the Jewish prefect to steer the middle course and to find, propose, and where necessary enforce arrangements that entailed the least possible dissatisfaction on both sides.

The concept of patriotism, which dominated Hungarian and Hungarian-Jewish life from the nineteenth century on, had not yet developed in the fifteenth and sixteenth centuries. But a precursor of the patriotic stance existed in that earlier period as the sense of duty to serve the king. Accordingly, one aspect of the split identity of the Jewish prefect was the role of the faithful royal servant who in his person embodied the loyalty that the Jews as serfs of the royal chamber were expected to have and display. In this capacity the Jewish prefect had a more subservient attitude to the throne than the nobles and the cities, for the simple reason that the position of the Jews was much weaker, and despite their internal divisions the Christian population elements together formed an overall unit from which the Jews, with their otherness, were excluded. It was the task of the Jewish prefect to demonstrate in his contacts with the king and the court that the Jews, though undeniably different from the Christians, were nevertheless as faithful and useful servants of the crown as any of its Christian Hungarian subjects.

While in his contacts with the crown and nobles the Jewish prefect thus embodied the Jewish community of Hungary, his role within that community brought into play the second part of his split identity. As a representative of the crown, the Jewish prefect had to see to it that the Jewish community lived up to its supreme duty toward king and crown: that it unfailingly paid the taxes imposed by the royal camera. For the Jews, therefore, the Jewish prefect represented the state authority. In their eyes he was part of the state machinery aiming at exploiting them by squeezing higher and higher taxes out of them, by making them pay by force of arms and under pain of imprisonment if necessary, and by appearing among them and behaving as if he were not a Jew at all but a member of the Hungarian high nobility. True, if a Jew or a Jewish community was in trouble, it was to the Jewish prefect that they could appeal, and it was he who could obtain redress through his influence at the court; nevertheless, the Jewish prefect was never an integral part of the Jewish community as was a rabbi or, in later centuries, a *shtadlan*, an intercessor (see chapter 19). Characteristically, while rabbis and Jewish communal leaders began by the late fifteenth century to leave behind halakhic or other religious writings, no writings of any kind were produced by the Jewish prefects (or at least none survived), as if the traditional Jewish pairing of leadership and scholarship could not extend into the high ranks of the Jewish prefects. Evidently, the Jewish prefect was not a Jewish leader in the traditional sense of the term but a Jew who, as representative of the Jewish community, achieved the highest position open for a Jew in the governmental hierarchy. Historical data are lacking, but one wonders to what extent the Mendels were observant Jews in a period and a community where strict orthodox observance was the rule. The role they were expected to play was essentially little different from that of their predecessors the Jew judges, who were non-Jewish Hungarian noblemen of high rank.

There can be little doubt that the tasks the Jewish prefect had to shoulder, and the position he occupied between the court and the Jews, produced in him an ambivalent attitude toward his own Jewishness and toward the Jewish community he headed. On the one hand, he could not deny his Jewishness and his identification with his people, whose representation was entrusted to him by the king, nor did he want to. All the Mendels, as far as we know, fulfilled their role faithfully, and their functioning redounded to the benefit of the Jews. But on the other hand, their position placed them outside their community and forced them to deal with the other Jews in a manner not too different from that of a great lord whose estates housed Jewish subjects. The Jewish prefects were the only Jewish magnates who are known to have resorted to armed force against Jews while carrying out their duties on behalf of the royal treasury. They were not only ambivalent, they were marginal men, standing between the crown and the Jews, and not belonging fully to either of them.

It is not farfetched to consider the possibility that the specific personality that must have characterized the Jewish prefects and enabled them to function as intermediaries left its mark on the history of the Hungarian Jews, and that perhaps in the nineteenth century, when the possibility again arose for Jewish leaders to play a role in Hungarian public life, similar types reemerged and were attracted by the double task of Jewish communal leadership and active participation in Hungarian politics and government. In the nineteenth century, of course, the dominant motivation in Hungarian public life was patriotism, and accordingly the new Jewish leaders of the period became the spirited spokesmen of Hungarian patriotism within the Jewish community as well as representatives of Jewish Magyar patriotism in the general social and political forums of the country. In any case, the historical antecedents from the 1400s and 1500s enable us to understand somewhat better the unique red-white-green coloration of the Hungarian Jewish establishment of the 1800s and 1900s that resulted in the virtual self-exclusion—until the Holocaust—of Hungarian Jewry from global Jewish affairs and its condemnation of Zionism as an unpatriotic and un-Hungarian movement.

9

The First Scholars and the First Blood Libel (Fifteenth and Sixteenth Centuries)

We have had occasion to mention that the Hungarian Jews were late-comers in producing religious or scholarly writings, or, for that matter, any other kind of writings. Their earliest contributions to Jewish literature date from several centuries after exegetical and halakhic writings began to flourish among Hungarian Jewry's Ashkenazi neighbors. And even then, the first known Jewish author who lived and wrote in Hungary around 1400 cannot be called a Hungarian Jew, because he was born in Vienna and moved to the Hungarian city of Nagyszombat only after completing his talmudic studies at the feet of several outstanding Austrian rabbinical scholars. Still, he spent enough time in Nagyszombat to be given the byname "Tyrnau," the German name of the city, and to become known as Isaac Tyrnau.

Isaac Tyrnau's teachers were the famous Viennese talmudist Abraham Klausner (d. 1407 or 1408), whom he calls his "chief teacher"; Klausner's brother-in-law, the martyr Aaron of Neustadt; and Sar Shalom of Wiener Neustadt. Tyrnau was in touch with other Jewish scholars as well, and in 1420, shortly before his death, he contacted Jacob Moellin ("Maharil") regarding a divorce case.

Isaac Tyrnau's renown in the world of Jewish scholarship rests on his *Sefer haMinhagim* (Book of Customs), first published in Venice in 1400, which he intended to be a guide for halakhically uneducated people, to enable them to follow the religious customs of the Jewish year. As he writes in his preface, since the Black Death (1348–50) decimated the Jewish communities of Germany, scholars became so few that in many places no more than one or two men remained with any real knowledge of the local custom. He states that "in this work I took note of the religious customs of our country, Hungary, Styria, and Moravia."

A manuscript of the book was in the hands of an unidentified Hungarian scholar who added glosses to it, and it was published together with them. From the sixteenth century on, it became very popular and

108

was reprinted frequently, often as an appendix to the Jewish prayer book. A German translation by Simon Günzburg was printed in Mantua in 1590, and it, too, was reprinted several times. The customs and rules of conduct as laid down by Isaac Tyrnau were subsequently adopted by most communities in Austria, Hungary, and Styria, and the book itself was widely used among German and Polish Jewry as well.

That the Hungarian sojourn of Isaac Tyrnau extended over many years is attested by an entry in his *Book of Customs* that shows that he had acquired a thorough mastery of the Hungarian language. He explains a rare Aramaic word by giving its Hungarian translation: he writes that the talmudic term *dohan* (a species of millet) is identical with the Hungarian *tatarka*. This name is still used in Hungary for buckwheat (*Fagopyrum tataricum*).

The Hungarian relations of Isaac Tyrnau laid the foundations of a legend about him, included in a booklet titled *The Finger of God, or a Wonderful Event That Happened to R. Isaac Tyrnau, the Author of the Book of Customs*. The son of the dowager duchess of Nagyszombat, so the story goes, fell in love with the beautiful daughter of R. Isaac and asked him for her hand. The rabbi was scared to death and tried everything to dissuade the young duke. But the duke persisted and did not give up his suit even when the rabbi finally stated that he could never agree to his daughter marrying anybody but a Jew and, what is more, an outstanding talmudic scholar. The love-smitten youth finally extracted a promise from the rabbi: "I shall let you marry my daughter if you fulfill my conditions." Soon thereafter the young duke disappeared. His mother searched for him, but in vain.

Years went by, and one day a young stranger appeared in the yeshiva of R. Isaac. He started to attend the rabbi's Talmud classes and before long manifested such broad knowledge and sharp understanding that he became the rabbi's favorite disciple. His diligence, piety, and modest and noble demeanor not only endeared him to the rabbi but also won the heart of his daughter. Finally, he made himself known: he was the young duke who had disappeared years before and now, having fulfilled the rabbi's conditions, came back to claim his bride.

The fame of the young couple's remarkable beauty spread abroad, and their wedding was attended by the dowager duchess, who, however, did not recognize her son. But sometime later his former nurse noticed a birthmark on his body, and thus his identity was revealed. He was thrown in jail but continued to deny his birth, even when his mother visited him in the dead of the night, begged him to admit the truth, and promised him full pardon. Since he remained unrepentant, the king sentenced him to death, and he was executed. His mother planned to take cruel vengeance on the Jews of Nagyszombat, and especially on R. Isaac, but her son appeared to her in a dream and his entreaty moved her to desist from her murderous plan, and she was satisfied with expelling the Jews from the city.

The legend may have something to do with the burning of the Jews in Nagyszombat in 1494 (see below) and their expulsion in 1537. However, it is possible that it developed in the wake of a wave of persecutions that swept over Nagyszombat in 1391, during the lifetime of R. Isaac Tyrnau, about which otherwise nothing is known, but which seems to be referred to on an old Jewish tombstone of Nagyszombat as "the year of woe."

Although R. Isaac Tyrnau was the first Jewish author domiciled in Hungary from whom a book has survived, several other Jewish scholars were his contemporaries but left behind no writings. One of them was Nathan of Buda, who lived prior to 1427 and is mentioned by R. Jacob Moellin ("Maharil"); another was R. Judah ("Mahari"), who also lived in the fifteenth century. Three other fifteenth-century rabbis, R. Meir, R. Koloman, and R. Goddel (or Gedel), may have lived in Ödenburg (Sopron), although the reading of their city's name is uncertain, and it could refer not to Ödenburg but Orenburg. These rabbis are known only from brief references to them by rabbinical authors who lived outside the borders of Hungary.

The sources that mention these names also inform us that the Hungarian rabbis of the age were in touch with Jewish scholars in other countries in connection with halakhic problems and that the Jews of Hungary meticulously observed the religious traditions and customs, were organized into communities with synagogues and other religious institutions, and had rabbis and other religious functionaries.

This sudden upsurge of Jewish scholarship and the parallel development of meticulous religious observance among the Jews of Hungary in the fifteenth century are remarkable phenomena, whose roots and the factors that produced them are still unresearched and hence can only be surmised. One of the factors undoubtedly was the arrival and settlement in Hungarian communities of learned rabbis from abroad, from countries where by the fifteenth century Jewish scholarship had a venerable tradition. Another must have been the relatively favorable conditions under which the Jews lived in fifteenth-century Hungary, which enabled them to build and maintain communities with synagogues, rabbis, and Torah schools, and which even improved in central Hungary after the Turks consolidated their rule over that part of the country. In any case, there can be no doubt that, compared to the period that preceded it, Jewish life in fifteenth-century Hungary became more religious, and developed an environment in which Jewish religious scholarship was able to flourish.

It is from the *Decisions* of R. Israel Isserlein (1390–1460), the foremost German rabbi of the fifteenth century, that we know of the type of halakhic problems Hungarian rabbis were faced with in that century. In one case, R. Abraham Hakohen of Buda felt that he had to consult Isserlein on a problem connected with a *get* (letter of divorce). What happened was that a Pressburg Jew had a *get* written for his wife, who received it in Buda, where she was living at the time. However, doubt was cast on the validity of the *get*, because it became known that the man was a renegade who used various aliases, which were not enumerated in the *get*. In the meantime, the man moved to Regensburg, and when the wife followed him there in order to have him acknowledge the *get*, he could not be found. The woman applied to R. Isserlein, requesting that he recognize the *get* as valid, but he, despite R. Abraham's authentication of the *get*, refused to permit the woman to enter a new marriage. R. Abraham's position was supported by one of his Hungarian fellow rabbis, Mahari, who seems to have been none other than R. Judah, the Pressburg rabbi before whom the *get* was originally written. Another Hungarian rabbi who lived in the early fifteenth century and is mentioned in the same decision of Isserlein was Maharam Hakohen of Buda, who was recognized there as the highest religious authority, possibly the *av beth din* of the community.

This single document, included among Isserlein's *Decisions*, is a most valuable source of information on the religious life of the Hungarian Jews in the fifteenth century. It shows that by that time, the Hungarian Jews had organized communities with official contact among their congregations, and rabbis functioning in widely dispersed cities with scholarly-religious contact between them and the leading rabbinical authorities in other countries. It also confirms what we know from other sources; that conversions to Christianity were occurrences that the rabbis had to deal with not infrequently.

Equally significant for our insight into the Jewishness of Hungarian Jews in this period is the fact that not only were the men, in general, able to read Hebrew, which is an indispensable prerequisite of living a Jewish religious life, but many of them could also write in it. They wrote their commercial and other notes in Hebrew, and even signed in Hebrew the Latin documents that attested to agreements between them and Christian Hungarians. This demonstrates that they were able to write only in Hebrew and not in Hungarian, which was the colloqial tongue, nor in Latin, which was the official language of documents.

We now turn to the tragic events that took place in Nagyszombat some seventy years after R. Isaac Tyrnau's death.

There is a curious parallel between the tardy beginnings of the production of scholarly books that characterizes Hungarian Jewish life until the fifteenth century and the late arrival in Hungary of those horrible incidents that caused the Jews so much suffering in many countries of medieval Europe: blood libels. It took 350 years for the infamous libel that Jews used Christian blood for ritual, medical, and other purposes to travel from England, where the first of such accusations took place in 1144, to Hungary, where the first blood libel was staged in 1494 (to be repeated in 1529, 1764, 1791, 1882, and 1891). On its way from west to east it brought torture and death to many Jews in France, Spain, Switzerland, Germany, Austria, and Bohemia before it penetrated the borders of Hungary and proceeded from there to Eastern Europe and the Ottoman Empire.

In 1494 the child of a Christian family of Nagyszombat disappeared. His parents searched for him in vain, but they found witnesses who stated that a day earlier they had seen the child in the Jewish street. This gave rise to the suspicion and allegation that the child had been killed by the Jews—a development that undoubtedly reflects familiarity on the part of some people in Nagyszombat with the blood libels and subsequent punitive proceedings that had taken place in other countries.

The major source of what happened next is the contemporary chronicler Bonfinius, who gives full credit to the accusation. He describes soldiers being sent to the houses of the Jews, in one of which fresh traces of blood were found, whereupon the owner of that house and his entire family were arrested. The women who were interrogated, "driven by the fear of torture," confessed in detail to the evil crime. According to them, he writes, twelve Jewish men and two women dragged the child into the nearby synagogue, where "they squeezed his throat, suffocated him miserably, cut open his veins, and partly drank his blood while his life ran out together with it, and partly put it aside for others, and then cut the body into pieces and buried them limb by limb."

This confession, says Bonfinius, was sufficient for the authorities to condemn the accused: upon the command of the palatine, István Szapolyai, who acted as the prefect of the city, they burned all of them at the stake set up in the marketplace, while other Jews, who appeared to be less guilty, were sentenced to paying large fines.

The chronicler also reports that "when they extracted from the old men the reasons for this foul deed by instruments of torment," they "confessed" that the Jews needed Christian blood for four purposes:

First, they were convinced by the judgment of their ancestors that the blood of a Christian was good remedy for the alleviation of the wound of circumcision. Second, they were of the opinion that this blood, put into food, was very efficacious for the awakening of mutual love. Third, they had discovered, since among them both men and women suffered equally from menstruation, that drinking the blood of a Christian was a specific medicine for it. The absurd beliefs and calumnies contained in this confession extracted by torture culminate in the assertion that the Jews were organized into a worldwide secret society that drew lots and imposed the performance of "religious" rituals on one of its member communities: "Fourth, they had an ancient but secret ordinance by which they are under obligation to shed Christian blood in honor of God, in daily sacrifices, in one place or another. . . . The lot for the present year has fallen on the Tyrnau Jews."

More details about the Nagyszombat auto-da-fé are contained in a Hebrew dirge written by a certain Joshua ben Ḥayyim, who either witnessed it himself or learned about it from eyewitnesses. According to it, the Jews were arrested on August 5 and burned on August 22; that is, the whole "legal" procedure, including the hearing, torture, sentencing, the erection of the stake, and the execution of the sentence, took a mere seventeen days. The poem has been preserved in an eleventh-century Cracow codex, on whose flyleaves the servants of the Old Synagogue entered memorable events of the period 1480–1576. The text of the dirge is accompanied by explanatory notes, likewise written in Hebrew, by the author himself, who states that "the burning took place on the twentieth of Elul [August 22], and I completed all the rhymes likewise." From these explanatory notes we learn that clemency was offered to the accused if they would accept Christianity, but they rejected it, and among the victims were two Kohenites and one Levite, as well as two elders who prayed fervently until the flames consumed their bodies.

After the auto-da-fé, the city of Nagyszombat set up a stone statue of the allegedly murdered child near one of the several monasteries of the city to serve as a memorial for him. This statue could still be seen in the early nineteenth century.

Despite this horrible experience, Jews continued to live in Nagyszombat for another thirty-four years, and their numbers even increased to such an extent that the crown felt the need to appoint a special Jew judge for the city. Up to the Mohács Disaster, the family of Palatine István Szapolyai controlled the city, since Ulászló II, who constantly suffered from a shortage of money, had given it as a pledge to the palatine. This being the case, the widow of the palatine, Hedvig Szapolyai, in her 1516 rescript to Nagyszombat disposing of the affairs of the local Jews, refers to them as "our Jews." Then in 1539, King Ferdinand I issued a decree expelling the Jews of Nagyszombat "for all times" from the city. In the event, it was not until some 250 years later that Jews returned to Nagyszombat.

Following the Turkish conquest of central Hungary and the capital city of Buda, the Jews, as we shall see in chapter 14, adjusted to Ottoman rule, and even found ways to prosper as intermediaries between Turkish Hungary and the two Christian-dominated parts of Hungary to its west and east. This was the period in which, stimulated by contact with more literate and scholarly Jewish communities, the Hungarian Jews under Turkish rule became full partners with their colleagues in other countries in engaging in halakhic work.

In the first half of the sixteenth century, R. Naphtali Herz Kohen functioned as rabbi of Buda. He was a relative of R. Meir of Padua (d. 1583), who speaks of him with the greatest respect. R. Naphtali, on his part, recognized R. Meir of Padua as the superior authority in religious law and appealed to his mastery of the Halakha. A case in point, known from R. Meir's *Decisions*, was the following. A deaf and mute woman, while still a minor, had been given in marriage by her father to a man who, years later, wanted to divorce her. The divorce proceedings in such a case were problematic, and R. Naphtali asked the advice of his kinsman R. Meir about it. The relationship between these two rabbis is known only from R. Meir's *Decisions*. R. Naphtali left no written documents at all.

Another rabbi of Buda, in the first quarter of the sixteenth century, was R. Joseph Zalmoni, who is mentioned in several contemporary sources as a leading halakhic authority, and to whom other rabbis submitted their own decisions for ultimate authentication.

An important center of Jewish life in Austrian-dominated west Hungry was the city of Kismarton (in German Eisenstadt, translated in Hebrew sources as 'Ir Barzel, that is, Iron City). In it during the first half of the 16th century lived a certain R. Solomon, son of R. Lieberman, who also had close contact with R. Meir of Padua, as shown by the latter's references to him and to the community of Eisenstadt. Occasionally R. Solomon disagreed with R. Meir, as happened in the following case: R. Solomon's stepdaughter picked up a few pennies dropped by a young man who thereupon, in jest, addressed to her the traditonal words of the betrothal formula, "Behold, thou art betrothed to me with this . . ." When R. Solomon was informed of this, he wrote to the young man, warning him that since he uttered the legal betrothal formula, he was not allowed to marry another woman unless he first divorced R. Solomon's stepdaughter. He added that the girl, however, could not be forced to accept a *get* [divorce letter] from him. R. Solomon insisted that this decision was the halakhically correct one even when R. Meir of Padua opposed it. When the young man and his father refused to accept his decision, R. Solomon put them under the ban.

In his old age, in about 1550, R. Solomon took an active part in an acrimonious controversy over the validity of a *get* in which rabbis from Bohemia, Poland, Austria, and Italy participated, siding with those who recognized the validity of the *get* written in Prague. R. Solomon spent the last years of his life in Posen (Poznań) as the *av beth din* (head of the rabbinical court) of that city.

These few references, found in the halakhic writings of rabbis outside Hungary, allow us to extrapolate and assume that, in addition to the rabbis who happen to be mentioned in these documents, there must have lived and worked in Hungary in the fifteenth and sixteenth centuries many other rabbis who left no traces in the contemporary literature but who served their communities as faithfully and effectively as those whose names survive in their writings.

10

Jewish Physicians in the Fourteenth to Eighteenth Centuries

This chapter and the next deviate from the chronological presentation of the story of the Jews in Hungary to sketch instead a diachronic picture of the development of two very specific aspects of Hungarian Jewish life through several centuries. The first, given in this chapter, is the work of Jewish physicians in Hungary, a subject on which the information, though extremely meager, is still sufficient to show that Jewish physicians played an important role throughout the five centuries that preceded the introduction of formal medical education in the country. A rapid overview of the services Jewish doctors rendered in Hungary from the fourteenth to eighteenth centuries permits us to conclude that the flocking of Hungarian Jews into medicine once the doors of medical schools were opened to them in the nineteenth century was but a sequel to the attraction medicine had held for them for several centuries already.

The next chapter discusses, likewise in a sketchy diachronic presentation, patterns of Jewish criminality from the sixteenth to eighteenth centuries. Here again we find a continuity: the almost total absence of violent crime among the Jews attested to by statistics from the nineteenth century on is preceded by a similar pattern in the three previous centuries, when, as in the nineteenth and twentieth, crimes committed by Jews were almost entirely confined to money matters. Whatever new features developed in the Hungarian Jewish character in the wake of the 1869 emancipation, in these two respects—their love of medicine and their specific crime pattern—they were very definitely the heirs of their own past.

While in several cities of Western Europe as well as in Vienna, Prague, and Cracow, medical schools were functioning by the beginning of the eleventh century, in Hungary the first such institution was not founded until 1769, when Empress Maria Theresa established one in the

city of Nagyszombat. Although prior to that time some medical education seems to have existed, Hungarian writers in the seventeenth and
eighteenth centuries complain that "in our country there are neither
medical doctors nor pharmacies." Even in the eighteenth century, the
usual procedure for taking care of ailments, wounds, and other physical
problems was to be treated by various types of traditional healers. These
healers are referred to by a wide range of names in the contemporary
German-language documents from Hungary—*Balbierer, Chyrurg,
Baader, Arzt, Feldscherer,* or simply "women who administer a *Cur*"
[cure]—but their precise areas of specialization are difficult to determine. In earlier centuries, the only persons in Hungary with access to
academically trained physicians were rulers and rich members of the
high nobility, who could invite doctors from abroad. Among the physicians who came to Hungary in this manner to treat kings and magnates,
Jewish doctors figure prominently.

The first Hungarian Jewish doctor known as an individual was
Moyses de Hungaria, whose name shows that he had become a permanent resident of the country. King Lajos the Great (r. 1342–82) seems to
have become dissatisfied with his work, for he expelled him from Hungary, whereupon Dr. Moyses went to Naples and opened a practice in
nearby Heraclea. We next hear of Jewish medical work in Hungary in
the year 1439, when the Jewish community of Sopron maintained a
hospital. For some reason, nearly a hundred years later (in 1530), the
Sopron community sold the building of this hospital to a Christian couple. Of the Azerbaijani-Spanish Jewish physician-diplomat who
sojourned at the court of King Matthias for about two years around
1472, we have heard above, in chapter 7. Matthias had also a Jewish
personal physician by the name of Salamon. Also in the second half of
the 16th century a Jewish woman doctor, referred to as "sydo doctor
azzony" (that is, "Jewish doctor woman"), worked in Sárvár, Komárom, and Sennye, and treated the wives of high Hungarian officials,
including the wife of the Palatine Tamás Nádasdy.

The son of King Matthias, János Corvinus, also had a Jewish per-
sonal physician. In 1491 he wrote to László Egerváry, the governor of
Croatia, Slavonia, and Dalmatia: "I would be glad to send you the Jew
Abraham, but at present I myself am sick. Let Your Excellency indicate
what medications you need, and we shall obtain them from the Jew
Abraham and send them to Your Excellency." After the death of János
Corvinus, Abraham went to Italy—he seems to be identical with the
Maestro Abraham Senior whose medical fame rapidly spread over the
entire peninsula. When Prince Louis Alexander Gonzaga was severely
wounded in the 1525 Battle of Parma, Abraham cured him, and four

years later when Giovanni de Medici sustained a life-threatening wound in the battle near Pavia, it was again Abraham who succeeded in saving his leg from amputation.

In 1492 an Italian Jewish physician, referred to in the sources as "Bracha doctor," was invited to cure the sick Pál Kinizsi (d. 1494), the commander of King Matthias's army in southern Hungary.

In 1511 the Pressburg Jewish physician and physicist Zacharias was invited to Buda to combat the pestilence raging in the city. As a reward for his services, King Ulászló II exempted him from wearing the Jewish badge. (The Jewish physicians of Rome obtained the same privilege from the pope.) Upon Zacharias's return to Pressburg, the city, as it often happened, did not obey the royal decree right away, and when the king was again in need of his services, Zacharias appeared in the court wearing the Jewish badge. Count Mózes Buzlay, master of the royal curia, therefore sent a second rescript to Pressburg reminding the city of Zacharias's privilege.

As with many royal heads all over Europe, the Hungarian king Ferdinand I (r. 1526–64), too, had a Jewish personal physician (name unknown) for his children and the personnel of the court. The Viennese medical faculty, motivated by jealousy, refused to permit this physician to treat other patients in the city.

Documents in the municipal archives of Hungarian cities provide scattered information on the work of Jewish physicians in the sixteenth century. One of them, from Pressburg, 1524, tells about a fee of one pound and two solidus denars the city paid to the Jew Michel of Austerlitz for restoring the eyesight of a blind purse maker. It is uncertain whether this man was a physician or a folk doctor. In 1540, one of the two Jewish families permitted to live in the city of Kőszeg was that of the Jewish physician Hatschl. In 1554, the Jewish physician Dr. Anselmus Ephorinus of Cracow sent the council of the city of Bártfa, which was smitten by pestilence, a "well-tried powder" and enclosed detailed instructions on its use and on what to do to protect themselves from the disease. He also suggested they take pills made of "aloe, myrrh, and saffron," and recommended other medications as well. In 1572, Maximilian I, king of Hungary, instructed the authorities in Vienna to issue a passport to "Jacobus Anselmus hebraeus, philosophiae et medicinae doctor," and his wife and family. Anselmus is identified as an Italian living in Poland.

Most interesting are three letters, written in 1559 and 1560, by a certain Ferenc Sennyei from Sárvár and Keresztúr to Palatine Tamás Nádasdy and his wife, about sending them an unnamed "Jewish doctor woman" to cure Nádasdy's wife. Evidently, the fame of that Jewish woman physician had spread beyond the area where she practiced, until her services were requested by the palatine, the highest official of the kingdom. In 1560, the sick wife of Kelemen Szalay, née Susanna Ghiczy, wrote to the wife of the palatine, begging her to send "the Jewish doctor woman," who was known to be able to cure a certain "illness in the head." Susanna vowed eternal gratitude to the wife of the palatine and added, "We shall pay for her trouble and work, not only as much as she will charge but, if with the help of God she should help, we shall give her even more." Soon thereafter, Mrs. Nádasdy herself tried to consult the Jewish doctor woman but could not locate her, and the palatine was advised to call in a Jewish physician from Vienna. (It is known that Jewish women physicians also worked in Germany in the fifteenth and sixteenth centuries.)

With the conquest of central Hungary by the Turks, Sephardi Jewish doctors, in the service of high Turkish officials, made their appearance in Hungary. Some of them, as we have seen in connection with King Matthias, combined the function of physician with that of international diplomat. Such a man was the physician (name unknown) who accompanied Grand Vizier Sinan on his incursion into Hungary late in the 1500s. That Jewish doctor played an important role in the court of the sultan, and it was he who obtained for Voivod Peter the position of prince of Wallachia. Subsequently, Voivod Michael of Wallachia had this Jewish physician captured, and even though the Jews offered him a ransom of 45,000 thalers (an unheard-of amount), he did not let him go but presented the physician as a gift to Prince Zsigmond Báthory.

Another important sixteenth century Jewish physician and diplomat was Solomon Ashkenazi, who at first was the personal physician of the Polish kings Sigismund August and Stephan Báthory; subsequently, he became the personal physician and confidant of Grand Vizier Mohamed Sokoli and then of Sultan Murad III (1575–95). As such, he negotiated the peace agreement between Turkey and the Venetian Republic and also influenced political relations between Turkey and Hungary.

To be the personal physician of a Turkish sultan was not without attendant dangers. In 1566, when the seventy-six-year-old Sultan Suleiman died while his army was laying siege to Szigetvár, his Jewish physician, who was with him, was put to death by strangling. Also in Christian Transylvania, the life of a Jewish doctor was not always easy. Several documents speak of a "Jewish Dr. Jacob," who came from Istanbul to Transylvania, was considered a man of evil character, owed money, was involved in lawsuits, and was imprisoned.

In the sixteenth century, most of the Jewish youths from all parts of Europe who wanted to become physicians studied at the university of Padua, where between 1517 and 1619 eighty Jews earned the medical doctorate. After graduation they settled in Italy, Turkey, and Poland, from where their fame reached Hungary as well. Several princes of Transylvania made use of their services, and the Hungarian cities and lords of estates near the Polish border frequently invited those who practiced in Cracow or Lemberg (Lvov). Quite often these doctors also engaged in diplomatic activity.

In 1606, when Prince István Bocskay of Transylvania contracted a serious illness, he dispatched two of his officers to King Sigismund III of Poland, to request the services of the king's famous Jewish physician Eleazar ("Medicus Iudaeus Doctor"). For a while Bocskay's condition improved under the ministrations of Dr. Eleazar, who prescribed a treatment called *manilla*, but a few months later Bocskay dismissed Eleazar and called in other physicians.

About 1619 two Jewish doctors functioned in Transylvania, possibly in the employment of the princely court of Gábor Bethlen. One of them was Dr. Abraham, the other Dr. Jacob. The latter seems to have been unsuccessful in covering his expenses with his patients' fees, for he incurred a debt of a hundred florins with a certain Lord Kamuti, and since he did not repay it even after being sued, he was imprisoned and kept in chains for a full month.

An influential person at the court at Gábor Bethlen, prince of Transylvania, was the Jewish physician from Constantinople Abraham Sarsa (or Sassa or Sarka; referred to as a "excellentissimus Abraham Szasza medicinae doctor Judeus Constantinopolitanus"). It was at his intercession that the prince in 1623 permitted the Jews, expelled from Transylvania earlier in the seventeenth century, to return and to bring along their physician, who was assured the right of unhindered movement including the freedom to travel abroad and to return again. Since Bethlen himself had a Jewish personal physician, Ryberius (or Riberius), Dr. Szasza must have been a consultant called in for some special reason. Riberius, who seems to have come to Transylvania from Turkey, was one of the three physicians who held a consultation over Prince Bethlen prostrated by a liver ailment. The three doctors could not agree on the cure: Riberius and one of his colleagues opposed the mineral water cure recommended by the third, a doctor from Moravia.

Prince George Rákóczi I also had a Jewish personal physician, with whom he discussed not only medical matters but also religious issues: once in 1635 he asked the doctor, "When do you expect the Messiah?" which the Jewish physician answered by shrugging his shoulder. The identity of this physician is not established, but he seems to be Dr. Valerius David, a Spanish Jew who immigrated to Translvania after 1623, converted to Christianity, and was appointed by Rákóczi *professor extraordinarius* of theology and philosophy at the college of Sárospatak. To take his place as his personal physician, Rákóczi appointed in 1639 another Jew, *Doctor Medicinae* Leon (Arye Yehuda) Sia. Dr. Sia, like many a Jewish physician before him, was also a philosopher and a Jewish scholar. He translated into Latin Judah Halevi's *Kuzari* and Baḥya ibn Paquda's *Hovot haLvavot* (Duties of the Hearts). He was in contact with Johann Buxtorf of Basel concerning the publication of these books, and in August of 1641, Prof. Hottinger of Zurich informed Buxtorf of a rumor that Dr. Sia had publicly converted to Christianity in Transylvania.

Another ruling prince of Transylvania, Mihály Apafi (r. 1661–90), also had a Jewish personal physician, Judah by name. We also know of a Jewish physician, Doctor Leo, who practiced in the 1640's in Kolozsvár.

That the Jewish physicians who put in an appearance in Hungary were able to administer psychological treatment as well becomes evident from a case in which the patient was Count Miklós Bethlen of Transylvania. Lovesickness caused the young count serious illness, and when the courtiers learned that the famous Jewish physician Máté (Mattheus), who had just cured the Wallachian voivoda of a dangerous disease, was stopping over in Segesvár on his way back to Lemberg, they called him to the eighteen-year-old count, whom he succeeded in restoring to health. Years later the count wrote an autobiography titled *Memoires historiques, contenants l'histoire des derniers troubles de Transylvanie* (published in Amsterdam in 1736), in which he described in detail the appearance of the famous physician—a big, fine-looking man, with the visage of a veritable Aesculapius—and the manner in which he had cured him. From the count's account of the treatment, it becomes clear that Dr. Mattheus, in addition to being a fine physician, was also a good psychologist.

The data referring to the work of Jewish physicians in Turkish-occupied Buda are few, but we know of at least one Jewish physician, a surgeon named Joseph, who lived in Buda in 1676 and was the son-in-law of the famous Belgrade physician Asher. Other data show that in the late seventeenth century some of the Jewish physicians of Buda treated their patients in consultation with visiting Christian physicians from Vienna and with Jewish physicians from Belgrade. Evidently, doctors maintained international contacts across the borders that separated the Christian and Muslim realms. We also happen to have knowledge of two Jewish midwives from the seventeenth century. The tombstone of one of them, Pserli bat Yosef, dated 1660, was found in Buda; the other midwife, aged eighty-seven, was among the victims of the 1686 battle for Buda.

In Royal Hungary, a Jew of Sopron, Andreas Loew, was the first academically trained physician. He earned his M.D. in 1682 in Jena with his *Inaugural Medical Dissertation on the Hungarian Disease*, and in the same year he published his *Medical Dissertation on Venereal Disease*, also in Latin, which he dedicated to the Evangelical Church Council of Sopron. It seems the council had helped him in his medical studies at the price of his conversion to the Evangelical faith.

In the early 1700s a member of the Italian Jewish Conegliano medical family practiced in Pressburg for some four years. His name was Joseph Stella, and like his Conegliano uncles and cousins on his mother's side, he was a graduate of the university of Padua. As a reward for his services in Pressburg during the 1711 plague, Emperor Charles III granted him the privilege of dwelling and practicing medicine in any place in Austria where Jews lived. Dr. Stella settled in Vienna and became a highly respected physician and a spokesman for the Jews of the empire. In his *Book of Saving Lives*, published in Hebrew in 1714, he describes the methods of protecting oneself against the plague and of curing those smitten by it, having in mind especially poor Hungarian Jews for whom it was difficult to consult physicians. Dr. Stella died in 1720 in Vienna at a young age.

By the early eighteenth century several Jewish physicians practiced in Pressburg, among them at least one surgeon. Because of the frequent epidemics, in 1710 the Jews of Buda were ordered by the commander of the fortress of Buda to build a *lazaret* (a hospital for contagious diseases) at the foot of Mount Gellért. In 1713 the city council of Pressburg put a building called Gunpowder Barn at the disposal of the Jews for their plague-stricken sick. In 1739, at the time of the plague epidemic that struck Hungary, the city council of Buda permitted the Jews to build another *lazaret*, which would become the property of the city once it was no longer needed. It seems the earlier plan had not materialized.

In the 1710s and 1720s a Jewish medical doctor, Marcus Mentzer, lived and practiced in Pressburg. This doctor must have been a well-to-do and sociable person, for he played host to the Jewish actor Jacob Joseph (see chapter 19). From documents relating to Dr. Mentzer we also learn that in those days physicians had to accept, occasionally at least, promissory notes from their patients in payment of their fees.

In 1733 Mihály Nathan Hirschel of Pressburg presented his doctoral thesis in Latin, titled *Pathological-therapeutic Inaugural Theses on the*

Cause of Intermittant Fevers to the medical faculty of Halle, and the next year he was awarded the M.D. degree. By that time young Hungarian Jewish men studied medicine abroad in Padua, Halle, Leiden, and Utrecht, but in the Austrian Empire they were not yet admitted to medical schools. After graduation, many returned to Hungary and practiced there. Among them were several who specialized in surgery. The Jewish physicians soon began to arouse the envy of others—one example appears in County Nyitra, whose council resolved in 1733 to employ a county physician, stipulating that he could not be a Jew. Nevertheless, in litigations the county accepted medical-legal depositions prepared by Jewish physicians.

By the middle of the eighteenth century, together with university-trained Jewish doctors, Jewish medical charlatans also made their appearance in Hungary. An example of such unlicensed practitioners was Isaac Lebel of Péczel, who, when called to account by the authorities, produced many testimonies from patients stating that he cured them of dangerous diseases. He was escorted to Pest to be examined by a leading physician and, failing in the exam, was forbidden to practice.

From the second half of the eighteenth century comes an example of collaboration between Jewish and Christian physicians in treating a Hungarian Jewish patient. The patient was Rabbi Isaac of Pressburg, and in 1761 he was treated by the Jewish doctor Israel Valmarin ("medicus physicus") jointly with two Christian "chyrurg"s for an infected abscess.

In 1764, Moses Markus, the son of a Pressburg rabbi, earned his M.D. degree in Butzow, Mecklenburg, with a Latin thesis titled *Philological-Medical Inaugural Dissertation on the Formerly Practiced Care of Hebrew Newborn Infants*, based on biblical studies, in which he engaged while a student. In 1773 the Royal Hungarian Lord Lieutenancy permitted Samuel Bernard Oppenheimer of Pressburg and Mendl Loebl of Holics, who had studied in Padua and Halle, respectively, to sit for their medical examinations at the university of Nagyszombat, enabling them to practice in Hungary. However, throughout this period, no Jew had yet been accepted as a student in the medical faculties of the Hungarian universities.

For years after being established, the medical faculties of Buda and Nagyszombat did not admit either Jews or other non-Catholics to examinations. Finally, in the fall of 1772, a governmental decree forced them to let non-Catholics take the exams. Nevertheless, it took ten more years before the first Jew earned the M.D. in Hungary: Joseph Manes Österreicher (b. Óbuda, 1756; d. Vienna, 1832), at the express order of Emperor Joseph II, was allowed to sit for the M.D. exam at the Buda faculty and earned his degree in 1782. His interest was in the medical use of mineral waters, and his dissertation dealt with the chemical composition of the waters of Buda and other spas in Hungary. The journal *Magyar Hirmondó*, reporting the event, noted: "The Royal University of Buda received special orders from His Majesty that the main medical freedom, that is, the doctorate in medicine, should from now on be given to non-Catholics in the same manner as to Catholics. Now, on the twenty-first day of the pre-fast month, a Jew, Mr. Manes Joseph Österreicher, was awarded this honor. There is no doubt that this new rule will serve the flowering of the university." Following his graduation, Joseph II appointed Dr. Österreicher physician of the Balatonfüred spa, which he developed into an important center of water cure. In 1792 Österreicher published in Vienna a study titled *Nachricht von den Bestandtheilen und Kraften des Füreder Sauerbrunnens*, which spread the fame of the spa abroad. Subsequently, he published several reports, in Hungarian, on the methods he developed for using "the wonderful Hungarian salt" for medical purposes. Apart from their medical interest, these papers are noteworthy in that they constitute the earliest writings by a Jew in the Hungarian language. In recognition of his services, Francis I (r. 1792–1835) awarded Dr. Österreicher a gold medal (which he proudly wore on a chain around his neck) and gave him the title "imperial-royal chief chamber physician."

Once medicine opened its doors to Hungarian Jews, it became their favorite specialization, and before long they were the dominant element among Hungarian physicians.

All one can learn from the above scanty data on Jewish physicians in Hungary and Transylvania from the fourteenth to eighteenth centuries is that both the rulers of the land and the people made use of the services of Jewish physicians (of both sexes) most of whom, until the eighteenth century, were foreigners visiting in Hungary or invited from abroad to settle. The history of Jewish physicians in Europe in general has been thoroughly investigated; in contrast, the history of Jewish physicians in Hungary has been woefully neglected. Hence, we do not know whether the Jewish predominance in the medical profession that characterized Hungary in modern times had any antecedents in those earlier centuries. The role of Jews in Hungarian medicine from the late nineteenth century on matched the general Jewish breakthrough into all academic fields, as well as all branches of commerce and industry, that took place after emancipation and that contributes to the picture we shall try to paint in later chapters of Jewish life in the hundred years before the Holocaust.

11

Jewish Criminals in the Sixteenth to Eighteenth Centuries

As we have seen in several preceding chapters, legal restrictions that barred them from most occupations forced many Jews in Hungary into the money business. Those Jews who had sizable sums at their disposal made loans to the royal treasury, to princes and magnates, and to cities and owners of landed property, and they secured their loans by mortgages or letters of indebtedness. Small-scale Jewish moneylenders had to be satisfied with pawnbrokering; the Christian borrowers deposited with them pieces of jewelry, candlesticks, even books, as security for the loans the Jews gave them. There were times when the Jewish pawnbrokers were then able to deposit the objects they thus received in the vault that was part of the jailhouse of the Jewish prefect in Buda, and leave them there for safekeeping until the borrowers redeemed them by repaying the loan. Mostly, however, they had no choice but to keep the pledges in their homes, which was known not only to the borrowers but also the local criminal element, making such houses the favorite target of breaking and entering. That such burglaries occurred not infrequently is known from the legal proceedings that took place when a borrower was ready to redeem a pledge and the Jewish pawnbroker was unable to produce it because it had been stolen from his house.

The minutes of criminal proceedings preserved in the archives of Hungarian cities show that criminality was not absent among Jews either. However, with the exception of a few trumped-up charges of ritual murder, the crimes for which Jews were arrested and tried did not, as a rule, include murder, kidnapping, or other violent crimes but only theft, the purchase of stolen property, and occasionally nonrepayment of loans. In the absence of relevant data we have no way of estimating the relative frequency of thefts committed by Jews compared to all the thefts perpetrated—in other words, whether this crime was more or less common among the Jews than among the general population. What the records show is that in the seventeenth and eighteenth centuries several hundreds of Jews were arrested and tried for theft.

Since the Jews were a disliked population element in Hungary, often aliens and newcomers, for whom the courts could be expected to have less sympathy than for indigenous Christian Hungarian offenders, the question inevitably arises whether a Jew stood less of a chance of being found not guilty by the Christian law courts of the country than a gentile. The available records do not permit us to draw any conclusion, but the few cases on record in which a Jew and a gentile jointly committed a crime and were jointly tried give the impression that the judiciary was by and large evenhanded and the scales of justice were not weighted a priori against Jewish suspects. Also, it is noteworthy that even in times of strong anti-Jewish prejudice when Jews were subject to many legal restrictions, recourse to the law courts was as open to the Jews as to non-Jews. A few of the cases that follow will illustrate these general observations.

Let us begin with the most serious of all crimes, that of murder, of which Jews were accused extremely rarely, and when they were, the accusation was, typically, in the nature of a blood libel. Of the first Hungarian blood libel, that of Nagyszombat of 1494, we have heard above in chapter 9. Of the two subsequent ones, those of Bazin of 1529, and the second one of Nagyszombat of 1536, we shall hear below, in chapter 15. In addition to these cases in which entire Jewish communities were accused of ritual murder, occasionally also individual Jews were charged with having killed Christians for ritual purposes.

The first case on record is that of the Jew Rufus, who was hanged in 1539 in Galgócz for the crime of having killed a Christian boy. It is doubtful whether the sentence was a just one, or the authorities were influenced by the always present Christian suspicion that the Jews used Christian blood for ritual purposes. Following the execution a wave of anti-Jewish excesses swept over Galgócz, which was so violent that Emperor Ferdinand found it necessary to caution the city to refrain from all illegal steps against the Jews. A month later the widow of the executed Jew was accused of having led two old women and one young girl in setting fire to three places in the city in order to reduce the whole city to ashes and thus to avenge the judicial murder of her husband.

That the blood libel was part of the anti-Jewish atmosphere in the 16th century becomes evident, among other things, from the edict issued in Warsaw by István Báthory (1533–86), Prince of Transylvania and King of Poland, which states that having instituted an investigation, he found that this grave accusation was not true, and wishing to put an end to these calumnies he ordered that nobody should any longer accuse the Jews of a blood libel, that is, with acting against the law by killing Christian children and stealing altar sacraments; he who dared to do this will henceforth be punished severely.

No royal edict, however, could eradicate the blood libel. In 1661 the Jews of Nagymarton (Mattersdorf) were accused of having killed a Christian girl. Fortunately, however, the girl turned up alive and well a week later.

Another case, which too had the features characteristic of a typical blood libel, was much more serious. As far as one can reconstruct the events from the single document describing them, what happened was that a Jew of Buda sojourning in Vác purchased from some Turks a young woman captive and her small son, whose home was originally in the town of Ponik. Then, wishing to make a profit, the Jew sold them to a certain János Almássy, domiciled in Vác, who, pretending that he wanted to restore them to their home and become the child's guardian, took them to Ponik. Arriving there, the young woman complained to her relatives that while he had her alone on the way, Almássy tried several times to violate her and force her to commit adultery. On the basis of this complaint, both of them were arrested in Lipcse—we do not know how they got there—and in the course of their interrogation the suspicion arose that Almássy maintained a partnership with the Jew, who traded in Christian blood. The case was therefore submitted to the plenary session of County Zolyom, which resolved that Almássy would be set free only if he could prove with sufficient testimonies that he was not guilty. All this was reported to the chamber of Pressburg by Mihály Fischer, Jr., who added that the mentioned "Jew of Vác" (who remains unnamed) slashed the skin of the captive infant with his nails and squeezed blood from its body to wash his own face with, and now he was resorting to all kinds of stratagems to avoid being punished. How Mihály Fischer came by all these details is not stated, nor do we know what action, if any, the Pressburg chamber took after receiving this singular document. One thing, however, becomes clear from it: the allegation that the Jew washed his face in the blood of the Christian infant indicates the presence of the belief among the Hungarian Christians in the late seventeenth century that Jews used Christian children's blood for ritual (or other?) purposes.

It happened that even a Jew who had a personal grudge against another Jew made use of the prevalent Christian belief in the Jewish use of Christian blood, and accused him of having killed a Christian child. Such a case took place in Pressburg in 1698: according to the testimony of the Jew Marcus Teutsch, the Jew Simon Michl forced the Jew Adam Schneider to marry "his whore whom he had impregnated." For this reason Adam Schneider hated Simon Michl with such a fathomless hatred that he accused him of having murdered a Christian child, and threatened to "stick a knife into his body" and to burn down the house in which he lived.

For more than two hundred years after the execution of the Jew Rufus in Galgócz no Jew suffered the death penalty in Hungary. Then, in 1742, a Pressburg document states rather ambiguously that "because of the impending execution of a Jew the scaffold had to be somewhat repaired. . ." It seems that the city council promised clemency to Moises Isaac, the Jewish criminal who had confessed under painful questioning of the third degree, and was to be executed for an unnamed crime, if he converted to Christianity. When he refused to accept this generous offer, the council decided that the little bell which used to be tolled to accompany a Christian criminal to his execution should this time remain silent. Before his execution Moises Isaac was questioned about other Jewish criminals sought by the city.

In the same year of 1742 ten Jews of County Nyitra were sought by the city of Pressburg for having allegedly murdered Judge Wolfgang Mikl of Ebenfurth, Austria, and his wife, and for having robbed them of more than 6,000 florins cash and several valuables. The warrant issued by the Royal Hungarian Council of the Governor General contains the names and detailed descriptions of the ten suspects, and states that they "don't walk together, and represent themselves as horse dealers." There is no information as to whether the suspects were apprehended.

Another capital case, which took place in County Sáros in 1764, had again definite connotations of a blood libel. A Christian infant was found cruelly murdered, and more than thirty Jews were accused of the crime and imprisoned. The Jews of Pressburg requested the Council of the Governor General to intervene, and to put a stop to the intense anti-Jewish agitation that swept the county. Three weeks later the city council of Sopron informed the Governor General that no suspicious phenomena that could in any way endanger the safety of the Jews could be observed in the city.

Rare as cases of murder committed by Jews were, physical violence perpetrated by them seems to have been even rarer. In fact the 18 volumes of the *Magyar Zsidó Oklevéltár* contain only two cases of legal proceedings against Jews and two against ex-Jews for physical violence. One involved a converted Jew of Buda, who in 1719 beat up a Christian woman, the owner of the White Wolf Inn, attacking her in the street. He was sentenced to two weeks imprisonment and the payment of the cost of her treatment by the *Baader* (bath-master).

The second case involved the Buda Jew Sabl Leidersdorfer, who was accused in 1722 by the Jewess Brindl David of having committed adultery with a certain Mrs. Schlesinger (a Jewess), whereupon Leidesdorfer beat up Brindl, and was duly sentenced to paying her 12 florins as damages. Two days later the same young Leidersdorfer attacked and wounded a city guard with his own sword, for which crime he was sentenced to a total of 88 florins. Evidently this young Jew had a problem in controlling his violent temperament.

The third case was that of a Jewish storekeeper of Tata who in 1726 caught a boy in the midst of stealing items from his store, and administered him such a beating that the boy subsequently died.

The last case on record is that of the musician Joseph Jordan, a converted Jew, who with his sword seriously wounded the head of a young Christian, and was sentenced to paying the injured man punitive damages and the cost of treatment by a *feldscherer* (surgeon-barber).

Let us now mention briefly some of the cases of theft and other crimes against property, which constituted, as stated above, the overwhelming majority of the criminal acts committed by the Jews. In chapter 8 we heard of two. In 1585 in Pressburg, and in 1615 in Kőszeg, Jews were accused of having purchased stolen oxen from criminals who were condemned for the theft. In 1650, the Jews of Wolfsthal were accused of having bought items stolen from the store of a Pressburg locksmith. In 1664 the Jews of Wolfsthal were again accused of receiving stolen property. The outcome of these cases is not known.

In looking over the seventeenth and eighteenth century records of the criminal proceedings against Jews, the first thing that becomes evident is that only a very small percentage of those accused and tried were actually convicted. From this fact two conclusions can be drawn: first, that Jews were frequently accused by their Christian neighbors of having committed thefts when in fact they had nothing to do with the crime; and second, that the courts of justice were fair in trying the Jewish accused and, if no evidence was found against them, pronounced them not guilty and released them.

The court records also show that the Jewish accused frequently managed to escape from prison and disappear so that the arm of justice could not reach them. We have no information as to whether those who resorted to this step were guilty or not of the crime they were accused of, but that they did so is readily understandable given that beating, flogging, and even torture were regular parts of legal procedures. There can be little doubt that the fear of painful interrogation motivated not only the guilty but also the innocent to try to escape.

Much material on court proceedings is available from the city of Sopron (Ödenburg) from 1600 to 1740. From 1700 on, cases against Jews accused of theft figure in it quite frequently. In 1702 the Jew Marx was accused of having stolen money from a market woman in Pressburg. He allegedly admitted the crime at the time of his arrest but subsequently denied it. It is not known what happened to him thereafter. In

1706 the Jew Balthasar Membler of the Jewish quarter of Sopronkeresz-túr was found guilty of stealing the key to the gate of a house and five florins cash. His punishment was relatively mild: expulsion from the city of Sopron. In 1708, the Jew David Salomon, accused of purchasing two stolen rings, was imprisoned. However, three other Jews stood bail for him, whereupon he was released with the understanding that within fourteen days he would clear the matter up with the man to whom the stolen rings had belonged.

Remarkable for its mildness is the sentence imposed upon the Jew Joseph of Buda in 1709 for having stolen from Dionis Kundorffy a black velvet cap, which was found in the Jew's possession: he was sentenced to pay a fine of six reichsthaler and to beg forgiveness.

Good relations between Jews and non-Jews are indicated by records of cases where non-Jews put up bail for a Jew accused of theft. For example, the Jew Lovel (Lobel) of Boldogasszony, accused of theft, was arrested in 1716 but was released when two Christian hatters put up bail for him in the amount of one hundred florins.

In 1717 the Jew Jacob Joseph was arrested on suspicion of thievery, but he was released six weeks later for lack of evidence against him. In 1718 three Jews of Pressburg were accused of having committed a theft in the house of the city's vicar, and investigations were launched to find out whether the Jewish community as whole was an accomplice in the crime. The result was that only one single Jew, by the name of Jacob, was implicated. All the other Jews arrested in connection with the case were then set free. However, four months later, just two hours before the public execution of Josia Maximilian Veiser and his wife Anna Maria for crimes not specified in the documents, the woman said she did not want to take with her to the grave something she knew about the theft from the vicar's house. She made a deposition to the effect that the same Jews who committed that theft, whose names she did not know, were also responsible for an earlier theft from the big church and she hoped that the Jewish criminals would be duly punished.

In 1721 the Viennese city court asked the Pressburg city council to examine the former Jew Jacob Moyses, who had converted to Christianity and taken the name Franz, arrested because he stole one hundred thalers from another Jew and buried the money in a cellar. More serious was the charge levelled against the Jew Schmule of Szakolcza in the same year: he was accused of having stolen "sacred objects." From several documents from the same period we learn that Jews were imprisoned, in the city of Pressburg and elsewhere for participation in thefts.

In 1724, a Jew, Simon Hirschl, pretended to have been in the employment of a Pressburg senator and on this basis got employment as a waiter in the Golden Deer Restaurant of Pressburg. While there, he stole shirts, pants, and other things from another waiter, a Christian, whose complaint brought about Hirschl's arrest. Hirschl at first denied but subsequently admitted the crime. He was arrested, and the stolen goods were recovered from him, after which he was expelled from the city. He went to Nagyszombat, where it was discovered that he was a Jew. He succeeded in escaping but was again apprehended and jailed in Pressburg. While he was in jail, it became known that Hirschl had also stolen clothes from a patron of the Golden Ox Restaurant in Pressburg. Hirschl converted to Christianity, confessed to a series of crimes in abject contrition, and asserted that he had no accomplices. When asked about the marks of "the French disease" visible on his neck, he insisted that he did not know how he had gotten it, since he had never committed debauchery.

In 1725 three Jews—Handl, widow of the Jew Mischl, her fiancé Volck, and one Itzig—were arrested in Pressburg for theft. All three insisted that they were innocent, but Matthias Wallner, a Christian suspect likewise imprisoned, testified against them and stuck to his testimony even in the course of a confrontation with them. Two months later the Jewish suspects were released, because the testimony of Wallner was considered unacceptable in view of his prior convictions, and because during the two months of their imprisonment nothing incriminating could be discovered about them. They were ordered not to enter Pressburg again.

In the same year, a Jew from Eibenschütz, Moravia, Isaac Leeb by name, was arrested in Pressburg on suspicion of having burglarized, together with another Jew, Philipp Jacob of Trebitsch, Moravia, the church of Preelenkirchen, and the nearby inn across the Danube. However, the accusation was not proven, and Leeb was released without punishment. At his request the city council issued him a certificate attesting to all this.

Still in the same year an old Jewish butcher, Jacob Lebll, was accused by the authorities of County Komárom of having blasphemed, and was sentenced to death. However, since he was the subject of Baron Franciscus Szluha of Csúz, the baron petitioned Emperor Charles III to intervene, arguing that Lebll was innocent. The Emperor in turn ordered County Komárom to submit the case to his decision. There is no information as to what happened to Lebll thereafter.

In 1726 several Jews of Eisenstadt were accused of having robbed the salt-office of Győr. A tantalizingly brief document from 1727 reports that the council of Pressburg sentenced the Jew Alexander from Mattersdorf to a fine of twelve florins for the crime of theft. In 1728 three

Jews from Masrich (Mezerich), accused of breaking and entering, were jailed in Pressburg. They submitted a petition to the Emperor requesting that before they were subjected to painful questioning their case be investigated by the Hungarian Lord Chancellery. The Chancellery instructed Pressburg not to torture the three Jews and to re-investigate the charges brought against them.

The following year another Jew, arrested for robbery and theft, managed to escape, and it was assumed that he had fled to Pressburg. A warrant was issued for his re-arrest. That same year a Jewish tailor who was imprisoned in Eisenstadt as a result of an accusation made against him by another Jew (who himself was charged with robbery) petitioned the emperor to order the authorities to free him, or at least to ease the conditions of his imprisonment, so that he should be able to continue his tailoring work and thus support his family. The Emperor ordered that he be informed of the case.

Also in 1729 the Jew Marcus (or Moyses), domiciled in Legend, was accused of having stolen about 700 florins from the sacristy of the church of Gyöngyöspata, as well as 150 *aurei cremnicienses* (Cremnitz gold pieces) from the parish priest. The Jew, however, produced three witnesses who testified that at the time of the theft he was at home in Legend, and that he had already owned the Cremnitz gold before the date of the theft. On this basis he was found not guilty.

In 1730 two Jews who, accused of theft, had been kept shackled in the prison of Lakompak for two years appealed to the Royal Hungarian Court Chancellery, arguing that they were innocent and requesting the removal of their shackles. The very same day the Chancellery instructed the County of Sopron to remove the shackles from the legs of the two suspects, but to retain them in custody.

An interesting case, whose trial lasted over four months, took place in Sopron in 1731. An unemployed Christian baker's journeyman, János Schmid, and a Jew, Moyses Salomon, were accused of having stolen seventy guldens from the master tailor Johann Georg Pauer on May 1. What happened, according to the testimony of Mrs. Pauer, was that at five o'clock in the morning, three Jews came to their house and asked the Pauer couple for change for several guldens, offering to take nineteen groschen per gulden. When the Pauers counted out the money, it turned out that they did not have enough small change for all the guldens the Jews wanted to exchange, and the Jews said they would come back the next day for the balance. However, after the Jews left, the Pauers found that while they were pouring the contents of their money bag onto the table, the Jews had managed to steal seventy-three guldens. They decided to wait and see whether the Jews would return the next day.

The next afternoon at three o'clock, only one of the Jews returned. He seemed to suffer from the falling disease (epilepsy). He asked Mr. Pauer whether he could make him a jacket right away; if not, he would get one from a local Jewish tailor, for he had to go to Eisenstadt the same day. Pauer agreed to make the jacket, and the Jew came for it at seven in the evening, paid, and went away.

The following morning, between seven and eight, while Mrs. Pauer was in their second-story room, she heard knocking on the door and, looking through a peephole, saw two of the Jews who had visited them two days earlier trying to break into the room. Mrs. Pauer ran to the window and cried for help, whereupon the two burglars ran away but were caught by people in the street. It turned out that one of the men apprehended was János Schmid, who, however, denied everything, despite torture by the local executioner. Eyewitnesses testified that they had seen Schmid in the Red Ox Inn in the company of two Jews, but he persisted in his denial.

On May 16 the interrogation began of Moses Salomon, the other man arrested in the street. He testified that he was originally from Offenbach near Frankfurt am Main, was about twenty-eight years old, and was married, with a wife in Magerdorff, some four miles from Pressburg. He was a horse dealer by profession. He was staying at present in the Red Ox Inn. He did not go to the house of Pauer on May 1, nor on May 3. On that day, as he was passing by the street, a woman cried from a window for help, whereupon he, among several other people, ran toward that house, but he never went up the stairs. He did not know the other man, who was arrested together with him.

At the conclusion of the hearing, the accused was warned to admit the truth or face painful questioning. On June 19, both suspects were again sternly warned to tell the truth, but both maintained they had never met. Moyses Salomon was confronted with Mr. and Mrs. Pauer, both of whom testified to recognizing him as one of the three Jews whose money they changed on May 1. Moyses, however, amidst "many avowals and shedding of tears," continued to deny that he had been there. Subsequently, Moyses succeeded in escaping from the city prison, and since during his imprisonment his wife Esther had moved from Magerdorff to Buda, the council of Sopron suspected that Moyses went there, too. On August 18 the council wrote to the Buda council asking it to apprehend and jail him. This is the last we hear of the case.

Also in 1731, the Jew Joachim of Bisancz, Moravia, was arrested in Pressburg on charges of stealing two bolts of linen from a Silesian merchant. In the course of his interrogation he pleaded not guilty and testified that he had come to Pressburg to seek work, and a Jew whom he did not know offered to provide him with meals during the Jewish holidays, then took him to a stall, gave him the two bolts of linen, and told him to take them to the inn of the Castle Hill. Joachim had no inkling that the linens were stolen goods. He was kept in custody for some ten weeks, during which he was beaten several times but did not confess. Finally, at the intervention of other Jews, he was freed.

Most interesting is a third document from 1731 in which the Hungarian governor-general's council describes eleven thieves, nine of them Jews, to the sub-*ispán* of County Sopron, asking him to institute secret investigations and arrest those whom he found. The first, named Jakubeckh, is described as short of stature, with a yellowish *camisoll* (doublet) and a scar on the lower part of his face. It is not stated that he is a Jew. The second is "Mahol, actually, however, called Gabriel, a Jew, black-brown of face, of middle height, with black hair on one of his hands, not known whether on the right or the left, about thirty years old, occasionally wearing a small beard, occasionally none. He lives in Veszprém with his wife. He stole goods from the vicar of Stinkebrun and Mr. Rossner of Pressburg."

The third is "Mayrl, tall of stature, a Jew, has a nice white face, a yellow beard, about thirty-two or thirty-three years old, brown, somewhat unruly hair . . . was arrested in Sommerein and Nicolspurg, and has got gallows written all over his face." Fourth is "Stephan, a converted Jew, domiciled nowhere but of Moravian extraction, small of stature, quite thin in body. . . . He was arrested the first time in Moravia, where, together with his comrades, as he himself admitted, he stole 2000 florins from a Jewish woman and, in addition, murdered her. The second time [he was arrested] in an unknown place. The third time in Ödenburg, where he wanted to rob a certain woman tailor and had broken open the door when he was caught. Twelve witnesses, who stood the test of torture, testified [against him]. He has nice yellowish hair. . . . Now he escaped together with the Jew Mahol, with whom he had much contact. He is about thirty-four or thirty-five years old." Note that this is the only case on record of a Jew being accused of murder (again with the exception of blood libels).

The fifth man described is Isaac Beckh, a resident Jew, born in Moravia, "tall of stature, has short, gray hair, is about fifty years old, is reputed to have been a *Rittmeister* [captain] in the *Kurucz* war . . . last time was arrested in Brünn, Moravia." The sixth is Hans Michael, a converted Jew, married, residing in Weizen (Vác?), by profession a merchant, about forty years old, "of small *ronner* [?] stature, with short, curly, black hair."

Next is Katalje, a black-bearded Jew, married, residing in Alt-Ofen [Óbuda], about thirty-five years old, by profession a barber, "has a black beard, nicely groomed short, black hair, is black-brown in the face, of small stature, came up together with the Jew Mahol from Veszprém." After him comes David, a Jew from Breslau, who "wears a brown goatee, has straight, short, brown hair, is about forty years old, married, of average stature, wears brown German clothes . . . stated to ride a *schimmel* [white horse]." The ninth is the Jew Wolff, "no domicile, has a red goatee and straight, red hair, about thirty-five years old, is married, of average stature, lean and lanky of body." Tenth is Moises Schneiderl, "a Jew, small of stature, has short, curly, black hair, a small beard, about forty years old, does not live with his wife . . . wears new brown clothes, was born in Moravia, kept company with Mayrl and Mahol." And last of the eleven is Kreutzer Hiessl, who had already been arrested in Gran (Esztergom). This is the second non-Jew of the eleven criminals whose arrest is requested.

The fact that five of the Jewish criminals—Mahol, Mayrl, Stephan, Katalje, and Moises Schneiderl—were known to have kept company with one another suggests that they were members of a kind of criminal gang. Among the Jewish criminals, it is conspicuous how many were of Moravian extraction.

In 1735 the Hungarian Royal Chancellery requested the Bohemian Royal Chancellery to apprehend "the Jew Jacob Mark alias Bünö," who was guilty of having participated in the robbery of the church of Göncz.

In 1737 a Jew of Pest was arrested, accused of theft, and tried in the presence of six city fathers, each of whom received a fee of one florin for each of the sessions he attended.

In 1739 a Jew, Solomon, was sentenced to death for having participated in the burglarizing of the Catholic church of Szenic and robbing several sacred objects. While the proceedings against him were in progress, he converted to Christianity, took the name of János (the Hungarian form of John), and petitioned the Emperor for clemency. The archdeacon of Szenic testified that "the new Christian Joannes Baptista" had indemnified the church, which seems to indicate that the culprit did escape the death penalty.

The above listed cases are merely samples. In the city of Sopron alone, in 1600–1740, many more Jews were apprehended and tried for theft, smuggling, or receiving stolen goods. In addition, there was an even larger number of cases in which Jews were imprisoned for non-payment of debts. We must also remember that records survived only of those cases involving Jews in which at least one of the two litigants was a non-Jew, or in which Jews committed crimes against Christian individuals, bodies, or institutions, and thus were tried by a secular court.

Very rarely, nevertheless, it did happen that the judicial authorities of a city handled litigations between two Jews. Such a case took place in Buda in 1739: the Jew Jacob Hirschl was ordered by the city court to pay the Jewess Mari Moysin six Dutch ducats, while the woman was ordered to return to him the corset with silver buttons that she had taken from him and which was valued at 25 florins. Another case between two Jewish litigants was decided by the city court of Sopron in 1749.

The Presssburg city archives record a case in which a Christian lawyer was disbarred for having declared a Jewish suspect innocent without the consent of his client. What happened was that in 1739 fifty-one florins were stolen from the wife of the Ivanka innkeeper, Catharina Barbara Muncker. Suspicion fell on her maid, Maria Anna Reminger, and the local distiller, the Jew Hirschl. One of the witnesses in the trial was the Jew Nathan Jacob, who testified that he was employed by Hirschl but knew nothing of the theft. What he did know was that Hirschl was arrested and beaten. The court servant (*Gerichtsdienerin*) Anna Barbara König testified that Hirschl's wife came and asked her to persuade the maid to implicate not her husband but rather the local butcher, who in the meantime had absconded, and "promised the maid to give her something." Hirschl denied everything. Within four weeks, the lawyer Samuel Huber (not Jewish), who seems to have been retained by Mrs. Muncker, submitted a memorandum to the city council of Pressburg, accusing the maid of the theft and arguing that Hirschl was innocent. Mr. and Mrs. Muncker then declared that they did not subscribe to Huber's views, and they left it to the council to decide who was guilty. In view of this development, the city council found that Huber had committed an unauthorized act, and they barred him from further legal practice.

In 1740, a young man of Corsican birth, Peter Fischer of Savinetz, of the Catholic faith, was apprehended in Nádszeg for having stolen money from his master, Baron Captain Ingenheim, on three occasions. Under questioning Fischer testified that he had committed the thefts at the instigation of the Jew Jacob Schneider, a tailor of Dunaszerdahely, to whom he delivered part of the money for safekeeping. The minutes of Fischer's confession were sent to the county attorney of Pressburg with a request to arrest the Jewish tailor, examine him, and conclude the case as soon as possible so the captain could recover his money. Three weeks later the county magistrate of Pressburg examined the Jews Jacob Schneider, Lobl, and Isaac, all of whom denied complicity in the thefts committed by Fischer. The last record of the matter is a rescript sent by Count János Pálffy, chief *ispán* of County Pressburg, to the magistrate, asking him to pursue the case of the Dunaszerdahely Jews and bring a just verdict.

One of the few lawsuits involving a Jewish woman defendant occurred in 1743 in Buda, when the wife of a Jew named Hirschl was accused of having stolen a woman's cap.

A case where Jews accused of theft were released for lack of proof took place in 1749 in Sopron. While attending the fair, Péter Csapó, the *ispán* (bailiff) of Captain Zichy's estate, lost thirteen florins from his coat pocket. He suspected three Jews from Stomfa of having stolen the money and threw them into the Sopron city jail but was unable to produce two witnesses to prove his accusation. Hence, the Jews were set free. This is of special interest because the accuser was an official of high standing while the accused were lowly Jewish merchants, and nevertheless the law took its proper course.

The municipal archives of Sopron contain records of several other cases that attest to the proper functioning of the Hungarian courts in the eighteenth century. When Christian burghers charged Jews with wrongdoing (in most cases, theft), the accused were imprisoned, but if no proof of their offenses was brought forth, they were set free and could even sue the person who caused their arrest; such a case took place in 1750. In 1761, a noblewoman, Rosina Csóy, was sued by the Jew Benedict Hirschl for nonpayment of merchandise she had bought from him. She was sentenced to paying the amount she owed plus the legal expenses of the Jew.

It has already been mentioned above that in many cases the crime Jews were accused of was having bought stolen property. If it could not be proven that they knew the purchased property had been stolen, as a rule they were not punished but only warned not to commit such an offense again. Those who were found guilty of theft were sentenced either to pay a fine or to receive a number of strokes, or both. If the culprit was physically too weak, he was let go without beating.

Occasionally, as a precautionary measure, the law court took some Jews, and especially foreign Jews, into preventive custody. Thus, in 1750 the Jew Wolff Abraham from Lofftsitz was arrested in Pressburg at 11 o'clock at night, and accused of "*nocturna divagatio*" (nocturnal loitering); but, after a hearing, he was released. Again, in 1765, to prevent thefts during the fair of Sopron, the court had seven Jews, all from Moravia, arrested as "suspects and vagabonds," and after the end of the fair it released them without any punishment. The minutes of the courts indicate that in the eighteenth century Jewish merchants from Nikolsburg, Bohemia, Turkey, and other places frequently came to Hungary to engage in trading, and in most criminal proceedings against Jews the culprits or suspected offenders were Jews who were visitors from countries to the north.

All the criminal cases referred to in this chapter are known to us due to the fact that many of the documents pertaining to the functioning of Hungarian courts have been preserved, and the material they contain in reference to Jewish suspects or litigants has been presented in the eighteen volumes of the *Hungarian Jewish Archives*. No corresponding documents attesting to proceedings before the *Bate Din* (rabbinical courts) are available, either because the rabbinical courts did not keep minutes, or because whatever minutes they did keep were lost. This being the case, the available material creates the impression that all the cases in which Jews were involved were adjudicated by the Hungarian courts and not by the Jewish rabbinical law courts. This impression is, of course, false. Typically, the Hungarian courts dealt only with cases in which both Jews and non-Jews were involved, while cases in which both sides were Jewish, or in which a Jew was accused of being guilty of a sin, were almost always dealt with by the rabbinical courts.

Very few references to such cases have survived. One comes from Eisenstadt, from 1649, in which a rabbi decided that a debt owed by the Christian hatmaker Johannes Fanger of Kőszeg and claimed by two separate parties of Jewish creditors should be paid to the Jews Moyses Jacob and Abraham Mathias, and not to the Jew Wolf Scheuch. The accountant Wolf Schonauer requested the municipal judge of Kőszeg, István Hosszthoti, to endorse this decision. The judge, however, felt that he wanted to give a hearing to the two claimant parties before making a decision. His disposition of the case is not known.

Another case has been preserved in the minutes of the Sopron municipal council. Its unique nature warrants a full presentation of the document. Entry no. 786, dated April 3, 1786, in the Sopron municipal minute book reads:

> Decree of the Council dated March 14, [1786] no. 11669, according to which it is ordered that since a Jew living in [County] Zala was punished by the rabbi because of physical [*fleischlich*] transgression to the effect that he can no longer enter any synagogue [*Tempel*], is excluded from all Jewish ceremonies, is incapable of any dealings, and that nobody has to repay him debts owed to him, therefore in case such abuse should occur also among the local Jews, it should instantly be annulled and the honorable Council should be notified. Since here there are no rabbis, nor any other Jews except owners of eating-houses, therefore in case of such an abuse the ordered suppression should be effected and notification of it given.

Although many particulars of this decree are unclear, one thing

138

becomes evident from it: the rabbi of the Jewish community of which the culprit was a member had the power to impose upon him not only punishments of a ritual nature, but also the secular financial penalty of declaring all debts owed to him null and void.

The foregoing selection of archival material relating to Jewish criminality in sixteenth- to eighteenth-century Hungary, despite the fragmentary nature of the information it provides, sheds some light on the social conditions of the Jews in the country in those two centuries. First of all, we find that Jews were much more frequently the victims of petty theft than its perpetrators. Second, the documents make it clear that Jews committed practically no violent crimes. Third, most of the crimes that Jews were accused of and tried for were theft and possession of stolen property. Fourth, if a Jew was accused of having committed theft, or if stolen property was found in his possession, his chances were good of being given a fair trial and, if no proof of his guilt was found, of being released. Fifth, most of the Jews arrested and accused of crimes were foreigners, visitors to Hungary in connection with trading activities. Sixth, the sentences passed on suspects found guilty consisted mostly of fines, flogging, and expulsion from the city where they were arrested.

All in all, one gets the impression that despite their much greater involvement in the money business, pawnbrokering, and other commercial activities than the Christian Hungarians—occupations where the chances for cheating were certainly greater than in other fields such as agriculture—the Jews were by and large a law-abiding element, conscious that any infringement of the law on their part would increase the antipathy of the Christian majority toward them and make their continued living and prospering in Hungary more difficult. The same awareness, added as it was to the almost instinctive aversion to violence acquired by the Jews in their long European Diaspora, made it almost unthinkable for Hungarian Jews to perpetrate violent crimes. They knew that they had no choice but to conduct their lives within the confines of the law, which was the only protection they had in a society that never let them forget their onus of otherness.

One more point requires brief comment. Moises Isaac, as we have just seen, was subjected to interrogation and was sentenced to death but was offered a reprieve if he would convert to Christianity. He refused and was executed. This is remarkable. Since Moises Isaac confessed to the crime he was accused of, we must assume that he was a criminal (perhaps a murderer), and yet he refused to save his life by converting. One is tempted to see this as an example of the powerful hold Jewish religion had in Hungary even on individuals whose inclinations, temperament, or circumstances made them commit a felony. Other instances are also known in which innocent Hungarian Jews accused of having murdered a Christian child (as in the blood libel of Nagyszombat) chose to be burnt alive rather than convert. Evidently, the Hungarian Jewish community comprised men and women for whom adherence to their faith was more precious than life itself, while at the other end of the social spectrum it also produced individuals who in their search for fame and fortune voluntarily abandoned their religion. It is to the most famous of the latter type that we turn in the next chapter.

12

Emericus Fortunatus
(Fifteenth and Sixteenth Centuries)

In the early sixteenth century, three of the foremost rabbinical authorities of the age were seized with an unusual halakhic problem presented to them by R. Naphtali Kohen, rabbi of the Jewish community of Buda, capital of Hungary. The problem was this: Jewish custom was that if a man converted from Judaism to another religion and his son, who had remained Jewish, was honored with an *'aliya* to the reading of the Torah on the Sabbath in the synagogue, he was called not by his name and the name of his father, as was otherwise customary (since the name of an apostate was anathema), but rather by his name and the name of his grandfather. The Buda congregation had two pious members, Abraham and Ephraim, whose father had converted to Christianity and who therefore, rather than suffer the public humiliation of being called by their grandfather's name and thus being stigmatized again and again as sons of a *m'shummad*, a traitor to Judaism, refused to be honored by an *'aliya*, and even refused to attend the Sabbath services altogether. The issue was compounded by the fact that not only was the apostate father the richest and most influential Jew (or ex-Jew) in all Hungary but he continued to support the Jews financially and to protect them vis-à-vis the Hungarian authorities, thus rendering services essential for the very survival of the community.

In view of these circumstances, the rabbi of Buda permitted the synagogue to deviate from the established custom and call the two sons to the Torah reading by their father's name. The congregation, however, still had its scruples and some time prior to 1525 sent an inquiry to R. Meir ben Isaac Katzenellenbogen (1473–1565), known as the "Maharam of Padua," one of the greatest Italian rabbis and halakhists of the time, requesting his opinion on the problem. R. Meir's responsum confirmed R. Naphtali Kohen's decision and supported it with additional arguments. He wrote:

Apart from all this, there are also other reasons why we can decide that the brothers should be called to the Torah by their father's name, as before [his apostasy]. Their father is a respected man, one of the great ones in the country, to whom can be applied also those rules that are in the interest of peace in the community. In all these countries [i.e., the Italian and neighboring states] it is an accepted religious custom that the *ḥazzan* [cantor], when he holds the Torah scroll in his hands, pronounces a blessing on the king or the ruler of the province and the great ones of the country. In doing this, the *ḥazzan* has the Torah scroll in his hands, and nevertheless we do not hesitate to mention their names in the synagogue. . . . If, therefore, in the interest of communal peace, the names of those men [who are obviously non-Jews] are mentioned next to the Torah scroll, and such names were mentioned even in the Temple of Jerusalem, it is certainly not permitted to deny the mention of the name of this man next to the Torah scroll. . . . And the more so since the father of the aforementioned brothers, even though he lives among Christians, is known to be "seeking the good of his people" [Esther 10:3] with his personal influence and his fortune, and does good to those near and far and to those who are true in heart. In this manner we can recognize his feelings from his acts, that is, that he repents his apostasy and is a God-fearing man. All this I heard about him from a reliable person. . . . Hence, based on the abovementioned reasons, I say in haste that the brothers should be called up to the reading of the Torah by the name "son of Shneur," as before. Thus speaks the small one among his scholarly contemporaries, who is troubled by the events of the times,

Meir ben Yitzḥaq Katzenellenbogen

Within a few months after the issuance of this responsum, all of central Hungary, including the city and fortress of Buda, was conquered by the Turks, in the event that went down in Hungarian history as the Mohács Disaster. The two brothers Abraham and Ephraim were among the Buda Jews forcibly taken by the victorious Ottomans to Turkey. The problem of whether the brothers could be called in the synagogue services by the name of their father (who had passed away in the meantime, after converting back to Judaism on his deathbed) continued to preoccupy the Buda Jews even in Turkey. They applied to R. Elijah ben Benjamin Halevi (d. after 1540), rabbi and *paytan* (author of liturgical poems) in Istanbul and a famous halakhic authority whose responsa were considered the last word in deciding hundreds of religious questions. R. Elijah's responsum is contained in his *Decisions* (number 95), and conforms in every respect with the view of the rabbis of Buda and Padua.

The same opinion was expressed by R. Moses Isserles (1525/30–72) of Cracow, usually referred to by the acronym "Rama," one of the greatest halakhic authorities and an outstanding *poseq* (arbiter), to whom all the great rabbis of the time addressed their problems. Isserles, in his *Decisions* (number 41), discusses the problem, cites the opinion of his relative R. Meir of Padua, and supports it with additional arguments. Thereafter, we hear no more either of the case or of what happened subsequently to the two brothers Abraham and Ephraim in Istanbul.

Who was this Hungarian Jew Shneur, whose apostasy preoccupied three of the greatest halakhic authorities of the age in Italy, Istanbul, and Cracow? We do not know much about him, but some information can be pieced together from the sources that refer to him. They show him as a man of reckless daring, great financial talent, and ruthless egoism, a schemer and intriguer, who lacked all moral restraint and yet, despite his apostasy, had a lifelong commitment to the Jewish people.

His name was Shneur Zalman. In documents he is referred to as Etil (or Eitel, or Etel), Shneur. The date of his birth is unknown, but since in around 1501 he had two married sons, he must have been born in roughly 1460. Nothing is known of his father except that his name was Ephraim. That Shneur Zalman received a good Jewish education is indicated by the fact that to the end of his life he wrote his notes in Hebrew; this feature is so important in attesting to his lifelong Jewish identification that to illustrate it we briefly abandon chronology to present an example from his very last years. On May 25, 1525, shortly before his death, Shneur Zalman, known since his conversion by the Hungarian name Szerencsés (that is, Fortunatus), received an order from Elek Thurzó, the royal treasurer, to pay 4,000 florins on account of the taxes he had collected in his capacity as *tricesimator* (collector of the one-thirtieth tax) to certain merchants whom the queen owed that amount for her purchases of cloth and silk. The order is in Latin, but the name of Fortunatus is given in Hungarian as "Zerenchees." On the outside of the document there are a few Hebrew words in cursive characters, written either by Fortunatus himself or by an official in his employ who summed up for him the contents of the document. They read: "Writing of Thurzo about 4,000 of the queen from the *dreissig* [thirty]." The last word is in German, in Hebrew characters, certainly not because the writer did not know the Hebrew word for thirty but because *dreissig* was the technical term for the type of tax referred to.

But let us return to the youth of Szerencsés. His father, Ephraim, must have been a wealthy man, for young Shneur Zalman was able to engage in the money business at a relatively young age, with investments financed, in all probability, by his father. With his business acumen he made himself indispensable to Palatine Emeric Perényi, the highest administrative dignitary in feudal Hungary, and even established close friendly relations with him.

Shneur Zalman married at a traditionally youthful age and had two sons, one of whom, according to the long-standing custom among the

Jews, he named after his own father, Ephraim. Years later, having gained entry into high Christian society, he had ample opportunity to meet Christian women, and when he was about forty he fell in love with a lady of Buda, Anna Held. She could not resist the advances of the rich Jew, who must have been an attractive man of much personal charm, and became his mistress. For a Jew to have sexual relations with a Christian woman was punishable by execution in a most painful and horrible manner, and to escape death Shneur Zalman converted to Christianity. His friend the palatine undertook to be his godfather, endowed him with his own name, Emeric (Imre in Hungarian), and added to it the epithet Fortunatus as an indication that the man was indeed fortunate to have embraced the true religion. Thus Shneur Eitel Zalman became known all over Hungary under the name Emericus Fortunatus (or Szerencsés Imre in Hungarian).

When he converted to Christianity, the marriage of Fortunatus became null and void, and nothing is known about whether he maintained any contact with his Jewish wife and sons, who continued to live in the Jewish street of Buda. What is known, however, as we have seen, is that his sons insisted on being referred to in synagogue services as "sons of Shneur." It is likewise known that Fortunatus continued to extend his help and protection to the Jewish community as a whole, which he had been forced to abandon, formally at least. Fortunatus subsequently married his Christian mistress and had a son by her, who was later murdered in Breslau. (After the death of Fortunatus himself in 1526, his Christian widow remarried in Vienna. While celebrating the wedding banquet, her bridegroom was arrested, and shortly thereafter he was murdered in Pressburg. The woman who, as the chronicles relate, "was accustomed to walk about in Buda like a princess in precious finery" lived in Vienna in great misery, and died of dropsy.)

After his conversion, Fortunatus's star continued to rise. His expertise in finances and the large loans he provided to the treasury made him a highly influential personage in the royal court, and he gained even the favors of King Lajos II (r. 1516–26) and Queen Maria. He was an especially great favorite and friend of László Szalkay—bishop of Eger, archbishop of Esztergom, and treasurer and chancellor of Hungary— who had risen to these high positions from the most humble origins as the son of a shoemaker. Fortunatus became a devoted supporter and advisor as well as an unscrupulous instrument of this man, participated together with him in the self-seeking schemes of the power-hungry and gold-thirsty upper nobility, and was accepted as a member of the glittering, corrupt high society of Buda.

Due to Szalkay's influence, Fortunatus was appointed sub-treasurer of the country, and in this capacity he virtually controlled the state treasury. Those were the days of increasing Turkish pressure on the southern borders of Hungary, and when in 1521 Nándorfehérvár fell to the Ottoman power, Fortunatus was accused of partial responsibility for the defeat by dispatching money and military equipment too late for the relief of that important border fortress. The historical sources covering this incident are not sufficiently detailed, but it seems that if the accusation was based on fact, its cause was not negligence on the part of Fortunatus but rather lack of funds in the royal treasury.

The fall of Nándorfehérvár caused near panic in the country. The emptiness of the treasury, it was felt, had to be remedied instantly, and it was Fortunatus who suggested to the king how it could be done. His advice was that the king issue an order to the treasury counts to mint new coins that would have the same denominations as the old ones and look exactly like them but contain only half as much precious metal. In November 1521 the Diet of Buda passed a resolution to adopt his proposal, stipulating that the king ensure that the new currency be forced upon the neighboring provinces as well. At the same time, the taxes imposed upon the people were increased considerably.

From this time on, the influence of Fortunatus continued to grow. He was the trusted advisor of László Szalkay, the effective power in the country; he enjoyed the full support of István Báthory, the state palatine who was responsible for the affairs of the Jews in Hungary and for whose "protection" the Jews paid 400 gold florins annually; and he was energetically active on behalf of the party supporting the royal court.

However, the more influential Fortunatus became, the more hateful he was in the eyes of the opposition party. This party was led by János Szapolyai, voivod of Transylvania, whose great ambition was to achieve control over Hungary by replacing Szalkay. Things came to an open clash at the Diet convened in Buda in September 1524. István Werbőczy, leader of the lesser nobility and the most astute suporter of Szapolyai, delivered an impassioned speech attacking the men in power, who, he argued, had brought the country to the brink of disaster. "Even the most rapacious and most cruel men," he thundered, "even half-Jews, are no longer excluded from public office, and since their evil has exhausted the treasury, we are forced to apply to them in the case of the smallest need that they lend us money with great usury." He concluded by exhorting the estates to liberate the country "from the insatiable blood sucking of these vipers."

István (Stephan) Werbőczy (or Verbőczy), who figures prominently in the life story of Emericus Fortunatus, was the author of the basic Hungarian law code known as the *Codex tripartitum* of 1514. This law code contains a secondary Hungarian adaptation of the Jewish oath of Erfurt, formulated about 1160–1200 by Archbishop Conrad of Mainz and adopted by the 1421 *Law Book of Buda*, which contains many restrictive and humiliating regulations applicable to the Jews. Werbőczy's *Codex* requires that a Jew, when rendering an oath in connection with a lawsuit, should wear his "Jewish cape" and the pointed Jewish hat, be barefoot, turn toward the sun (that is, to the east), and recite the oath, which reads as follows:

> I, So-and-So Jew, swear on the living God, the holy God, who created heaven and earth and the sea and everything that is in them and on them, that I am innocent in this matter of which this Christian accuses me. And if I am guilty, let the earth, which swallowed Dathan and Abyron [Abiram], swallow me. And if I am guilty, let apoplexy and leprosy seize me, which upon the supplication of Elizeus [Elisha] left the Syrian Naaman, and possessed Gehazi, the servant of Elizeus. And if I am guilty, let falling sickness, hemorrhage, and sudden apoplexy strike me, and let accidental death carry me off, and let me perish in body, soul, and fortune, and may I never attain to the bosom of Abraham. And if I am guilty, let the law of Moses received at Mount Sinai annihilate me, and everything written in the Five Books of Moses put me to shame. And if this oath is not true and honest, may the power of Adonai and his godhead be wiped out.

Since this oath is an almost word-for-word adaptation of the twelfth-century German Jew oath, it does not reveal much about the situation of the Jews in Hungary in the fifteenth or sixteenth century, except that the public humiliation of the Jews it represented was considered as much part of Jewish life in Hungary as it had been in German lands three or four centuries earlier.

But to return to the September 1524 Diet of Buda, among the resolutions passed by it (but not confirmed by the king) was the demand that Fortunatus, under whose management the treasury was becoming more and more impoverished and the public revenues were being shamefully squandered, be removed from his office of sub-treasurer.

While this internal struggle was taking place in Hungary, the Turks made additional advances and took the fortress of Szörény. The tension between the court and Szapolyai's party increased, and at the Diet of May 1425, in the course of discussing the new coins of lesser value, the nobility focused its attack on Fortunatus, whom they accused of causing the troubles of the country. They also accused Szalkay of having a Jew as his advisor (characteristically, despite his conversion, Fortunatus remained for them a Jew) and expressed their consternation over the respect and honor shown to Fortunatus by the king and queen. They dispatched a deputation of sixty men to the king that submitted to him several demands, the last of which was "that His Majesty should have the Jew-turned-Christian Emericus Fortunatus burned at the stake, and let him be punished for his evil life and bad acts." The king's response, given three days later, was that he would initiate inquiries into the affairs of Fortunatus and, should he be found guilty, mete out just punishment to him.

Fortunatus instantly went into action to quiet the passions aroused against him. He acquired spokesmen among the Estates who effectively spread the view that the monetary disarray of Hungary was caused not by him but by the House of Fugger, the great south German banking family that was the financial power behind the Austrian Empire and which, the pro-Fortunatus people tried to prove with a series of financial data, committed a series of damaging frauds against the Hungarian treasury.

On May 18, 1525, King Lajos (all of nineteen years old at the time) was induced to appear personally before the Estates, where the nobles repeated their demand that he "punish the Jew." Two days later, the nobles sent another delegation to the king again urging him "not to protect the Jew but to punish him." Cardinal Campeggio, apostolic delegate of the Vatican, advised the king to appease the nobles by arresting Fortunatus. The king did so, and on May 20 (a Saturday) had Fortunatus imprisoned in the so-called Ruined Tower.

The friends of Fortunatus hurried to his rescue. As the Jewish chronicles of Buda report, two weeks later, "at the price of great monetary sacrifices" on Fortunatus's part, he was released thanks to the intervention of Palatine Báthory. The court party made use of the opportunity to organize a demonstration against the nobles (most of whom had dispersed in the meantime upon the conclusion of the Diet). When Fortunatus was released from the prison on June 5, officers of the royal court, among them Chamberlain Bernard Boeheim, and Pock, the queen's majordomo, accompanied him in a festive procession, and attended the boisterous banquet with which Fortunatus was received at his home.

The house of Fortunatus on St. George Square was a veritable palace, located next to the royal residence on top of the Castle Mount. It hugged the wall of the fort of Buda, with its back over a sheer drop down to the moat far below. It had a cellar stocked with the finest wines, was served by a veritable army of servants, and was the scene of many luxurious banquets. Among the guests who frequented the Fortunatus palace was George of Brandenburg, the king's uncle and former guardian.

To celebrate the release of Fortunatus with an ostentatious gathering and repast was considered by the opposition party an open provocation.

Several of the nobles were still in Buda with their servants and armed retinue, and this crowd, joined by the rabble that was always ready to jump into violent action, surrounded the house and, using the carriages left in the street as battering rams, broke through its fortified gates. Fortunatus and his reveler friends were able to get away by sliding down ropes from the top of the wall into the moat and thus escaped unscathed, except, as one of the chronicles mentions, by the deep wounds cut into their hands by the ropes.

At that point the rabble was more interested in looting than in pursuing Fortunatus and his friends. It ransacked the house, which as described by a chronicler, was a veritable treasure trove, "full of endless riches: jewels, gold-embroidered materials, velvets, silks, cloths, money, all kind of domestic utensils, horses, and much Syrmian wine." Within a few hours the house was completely emptied. The loot comprised huge treasures, including 60,000 old gold florins of full value. The foot soldiers, hussars, and servants of the nobles, who wore short, tight clothes, were unable to hide much money on their bodies and filled sacks with the coins, while others carried away the wine in vats. The king, unable to intervene, impotently had to witness the robbery taking place right next to the royal palace. The authorities did not even try to put an end to the rampage.

Next day the plundering crowd set to work to demolish the empty shell that remained of the Fortunatus palace. But Francis (Ferencz) Bodó, captain of the Szapolyais, advised them rather to attack the houses of the noblemen who belonged to the court party. Bodó subsequently suffered harsh punishment for this act: he was imprisoned and died in jail. Since the houses of the court nobles were well protected by their own armed guards, the rabble was unable to break into them, whereupon they moved to attack the houses of the Jews. By that time the Jews, too, were prepared to defend themselves, with the help of hired troops. They locked the gates of the Jewish street, erected barricades behind them, and held out against the mob, which throughout the night launched repeated assaults. Finally, at dawn, the superior numbers of the attackers forced the Jews to retreat. They withdrew into their tower and the one fortified house in their street. The mob, after breaking down the gates, attacked all the other Jewish houses and looted them. An Italian eyewitness reported that "the scene was like the sack of Troy: there was not a man who did not carry off something. They found enormous fortune, left behind nothing, not even a single window lock. Then they started to attack the tower and the fortified house in which the Jews had taken refuge with a great part of their fortune." At this point, finally, the Szapolyais felt they had to put an end to the riots. György Szapolyai, younger brother of the voivod, saved the Jews gathered in their tower by dispersing the attackers and chasing them out of the city.

Although attacks on the Jews of Buda by plundering rabble were nothing unusual, this particular rampage was unquestionably provoked by the comportment of "the Jew Fortunatus." In the eyes not only of the nobles but also of the common folk, he remained a Jew despite his conversion to Christianity, his marriage to a Christian woman, and his achievement of power in the court party.

As for his own attitude, even though his conversion effectively and formally excluded him from the Jewish community, Fortunatus never ceased feeling and acting as a Jew. He used his influence with the court and the grandees to help the Jews whenever and wherever they were in trouble, even outside the borders of Hungary. The fame of his work as protector of the Jews spread abroad, and R. Elijah Halevi of Istanbul summed it up as follows shortly after Fortunatus's death:

He was imprisoned, and was condemned to being burned, for they said that he was still a Jew; only with great financial sacrifice was he able to escape from their hands, for God was merciful toward him. And after he was freed from prison, he did not cease to do good for the Jews with his person and his money, as before, or even more so, until the very day of his death.

And now let me mention some of the things he did. The entire community of Buda—may God protect it—knows that a calumniator appeared who accused the Jews of having killed a Christian child; however it was he himself who hid the blood among the Jews. The mentioned Shneur, having found out about it, intervened with the king and the nobles, so that the calumniator was delivered into his hands, and he delivered him to the Jews, who strangled him. [This detail indicates that the calumniator was a Jew or converted Jew, over whom the Jewish community had jurisdiction, even in capital cases.] The money that he spent on this was his own. After he did this, all the rabbis in the synagogues of all the communities announced that anyone who called him an apostate would be punished in person and property.

Thereafter he again brought great succor to Israel in Bohemia, which kingdom is also under the rule of the Hungarian king, in the community of Prague, where more Jews lived than in Buda. Angry demands were lodged against them, that they should be expelled, but he intervened in person and with his fortune, until, with the help of God, he succeeded in averting this disaster as well.

On another occasion he saved a Jewish woman who was imprisoned and condemned to burning, and likewise saved from hanging a youth who was imprisoned because of theft. Every Friday afternoon, until the day of his death, he had alms distributed among poor Jews. And then there was an evil man in foreign lands who brought his small son and daughter to Austria and there converted, together with his son, and dedicated his daughter to the service of a foreign god [possibly: sent her to nunnery]. When this evil man—may his name and memory be wiped out!—died,

Shneur sent for his children and brought them back into Judaism, which cost him close to 200 florins. He did many more such things, for whose description there is no space on this paper. In the hour of his death, in the presence of many Jews, amidst crying and praying, he repented of his sins, and died in repentance.

Since apostasy has always been one of the gravest sins in Judaism, for a rabbi of the stature of R. Elijah Halevi to speak in such terms of a convert is proof that Fortunatus was indeed all his life a devoted and effective protector of the Jews, and was recognized as a benefactor who saved countless Jewish lives.

Little wonder that this man, considered by everybody a Jew and known to be a protector of the Jewish community, should be hated as a Jew by those jealous of his fortune, power, and position. Some Hungarian noblemen even accused him of Marranism: even though he was baptized, they said, in secret he remained a Jew. This was the basis of the nobles' demand that the king have him burned on the stake: death by fire was the usual punishment meted out to a Jew who converted to Christianity and was discovered to have secretly adhered to Judaism.

Characteristic of the resilience of Fortunatus was his reaction to the mob attack on his house and the looting of everything in it. Not only did he continue to work as financial advisor to the king and the treasury but he managed to carry out the adage, "If you can't defeat your enemy, buy him." He found a way to approach Szapolyai himself, as well as his chief aide Werbőczy. He let them share in various advantageous financial schemes and was able to convince them that he knew of new, rich sources of revenues, with which he could replenish the empty treasury if they only allowed him to act. The sources, as usual, are incomplete, but they clearly show that within a month after his liberation from jail, Fortunatus was more powerful and influential than ever.

The next session of the Hungarian Diet convened early in July in the city of Hatvan. It was largely dominated by the Szapolyais and Werbőczy, under whose leadership Palatine Báthory and his allies Sárkány and Thurzó were sharply attacked from the floor. More remarkable is that the same group of nobles who only a few weeks before had tried to force the king to put Fortunatus to death now uttered not a single word against him. On the contrary, as the Vatican delegate who was present reports skeptically, it was decided that "the copper mines that were in the hands of the Fuggers should be handed over to the same Jew whom the recent session wanted to condemn to the stake. He promised great revenues from the mines, but many believe that the revenues will consist of his acquiring twice as much as was looted from him, and then he will clear out of the country."

These misgivings, however, were not shared by Werbőczy, who moved that the control of the state treasury be entrusted to Fortunatus since he promised great revenues to the country. Fortunatus not only was appointed treasurer but also became a member of the council of state. His own financial affairs prospered, and he was named tax farmer of the city of Buda. In April 1526, King Lajos II mortgaged to him the income from the taxes of Pressburg to enable him to recover the 1,500 florins he had loaned the king. In July, when the Turks laid siege to Pétervár and the treasury was unable to pay the army sent to relieve it, Fortunatus, as the king himself acknowledged it, "wishing to alleviate the endangered country's need," gave the king another loan of 10,000 florins. In documents dating from this period the king refers to him as *egregium consiliarium nostrum*, that is, "our distinguished counselor."

Fortunatus was by now an old man and had only a short time to live. But his ability to stand up to the Diet and confront it with outright accusations was not diminished in the least. Nobles who convened at Rákos in May 1526 were so confused about the treasury's involved and dismal financial situation that they asked King Lajos and Queen Maria to send Fortunatus to explain the state of affairs to them and suggest what should be done, since "he is the one who knows all the tangles of the country." Fortunatus appeared the same day at the Diet and presented the accounts of the royal revenues. He then went on to confront the Diet with such disclosures of fraudulent acts and details of shameful profiteering by several of the country's grandees, and especially by the House of Fugger, that the most vehement scenes disrupted the proceedings of the Diet, and the estates dispersed without concluding their agenda.

This is the last episode known about the public life of Fortunatus. What remained for the sources to tell about him was the scene at his deathbed that took place soon thereafter, quoted above.

Soon after Fortunatus's death, Anna Held remarried. Her new husband was a burgher of Pressburg, Marton Khle (Klee). In July 1530, Anna gave two powers of attorney to Khle to represent her and her son George in claims they had on the estate of Fortunatus. In September, King Ferdinand ordered the city of Buda to give justice to Anna and George against a certain Johannes Pook, whom Queen Maria had instated into the Buda house of Fortunatus. The outcome of the suit is not known. About the same time, Queen Maria, as heir to King Lajos II, demanded from King Ferdinand I the repayment of two loans, one of 10,000 and the other of 1,500 florins, which, she argued, were assigned to her.

The last time we encounter the name of Emericus Fortunatus is in 1532, when King Ferdinand I gave a son of Fortunatus, known as Abraham Balgel (Palgel, Belgel), a recommendation to the city of Breslau. Since, however, the city was not forthcoming, Abraham purchased a house in the city of Oels.

13

Transylvania and the Sabbatarians (Sixteenth and Seventeenth Centuries)

The 1526 defeat at Mohács lived in the history of Hungary and in the national consciousness as the Mohács Disaster, the greatest national catastrophe until the loss of two-thirds of the country after World War I. As a result of the Ottoman victory, historic Hungary came to be divided into three parts, among which there were tensions, enmity, and even armed clashes most of the time. The only one of the three where a semblance of independence survived was the eastern part, the principality of Transylvania (Erdély in Hungarian), recognized by the Ottomans as a quasi-vassal state and ruled by a succession of Hungarian-Transylvanian princely houses.

The southern and central parts of Hungary, as far north as the cities of Vác and Miskolc, were under Ottoman rule, with the pasha of Buda as the governor of the entire Hungarian *vilayet* (province). In a sweeping half circle to the northeast of Transylvania and the north and east of Ottoman Hungary stretched so-called Royal Hungary, which became in effect a Habsburg province. Although the Hungarian Estates retained their traditional right to "elect" their king in this province, the election of the Habsburg heir to the Austrian throne as king of Hungary was always a foregone conclusion.

In this period the Reformation penetrated into all three parts of Hungary. By the end of the sixteenth century, some 90 percent of the population of Ottoman Hungary was Protestant, with Calvinism predominant, while in the mountainous regions of northern Hungary (under Habsburg rule) the Lutheran dioceses commanded the adherence of the majority. One of the major religious-cultural achievements of this period was the translation of the Bible into Hungarian.

As for the position of the Jews during the century and a half of Ottoman rule, it differed greatly in the three parts of the country. Hence it seems appropriate to discuss Jewish life in each of the three separately. We begin with Transylvania.

Whether Jews lived in Transylvania prior to the sixteenth century is unknown. The first reference to their presence is found in the records of the 1578 Transylvanian Diet of Kolozsvár (German Klausenburg, Rumanian Cluj), which state that "never before have so many suchlike Greeks, and even Jews" entered the city as in those days.

In the early seventeenth century, Gábor Bethlen (r. 1613–29), prince of Transylvania and patron of arts and commerce with close ties to Istanbul, wishing to promote trade in his principality, settled Turkish Jews in Gyulafehérvár (Roman Apulum, Alba Julia; in Hebrew documents 'Ir L'vana, that is, White City), an important center in south central Transylvania. On June 18, 1623, he issued a letter patent in which he assured the Jews of the right to engage freely in trading and of several other privileges. In article 5 of this letter patent, the prince proclaims that the Jews could practice all occupations freely and could live in accordance with the customs of their religion, provided these observances did not become a burden (*molesta*) for others and the Jews did not make themselves conspicuous. Article 6 states that the Jews who had come to Transylvania from Spain or other countries should not be hindered in pursuing their occupations and accords them his princely protection. Article 8 permits them to take money out of the country, and article 9 allows them to emigrate from Transylvania if difficult conditions should prompt them to do so.

In October 1627, Prince Gábor Bethlen engaged in a classic example of price fixing: he issued what was called a *limitatio* of the prices that Turkish, Greek, and Jewish merchants were allowed to charge for merchandise they imported into the country. Many of the listed items were from Turkey, such as silk, clothing materials, buttons, stirrups, leather goods, paper, and so on. The documents show that the Jews were but one of three mercantile minorities in Transylvania, and that the country as a whole acted as a market for the manufactured goods of the more advanced Turkish economy.

More information about the Jews' activities in the import business is contained in a report issued by the tax office ("thirtieth office") of Kolozsvár in 1631. According to it, the Jews imported ironwares and textiles—the most important types of import—from Nagykároly (Carei Mari, Rumania) to Kolozsvár. It seems that by the early seventeenth century, in some cities the Jews actually dominated the import business. In any case, in 1648 the Greek merchants lodged a complaint with Prince George Rákóczi I (r. 1630–48) alleging that the Jews of Gyulafehérvár had gained control over commerce, and especially over merchandise imported from Turkey to the cities of Szászsebes, Szeben, and Gyulafehérvár. A similar grievance was lodged by the burghers of Gyulafehérvár itself, who complained that the Jewish merchants would go to meet the foreign traders, buy up their merchandise, and then sell it to the local citizens at inflated prices.

As could be expected, the activities of the Jews were repeatedly the subject of regulations and laws passed by the Transylvanian Diet or issued by the princes. The Diet of 1650 imposed (or reimposed) upon the Jews and Greeks the wearing of special garb. This law speaks of the Hungarians, Greeks, and Jews as "three nations"—the Turks seem to have lost importance.

Three years later, Prince George Rákóczi II (r. 1648–60) issued a decree granting Jews the right to trade freely in Transylvania and permitting them to settle at Gyulafehérvár as tenant farmers. Although the Jews stood under the protection of the prince and paid their taxes to him, it was the Diet that determined the amount of their taxes, as well as those of the Greeks, the Armenians, and the Serbians. The 1662 Diet differentiated between indigenous and nonindigenous Jews for purposes of taxation: the former had to pay 10 percent, the latter 1 percent. The 1665 Diet of Gyulafehérvár imposed an annual head tax of five thalers on the Jews and Greeks, and in 1669 the Jewish, Greek, Armenian, and Serbian communities, "and all other foreign nations trading in this country," were required to pay a tax of 2,000 thalers each. The allocation of the tax within each community was to be the task of its own judge.

The close connection between the Jews of Transylvania and those of the Ottoman Empire explains why the community of Gyulafehérvár followed the Sephardi rite. In 1637 the chief judge of the city sold the community a plot of land to be used as a cemetery. In 1661 Prince Mihály Apaffy (or Apafi, r. 1661–90) permitted them to purchase cattle freely for the purpose of ritual slaughtering, and to sell freely those parts of the carcass whose consumption was forbidden by their ritual laws. Four years later he reconfirmed these privileges.

Under this prince the Jews of Transylvania had their own judge. He was Juda Melemet of Gyulafehérvár, a Sephardi Jew from Turkey. In 1662, for valuable services rendered by Melemet, the prince gave him and his heirs of both sexes the Omponicza estate (in County Fejér) with all its appurtenances, including arable fields, pastures, camps, forests, mountains, valleys, vineyards, rivers, and lakes, against the payment of one thousand Hungarian florins. Melemet served the prince as his Turkish interpreter, and when appointed to that position he had to render an oath whose text is preserved in a Hungarian-language document dated October 12, 1671. In it Juda Melemet swears to be a faithful servant of Prince Mihály Apafi and his beloved wife, Princess Anna Bornemisza, and to translate everything accurately, without any changes. "Should I commit any falsehood . . . let the earth that swallowed Chore [Korah], Datan, and Abyron [Abiram] swallow me, let leprosy smite me . . . let me die a sudden death, and let me perish in both body and soul, and let me never reach the bosom of Abraham, and let the Law of Moses revealed on Mount Sinai be wiped out, and all the writing written in the Five Books of Moses collapse, and if I should not be true let Adonai and the great power of his divinity wipe me out."

Transylvanian Hungarian squires occasionally made use of the contacts Jews had with Turkey. Thus, in 1666, the Jew Samuel of Gyulafehérvár was offered 200 thalers "or somewhat more" by the knight (vitézlő) István Nagy if he could succeed in redeeming from Turkish captivity the wife and small son of András Komáromi, resident of Kisperi—or 100 thalers in case he redeemed only the wife.

In general, the Transylvanian princes related to the Jews under their rule with the same mixture of benevolence and exploitation that had long characterized the attitude of the Hungarian kings to "their" Jews. Prince Mihály Apafi issued no fewer than three decrees (in 1661, 1673, and 1678) instructing the authorities to protect the Jews against the arbitrariness of the city of Gyulafehérvár, emphasizing that the city had no jurisdiction over them because the Jews depended only upon the prince himself. The street of the Jews, the prince stressed, lay not within the city itself, but in the princely domain, in the external customs area, even though located within the city walls.

As far as taxation was concerned, the position of the Jews became more and more difficult as time passed. At first they paid taxes only to the prince, as their liege lord; then all kinds of special taxes were imposed upon them, for example, contributions toward building the Transylvanian House in Istanbul, which housed the Transylvanian embassy, and the ransom of soldiers who were captured in the Polish campaign of George Rákóczi II. Of other taxes and levies imposed on the Jews we have already heard above. In this respect, as well as with regard to the functions of the Jew judge, the situation in Transylvania closely resembled that in pre-Mohács Hungary. The ability of individual Jews to overcome discrimination and restriction in Transylvania is also reminiscent of Hungary. In both countries, some Jews of outstanding ability could and did rise to highest positions at court.

The Transylvanian Diet also behaved in a manner familiar to us from the Hungarian scene in pre-Turkish times. Its main concern was usually to protect the interests of the city people against the "foreign" merchants. In 1678 the Diet prohibited Greek, Jewish, Armenian, and Serbian merchants from buying up merchandise imported from abroad at the frontiers of the principality and then reselling it at higher prices. In 1685 the Diet of Fogaras reconfirmed this prohibition. From these and similar laws it becomes evident that at the time the Jews were considered foreign residents, having the same status as the other non-Hungarian speaking population elements of the principality. In view of the fact that many Jews were actually of Turkish provenance, lumping them together with the other foreigners must have seemed just and equitable to the Transylvanian lawmakers.

As in Hungary, so too in Transylvania the Jews suffered many forms of local discrimination against which only the ruling prince could protect them. Hence, they frequently appealed to the prince by submitting to him humble *supplicationes*. In response to such a petition Price Apafi issued on July 4, 1680, a rescript to the council of Gyulafehérvár admonishing it to cease inflicting any damage, hurt, or injustice on the Jews, not to demand from them higher interest than was customary, and not to disturb them in any way. Such a document shows that Jews were not always at the lending end of the money business: there were also those among them who were short of money and had to obtain loans from Christian lenders.

The spread of the Reformation in Transylvania created fertile ground for the burgeoning of the Sabbatarian (Hungarian *Szombatos*) sect in the late sixteenth century. Prior to that time Judaizing movements had emerged in England, Bohemia, Poland, and Russia, where their adherents came to constitute sects whose doctrines and practices were varying mixtures of Judaism and Christianity. Christians by origin, most of them retained the belief in Jesus as the messiah, the redeemer, and the son of God, but rejected the teachings of the Church as they had developed in subsequent centuries and based their practices on the commandments contained in the Old Testament. As the day of the weekly rest they observed not Sunday but Saturday (hence they were in several places called "Sabbatarians"), they celebrated the Jewish holidays, they obeyed the Jewish dietary laws, and so forth. Some of them, such as the Subotniki of Russia, where the movement started in the second half of the fifteenth century, actually converted to Judaism.

In Transylvania, the origins of the Sabbatarian sect go back to the initiative of the Székely magnate Andreas Eőssi, who in 1567 converted to Unitarianism together with several other Transylvanian nobles. From Unitarianism they proceeded to an observance of the Sabbath and the commandments specified in the Five Books of Moses. Eőssi laid down the dogmatics of the Sabbatarian faith, which were subsequently elaborated by his disciples, first among whom was his adopted son, Simon Péchi.

Simon Péchi (ca. 1565–ca. 1643) was a man of great talent who mastered several languages, among them Hebrew, and made a brilliant political career, becoming at a relatively young age the chancellor of the principality under Gábor Bethlen. He composed a Sabbatarian prayer book (in Hungarian), basing it largely on the Sephardi rite. Under Péchi's inspired and inspiring leadership some 20,000 Székelys converted to the new faith. Their major concentrations were in the cities of Kolozsvár, Torda, and Marosvásárhely. Sabbatarianism spread so rapidly that the 1595 Székesfehérvár Diet felt compelled to pass a resolution condemning it and its followers. In 1618 Prince Gábor Bethlen severely restricted all freedom of religion, a serious blow for the Sabbatarians in particular. All over the principality they bitterly lamented their fate, but at the same time the new faith continued to make converts in all layers of Transylvanian society, including leading members of the prince's government. Sabbatarian preachers working among the simple people spread the faith, which was a unique combination of strict adherence to the laws of the Five Books of Moses and a purely Hungarian protonationalist theology.

Finally, in 1621, Péchi's Judaizing became intolerable to the prince, who had him arrested. Péchi spent four years in prison, and when he was released and confined to his village, he devoted himself to literary work in the service of Sabbatarianism. The immigration of Sephardi Jews in the 1620s had a decisive influence on Péchi's and the Sabbatarians' further rapprochement with Judaism, as can be seen from the content and purpose of Péchi's books from this period, which included a study of Jewish ethics and a translation with commentary of the Book of Psalms. The degree to which Péchi acquired Jewish knowledge and internalized Jewish attitudes was nothing short of remarkable. He found a parallel between certain phases in the history of the Jewish and the Magyar nations, and attributed the disaster each of those two peoples suffered to their transgression of the Law and the Commandments. He even followed in the footsteps of the Kabbalists, discussed the meaning of the divine name *Shaddai*, and interpreted the connections between the names *Yahweh* and *Adonai*. In his "Prayer Against Weapons," which he composed when he was in his sixties, he referred to the Kabbalistic Jewish method of interpretation known as *Gematria*, and wrote that "it is proven from the Gymatria" that Satan has constant access to Heaven, and "can proceed freely in his evil function, except for one day in the year, "the Day of *Kippur*, of atonement, when Heaven is closed to him . . ." Péchi was also familiar with, and quoted, medieval Hebrew philosophers, incuding Solomon ibn Gabirol's *Keter Malkhut* (Crown of Kingship), and Maimonides's *Guide of the Perplexed*.

Gábor Bethlen died in 1629, and in 1631 the heads of the Reformed (Calvinist) Church lodged a complaint against Péchi with the new prince, George Rákóczi I. For a number of years Rákóczy was preoccupied with major problems that threatened his rule, but in 1639 he took ruthless measures against Péchi and the other leaders of the Sabbatarian sect, including members of their familes. Elaborate legal proceedings were instituted, with the outcome that all the accused were sentenced to loss of life and property. The estates confiscated from Péchi alone included some thirty-six villages, all of which became the property of the princely treasury.

An individual case illustrating the attraction Judaism held for ranking Transylvanian Christians in the early seventeenth century is referred to in letters exchanged between the Transylvanian embassy in Istanbul and Prince George Rákóczi concerning a certain Péter Bakó, who served as an official in that embassy. The circumstances are not clear, but it seems that Bakó had learned about the Sabbatarian sect from his father, who was an adherent. While in Istanbul, the younger Bakó became acquainted with local Jews, and under their influence he decided to convert to Judaism. This became known to the Transylvanian ambassador, who reported it to Prince Rákóczi, stating that Bakó was studying "Jewish writing" (Hebrew), was simultaneously teaching two Jewish children, had obtained Jewish books, and even though "he will not become a Turk, it is to be feared that he will join the Jews . . . for he has already absorbed much of their faith." The response of the prince was to instruct the embassy to withdraw its protection from young Bakó. Bakó proceeded to "a Jewish village named Ortaköy on the shores of the Black Sea" and had himself circumcised in secret. This, too, became known to the embassy, and one of Bakó's colleagues informed the prince (on July 20, 1637) of this development, adding that Bakó did not intend to remain in Turkey. In view of the mass conviction and execution of the Sabbatarian leadership in 1639, it is doubtful whether Bakó actually returned to Transylvania.

The events of 1639 were a terrible blow to the Sabbatarians but not a mortal one to the movement. Deprived of their leadership and facing the death sentence, most of them had no choice but to convert (actually reconvert) to one of the established religions. Nevertheless, a few of them remained faithful in secret to Péchi's religion and kept its traditions alive in a handful of isolated localities. Among these was the village of Bözödujfalu—once owned by Péchi—whose inhabitants were still Sabbatarians two centuries later. After the 1867 emancipation of Hungarian Jews (see chapter 29), Baron József Eötvös, the minister of religions, granted them a special permission to convert to Judaism, and the remaining 105 Sabbatarians of Bözödujfalu actually converted, creating, in 1868, the only proselyte Jewish congregation in modern European history. They built themselves a *miqveh* (ritual bath) in 1870, a synagogue in 1874, and became in every respect a strictly orthodox Jewish congregation that also attracted a few originally Jewish families. By the late 1920s the convert community of Bözödujfalu consisted of fifty to eighty families, most of whom had the surname Kovács (the Hungarian equivalent of Smith). Their garb was that of the typical Székely peasant, over which the men wore the traditional Jewish *tallith qatan* with the four fringes. The men also wore the orthodox Jewish *pe'ot* (sidelocks), and the women kept strictly kosher kitchens.

The cruel treatment meted out to the Sabbatarians by the prince, Diet, and judiciary of Transylvania in the seventeenth century presents a remarkable contrast to the toleration and protection the same powers accorded the Jews at the same time. Although Jews were restricted in the rights they enjoyed—their movement, occupations, rights of residence, and the like were limited, often quite severely, and they were oppressively taxed and often treated harshly—their adherence to Judaism was never pronounced a crime, they were never forced to convert to Christianity (as Jews had been in Spain and in several other countries), and they were never prevented from practicing their religion or living according to its tenets. The "otherness" of the Jews was recognized as an inalterable fact, regrettable and even deplorable, that brought with it certain disabilities and condemned them to a lower status than Christians and to being disliked and, by at least some Christians most of the time, also despised and hated—but they were allowed to continue their lives as Jews.

The Sabbatarians were, in the eyes of the Transylvanian Christians, a different case altogether. They were Christian Székelys, who committed the unforgivable crime, or even sin, of becoming renegades, of denying the most sacred tenets of Christianity, of voluntarily adopting and stubbornly following teachings of the unregenerate, perfidious Jews. This was something that simply could not be tolerated but had to be extirpated. The Sabbatarians were persecuted not because they Judaized but because they abandoned Christianity. Had they, instead of Judaizing, engaged in Islamizing, the reaction on the part of the faithful Transylvanian Christians would have been the same: such sinful sectarians must be forced to return to Christianity or must face death.

All this does not mean that the anti-Sabbatarian actions of the prince and his subordinates in the judiciary were not also influenced by materialistic, that is, financial, considerations. Some of the leaders of the Sabbatarians were enormously rich magnates. Simon Péchi himself, as we have seen, owned huge estates incuding dozens of villages. To acquire these holdings in a legal way for the princely treasury was certainly a great temptation, and one cannot help suspecting that had the Sabbatarian leaders been as poor as most of their followers, their apostasy would have been dealt with less harshly. The combination of religious zeal with cupidity has other examples as well in both the Christian and the Muslim worlds. In Hungary, as we have seen, born Jews, not guilty of any religious transgression such as the Sabbatarian apostasy, were also summarily deprived of their estates or the monies owed them by Christian debtors. Still, the prime motive for condemning the Sabbatarian leaders to loss of life and property seems to have been the painful affront caused to a Christian realm by Christian magnates who abandoned the faith of salvation for a quasi-Jewish sectarian doctrine.

We have no information about the reaction of the Transylvanian Jews to the emergence of the Sabbatarian movement and its persecution by the prince and his judiciary. One must assume that they knew about it and felt it was the better part of wisdom to lie low and keep their distance from what was, after all, an internal Christian issue.

14

The Jews in Turkish-Occupied Hungary (1526-1686)

The story of Jewish life in the central part of Hungary, which was under Turkish rule for 160 years, must begin with a brief acccount of what happened during and immediately after 1526, when the Ottoman armies defeated the Hungarian forces at the southern Hungarian city of Mohács. The Mohács Disaster opened the road to the Turks to occupy all of central Hungary and thus to achieve the deepest Ottoman penetration into Christian Europe to date. The capital city and fortress of Buda fell to the Turks in September 1526, and a few years later the Sephardi historian Joseph Hakohen (1496–1578) described the event in his Hebrew book *Chronicle of the Kings of France and the Kings of the House of Ottoman the Turk* as follows:

> The inhabitants of Buda were seized with dread coming from God. They left the city and ran away. But the Jews remained in the city, cried to God, and he in his holy place listened to their supplication. [Sultan] Suleiman, who did not yet know of this, approached the city. The leaders of the [Jewish] community went out to receive him, prostrated themselves before him, delivered the city to him, and he entered the city. He said not a word against the children of Israel and took not even a shoelace from their possessions. Because Suleiman was merciful toward them, he sent them by ship to his country, where they live even to this day.

This almost idyllic picture of the first encounter beween the Turkish conquerors and the Jews of Buda is evidently colored by the strongly Turkophilic sentiments of its author and is not borne out by the accounts of other contemporary chroniclers. According to the Swiss humanist Johann Kessler, what happened was that in September 1526, when the Turks penetrated Buda, they killed all the Christians—men, women, and children. Then they attacked the Jewish street, which was protected within the city by special walls and fortifications and was defended by the Jews with such vigor that the Turks lost 2,500 men in taking it. The Turks brought up their artillery, broke down the gates, stormed the quarter, and "hacked to pieces whatever had breath, and dealt with them in such a manner that of the 3,500 Jews not more than twenty escaped."

That Kessler's report exaggerates in the opposite direction from that of Joseph Hakohen becomes evident from a third one, contained in the eyewitness account of the Turkish historian Ferdi Efendi. He writes:

> Since the unbelievers living in the fortress of Budun did not trust in their fortress and had no strength to oppose the attack of the army engaged in the holy war, they were forced to escape, leaving the fortress empty. Most of them, trembling only for their lives, cared nothing for their goods and property, so that of the profligate unbelievers nobody except the poor remained there.
>
> When the flags, sparkling like the sun, shed their light upon the environs of this city, the mentioned Jews, wrapped in shrouds, came out to receive the victorious army and, rubbing their faces into the dust of the earth, beseeched us for mercy. Their humble request having reached the place of compassion, they were granted mercy for their person and property, and the mentioned Jews, whose number was greater than 2,000 families, were sent on ships to the land of Islam.

Other historical sources, too, make it clear that a considerable number of Jewish captives were removed from Buda and settled in Turkey, in Istanbul and elsewhere, so that the report about the slaughter of all the Buda Jews except twenty simply cannot be true.

After 1526 the fort and city of Buda were fought over several times, and it was not until 1541 that the Turks definitively established themselves there and made Buda the capital of their newly won Hungarian province. Not only in Buda but in the country as a whole, there followed after 1526 fifteen years of armed struggle beween the Turks, the Austrians, and the Hungarians, in which the two Christian forces not only fought against the Turks but more than occasionally also fought one against the other. Even the 1538 Treaty of Várad did not ensure peace between the Hungarians and Austrians, and tension between them continued. In 1540 and 1541 Ferdinand's armies made unsuccessful attempts to retake Buda. In August of 1541 the sultan assigned to the infant king János II and his mother Isabella the lands east of the Tisza River and Transylvania, thereby creating a new state, the Principality of Transylvania.

In the early years after Mohács the Ottoman army, expanding its hold on the central part of Hungary, behaved like all conquering armies, killing and destroying. Whether the people they encountered on the way were Christians or Jews made no difference: they were the enemy and had to be eliminated. Thus, when Pécs, lying only a few miles west of Mohács, fell to the Turks, they slaughtered the entire Jewish population of the city. The Turkish advance spread such fear in the land that the approaching Turkish armies were preceded by streams of refugees fleeing in the opposite direction. From Buda, a whole armada of river-boats carried all those who could afford to leave to the safety of Vienna.

However, once the first frenzy of conquest was over, the Ottoman penchant for peacefully controlling subject populations and providing them with security—in which the ever-present interest in being better able to squeeze taxes out of them played a main role—gained the upper hand, and conditions gradually returned to "normal." The Turks also followed the millennial Near Eastern method of securing newly conquered territories by removing parts of their populations to other areas —this was the origin as early as 586 B.C.E. of the Babylonian Jewish community, established after the conquest of Jerusalam by Nebuchadnezzar. Likewise, after the conquest of the Hungarian capital, Buda, the Turks transported some 2,000 Jews of the city and its environs to Istanbul and other cities of the Ottoman Empire. There the Hungarian Jews established themsleves as separate communities and preserved their Hungarian identity and customs for several generations, until they gradually assimilated to the preexisting Ashkenazi and Sephardi communities.

Once the situation was more or less under control within the Turkish-occupied area, the wide Turkish practice of enabling non-Muslim populations to live under the *millet* system came into play. This meant giving the *millet*s, recognized non-Muslim communities, internal autonomy, including the freedom to practice their religion, while circumscribing what they were and were not allowed to do, and what duties they owed to their Turkish overlords. The nature of the religious persuasion of the *millet*, whether the "infidels" constituting it were Christians or Jews, was a matter of indifference to the Turks.

For the Christian Hungarians, both Catholic and Protestant, to have to live under Muslim Turkish overlordship was, of course, a traumatic and humiliating experience. It was less so for the Jews, who had long been inured to living under the dominion of gentiles, to being restricted, discriminated against, looked down upon, oppressed, and even persecuted, whether by the power of Edom (Christianity) or Ishmael (Islam). In fact, once the situation quieted down within the Turkish-dominated territory, some Jews felt that it was more desirable to live under Turkish rule than in a Christian country.

By the 1530s Jews again lived in the walled city of Buda, and by the 1580s their number had grown to 88 families (or some 500 individuals). The oldest known list of Turkish tax assessments enumerates among the inhabitants of Budin (Buda) 238 Christian Hungarian, 75 Jewish, and

60 Gypsy heads of families; that is, some 20 percent of the civilian population of the city was Jewish. (Incidentally, this remained the percentage of Jews in Budapest until the end of World War II.) In addition, at the beginning of the Turkish period, the city had a Turkish military population of 2,000, so that it was predominantly a military outpost of the Ottoman Empire. The growth of the Buda Jewish community was the result of immigration not only from the territory of Royal Hungary (under Habsburg rule) but also from other parts of the Ottoman Empire, including Istanbul and even the Galilean city of Safed.

Most of the Jews in Turkish Hungary were engaged in trading and played an important role in the commerce between various regions of the Ottoman Empire, on the one hand, and the Western Christian countries, on the other. They bought the products of the more developed Western industries and handicrafts, such as military supplies and equipment, metalwares, and so on, and shipped these to the East, while in the Turkish Empire they purchased various agricultural products and so-called Turkish wares, including textiles woven through with metal threads, cordovan leather, coffee, and tobacco, for which there was a market in the West. Of course, the Turkish rulers of the country skimmed off considerable taxes from the top of all these export-import and middleman businesses.

Some of the Jews of Buda were artisans: contemporary sources mention passementerie makers, glassworkers, and purse makers. In addition, they were also engaged in renting taverns and exchange houses—in the 1580s they were in charge of the royal taverns and exchange houses in Buda and Pest, for example—and they rented the bridge toll of Buda and served as supervisors of rents and as tax gatherers. We also happen to have information on an income-producing occupation in which some Jewish women of Buda engaged: they made simple broadcloth, known as *shayaq*.

As far as commercial activities were concerned, it was in the interest of the Turkish authorities to allow merchants to pursue their trade without undue interference. On occasion the Turks could even point with pride to the better conditions the merchants enjoyed in the Turkish region than in the Austrian-dominated area. In 1581 the Habsburg Holy Roman Emperor Rudolf II (king of Hungary 1572–1612) closed down the weekly market of Győr (an important city in royal Hungary) in order to increase the revenues from the markets of Vienna and other cities, which went directly into the imperial treasury. This was a serious financial blow to the treasury of Royal Hungary, and it also affected commercial activity between it and Turkish Hungary. Ali, the pasha of Buda, therefore sent a letter to Archduke Ernest, alerting him to the damage this would cause to the Hungarian economy, and stating: "We request Your Highness to issue an order to the frontier officials that they should not perturb the poor merchant people, not arrest them, but let them trade, which would redound to the profit of both our gracious Sovereign and Your Highness. See, in our domain we do not arrest, nor disturb, anybody."

Not only did the Turkish rulers make sure that commercial activities could proceed unhindered by providing security of roads, of markets, and of credit arrangements; they also made a point of emphasizing their tolerant attitude toward religions other than Islam. In several extant letters written by the pashas one reads statements such as "We have one God, we are one man, even if we differ in faith."

Having lived for several decades under Turkish rule in Buda, the Jews developed the same loyalty toward their overlords that was characteristic in every country where they were tolerated and enabled to earn a livelihood. This explains the fervor with which they participated in the defense of Buda when the city was attacked in 1598 by the imperial Austrian forces. A quasi-contemporary account of what happened was added by an anonymous chronicler to the book *Emeq haBakha* (Valley of Tears) by Joseph Hakohen (whose earlier book was cited at the beginning of this chapter):

> At this time a cruel war raged in the territory of Hungary. The armies of the emperor [Rudolf II] penetrated as far as Buda and occupied by storm the suburbs all around, and the Turks who were there sought refuge in the castle. When the Jews who lived there saw this, they arose to defend their lives, saying, "Let us fight with courage for our children, our wives, our possessions, and let God do what seems good in his eyes." They fought against the emperor's armies with great power and a strong hand, beat and scattered them, so that they had to retreat in great shame.
>
> Then people arose who slandered the Jews in the [Viennese] palace and said: "Our lord, our emperor! The Jews sided with our enemies, so that we were unable to take the city of Buda. Therefore, they deserve that all the Jews living in our country be expelled."
>
> Whereupon the emperor, as a wise man and like an angel of God, answered: "On the contrary! It should be counted as a merit for them that they fought faithfully for their ruler. I doubt not that our Jewish subjects, if the time for it should come, would fight faithfully also for us. For this, therefore, no reproach should reach them." Praise be to him who put this into the heart of the emperor!

Other reports, too, attest to the help the Jews of Buda rendered to the Turks in the defense of the city. The exchange between the emperor and the anonymous accuser of the Jews is, of course, fictitious. If the Jews in Turkish Hungary were exposed from time to time to suffering, attack, mayhem, and murder, this was largely due to the continuing armed struggle between the Turks and Austrians. In 1602 the Austrian imperial army again besieged Buda, and many Jews fled the city while escape was still possible. The Austrians managed to penetrate the city temporarily, killed many of the Jews who had remained there, captured twenty-two wealthy Jews, and abducted them with the intention of extracting a rich ransom for them. Despite this setback the city remained in Turkish hands for another eight decades, and the Jewish community in it not only continued to function but grew in size. Jewish immigrants were attracted from the Ottoman Empire, as well as from various European countries where the position of Jews had become untenable owing to expulsions and attacks such as those perpetrated in the Ukraine by Chmielnicki.

As was the case in pre-Mohács days, the Jews continued to live on the Castle Hill of Buda, in the so-called Jewish Street, where they also had their synagoue. (This synagogue was excavated in recent years at 23 Michael Táncsics Street.) Near it, where today the Viennese Gate Plaza is located, was the marketplace, known as the Jewish Market. Other Jews lived beneath the Castle Hill, near the Danube harbors, in *Vizivá-ros* (Water Town), which was also called Jew Town.

During the decades of Turkish rule in central Hungary, the Jewish communities achieved a degree of economic well-being that enabled them to lend their support to the charitable institutions of the Jews in the Holy Land. The Jewish community of Buda sent several hundred florins every year to the pious poor in Jerusalem, Safed, and Hebron, and from time to time emissaries from those cities would visit Buda. The intensity of the religious feelings of the Buda Jews is indicated by the fact that some of them had themselves laid to rest in Safed.

An interesting glimpse into conditions in sixteenth-century Buda and the relationship among the adherents of the three religions to which its inhabitants belonged, Islam, Christianity, and Judaism, is afforded by the travelogue of a German traveler who passed through the city prior to 1578. He writes that in Buda there lived many Jews, whose occupations were "commerce, usury, and betrayal." When the city suffered a drought, the commander of Buda, Mehmet Pasha, took the opportunity to find out which one of the three groups was in the possession of the true faith. For this purpose he staged what was in effect a rain-making competition among the three religions. He first commanded the Turks to bring out all their children from the schools and let them pray for rain under the open sky. This had no effect on the weather. Likewise, nothing happened after the "poor, blind" Jews prayed. Finally, the Christian children were brought out of their schools, and as a result of their prayer rain fell. Thereupon the Pasha acknowledged the truth of the Christian faith.

The interesting point in this account is not whether the Turkish pasha actually recognized the truth of Christianity—it does not seem very likely, but then the account is written by a Christian traveler—but rather the recital itself of prayers for rain by children of the three religions. Prayers for rain, whose origin goes back to biblical times (see 1 Kings 18), were offered by the Jews and Muslims in the Middle East down to modern times, and more often than not it was the task of children to recite them. Evidently, the pasha of Buda was familiar with this ritual, hence his order to perform it. That he commanded the children of the three religions to recite them one after the other indicates that, as in Turkey itself, so in Buda the Jews and Christians constituted recognized *millets*, religious communities, assured of the freedom to practice their religion.

One of the most serious dangers that threatened well-to-do Jews living in the Turkish-dominated part of Hungary was being kidnapped and held for ransom by Hungarians. A case recorded in surviving documents was that of the Buda Jew Moyses in 1567. In July of that year a certain Gergely Szücs, a soldier of Eger, entered into a contract with Baron Simon Forgács, chief *ispán* of Counties Heves and Borsod and military commander of the city of Eger, to the effect that if Szücs kidnapped the Jew Moyses, one of the richest Jews of Buda, and obtained ransom for him, one-third of the ransom would go to Baron Forgács, while two-thirds would be the Szücs's share. Szücs, born in Ráckeve, knew well the local conditions of that town and planned to carry out the abduction on the occasion of Moyses's visit there in connection with his business. The opportunity arose in September, when Moyses went to Ráckeve with a considerable amount of merchandise. He was kidnapped by Szücs and spirited away to Eger, where, it seems, he was kept in the prison of the chief *ispán*'s castle. On September 9, 1567, Mustafa, the Turkish pasha of Buda, wrote letters to two high Hungarian officials, Count Salm and János Trautson, informing them that "again a Jewish merchant was kidnapped from Ráckeve," asking them to arrange for the release of the kidnapped Jew, and reminding Trautson that Mustafa had himself only recently released three Germans who had been abducted at Komárom from aboard a ship. Moyses, however, was not immediately released, and Mustafa, who in the meantime found out that the kidnapping was engineered by Forgács of Eger, wrote on February 14, 1569, to Emperor Maximilian, asking him to order Forgács "to release to me the Jew in all neighborly friendship," otherwise the wife, children, and friends of the Jew would betake themselves to "the mighty emperor" (the sultan) crying and complaining, which would cause him, Mustafa, "great worry."

It so happened that by the time Mustafa wrote this letter Moyses was no longer in captivity, as we learn from his petition on February 16, 1569, to Emperor Maximilian. In it he describes himself as "a poor captured Jew" who had been imprisoned by Baron Forgács in Eger. He tells him that when Forgács learned that the emperor was trying to find Moyses, he moved him to Szarvaskő, had him tortured twice, and then sent him to the Turutza castle, where the nobleman István Liputi kept him imprisoned through the winter. When officials of the emperor came to look for him, Liputi hid him, and once they left, he sent him back to Forgács. Forgács in turn sent Moyses to Transylvania, to his friend István Báthory, who, however, was away, and his servants did not want to accept Moyses. Now Moyses was taken back to Eger, where he was again imprisoned. Knowing that the men of the emperor were looking for him, Moyses tried to call attention to himself by crying and shouting, whereupon Forgács had a chain put around his neck and threw him in a deep dungeon so his voice could not be heard. Moyses was kept there until three days before Christmas 1568, when Forgács sent him under guard to Fischamend near Tyrnau (Nagyszombat). There it seems Moyses was able, through the good offices of the judge of Jászberény, to arrange for the payment of the ransom Forgács demanded of him, after which he was kept in custody for five more days to prevent him from going to Vienna and lodging a complaint against Forgács. We have no information as to what happened to Moyses between the end of December 1568 and February 16, 1569, when he wrote his petition to the emperor, which he concluded by requesting an audience to be able to tell the emperor of his captivity and sufferings.

From this point on the documentary evidence is confusing. Moyses's February 16, 1569, petition is clear evidence that by that time he was no longer in the power of Forgács, but on June 22, 1569, Gergely Szücs wrote a promissory note to Simon Forgács, in which he undertook to hand over to Forgács 4,000 florins in cash and 500 florins in merchandise out of the total of 8,000 florins cash and 2,000 florins in merchandise he had received as the ransom for Moyses. It seems unlikely that Szücs kept the entire sum of the ransom for more than four months before paying Forgács his agreed-upon share.

Nor did the matter rest here. On March 31, 1570, Mustafa Pasha again wrote to Emperor Maximilian an exasperated letter in which he reproaches the emperor for not having punished Forgács for the kidnapping, and for having "elevated him in great honors." Furthermore, the pasha requests that the emperor recover from Forgács the 9,000 florins the Jew Moyses paid Forgács as ransom. This should be done in view of the peace concluded between "the two emperors" (Maximilian and the sultan); if not, the pasha would extract the money from the merchants who would fall into his hands. At this time Moyses was safely back in Buda. What happened thereafter, whether the ransom money was returned to the pasha, and whether he in turn refunded it to Moyses— about all this we have no information. What we do know is that the Jew Moyses was far from the only Buda Jew to be kidnapped and held for ransom by Hungarian soldiers.

In 1582, István Nyáry, Hungarian extraordinary envoy to the court of the pasha of Buda, wrote to Archduke Ernest about the capture by Hungarian soldiers from Palota of three poor Jewish servants of well-to-do Buda Jews, probably for the purpose of extorting ransoms from their masters. In retaliation, the pasha of Buda had three Christians impaled for each of the three Jews, and was about to execute another six. Nyáry begged the pasha not to commit such unheard-of cruelty and suggested to the archduke that the three Buda Jews be released, informing him of the names of the Hungarian offices holding them for ransom. In addition, wrote Nyáry, Gen. Rueber was also holding a Buda Jew, whose brothers obtained a rescript from the sultan to the pasha of Buda, ordering him to retaliate by executing sixty prisoners held as hostages in Buda. However, the Jews of Buda, motivated by pity, decided to redeem Rueber's prisoner, and offered him 200 Christian prisoners in exchange for the one Jew. (The exchange of one Jew for 200 Christians reminds one of the exchanges in the 1980s and 90s of one or two Jews held by Arab states or terrorists for several hundreds of Arab prisoners held by Israel.)

The change of ruler from Austrian emperor to Turkish sultan did not prevent the Jews of Buda from continuing their money business and their wholesale commercial activities. A case in point is that of the Jew Jacob son of Bereczk, a Buda wholesale merchant. This Jacob entered into a barter arrangement with János Trombitás of Nagymaros: Jacob gave him merchandise in the value of 1,300 florins, against which Trombitás undertook to deliver to Jacob one hundred quintals of copper within three months, or, if he did not deliver it, to pay him 1,300 florins in cash, and as security he mortgaged his house and vineyard to the Jew. Shortly thereafter, however, Trombitás absconded, whereupon (in 1582) Ali, pasha of Buda, wrote several letters to Archduke Ernest asking him to see to it that the debt of Trombitás be paid to the Jew. Jacob could not obtain satisfaction of his demand from the mortgaged property of Trombitás, because according to the law, if a person absconded, his property passed to "the mighty emperor," that is, the sultan. Settling this debt was the more urgent since Jacob himself owed large amounts of money to the sultan, which he was unable to defray

170

until he got what Trombitás owed him. Should the archduke not settle the matter, Ali Pasha wrote, he would imprison the next merchants from Vienna, Nagyszombat, or Komárom to visit Buda. Despite the pasha's repeated demands and threats, the matter was not settled, and two years later Ali's successor, Sinan Pasha, repeated the demand, asking by that time not 1,300 but 1,500 florins for Jacob son of Bereczk. What ultimately happened is not known, but the extant letters show that the Jew Jacob enjoyed the protection of the pashas of Buda and that he owed money (possibly taxes) to the Sublime Porte. He was certainly not the only Jew engaged in large-scale business transactions, and his case, taken together with the abductions of rich Buda Jews described above, testifies to the existence of a well-to-do and influential class of big Jewish merchants in the capital of Turkish Hungary.

We have seen that when Sultan Suleiman conquered Buda and the central part of Hungary in 1541, he removed to Constantinople some of the Jews who lived in Buda—probably the gold- and silversmiths and other craftsmen—but the rest were enabled to stay and to live in safety in the city. They were concentrated in the *mahalle-i yahudiyan* (Jewish quarter), where they enjoyed a certain internal autonomy. Consequently, a number of Jews from other parts of Turkish Hungary moved to Buda. The Turks themselves settled Jews from the Balkans, probably from Edirne and possibly also from Salonika, in Buda. These newcomers replenished the community, many of whose members had moved to Istanbul, Edirne, and other Turkish cities.

From Turkish *defters* (tax lists) enumerating the Jews who paid the *jizye* (head tax), it is known that between 1546 and 1633 the number of Jews in Buda fluctuated greatly: the number of tax-paying heads of families was between 11 and 103, with a total number of persons between 110 and 1,030. Of the customs duties paid by merchants in 1571, 7 percent was paid by Jews, a fraction that increased by 1573 to 17.07 percent and went down in 1580 to 13.74 percent. The merchandise the Jews traded from 1550 to 1580 included foodstuffs (flour, wine, brandy, fat, honey, pepper imported from Turkey, ginger, chestnuts, poppy, cloves), cloth and dry goods, leather goods, slippers, ammonia (called *nishadir*), soap, and metal items (so-called Hungarian knives imported from Styria, razors, tin, copper, wire). Several of these items were imported only by Jewish merchants.

It is partly from the Turkish *defters* that we know of the occupations of the Buda Jews. They were headed by a *kiaya* or *kethüda* (head of the Jewish quarter), who was free from paying the tax. They had three rabbis, Moses, David, and Abraham by name, who may have been the respective rabbis of the Spanish, Syrian, and German Jews who lived in

Buda, and constituted the *Jema'at Yahudiyan*, the Jewish Community. Two butchers, Kohen and David Moses, may have functioned also as ritual slaughterers. Five Jews had the name Meir, one or more of whom may have been synagogue servants. There were also two physicians, Moses and Abraham. One Jew, Joseph, was a glazier. Several Jews served as customs officials, not only in Buda but also in provincial cities all over the country.

As early as the 1540s, some Edirne Jews engaged in the money business settled in Buda. In 1542, two Jews, Musa ben Baliko of Szendrő and Zakaria Dobos of Istanbul, rented the candle works and the money exchange of Buda and Pest from the Turkish government, for three years, guaranteeing an annual income of 51,000 akchas (small silver coins) with all their assets. In 1556, the Jew (Yahudi) Salimun, together with several partners, was entrusted with the management of the Turkish *muqataa*. This was the financial office established for controlling, in behalf of the Turkish treasury, the finances of merchants' rent for their stalls in the markets of Buda and Pest, the payments to courts of justice for issuing summonses, fees for selling beer, wine, and sheeps' heads, ferry dues, tolls collected at the city gates, and taxes on candle making. Salimun Yahudi functioned as *bashamil* (chief revenue manager), and several *amil*s (revenue managers) worked under him. The income Salimun paid into the Turkish *defterhane* (treasury office) of Buda in a year amounted to about 600,000 akches. He himself received for his work a daily salary of seven akches.

In the 1550s other Jews also functioned as managers of Turkish revenues in Pest, Buda, and elsewhere. One of them was the Jew Simon, another the Jew Kelemen, who in 1548 became the comptroller of revenues of the *muqataa* established in Buda for handling the wine taxes. In 1600 and 1601, the Jew Musa was the *emin-i mültezim* (contractor-commissioner) in charge of the revenues Buda received from its Danube harbor. After 1667, Ephraim Kohen, rabbi of Buda, reported the Buda Jewish merchants' practice of sailing to the fairs of Eszék, located on the upper reaches of the Tisza River. The Turkish customs logs mention Jewish merchants of Nikopol, which also indicates riverine commerce. Jewish merchants from Turkey itself were frequent visitors in Buda for commercial purposes. Jewish merchants of Buda, on the other hand, regularly sailed up the Danube as far as Pressburg and down as far as Belgrade. Evidently, they were permitted to cross the international border between Turkish and Austrian Hungary, which was closer to Buda than to Pressburg.

A smaller but still significant Jewish commercial center was Vác, located at the big bend of the Danube to the north of Buda, from where the names of several Jewish wine merchants have survived. The Vác trade was also under the supervision of the Jew Salimun as *amil*. Under his administration the income produced by that city rose from 459,819 akches in 1558 to 1,985,421 akches in 1560.

Among the other cities in Turkish Hungary where Jews lived and engaged in commercial activities were Szeged, Szerémség, Székesfehérvár, Ráckeve, Báta, and Solt-Révfalu, and in several of them Jews functioned as *amil*s.

Not all the Jews were honest all the time. The records tell us that in September 1558, the Jew Ibn-i Yafes of Ráckeve, who had been in charge of the local revenue office of Paks and then that of Ráckeve for more than two years, suddenly absconded to Belgrade without paying what he owed the *defterhane*. The Turkish authories went after him in a fast boat down the Danube, apprehended him, and brought him back to Buda. There he was able to obtain loans and guarantees from some Jews (among them Baruḥ Yahudi) and Turkish soldiers and thus to pay the monies he owed the treasury. He was dismissed from his post but went to Tolna and there, within ten days of his dismissal, became the *amil* of the local *muqataa*. We lose track of him after that, but a year later he was no longer in that post, which was filled at that time by Kaleman ben Asher Yahudi. From these and other similar data it appears that the post of *amil* was frequently held by Jews.

Although the Jews of Turkish Hungary were active in commerce and officialdom and had synagogues and rabbis, they were deficient in producing any scholarly or literary works. Because of this absence of writings and records of their own, what we know about them comes either from the Turkish official documents discussed above or else from references found in the writings of Jewish scholars from other countries who happened to have contact with their Hungarian coreligionists. As before the Turkish period, it happened occasionally that Hungarian rabbis turned to their colleagues abroad to obtain opinions on legal questions they did not feel competent to decide on their own. The responsa of the learned foreign rabbis shed some light on the conditions of Jewish life in Hungary, and the relations between the Jews and the Turkish masters of the country in this period. Take, for example, the following responsum from R. Elijah ben Ḥayyim, who from 1575 was chief rabbi of Istanbul.

> In 1586 quarrels broke out between a Jewish husband and wife who had been married since 1581 and lived in Buda. The uncle of the woman came from Sofia to Buda to settle the matter, and demanded that the husband give a *get* to his wife and pay her 80,000 silvers [*l'vanim*, "whites," in the Hebrew original; also called *aspers*; in Turkish *akche*]. The husband refused, whereupon the woman's uncle bribed the Turkish "little judge" [*dayyan qatan*], who had the husband and his father jailed. The husband

and wife came to an agreement about the payment, but the husband continued to refuse to give a letter of divorce to his wife.

At this point Asher, the uncle of the woman, and her brother went to the house of the "great judge" [*dayyan gadol*], Baha ed-Din Zade by name, and pressed 200 ·*shāhi*s (Persian coins) into his hands, whereupon the judge asked Asher, "How do they treat the husband in the jail?" Asher replied, "The husband lives and walks about in jail as if it were his own house. This is the reason why he cannot be induced to give a letter of divorce."

The judge ordered the prison commander to be brought before him, and instructed his police officer [Arabic *kāshif*] to give him a thorough beating. When the prison commander arrived, the Turks present asked the chief judge not to have him beaten, whereupon the chief judge commanded him not to let the husband out of the inner part of the jail, where the prisoners were kept, and not to let him sit around in the outer courtyard, where the prison commander lived, so that the husband should pay his wife whatever he owed. Then turning to Asher he said, "According to our laws the divorce has already taken place, but not according to your laws; but I shall see to it that within eight days the divorce should be effected also according to your laws."

Subsequently, after the issuance of the *get*, the judge said to the witness: "Why don't you see to it that the uncle of the woman give me the reward promised, since I made every effort to have his niece receive the letter of divorce?" The witness reported this to the woman's uncle, who asked him: "What do you advise, shall I give the judge a silver cup, or a robe [*dunluq*, from the Turkish *tunluk*] made of Venetian cloth?" The witness answered: "Would that he were satisfied with both!" All this was described in the question sent to R. Elijah Hakohen and supplemented by several other testimonies to the effect that the chief judge was a man easily bribed, who, if bribed, suppressed the truth. The question asked of the Constantinople rabbi was whether the *get* obtained in this manner was valid according to halakhic law. R. Elijah studied the matter and declared the *get* valid.

Another leading rabbinial authority with whom the Buda rabbis maintained frequent contact was R. Ḥayyim ben Shabbetai (before 1555–1647), rabbi and from 1640 chief rabbi of Salonika, from whose responsa we learn some interesting details about the position of women in the Jewish community of Buda and about the conditions in the city contested between the Turkish and Austrian powers in the early seventeenth century. In one of his responsa R. Ḥayyim ben Shabbetai writes:

The people of the community of Budun [Buda], in German Ofen, turned to me with a question. The following events took place in that community: "Rachel" for several years had a seat in the synagogue, as is the custom in all Ashkenazi communities, where each person acquires for himself a place in the synagogue, where he sits, and which is his property, and which he can rent out to anybody, or sell in perpetuity for a price, or give away as a present. It happened that while the [Austrian] enemy was besieging the city, and outside it there was heavy fighting and inside it there was famine, Rachel could not go to the synagogue because she had become totally impoverished and was able to maintain her house only with great difficulties, as a result of which her seat remained empty. Now "Leah," seeing this, occupied the seat, and when her neighbors asked her, "What are you doing here? This is not your seat!" she answered that it was her intention to purchase the seat from Rachel. Since at the time the city was increasingly threatened by war and famine, many fled from the city to the countryside. And the community was forced to expel especially those poor people who had no livelihood, to go elsewhere. Thus, Rachel was also sent away so as to save her life and the lives of the people of her house. In the meantime Leah died, and left her seat to her daugher "Dinah" as an inheritance. After a long time, when Dinah had already been sitting in her seat for more than three years, Rachel returned to the city, where she found Dinah sitting in the synagogue in her seat.

In the ensuing lawsuit between the two women, Dinah argued that her mother, Leah, had purchased the seat from Rachel. Nevertheless, the decision of the Buda rabbi, R. Gedaliah, was that Rachel was the legal owner of the seat. The decision was appealed to R. Ḥayyim ben Shabbetai, who confirmed R. Gedaliah's decision.

We learn from this case that the Jewish women of Buda owned houses and permanent seats in the synagogue, and that those of them who stayed in the city during its siege by the Austrian army (in 1602) and the consequent famine piously continued to attend synagogue services. It is also interesting that the council of the Jewish community had the power to expel its poor members from the city, which it evidently did in order to save them from starvation, and to alleviate the situation of others suffering from the famine. The expellees managed to survive in the other Turkish-held parts of the country, and when the Austrian army withdrew, following its unsuccessful campaign, they returned and claimed possession of their abandoned property.

That the Jewish community of Buda did not always behave entirely charitably toward its members who fled the city and then returned is known from another of the responsa of R. Ḥayyim ben Shabbetai:

A question addressed to my lord. The city of Buda having been besieged and stricken by arms, pestilence, and famine, most of the inhabitants of the city had to flee the rage of the besiegers and seek repose together with their families wherever they could find it, one here, one there. Only a few who could not escape remained. Among those who fled were [Jewish] inhabitants of Buda whose ancestors, too, had lived there, and who even today own houses, stores, and other real estate, for which they still pay taxes. Now, when they heard that the Lord had remembered his people and that the Christians and Turks had made peace, they returned, together with their families, to their old dwelling places.

But that part of those who had remained in the city who are friends of quarrel passed a resolution to the effect that those who wanted to return to the city should not be allowed to do so, and especially should not be admitted into the community until they paid an amount determined by the former. But the returnees said that they did not leave of their free will and that it had not been their intention to leave Buda, but they were forced to do so in order to save their lives and to escape from pestilence, arms, and famine until the wrath passed.

The decision of R. Ḥayyim ben Shabbetai was that the law supported the returnees, and those who had remained in the city throughout the siege could not prevent them from returning. The inquiry seems to have been sent to Salonika following the 1607 peace agreement of Zsitvató-rök between the Austrians and Turks.

An interesting piece of anecdotal information about the help the Jews of Buda rendered the Turks during a later siege of the city by the Austrian army is found in the travelogue of the famous Turkish seventeenth-century traveler Evliya Chelebi, who passed through Hungary several times. He writes:

> During the third siege [of Buda], when the enemy burst through this gate [Chelebi refers to the Viennese Gate, in Turkish *Bech Kapusi*, located at the western part of the fortress of Buda], and was about to occupy the fort, the Jews took pieces of rat poison [in Turkish: *sülmen ve sicān otu*, literally: quicksilver and arsenic] and said to one another in the Jewish language: "If the enemy enters the fort, we shall lick [i. e. swallow] the poison; we shall either die or escape." Among the Jews of Buda there is to this day the saying, "Shall we lick?" Inside the Viennese Gate there is still a cannon from the times of hostility, in which a man can find room [i.e., of a very large caliber]; when the enemy was rushing straight in at this place, a Jew suddenly fired this canon, and it hit the unbelievers who were standing tightly packed between the gates and outside them, so that, according to what is told by the Christians themselves, a few thousands of their choice soldiers were struck down into the dust of death. For this reason the Jews of Buda now are exempt from all provincial taxes. They live inside the Viennese Gate in several stone buildings, but if a Jew from this neighborhood falls into the hands of Hungarians, Germans, or Czechs, they roast him on a spit . . .

Evidently, the Jews of Buda threw in their lot with the Turks, and when the Austrians finally did take the fort they were massacred by them.

Among the other details we learn from Chelebi is that there were several synagogues in Buda, and that the Jewish women engaged in cloth weaving.

In conformity with the mores of the times and place, the Jews of Buda owned slaves. Under Turkish rule it was possible for them to own Christian male and female slaves, whom they could convert to Judaism, and marriages between such converts and Jewish-born men and women could and did take place. Several such cases are referred to in contemporary responsa literature, especially in the *Sha'ar Efrayim* (Gate of Ephraim) of R. Ephraim haKohen of whom more will be said below. The same source also mentions cases of Jews who converted to Islam.

We also learn from the contemporary responsa literature that some Jews maintained friendly relations with Turks, some of whom were frequent guests in Jewish houses. Jews also sold merchandise to Turks on credit and lent money to Turks, which led to this warning by R. Efrayim haKohen: "It is an especially dangerous thing, and liable to violence, to lend money to Turks. Such a business results in many evil calumnies, which they raise even after the passing of several years. It is impossible to pressure the debtors to pay, because they can come forward with such evil calumnies that the principal with the interest is lost."

The friendly relations between the Jews of Buda and the Turkish authorities in control of the city did not remain a secret to the Austrians. In fact, during the 1684 Austrian siege of Buda it was rumored in Padua that the Buda Jews paid huge amounts of bribes to the pashas who headed the Turkish army defending Buda in order to keep them from entering into peace negotiations with the Austrians.

The data presented above are scanty and scattered, but they are sufficient to show that in Turkish-ruled Hungary the Jews were a religiously observant, well-off, and well-organized community whose members could pay large dowries, had synagogues and rabbis, suffered the internal squabbles that inevitably accompany congregational life, had professional physicians, and established well-oiled communications with the local representatives of the Turkish power, including the judges, to whom they gave lavish bribes. They could travel freely all over the Ottoman Empire, and their rabbis corresponded in halakhic matters with colleagues in Istanbul and Salonika, whose superior expertise they ungrudgingly recognized. Despite the enmity between Turkey and Austria, the Jews of Buda also maintained close contact with the Viennese Jewish community, and in many cases their rabbis appealed to Viennese rabbinical authorities for decisions in difficult halakhic questions.

Material well-being and communal organization were accompanied by intellectual-religious development. The community of Buda attracted scholarly rabbis from abroad by offering them important and prestigious positions. Some of its rabbis achieved renown throughout the Jewish world. The best known among them was R. Ephraim ben Jacob haKohen (1616–78), who first was rabbinical judge in Vilna, then served in Velke Mezerici (Moravia), Prague, and Vienna, and in 1666 was appointed *av beth din* in Buda. Here he established a yeshiva that soon became famous, and he corresponded with some of the most prominent rabbis of his time, including those of Turkey, Palestine, Italy, Moravia, and Germany, who addressed questions to him. R. Ephraim's decisions on civil, domestic, and religious issues influenced Jewish life in several countries. Toward the end of his life he was invited to be rabbi of the Ashkenazi congregation in Jerusalem, but he died before he could take up the position. His responsa, *Sha'ar Efrayim*, were published by his son Arye Löb in Sulzbach in 1689; other works of his remained in manuscript.

The defeat of the Turkish army at Vienna on October 12, 1683, was the beginning of the end of Turkish rule in Hungary. At that time the total population of the twin cities of Pest and Buda was 28,000, of whom about one thousand were Jews. They had three synagogues, and the commerce of Buda was almost entirely in their hands. In 1684 the Austrian army laid siege to Buda unsuccessfully, but when, on August 16, 1685, Érsekujvár fell to the imperial army, the Turkish forces were totally demoralized, and many of them escaped toward the Balkans. At the same time, a great number of Jews left Buda and settled in Constantinople, where an 1688–89 census of the Jews lists sixty-four family heads, who were members of the society of Buda Jews and had immigrated voluntarily. Other Buda Jews who escaped in time settled in Belgrade. All of these must have left Buda prior to June 16, 1686, because on that day the Austrian forces surrounded Buda, and thereafter nobody was able to leave the city.

While the struggle for Buda was in progress, a young Prague Jew, Sender Tausk, embarked on a grand and urgent project to save the Jews of Buda from falling into captivity. Armed with a letter of recommendation from the chief rabbi of Prague, he went to Vienna to contact Samuel Oppenheimer, the main supplier of the Austrian army, who was not only the most outstanding Jewish leader of the age but a man of extraordinary influence in imperial government circles. Tausk succeeded in convincing Oppenheimer of the practicality of his plan, and Oppenheimer referred to him one of his chief officials, who had entry to the commander-in-chief. The commander-in-chief received the two men and at their request gave orders that the Jews captured at Buda should be collected in one place and released.

On September 2, 1686, the Hungarian and Brandenburgian units broke through the Turkish defenses and captured Buda. A horrible massacre followed. About one hundred Jewish men, women, and children sought refuge in the synagogue near the Vienna Gate, and the Hungarian Hussars and Brandenburgian soldiers slaughtered seventy-two of them. They put the bodies into the *geniza* chamber of the synagogue, intending to bury them next day, but the commanders, Prince Charles of Lothringen and the Bavarian elector Maximilian Emmanuel, gave their soldiers free hand. In the course of the brutal looting that ensued, several houses caught fire, so that during the night much of the city, including the synagogue, burned down.

The next morning (September 3, 1686) Sender Tausk, accompanied by an officer and soldiers, was able to enter Buda, where they announced next to every city gate, to the accompaniment of drumming, that even though it was permitted to capture Jews, it was forbidden to kill them. Some children showed him the location of the Jewish street and the synagogue. Tausk and his company gathered every person who could recite the *Sh'ma Yisrael* into the burned-out ruins of the synagogue and, by way of protection, hoisted the imperial flag over it. By nightfall he had assembled 274 Jews and also saved thirty-five Torah scrolls.

As soon as Tausk was convinced he could find no more Jews alive in the ruined city, he set out with them, under the protection of a contingent of thirty-four soldiers, along the Danube, toward Pressburg. Contemporary sources report that the provisioning of the thirty-four soldiers cost thirty florins daily, while the Jews fasted on bread and water. Tausk ransomed six Jews from captivity for eighty thalers in Pressburg and hurried on to Vienna, where with Oppenheimer's help the committee for the war prisoners agreed on a ransom of 21,000 florins for the rest of the Jews. Tausk undertook to raise the money and pay the ransom within a certain period. Returning to Pressburg, he put the old people and children on fifteen wagons, while the rest had to continue on foot, this time accompanied by forty horsemen. They proceeded to Nikolsburg, the most populous and richest Jewish community of Moravia, where the refugees found a new home.

Tausk was unable to raise the ransom money in time and was put in debtors' jail, where he remained for thirty-nine weeks until finally the committee recognized that with Tausk in jail they would never get the ransom. They released him, holding his mother and brother as hostages. Tausk went from city to city, visiting Cracow, Metz, Frankfurt, Amsterdam, Cleve, and other places, until through desperate efforts he succeeded in raising the ransom money and secured the release of his mother and brother.

Shortly after the Tausk group left Buda, another twenty-five Jewish men, women and children had emerged from hiding and were captured. They somehow had found hiding places that were not reached by the conflagration, nor found by the looting soldiers, and came out only when driven by hunger to do so. By that time Baron General Beck was in command of the Hungarian army in Buda. Aware of the arrangement for the ransoming of Jewish prisoners, he sent the Jews on to Györ, where they were given shelter and minimal food. Samuel Oppenheimer was informed of the plight of these Jewish refugees in Györ, and offered to pay the royal treasury of Vienna a thousand florins and to supply one well-armed soldier for every poor Jew liberated, while the rich Jews woud pay for their own ransom. On January 4, 1687, the treasury accepted this offer, and some two weeks later the Jews were actually released and sent to Vienna. Large-scale exchanges of Turkish and Austrian war prisoners subsequently also took place.

The recapture of Buda did not signal the end of Turkish rule in Hungary as a whole. The southern part of the country remained under Ottoman occupation for another fifteen years, and the *beglerbegilik* (county) of Temesvár remained Turkish until 1718. During those decades the struggle continued between the Turks, on the one hand, and the Austrians and Hungarians, on the other, bringing much suffering to the population. For the Jews, the replacement of Ottoman by Austrian rule meant a marked deterioration in their position, culminating in many places in expulsion.

The liberation of Hungary from the Turks concluded a chapter that was unique not only in the eighteen-century sojourn of the Jews in the Carpathian Basin but also in the history of Ashkenazi Jewry in general: for 160 years a major part of the Hungarian Jews constituted the only Ashkenazi Jewish community to live not under Christian but under Muslim rule. This fact poses a number of questions that have not only remained unanswered by historians but even have yet to be asked. The foremost among them are these: What influences did Hungarian Jewry absorb from its Muslim Turkish overlords during those five generations? Are those influences paralleled by Turkish influences on the Hungarian Christians? What survived of those influences among the Jewish and Christian Hungarians after the reconquest of Hungary from the Turks? Are there any traits in the Hungarian and specifically the Hungarian-Jewish "national character" that can be considered as having emerged in consequence of the Turkish domination? Could, for instance, the well-known Hungarian and Hungarian-Jewish over-emphasis on patriotism have anything to do with the historical experience of Turkish domination? Can the cultural differences between Hungarian Jews and the Ashkenazi Jews of neighboring countries be correlated in any way with influences absorbed during the Turkish domination of Hungary? Answers to these and other such questions could, I believe, contribute to a better understanding of the cultural specificity that made Hungarian Jewry different from the neighboring Jewish communities.

15

The Jews in Royal Hungary (1526-1686)

Within a few weeks of the Mohács Disaster, the Hungarian Diet convened in Székesfehérvár (Stuhlweissenburg), where the majority of the nobles elected János Szapolyai, the vajda (voivod) of Transylvania, king of Hungary. At the same time, the Diet resolved to expel all the Jews from the entire country that had remained under their control. However, this resolution could not be carried out because Szapolyai withheld his approval, and soon thereafter the Habsburg archduke Ferdinand, king of Bohemia, who was elected king of Hungary by the Pozsony Diet, annulled all the resolutions of the Székesfehérvár Diet.

Nevertheless, the Jews were expelled from several cities in western Hungary, where the burghers increasingly resented the successful activities of Jewish merchants and moneylenders. The first city to eject Jews soon after the Mohács Disaster was Sopron (Ödenburg), where the citizens owed the Jews 4,000 florins and got rid of this debt by the simple expedient of getting rid of the creditors. Several Jews of Sopron, foreseeing the danger, fled in time to neighboring Kismarton (Eisenstadt, *'Ir Barzel* in the Hebrew documents). To forestall royal intervention in the interest of the Jews, the burghers of Sopron informed Queen Maria, the widow of King Lajos II, who had been killed at Mohács, that the Jews wanted to leave the city voluntarily and petitioned her for her consent.

This calculated step had adverse consequences for Sopron. The queen gave her consent but stipulated that the city would have to defray within a year the taxes owed by the Jews, purchase from the Jews their houses at an officially established price, and repay them the principal of the debts. The only concession she made to the city was to annul the interest on the debts. Without waiting for the royal permission, therefore, the city expelled the 400 Jews who lived in Sopron, retaining all their movable and real property and removing the lists of debtors from the Jewish houses. The Jews lodged a complaint (by that time Ferdinand I had become king; r. 1526–64), but the repeated royal interventions were of no avail, and the Jews obtained no redress.

By the merest chance, evidence has survived as to the intellectual life of the Jews of Sopron prior to the expulsion. When the Jews were expelled and their houses ransacked, the looters grabbed the Hebrew parchments they found, which were subsequently used in binding books. Several of these have been preserved in the Sopron city archives, and from them we know that some of the Jews of Sopron were engaged in biblical exegesis, in talmudic study, and in studying the halakhic law code of Maimonides. Also known are the names of several Sopron rabbis who, in all probability, maintained a yeshiva.

The conflict between the burghers and the Jews of Pressburg had a similar outcome. Prior to Mohács some 800 Jews lived in Pressburg, but in the wake of the Disaster many more fled into the city from the territories overrun by the Turks. It is estimated that in 1526 the city sheltered some 3,000 Jews. In the fall of 1526 Pressburg, too, decided to get rid of the Jews, whose financial strength, as a result of their mercantile relations with the West, had become considerable. The disturbances that followed in the wake of the Mohács Disaster increased anti-Jewish sentiments. The citizens of Pressburg applied to Queen Maria and obtained her permission to expel the Jews, provided they let the Jews sell their houses and take the money with them. The citizens, however, managed to prevent these transactions, and the Jews had to depart without their money. King Ferdinand approved the fait accompli, holding the citizens only to paying the royal treasury the taxes the expelled Jews had paid.

The expulsion of the Jews from the two most important west Hungarian cities was a heavy blow to the Jewish community of Royal Hungary, but it entailed only financial losses and other practical hardships. Much more tragic, involving the loss of thirty Jewish lives, was the 1529 blood libel of Bazin (Pösing). It was initiated by Ferenc (Francis) Wolf, count of Pösing and Szentgyörgy, who sought a way out of having to repay his sizable debts to the Jews of Bazin and Marchegg. At first, in 1521, he imprisoned several Jews a number of times. When Isaac Mendel, the Jewish prefect from 1526 on (see chapter 8), heard what was happening in Bazin, he appealed to King Ferdinand, asking him to protect the Jews. However, despite royal intervention, the count carried out his diabolical plan and proclaimed in public that the Jews had killed a Christian child in order to use his blood for ritual purposes. Thirty Jews of Bazin were apprehended, among them the leaders of the community, including R. Moses ben Jacob Kohen and his children, as well as other children and two pregnant women. The city council subjected them to interrogation, and on the basis of confessions extorted by cruel torture, all of them were condemned to death and burned at the stake. The remaining Jews were summarily expelled from the city. When the count imprisoned the Jews of Marchegg as well, they applied to Ferdinand, who ordered their release and opened an inquiry. In the meantime, the boy whose murder the Jews were accused of was found: it turned out that the count himself had the child hidden by a dim-witted woman accomplice. A few years later the Protestant reformer Andreas Osiander subjected the Bazin blood libel to a minute investigation that clearly incriminated the count, and published the results in a booklet about 1540. Thereafter, no Jews lived in Bazin until the middle of the nineteenth century.

In 1536 the trauma of blood libel was visited upon the Jews of Nagyszombat (Tyrnau) a second time. We saw above (in chapter 9) that in 1494 in Nagyszombat fourteen Jews were burned at the stake in the first blood libel in Hungary. Now, after the Bazin Jew-burning, the burghers of Nagyszombat decided that they, too, would get rid of their debts to the Jews by raising another blood libel against them. They accused the Jews of having killed, for ritual purposes, a small child who had disappeared two years earlier. The Jew Moses was tortured on the rack, until he "confessed." In 1537 King Ferdinand I granted the request of the city and ordered the expulsion of the Jews from Nagyszombat, again with the proviso that the city pay one-half of the Jews' taxes into the royal treasury.

Faced with increasing harassment and the acute danger of the proliferation of the blood libel, in 1540 the leaders of Hungarian Jewry appealed to Pope Paul III (r. 1534–49). They emphasized that "the rules of their religion prohibited them from committing the inhuman deeds of which they were accused, to the same extent to which the Christians were by their laws." They requested that the pope extend to them his apostolic grace and protect them against the terrible persecutions. The pope, in his encyclical of May 12, 1540, condemned the blood libel. He confirmed the privileges issued by his predecessors and ordered the clergy to protect the Jews, as far as possible, against everybody who might intend to harm them unjustly. He called upon the kings, princes, barons, and nobles of Hungary, Bohemia, and Poland to use their influence to prevent the persecution of the Jews. Whether or not it was the effect of the papal letter, the fact is that for several centuries thereafter no case of blood libel was to arise again in Hungary. On the other hand, expulsions of Jews, or restrictions of their rights of residence to certain limited areas and localities, continued to occur in Royal Hungary during this period, as well as after the defeat of the Turks.

Some of the Jews who were forced out of the cities settled on the estates of the great magnates. There they engaged in selling the agricultural products of the estates, renting the customs and the taverns, distilling brandy, and providing loans to the estate owners. Others worked as peddlers or purchased the products of the peasants who lived on the estates (rawhides, animals, and so on). In pursuing these activities, the Jews were caught between the often conflicting interests of the landlords and the peasants, the landlords and the cities, and even the landlords and the royal treasury.

Some Jews worked for the treasury collecting silver and other metals. When the customs officer of Vágujhely confiscated from Jews who passed through the city the old silver coins they had collected for the treasury, Ferdinand II (r. 1618–37) instantly ordered him to return the coins he had seized. Other Jews participated in supplying provisions to the army: cereals, cattle, skins, and so forth. This activity especially gained in importance in the late seventeenth century during the wars that resulted in the expulsion of the Turks.

The historical data that underlie the above brief overview of the developments during the 150 years in which Hungary was divided into three parts—Royal (Habsburg) Hungary in the west and north, Turkish Hungary in the center, and the Transylvanian principality in the east—leave us with the definite impression that Jewish life was least onerous in the Turkish area, somewhat more so in Transylvania, and most difficult, with the ever-present danger of persecution, in Royal Hungary. For one thing, while in Royal Hungary the Jews were several times expelled from this or that city and in Transylvania their right to settle was severely restricted (for example, in 1653 Prince George Rákóczi II [r. 1648–60] allowed them to live only in the single city of Gyulafehérvár), no such expulsions or restrictions took place in Turkish Hungary. For another, in Turkish Hungary (or in the whole Ottoman Empire, for that matter) the Jews were never subjected to a wholesale deprivation of rights like the one ordered by Ferdinand III (r. 1637–57), who in 1647 removed the Jews from renting the customs revenues and declared that they had no share in the rights of the country.

It seems that the difference between the position of the Jews in Turkish Hungary, on the one hand, and the two Christian Hungarian countries, on the other, was due primarily to the accommodation the Turks reached with their non-Muslim minorities under the *millet* system, which worked well in both the central area and all the far-flung provinces of the Ottoman Empire. Throughout the Ottoman Empire there were several *millets*, that is, religious communities (e.g., Greek Orthodox, Armenian, Jewish), which were treated more or less equally, as subject people. Since they were not Muslims they were inferior in their religious position but were nevertheless considered integral parts of overall Ottoman society, with definite tasks and functions wherever they lived. The *millet*s, although not liked in particular, were not merely tolerated but accepted as parts of the human mosaic that constituted the empire. They were also welcomed when they asked for admission into the Ottoman realm (the reception of the Spanish Jewish expellees in 1492 is the most telling example) and were occasionally even brought into Turkey against their will (as with the Jews of Buda after its Turkish conquest).

No such accommodation was worked out in the two Christian parts of Hungary. There the Jews were perceived to be a foreign element, in fact, the only sizable non-Christian and therefore alien element, whose economic achievements in fields where Christian Hungarians were either unable or unwilling to work were resented by the majority population. As for the rulers in the two countries—the kings, nobles, and city elders—though they derived definite and even substantial financial benefits from the Jews' activities, the tensions among them and the desire to enjoy a momentary advantage resulted from time to time in harassments, persecutions, and expulsions of the Jews.

The contrast between conditions in Royal Hungary and the Turkish-occupied area was not confined to the treatment accorded the Jews but affected the entire population in both territories. Contemporary reports paint a dismal picture of the conditions in Royal Hungary: the roads were unsafe; the German imperial soldiers engaged in looting; the free hussars and unsalaried Hungarian soldiers of the borderlands, the free Haiduks, whose numbers had greatly increased, roamed the countryside marauding and falling upon the markets; while the court in Vienna remained totally unaware of the advantages well-ordered commerce could constitute for the royal treasury and the country as a whole. In addition to the uncontrolled rabble, lordly plunderers also made traveling dangerous: they would capture travelers and keep them in detention until ransomed for exorbitant amounts. A few such cases were presented above in chapter 14.

In contrast to these conditions, Turkish Hungary proved attractive to the Jews who had to suffer the restrictions and insecurities of Royal Hungary, and thus a certain Jewish movement took place from the Christian regions into the Muslim parts of the divided country.

16

The Jews in Reunited Hungary (1686-1740)

The reconquest of Buda in September 1686 by the imperial Austrian forces, which opened the door to the reestablishment of Hungarian rule over much of central Hungary, was celebrated as a great victory in Hungary and, in fact, throughout Europe. A year later, the Hungarian magnates at their meeting in Pressburg expressed their gratitude "for His Majesty's successful action against the Turks" by recognizing the House of Habsburg's hereditary right to the Hungarian throne and giving up the right of resistance they had had since the Golden Bull of Endre II in 1222.

For the Jews of Buda, however, the "liberation" of the city was nothing short of a total catastrophe. It meant death and destruction. The Austrian soldiers who forced their way into the city and enjoyed several days of free looting killed many of the Turks and Jews who were still there, and either ransacked or destroyed all property they found. In a great conflagration, which may have broken out spontaneously or possibly was the result of arson, a large part of the city was destroyed, including the synagogue, with all its Torah scrolls and holy books. It has been estimated that of the approximately one thousand Jews who were found in the city on the day it was taken, about half were massacred and the other half were captured and held for ransom. One of the survivors, Isaac Schulhof (d. 1733), son-in-law of the famous R. Ephraim Hakohen of Buda, left behind a description, partly in Hebrew verse, of the horrors of the siege, the destruction after the conquest of the city by the imperial forces, and the sufferings of the Jews captured by them.

The reconquest of Buda meant the end not only of the Jews' presence in that city but also of Jewish life in all of Turkish-dominated Hungary. It took several decades before some Jews again wanted to settle in Buda and actually obtained permission from the central authorities to do so. This was granted them with the explanation that the mercantile activities of the Jews would help to repopulate and develop the city. From the other free royal cities of the liberated area the Jews were kept out by the will of the burghers.

As for the position of the Jews in the Habsburg Empire in general, two opposite tendencies were evident. On the one hand, the Counter-Reformation, which began to make headway in the Habsburg realm in the latter part of the seventeenth century, persecuted not only Protestants but also Jews. Its anti-Jewish stance was exemplifed by the plan Count Leopold Kollonich, bishop of Győr, proposed for the reconstruction of Hungary. He advocated gradually displacing the Jews from the country and preventing their settlement in the newly liberated areas. Nor did the cities, as shown by the examples of Sopron and Pressburg, want to tolerate Jews in their midst.

On the other hand, the financial interests of the Habsburg Empire prompted Vienna to take a more positive stand toward the Jews. The court was in need of money and supplies for its armed struggle against the Turks, and hence it needed Jewish moneylenders and merchants. Among these, Samuel Oppenheimer (1630–1703) stood out as by far the greatest large-scale supplier of the army, providing it with such basic essentials as flour, oats, horses, gunpowder, and ammunitions. In 1695 alone, Oppenheimer supplied 122,146 quintals of flour (1 quintal is 100 kilograms or around 220 pounds) and 155,234 quintals of oats to the army in Hungary, and similar amounts to the German contingents.

Oppenheimer's younger partner, the financier and banker Samson Wertheimer (1658–1724), perhaps played an even more important role in supplying credit to the Viennese court, as well as to Hungarian counties. His lifestyle in Vienna was that of a great lord: his palace was protected by a detachment of ten imperial guards. From 1694 to 1709 he was chief administrator of the financial affairs of emperors Leopold I, Joseph I, and Charles VI. He was a great favorite of Leopold I (r. 1657–1705), who entrusted him with diplomatic missions and, at his request, issued a letter patent for the protection of the Jews of Kismarton (Eisenstadt) and Pressburg. In addition to an outstanding financier and courtier, Wertheimer was a Jewish scholar (in his youth he had studied in the yeshivas of his hometown Worms and of Frankfurt). In his capacity as the head of the Viennese *beth din*, he shared his opinion in halakhic matters with rabbis all over Europe who sought it. In the synagogue he maintained in his palace in Vienna, he would give the *derashot* (sermons), some of which survive in manuscript. He financed and proofread the 1712–22 Frankfurt edition of the Talmud and wrote introductions and approbations to several halakhic works. Wertheimer's financial and political support of the Jews was as generous as it was effective: with his great influence he succeeded in 1700 in having the emperor forbid the circulation of the notorious anti-Semitic book *Ent-decktes Judentum* by Johann Eisenmenger. In Hungary he reestablished and supported forty Jewish communities, founded yeshivas, set up foundations, and built a great synagogue in Kismarton (Eisenstadt). In gratitude, some of the Jewish communities of Hungary awarded him the title *Landesrabbiner* (roughly "national chief rabbi"), and this title was officially confirmed by Emperor Charles VI (r. 1711–40) upon his accession to the Austrian throne.

While Oppenheimer and Wertheimer were *grands seigneurs* whose position was entirely exceptional in the Jewish life of the period, there lived in Hungary itself several smaller Jewish wholesale merchants who supplied arms, ammunitions, cereals, fodder, and other articles to the army and collected metals it needed. Their services were appreciated by the governmental authorities, and they were generally protected and supported by the royal treasury and war council whenever they suffered restrictions or abridgements of their rights by the citites and counties. For the same reason, both the treasury and the owners of the big estates were more inclined to permit Jews to settle in the depopulated or sparsely populated areas of the country than were the cities to allow them to immigrate. Thus, in 1690, the palatine, Prince Paul Eszterházy (1635–1713), settled Jews in the city of Kismarton, which belonged to him. They became his *Schützjuden* (protected Jews) and he granted them freedom to practice their religion and to engage in commerce and crafts. In 1698 Emperor Leopold I tried to introduce a *taxa tolerantialis* (toleration tax) that the Jews were to pay for permission to live in the cities and other localities, but the objection of the Hungarian counties prevented it. The minute book of the *Ḥevra Qadisha* of Nagykálló (County Szabolcs) dates from about 1700 and shows that the Jewish community there was the center of the county's Jews, headed by a county chief rabbi. From the 1710s on, the Count Zichy family permitted Jews to settle in Óbuda (today part of Budapest), where their number increased rapidly, reaching 285 families by 1785. In 1724, Count Sándor Károlyi had a rabbi sent from Pressburg to the Jews of Nagyká-roly; this indicates that by that time a sizable Jewish community must have existed in that city.

In 1725 the Royal Hungarian Lord Lieutenancy (*Consilium Regium Locumtenentiale Hungaricum*), wishing to limit Jewish immigration, ordered as a preliminary step a general census of the Jews in the country. Not all the counties carried out the census, but from the data of those that did it appears that most Jews lived on the estates of the big landlords, primarily in the west Hungarian "Seven Communities" of Boldogasszony (Frauenkirchen), Kabold (Kobnersdorf), Kismarton (Eisenstadt), Köpcsény (Kittsee), Lakompak (Lakenbach), Nagymarton (Mattersdorf), and Németkeresztúr (Deutschkreuz), all of them located in the Moson and Sopron counties, on the estates of the Kanizsai family, and later of the Eszterházys. Already in the sixteenth century each of these Seven Communities had a rabbi of its own, and all of them recognized the rabbi of Kismarton as their chief rabbi. The Jews of that city, as well as those of Nagymarton, enjoyed special privileges. The total number of Jewish heads of households in parts of the country where the census was carried out was over 1,700, and the number of localities with more than ten Jewish families was close to forty. In addition, in many villages and other localities, especially in the northern and northeastern counties, there lived one or two isolated Jewish families, making a living mostly by distilling brandy or renting taverns from the local landlords.

Within the next few years the number of Jews in Hungary increased considerably. Another census, likewise incomplete, was carried out in 1735, this time primarily for purposes of taxation. It showed that in addition to the free royal cities that mostly belonged to the great magnates' estates, Jews lived also in thirty counties (*vármegye*), and they numbered 11,621 souls or 2,531 families. Of the heads of these families, only 885 identified themselves as being of Hungarian origin, which means that the rest, around 65 percent, were newly settled immigrants from other countries. This sizable immigration was at least partly triggered by the 1726 edict of Emperor Charles VI, which aimed at limiting the number of Jews in Austria by permitting only one man in each Jewish family to marry. One of the consequences of this edict was that young Jews, to be able to marry, migrated from the Austrian domains to Hungary. This explains why, in the 1735 census, 961 heads of Jewish families were of Moravian, 77 of Bohemian, and 133 of other Austrian origin.

The above details are but examples of the trials and tribulations the Jews suffered in the early eighteenth century in their attempts to settle in Hungary and, once settled, to make a living despite the limitations imposed on them. Fortunately for them, the country contained several authorities with conflicting interests. The generally anti-Jewish attitude of the cities—with their fanatical clergy, jealous craft guilds, selfish burgher merchants, and power-hungry municipal councils—was counterbalanced by the economic and financial self-interest of the great landlords and the royal treasury, for whom the rents, taxes, and levies paid by the Jews constituted a reliable and expandable source of income. Also, the never-ending power struggle between the imperial court and the great magnates, who in many cases were able to act as independent rulers within their huge estates, redounded to the advantage of the Jews: one of the two sides was usually willing to extend its protection when the other side found that its interest of the moment required the oppression or expulsion of "their" Jews.

As against this, the lack of one single decisive power center—to which the Jews would have been beholden and which would have determined their status, including their duties and rights (or, if you wish, their servitudes and privileges)—made the position of the Jews uncertain, hazardous, and lacking in clear-cut continuity. Having no power of their own, the Jews were exposed to the whims of whoever had power, and all they could do if members of their community were attacked, harmed, robbed, imprisoned, or even tortured and murdered was to request, and pay for, the protection of a stronger power, whose intervention often came slowly or too late.

The Jews thus had to wend their way with utmost caution and circumspection. They had to learn to pacify would-be actual opponents, to bend their necks uncomplainingly under the yoke of multiple taxations, and to do whatever they could to convince powers of various grades and strengths that letting them live and work, and not imposing upon them levies greater than they could bear, was more advantageous than robbing them of everything they had, destroying them, or expelling them. Having said this, we must not lose sight of the significant fact of immigration from neighboring countries, which proves that in many periods the position of the Jews in Hungary was better than that of their coreligionists in adjacent countries, especially in the provinces of the Habsburg Empire.

The attraction Hungary held for Jews in other countries is exemplified by the history of the Eisenstadt community. In 1626 the city came under the rule of the princely Eszterházy family, who accorded their protection to its Jews. In 1670, when Leopold I expelled the Jews from Austria, they also had to leave Eisenstadt, but within four months the prince was able to secure their return, assigning them new quarters next to the palace. In 1675 the Jews who had immigrated from Mikulov (Nikolsburg), Moravia, were granted a letter of protection. In 1690 it was renewed and served as model for all the Seven Communities. In return for annual taxes and lavish gifts on all possible occasions, the Jews enjoyed substantial political autonomy. They had the right to close off their streets with chains on Sabbaths and holidays, and from 1732 a mace was carried before their leader, the *Judenrichter*, as a symbol of his function. In 1704 and 1707 the community was destroyed during the Kurucz revolts and the Jews had to seek refuge in Wiener Neustadt, inside the Austrian borders, but soon thereafter they returned and rebuilt their community with the help of Samson Wertheimer.

The fact that many foreign-born rabbis served in Eisenstadt testifies to the appeal of the community. In 1526 R. Jacob Margaliot became its rabbi; he came from Prague. After him, a series of rabbis from various parts of the Habsburg Empire functioned in Eisenstadt, and at the same time as chief rabbis of the Seven Communities. Of them, two, Mordecai "Mokhiah" and Meir Eisenstadt ("Maharam Esh"), were outstanding and became known all over the Jewish world.

Mordecai "Mokhiah" ben Hayyim of Eisenstadt (1650–1729) was an ascetic preacher (*Mokhiah* means "reprover"), an adherent of the false messiah Shabbatai Zevi (1626–76). After Shabbatai Zevi's conversion to Islam in 1666, to which Mordecai, like Nathan of Gaza before him, attributed a mystical significance, Mordecai wandered all over Poland, Moravia, Hungary, and Italy, preaching, warning, and spreading the faith in Shabbatai Zevi. During his stay in Italy, he claimed that while Shabbatai Zevi was the Messiah Son of Ephraim, he himself was the Messiah Son of David. Mordecai spent long enough in Eisenstadt to have the name of that community permanently associated with his own name, and to be called Mordecai Eisenstadt. His son, Judah Mokhiah (Berliner; d. 1742), was rabbinical judge in Eisenstadt and the author of several halakhic works.

Meir ben Yitzhaq Eisenstadt (1670–1744) was born in Lithuania and became rabbi in Poland and then in Worms, where Samson Wertheimer appointed him head of the yeshiva. In 1701, when the French occupied Worms, he went to Prossnitz, Moravia, where he founded a yeshiva, and had Jonathan Eybeschütz (see chapter 21) among his pupils. In 1714, again with the support of Wertheimer, he was appointed rabbi of Eisenstadt and the Seven Communities, which by that time had recovered from the 1670 expulsion and the havoc wrought by the Kurucz uprising. On that occasion R. Meir assumed the Eisenstadt surname, which was abbreviated "Esh." He established a yeshiva, which soon attracted students from many countries. However, he did not lack opponents, and in 1723 he had to leave the city because of "informers and calumniators." During his absence of three years, his son substituted for him. After his return he remained in Eisenstädt to the end of his life. Under his leadership the community became so famous for its piety that men of wealth and influence in nearby Vienna sought "right of residence" there. Meir Esh authored several halakhic works, among them responsa to questions from such leading rabbinical luminaries of the age as R. Akiba Eger, R. Moses Harif, and others from Italy and Turkey. These questions testify to the great halakhic authority R. Meir wielded in both the Ashkenazi and Sephardi worlds.

It was largely due to the activities of Meir Esh that the community of Eisenstadt became, from the late seventeenth century on, one of the leading centers of Jewish life in Europe. It was referred to as Little Jerusalem, and there were many customs peculiar to it. By 1735 it numbered 113 families, 24 of them living in Vienna.

17

Jewish Women in the Sixteenth to Eighteenth Centuries

The available historical sources contain some information on the role and position of the Jewish women both within the Hungarian Jewish community and in their contact with the Christian environment. The data are haphazard and meager, but still provide us at least with some idea on this important subject.

The most unusual profession a Jewish woman engaged in was that of a physician: we learn of one Jewish woman doctor who, in the middle of the sixteenth century, treated the wives of high Hungarian lords in the towns of Sárvár, Komárom, and Sennye. Her name is not known: she is referred to merely as "doctor woman."

Women, like men, could be bought and sold as slaves: we hear of at least one Jew of Nikolsburg who in 1696 bought a Turkish Jewish woman from a Christian, who, in turn had purchased her in Belgrade. On the other hand, some of the Jewish women were extremely energetic, active, and independent even in Turkish-ruled Hungary. From a brief reference we know that in 1598, while the Austrian imperial army besieged the Turkish-held fort of Buda, a Jewish woman fired a big gun that was located in the Jewish street, thereby forcing the imperial army to retreat. The well-to-do Jewish women of Buda dressed very luxuriously, as mentioned in the diary of a German traveler from the mid-16th century.

We hear of several Jewish women who engaged in money lending, some of them on a large scale. Thus in 1526 a Pressburg Jewish woman by the name of "Manndel judin" (i. e. "the Jewess Manndel") gave sizable loans to Count Farkas of Bazin and Szentgyörgy against pledges consisting of valuable jewelry.

A businesswoman and large-scale moneylender in Pressburg from 1692 to 1709 was "the Jewess Eva Lewin" or "Lovlin," who in connection wih her business dealings was involved in several legal proceedings she instituted against debtors who refused to repay, or were late in repaying, loans she had given them. Some of her loans were quite sizable: thus she gave a loan of 2298 florins to a certain Christian woman, Susanna Dorotha Plankenauer. As part of her business, probably in order to have more money to loan out, Eva Lewin also borrowed money from Christian lenders. It seems that the business acumen ran in the family of Eva Lewin, for her daughter Johanna, wife of Isaac, also engaged in money lending. Another Jewish businesswoman who worked in Pressburg at the same time was Elisabeth, wife of the Jewish doctor Marcus, who also gave loans and had to sue at least one of her debtors. On the other hand, she too took loans, and secured them with depositing valuables as pledges with her creditors.

Other Pressburg Jewesses of the same period who engaged in money lending were Magdalene, wife of Joachim, Eva (or Susanna) Bethlehem, and Anna Goldschmid.

Yet another Pressburg Jewess, Maria, the wife of Moyses, engaged in brandy distilling. We happen to know about it because her distilling kettle was stolen, and she sued the thief, a young coppersmith, who broke the kettle into pieces.

Some of the Jewish women who had direct business contact with gentiles impressed them with their beauty. Thus the wife of the Pressburg Jew Michael Simon, who was engaged in the money lending and borrowing business, was known among the gentiles as "the beautiful Jewess."

According to the testimony of the Jewish traveler Moses Cassuto, who visited Pressburg in 1735, at that time many Jews lived in the city, they were rich, and more women than men were engaged in trading, and worked in stores as salespersons "with a happy mien." Some Jewish women were engaged in the wholesale wine business, others in selling brandy.

One of the ways in which Jewish women could independently support themselves was to own restaurants or to work as cooks. In the early eighteenth century among the Jews of Buda there were several women who made a living by cooking for wedding banquets, making and selling lace, and working as midwife. Occasionally, to enable a poor woman to earn a livelihood, the municipal council of Buda gave such a woman a subsidy, as it did, for example, in 1720, when it allocated a quarterly subsidy of six florins to the converted Jewess Maria Theresia to enable her to learn cooking. In 1769 a Jewish widow by the name of Hirschl was the owner of a restaurant in Sopron.

Some Jewish women even played a role in communal and public affairs, as one can conclude from the fact that one, a certain Hirschlin (that is, Mrs. Hirschl) of Buda intervened in 1718 at the city council in behalf of a poor Jew of Óbuda, and was herself arrested two years later because she undertook a guarantee for a debt contracted by her stepson. Also, among the thirteen Jewish signatories of an agreement concluded in 1731 between Count Sándor Károlyi, lord of the city of Nagykároly, there was one woman. Incidentally, all those signatures are in Hebrew.

Nothing indicates more the ability of women to act independently than legal proceedings they instituted against their own husbands. Such a case took place in Buda in 1725, when the Jewess Mrs. Ofner ("Ofnerin") lodged a complaint (nature unknown) against her husband with the city judge.

Since the sojourn of Jews in Buda was dependent on special permits they had to obtain, widows had to learn how to apply for such permits to the city council. This was done by the Jewish widow Cyboria in 1726, but her application was denied.

In the course of the eighteenth century Jewish women of Buda were quite frequently engaged in litigation over debts and other money matters with Jewish and Christian creditors and lenders, which is an indication of their business activities. In several cases Jewish businesswomen were imprisoned for non-payment of their debts. Some Jewish women were even found guilty of theft, as the one who in 1771 was imprisoned in Sopron for having stolen a few silk handkerchiefs.

Business contact between Jewish women and men inevitably led to occasional extra-marital sexual relations between them. In 1734 the Jewish widow Lea accused the Jew Anschl Gans of Viziváros (part of Buda) of having had sexual relations with her and having impregnated her. Anschl, in his response, demanded that she prove her charge. The city council opined that a rabbi and two other Jews should mediate between the two litigants, and that Anschl should be persuaded to marry Lea.

Since the business dealings of Jewish women brought them in direct contact with gentiles, it happened that they came under the influence of one or the other of them and converted to Christianity. One of such converts was Anna Maria Rachel of Nagyszombat (Tyrnau), in 1720.

The above is but a rapid and cursory survey of the historical documents that testify to the position and activities of Jewish women in Hungary in the sixteenth to eighteenth centuries. A thorough study of this subject is one of the highest desiderata of Hungarian Jewish historiography.

18

Conversions in the Seventeenth and Eighteenth Centuries

Conversion to Christianity was a fringe phenomenon that nibbled at the body of the Hungarian Jewish community throughout its history, and occasionally, especially in times of anti-Semitic excesses, made serious inroads into it. Until the introduction of the German-type racial anti-Semitism into Hungary, and the promulgation of the 1938 and subsequent Jewish laws, the Hungarian Churches openly welcomed Jewish converts, and even made efforts to spread the faith among the Jews. Even though socially Jewish converts were not accepted as full and equal Magyars by the Christian Hungarians, as far as the Catholic and Protestant Churches were concerned, once a Jew converted he became a full member of the Church of his choice. Employment at both religious and secular institutions of higher learning, as well as in state, county, and municipal offices, was closed to Jews until the end of the 19th century, but once a Jew converted there was no longer any obstacle to his penetration into those traditional bastions of Hungarian Christian clergy, nobility, and intelligentsia. In chapter 12 above we heard of Emericus Fortunatus, the earliest famous Jewish convert to make a fabulous career in Hungarian government circles in the fifteenth and sixteenth centuries, and in our chapters dealing with the nineteenth and twentieth centuries we shall learn of many Jewish converts who rose to the top of their profession and became leaders in Hungarian economy, industry, finance, the arts, literature, science, scholarship, politics, the military, etc., were ennobled, and/or intermarried with the old Christian Hungarian nobility. The examples of these men demonstrate that if a talented Jew was willing to jettison his formal adherence to the community of his birth he stood a good chance to rise to the top of Hungarian society. The case of Emericus Fortunatus indicates that this was a possibility long before the emancipation of Hungarian Jews, but developments in the nineteenth and twentieth centuries show that one of the consequences of emancipation, when finally achieved, was to lead many

197

ambitious Jews not only to assimilation, but also to conversion for the sake of career and hoped-for social acceptance.

It so happens that from the seventeenth and eighteenth centuries several dozens of documents survived which allow us to conclude that in that period, too, a number of conversions to Christianity did occur. The documents pertain only to cases in which, for some reason, the authorities became involved. One is therefore justified in concluding that a much larger number of conversions must have taken place without such involvement, and hence without leaving behind documentary evidence.

In several cases, if an individual accused or suspected of criminal activity, was a convert to Christianity from Judaism, this fact was stated in the document pertaining to his case. Some of these cases were mentioned in chapter 11 on Jewish criminals. A few more can be added here. In 1719 a converted Jew in Buda beat a Christian woman in the street, for which crime he was sentenced to two weeks in jail. Another Jew, Aron Hirsch, who converted to Christianity and took the name of Tamás Hieczinger, was imprisoned in 1740 for having defaulted on a debt. In 1763 a converted Jew was expelled from County Sopron. Several more similar cases are known.

In some cases the conversion of Jews was considered a triumph for Christianity and the new Christians were feted in a celebration. This happened in Sopron in 1661, when the city council spent 132 florins on a lavish banquet in honor of three Jews, two from Posen and one from Cracow, who converted to the Evangelical faith.

It also was customary that if a Jew converted the authorities gave him a gift of a few florins. When the Jew Hirschl of Buda converted in 1726, the city council of Buda helped him financially. When the Jesuits coverted a Buda Jew in 1728, the city council gave him a suit of clothes and some money. In 1735 two Jews obtained financial help from the city of Buda, one before and one after the act of conversion. There was even a case in 1733 in which a converted Jew of Buda was supported by the city council so as to enable him to learn the trade of cobbler. More interesting is the case of the Jew Samuel Rátz, who had lost all his property in the last Turkish war, and after having produced authentic attestations that he had converted to Christianity, received in 1745 17 *Groschen* (pennies) alms from the city of Pest so that he should pray for the city.

Some Jews converted in order to facilitate their professional advancement. Thus in the 1630s a Jew of Kolozsvár, David Valerius, converted to the Reformed Church, and became a professor at the Reformed College of Sárospatak.

Occasionally the missionary zeal of Christian clergymen induced them to baptize Jewish children without the consent or knowledge of their parents or guardians. Such cases were frequent enough for the authorities in Pressburg to issue in 1762 a decree to the effect that he who baptizes a Jewish child against the wishes of its parents will be severely punished. Despite this edict, in neighboring Sopron, two Jewish children were baptized in 1698. The problem of the conversion of Jewish minors continued to preoccupy the Hungarian authorities, and in 1782 the Royal Hungarian Council of the Governor-General issued detailed instructions as to how to proceed in connection with the conversion of a Jewish minor or orphan to Catholicism. In 1786 the same council strictly prohibited the conversion of Jewish or other non-Catholic minors without their parents' consent. It emphasized in particular that it was forbidden to try to influence such minors by enticing, threatening or frightening them with punishments. To this was added in 1789 a prohibition that roundly forbade the conversion of any Jewish minor younger than 18, unless he requested it on his deathbed. This prohibition was communicated to the two Catholic priests, the Evangelical minister, and the Greek "pope" of Sopron.

Another impetus to conversion was love. If a Jewish woman became the lover of a Christian man, there was a likelihood that she would convert for his sake. Thus in Buda in 1706, a Jewish woman who had not only become the lover of a Christian man but was also impregnated by him converted. We also know of cases in which a Jewish man converted because he fell in love with a Christian woman: the Jew Moses Abraham of Nemesszalók fell in love with the Christian widow Susanna Sikós, was converted to the Evangelical faith by the minister István Horváth, married his lady-love, and had a child by her.

Let me add here in conclusion that the converse step, that is conversion of Christians to Judaism, was prohibited in the Christian parts of Hungary in the period in question and after it, until the 1895 *recepció* of the Jewish religion (see chapter 32), and as far as we know, did not occur. In Transylvania, as we have seen in chapter 13, members of the Sabbatarian sect, even though they were greatly attracted to Jewish religious observances from the early 17th century on, were given the exceptional permission to convert to Judaism only in 1868. In the Turkish-ruled central part of Hungary the situation was different. There, it was Muslims who could not convert to Judaism; Christians could. In chapter 14 we heard of a Jewish master in Turkish-ruled Buda, who converted his Christian slaves to Judaism. The same was, of course, the situation in Turkey itself, where, as we learned in chapter 13, a Christian Hungarian official of the Transylvanian embassy in Constantinople, who had come under the influence of the Sabbatarians, converted to Judaism in 1637.

Of the epidemic of apostasy that hit Hungarian Jewry in the late nineteenth century and extended into the twentieth we shall hear in chapters 32 and 46.

19

The Jews Under Maria Theresa (1740-80)

The war leading to the expulsion of the Turks, and Ferenc Rákóczy II's long and ultimately unsuccessful war of independence (1703–11) against Habsburg rule, drastically reduced the population in many parts of Hungary. It was estimated that as against a population of about 4 million under King Matthias (in the fifteenth century), in 1720 only 3.5 million lived in the country, while in the same period the total population of Europe increased from 80 to 130 million. Even of this diminished population, more than two-thirds were concentrated in the western and northern counties, which means that other parts of Hungary were seriously underpopulated. In this situation, the prime task facing the landlords and the authorities was to find settlers and workers for the newly reconquered lands. To attract immigrants, the newcomers were promised ample land for cultivation, as well as farm animals, tax concessions, and light corvée obligations. These policies gave rise to increased immigration and settlement, especially in the southern and eastern (Transylvanian) parts of the country, resulting in a rapid increase of the total population to no less than 9 million by 1787.

This is the background against which the immigration of Jews into Hungary from the countries to the west, north, and northeast must be viewed. At first, Jews came mostly from the west and were admitted primarily into the cities and villages of the estates of the great landlords. Also, in this period many Jews moved from west Hungary into the more southern and eastern parts of the country, where the depopulation was especially severe. The increase of the Jewish population in Hungary provided the occasion for the government of Maria Theresa (r. 1740–80), empress of Austria and queen of Hungary, to impose in 1746—the very same year in which she gave her consent to the expulsion of the Jews from Buda—a new kind of tax on the Jews in the form of the so-called toleration tax. This was a head tax of two florins annually, payable to the imperial treasury, for every Jewish man, woman, and child, for permission to reside in the country. Following the example of the old Hungarian kings, the queen-empress imposed her tax, popularly referred to by the Jews as *malke gelt* (queen money), on the Hungarian Jewish community as a whole, and left it to the Jews themselves to apportion the sum among the congregations.

In 1749 the toleration tax was set at 20,000 florins; by 1760 it was raised to 30,000, by 1772 to 50,000, by 1778 to 80,000, and by 1813 to 160,000 florins. These figures show that the Viennese government estimated the number of Hungarian Jews at 10,000 in 1749; 15,000 in 1760; 25,000 in 1772; 40,000 in 1778; and 80,000 in 1813.

However, the imperial government was not satisfied with its own estimates and therefore ordered a census of the Jews of Hungary that was to count not the number of families but the number of Jewish persons in every locality. The counties, controlled by the nobles, resisted both the census and the tax, ostensibly because they considered the imposition of a special head tax on the Jews illegal, but in reality because it was contrary to their interest: they wanted to be the sole beneficiaries of every tax the Jews were able to pay. Consequently, the census was carried out only partially, and its results give no full picture of the number of the Jews in the country. However, what they do show is that in 1746–48, of the 43 Hungarian counties (outside Transylvania and Partium) Jews lived in 36, and of the 37 free royal cities in 9. The total number of the Jews is given by the census as 14,847. It also shows that of this number, 5,787 lived in the westernmost three counties of Nyitra, Sopron, and Pressburg, next to the Austrian border. In the course of the eighteenth century the greatest increase in the Jewish population took place in central Hungary, especially in the city of Óbuda, which belonged to the Zichy domain and which, before the end of the eighteenth century, became the largest Jewish community in the country.

Most of the Jews in Hungary in this period were merchants and traders of the most diverse sorts. The great majority were peddlers who went from village to village on foot, selling small wares to the villagers and buying up what the villages had to offer: rabbit furs, sheepskins, old clothes, scrap iron. Above them ranked the merchants who had their own shops, in which they sold either common or finer merchandise. Many Jews went from market to market, selling local or imported wares. The highest sector consisted of wholesale merchants, who imported merchandise from abroad or worked as military suppliers. Others functioned as "house Jews" for the big landlords, who bought up the produce of the estates, imported textiles from abroad, and in many cases provided loans to the landlords and the counties. A smaller part of the Jewish population made a living of handicraft and artisanship:

among them were tailors, glaziers, gold- and silversmiths, bookbinders, pipe makers (for smoking), seal engravers, and the like. In the eastern and northern Hungarian counties most Jews were renters of the landlords' taverns and distillers of brandy. Some Jews leased the landed properties of magnates (in 1752, for example, the Jew Solomon Jakab leased the entire estate of Count Ignác Forgách); others were owners of vineyards and plow lands (as shown by 1774 data from the counties of Zemplén and Sáros).

We mentioned above the Jewish immigration from Moravia that resulted from the marriage restrictions imposed on them in that country in 1726. From the mid-eighteenth century on there was also an increase in the immigration of Jews from Poland, who settled mostly in northeastern Hungary and the eastern part of the Great Hungarian Plain. It has been estimated that as a result of continued immigration, the number of Jews in Hungary grew no less than eightfold in the course of the eighteenth century.

In view of the general underpopulation of the country, it is understandable that the owners of the great estates, for whom more Jews meant more income in taxes and services, were interested in having Jews settle on their lands. These great estates included not only those of secular magnates but also estates of church lords. The latter also controlled cities, and welcomed Jewish immigrants there as well. On the other hand, those for whom the Jews meant direct competition—the burghers of the free royal cities, and in general the non-Jewish merchants and craftsmen—did everything they could to prevent the settlement of Jews in their midst.

In the third decade of her reign, Maria Theresa issued several edicts that provided a modicum of protection to the Jews. In 1762 she prohibited the forceful conversion of Jewish children to Christianity; in 1763 she called upon the Catholic clergy not to extract the "surplice fee" from the Jews; and in 1764 she ordered the release of those Jews who had been thrown in jail on the basis of a blood libel in the village of Orkuta. The queen-empress's decree in that affair was the result of the intervention of the "court Jew" Abraham Mendel Theben, who was a special favorite of hers (see chapter 21). The story of the Orkuta blood libel throws additional light on the condition of the Hungarian Jews under Maria Theresa and deserve to be told in some detail.

What happened in that village was that on June 3, 1764, a five-year-old Christian boy named István Balla disappeared, and two days later his naked body, with a rope around the neck, was found just outside the village. The Jews were accused of having killed the boy in order to use his blood for ritual purposes. The blood libel of Orkuta was neither the first nor the last of such accusations in Hungary, but it had a special twist: witnesses were produced who testified that they had seen Hebrew letters tattooed on the body of the boy. The authorities sent troops to surround the synagogue of the neighboring village of Szedikert, where the Jews were assembled in celebration of Shavu'ot, the Feast of Weeks. Thirty Jews were arrested. The judge had a life-size painting made of the murdered boy's body, which he sent to Vienna to the Hungarian court chancellery. The empress herself had a look at the painting, which thereafter was deposited in the National Archives.

The Jews of Szedikert sent a delegation to Pressburg to ask for the help of the congregation and its influential president. Abraham Mendel Theben himself proceeded to Vienna and was received in audience by the empress, who, though not a great friend of the Jews, listened with sympathy to the representations of the man whom she liked personally. It is not known precisely what the empress did, but twenty-one of the arrested Jews were released, while nine were detained and the proceedings against them continued. One of the chief "suspects," Samuel Shapse, converted to Christianity, whereupon he was immediately released. Another, Jacob Lefkovitch, together with his twelve sons, sought out Count László Bornemissza in his castle and asked to be accepted into the Christian faith. Their conversion was celebrated in a great fete on June 27. The Pressburg community thereupon lodged a complaint against the count for forcible baptism, and at the insistence of R. Meir Barbi of Pressburg (see below), who was received in audience by the empress, investigations of the count's actions were initiated. However, even this was of no avail, and the proceedings against the Jews still in prison continued. The judge ordered two of them, the lease holders Moses Josefovitch of Gombosfalva and Jacob Joseph Lefkovitch of Ádámföld, to be subjected to harsh questioning. On January 25, 1765, the executioner of Eperjes tortured them for ten consecutive hours. Josefovitch survived without admitting guilt; Lefkovitch died on the rack. A few weeks later the sentence was passed. It stated that the two who were tortured had received the punishment due to them; the rest were found not guilty. (This was the last time torture was used in legal proceedings in Hungary; in 1790 the Diet prohibited it.)

As for the life and work of Abraham Mendel Theben, nothing more is known, although the high title he was given in Jewish sources indicates that his activities must have been of great significance and redounded to the benefit of the Jews of Pressburg, and perhaps of Hungary as a whole. Much more is known about his son, Koppel Mendel Theben, who was highly influential with Maria Theresa's successors on the throne (see next chapter).

That the conditions of the Hungarian Jews improved under Maria Theresa, despite the horrors of the Orkuta blood libel and the imposition of the toleration tax, which the Jews perceived as increasingly intolerable, is indicated by two more phenomena in addition to the rapid growth of their numbers: the awakening Jewish interest in the civic affairs of the country, and the development of Jewish scholarship and literary activity.

As for the former, its inception can be dated from 1703, when Michael Simon, a Jew of Pressburg, requested permission to found a bank to provide capital for opening up the country only recently liberated from Turkish rule for foreign trade, and for increasing the circulation of money among the people in general. This, the first plan for a bank in the country, was rejected.

In 1755 the Jew Jacob Simon and five associates founded a factory near Trencsén for producing oil out of birch bark. Oil was indispensible for the tanning industry and up to that time had been available only as an import from Russia. The factory actually opened, but it encountered such obstacles in shipping the merchandise that before long it had to close down again.

In the course of the eighteenth century, several Jewish entrepreneurs put forward plans for the improvement of the waterways of Hungary. About 1720 a Jew of Vágszered, Solomon Beer by name and salt supplier by profession, together with several other Jews worked out a plan to make the river Vág navigable. In 1774 the Jew Elias Loebl of Dombóvár suggested to the Viennese court that a canal be built to connect Lake Balaton with the Danube. In 1782 Moses Lazar Österreicher of Óbuda requested permission to carry out a plan that would make the Danube between Pest and Vienna navigable even at low water. In that year the Hungarian journal *Magyar Hirmondó* (Hungarian Gazette) recommended the project, but in the event nothing came of it.

As for Hungarian Jewish halakhic, scholarly, and literary activity in this period, it actually began in western Hungary even before the expulsion of the Turks from Buda. The first among the authors of the age was R. Meir Katzenelbogen (Eisenstadt), who studied in Metz and settled in Eisenstadt prior to 1670. In that year, when the Jews were expelled from the city, he moved to Stomfa (today Stupava, Slovak Republic), a part of the Pálffy domain. In Stomfa lived several rich and influential Jews, among them Lazels Hirsch, silver supplier to the Viennese mint, and Moses Stambe (Stampfen), supplier of the Komárom garrison, who wrote glosses to the *Sefer haGilgulim* (Book of Transmigrations, Frankfurt, 1684).

Another rabbi of Eisenstadt was R. Simon ben Ephraim Yehuda Eisenstadt, of Viennese birth, who was also among those expelled from Eisenstadt in 1670. He settled in Poland, and wrote *Hiddushim* (Novellae) to the Talmud (1677), a homiletical work titled *Heleq Shim'on* (The Portion of Simon), and a kabbalistic study titled *Gilgule N'shamot* (Transmigration of Souls, Prague, 1688).

Mordecai Deutsch (d. Galgócz, 1773) became rabbi of Galgócz in 1740, after serving in Bohemia. His talmudic study *Mor D'ror* (Flowing Myrrh) was published in Prague in 1738. Halakhic studies were also published by three rabbis of Pressburg: Joseph ben Samuel (1737), Isaac Schacherles (1777), and Solomon Zalman Joseph (1780). Meir Barbi (1725–89) spent the last twenty-five years of his life as rabbi of Pressburg and head of its yeshiva. His novellae, titled *Hiddushe Maharam Barbi*, were published in two volumes (Dyrhenfurth, 1785, and Prague, 1793). He was exceptional among the talmudists of the age in that he took an active interest in secular sciences, especially medicine, and recommended music, which he loved, to his students. Among the others who produced rabbinical writings were Benjamin Zeev Rapaport, rabbi of Pápa (1971), Barukh Leipniker, rabbi of Zimony (1786), and Jeremiah Auspitz, rabbi of Nagymarton and later of Szántó (1798).

All of these authors were far outshone by R. Akiba Eger the Elder (b. Halberstadt, ca. 1720; d. Pressburg, 1758), rabbi and yeshiva head in Pressburg, author of novellae and responsa, and founder of a rabbinical dynasty of great fame, who despite his short life achieved recognition as one of the foremost rabbinical authorities of the age. Only his grandson, R. Akiba Eger the Younger (b. Eisenstadt, 1761; d. Frankfurt, 1837), and the husband of his great-granddaughter, R. Moses Sofer (Schreiber; b. Frankfurt, 1762; d. Pressburg, 1839), two generations later, did outshine him in authority and renown.

Most interesting are the beginnings of nonhalakhic literary activity among the Hungarian Jews of the eighteenth century, several of whose works antedated the inception of the German-Jewish Haskala (Enlightenment) movement initiated by Moses Mendelssohn. The brother of R. Meir Katzenelbogen, R. Moses Eisenstadt, was among those who had to leave Eisenstadt in 1670; he went to Prague, where he became a teacher and a prolific author. He wrote a humorous commentary on the book of Esther titled *Mishte Yayin* (A Feast of Wine, Fürth, 1695 or 1797) and a book of poems *Zemer* (Song, Prague, 1703), translated medieval Hebrew poets into German (published in 1705), authored a Hebrew mathematics textbook, *Hokhmat haMispar* (The Science of Numbers, Dyrhenfurth, 1712), and commemorated the victims of the 1712–13 Prague pestilence in a poem titled *Ein neu Klaglied* (Amsterdam, 1714).

R. Eliahu Zahlen (or Zalin), rabbi of Nagyvárad and later of Bátorke-szi (where he died in 1786), wrote, in addition to several Hebrew halakhic and related works, a mathematics textbook in Hebrew titled *M'lekhet Maḥshevet* (Artistic Work, Frankfurt, 1766). Judah Loeb Oppenheimer (d. Galgócz 1803), rabbi of Galgócz, left in manuscript several studies dealing with the holidays and one on the talmudic rules touching upon money matters. In 1777 R. Jacob Kunitz, a private scholar of Óbuda, having authored in 1765 a biblical commentary, published an ethical study on calumny and peace. In 1790, Yehuda ben Leib, a teacher in Pressburg, published a Hebrew methodology of teaching.

This is far from a complete list, but it suffices to show that by the eighteenth century some Hungarian Jewish scholars and literati began to strike out beyond the traditional "four cubits of the Halakha."

Here is the place to insert a comment on the use of Hebrew by the Jews of Hungary in the seventeenth and eighteenth centuries. In chapter 14 we saw that Hebrew was used occasionally in documents signed or written by Jews in the early sixteenth century. In the seventeenth and eighteenth centuries the average Hungarian Jewish men seem to have had a working knowledge of Hebrew, or, possibly, Hebrew was often the only language they could write or in the writing of which they were most fluent. This can be concluded from the fact that many commercial, legal, and other documents, written by various secular Hungarian authorities, which required the signature of Jews, were signed by them in Hebrew. Often, prior to appending their signatures they wrote the Hebrew word "*n'um,*" meaning "the word of . . ." Other such documents carry not only Hebrew signatures, but also full sentences in Hebrew, summarizing the contents of the document which itself is written in Hungarian or German. Occasionally, the signature and a brief note accompanying it are in Hebrew characters but in the Yiddish language. Still other documents have notes written in a mixture of Hebrew and Yiddish. More rarely the surviving documents indicate that entire business ledgers were written in Yiddish.

Also in the seventeenth and eighteenth centuries there was some interest in the Hebrew language among the Christian Hungarians as well. Thus in 1633 a Christian printer in the city of Sárospatak had Hebrew type fonts (called in Hungarian "*Sido beuteuk,*" that is, in modern Hungarian, *zsidó betük,* or "Jewish letters"), and in 1723 the city council of Buda voted a subsidy to a man by the name of Neugebohrn, a converted Jew, who is identified as a professor of *linguae sacrae* (the holy language), that is, Hebrew. By the late eighteenth century the Hungarian government permitted Jews to establish presses for the printing and sale of Hebrew books.

One of the most interesting Yiddish documents surviving from the mid-eighteenth century contains the resolutions passed by the Pressburg Jewish community in 1766 concerning itinerant beggars who flooded the city, and the luxurious clothes worn by the women and their immodest behavior in public. As for the beggars, the resolution strictly limits the amounts they could be given in alms and how long they could be allowed to stay in the hospice the community maintained (as a rule from Friday afternoon to Sunday morning, during which time they were to be given meals as well). As for the women, they are reproached for wearing luxurious colored silk and knitted clothes in which "they walk tripping along according to the custom of the pagans, which is most detrimental to the sons of our people." All this must be discontinued forthwith, under severe penalty. A disobedient woman will be publicly named and shamed in the synagogue, and summarily ejected. Moreover, women and girls are forbidden to walk about in groups on the banks of the Danube, and both men and women are strictly forbidden to visit a "*komedi*," that is, a theater. He who transgresses this last prohibition has to pay a fine of six florins to the lord of the city, and six to the community. If the culprit is a member of the community, he loses his election rights for six years. All this is being resolved in order "to serve the welfare of the members of the community, so that they should exhibit no ostentation to the people and the princes. . . ."

As this document shows, the Jews of Pressburg in the eighteenth century were a rich community, and as such attracted itinerant beggars. The clothing worn by the men seems to have been unexceptional, but the women indulged in luxuries and imitated the customs of the Christians. The motivation of the resolution, as stated in the concluding words, indicates that the Pressburg community leaders were concerned lest the luxurious clothing and immodest behavior of the well-to-do Jewish women arouse envy, resentment, and wrath among the Christian citizens and rulers of the city. The Jewish leaders knew only too well that the Jews were seen as a people apart by the Christian majority, and felt that modesty in clothing and comportment was required in order to prevent any unintended provocation. The prohibition of attendance at theatrical performances had, in addition, a second motivation anchored in an old religious-traditional position. In the eyes of the conservative leaders of the community theatrical performances were highly immoral affairs: women appeared on the stage with indecently exposed necks, chests and arms, behaved provocatively, and, to cap it all, raised their voices in song! Since Jewish tradition held that *qol ba'ishah 'ervah* (voice in woman is a shameful nakedness), to watch and listen to such things was definitely a scandal and a sin they felt they had to prevent as best they could, and they tried to do it by depriving the culprits (they evidently had men in mind) of communal election rights and by imposing heavy fines upon them.

As for the performing arts, in which from the nineteenth century on the Jews were to become so prominent, the documented beginnings of active Jewish participation in Hungary go back to the early seventeenth century. In 1619 Jews participated in the performance of a comedy in Italian in the court of Prince Gábor Bethlen of Transylvania. In 1717 a Jewish *histrionus et lusor* (player and comedian) by the name of Jacob Joseph sojourned in the house of the Jewish physician Marcus Mentzer in Pressburg. For some unstated reason this Jacob Joseph was subsequently imprisoned in Buda.

However, it was not the theater but musicianship that, as far as we can judge from the available documentation, exerted the greatest attraction on Jews interested in practicing a performing art. In fact, as early as 1716 there were so many Jewish musicians in the city of Kőszeg that its council found it necessary to prohibit them from playing in hostelries. Some of the Jewish musicians converted to Christianity to be better able to pursue their careers. In 1731 the converted Jewish musician Joseph Jordan of Buda was fined and jailed because he seriously wounded with his sword a journeyman working for the Christian tanner Jacob Matthy. Four months later the tanner himself accused Joseph Jordan of having seduced his wife. Three years later we again hear of Joseph Jordan: this time he petitioned the city council of Buda to enable him to study military music by allocating him the 150 florins required to defray the tuition fee for those studies.

By the late eighteenth century there were so many Jewish musicians in Hungary that a keen competition developed among them. In 1781, at the urgent request of the Jewish musicians of County Somogy, the county authorities issued a decree preventing the Jewish musicians resident in the neighboring County Tolna from playing at weddings in County Somogy. Thereupon the Jewish musicians of County Tolna retaliated by requesting their own county authorities to exclude the Somogy Jewish musicians from playing in Tolna.

As the paucity of the above data shows, the role Jews played in the theatrical and musical life of Hungary prior to the nineteenth century is an as yet entirely unexplored field. It would be highly desirable that researchers should devote attention to it.

In the preceding chapters we repeatedly noted better Jewish conditions in Hungary compared to the other realms of Christendom, or, to express it more circumspectly, the generally less harsh treatment accorded to the Jews in Hungary than in the other European countries.

While one or two cases of the blood libel did occur in Hungary as well, it is a fact that until the Holocaust the Hungarian Jews never experienced massacres like those visited upon the Jews of France and Germany by the Crusades or upon the Jews of the Ukraine by the Chmielnicki's hordes in the seventeenth century and the Haidamaks in the eighteenth. We also recall the remarkable phenomenon of several Hungarian kings who treated the Hungarian Jews much better than the Jews who lived in other provinces of their domains. Also, the periodic migrations of Jews from other countries into Hungary testify to the attraction Hungary exerted on Jews whose position elsewhere was more difficult. A case in point is the semi-internal migration that went on for centuries during the Habsburg era and brought large numbers of Jews from other parts of the monarchy (Galicia, Moravia, etc.) into Hungary. We shall do well to keep in mind this differential when we come to try to understand both the fervent patriotism that characterized the official Hungarian Jewish position and the total identification with Magyardom embraced by the Hungarian Jewish establishment from the nineteenth century on. First, however, we continue our survey of the late eighteenth century.

20

The Jews Under Joseph II (1780-90)

When Maria Theresa's son, Joseph II (r. 1780–90), succeeded his mother as emperor, he was a mature man (thirty-nine years of age) with a complex program of political, economic, social, and cultural reforms that he had formulated under the influence of theorists whose works were published in France, Great Britain, and the German lands, which he was impatient to initiate. He was a levelheaded, pragmatic ruler who believed in the absolute power of monarchs and was opposed to the nobility's privileges and all regional rights and institutions. He wanted to carry out his program by means of a centralized administrative organization that ideally, was to serve the good of all the inhabitants of his domains. To realize his plans he issued, as one of his earliest and best-known edicts, the so-called Toleration Patent (1781). This edict extended the "free practice" of religion to all confessions—except the Jews—and though it left in place some restrictions on non-Catholic practices, it in effect granted full rights as citizens to all non-Catholics. In the crafts, they could become guild masters, in the professions they could earn university diplomas (formerly they had to go abroad to study), and they could enter service in state offices.

This is not the place to discuss the wide-ranging reforms Joseph II introduced into the civic and religious life of Hungary, nor the opposition that greeted them and forced him to retract practically all his rescripts and enactments shortly before his death. But it should be noted that his dispositions also granting the Jews the right to practice their religion freely were part and parcel of his overall reform plans, which restricted the rights of the Catholic Church, on the one hand, and, on the other, increased the central government's control over all aspects of civic and religious life in the country.

Joseph II began issuing special edicts dealing with the Jews soon after his accession to the throne. On May 13, 1781, he sent a rescript to the Hungarian Royal Chancellery stating that it was his intention that "the

211

numerous Jewish nation should become of greater advantage to the country than it has been heretofore, owing to its limited commerce and enlightenment." For this purpose he urged lifting the prohibitions limiting Jews' economic activities "so that, at long last, by increased and broadened sources of income, they should be diverted from the usury and cheating commerce characteristic of them." Jews should be permitted to engage in agriculture as tenants for twenty years, if they employ only Jews to cultivate the land. If they converted to Christianity, they should be allowed to acquire landed property. Jews should be permitted to engage in transportation, tailoring, shoemaking, stonemasonry, and carpentry. If they studied mathematics, they should be allowed to work as architects. They should be able to become cabinetmakers, painters, sculptors. They should be permitted to establish factory industries, "since they are very inventive," to become weavers, and to engage in other similar crafts. All humiliating garb and marks should cease.

In order to obtain up-to-date information on the Jews in Hungary, Joseph II ordered the Hungarian chancellery and lieutenancy, and through them the individual counties, to furnish the court with details on the actual condition of "the Jewish nation" in the country. The responses stated that the Jews wore no distinguishing marks and were not prohibited from being tenants of landed property. The first to respond was the chancellery of Transylvania. It supplied the information that the Jews were permitted to engage in commerce everywhere but were allowed to settle only in Gyulafehérvár; on the estates of some magnates they had been regalia renters, but since they thereby deprived Christians of that income and paid only 1,119 florins in taxes, the Transylvanian chancellery had ordered the expulsion of the foreign Jews in 1780 and confined the indigenous Jews to Gyulafehérvár, where they could practice their religion freely, become craftsmen, and even attend public schools.

The chancellery of Hungary proper responded to the royal order with considerable delay. It stated that the Jews were free to rent real estate and to engage in crafts outside the royal cities, and that many of them were innkeepers. The reports of the counties paint a dismal picture of the Jewish condition in several of them. In County Ung their income was so poor that they paid no taxes at all, and their synagogue and school were located in a rented building. In County Máramaros, they had no synagogue or school at all. In general, the counties did not object to the improvement of the Jews' condition, even though County Somogy requested that a separate guild be established for the Jewish artisans.

A favorable development of those years took place in the city of Nagyszombat, which, on the occasion of the 1539 blood libel, had expelled the Jews: about 1780 they were permitted to return. The emperor himself subsequently refused to reconfirm the privilege of several free royal cities to exclude Jews.

Finally, on March 13, 1783, one year after the issuance of the toleration decree for the Austrian Jews, Joseph II issued a new patent titled *Systematica Gentis Judaicae Regulatio* (Systematic Regulation of the Jewish Nation). While this new patent did not grant the Jews full citizenship rights, as the other non-Catholics had received two years earlier, it granted them several extremely important new rights they had not enjoyed before. It ended the special regulations dealing with them, and they became subject to the general laws of the country. Specifically, the *Regulatio* opened up the royal free cities to the Jews and enabled them to rent lands and to engage in crafts and commerce. It put an end to the distinguishing marks the Jews had been forced to wear and permitted them to carry swords. It abolished the prohibition that up to that time barred the Jews from working as seal engravers, gunpowder manufacturers, and saltpeter producers. It gave them the right to become members of the guilds, and to apprentice their children to Christian guild masters, at the same time warning the latter not to treat the Jewish children more roughly than the Christian apprentices, and to permit them to observe their dietary laws.

On the other hand, the *Regulatio* contained a number of prohibitions, several of which interfered deeply and disturbingly with old customs and religious-cultural values dear to most of the Jews in Hungary. The Jews were ordered to write all contracts, undertakings, testaments, account books, certificates, and all other documents in the languages of the area, meaning German or Hungarian, or in Latin; documents written in other languages, i.e., Hebrew or Yiddish, were declared null and void. Moreover, Jews were forbidden to use Hebrew and Yiddish except for prayers. The imperial argument for prohibiting the printing of books "in their languages" and importing them from abroad illuminates the religious and cultural condition of the Jews in late-eighteenth-century Hungary. It states:

> Since it is generally known that especially the more lettered Jews acquire proficiency in the use of their language by reading such books, therefore, in the interest of expediting the extirpation of the Jewish languages, and at the same time expediting the spread of the languages used in the dominions, it is graciously ordered that, with the exception of books written in the pure Hebrew language, which belong among the Jews in the strict sense to the group of the holy and ritual books and are needed for the performance of the divine services, ceremonies, and prayers of this people,

the printing in and import into our countries of all other books classifiable to any group—whether written in pure Hebrew, or in the corrupt Jewish language [Yiddish], or merely written in Jewish letters—will be totally and most strictly forbidden.

In the economic area, the Jews were not allowed to engage in a craft if by doing so they infringed on the interests of a noble or the privileges of the guilds. They were allowed to rent village lands only if they employed Jewish hands to work them. The exclusion of Jews from the mining towns and their vicinity remained in effect. They were ordered "to divest themselves of wearing beards and all external signs of their religion," that is, their traditional specific Jewish attire.

The major part of the *Regulatio*—some 90 percent of its roughly 3,500 words—is devoted to the education of the Jews. It decrees that wherever Jews live in sufficient numbers, they should establish schools, including high schools, and should cover their own expenses. In these Jewish schools the pupils should be instructed in "the languages living in these countries, as well as in German, Hungarian, and Slavic, and also in mathematics and other subjects that are of general use to people whatever their religion, and which are taught in the Christian national schools." It provides that during the periods when the catechism is being taught in the Christian schools, all the Jewish children should assemble in the Jewish schools to be instructed there in the Jewish religion. To gather the Jewish children outside these periods is strictly forbidden. The Jewish pupils are given the right to study in Christian schools. Christian teachers should gain employment in the Jewish schools only if the Jews do not produce Jewish teachers within two months after the issuance of the patent. In order to force the Jews, even against their will, to send their children to the newly established Jewish schools, they are forbidden to employ private tutors; should the Jews transgress this prohibition, the local authorities can punish them in whatever manner they see fit. After a certain time,

> for instance after ten years, . . . no Jew under the age of twenty-five will be allowed to engage in any craft, to keep a tavern, to acquire a leasehold, or to engage in any commerce yielding significant profit, for example, of wool, leather, tobacco, cereals, etc. (that is, those which constitute the significant sources of income of this people), unless he can produce authenticated testimony from the leadership of a Christian or Jewish national school that he had attended a Jewish or Christian national school and received the requisite training in it.

Most interesting from the point of view of the impression the mentality of the Hungarian Jews made on the authorities who formulated the *Regulatio* is this paragraph:

The widespread demand that in the more significant cities, where there
are universities, the better-to-do people should not be excluded either
from the schools of higher grade or from any branch of science (with the
exception of theology) constitutes no difficulty, all the less since the Jewish
people are forbidden neither by their paternal laws nor by the benevolent
royal regulations to attend schools of higher degree and, furthermore,
since it can be hoped that their graciously influenced education of a better
direction and the moral cultivation of their character will make them duly
suitable for the acquisition of higher sciences.

As against the seemingly inadvertent compliment paid in this paragraph to the mental abilities of the Jews, who are said to need only
proper direction to "make them suitable for the acquisition of the higher
sciences," the framers of the *Regulatio* found repeated opportunities to
express forcefully their low opinion of the Jews' character, inclinations,
and morals. They warn the circuit supervisors of education that the
establishment of the new schools, "because of the well-known obstinacy
and inborn prejudice of the Jews, will not lack difficulties," and that
they should see to it that "this people, owing to its innate shrewdness
and deceitful conduct, should not be diverted from the target graciously
set by His Holy Majesty." The Jews are a people "inclined to distrust
and suspicions," and characterized by "habitual subterfuges." Hence,
everything must be done so that the Jews, "with their usual reluctance,
should not elude and delay" the execution of these laws. It is necessary
to prevent all "fear and suspicion originating from their innate
prejudices" concerning the establishment of the new schools. The Jews
are thus represented as having inborn and innate prejudices, and being
shrewd, stubborn, treacherous, distrustful, and suspicious, and this only
serves to throw into bolder relief the graciousness of "His Holy
Majesty" in wanting to lift up and improve this people of low morality
and deficient character.

In unabating determination to improve the condition of the Jews, in
1787 Joseph II decreed that, as of January 1788, all Jews must select for
themselves a German family name, which from then on will remain
their names all their life. Even though some Hungarian Jews did have
family names earlier as well, most did not, and now this decree imposed
on the local officials the task, by no means easy, of providing names to
tens of thousands of Jews within a few short weeks. The result was that
most Hungarian Jews were assigned simple names referring to their stature, such as Klein and Gross, or to colors, such as Weiss, Gelb, Braun,
Roth, Blau, Schwarz, and the like. These remained the characteristic
Hungarian Jewish names until the late nineteenth and early twentieth
century, when many of them officially "Magyarized" their names, selecting in most cases Hungarian names that began with the same letter of

the alphabet. Thus Klein became Kelen; Gross, Garai; Weisz, Vészi; Gelb, Gerö; Braun, Barna; Roth, Radó; Blau, Balog; Schwarz, Sajó. On more than one occasion the officials bore ill-will toward Jews and assigned them names with unpleasant connotations, which the Jews tried to change by offering them bribes. The great Hungarian novelist Mór Jókai (1825–1904, not a Jew) describes such a case in one of his novels: a Jew is given the name Rothesel, meaning "red donkey," and makes efforts to have it changed instead to Rotheisel.

The Jewish reaction to the Josephine reforms was mixed. The broadening of the Jews' rights in the economic area was, predictably, greeted with general satisfaction. On the other hand, the decrees touching upon education were welcomed only by the relatively few modern-minded Jews in the country, while the orthodox, still the majority at the time, saw in them a danger to traditional Jewish life. Nor did the abolition of the traditional Jewish apparel sit well with most Hungarian Jews. However, the single decree that created the greatest Jewish opposition and, in fact, for the first time united all Hungarian Jews to undertake common action, was the prohibition of wearing a beard. They submitted an application to the king-emperor in the name of "the totality of the Jewry of the Kingdom of Hungary," pointing out that the outlawing of beards was injurious to their religious customs, and as such contradicted the spirit of the toleration decree. Joseph II graciously retracted this decree.

The traditional Jewish educational system in Hungary was already sizable in the early eighteenth century. According to the 1735–38 conscription there lived at that time 2,498 Jewish families in Hungary, and they employed 203 teachers, that is, one teacher per every twelve families. Most of those teachers whose birthplaces are known had come to Hungary from abroad: from Moravia, Poland, Bohemia, Silesia, the German lands, and even France and Russia. In view of this preexisting situation, in which most Jewish boys received a traditional Jewish education, many of them from private tutors, it is understandable that the more conservative Jews in the country considered the Josephine educational reform a danger to the continued Jewishness of their community. Nevertheless, most of the Jews complied with the new law, and within the seven years that still remained of Joseph's reign after the issuance of the *Regulatio* more than twenty Jewish schools were opened, and about 2,000 Jewish children attended them.

Joseph II persevered in pressuring the Hungarian Jews to conform to his education law. In 1786 he extended to Hungary the law already introduced in Austria in 1783 that provided that only those Jewish youths would obtain permission to marry who could prove that they had completed their primary ("normal") school studies, which were thereby made obligatory for all boys and girls aged six to twelve. He promised teachers exemption from paying the toleration tax (which amounted to between four and forteen florins per person). He also issued regulations to ensure that the Jewish children attending public schools were treated properly, were not seated in separate benches, and were free not to attend school on Saturdays and Jewish holidays, and that everything that could be offensive to Jews would be deleted from the textbooks. More than that: in schools where the school day started with prayers, the Jewish children should be required to arrive only after the prayers were finished and were allowed to leave school before the noonday prayers.

The school issue aside, Joseph II's decrees resulted in several significant changes in the life of the Hungarian Jews. First of all, the relatively favorable conditions they created induced many Jews from abroad, in addition to teachers, to immigrate to Hungary. The Jews had to pay a toll of one florin when crossing a border, and the revenues produced by these tolls amounted to 14,000 florins annually. Since there is reason to assume that most of these border crossings were those of Jews coming *into* Hungary from countries lying to its northeast, north, and northwest, this figure in itself points to a considerable Jewish immigration. In fact, this movement had started in the latter years of the reign of Maria Theresa, as shown by the increase of imperial revenues from the toleration tax, which amounted to two florins per person and whose total rose from 50,000 florins in 1771 to 80,000 in 1778: this corresponds to a rise in the Jewish population from 25,000 to 40,000 in those seven years. In 1780, when Joseph ascended the throne, there were 46,166 Jews in Hungary, and under him Jewish immigration into Hungary accelerated. This trend continued for several decades after his death, so that in 1813 the number of Jews in Hungary reached 80,000.

Within the borders of Hungary, the decrees of Joseph II opened up the possibility of settlement in several cities that up to that time had insisted on excluding Jews. Thus, royal permission enabled the Jews to return to Buda in 1783; in the same year they obtained permission to settle in Pest, the rapidly developing city on the left bank of the Danube opposite Buda; and in 1784 they were admitted into the southern Hungarian city of Szeged. The development of the city of Pest attracted many Jewish merchants, who came to spend a shorter or longer time in the city. At first they were unable to obtain kosher food, but in 1783 a kosher restaurant was opened in Pest, followed by a similar restaurant in Buda in 1787, despite the objection of that city.

The most important internal Jewish development during this period, which was to have a long-range effect on the history of the Jews in Hungary, was the emerging sense among them that their position in the country was unjust, demeaning, and intolerable, and that it was up to them to do something about it. We have no historical data about how they felt, but there are records of what they did, and what they did indubitably flowed from such feelings of dissatisfaction and indignation. To be sure, individual efforts by Jewish leaders who had the ear of the rulers and great lords of the country did take place in earlier times as well, but organized communal action started only in this period. We heard above of the common effort to have the beard prohibition retracted, which was successful. Now the Jews of Hungary requested the abolition of the one-florin toll they had to pay when crossing a border, which they felt was worse than an economic hardship—it was a humiliation. This request was opposed by the royal chancellery, apprehensive lest it result in the increase of the immigration of poor Jews. Nevertheless, in 1785 the emperor ordered the abolition of the Jewish toll at borders between the various provinces of the empire, so that from then on Jews could come from Bohemia and Galicia into Hungary without paying the toll. The toll remained in effect on the borders between Austria-Hungary and other countries. In the same year, out of consideration for the sensitivities of the Jews, Joseph II changed the name of the hated toleration tax to "chamber tax."

These were relatively minor matters, small victories and small defeats, for the Hungarian Jews, but they contained an important lesson for them: that communal action had a chance of succeeding. In June 1790, a few months after the death of Joseph II, the Hungarian Diet was scheduled to meet in Pest, and its agenda included the further regulation of the position of the Jews in the country. The Jewish communities prepared a detailed application, in the name of "the community of the Jews living in Hungary," and sent their representatives from fifty-four counties to Pest to submit it to the Diet. The application, written in Latin, is a remarkable document, not so much for the reform requests it contains as for its description of the conditions of Jewish life in Hungary in the latter part of the eighteenth century and, even more, for the feelings of the Jewish community it reveals. Those feelings, the document shows, included embitterment and resentment over the treatment accorded the Jews up to that point by the Hungarian people and government, and at the same time manifested a deep sense of Hungarian patriotism, expressed, for the first time in Hungarian Jewish history, with the same emphasis and enthusiasm that were to remain characteristic from then until the catastrophic years of World War II. In fact, the rare psychological insight this document affords into the Hungarian Jewish mentality in the formative period of the late eighteenth century makes it so valuable that we present it here in considerable detail. It addresses the diet with a unique combination of humility and self-assurance:

> Now that the Estates of the Realm, with the mutual will of the Emperor and King Leopold II, after a cessation of twenty-five years, again hold a national assembly, and the desire, endeavor, and activity of all of them is directed to making the much troubled Hungary strong, based on a safe system, happy, and fortunate, and to let all inhabitants equally, without distinction of station and class, have a share in the public welfare, let it be permitted also to us, the seed of Abraham, who because of the various misfortunes of adversity have been suffering for many years, to come before you and to hope for a minute share in the happiness that the whole fatherland now expects from you and from our new king. To our greatest pain, we have been despised until now, but not because of our own fault; here and there they treated us not as is customary to treat humans and the inhabitants of the same country but like slaves, not to say draft oxen. We have been driven from city to city, from village to village, often exposed to the ridicule, derision, insult of the mob; even on the highways and the crossroads, though it is necessary that every traveler should have secure and safe journey on them, the mischievous youths not infrequently threw stones at us, unpunished.

It goes on to refer to the changes that had recently occurred in Europe under the influence of the Enlightenment:

> But now, the happy sun of all Europe has arisen, so to speak, so that there is no longer anyone so savage and uneducated as not to know those duties that man naturally owes to man. Now already, everywhere the more sober philosophy has raised its head, so to speak, that philosophy which, with clear and understandable words, teaches everybody that no single inhabitant of the state, whatever his religion, status, and manner, can be insulted unpunished, and that among all the inhabitants of any state there is not a single one who should not be able to obtain the proper right of sustaining life and body, of acquiring fame and fortune. Christian faith itself, whose followers in former centuries had not shrunk from persecuting with fire and iron those who did not belong to the Roman Church, now lets the mild spirit of Christian charity trickle into everybody, and either privately or openly proclaims that all men are brothers, and that therefore it is forbidden to leave unpunished lawlessness, the persecution of anybody, the deprivation of anybody of his fortune, and, what is more valuable than anything else, of his faith. In this enlightened century, should we not be allowed to give room to the certain and undoubted hope that, through the generosity of our most excellent King and the noble Hungarian Estates of the Realm, we should gain that for which in those dark centuries we barely dared to hope?

The application then mentions the important role the Jews played in the history of Hungary:

The Jews of Hungary

Ever since the beginning, the Jewish people have lived in the Hungarian kingdom. This is amply attested by the old annals of events, as well as by the Hungarian laws, whether they were enacted in favor of the Jews or for their restriction, according to the views of the people in a certain century. And if at times it did happen, as old memories tell us that it did under Lajos I, that religious hatred forced our people to emigrate from the country, shortly thereafter, with a change of circumstances, they not only obtained the freedom to return but were showered with greater favors than previously. And truly, if the Jew does differ in custom and religion from the multitude of the people, it is certain, experience confirms it, that throughout those many centuries he did not fall behind the citizens in faithfulness and reliability toward the kings and the fatherland. Moreover, if one examines the Hungarian annals, the undoubted documents of past events, there is scarcely an age in which our ancestors had not courteously helped the Hungarian state, which suffered the greatest need, with great amounts of cereals, often purchased with money, or had not straightened out and restored, with tremendous effort, advice, and useful collaboration, the royal treasury itself, which in various cases was completely exhausted by cruel fate. Who does not know what a sorry state the treasury was in under Endre II, Béla IV, Sigismund, Ulászló II, Lajos II? In the extreme peril of the shaky state, what else did those kings of superior wisdom consider the best remedy but to vest in the Jews various positions of the chamber, and to entrust the treasury of the king and the country to their fidelity and fervor. We do not deny that our ancestors often suffered persecution, visited upon their heads by envy or by the fanaticism of the defense of religion, and at times—we are convinced of this—also by too intense greed, of which many of our ancestors were not free. But meanwhile most Hungarian kings who saw at close quarters the outstanding services the Jews rendered to the state, which often struggled against the greatest disturbances—and how, indeed, could they have observed with an indifferent soul how great a profit was derived from their intelligence, fervor, astonishing adroitness, for the entire country and the royal house? —not infrequently adorned the Jews with grace, favor, and privileges and accorded them permanent protection. The memory still exists of those privileges, which Béla IV and Sigismund, those two fervent champions of the Christian faith, granted to the Jews, and which Albert, László V, and Matthias Corvinus did not hesitate to reconfirm with solemn documents. Well known to us also are the various decrees of the later kings, and mainly those who descended from the Austrian house, which were given at various times, repeated, and more than once broadened by various additions.

But our endeavor on this occasion is not to demand the resuscitation of the old privileges of our people, which are buried in our archives and are no longer suited to the changed conditions of today. We request of the King and the estates only that which one is entitled by holy nature and the law of the nations to demand. Since the grace of the King and the favor of the Estates of the Realm have permitted us to live in Hungary, as a result of which we can count on being considered, and must be considered, the oldest inhabitants of Hungary and, in addition, an incorporated nation; since the experience of years, even centuries, teaches that we do not take provinces but consume it in the country or keep it in constant circulation; since we and our families belong in the ranks of the taxpayers and, beyond that, must pay, in addition to the public burdens, also a royal census, that is, a toleration tax; since we are obliged to carry a *subsidum* of all the needs of the kingdom, the supply of food, and all kinds of burdens; since we comport ourselves always and everywhere with due obedience to the authorities and superiors, and pay promptly and without complaints or resistance the taxes to the landlords, which often are heavy and exceed our ability; since we live peacefully and quietly in the midst of the Hungarian nation, offend nobody, tolerate everything peacefully, do not decline any burden—therefore, why should we not be able to demand of the most gracious King and the Estates of the Realm at least the right to live in the confidence that we, too, should be given the same kinds of subsistence as the other inhabitants of Hungary, and that every obstacle that either restricts our livelihood or impedes the customary practice of our faith according to the Laws of Moses should cease? Animated by this hope, we present a few of our requests to the King and the Estates, with proper humility, begging that they should graciously include our just requests with approval among the provisions of the country in legal form.

Before listing the nine requests that follow, we should point out that the foregoing section is truly remarkable for the historical information it contains. When the application was written, there existed no study on the history of Hungarian Jewry, and nevertheless the authors of the application were able to give a brief but adequate overview of the relationship between the Jews in the country and its kings and treasury. This indicates that there were among the Jews of Hungary scholars who, though they did not leave written works, had a thorough knowledge of the history of the Jews in Hungary and were able to supply the data for this part of the application.

The nine points themselves are as follows:

1. The Jews should be allowed to practice their religion freely, and nobody should be forced to convert to Christianity.
2. They should be allowed to settle everywhere and purchase or rent houses and lots.
3. They should be allowed to transact business undisturbed at the national and weekly markets.
4. They should be free to practice handicrafts and to purchase or rent lands.
5. The source of income of the free royal cities, the renting of Jewish restaurants, should cease.
6. They should be able to attend lower and higher educational insitutions without being hindered in the practice of their religion.
7. In lawsuits between Jews and Christians, not the city or the village judge should be competent to pass judgment but only the manorial court or the county court.
8. In lawsuits among Jews, the rabbis, the experts in Jewish law, should decide.

9. The rabbis should be given the power to prevent acts contrary to Jewish religion.

Having thus enumerated the reforms they wished to see, the authors of the application appeal to the humanity of the Estates. They write:

These are our humble desires, these are the questions which we have the temerity to bring before the Diet. We do not belong among those who request exception from the law, privileges, extraordinary favors. We only wish that those rights that are the dues of every man in general, that can in no cultured state be denied to any citizen, should be given to us as well, wholly, soundly. In conclusion we also request that we should be treated humanely, that we should be considered brothers, the descendants of Adam, of one and the same tribe, believers in the same Supreme Being who is adored by the Christians as well; at long last let it be permitted to us, too, to be citizens, useful citizens of the fatherland. In the whole world we have outside Hungary no fatherland, no other father than the King, to whose rule the Lord of the Universe entrusted Hungary and its peoples; we have no other protectors than the public authorities and our landowners, no other brothers than those with whom we live and die in one society; we have no other protection than the laws of the fatherland, no other refuge than the duties of humanity that man owes to man without exception.

After all, we are but those kinds of vine tendrils which, because of their very nature, creep along the ground, and cannot rise up unless a neighboring tree gives them support, or the beneficent hand of man places a stick next to them on which they can raise themselves. To whom should we appeal in our need if not to the common father of all of us, the King, and to those who are entrusted with the governing of the state? From where should we expect peace, tranquility, courage, if not from the state, which has long since received us like a mother, which nourishes, clothes us, and which yet rightly demands of us to fulfill the duties of good citizens? Where should we find support if not in you, to whom the will of the ruler and the mindful disposition of your ancestors have entrusted the power of legislation and of making the peoples happy? Do strive, therefore, Your Majesty the King, you illustrious magnates and emissaries of the provinces, to clear away the fog of prejudices with which many of the people do not shrink to persecute the Jews, so that the obstacles suppressing the efforts of the Jews should disappear, so that security be given to our persons, freedom to commerce, and the ability of decently earning a living to everybody. Do strive that we should not be treated worse than the other inhabitants of the country, that people should not be able to insult, beat, oppress us unpunished, that access to the free royal cities, the country towns, the villages not be restricted for us, that we should not be exposed to derision on the highways and public places. Do strive to place us in a position where we do not have to neglect ourselves, our wives, our children, that we should not collapse under the weight of public and private burdens, or that the state should not be able to say with justification that we are not as useful for it as we should be and as we ourselves desire to be.

And as for us, we shall always consider it our task to direct our endeavors, our strength and our work to making everybody recognize that we are worthy of the grace that we expect today from you, and the hope of attaining it that fills us. Our task will be to request in our unceasing prayers of the Supreme Judge of all beings, Jehova, who unites peoples and disperses them, and whose will makes all kingdoms of the world stand and fall, that he keep our most gracious King to the longest age, in health, glory, and good fortune, together with his imperial house, and grant the Hungarian kingdom peace, tranquility, concord, splendor, and all happiness. Our task will be finally everywhere and always to prove with deeds that we have no other desire than to live and die in eternal devotion.

The Latin text of this remarkable document was, in all probability, prepared by a non-Jewish expert. It is unlikely that any Jew at that time had such a command of Latin, nor would a Jew have used the divine name Jehova. The reaction of the Estates, and the subsequent development in the history of the Jews in Hungary, will be dealt with in the next chapter.

However, first a few words need to be said about the internal situation in the Jewish communities of Hungary in the times of Maria Theresa and Joseph II, or roughly the second half of the eighteenth century. It is noteworthy that despite the restrictions under which the Jews labored in those decades, they nevertheless were capable of important achievements in their inner life.

For one thing, the 1780s were the decade when the first Jewish printing press was established in Hungary: it was set up in Pressburg. Although this item in itself does not seem crucial, it testifies to the burgeoning of interest among the Jews of Hungary in Jewish-Hebrew culture, and therefore it deserves notice.

In the same period the internal organization of the Jewish community of Óbuda occurred, at the time one of the largest Jewish communities in the country. The Jews of that city constituted themselves formally as a congregation, headed by a council that was elected annually, consisted of twenty-four members, and met as frequently as twice a week. It had detailed statutes that specified, for example, that delegations to the royal court in the name of the community could be sent only when the council unanimously decided to do so. The statutes also called for decorum at its meetings: no smoking was allowed, and noisy behavior was prohibited.

On June 2, 1783, the Óbuda congregation together with the Jews of County Pest, solemnly undertook to comply with the decree of Joseph II by establishing a Jewish school in the city and covering its expenses. At the same time, they requested that the language of tuition in the new school be German, but that the teachers to be employed should also be able to teach Hungarian, Slavic, and Latin. If no Hebrew is mentioned, the reason is that the congregation by that time had a functioning Talmud Torah (school for teaching the Hebrew prayers and the Bible in Hebrew). They also carried out a census of children of school age, and actually opened their school on June 22, 1784. The dedication address was delivered by Dr. Joseph Manes Österreicher, whom we met above (in chapter 10).

The Óbuda congregation could boast of other communal institutions as well: it maintained a private commercial school, a kindergarten, an educational society, a society for the distribution of bread and for the support of widows and children, and a *Hevra Kadisha* (traditional society whose main task was to oversee burials). In 1794 they were to organize a *Biqqur Holim* (Visiting the Sick) society to take care of the medical treatment and support of indigent, sick young men and to perpetuate the memory of the deceased.

At this time the Óbuda congregation was well enough off to be able to invite the greatest rabbinical authorities of the age and offer them high salaries. In 1743 they elected R. Matityahu Günsburg (or Günsburger) of Belgrade to be their rabbi. He accepted and served until 1783. Following his death, they asked (in 1786) Wolf Mendel Theben of the famous and influential Pressburg *shtadlan* (interceder) family to persuade R. Wolf Eger, son of the great R. Akiba Eger (see above, chapter 19), to accept their invitation to be their rabbi, offering him a salary, lavish at the time, of ten florins per week or some 500 florins annually. When Wolf Eger nevertheless refused, they invited (in 1789) R. Moses ben Isaac Halevi Muenz (ca. 1750–1831), rabbi of Brody. R. Muenz accepted and served the community to the end of his life. In 1793 the government appointed him chief rabbi of the entire Pest region and Jewish judge in all the affairs of the Jewish communities of the area. He was greatly respected, had considerable influence, and it was upon his initiative that a beautiful synagogue was built in Óbuda in 1822. (After World War II this synagogue was proclaimed a historic building by the Hungarian government, and as of 1995 it was still standing.)

The Pest congregation was founded in 1787. It began modestly, with a rented building as its synagogue and a Torah scroll lent it by the Óbuda congregation. A year later it received a plot of land from the city to serve as its cemetery. Having no school, for several years the Jews of the city had their children taught by private tutors. They recognized R. Muenz of Óbuda as their rabbi, but the relationship between them and Muenz soured after 1793, when the house of R. Wolf Boskowitz (1740–1818), who had lived in Buda since 1769, burned down, and he settled in Pest. In that year Boskowitz was elected rabbi of Pest, subject to the

superior authority of Muenz. Both Muenz and Boskowitz were important Jewish scholars, but their personalities clashed, and a bitter opposition developed between them. In consequence of the disagreements, R.
Boskowitz was forced to resign two years later. He left Hungary but
returned in 1809 to become rabbi of Bonyhád, where he remained to the
end of his life.

The ten years of Joseph II's reign introduced limited but nevertheless
significant civic improvements into the life of Hungarian Jews, and,
what was equally important, opened before them the road toward linguistic and cultural assimilation to the Hungarian environment. As a
result, an alienation developed between the conservatives and the liberal-minded Jews in Hungary, which, two generations later, was to lead
to a formal schism between the former who called themselves
"Orthodox," and the latter, who adopted the designation "Neolog." (See
chapter 29.)

21

The Theben Story
(Eighteenth and Nineteenth Centuries)

This is the point in the history of the Jews in Hungary at which mention must be made of the members of the Mendel-Theben family, one might say dynasty—leaders of the Pressburg community and *Hoffaktors* (roughly "court Jews"), who played an important role in representing the interests of the Hungarian Jews at the Habsburg court in Vienna. The original name of the family was Mendel (also spelled Mandel, Mandl, etc.), and it seems they were the descendants of the Mendels who had been the Jewish prefects in fifteenth- and sixteenth-century Hungary (see above, chapter 8). The name Theben was attached to them because their first definitely known ancestor came from the town of Dévény (German Theben) to Pressburg. He was David Eben Divinien-sis (i.e., "of Theben"). All I could find of him is that his life ended in murder. His son, Menahem Mendel Theben (d. 1730), was an older con-temporary of Rabbi Akiba Eger (d. 1758) and a leader of the Pressburg Jewish community. His son, in turn, was Abraham Mendel Theben (d. 1768), who is referred to in Jewish sources as *manhig ufarnas ham'dina*, that is, "leader and chief of the country," meaning that he was the recog-nized head of the Jews of the whole country. He had for forty years the monopoly of buying up the entire output of the imperial cloth factory, and he maintained close relations with the court and the Austrian aris-tocracy. He used his influence for the good of Hungarian Jewry, and intervened with Empress Maria Theresa on the occasion of the blood libel of Orkuta (see above, chapter 19).

His son was Koppel (diminutive of Ya'aqov) Mendel Theben (1732–99), the most outstanding member of the Theben dynasty. He joined his father's firm, which from that time on became known as Abraham Koppel Mendel. In 1773 he became head of the Jewish community of Pressburg, and it was in the last year of his life that the community became the seat of the great Moses Sofer (1762–1839), who with his yeshiva made Pressburg one of the most imporant centers of talmudic learning. As head of the Pressburg community he was was also a spokesman of all the Jews of Hungary and the foremost *shtadlan*, representing their interests at the Vienna court and doing whatever he could on his own to help them. Thus, when the Jews were expelled from various places in Hungary (see above, chapter 15), Koppel used his own money to support hundreds of them. When Joseph II's toleration decree prohibited the wearing of beards (see above, chapter 20), it was Koppel who used his influence with the emperor to make him rescind (on April 28, 1783) the prohibition, which was considered by all the Jews of Hungary an arbitrary and vexing interference with their religious life. When the toll on bridges was made twice as high for Jews as for non-Jews, Koppel invested a sizable sum into purchasing the total bridge revenues and then reduced the humiliating extra toll. At the coronation of Leopold II in 1791, Koppel led the Jewish delegation of Pressburg, and the emperor, who must have been appraised by his counselors of the services Koppel had rendered to the imperial treasury, presented him with a gold medal weighing sixteen ducats.

But over and above these activities, which followed the beaten path of the usual *shtadlan*s, Koppel gave evidence that his thinking was far ahead of his age, and he dreamt of attaining equal rights for the Jews. In 1799 Koppel was entrusted by the Jews of Hungary with the task of asking Emperor Francis I (r. 1792–1835) to refrain from repealing their old exemption from military duty. To lend weight to their request, they provided Koppel with a gift of 21,000 gold ducats to deliver to His Majesty. But Koppel did something unexpected and unheard of: instead of submitting the Jews' humble request to the Emperor, he had the temerity to argue that if the Jews were fit to serve as soldiers in the army, like the other subjects of the emperor, they should be allowed to enjoy the rights His Majesty's other subjects had. Koppel must have planned in advance to confront the emperor with this daring request, for in preparation for the audience he had fasted all day long. Weakened by the fast, he was so carried away by the emotion of his impassioned plea that he raised his voice in the imperial presence.

According to the account of this audience given by the Hungarian Jewish historian Ignaz Reich some half-century later, Koppel lost his self-control to such an exent that he uttered words amounting to a threat: "One thing I can tell Your Majesty in all humility: until now no oppressor of the Jews came to a good end; thus Pharaoh, Nebuchadnezzar, Haman, Titus, and———" At this point the excitement was too much for Koppel: he lost consciousness and fell flat on his face. The attendants present quickly carried him out and had him taken home. Barely an hour later, as soon as he regained consciousness, a messenger came bringing the decision of His Majesty: the Jews were to continue to be exempt from military duty—a victory for the Hungarian Jews who sent him, but a defeat for Koppel. It seems that his fainting was caused by a stroke. At his doctor's advice, he was taken to Karlsbad for the healing waters of the famous spa, but his condition deteriorated while on the way, and he died in Prague.

Koppel Theben had a sister who was married to Mordecai Eybeschütz, son of the famous talmudist and kabbalist Jonathan Eybeschütz (1690/95–1764), one of the central figures in the celebrated early-eighteenth-century Shabbatean controversy (whom we met in chapter 16). Leopold Löw, the great Hungarian rabbi, scholar and religious reformer, of whom we shall hear more later, tells about this marriage somewhat scornfully: "Abraham Theben, the richest and most respected member of the Pressburg Jewish community, decided to make a fine *baḥur*, i.e., an outsanding Talmud student, happy with the hand of his daughter. Among the many suitors, of whom, of course, there was no dearth, Mordecai Eybeschütz was given preference. . . . He was the son of R. Jonathan, who had thousands of pupils, and whose name was celebrated all over Israel!" The wedding took place in Pressburg with all due pomp and circumstance, but before long trouble started. Young Eybeschütz became suspected of Shabbateanism, that is, belief in the messiahship of Shabbatai Zevi, whom some of his followers continued to consider the Messiah despite his patent failure to restore the throne of David in Jerusalem, and even despite his apostasy. When Shabbatai Zevi, in order to save his life, converted to Islam (in 1666), a group of his disciples followed him being persuaded that Shabbatai's embracing Islam had a deep mystical significance. Although Jonathan Eybeschütz was among the Prague rabbis who in 1725 excommunicated the Shabbatean sect, later in his life, when he served as rabbi of the "Three Communities" of Hamburg, Altona, and Waldbeck, he himself was suspected of Shabbateanism. This gave rise to a great public controversy between him and his chief opponent, R. Jacob Emden (1697–1776), which did not end even after Eybeschütz's death in 1764. In its very midst, Eybeschütz's younger son Wolf presented himself as a Shabbatean prophet, and more than a shadow of suspicion of Shabbatean sympathies also fell on his elder brother Mordecai. Despite the great influence wielded by Abraham Theben, in the spring of 1761 Samuel Sabel (Zanwil) Leidesdorfer, president of the Pressburg Jewish community, had Mordecai Eybeschütz imprisoned. Jonathan Eybeschütz appealed to Empress Maria Theresa, and subsequently Leidesdorfer himself admitted that Mordecai was innocent. Somewhat later both Eybeschütz brothers, Mordecai and Wolf, moved to Dresden, where they founded a synagogue.

Another son of Abraham Theben was Mendel Theben (d. 1824; in his case Mendel was a first name), who attained fame for both his scholarship and his charity. He had the book *Sefer haYashar l'Rabbenu Tam* (The Book *Yashar* by Rabbenu Tam) published at his own expense. Yet another member of the Theben family was Wolf (Zeev) Theben (1734–1806), who served as rabbinical assessor and *mohel* (ritual circumciser) under six rabbis. He circumcised 1,300 Jewish boys, and the records he kept of these circumcisions constitute an important historical source. He also acted as a *shtadlan* and was received by the emperor in Vienna several times. A daughter of Koppel Theben was married to R. Yisrael Hayyim Boskowitz-Braun, son of R. Feivel Boskowitz, rabbi of the city of Gyöngyös. Their son, Feivel Braun (1826–82), was my father's maternal grandfather. Other descendants of the Mendel-Theben dynasty include the Brüll-Schossberger, Dukesz, Gomperz-Kaufmann, Leidesdorf, Lemberger, Mandl, Mandelly, and Mendel families.

The Mendel-Theben Dynasty

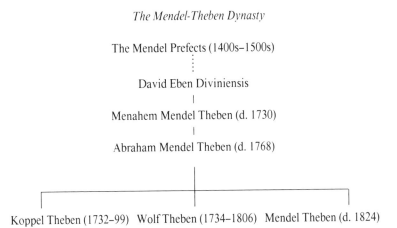

The Mendel Prefects (1400s–1500s)
⋮
David Eben Diviniensis
|
Menahem Mendel Theben (d. 1730)
|
Abraham Mendel Theben (d. 1768)

Koppel Theben (1732–99)   Wolf Theben (1734–1806)   Mendel Theben (d. 1824)

22

Early Struggles for Emancipation (1790-1848)

The fifty-eight years that passed between the death of Joseph II and the outbreak of the revolution of 1848 were a time of dramatic changes in the history of Hungary. Not least important was the growing challenge to Habsburg royal absolutism, and at the same time to traditional Hungarian feudalism, by the autochthonous Hungarian forces whose ideas and aspirations increasingly echoed Western ideas of liberalism. The rising spirit of liberalism provided the historical setting in which two movements converged toward the common goal of Jewish emancipation: the endeavor of the Hungarian liberal leadership to achieve the emancipation of *all* the varied ethnic elements of the country, on the one hand, and the increasingly courageous efforts of the Jews themselves, on the other.

The process began timidly and hesitantly. Late in 1790 the Hungarian Jews submitted an appeal to the Diet (see above chapter 20), which was presented by Baron Ferenc Splényi, bishop of Vác, and was acted upon on December 2, 1790. The resolution as passed was a watered down version of the original petition: it roundly disregarded most of the points contained in the application, and all it said was:

> So that the situation of the Jews should be taken care of even before their affairs and several of the privileges of the royal free cities pertaining to them will be discussed by a national commission that will report to the next Diet, and the joint will of His Majesty and of the Realm will decide on the position of the Jews, the Estates of the Realm have decided with the approval of His Majesty that the Jews living within the borders of Hungary and the attached Parts should be maintained in all the free royal cities and the other places (not including the royal mining towns) in the same condition in which they were on January 1, 1790, and if by any chance they were expelled, they should be reinstated in them.

This resolution was duly sanctioned by the emperor on January 10, 1791.

In preparation for the promised discussion of the situation of the Jews, the Diet actually appointed a commission, and Count Joseph Haller, having studied the matter, reported: "Jewry does have its faults, because until now it was despised; bad manners are general, but this does not prove anything against them, since formerly even the belief that the sun revolved around the earth was general; one cannot suppose that the true God, whom they worship, should have commanded them to commit crimes." Haller proposed that everything the Jews asked in their application should be granted them, and even suggested permitting them to participate in the weekly markets of the mining towns. However, these recommendations were not put on the agenda of the Diet, and thus the article identified as 1790:XXXVIII, "De Judaeis," was to remain the basis of the legal position of the Jews in Hungary until 1840. This meant that the Jews who had settled in the cities during the reign of Joseph II could remain living there and could attend schools, even universities. A minor improvement of the Jewish condition was contained in the 1807 and 1808 decrees of Francis I (r. 1792–1835), which provided that "Jews should be capable of being admitted and accepted among the recruits" of the army, and that "the competent local authorities should impose contributions upon the Jews in proportion to the part of the population they represent, and the individuals produced by the Jewish communities from among their own members must be accepted into the number of recruits offered."

The gradual softening of the Estates' attitude toward the Jews alarmed the cities for whose merchants the Jews constituted unwelcome competition. After the 1825 Diet again considered the improvement of the Jewish situation, even though it adjourned without any positive resolution, the merchants of Pest were apprehensive "that the Estates, which in 1790 thought very favorably about the Jews, could grant them such favors as will be damaging for the civil merchants." To forestall such a development, they convened in 1829 a meeting of all the merchant bodies of the country, which adopted a memorandum complaining of the rapid increase in the number of the Jews, and requesting that Jewish peddling be limited and the Jews not be allowed to acquire landed property. However, the submission of the application would have cost 3,000 florins, which the merchant societies were unable to raise, and thus the whole movement petered out.

Even Count István Széchenyi—the leading liberal and reform-minded Hungarian statesman of the age, founder of the Hungarian Academy of Sciences, and builder of the first bridge across the Danube between Buda and Pest, who earned the epithet "the greatest Magyar"—was no supporter of the emancipation of the Jews. Although he advocated "equality before the law of everybody in the country," his concept of "everybody" did not include the Jews, of whose emancipation he said in one of his speeches in the Diet, "We cannot follow the examples of other countries, for in them the matter is like pouring a bottle of ink into the sea, while here at home we would pour a bottle of ink into a plate of soup." As this ingenious simile shows, Széchenyi evidently considered the Jews a contaminating element whose absorption into the body politic of Hungary the nation could not afford because of the much larger proportion of Jews in the country compared to the countries of the West in which the Jews were treated more liberally.

Still, in his book *Hitel* (Credit), published in 1830, Széchenyi grudgingly recognized the role the Jews played in providing an economic basis for the existence of the nobility, whose backward economic views and practices he sharply condemned: if the Jews did not buy up the product of the nobles' estates, he wrote, "it would dry in their houses." In his subsequent polemical work titled *Világ* (The World), published in 1831, he referred several times to the Jews' role as suppliers to the army, and took the nobles to task for saying that supplying horses to the army was not their task but the Jews'.

In the 1830s a brilliant young patriot, László Lovassy, was first to come out openly for the emancipation of the Jews at a meeting of the law students' casino. The humiliating toleration tax was the subject of deliberations at the 1832–36 Diet, where the issue was raised by the leader of the Liberal Reform Party, the poet Ferenc Kölcsey, and by the foremost spokesman of the liberal gentry, Ferenc Deák, whose domination of Hungarian politics dated from that Diet. They fought valiantly for the abolition of the tax, but the majority of the nobles, under the influence of the court, opposed the motion, so that only after sustained effort did the Diet agree on the formulation of a resolution to be presented to Vienna. The resolution requested that the toleration tax be abolished and that "the Israelites be placed on the same footing in carrying the public burdens as the other taxpayers of the country." The emperor did not sanction the bill—the court was unwilling to forgo the revenue the tax represented.

Further important steps were taken by the 1839–40 Diet, at which the representatives of two counties, Vas and Pest, submitted motions aiming at the emancipation of the Jews. County Vas moved that all the civil rights possessed by the nonnobles should be granted to the Jews as well, and County Pest argued that "the Jews are not a separate nation, and therefore should be awarded the rights due to the Hungarian citizens." The representative of Pest, moreover, demanded that "the Jewish religion should be counted among the accepted religions, its followers should have equal rights and, if they are worthy, should even be able to receive noble rank." The counties of Komárom, Arad, and Tolna jointly renewed the motion to abrogate the toleration tax.

Some of those who supported these motions in the Upper House favored the emancipation of the Jews because they saw it as a measure that would increase the number of Hungarian nationals in a country faced with the problem of large non-Hungarian nationalities within its borders. Count Aurel Dessewfy, the new leader of the young conservatives in the Upper Chamber, argued, "I already now know, in the Plain, Jews who with regard to language have totally become Magyars." Yet at the same time he urged tightening immigration laws, for "otherwise the country will be flooded with a multitude of immigrant beggar Jews . . . which is in the interest of neither the country nor the homeland's Jewry." Lajos Kossuth (1802–94), the rising young leader of the Hungarian reformers, while he spoke of "the dregs of the Máramaros Jew crowd . . . from whose crimes we cannot protect the country," nevertheless urged the elimination of distinctions between the Hungarian and the immigrant Jews.

After much back and forth between the Lower and Upper Chambers, a compromise bill was worked out and submitted to the court, which effected further curtailments of the rights it granted the Jews and then issued the act 1840:XXIX. This law granted Jews who either were born in Hungary or had obtained legal residence permission the right to live freely in the country and the attached lands, with the exception of the mining towns, to practice manufacture with the help of Jewish journeymen, and to establish factories. The law also obliged the Jews to use permanent first and family names, to register all births in registers to be kept by the clerics of their religion, and to use in their documens and contracts the living languages current in the fatherland and the attached parts. It also confirmed their right to acquire "civil plots of land" in cities in which they enjoyed this right at present.

Although this law was a far cry from what the Jews desired, even the limited improvements in their situation it provided were greeted by them with satisfaction, since they incorporated into law their right to live in all parts of the country. Thus, they were also in firm possession of the right to move anywhere, even into the free royal cities.

Also in 1840, Baron Joseph Eötvös (1813–71), a sensitive poet, fine novelist, noble liberal leader, and true friend of the Jews, of whom we shall hear more later, published two political essays arguing the need to alleviate human suffering in Ireland, caused by a century of oppression, and to emancipate the Jews, persecuted through the ages. These publications contributed substantially to creating a proemancipation atmosphere in Hungarian political circles.

233

The actual number of Jews in the country, whose problem so preoccupied the Hungarian lawgivers, was rather small. A census carried out in the 1830s counted 202,876 Jews, or 2.34 percent of the total population. The number of Jews in Pest, which was rapidly developing into the uncontested economic and cultural center of the country, was 6,031.

In the eight years that remained between the passage of the 1840:XXIX law and the 1848 revolution, the Jews, often protected by the owners of large estates and local administrations, made significant advances in business, the professions, and their adoptive Magyar culture while still waiting and hoping for full emancipation. By the middle of the nineteenth century, hundreds of Jewish communities had developed in the cities and villages and on the estates of the secular landowners, as well as on those of church leaders, mostly bishops. The Jewish communities employed rabbis, many of whom introduced the custom of frequent sermonizing in their synagogues and also engaged in the writing of scholarly studies, which began to make their names known beyond the borders of Hungary as well.

After the 1840 Diet, Kossuth's interest in the Jewish question increased. That Diet granted the Jews the right to engage freely in commercial activity, and Kossuth found reason to reproach County Zemplén for barring the Jews from commerce in wine and the manufacture of *aszubor* (a Hungarian specialty, sweet wine made by the addition of choice grapes dried on the vine to the ordinary must), whereby the County "in practice frustrated the noble principles adopted by the Diet." However, at the same time, Kossuth became convinced that for the Jews to take their position as equal members of the Hungarian nation, first their religion must be reformed. In 1844 he wrote in the *Pesti Hirlap* (Pest Gazette), which he had edited since 1841, that he considered indispensable the convening of a *Sanhedrin* (Jewish national council) to reform the Jewish religion. He wrote in the May 5, 1844, issue:

> As for us, we believe and proclaim that, first, to exclude anybody from civil rights merely because of religious differences, merely because he worships the God of the great universe in another temple than we, is contrary to the law of God, to truth, and to politics. Second, we believe and proclaim that Jewish emancipation has two branches: political and social. The former depends *entirely* on the power of the legislator; the latter only inasmuch as the legal limits of social merging must be removed so that the slow process of social emancipation should take place. Hence, third, we believe and proclaim that, even though political emancipation will not put an end to the question, its time has come, and we believe, fourth, that every counterargument based on the alleged immorality of the Jews is powerless, weak, and unloving. Thus far goes our opinion when we proceed from the point of view that the Jews in our fatherland must be con-

234

sidered no differently than as a fraction of all the inhabitants of our homeland that differs from the others only in religious faith. Accordingly, the
Jews in our country are a religious denomination. . . . But Moses was not
only a creator of religion, he was also a civil legislator. . . . The Jews therefore cannot be emancipated, because their religion is a political institution
based on theocratic foundations, which cannot be reconciled politically
with the existing governmental order. . . . Yes, let us look around and we
must admit regretfuly that sympathy for Jewish emancipation has constantly diminished since 1840. It is therefore necessary that the more spirited Jews should endeavor, insofar as it depends on them, to clear away
the pretexts of the deficiencies of this sympathy. If somebody casts suspicion on their morals, the proud word of noble indignation behooves them
that seriously rejects the calumnies, because their ethics are just as pure as
those of anybody else. But if the criticism against them is that their religion is not only a religion but also a political organism, that one cannot
give civil validity to theocrcy, that they are not only a separate religion but
also a separate people, then, truly, this objection, if it is based on prejudice, deserves to be benevolently enlightened and, if it is something more
than prejudice, to be averted by appropriate reforms.

Following these elucidations Kossuth suggested that the Jews should
convene a universal conclave, which should determine what in their
faith is religious dogma and should "lay the cornerstone of social amalgamation."

This view of the foremost leader of the Hungarian opposition was
countered by Leopold Löw (see chapter 23) with a spirited defense of
Judaism, but Kossuth did not let himself be swayed. In his rejoinder he
stated:

As long as the Jews cannot eat together with their fellow citizens of
other religions a little salt, a piece of bread, cannot drink one wine with
them, cannot sit at one table, so that these and other similar things hinder
the social amalgamation of the various religious denominations, as long as
these things are not declared not to belong to the essence of Jewish religion
—not only by the practice of the more educated ones, who thereupon are
considered by their coreligionists bad Jews, but by solemn ecclesiastical
declaration of faith—the Jews will not be emancipated *socially*, even if
they should be emancipated politically a hundred times.

In thus tying the political emancipation of the Jews to their religious
reform, Kossuth opposed the views of the other political leaders of
Hungary, foremost among them Ferencz Deák and Baron Joseph Eötvös, who felt that granting human rights to the Jews by politically emancipating them was a move that did not brook delay.

Kossuth's demand of reform of the Jewish religion in connection with
Jewish emancipation had repercussions among both the country's political leadership and the Jewish community itself. At the 1843–44 Diet,
the Lower House was addressed by representatives of several counties

who vociferously demanded radical reforms in the Jewish religion as a precondition of emancipation. County Ugocsa demanded, "the Jews should not be emancipated until they chisel off the trappings from the formalities of their religion." County Komárom likewise argued that "the eccentricities of the Jews in religious matters should be smoothed away." The delegate of County Györ even went so far as to demand that the Jews "contradict the principles of their religion."

These parliamentary utterances were paralleled by opposition to the emancipation of the Jews voiced in the press. In 1844, when Jews expressed their dismay over the apostasy of Mór Ballagi (see chapter 24), Joseph Székács, Evangelical minister of Pest, attacked the Jews in an open letter for daring to fret over that conversion, and concluded that this showed how immature they still were and how far from deserving emancipation. In the same year, a certain Dr. J. G. published a pamphlet titled "Some Modest Views from the Religious Perspective Concerning the Naturalization and Amalgamation of the Jews with the Hungarian Nation." In it he argued that "the emancipation of the Jews not only is not favored but is opposed by common sense," because the Jews constitute a separate nationality, they look to Palestine with the most fervent desire, and their messianic faith is tied to their return to the Holy Land. In the May 5, 1844, issue of the *Pesti Hirlap*, Gábor Fábián, a member of the Hungarian Academy of Science, published a lead article titled "Jewish Emancipation," in which he stated that "no bastard generation has ever ennobled itself" and that "an indispensable condition of emancipation is the liberation of marriages between Jew and Christian."

Demands and arguments such as these could not but alienate the conservative element among the Jews of Hungary. The Jews of Ugocsa responded to the speech of their county's representative by stating that "they would rather forgo the happy future if the improvement of their civic condition were to be made dependent on the slightest change in their religion." And the rabbinate of Pressburg, that citadel of orthodoxy still under the influence of the great personality of R. Moses Sofer (1762–1839) and led by his son, R. Abraham Samuel Sofer ("the K'tav Sofer," 1815–71), reacted to Kossuth's 1844 article in the *Pesti Hirlap* by openly taking a position opposing emancipation. By 1847 it appeared that, as Lajos Venetianer put it, "the majority of Hungarian Jews were prepared to give up the blessings of emancipation rather than deny the values contained in the millennial traditions of their religion, which educate to pure humanity and ethical ideals."

At the other extreme of the Hungarian Jewish spectrum stood those educated Jews who drew the opposite conclusion from the hope of

emancipation that was dangled before their eyes, and left Judaism altogether. The 1840s saw a veritable epidemic of apostasy. We have mentioned Mór Ballagi, the first to convert to Christianity. He was followed
by the Ullmann (Szitányi), Kanitz, Finaly, and other families. One conversion was especially painful for the Pest congregation: that of its president, Jónás Kunewalder, a spirited leader of Jewish movements who
converted shortly after submitting, on September 23, 1847, an application to the Diet in the name of "the Israelites of Hungary and attached
Parts, in behalf of the aldermen and elected directors of the Israelite
Congregation of Pest." In his application Kunewalder painted a touching picture of the devotion of the Hungarian Jews to the fatherland, and
complained that while foreigners coming into Hungary could become its
citizens, the Jews, who had been born in this country and all of whose
endeavor was to be citizens of their beloved fatherland, were denied this
right. "This hard punishment," he wrote,

> to be forced to be a stranger in his own fatherland, is meted out not to the
> guilty but is inflicted on all of those who by the will of divine providence
> were born as Israelites, that is, on our innocent newborn children, on
> whose foreheads it stamps the mark of rejection the moment they are
> born, even though no other accusation can be made against them except
> that they came into this world in the faith of Moses, in that faith whose
> principles are elucidated in the attached enclosure. This enclosure . . . was
> unanimously approved by the general assembly of all the representatives
> of the Israelites of Hungary and the attached Parts, and can hence be con-
> sidered the synopsis of our specific creed. [There follows a detailed enu-
> meration of all the arguments that could be marshaled for the emancipa-
> tion of the Jews, and the petition concludes with the request:] Kindly
> favor these comments of ours with your attention and thorough examina-
> tion, so that the well-understood interest of the fatherland should be
> served by all the forces that can contribute to the flowering of our joint
> fatherland, and so that nobody should be prevented from the cultivation
> of his God-given qualities and their utilization for the common good.

Soon after signing this self-assured, dignified, and at the same time
embittered application, "Jónás Kunewalder, president," converted to
Christianity.

The 1847–48 Diet heard many arguments both for and against the
emancipation of the Jews. Kossuth and his liberal colleagues spoke
about the merits of the Jews and the injustice of their rightless status;
the representatives of the cities and the counties, for whose constituents
the Jews represented serious economic competition, repeated the argument that emancipation should be granted the Jews only after they
prove their religion to be in harmony with the interests of the state.
Much emphasis was put on the dangers the "streaming of foreign Jews"
into Hungary represented for the fatherland. In the end, the Lower

House passed a bill that, while it did not infringe on the right of the indigenous Jews to live wherever they chose, did include the clause that "maintaining the provisions of the 1840:XXIX law, foreign Jews are allowed neither to immigrate nor to settle" in Hungary. The Upper House discussed this bill briefly and returned it to the Lower House for modification, but limitations of time did not allow it to be reconsidered, and thus it did not become law. However, a decision was passed resolving that the next Diet would discuss the full emancipation of the Jews.

At that point historical events intervened: the 1848 revolution broke out, was defeated, and was followed by almost two decades of auto-cratic, absolutist Austrian rule during which all Hungarian legislative activity was suspended, and the condition of the Jews remained as it had been before 1848.

What the Hungarian Jews could not help noting was that the Hungar-ian legislators, in their discussion of the Jewish question, made a sharp distinction between them and the immigrant Jews (read "Galician Jews") who either sojourned in Hungary illegally or clamored for entry permits. The indigenous Hungarian Jews, they understood, were consid-ered by the Hungarian legislators good Magyars who merited emancipa-tion; the "streaming in" of foreign Jews was felt to be a danger for the cultural and ethnic integrity of Hungary, and emancipation or no eman-cipation, they had to be kept out. Many, if not most, of the foreign Jews came from Galicia, that part of Austria which adjoined Hungary to the north-east across the Carpathian Mountains. These immigrants, as a rule, were ultra-religious, with a major part of them Hasidim. They tended to retain their traditional garb, the long black kaftan reaching down to the ankles, wore long, uncut beards and sidelocks, and the strange impression their appearance made was augmented by the fact that even if they learned Hungarian, their speech remained colored by what was identified as a Yiddish accent. Most of them were products of Yeshivas, without any secular education, and could read and write only Yiddish and Hebrew, and the only occupation in which they were able to eke out a living was petty trade, peddling, buying and selling old clothes, and the like. They were considered dirty and dishonest, people with the worst possible manners and mentality—a stereotype to which many of both the gentile and the Jewish society of Hungary subscribed. The more narrowminded among the indigenous Hungarian Jews looked askance at these foreign coreligionists, had contempt for them, and tried to play up the differences and the lack of commonality between them-selves and these newcomers. The term *Galizianer* (German for Gali-cian) or *galiciai* (the same in Hungarian) became a term of opprobrium and disdain, that was to remain in use among the Hungarian Jews well into the interwar years of the twentieth century.

This differentiation between the native Hungarian Jews and the foreign "Galician" Jews was on the legislative agenda for some two decades prior to the 1848 revolution, and the Hungarian Jewish leadership was impressed with the necessity of going along with it if they wanted to succeed in their great quest for emancipation. Hence, even after emancipation was granted, whenever anti-Semitism raised its head—as happened frequently enough—many leaders of Hungarian Jewry tried to defang it by arguing that whatever undesirable traits the anti-Semites attributed to the Jews to justify their anti-Jewish stance were found only among the foreign Jews (again, read "Galician Jews"), but not among the indigenous Hungarian Jews, who were as Magyar in language, behavior, feeling, and patriotism as any non-Jewish Hungarian.

Whether any Hungarian anti-Semite went along with this argument is a moot question. What historical evidence documents is that as late as during World War I, when the Russian advance on the eastern front forced Galician Jews to seek refuge in Hungary, some Hungarian Jewish leaders asked (or suggested) that the Hungarian government not allow them into the country. They did this not for lack of sympathy for the plight of those unfortunate Jews, but because they feared the adverse reaction of the Hungarian people to the influx of "the Galicians" and the extension of that reaction to indigenous Hungarian Jews. Their fear was greater than their humanitarian readiness to help the refugees. In a later chapter we shall have to return to this issue.

23

Religious Reform (1798–1852)

It was while R. Muenz held office in Óbuda (see chapter 20) that the first stirrings of Jewish religious reform took place in Hungary. Its first representative in the country was Aaron Chorin (1766–1844), rabbi of Arad. Chorin was born in Moravia and studied at the yeshiva of Nagymarton and subsequently under the great Ezekiel Landau of Prague. He married at the age of seventeen, became a merchant and, failing in that profession, accepted the invitation of the Jewish community of Arad to become its chief rabbi. (It should be noted that in Hungary every rabbi, unless there was another rabbi in the same congregation superior to him, could boast the title "chief rabbi.") His first piece of writing, a pamphlet titled "Imre No'am" (Pleasant Sayings) was published in 1798. In it he dealt with religious questions, and stated inter alia that the consumption of sturgeon was permitted because the halakhic prohibition related only to fish having no scales. Even though Ezekiel Landau concurred with his opinion, Chorin was attacked by R. Mordecai Benet, chief rabbi of Moravia, and R. Isaac Krieszhaber of Paks. Chorin refuted the latter's arguments in 1799 in a pamphlet titled "Siryon Qasqasim" (A Coat of Mail) and in 1803 his book *Emeq haShave* (The Valley of Equality") was printed in Prague. In it he openly professed to be a reformer, argued that the Talmud was not incompatible with rationality, and advocated the adaptation of Judaism to modern times. The book manifested great scholarship, especially in its criticism of Maimonides, the Halakha, and the Aggada, as well as the Book of Zohar, from a philosophical point of view. Chorin only touched upon theoretical issues, rejecting practical Kabbala as contrary to common sense. He submitted his manuscript to R. Muenz, who was sixteen years his senior and whom he highly respected, and Muenz wrote an introduction to it, which was printed in the book. Nevertheless, the book created an uproar in orthodox circles, with some even demanding that it be burned, so Chorin voluntarily made alterations for its second edition.

When the controversy reached Arad, Chorins's own congregation, and he was publicly insulted in his synagogue while preaching a sermon, the heads of the congregation turned to Muenz for his opinion as to whether or not the book contained heresies. Since Muenz had given his *haskama* (approbation) to the book but was himself strictly orthodox and a determined opponent of radical reform, he faced a dilemma. He solved the problem by inviting to Óbuda in 1805 two other rabbis to constitute, under his chairmanship, a three-man *beth din*, which took testimony from Chorin. But on the second day of the hearings, Muenz did not appear, whereupon the senior rabbi, R. Samuel Butchewitz (or Budaspitz) of Aszód, pronounced judgment that Chorin had to retract the contents of his book, and should he refuse to do so, as a punishment for taking a position bordering upon heresy his beard should be cut. In addition they ordered a reduction in Chorin's salary; this, however, the Arad congregation rejected. The affair reached the government, which, in 1806, invalidated the judgment of the *beth din*.

Chorin remained a partisan of reform, especially after he read of the innovations introduced by the Jews of Hamburg. In papers titled "The Spendor of Truth" and "The Dirge of Truth" he advocated reforms in the synagogue services and permitted the introduction of German prayers, German sermons, and organ music. However, around 1829, at the request of R. Muenz, who maintained desultory contact with Chorin, he withdrew his suggestions. Still, his reforming spirit could not be squelched, and the very next year he resumed writing on the subject. This time his work was translated into German in Vienna, bringing him to the attention of the reform party of the Austrian and German Jews. They offered him the newly created rabbinical post in Vienna, but the government withheld its required consent.

In 1821 the State of Baden requested Chorin's expert opinion concerning the duties of rabbis and the reforms. Chorin responded in a pamphlet (in German) titled *Iggeret Elassaph: Letters of an African Rabbi to His European Colleagues* (1826), proposing further reforms. As an advocate of reform he wanted to establish secular and trade schools and to see the Jews take up handicrafts and agriculture. He did not go as far as some of the German Jewish reformers and suggest the substitution of Sunday as the Sabbath. But he did propose that the religious laws he considered too strict be mitigated, for example, that travel by railroad be permitted on the Sabbath, that the organ be introduced into the synagogues, that the religious duty of eating matza during the eight days of Passover be abolished, that a psalm be substituted for the Kol Nidre prayer on the eve of Yom Kippur, and the like. In his article "Hillel," published in 1835 in Óbuda in the journal *Bikkure ha'Ittim* (Firstfruits of the Times) he put forward quasi-Zionist ideas, urging the union of world Jewry and the establishment of a supreme religious authority with its seat in Jerusalem. He played a role in launching the movement for the emancipation of Jews in Hungary, and was greatly respected in non-Jewish circles as well.

Simultaneously with the early years of Chorin's struggles for religious reform, another advocate of similar ideas made his appearance in Hungary. He was Marcus (or Mordecai) Nissa Weisz (dates unknown), who in 1792 had a store in Pest and thereafter was a renter of land near Munkács, where he employed Galician Jews but treated them so harshly that they rebelled. In 1802 Weisz published a German treatise titled "The Jew As He Is" in which he discussed the transformation of the "moral sentiments" of the Jews. He considered the strictness of rabbinical law the source of the crisis in Jewish religious life, and argued that the rabbis and the talmudists misinterpreted the divine laws, and the rules of kashrut and clothing were outdated and antiquated. He gave vent to very dim views of orthodox Judaism: it totally subordinated its life to tradition and thereby isolated itself from the environment. As could be expected, he was sharply attacked for his views, and the next year he published another broadside titled "The Harassed Marcus Nissa Weisz and the People." Embittered by the reaction to his ideas and the personal attacks upon him, he converted to Christianity, which step, however, did not keep him from continuing to publish his views. After printing a mathematical work in 1805, he returned to discussing the Jewish question in 1807 in a treatise titled "Impartial Reflections on the Great Jewish Sanhedrin of Paris." In it he presented a detailed description of the reforms he advocated, and discussed the problem of Jewish emancipation in its relationship to Jewish religious reform. He envisaged the possibility of partial emancipation, which would reward reformed Jews with the rights enjoyed by the general society while traditional orthodox Jews would be excluded from it. He tried to submit his writings to the king and the Estates but did not succeed.

Another early advocate of Jewish religious reform in Hungary was David Friesenhausen (ca. 1756–1828). Born in Friesenhausen, Franconia, he studied Talmud in Furth, and it was only when he reached the age of thirty that he began to take an interest in secular sciences. He lived in Berlin from 1788 to 1796, when his Hebrew book *K'lil haHeshbon*, an introduction to algebra, was published there. Shortly thereafter, Friesenhausen embarked on a European tour with the double purpose of selling copies of his algebra book and soliciting advance subscriptions to another book, *Mosdot Tevel* (a presentation of the structure of the universe according to Copernicus), which he had ready in manuscript. Around 1800 he settled in Hunfalu (in the Jewish sources Unsdorf), a small village in northern Hungary, where he became *day-yan* (rabbinical assessor) and also worked as a merchant. Unhappy in the isolation of the Carpathian village, he moved in 1806 to Pest, where he continued to work on *Mosdot Tevel* and on a memorandum, in German, discussing the establishment of three rabbinical seminaries, in Hungary, Galicia, and the Czech lands. The curriculum Friesenhausen envisaged included not only talmudic but also biblical subjects and was radically innovative in that it also incorporated secular studies. His idea was that fifteen years after the establishment of the rabbinical seminaries, no person should be allowed to serve as rabbi unless he had completed this course of studies.

Friesenhausen's plan was to submit his seminary proposal to the palatine, Archduke Joseph. On July 26, 1806, he was received by the palatine, who graciously promised him to bring the matter before his brother the emperor. Unable to secure a rabbinical position in Pest, Friesenhausen returned to Hunfalu.

The office of the palatine considered Friesenhausen's plan and obtained information on the status of Jewish education from the Governorate of Galicia, but in 1813 it "closed" the Friesenhausen file, that is to say, resolved not to act upon it. Its reasons for doing so were: first, the plan could not be executed, because the Jews had no funds for financing it, and no additional burden could be imposed upon them, especially now when the toleration tax had been increased; second, the policy of the state was to diminish the separateness of the Jews, and the establishment of rabbinical seminaries would augment it; and third, there was no need of a Jewish school, since the Jews were permitted to study in the Christian schools.

Despite the rejection of his project, the very fact that Friesenhausen dared to approach the highest governmental authorities without the permission of the leading Hungarian rabbis made him a persona non grata among them. The rabbis accused him of undermining their position and of being a dangerous reformer. The controversy led to mutual recriminations and did little to enhance the public's respect for the rabbis.

In 1808 Friesenhausen became a *dayyan* in Sátoraljaujhely, where he remained until 1816. While there he went on record criticizing the growing Hasidic movement, although, curiously, he did believe in the efficacy of *qame'ot* (amulets) if they were written by experts who knew the secret of the *shemot*, the sacred divine names. In 1816 he undertook a second international tour to recruit subscribers for his *Mosdot Tevel*. He visited some 130 congregations in Hungary and thirty in Moravia;

among the subscribers were rabbis from all the hues of the religious rainbow, including the great halakhic authority R. Moses Sofer of Pressburg, the Hasidic rabbi Moshe Teitelbaum, the *tzaddiq* of Nagykálló (in the Hebrew sources Qalov), and the reformer rabbi Aaron Chorin of Arad. The subscriptions he collected enabled him to have his book printed in Vienna in 1820.

Little is known of the last years of Friesenhausen's life, except that he seems to have lived with his son, Dr. Meir Friesenhausen, who served as the physician of the Jewish community of Gyulafehérvár (Alba Julia, Karlsburg). Whether he was basically a reformer or an adherent of Hasidism became a controversial issue among those Hungarian Jewish historians who later studied his life and work.

One more early advocate of Jewish religious reform in Hungary must be mentioned. He was R. Eliezer Leibermann, rabbi of Homonna (County Zemplén), who in a paper attributed the crisis in religious life to the fact that the Jewish youth grew up without acquiring familiarity with the contents of their faith or an understanding of what the rabbis were speaking about. He called upon the rabbis to introduce timely reforms, and held up as a guiding example the quiet devotion that characterized the services in the Christian churches, in contrast to the relative noise and disorder of traditional Jewish worship.

In the early nineteenth century the Jewish community of Pest was well on the way to becoming the largest in the country, and its first chief rabbi, Israel Wahrmann (1755–1826), took steps to organize congregational institutions along the lines of the modern West European Jewish communities. He considered it his first and foremost task to establish a Jewish school, to be patterned after that of the Amsterdam community, and this initiative in itself embroiled him in a fight with the conservative camp of the Pest Jews, who strenuously objected to any modern Jewish school. The school was nevertheless opened in 1814. R. Wahrmann also established other religious and charitable institutions, such as the Society for the Relief of the Bashful Jewish Poor of the City. He organized special Sabbath services for the schoolchildren, and it was thanks to his intervention that in 1825 the chancellery made instruction in the Jewish religion obligatory for Jewish *gimnázium* students.

In 1830, well-to-do members of the Pest Jewish community, led by Gábor Ullmann, founded the Cultus Tempel, which followed the example of the Viennese modern Tempel (established in 1826) in reforming the services: a choir was introduced, the language of the sermon changed from Yiddish to German, and (from 1832 on) weddings were solemnized not in the courtyard but inside the synagogue. These innovations occasioned sharp clashes with the orthodox, who considered

them attacks on traditional Jewish religion and tried repeatedly to liquidate the Cultus Tempel.

The breach was temporarily healed by R. Löb (Arszlán) Schwab
(1794–1857), who became chief rabbi of the Pest congregation in 1836
after the position had been vacant for ten years following the death of R.
Israel Wahrmann. We shall hear more of R. Schwab in chapter 25, when
we come to discuss the phenomenon of the Hungarian Jews' "patriotic
imperative."

While the conservative and progressive elements in Hungarian Jewry
girded for the struggle that was to lead to schism at the 1868–69 Jewish
National Congress, the modernization and Magyarization of the community as a whole continued unabated. One of its salient expressions
was the increase in the numbers of Jewish children attending not religious Talmud Torah schools or heders but modern elementary schools,
so that by the early 1840s the Jews were the country's denominational
group the highest percentage of whose children received institutionalized education. According to the statistical research published in 1842
by Elek Fényes, in the country as a whole, one out of every seventeen
children of primary school age attended school, while the corresponding
figure for the Jews was one out of ten. Although most of the schools
maintained by the Jews were still Yiddish speaking, the secular subjects
were taught mainly in Hungarian. Evidently, by the mid-nineteenth
century the Hungarian Jewish community was well on its way to
becoming a Magyar denomination through and through, Hungarian in
language, and as we shall soon see, fervently Magyar in sentiment.

It was in the decade preceding the 1848 revolution that Lipót (Leopold) Löw (b. Czernahora, Moravia, 1811; d. Szeged, 1875) began his
rabbinical work in Hungary. He was a descendant of the famous R.
Judah Loew ben Bezalel (to whose name is attached the golem legend),
studied in Moravian yeshivas, and also acquired a thorough knowledge
of Italian, French, Latin, and Greek, and later in life also Hungarian. He
married the daughter of R. Schwab, who was one of the rabbis to ordain
him, and in 1840 he became rabbi of Nagykanizsa, where from 1844 he
began to preach in Hungarian, the first rabbi to do so. He was convinced
that Magyarization was a vital issue for Hungarian Jewry, and one of his
first acts in Nagykanizsa was to introduce two weekly hours of instruction in the Hungarian language in the school of the Jewish congregation.
In 1845 he published a sermon in Hungarian, "Isaiah, Teacher of Our
Age," in which he wrote: "Where morality must be awakened, evil
reproached, invective answered, calumny refuted, there raise your Hungarian voice! Speak courageously; speak resolutely! Speak to the Hungarian in his language, even if weakly; he will understand you, and our

word will reverberate in his sympathetic bosom." The sermon was given an appreciative review by the *Pesti Divatlap* (Pest Fashion Journal), which concluded, "May God give our fatherland many such stalwart Hungarian clergymen."

From 1846 to 1850 Löw served as rabbi of Pápa, and from 1850 to his death, as that of Szeged. He was at the forefront of the Jewish fight for emancipation in Hungary, he participated in the rabbinical conferences of Breslau (1845) and Leipzig (1870), and he was entrusted by the 1851 Viennese Hungarian Jewish rabbinical conference (convened by the Austrian government) with preparing detailed statutes for a country-wide organization of the Hungarian Jews. His personality, his scholarship, and his religious and political leadership earned him the greatest respect and admiration of both the Jews and non-Jews of Hungary.

Leopold Löw was the first to suggest the establishment of a Hungarian Jewish literary society and the preparation of a Jewish translation of the Bible into Hungarian. He advocated the founding of a rabbinical seminary, and in 1859 launched his journal *Ben Chanania*, which he edited until 1868. It was a monthly, in German, dedicated to Jewish history, archeology, society, politics, religion, ritual, and education, and it paid special attention to the struggle for emancipation. Its contributors included the foremost Jewish scholars in Hungary and abroad, who published in it the results of their research. Löw also wrote an impressive number of scholarly studies, among them several dealing with the history of the Jews in Hungary. During the 1848 revolution he served as military chaplain, and delivered inflammatory speeches for which he was imprisoned for three months after the defeat of the revolution.

In chapter 22 we mentioned that Löw rose to the defense of Jewry and Judaism when Lajos Kossuth suggested that emancipation of the Jews be made contingent on their internal religious reforms and Magyarization. Löw had many other occasions as well to use his scholarship for the defense of the Jewish people. When the anonymous Dr. J. G. opined that the Jews constituted a separate nationality (see chapter 22), Löw published a scholarly response arguing that ever since their scattering in the Diaspora the Jews had ceased to be a nation, that they lived among the nations as a denomination only, their messianic beliefs about the Holy Land had no political but only religious significance, and Jewish messianic beliefs were identical with the Catholic belief in the coming of the kingdom of God and the eastward orientation of the Christian Church.

As for religious reform, Löw supported it, but he was a moderate reformer. In 1847 he issued the following appeal, calling upon his colleagues to sign it with him:

We, the undersigned Hungarian rabbis, in harmony with our sacred religion, solemnly declare:

1. All the duties toward fellow men that are taught in our sacred writings have to be solemnly fulfilled not only toward Israelites but equally toward non-Israelites, because we consider every man, whatever religion he follows, our true brother.

2. Recognizing that Hungary is our true and only fatherland, we shall endeavor to instill its love and the fervor for its patriotism into the hearts of our adherents.

3. Appreciating the value of popular education, we shall use all our influence as clergymen to establish good and effective elementary schools.

4. Everything contained in our casuistical works that does not agree with what is said above, we declare as being outmoded and invalid, and we shall endeavor with all our strength to have our principles as presented spread among our people through both the living word and the textbooks to be written and approved by us.

Everybody will gain through the realization of these suggestions. The government will gain intelligent and educated citizens; the fatherland will gain honest sons; patriotism will gain enthusiastic and fervent cultivators; and we ourselves will gain peace of mind, the approval of our God, and recognition, so that the Jewish question will no longer be like the dress of Penelope, which is woven today only to be unraveled tomorrow.

The operative paragraph, which aroused the ire of the tradition-bound elements in Hungarian Jewry, was of course number 4. From the traditional point of view it was little short of apostasy to arrogate to oneself the right to abolish *any* part of traditional halakhic literature, and what else could the reference to "casuistical works" mean? The traditionalists could also point to the increasing number of Jews who left the fold and attribute that painful phenomenon to the loosening of the ties that for millennia had bound Jews to Judaism. Löw's appeal thus became one more factor in the developing split between the liberal and the tradition-bound, which was to take center stage at the 1868–69 Hungarian Jewish National Congress.

An attempt to establish a Reform congregation took place in Pressburg in 1844. In that year, influenced by the political atmosphere, members of the Jewish merchants' *kaszinó* (social club), with the support of R. Manheimer of Vienna and R. Leopold Löw, at the time rabbi of Nagykanizsa, wanted to secede from the mother congregation in order to hold thanksgiving services. However, the Hungarian authorities withheld their approval. In 1847, in Arad, Nagybecskerek, Nagyvárad, and Pécs, "Israelite Reforming Societies" were founded, which, however, ceased functioning after the revolution of the following year.

In 1848 the reform-minded Jews of Arad issued a call to the Jewish communities of the country, suggesting a series of reforms to invalidate the accusation that the Jews "stubbornly kept themselves apart from the other denominations." To wit:

1. The Sabbath, as a day of rest, should be transferred to Sunday, so that with regard to contact the Jews should be brought into harmony with citizens of other faiths; nevertheless, for those who wish to continue to adhere to the old system, divine services should be held also on Saturdays.
2. The existing, exceedingly purposeless dietary laws, which have until now had an impeding effect on the Jews' social relations, should be abolished.
3. Since the differing and uncertain calendar makes it impossible to celebrate Jewish holidays at the same time as the other denominations', these, which mostly have only the character of memorial observances, should be reduced to the shortest possible time; the so-called half-holidays and the fast days—with the exception of Yom Kippur—should be abolished.
4. The divine services should be brief and, so that what the mouth utters should be comprehended by the mind with proper devotion, celebrated with prayers composed in the living language, without any external symbolic clothes and with uncovered heads. However, those who adhere to the old system should not be hindered in observing, according to custom, the holidays to be abolished.
5. Since circumcision cannot be counted among the main tenets of Mosaism and, besides, cannot be compatible with human feelings and dignity, it should be proclaimed that its nonobservance should not be a hindrance to being accepted into the bosom of the Jewish religion.
6. Since it is stated in the Bible that with regard to the Jews only the Ten Commandments serve as the basic religious principles and are obligatory as the revelation from God to Moses, it follows of itself that all other existing commandments, religious ceremonies, the Talmud, and other introduced customs are invalid.

The Jews of Pest collected signatures for similar appeals for the purpose of religious reform, which inevitably inflamed the more observant element. These were largely the principles adopted by the Reform Society organized in Pest in 1848 by Ignác Einhorn (later Ede Horn; see chapter 24), who also served as its first rabbi. It seceded from the Israelite Congregation of Pest, depriving it of its most affluent members.

In 1851 the government convened a Jewish conference in Buda to put in order the internal affairs of the country's Jews, and the representatives of the Pest congregation took that opportunity to combat the Reform Society. The conference declared that the reform trend, like Hasidism, was a sect, and resolved that "as sects, in particular societies or associations that band together for the purpose of communal prayer, eliminate from their liturgy the typical temple prayers, or in general perform their services in the fashion of reform societies, cannot be tolerated." This condemnation of the Reform Society was approved by the Viennese government, and in 1852 the Minister of Education dissolved the society.

A few months before the government decree forced it to close its temple, the Reform Society invited David Einhorn (b. Dispeck, Bavaria,

1809; d. New York, 1879) to serve as its second (and last) rabbi, succeeding Ignác Einhorn (no relation), who had to flee Hungary because of his revolutionary activities. It was during his sojourn in Pest that David Einhorn began to work on his book *Das Prinzip des Judaismus*, published in 1854. After leaving Pest, Einhorn moved to America, where he became one of the most important leaders of the Jewish Reform movement.

In November 1852 the Pest mother congregation readmitted the members of the disbanded Reform Society. Thus, it was able to count on the contributions of the affluent Jews who rejoined the congregation, and to proceed with its plans to build a central synagogue for the large Jewish community of Pest. Work on the synagogue began in 1854 and was completed in 1859. It was to become known as the Tobacco Temple (in Hungarian Dohány Templom), after the name of the street (Dohány) on which it was located. It still stands (as of 1995) and with its 3,000 seats is the largest synagogue in Europe, perhaps in the world.

24

New Horizons (1800-48)

The first half of the nineteenth century was not only a time of outpouring of patriotic sentiment from the hearts, mouths, and pens of the Jews in Hungary, it was also a period of intense cultural, literary, scientific, and economic activity, into which they threw themselves with the same energy and enthusiasm that characterized their simultaneous struggle for equal rights. In this chapter I shall give a series of very brief portraits, in chronological order by birth date, of those Hungarian Jews who were most acclaimed by their contemporaries for outstanding achievement in one of these fields. The sum total of these sketches amounts to a panoramic view of a community that found itself in a paradoxical situation. On the one hand, the Jews counted as second-class human beings, were denied the most elementary rights enjoyed by the rest of the population, and were looked down upon either as foreigners or as individuals whose "otherness" stamped them as inferior. On the other, the Jewish community included a high percentage of men of great talent, who penetrated, and achieved leading positions in, diverse fields of activity, and contributed substantially to raising Hungary out of its backwardness and enabling it to become a force not only within the Habsburg Empire but also in the European community of nations.

In the early 1800s, Hungarian Jewish authors—most of them rabbis—wrote in either Hebrew, Yiddish, or German. Most of their published writings were of a religious character, with only a few treating secular subjects. Only in 1840 did the first Jewishly authored publication in the Hungarian language make its appearance: an anonymous patriotic pamphlet titled "The Feelings of an Israelite on the Occasion of the Conclusion of the Glorious Diet of 1840." It was also in the 1840s that the chief rabbi of the Pest congregation, Löb (Arszlán) Schwab, started to publish writings in Hungarian.

Because of the legal disabilities of the Jews in Hungary and the prejudices they encountered on the part of the general population and its leadership, it was not easy for even the most talented of them to achieve the positions they aspired to or the scope of activity that would have satisfied them. These were the circumstances that, already by the early 1800s, motivated many talented Hungarian Jews either to convert to Christianity or to emigrate and try their luck in other countries—or, in some cases, to take both steps, in either order. Statistical data are lacking, but one gets the definite impression that both conversion and emigration were much more frequent among the highly talented Hungarian Jews than in the Hungarian Jewish community as a whole, or, for that matter, in the general population in the case of emigration.

Writers and Literary Historians

To this group of individuals, who put a double distance between themselves and their Hungarian Jewish origin via conversion and migration, belongs the oldest of the litterateurs who must be mentioned here, the satirist Moritz Gottlieb Saphir (b. Lovasberény, 1795; d. Baden, 1858). Born into a Yiddish-speaking Orthodox family, he studied Talmud in Pressburg and Prague, and before age twenty he settled in Pest. There he learned French, English, and Italian and wrote his first work, a biting satirical farce in Yiddish, titled *The False Kaschtau*, which was lost for several decades until rediscovered by Bernát Mandl, who published it in the 1900 volume of the eminent *Magyar Zsidó Szemle* (Hungarian Jewish Review). Another similar farce by Saphir, *The False Catalini*, is definitely lost. His first work in German, *Papilloten*, was published in Pest in 1821 and achieved considerable success. Soon thereafter Saphir moved to Vienna, where his satirical and sensational articles in the *Wiener Theater-Zeitung* became such a source of scandal that in 1825 he felt it was better to move to Berlin. There he edited the journals *Berliner Schnellpost für Literatur, Theater und Geselligkeit* and *Berliner Courier*, earning many friends as well as enemies, who attacked him in a pamphlet titled *Saphir in Berlin*. He responded sharply in his book *Der getötete aber dennoch lebende Saphir*, which reached three editions. His conflict with the Berlin literary elite intensified to the point that he found it advisable to take refuge in Munich, where he became editor of the journals *Bazar für München* and *Deutsche Horizont*. His satire of the Bavarian king led to his expulsion from Munich, and the next stop in his peregrinations was Paris, where he joined two famous ex-Jewish German exiles, Heinrich Heine and Ludwig Börne. However, a royal command called him back to Munich, where he was awarded the honorary title of Councillor to the Administration of the Royal Theater, and he became editor of the *Bayerische*

Beobachter. In 1832 Saphir converted to Lutheranism, and in 1835 he returned to Vienna, where he edited the *Theaterzeitung* and in 1837 founded his own periodical, *Der Humorist*. In it, Saphir's biting wit, much feared in his time, was no longer directed at Metternich's reactionary policies but rather at general human foibles and follies.

Saphir's voluminous literary output includes humorous and satirical poems, essays, feuilletons, literary criticism, comedies, short stories, and reviews of plays. For decades his witticisms circulated throughout the German-speaking world and his satirical sketches were recited by actors. It was only after the 1848 revolution that his popularity and influence began to wane, but then, from 1887 on, his collected works were published in twenty-six volumes. His attitude to Judaism was negative: while Heine said that the baptismal certificate was the passport to Europe, Saphir quipped that his Jewish origin was a birth deformity corrected by a baptismal operation.

A peculiar character, and likewise a convert to Christianity, was Leopold Julius Klein (1804–75), a linguistic genius, poet, and literary historian. Born in Miskolc, he studied there and in Pest and earned his M.D. at the University of Vienna but never practiced medicine. At the inauguration of Count Adam Reviczky as *főispán* (lord lieutenant) of County Borsod, Klein greeted him with a poem written in nine languages: Hungarian, German, English, French, Italian, Spanish, Latin, Greek, and Hebrew. Subsequently, he studied art history in Italy, and started writing plays. He was still a young man when he converted (prior to 1830), after which he became a tutor for families of several Hungarian princes and counts. When his mother died of sorrow over his conversion, he wrote seven sonnets in her memory (published in Miskolc in 1830). He moved to Berlin, where he lived in seclusion, suffering constant hardships while producing tragedies, the first of which was *Concini* (1841), whose title he later changed to *Maria von Medici*. His tragedy *Kavaliers und Arbeiter* (1850), inspired by the 1844 revolt of the Silesian workers, was the first serious attempt in German drama to portray the proletariat and the new problems created by the Industrial Revolution. Klein's real claim to fame is his fifteen-volume *Geschichte des Dramas* (1865–76), a general history of drama up to Shakespeare, which was a landmark in the history of aesthetics. His own plays were collected in seven volumes in his *Dramatische Werke* (1871–72). Although he had nothing to do with Hungary or Hungarian literature, the prestigious Hungarian Academy of Sciences elected him a member in 1869.

Yet another Hungarian Jewish author who converted to Christianity was Karl Beck (1817–79). Although he spent the twenty most creative years of his life abroad—he lived from 1835 to 1855 in Vienna and Leipzig—and wrote all his works in German, his writings were suffused with the Hungarian national spirit. His lyric poem *Janko the Hungarian Horseherd* depicted the life of the Hungarian *csikós*. His play *Saul* was performed in Pest, and his novels achieved great popularity. His contemporaries regarded him as an enthusaist and dreamer, an exponent of true Hungarian inclinations and feelings, a poet of rich imagination, with an overstrung, restless temperament, a stormer of the gates of heaven, a Hungarian (actually German) Byron, and he was generally loved, esteemed, and even revered.

Márton Diósy (1818–92), of whom we shall hear more in chapter 25 as the editor of the *First Hungarian Jewish Calendar and Yearbook*, was the first Hungarian Jewish author to write all his works in Hungarian. His play *Old Arszlán and His Son* was performed at the Hungarian National Theater in 1844. The same theater also performed his Hungarian translation of the play *Don Cesar de Bazan* and published it in its Library of Plays. During the 1848 Hungarian War of Liberation Diósy was Lajos Kossuth's secretary. After the revolution he emigrated to England and became a wine merchant, but he maintained an interest in promoting British-Hungarian relations and even published a series of articles in the Hungarian periodical *Gazdasági Lapok* (Economic Papers, 1861–69) on the Hungarian wine business in England.

Adolf Dux (b. Pressburg, 1822; d. Budapest, 1881) studied law and philosophy at the University of Vienna and became chief contributor of the *Pressburger Zeitung* and, from 1855, correspondent of the *Pester Lloyd*. Although he lived in Vienna, his interest in Hungarian literature and poetry persisted, and he translated into German the poems of Sándor Petőfi and Joseph Eötvös and the drama *Bánk Bán* by Katona. His feuilletons were published in several volumes.

A foreign-born Jewish author who lived for several years in Hungary and, though he wrote in German, devoted much of his writing to Hungarian subjects was Leopold Kompert (b. Munchengraetz, Bohemia, 1822; d. Vienna, 1886). He was editor of the Pressburg German-language literary periodical *Pannonia*, in which he published his first articles on the Hungarian scene; *Pannonia*'s strongly Hungarian patriotic stance brought about its suspension in 1848. The most successful of his novels was titled *Roman der Puszta* (*puszta* is the Hungarian equivalent of the prairie). He was an enthusiastic supporter of the 1848 revolution, but, disappointed by the anti-Jewish outbreaks that accompanied it in Hungary, he wrote an article urging the oppressed and plundered Jews to emigrate to the United States. Kompert himself settled in Vienna after the revolution, and continued to produce a series of novels on Jewish life, which were widely acclaimed. He was also co-editor of the journal *Neuzeit* with Simon Szántó, a Hungarian Jew. Two editions of his collected writings were published in 1882 and 1906.

Editors and Journalists

It was during the decade preceding the 1848 Hungarian revolution that Hungarian Jews began to work as newspaper editors. The first of them was Zsigmond Saphir (1806–66), who edited the *Pester Tageblatt* from 1839 to 1845, the poetry annual *Iris* in 1840–41 (with Count Majláth), and later the weekly *Pester Sonntagszeitung*. He was followed by Herman Klein, who in 1842 launched the German-language literary journal *Der Ungar*. In 1846, the painter Vilmos Beck edited in Pest the first comic periodical, titled *Der Zeitgeist*. Lipót (Leopold) Jeiteles (Jeitteles; b. Prague, 1812; d. Arad, 1871) edited in Arad the liberal journal *Der Patriot*, devoted to politics and belles lettres, and he contributed his own poems to it. After the Hungarian surrender of 1849 he escaped into the mountains but was apprehended and was set free only after a long and painful imprisonment. Upon his return to Arad he edited the *Arader Zeitung*.

An author who lived in both Hungary and other countries was Adolf Neustadt (b. Prague, 1812; d. Vienna, ?). He started his career as a journalist in Vienna but suffered harassment from the authorities because of his radical views, so he moved to Pressburg, where he contributed to Leopold Kompert's *Pannonia*. Moving on to Pest, in 1839 he joined the staff of Zsigmond Saphir's *Pester Tageblatt*. After acquiring Hungarian citizenship, Neustadt became editor of the *Pressburger Zeitung*, one of whose contributors was Count István Széchenyi. The anti-Austrian tone of his paper again brought down the wrath of the Viennese police on Neustadt's head, but Baron Joseph Eötvös extended him his protection, which enabled him to continue his work of preparing the ground for the revolution. He was one of the main sources for politicians and journalists abroad who wanted information about political developments in Hungary. His strongly nationalist position brought about the suspension of his paper by Chancellor Metternich (who was in charge of Austrian foreign policy from 1809 to 1848). In 1848, when the mob attack on the Pressburg Jewish quarter took place, Neustadt moved back to Vienna, then went on to Prague, Italy, the Levant, England, and France. Returning to Vienna, he edited the *Österreichische Zeitung* and took active part in the leadership of the Viennese Jewish community. His early books, published in Hungary, included *Die erste Eisenbahn in Ungarn* (1840) and *Litteratur und Kunst in Ungarn* (1843). Among the books he published abroad were *Aus dem Leben eines Honveds* (on the life of a Hungarian soldier), *Maissim und Schnokes* (on Jewish books), and *Das Gebahren der Österreichischen Creditanstalt*.

Six years younger than Neustadt, R. Jacob Steinhardt (b. Makó, 1818; d. Arad, 1885) was the first Hungarian Jew to edit a Hungarian-language periodical. Its title was *Hirnök* (Messenger), and it was a modest mimeographed news bulletin in which he reported on the proceedings of the 1843 Diet of Pressburg. After the death of R. Aaron Chorin (1844), Steinhardt was elected chief rabbi of Arad, which post he filled for forty years. At the 1868 Hungarian Jewish Congress he was a leader of the Progressive Party, and played an important role in the establishment of the rabbinical seminary in Budapest. He became known all over the country for his outstanding oratory in Hungarian and German, and many of his sermons appeared in print.

An editor, writer, politician, and important public figure was Ede (Eduard) Horn, whom we met above under his original name, Ignác Einhorn (b. Vágujhely, 1825; d. Budapest, 1875). His parents planned a rabbinical career for him, and he studied in the yeshivas of Nyitra, Pressburg, and Prague before moving on to the University of Pest. While still in his early twenties, he was one of the founders of the Israelite Magyarizing Society, published a pamphlet titled *Zur Judenfrage in Ungarn*, founded a radical Jewish Reform congregation in whose temple he was the first preacher, and edited the short-lived weekly *Der ungarische Israelit*, in which he advocated religious reform. In 1848 the twenty-three-year-old Einhorn became co-editor with Marton Diósy and Mór Szegfy of the *First Hungarian Jewish Calendar and Yearbook*. He participated enthusiastically in the Hungarian revolution, gave rousing speeches, and served as military chaplain in the army of Gen. George Klapka. After the defeat of the Hungarian uprising in 1849 he had to flee the country, seeking refuge in Leipzig, where he devoted himself to literary work. It was during his Leipzig sojourn that he Magyarized his name. In 1851 he published a treatise on Kossuth, the great Hungarian revolutionary leader, whereupon the Austrian-dominated Hungarian government demanded his extradition. Horn fled to Brussels, where he remained until 1855, producing a number of studies in the field of political economy. In that year, on the occasion of the first Exposition Universelle, a German paper sent him as its correspondent to Paris, where he stayed on, becoming a contributor to the *Journal des Débats* and participating in 1863 in the foundation and editing of *L'Avenir*. In 1867 he received the Grand Prix of the French Academy for his study *L'économie politique avant les physiocrates*. Having become famous as a political economist, he was called home several times, and did actually return in 1869. He was elected to the Diet of Pressburg and settled in Budapest, where he edited the short-lived *Neuer Freier Lloyd*. In 1875, shortly before his death, he was appointed undersecretary of state for commerce in the Hungarian government. The city of Budapest honored him by naming a street after him.

Ede Horn remained Jewish all his life, but his life history nevertheless shows a certain conformity with the pattern of emigration or conversion that emerges from all these thumbnail biographies. He achieved recognition and honors in Hungary after, and probably in consequence of, his successes as an economic writer abroad, where he spent the most productive twenty years of his life. While he himself never converted, his brother, the economic writer Antal Horn, and his sons Emil Horn, a historian and banker, and Ödön Horn, an author of military writings, each of whom also spent considerable parts of his life abroad, all became Christians.

The above sampling of early Hungarian Jewish writers and editors—and it is definitely only a sampling—is indicative of the trend that was to remain characteristic of the literary careers of talented and ambitious Hungarian Jews until the days of the Second World War: a remarkably high proportion of them found the Hungarian language and the Hungarian cultural and social ambience too confining and so tended to leave the "fatherland," to write in one of the great European languages, and also to convert to Christianity. This phenomenon was paralleled by similar ones in the fields of the arts and sciences, to which we now turn.

Artists and Scholars

The prerevolutionary decades were also the time when Hungarian Jews started to work in the arts. As with several of the writers and journalists discussed above, these early Hungarian Jewish artists also frequently achieved recognition not in Hungary but abroad. The earliest among them was the sculptor Joseph Engel (b. Sátoraljaujhely, 1815; d. Budapest, 1901), who started out as a student of R. Moshe Sofer in Pressburg but had to leave the yeshiva because the master would not countenance his also busying himself with wood carving. Engel went to Vienna, where he became an apprentice to a wood sculptor and showed such talent that in 1834 he received a scholarship from Cardinal Schwarzenberg, which enabled him to study at the Viennese Academy of Fine Arts. In 1837 he continued his studies in Paris, and in 1838 he moved to London, where he became a protégé of the Hungarian ambassador, Prince Paul Eszterházy; received support from Sir David Salomons, the (Jewish) lord mayor of London; and executed busts of Queen

Victoria and Prince Albert, the latter also commissioning several other works from him. From London he went on to spend twenty years in Rome (1846–66), during which he became a favored portraitist of the international aristocracy, including several crowned heads. While in London and Rome he created his major works in the classicist spirit, including *The Amazons' Fight with the Argonauts, Apollo and the Horae, Achilles and the Body of Penthesilea, The Awakening Eve, Amor Recumbent, Before the Hunt,* and *After the Hunt.* In 1866 he won first prize in the competition for the Széchenyi memorial statue, prompting him to return to Pest. Some years later he also won the competition for the sitting figures of the base of that monument (Minerva, Neptune, Vulcan, and Ceres) and the gold medal of the 1873 Viennese World Exposition. Following these successes, his star began to set, and even though he still won the bronze medal at the Paris Exposition of 1899, by that time he had practically ceased working, and in light of the incipient naturalistic-realistic trends that became dominant in the art world in the late nineteenth century, his whole oeuvre came to be considered representative of an earlier, outmoded classicism.

Another Hungarian Jewish sculptor who was a contemporary of Engel but died tragically in his early forties was Jacob Guttman (b. Arad, 1815; d. Döbling, 1858 or 1861). When he was thirteen, his destitute parents apprenticed him to a gunsmith. Five years later, upon completing his apprenticeship, he went on foot to Vienna and there found employment with the gunsmith Marton Meyer, who also taught him carving. A year later he started working as an independent master carver, and that same year he exhibited, at the Viennese Exposition of Industrial Arts, a weapon he had decorated with carvings depicting the procession of the Argonauts. This work caught the attention of Metternich, who was so impressed that he awarded young Guttman a scholarship to the Viennese Academy of Fine Arts. In 1841 Guttman submitted to the exhibition of the Academy a bust of Metternich, a wax statue of the mythical Paris, and a plaque portrait of the Emperor Joseph II, likewise in wax. In 1843, on the basis of a picture, he sculpted a bronze bust of Salomon Mayer Rothschild (1774–1855), the powerful head of the Viennese House of Rothschild, who was friendly with Metternich. When this work was brought to Rothschild's attention by his secretary, Leopold Wertheimstein, Rothschild granted Guttman an annual fellowship of one thousand florins to enable him to continue his studies in Rome. Guttman showed his gratitude by executing a coat of arms of the House of Rothschild (1844). He also made a bust of the satirist Moritz Gottlieb Saphir. He spent five years in Rome (1845–50), where he became friendly with Joseph Engel and two other Hungarian sculptors who worked there at the same time.

Guttman was a diligent correspondent, and the letters he wrote from Rome to his friends and relatives paint a fascinating picture of the artistic and other attractions of the Eternal City, including the life of the Jewish ghetto. It was in Rome that Guttman created most of the statues that won the admiration of his contemporaries, including his *Moses, Samson and Delilah, Psyche and Amor, The Genius, The Statue of the Youth, The Little Girl,* and the *Tomb of R. Aaron Chorin.* In 1848, commissioned by the Naples House of Rothschild, he executed a marble bust of Pope Pius XI whose original is in the Museum of fine Arts in Budapest, while thousands of copies were purchased by art lovers in Italy. The success of the bust of the pope prompted Rothschild to commission Guttman with the execution of five reliefs depicting the revolution. At the same time, Guttman also created a statue group in which he presented the life of the pope, showing *The Conclave, The Mission of the Pope, His First Act,* and *The Uprising of the People and Its Consequences.* All these works are lost, and we know of them only from Guttman's letters.

Between 1850 and 1852 Guttman was back in Pest, then went on to London, where he stayed about a year and a half. In one of his letters from London he mentions selling a statue titled *Peasant with the Plough.* In 1853, disappointed with the British capital, he moved to Paris, where, among other works, he executed a group titled *Ceres: Faith, Hope, and Love* (whereabouts unknown). While in Paris, Guttman fell in love with the great French tragic actress Rachel, and his unrequited passion led to a mental breakdown. He was brought back to Pest in 1857 and a year later was admitted to the Döbling mental institution, where he died soon after.

Another Hungarian Jewish artist of the period who during his very short lifespan achieved extraordinary successes was the graphic artist Joseph Tyroler (b. Alsókubin, 1822; d. Pest, 1854). At the age of fifteen he was sent as an apprentice to Pest, where a music publisher employed him as a draftsman-illustrator. He rapidly learned the arts of lithography, wood engraving, and copper plate etching and within a short time became one of the two most sought-after illustrators of Hungarian and German magazines. His portraits of the royal couple, Palatine Archduke Joseph, Lajos Kossuth, poet Sándor Petőfi, composer Franz Liszt, Hungarian kings and heroes, and others won him wide acclaim. A specialty of his creative work was caricature, which he pioneered in Hungary and which greatly contributed to his popularity. During the revolution he was entrusted with preparing the plates for the Kossuth banknotes, for which illicit activity he was imprisoned by the Austrian authorities and was released only after intervention by people of influence.

While in the visual arts the work of many Hungarian Jewish artists in this period was of major significance within the general Hungarian and even European context, in the vocal arts there was only one Hungarian Jewish artist whose contribution truly stands out from a historical perspective. He was Mark Rózsavölgyi (originally Marcus Rosenthal; b. Balassagyarmat, 1787; d. Pest, 1848), who did more than any other Hungarian musician or composer until Bartók and Kodály to give an art form to traditional Hungarian folk music. Young Marcus worked as salesman, but already in his youth he tried to write out Hungarian dance melodies, and he was the first to compose *csárdás* music. His very first public appearance was such a success that he set out right away on a concert tour all over the country. In 1814 he settled in Baja, and in 1819 in Pest. He got a contract from the Hungarian National Theater in 1837, but shortly thereafter he left the theater to be able to accept the frequent invitations he received to give concerts. On his concert tours he performed exclusively his own compositions based on Hungarian folk melodies. When he died, Sándor Petőfi bid him farewell in a beautiful poem. His compositions were collected and published by his son, Gyula Rózsavölgyi, who was the founder and owner of the most important Hungarian music publishing house.

The peak period of the scholarly and scientific achievements of Hungarian Jews did not start until the early twentieth century, but their contribution to many areas of science and scholarship began almost a full century earlier. Likewise, the tendency of the early-twentieth-century Hungarian Jewish scientists and scholars to emigrate and pursue their work abroad was already evident in the first half of the 1800s. Another characteristic of the Hungarian Jews' move into academic disciplines was that their interest was about evenly divided between Jewish and secular studies. We must confine ourselves to mentioning only a very few of these many scholars.

The earliest of them was David Mandelli (original name Mandel; b. Pressburg, ca. 1780; d. Paris, 1836), whom his contemporaries considered the greatest philologist of his age. At the age of twelve his parents sent him to Rajka, County Moson, to study Talmud, but he was a student in Prague by 1799 and by next year in Berlin, at the university. From 1805 he worked as a tutor in Offenbach, until he saved enough money to go to Paris, which he did by walking all the way. (Such long-distance walks from city to city were undertaken, as we shall see in chapter 30, by other young Hungarian Jews as well.) In Paris he supported himself by giving lessons in mathematics and Arabic. In 1822 the French government entrusted him with cataloging the rare oriental manuscripts and books in the Bibliothèque Nationale, with an annual stipend of 1,800 francs. Mandelli accomplished the huge task within a month, and after taking his salary for that single month only he resigned, and thereafter lived the life of an ascetic in the cellars of the Arsenal, subsisting only on vegetables. He wrote his mathematical notes on slate tables, which he erased after solving a problem.

The French linguists unanimously admired his phenomenal knowledge of languages and considered him a greater master than the famous Italian philologist Cardinal Giuseppe Mezzofanti, who was reputed to have spoken fifty languages. One day Mandelli walked down to the Seine, barefoot, to draw some water in a jar, lost his balance, fell into the river, and drowned. The journals of the world noted his passing in obituary articles, and in the French Academy the famous poet, writer, and critic Charles Nodier gave the memorial address in his honor.

An early Hungarian Jewish representative of the scholarly movement known as *Wissenschaft des Judentums* (scientific study of Judaism) was Lipót, or Leopold, Dukesz (b. Pressburg, 1810; d. Vienna, 1891), a cousin of Adolf Dux (see above). He studied at the yeshivas of Pressburg and Würzburg and devoted himself to the history of medieval Hebrew literature. He spent years working in the important libraries of Central Europe, where he discovered formerly unknown Hebrew and Jewish manuscripts and edited them with scholarly annotations. His work opened up treasures of medieval Hebrew literature and was applauded by both Jewish and Christian Hebraists. His books include studies of Hebrew poets, Rashi, Moses ibn Ezra, the language of the Mishna, Solomon ibn Gabirol, Hebrew exegetes, grammarians and lexicographers, and so on. He contributed papers to *The Orient* and to *Ben Chanania*, edited by Leopold Löw (see above, chapter 23).

A Hungarian Jew who made a noteworthy career in Paris, though more as a fighter for Jewish rights than as a scholar, was Albert Cohn (b. Pressburg, 1814; d. Paris, 1877). He studied in Vienna, specialized in oriental languages, became fluent in Arabic, Hebrew, German, French, and Italian, and moved to Paris in 1836. There he became a tutor to the Rothschild family and then was put in charge of the philanthropic works of James de Rothschild. He reorganized the Paris Jewish community and became its president. From 1845 on he fought for the interests of Algerian Jewry, and reported on its condition to King Louis Philippe. In 1860 he visited Morocco, obtaining for its Jews the protection of Spain's Gen. Prim. He visited Palestine five times, each time in connection with the protection of the Jews, and promoted the establishment of Jewish hospitals in Jaffa and Jerusalem. From 1860 to 1876 he taught at the Rabbinical Seminary of Paris and was a member of the central committee of the Alliance Israélite Universelle. One of his achievements was the improvement of the legal status of the Jews in the Ottoman Empire. In a sense, in intervening with crowned heads in the interest of the Jews, he was a forerunner of Theodor Herzl, the founder of political Zionism. He also wrote various scholarly and religious works.

A Hungarian Jew of a very different ilk was Mór Ballagi (originally Móric Bloch; b. Inóc, County Zemplén, 1815; d. Budapest, 1891), who not only spent much of his life abroad and converted to Christianity but also purposely alienated himself from Judaism and identified himself emotionally with Protestantism. A son of destitute parents, young Móric was introduced to the Bible and Talmud by his father, then studied in the yeshivas of Nagyvárad and Pápa. While making a living as a tutor in Jewish families in Mór and Surány, he began to take an interest in Greek and Latin, as well as modern European languages. In 1837 he went to Pest, studied mathematics at the University, and began to contribute patriotic articles to the *Pester Tageblatt*. Since a Jew could not earn a diploma in Hungary, Bloch went in 1839 to Paris, and while studying there wrote a pamphlet, "A zsidókról" (On the Jews, published in Pest in 1840), in which he advocated Jewish emancipation. This treatise caught the attention of Baron Joseph Eötvös, the great liberal leader of Hungarian reform, who called him back home and asked him to urge the Jews to Magyarize and to foster Hungarian literature. Ballagi returned and published in 1840–41 an annotated Hungarian translation of the Pentateuch, which earned him election as a corresponding member of the Hungarian Academy of Sciences. Within the next two years he published several more books (in Hungarian and German) on Jewish and Hungarian subjects, including a Jewish prayer book (1841). He won Count István Széchenyi's support for his idea of establishing a Jewish teacher training college but, disappointed by the lack of Jewish response, he again left Hungary and went to Tübingen, Germany, where he studied with the foremost Protestant theologians of the age. In 1843, in Notzingen, he converted to the Evangelical and later to the Protestant Reformed religion. Returning to Hungary in 1844, he became a fervent fighter for Protestantism and made a meteoric career as a professor at Protestant theological schools, secretary to general Görgey, and a high official in the Hungarian Ministry of War. Above all, however, he became the foremost intellectual representative and spokesman of Hungarian Protestantism. He also founded and edited the *Protestant Scientific Review* (in Hungarian) and authored scholarly studies on Protestantism and the Hungarian language, a Hebrew grammar, and so on.

The last scholar we can mention in this highly selective series of sketches is one whose lasting fame rests on his biographical lexicon of Hungarian Jews. Ignác Reich (b. Zsámbék, 1822; d. Budapest, 1887) studied in the yeshiva and later the high school (*gimnázium*) of Nagy-várad, and served from 1851 as teacher of religion for the Israelite Congregation of Pest, introducing the teaching of the subject in Hungarian. He wrote poetry, translated into Hebrew Ferenc Kölcsey's national anthem, and contributed articles to various Jewish periodicals, His volume of Hungarian poems, *Honszerelmi Dalok* (Songs of Love of the Fatherland), was published in Buda in 1848. In 1872–73 he published two volumes titled *Besz-Lechem, Jahrbuch zur Beförderung des Ackerbaues, des Handwerks und der Industrie unter den Israeliten Ungarns.* By far the most important of his works is his *Besz-El: Ehrentempel verdienter ungarischer Israeliten,* five volumes of which were published in Pest in 1856–65. This rich collection of biographies of Hungarian Jews is indispensable to this day for any study of Hungarian Jewish history.

Physicians and Lawyers

The law 1790:XXXVIII, "De Judaeis" made academic careers accessible to the Jews of Hungary, and of all the specializations it was medicine that attracted them most. Medical students, at the end of their university studies, had to write a thesis, in Latin, in order to earn the M.D. degree. The printed medical dissertations (preserved in the Hungarian National Library in Budapest) constitute a record of the extent to which members of the young Hungarian Jewish generation entered the field of medicine in 1820–40. In those twenty years, eighty or more medical dissertations were written by Hungarian Jews. In the remaining eight years until the 1848 revolution, another fifty Hungarian Jews entered the field of medicine, several of them engaging also in medical research. Here we have the actual beginnings of the movement into medicine by Hungarian Jews which in the late nineteenth and early twentieth century led to a domination of Hungarian medicine by Jews.

Jews became active also in providing medical and related services to the public and founding hospitals, clinics, and other institutions serving the public welfare. The ophthalmologist Dr. Frigyes Grosz (1798–1858) founded in 1830 a hospital for eye diseases in Nagyvárad; Móric Mauksch (1806–48) established in Liptószentmiklós the first Jewish institution for the deaf-mute; in 1825 Rafael Kastenbaum of Sátoraljaujhely left in his will 20,000 forints for a municipal hospital and 100,000 forints for the establishment of a Jewish school "so that the Jews should become educated." In 1841, the Jewish Hospital of Pest was opened. Founded in 1846, at the initiative of Manó (Emanuel) Kanitz, was the Mercantile Society for Pension and Care of the Sick, whose hospital was later reorganized by Jacob Kern. Hungarian Jews established the first sick fund in the country, in which medical care was provided by several of the dozens of doctors who by that time practiced in Pest.

As in many other fields, so too in medicine, some of its most outstanding practitioners of Hungarian Jewish birth made their careers not in Hungary but abroad. We shall hear later (chapter 30) of Max Nordau, one of the most famous representatives of this group (although his fame rested not on his medical work but on his sociological studies). One of the earliest of these doctors was Louis Mandl (b. Pest, 1812; d. Paris, 1881), who started studying philosophy, astronomy, and medicine in Vienna, then returned to Pest, earned his M.D., and in 1836 moved to Paris. There he became a highly sought physician, a teacher of physiology and anatomy at the Collège de France, and a member of the leading scholarly societies of Europe, including the medical societies of Paris, Munich, Vienna, Naples, and Pest. In 1846 he was elected a member of the Hungarian Academy of Sciences. He edited the *Archives d'Anatomie* and published important medical studies in it, as well as a series of books on anatomy, microscopy, and blood analysis, which made his name familiar in medical circles all over Europe.

In contrast to medicine, in which Hungarian Jews began to shine in the prerevolutionary decades, they entered the field of law relatively late. In 1853 the Hungarian Ministry of Justice rejected the application of a Jewish candidate to sit for the bar examination, but three years later, responding to a question by the University of Pest, it stated that there was no law that would prevent Jews from becoming lawyers. In 1858 one Jewish lawyer settled in Nyitra and another in Kassa, but in 1861 the Royal Court of Appeals decided to permit no more Jews to sit for the law examination. The Jewish law students who had completed their studies at the University of Pest thereupon appealed to the court chancellery, to the Supreme Court, and finally to the Emperor Francis Joseph himself, requesting a reversal of the decision. The Emperor did not annul the decision but did grant several candidates the royal privilege of practicing law. On this basis, from 1861 on, several Jews practiced as lawyers in Hungary, while others contributed significantly to the development of legal literature, edited law journals, filled high posts in the Ministry of Justice, and taught at the universities and legal academies. A high percentage of them converted to Christianity.

Industrialists and Merchants

In would burst the covers of a survey history of the Jews in Hungary to tell in detail about their early participation in the industrialization of the country, but the broad picture of Jewish life in prerevolutionary Hungary would not be complete without a few general observations on their share in developing various industries in what was in the early nineteenth century a largely agricultural economy.

In chapter 19, mention was made of the unsuccessful joint attempt by Jacob Simon and five Jewish partners to establish an oil factory in Trencsén in 1755. The Jewish laws issued in 1781 and 1783 by Joseph II had opened a small door through which Jews could enter the fields of industry, although even after that Jewish manufacturers were not admitted into the guilds and hence could sell their products only to other Jews. The legal situation did not change with the 1790 "De Judaeis" law, and only in 1840 did a new law permit the Jews to "engage in manufacture either with their own hands or with the help of journeymen of their own religion." This law encouraged the Israelite Congregation of Pest to establish, in 1842, the Pest Society for the Spreading of Heavy Handicraft and Agriculture Among the Israelites, which soon thereafter was renamed the Hungarian Israelite Handicraft and Agricultural Society, known by the Hungarian acrostic as MIKÉFE. Its program comprised four points, which combined practical, patriotic, and ethical purposes: first, the practice of heavy handicrafts and branches of industry; second, the fostering of the Hungarian language; third, the practice of agriculture; and fourth, the dissemination of useful knowledge and pure morals. Immediately upon its establishment, MIKÉFE participated in the founding of the Hungarian National Industrial Society. The first graduate of MIKÉFE was a Jewish locksmith who obtained his master's license in 1846, and in the following year the society provided ten Jewish youths with training in agriculture.

Despite considerable opposition on the part of the Christian guilds, by the early 1840s Jewish entrepreneurs began to establish factories. The earliest among them was the dye factory of Samuel Goldberger and Sons, which, although founded as early as in 1785, only became an important plant with large-scale production in the 1840s. In 1837 Bernát (Albert) Mandel founded the first steam mill of Hungary, and later he was the first to introduce the use of mechanical harvesters, steam-driven threshing machines, and chemical fertilizers, in working the estates he rented in County Szabolcs. Another important first by Mandel was establishing and maintaining a school for the children of agricultural workers.

Still in the first half of the nineteenth century, Jews founded a sugar factory in Tata and established opal mines in Vörösvágás. Móric Fischer founded the porcelain factory of Herend, which represented an entirely new industrial branch in the country and whose products won the bronze medal of the first Hungarian Industrial Exposition in 1842 and the gold medal in 1847 and became famous abroad as well. Also in the 1840s, the brothers Simon, Bernard, and Max (Miksa) Neuschloss established a wholesale timber and carpentry business, which they transformed in 1860 into the First Hungarian Parquetry Factory of Pest.

The industrial activities of the Jews were greatly facilitated by the 1851 Law by which the Viennese government provided that nobody could be excluded from practicing commerce and industry because of his religion, his nationality, or his parents' status. When this edict was first issued, the tailors' guilds of Pest and Buda requested its withdrawal, arguing that it threatened the interests of the Catholic faith, but upon the suggestion of the commercial and industrial chambers themselves the law was passed and definitively eliminated all religious discrimination. Subsequently, small-scale industries among the Jews developed to such an extent that when the building of the great Dohány Street synagogue began in the 1850s, the iron- and brassworks for it were done by Jewish artisans.

A Jewish industrialist who became the founder of a city in Hungary deserves special mention. Isaac Lőwy (1793–1847) studied in his youth in various yeshivas, and in 1823 took over the leather factory founded by his father in Nagysurány. Since he was constantly harassed because of his Jewishness in the neighboring city of Érsekujvár, the main outlet for his products, he decided to move his factory to Pest. However, a Jewish industrialist could get no permit at the time to settle in Pest, and hence Lőwy, in 1835, conceived the idea of founding a new town next to Pest and locating his factory there. He purchased a large, totally bare tract of land north of Pest from the Count Károlyi family and included in the deed the right of full religious freedom, the right to engage in industry, and the right of self-government. After building his factory and home on the tract, he gave the new quarter the name of Ujpest (New Pest), and this is how he had his mail addressed. He and his workers were the first inhabitants of the new town, and they soon formed a congregation that grew rapidly as the town developed. By 1839 they built themselves a synagogue for which the landowner family donated the land, and in 1840 they opened a school and employed a rabbi. By 1870 the congregation counted 1,525 souls; by 1895, 3,500; by 1908, 5,000; and by 1928, 15,000. The new town attracted Christian settlers as well, and soon after its foundation the Jewish and Christian inhabitants elected Isaac Lőwy judge of the new municipality.

Hand in hand with the founding of industries went the Hungarian Jewish effort to introduce modern wholesale establishments. By the early 1840s no fewer than 120 Jewish wholesale merchants were active in Pest, several of them forming the Association of Israelite Merchants. Two of them, Fröhlich and Ullmann, were elected members of the steering committee of the National Society for the Protection of Industry, founded in 1844, with Count Gábor Keglevich as president and Count István Széchenyi as vice-president. Members of this society had to promise to purchase nothing but Hungarian-produced merchandise for six years.

In 1842 the Christian and Jewish merchants of Pest jointly petitioned the palatine for a permit to establish an association of licensed royal wholesalers, to which members would be admitted without distinction of religion. The civic merchants of Pest objected, but after a delay of three years the association was approved by Emperor Ferdinand V.

Financiers and Bankers

The development of commerce and industry was accompanied by a growing need for modern financial methods, an important part of which was the utilization of deferred payment techniques in the form of promissory notes, or bills of exchange, as negotiable instruments. By 1840 the Jewish participation in issuing, accepting, discounting, and redeeming IOUs was such an important part of financial activity in Hungary that the government found it necesssary to regulate the days on which the Jews could not be asked to perform such transactions because they were religious holidays for them. Law 1840:XV, which deals with the subject, is titled "On Acceptation in General and on Honoration in Particular," and all of it, after a brief reference to Christians, deals with Jews. It reads (with the original spelling of the Hebrew terms retained):

54. The Christians on Christian Holidays and Sundays, the Israelites on Saturdays and on their holidays enumerated in the next paragraph, are not obliged to present bills, nor to make a declaration concerning their acceptance; if therefore the last day of the time limit falls on such a day, the presentation or the declaration about its acceptance can be postponed to the next workday.

55. In addition to the weekly Sabbath, the holidays of the Israelites are as follows:

a. Pessach [Passover]: Easter, that is, the feast of unleavened bread, on days 15, 16, 21, and 22 of the month of Nison, usually in the month of St. George; the intervening days 17, 18, 19, and 20 are half-holidays, on which presenting and declaring concerning acceptance not only is possible but is a duty.

b. Schebuos: Pentecost, that is, the feast of the first-born [sic], on the sixth and seventh day of Sivon, usually in the month of Pentecost.

c. Rosch-Haschana: the feast of the New Year, on the first and second day of the month of Tischri; commonly in the month of St. Michael.

d. Yom Kipur: the feast of reconciliation, ten days after the feast of the New Year.

e. Sukes (Lauberhütten): the feast of booths, on the fifteenth and sixteenth day of the month of Tischri, in the month of All Saints.

f. Schmini Azeres: The feast of the Ten Commandments, on the twenty-second day of the month of Tischri.

g. Simchas-Tora: the feast of joy, on the twenty-third day of the same month.

56. On the days preceding Saturday or the feast days enumerated in the preceding paragraph, the Israelite is obliged to declare concerning acceptance only until three o'clock in the afternoon.

This law is interesting on several counts. It shows, first of all, that the Jewish participation in the promissory note business was so substantial that special laws had to be passed about it; it also shows that the Jews observed the Sabbath and thirteen annual holidays to the extent of refusing to transact money business on those days; and finally, it shows that the legislators were aware of the Jewish custom of celebrating holidays beginning with the afternoon of the day preceding them. Evidently, while the Jews did not enjoy equal rights as citizens, the business world took their religious observances into account.

Within a year of the issuance of this law, the participation of Jews in the Hungarian banking business began. In that year Mór Ullmann, utilizing capital derived from the tobacco trade, founded the Hungarian Bank of Commerce of Pest. Four of the twelve members of the board of the First Hungarian savings Bank of Pest, headed by András Fáy, were Jews.

Limited Rights

The great strides the Jews made in the business, banking, economic, industrial, medical, educational, literary, and scholarly fields, as well as their wholehearted identification with the Magyarization movement and Hungarian patriotism—coupled with the interest of the Magyars in increasing the proportion of Hungarian-speakers in the country (see chapter 25)—were powerful factors that by the mid-1840s convinced the majority of the Hungarian political leadership that the emancipation of the Jews was inevitable and that its achievement was a matter of one or two years at the utmost. This is where things stood when the 1848 revolution broke out. Its defeat by the Austrians practically froze the Hungarian Jewish status quo for almost two decades. Consequently, up to the emancipation of 1867, the Jews of Hungary were forced to live with and under the 1840:XXIX law that granted them limited rights. Its full text reads as follows:

About the Jews

Until the law regulates the condition of the Jews in greater detail, it is herewith resolved:

1. All of those Jews who were born in the country or in the attached Parts, as well as those who in a legal way have obtained permission to live here, unless there is against them a proven well-founded objection as to their moral conduct, can live in the whole country and the attached Parts —excepting only the mining towns mentioned in the Law of 1790:XXXVIII and those places from which they are excluded at present in consideration of the mines and the mining institutions according to ancient custom.

2. Under the existing conditions the Jews can found factories, can practice trades, whether with their own hands or with the help of journeymen of their own religion, and can instruct their young people in them—and can hereafter also practice those sciences and fine crafts which they have practiced until now.

3. In addition, they are obliged to use permanent family names and first names, and to have their newborn registered in registries kept by the clergymen of their faith.

4. Furthermore, they are obliged to compose all documents and contracts in the language that prevails in the fatherland and in the attached Parts.

5. Inasmuch as the Israelites have the practice of freely acquiring civic plots of land (*fundus*), in such cities this practice is established for the future as well.

6. All laws, customs, orders, or decisions contrary to this law are herewith annulled and done away with.

25

The Patriotic Imperative (1800-48)

"Hungarian literary historians used to take special pride in arguing that Hungarian literaure is the record of Hungarian patriotism." While this observation, made in 1990 by historian George Barany, is undoubtedly valid even for earlier times, it was in the half-century preceding the 1848 revolution that the idea and sentiment of Hungarian patriotism became a virtual obsession with the Magyars in Hungary and, under their influence, with the Hungarian Jews. A discussion of why and how this came about would require a special political-psychological study, far exceeding the scope of the present book, but a few factors can nevertheless be mentioned. As a result of the historical and political developments of centuries, while in the central part of the Hungarian state the solid majority was Hungarian, this Hungarian core-territory was surrounded by areas in which the majority was Rumanian, Slovak, Croat, German, Serb, or Ruthenian. All in all, around 1840, of the 12.9 million inhabitants of Hungary only 4.8 million, or ca. 37 percent, were Hungarians. In this ethnic conglomerate the Jews constituted a special case: they were counted neither with the Magyars nor with the other groups.

Moreover, although Hungary enjoyed considerable autonomy, it was subject to Austrian (Habsburg) rule, which, from its seat in the glamorous political and cultural center of Vienna, also held sway over several other provinces with a non-German majority, including Bohemia and Moravia. In this situation, the energetic propagation of Magyar nationalist sentiment came to be considered essential by Hungarian politicians for the double purpose of maintaining Hungary's special status vis-à-vis Vienna and securing Hungarian supremacy over those provinces of the country in which the majority of the population was not Magyar.

A third factor in the emergence of Magyar patriotism was the language situation. Hungarian, until the eighteenth century, was spoken mainly by the peasants, who had the status of serfs, lacked representation in the Diet, and enjoyed no rights. The nobles, who constituted only 5 percent of the total population but who in effect were the exclusive members of the Hungarian *natio*, spoke mostly German, while the official language of communal life, political meetings, and documents was Latin. The political leadership now felt that in order to strengthen the Magyar nation, a feeling of Magyardom had to be inculcated into all layers of the population by making Hungarian the official language of the country (or at least one official language), thus forging a unity of purpose between the nobles and the rest of the people.

This was the background against which emerged the slogan (typically, in Latin) "Extra Hungariam non est vita, si est vita non est ita" (Outside Hungary there is no life; if there is life, it is not the same). This was the age when, as Hungarian literary historians later proudly argued, many Hungarians became obsessed with linguistic nationalism. It was the period of the launching of journals in the Hungarian language—the first was the Pressburg *Magyar Hirmondó* (Hungarian Courier), which became a focus of Hungarian cultural life and energetically propagated literature and scholarship in the Magyar tongue.

Patriotism was seen as the glue that could cement Hungarians of different creeds and make them citizens of the fatherland first and foremost. The Hungarian language was considered identical with Hungarian nationality, and the major means for spreading civilization, and simultaneously Magyar predominance, in the country. This situation inevitably led to the prevalence of Magyar nationalist trends. Those who fought to replace Latin with Hungarian felt that cultural life would thus become more democratic. They did achieve their goal, but at the same time they introduced an ethnocentric provincialism that thereafter was to remain characteristic of Magyardom's outlook.

Every activity deemed important was labeled patriotic, or at least given a patriotic coloration. To improve agriculture, to promote industry, to build canals and bridges, to regulate rivers and drain marshes, to engage in any of the arts or sciences, to write poems, novels, or any other type of literature—all this was done under the rubric of patriotism, and was considered valuable because it promoted the welfare of the fatherland. One could scarcely open a printed page in that period without encountering the claim of patriotism or reference to it. A few examples will have to suffice.

István Kulcsár, editor of *Hazai Tudósitások* (Reports from the Homeland), launched in 1806, summed up his program in 1823: "The foremost ornament of every nation is scientific learning. We must strive for this not only because we can thereby raise our human dignity and enrich our domestic condition, but . . . even more because through the diffusion of sciences in the nation we can make the country's strength more potent, the nation's glory more radiant."

270

The same ideas of enlightened patriotism were put forward by Count István Széchenyi, whom we have already met, whose achievements earned him the designations "the great patriot" and "the greatest Hungarian." In 1825, when he offered one year's income of his estates (60,000 florins) for the foundation of what was to become the Hungarian Academy of Sciences, he said that his purpose was to establish an institution "to propagate the national idiom [Hungarian] and to raise sons worthy of a fatherland like ours." Eventually, in 1830, Széchenyi became the first vice-president of the Academy. In the same year, in his book *Hitel* (Credit), he wrote: "Let us awaken our dear fatherland through purposeful patriotism and loyal unity to a brighter dawn." Again, when Széchenyi, in connection with his Tisza River project, stressed that the Tisza region was the "most Magyar" part of the fatherland, he argued that, this being the case, its welfare should be promoted by every patriot.

One of the few points on which both the neoconservatives, whose leaders included Széchenyi, and the liberal opposition, led by Lajos Kossuth, agreed in preparation for the 1847–48 Pressburg Diet was to stress the claims of Magyar nationality. Each of the two parties based its appeal for the support of the Magyar public on the claim that *it* was the truly patriotic party.

Such was the superpatriotic atmosphere in which the Jews conducted their fight for emancipation. In these circumstances it was almost inevitable that when they wished to demonstrate their deserving of equal rights, they did it by claiming and proclaiming they were as truly and fully Magyar patriots as the Christian Magyars.

In the unceasing declarations of the Magyar patriotism of the Jews, the rabbis played a leading role. They took every opportunity to preach patriotism and faithfulness toward the king and the authorities. As Lajos Venetianer, the historian of the period, remarked, "Without a doubt there was no single Jewish meeting in which, at the appropriate occasions, the rabbis would not have inspired the community to the fulfillment of civic duties and to faithfulness to king and country." Venetianer presents a long list of those sermons and addresses, which survived because they happened to be printed, as examples of this rabbinical exhortation to patriotism. For example, Aaron Chorin, whom we met in chapter 23 as a fighter for Jewish religious reform, gave a sermon in German on March 6, 1793, titled "Memorial Address About the Unfortunate Fate of Louis XVI, with an Appendix on the Love of the Fatherland." Israel Wahrmann (1755–1826), chief rabbi of Pest from 1796, delivered in 1814 a sermon titled "Patriotic Flower for the Victory Celebration of the Israelite Congregation of Pest." Other rabbis preached sermons whose titles described them as "expressions of feelings of joy" and the like, on occasions such as the inauguration of this or that nobleman as a county's *főispán* (lord lieutenant), the investiture of the provost of a chapter, the coronation of a king or queen, a royal jubilee, the conclusion of a Diet, or even the name day of a high official or simply the civil New Year. Almost all of these sermons were preached in German, with a very few in Hebrew or Hungarian.

A favorite subject of rabbinical preachment was Magyarization, meaning, foremost, the replacement of German by the Hungarian language in the synagogue and the schools. The first prayer in Hungarian was offered in 1840 in the synagogue of Szeged by Markfi Henrik Bauer, notary of the congregation. Most fittingly, it was a prayer for king and country. In the same year, R. Löb (Arszlán) Schwab, chief rabbi of Pest, who himself was of Moravian birth and was a student of Moses Sofer of Pressburg, urged (in a German sermon!) Magyarization on the members of his community. Also in 1840, the vice-mayor of Pest reported to the city council that in the city's Jewish school the pupils had made excellent progress in the Hungarian language.

Under the influence of R. Schwab's patriotic sermon, the Jewish students at the medical faculty of the University of Pest founded a society called Pest Society for the Spreading of the Magyar Language Among the Israelites of the Homeland. Its first meeting took place in 1844, and in the *First Hungarian Jewish Calendar and Yearbook*, published in 1848, Márton Diósy (note the Magyarized name), secretary of the society, proudly reported its achievements. He reminded his readers that at the Diet of 1840 the Jews were accused of "un-Hungarianness and unnationalism." While the accusation was not justified, he wrote, the demand of the nation was fair and reasonable, and the Jewry of the Hungarian homeland had hastened to respond to it: since then the Jews had established no fewer than thirty-five Hungarian schools, many Hungarian reading circles, and Magyarizing societies.

> We must prove that to be a Magyar-Jew is not a chimera. After all, Abraham and Árpád were fellow countrymen [?], so why then should their descendants not be able to unite in one idea: nationality. This should be our ultimate goal, so that the achievement of citizenship, which will unfailingly take place, should be given us not as a magnanimous handout but as a well-deserved reward. The purpose of the society is not only to spread the knowledge of the Hungarian language but also to enrich the circle of readers of the products of the Hungarian press, to win the intellectual talents slumbering in the Jews for the literature of our country, to introduce the national spirit into the Jewish public institutions; that is, by strengthening the temple of nationality with a not inconsiderable pillar, to increase as far as possible the factors of civilization in our sweet homeland. For this purpose our society maintains a reading room, a library, a

free Hungarian school, and a kindergarten, and awards prizes to those who excel in acquiring the fatherland's language.

An especially noteworthy development on the Hungarian Jewish scene of the 1840s was the establishment of a connection between patriotism and religious reform. Since a considerable part of the Hungarian political leadership felt that the emancipation of the Jews should be preceded by or contingent upon Jewish religious reform, and since emancipation was the common goal of all Hungarian Jews except the ultraorthodox wing and was considered by both the Hungarian and Jewish leadership a patriotic requirement, the reformers had a powerful weapon at their disposal in claiming the necessity of reform for the patriotic goal of emancipation. This was the political background that made the invocation of patriotism an inevitable ingredient in the program of the reformers.

However, it must be emphasized that the reformers we speak of here were not reformers of the extreme manner of Chorin or Friesenhausen, but very moderate innovators whose aims did not go beyond a few innocuous "improvements" in synagogue services. Their leader was the Moravian-born Löb Schwab, whose Hungarian patriotism and adherence to Magyarization was expressed, among other things, in the fact that in several of his published writings he substituted for his first name Löb ("lion" in German) the Old Hungarian form of the word "lion," Arszlán.

In 1839, at Schwab's initiative, a meeting of the Hungarian Jewish communities took place, in Pest, at which a petition Schwab had prepared was approved, and a committee of twelve was elected for the purpose of submitting it to the counties. This measure was taken in the face of strong opposition by the Pressburg community, under the leadership of the Sofer dynasty.

This is where things stood when Pinkas Horowitz, the conservative rabbi of Pápa, took the initiative in the wake of Kossuth's call for a Jewish Sanhedrin to convene in the city of Paks a Jewish conference to work out an understanding between the adherents and the opponents of religious reform and emancipation. Horowitz got in touch with Leo Hollander, a leading protagonist of the cause of Jewish emancipation (who was to become the quartermaster-general of the Hungarian revolutionary army), and, citing the rights of "science and patriotism," asked his help in convening a "synod," which should create a consistory composed of rabbis and laymen. Invitations were sent out to one hundred rabbis, but because of advance disagreements among the invitees, only twenty-five of them showed up in Paks.

Among those who did put in an appearance was R. Schwab, who represented a moderately reformist point of view, in opposition to Horowitz. He demanded that laymen be included in the rabbinical council to be founded, hoping thereby to ensure that the council not merely function as a sanctioning body but effectively represent the interests of Hungarian Jewry. His purpose was to use education for making the Jews not only religious persons but also good citizens. He called upon the meeting to declare the Jews' devotion as citizens and to proclaim that the Jew loved his fatherland, whose language he considered his native tongue. He urged the publication of Jewish religious textbooks that would contain the public creed of Jewry. However, the disagreements between the modernizers and the conservatives caused the meeting to break up the day after its opening without completing its agenda.

When the winds of the Haskala (The Jewish Enlightenment) reached Hungary and the Jewish literati began to write works of belles lettres in Hebrew and to move into areas of secular subjects, some Hungarian Jews made use of this newly developing facility to express in Hebrew their Hungarian patriotism. One of them was Henrik Jakab Löw, otherwise unknown, who in 1847 published in the Viennese annual *Kokhve Yitzḥaq*, the central organ of the Hebrew Haskala movement, a poem titled "*Ḥezyon haḤofesh*" (Vision of Freedom), which is an enthusiastic outpouring of overwhelming Hungarian patriotic sentiment.

In the 1840s emigration from Hungary to America increased enough to cause concern among the ranks of the Hungarian patriots, who considered leaving the country an unpatriotic act. Among those who spoke out on the issue was the Jewish activist Sándor Herczfeld, who in 1848 published a pamphlet in Hungarian titled "We Don't Go to America, But Shall Stay Here!" He dedicated it "to the great-hearted Herman Klein, editor of the Journal *Ungar*." Herman Klein, as we have heard above, was the first Jewish newspaper editor in Hungary, who launched his literary journal in 1842.

The patriotism of the Hungarian Jews was the basic argument utilized by the Representatives of the Israelite Inhabitants of Hungary and Its Attached Parts in their impassioned petition to the Diet in the summer of 1848:

> Hungarians! Extend a brotherly hand! It is in your interest as well as ours to count on brotherly bosoms. We are the born martyrs of freedom, our ancestors bled to death in their fight for this treasure, and therefore we can appreciate its value. That which the history of 3,000 years proved of our ancestors has been demonstrated by us, too, in the most recent events and in days rich in dangers: that we burn for freedom, that no social class exceeds us in patriotism, that no blow, no misfortune can shake our steadfastness, our perseverance. In attaining the freedom of Europe, our coreli-

gionists fought gloriously in each of its countries—victims also fell from our ranks on the altar of national sovereignty—and even though humiliated, rejected, trampled underfoot, upon hearing the words, "The fatherland is in danger!" many of our brothers entered the maw of death, while a great part of the other nationalities refused to do so, or even allied themselves with the enemy; many [Jews] hastened to contribute with their fortune to meeting the needs of the fatherland, with readiness, with enthusiasm. Convinced of the justice of our cause, we hope that you, too, will be led by justice toward us, by justice that dispenses not mercy, not awkward decrees, not rights and concessions, but equality before the law to all inhabitants without distinction.

Within a few weeks of the submission of this petition, historical events proved the truth of its basic argument. The Hungarian War of Liberation was launched in the fall of 1848, and while other non-Hungarian minorities of the country did not participate in it, the Jews joined the Hungarian army in numbers exceeding several times their proportion in the population (see below, chapter 26). During and after the war, Gen. George Klapka and other leaders of the Hungarian forces offered glowing testimonies about the heroism, self-sacrifice, and exemplary conduct of the Jewish recruits.

The war did not go as the Hungarians hoped it would, and the Diet had to flee to Szeged, a city far removed from the Austrian border. There, Prime Minister Bertalan Szemere in an address to the Diet fully acknowledged the Jewish participation in the fighting, and at the same time urged the recognition in principle of the Jews' equality:

I now imagine Hungary as if its various peoples were gathered around a big table for a repast. The table is loaded with fortune, life, peace, freedom, honor, glory, luck, hope for the future, blessing for the successors. All the peoples of Hungary are around the table, and protect it to the last drop of blood, to death. But aside and apart stands one class of people, which also rose up to the defense of the table loaded with treasures, even though its freedom is not on the table, its honor is not on the table, its rights in whose defense it participates are not among the rights assured on this table, so that it appears that it defends the rights, honor, and freedom of others, nevertheless shedding its blood equally with the others. This class is the social class of the Jews. Gentlemen! If the Jewish people is likewise there on the battlefield, and sheds its blood for a fatherland of which it is not yet a declared citizen, if it sacrificed joyfully its fortune, its life, for a freedom it can only hope for, for rights it does not yet possess while they are possessed by the others who fight alongside it, I do believe that justice requires it that even while the enemy oppresses [the Jewish people] with greater burdens than the other peoples, the time has come that the Diet should no longer postpone the sacred declaration in principle that the Jews, too, are citizens of the fatherland in law, in duty, equal with the others.

The bill, titled "Bill About the Jews," contains the "declaration in principle" that Jews (termed "residents of the Mosaic faith") born in Hungary, or settled in the country legally, have equal rights with the residents who follow any other faith, and that they can legally marry Christians. It also provides that "those of the Mosaic faith should convene an assembly of their clergy and elected representatives, partly in order to declare—or reform—their articles of faith, and partly in order to effect improvements in their future ecclesiastical organization conforming to the wishes of the age," and that "those of the Mosaic faith should be led to the practice of handicrafts and agriculture through suitable rules."

The Diet, without any debate, adopted the bill by acclamation. However, "the sacred declaration of principle" was destined to remain nothing more than a declaration on paper for eighteen years. On August 13, 1849, Görgey surrendered to the Russians, who fought for and with the Austrians, and not only did the Hungarian War of Liberation thereby end in total defeat, but a period of harsh absolutist Austrian rule over Hungary began, which was to last until the 1867 Compromise. In the fall of 1849 the Austrian power imposed a special tax of 2,300,000 florins, a huge fine, on the Jews of Hungary for their support of the Hungarian revolution, so that the first concrete reward the Jews earned for their fervent Hungarian patriotism was to be singled out for special punishment. The payment of this war indemnity meant nothing less than financial ruin for the Jews. The decree of the Viennese Council of Ministers stated that the fine was imposed "because the greatest part of the Israelites living in Hungary promoted, by their feelings and evil manner of acting, the revolution in that country, which without their participation could never have attained such dimensions." In these circumstances, whatever the Hungarian Diet had planned for the Jews had to wait until the Compromise of 1867.

As for the patriotism of the Hungarian Jews, it remained one of the most fundamental traits not only of their overt behavior but also of their culturally inherited character. It was Hungarian Jewish patriotism that was to prove the one major obstacle to the spread of the Zionist movement in Hungary, that was to limit the number of Jewish emigrants from Hungary in the years between the two World Wars when emigration was still possible, and thus was to be ultimately responsible for the presence in the country of some 600,000 Jews in the last few months of World War II, when joint action by the German occupiers and their Hungarian henchmen would exterminate some 500,000 of them.

26

The 1848 Revolution

The year 1848 saw a tide of revolutions against established authority sweep across Europe. On January 12 there was an uprising in Palermo, on January 27 in Naples, and on February 22–23 in Paris. Beginning in March, revolutionary activity and other forms of agitation broke out in the major states of Germany, the Habsburg Empire, and north and central Italy, as well as in Denmark, Sweden, Ireland, and Rumania. Although the revolutionary wave subsided by the end of the year and was finished off by the Austrian forces' defeat of the Venetian Republic and the Hungarian nationalists in August 1849, its impact on the political development of Europe was profound.

The Hungarian revolution, which broke out on March 15, 1848, followed a painful preamble for the Jews of the country. In February of that year, the Diet, sitting in Pressburg, had heard several motions (one of them by Lajos Kossuth) aiming at total or partial emancipation of the Jews. When news of what the Diet was discussing leaked out, as Mihály Horvát, a Hungarian historian of the period, put it: "The prejudiced lower classes of the Pressburg artisans, who had for a long time looked askance at the increase and progress of the capable Israelites, unable to tolerate that the latter should become through this law their equal in rights, attacked the homes of the Jews in enraged bands, destroyed their property, and assaulted their persons with savage violence. Only armed force was able to curb the bloody outbreak of prejudice and hatred born of filthy self-interest."

Within a day or two the anti-Jewish excesses spread to the other cities of Hungary, including Nagyszombat, Vágujhely, Székesfehérvár, Szombathely, and Pest. In view of these events, Kossuth stated on March 20, "One's soul is pained by seeing everywhere in the country the spread of freedom, from which it sees only the Jewish people excluded; but prejudice exists, and against its reality, as the poet said, 'even the gods fight in vain.'" On April 19 a mass meeting was held in Pest, which resolved that, first, one quarter-year's rents should be canceled, because in the eventful month [that passed] there were no earnings; second, the position of the workers must be improved; third, the Jews should be expelled from the country; and fourth, Jews should not be admitted into the National Guard.

Reacting to these outbreaks and demands, the great Hungarian national poet Mihály Vörösmarty, author of one of the two Hungarian national anthems, wrote in the June 4, 1848, issue of the *Pesti Hirlap*: "The blessings of equality and fraternity have left only one people untouched, the Jew, eternal in his sufferings. One thing is sure: that the sacred name of equality has never been a more monstrous lie than now."

Despite these manifestations of anti-Semitism, the Jews of Hungary participated in the popular uprising wholeheartedly and enthusiastically from its very first moment. On March 15 a young Jewish physician addressed the crowds in Pest; the Jewish students of the university volunteered for the National Guard, the president of the Pest Jewish congregation sent a circular letter to all the Jewish congregations of the country urging Jews to demonstrate their gratitude to the nation and joined the delegation of the city of Pest that went to Pressburg to greet the Diet. As Lajos Venetianer writes: "On March 15 the public intoxication was able to enrapture the Jews as well." True, under the impact of the anti-Semitic outbreaks a movement was initiated among the Hungarian Jews aiming at emigration to the free land of America, but within a few weeks its office became a recruiting station for participation in the fight for freedom.

Also in March 1848, the Diet resolved to prepare for its next session "a bill regarding emancipation and the elimination of those obstacles that at present prevent it." Accordingly, at the July session of the Diet, Ödön Kállay, acting upon the application submitted by the representatives of the Israelite Inhabitants of Hungary and Its Attached Parts, introduced this bill: "1. With the publication of the present law all Jews settled in Hungary and the attached Parts are declared equal with the other citizens of this fatherland in civic as well as religious respects. 2. Regarded as settled are all those who paid regular taxes prior to the publication of this law." However, the committees that had to pass the bill recommended that its adoption be made contingent on social and religious reforms within the Jewish community itself and thus effectively postponed its adoption.

In addition to the hesitance of the legislature regarding emancipation, the Jews had to experience other rejections, as well as humiliations, and even physical attacks by various groups whose passions were aroused by the revolutionary atmosphere. This was especially the case in those parts of Hungary inhabited by non-Hungarian minorities, which had little sympathy with the Magyar nationalist endeavor and resented the Jews' enthusiastic support of it. The "Illyrian" propaganda that stirred up anti-Hungarian feelings among the southern Slav population of counties of Bács, Torontál, Arad, and Csongrád contemptuously and threateningly addressed the Jewish inhabitants of those counties: "For what are you so zealous? Perhaps for the Easter of Pressburg and Pest? Be careful! Next time, when you are no longer needed, it will again be your turn!" (The mention of "the Easter of Pressburg and Pest" referred to the anti-Jewish outbreaks that had taken place in those two cities.) The Serbs not only tried to influence the Jews with inciting addresses but, when they saw that words did not shake their Magyar patriotism, resorted to violence and attacked the Jews in village after village. One victim of their brutality was R. Weber of Petrovoszelle, known for his patriotic speeches in many popular meetings: they assaulted him while he was in the midst of his prayers, cut out his tongue, and then hacked him to pieces.

On a different level, but no less painful for the Jews, was the official policy. Even the most liberal legislators hesitated to deal with the Jewish question for fear that any deliberation would fan the fires of anti-Jewish sentiments. Hence, on March 31, Kossuth declared in the Diet, "To legislate now concerning the Jews would be equivalent to throwing masses of this race victims to the fury of their enemies." In the hope of putting an end to the looting, on April 3 the government proclaimed that the legislature did not wish to change the situation of the Jews. The same purpose was supposed to be served by the ruling on April 22 by the Council of Ministers that barred the Jews from becoming members of the National Guard (neither could they join the guilds).

But neither atrocities nor indignities were able to dampen the Jews' enthusiasm for the revolution. When Kossuth appealed (on May 19, 1848) to the generosity of the nation and asked for gifts and loans, "the Jewish congregations, associations, and individuals offered up their ritual objects and fortunes on the altar of the fatherland" (Venetianer's phrasing). In the first days of June the Israelite Congregation of Pest made an offering of 50,000 florins in the form of a loan, and delivered respectable quantities of silver to the treasury. The congregations of other cities followed the Pest example. The Jews likewise took a leading part in establishing, developing, equipping, staffing, and maintaining several hospitals and field hospitals in various cities.

As for active service in the army, Jews flocked to the separate Jewish guard company organized by Michael Táncsics, that self-taught scion of serfs, and by the summer of 1848 one city after the other admitted them to its National Guard. In fact, the number of Jews in the local guard units soon became surprisingly large. By the end of June no less than one-quarter of all members of the National Guard of the city of Pápa were Jewish; in Lovasberény, 62 of the 411 National Guardsmen were Jews. In Székesfehérvár there were 59, in Szombathely 22, in Hódmez-óvásárhely 40, in Arad 120, and in Sátoraljaujhely 100 Jews who fought in the National Guard. As for Pest, it admitted Jews to its guard units only in October 1848, when Gen. Josip Jelačić (a Croatian), whom Vienna appointed supreme commander of Hungary, invaded Hungary with his Croatian army, initiating the Hungarian-Austrian war. Kossuth's *Pesti Hirlap* greeted the admission of Jews to the Pest guard by proclaiming, "Finally Pest is about to wash off a blemish from its conduct, we could say the only one, the intolerance towards the Jews. The officers' staff of the National Guard of Pest deserves for this gratitude in the name of humanity."

Gen. George Klapka in his memoirs stated that one-twelfth of the 800 men of the Veszprém battalion commanded by him were Jews. Just as many were the Jews, mostly from the Bánát region, in the Third (Szeged) Battalion. There were many Jews in the Fourth (Györ) Battalion, the Ninth (Kassa), and most of the other battalions. There are no statistics on the total number of Jews who fought in the Hungarian Revolutionary Army, but two contemporaries, Lajos Kossuth and Ignac Einhorn, both estimated it as 20,000, out of a total of 180,000 men in the whole army, that is, around 11 percent at a time when Jews formed around 2.5 percent of the population of Hungary.

Nor did the quality of the Jews as soldiers in any way fall behind that of their Christian comrades. Gen. Arthur Görgey offered this opinion in a letter: "In discipline, personal courage, and pertinacious endurance . . . that is, in every military quality, they competed bravely with their other comrades."

It is not easy to imagine the mental state of the Jewish soldiers fighting for a country that treated them unkindly, and in which many sectors of the Christian population hated them, abused them, and on frequent occasions attacked them. Having for decades declared their love of the fatherland, having comported themselves as true patriots, having made prodigious efforts to assimilate to the Magyar majority in language and culture, having deeply and sincerely felt that they were as true Hungarians as their Christian compatriots, having become convinced that being a Jew had no national but only religious significance, and having essentially become Hungarians of the Mosaic or Israelite persuasion—the Jews were conditioned by upbringing and the heritage of several generations to want to fight for the independence of the beloved fatherland. Yet, they had to do this while smarting under the indignity that the one thing they most wanted from Hungary—citizenship equal with that of the other denominations—that same fatherland withheld from them. To be denied equal rights was bad enough for the Jews in any country; but in Hungary, where patriotism was the reigning sentiment among Christians and Jews alike, it was doubly hard. Since being a Hungarian patriot was part of the essence of the Hungarian Jewish personality, it was impossible for them not to suffer acutely from the denial of full Magyardom. Psychologists know of cases of children whose parents abuse them, and who nevertheless are deeply devoted to their parents and ready to make the greatest sacrifices for them. Something like this was the attitude of the Hungarian Jews to Hungary. That they would be ready to fight for Hungary, to risk their lives for the harsh *patria*, was a psychological inevitability in 1848, and not for the last time.

The Hungarian uprising constituted such a danger to the Austrians that the young emperor, Francis Joseph, had to apply for help from the Russian czar. Once the Russian army entered the fighting, the Hungarians were hopelessly outnumbered, and on August 13, 1849, they were forced to capitulate at Világos. Ever since this experience the Russian power lived on in the Hungarian consciousness as an ever-present menace from the east.

27

Neoabsolutism I: The Harsh Years (1849-59)

The surrender of the Hungarian army at Világos signaled the beginning of a nineteen-year period of absolutist Austrian rule that considered all manifestations of Hungarian patriotism a treasonable and punishable activity. It began with several months of Austrian governmental terror in which more than a hundred persons, including the Hungarian prime minister and thirteen *honvéd* (Hungarian army) generals, were executed, more than a thousand condemned to twenty years of prison or forced labor, and 40–50,000 *honvéd* officers and soldiers forcibly inducted into the imperial army and stationed in Austrian provinces. An unknown number of leaders and simple soldiers of the revolution, including Lajos Kossuth, fled the country. The theory behind the reprisals and the new attitude of Austria to Hungary, advocated energetically by Prince Felix Schwarzenberg, the Austrian prime minister, was that by resorting to armed uprising against their king, the Hungarians had "forfeited" their historic rights, and this justified the emperor's absorption of Hungary into the Habsburg Empire. Thus, as far Hungary was concerned, the reign of the young emperor Francis Joseph I (r. 1848–1916) began most inauspiciously.

The Austrian control of Hungary in the 1850s, known as the Bach Period after Alexander Bach, the all-powerful minister of the interior, was characterized by unrestrained absolutism, a centralized legal system, and ruthless oppression of all Hungarian reform attempts. The Hungarian Diet was not allowed to meet; the governing institutions of the counties and cities were abolished. Politically, the country was totally shackled.

Side by side with these harsh measures, the Austrian government issued a series of regulations aimed at strengthening the civil, economic, and social institutions of the country. In 1853 the so-called Labor Statute Patent confirmed the liberation of the serfs, and in the same year the Austrian Civil Law Code was introduced, promoting the free disposition of personal property. Economically of greatest importance was the development of a railroad network, which boosted the production of coal and iron, and the growth of the machine industry, mining and metallurgy, and food processing. In all these economic developments the Jews, as we shall see, took an active and often leading part.

An important feature of the Austrian retribution was the exacting of a crippling war indemnity from Hungary. Since Jews had played a prominent part in the revolution, the Austrians punished them with separate reparations payments. In fact, they instituted this policy soon after the outbreak of the fighting. In November 1848, they decreed that the Jews of Temesvár had to make a special contribution of 1,000 florins toward the cost of strengthening the fortifications of the city, and in January 1849, another of 5,300 florins for equipping the cavalry. The Austrian military commander, Prince Alfred Windischgrätz (1787–1862), who arrived in Hungary in December 1848, issued an order on February 11, 1849, in which he dealt separately with the Jews suspected of sympathizing with the Hungarian revolutionary government that took refuge in Debrecen: the Jewish communities, he decreed, would have to pay a fine of 20,000 florins for each Jew who maintained connections with the Debrecen government by supplying it with merchandise or information. In March 1849, two Jewish military suppliers of Pest were caught furnishing equipment to the *honvéd* army; they were sentenced to hanging, but then the sentence was commuted to imprisonment, and the Pest congregation as a whole was fined 40,000 florins. For a similar offense by a Jew of Óbuda, that congregation, too, was fined 20,000 florins. Windischgrätz imposed other monetary punishments as well on the Jews of Hungary, and when he was removed, his successor, Gen. Baron Julius Haynau, the new commander-in-chief of Hungary, continued his policy of heavily fining the Jewish communities of those parts of the country that fell to his army. In the summer of 1849 he issued a proclamation in Győr, indicating what indemnities would be demanded of the Hungarian Jews, and began by imposing a fine of 80,000 florins on the Jews of that city. After conquering Pest, he imposed (on July 19) a huge tribute on the Jews of Pest and Óbuda, this time not in cash but in kind: they were required to furnish tens of thousands of uniforms for the Austrian cavalry and infantry, as well as large numbers of horses, saddles, harnesses, and the like. As Haynau's army advanced that summer in Hungary, he exacted similar tributes from the Jews of each city that fell to him. A large number of Jewish *honvéd*s were punished by being inducted into the Austrian army, and two of the most outstanding Hungarian rabbis, Löb Schwab of Pest and Leopold Löw of Pápa, were imprisoned for having hailed the Hungarian declaration of independence in their sermons.

The Hungarian Jewish congregations were simply unable to procure the huge amount of military equipment and materiel demanded, and their efforts to purchase the merchandise caused a rapid rise in its price, which also increased the expenditure of the Austrian government on supplies it had to purchase for the army. Bowing to these factors, on September 17, 1849, the Viennese Ministry of War issued an order that the six congregations involved (Pest, Óbuda, Kecskemét, Cegléd, Nagykőrös, and Irsa) could pay the tribute in cash instead. The total amount was set at 2.3 million florins, an enormous amount of money at the time. The congregations were stymied, and the Jews of Pest and Óbuda asked the military authorities for a reduction of the fine. In response, the emperor made a minor adjustment: on October 22, 1849, he decreed that the tribute should be paid not by the six congregations alone but by *all* the Hungarian Jews (with the exception of those of Pressburg and Temesvár, since those two cities had been mostly under Austrian control at the time of the revolution, and thus their Jews had little or no possibility of joining the Hungarian uprising).

The tribute continued to be a subject of negotiations and bargaining between the Jews and the Austrian government. In Pest a permanent committee was established for the purpose of allocating the tribute among the Jewish communities. However, the payments lagged behind, whereupon the committee suggested to Vienna that in exchange for a repeal of the tribute the Hungarian Jews would contribute to the setting up of a national Jewish educational fund. On September 20, 1850, the emperor did annul the tribute and instead obliged the Hungarian Jews —including those of the Banat of Temes and the Serb Voivodship—to pay one million florins to a school and educational fund.

The Viennese government appointed an Israelite National Committee for Establishing the School Fund, which allocated the amounts to be paid by each community. By 1855 the whole amount was actually collected, and on March 29, 1856, the government issued instructions stating that the purposes of the school fund were to be, first, the establishment of a rabbinical seminary; second, the opening of a Jewish elementary model school in each administrative district, and third, the education of poor blind or deaf-mute Jewish children. Accordingly, the government established model schools in Pest, Temesvár, Pécs, and Sátoraljaujhely, of which the one in Pest was subsequently developed into the Hungarian Jewish Teacher Training School, while the other three were closed down by resolution of the 1868–69 Hungarian Jewish Congress. The Rabbinical Seminary and an institution for the deaf-mute were opened in Budapest in 1877. Thus, it came about that the establishment of the most important Hungarian Jewish religious educational institutions resulted from the tribute imposed by the Austrians on the Hungarian Jews in 1849, and that they were set up as, and remained throughout their history, *governmental* institutions.

To return to the early 1850s, the dominant Austrian policy of governmental centralization and the transformation of Hungary into a German-speaking component of the Habsburg Empire meant, for the Jews, that the government was interested in their assimilation, which it tried to promote by establishing a network of Jewish schools. Prior to 1848 only twenty to thirty Jewish elementary schools existed in Hungary; by 1848, the Jews of Hungary maintained 304 elementary schools, all over the country. What was less than satisfactory was that on March 19, 1850, the Jewish schools came under the supervision of the Catholic clergy, and the Concordat of 1855 between the Austrian emperor and the pope subjected the entire school system of the empire to management by the Vatican. As a result, Catholic priests controlled the Jewish schools. The only Jewish school inspector of the period was Leopold Löw, who was appointed in 1857 supervisor of the Jewish schools of County Csongrád.

In 1858 the Viennese Ministry of Education ordered the unification, or rather homogenization, of all the schools in Hungary. With reference to the Jewish schools it decreed that: the Jewish public schools must follow the example of the Christian schools; instruction must take twenty hours weekly, including classes in religion but excluding those devoted to the Hebrew language; regularly paid teachers must be employed; a teacher could be required to teach in only one grade; a teacher could not be dismissed arbitrarily; and Hebrew language could be taught as a separate subject but must not burden the pupils.

Vienna took care of the question of uniform textbooks as well: it entrusted two Jewish teachers of Prague with reworking the texts prepared for the Catholic schools by substituting reading material with Jewish content for the Christian pieces. In 1856 it also entrusted Leopold Löw with writing a biblical history to serve as textbook in the Jewish schools. These steps undeniably introduced a certain order into the Jewish schools in Hungary, strengthened the position of the teachers, and created a uniform basis for Jewish education in the country.

The same period saw also an increase in the number of Jewish students in general high schools and higher education. By 1851, there were 584 Jewish students in the academic high schools (*gimnáziums*), and in 1858, 128 Jewish students attended universities.

One of the outcomes of the greater accessibility of education for the Hungarian Jews was, paradoxically, an intensification of the tendency of their talented element to go abroad, which, as we have seen, had been a

clear trend in the prerevolutionary decades. Under the Austrian absolutist rule more Hungarian Jewish youths than before were attracted by the
greater opportunities other countries offered for professional advancement. Some of them went abroad to study, others left Hungary after
graduating, and others began their careers in Hungary and then left for
abroad. Once having studied and started their work in Austria, France,
or England, only a handful returned to Hungary. A few examples of the
greatly varied careers of these talented young men will illustrate their
attraction to life outside Hungary and the positions they were able to
achieve abroad.

Two of the earliest men in this colorful group were the brothers
Fischhof, both born in Óbuda. The elder of the two was the physician
Ignác Vilmos (Wilhelm) Fischhof (b. Óbuda, 1814; d. Budapest, 1890s),
who began studying medicine in Pest, then continued in Vienna, where
he earned his M.D. He started practicing in Grafenberg near Priessnitz,
then worked as a doctor in Vienna. He was the first physician to recom-
mend the water cures available in the Hungarian spa Szliacs, about
which he published a study in 1847. He also wrote a medical study
about cold water treatment, published in 1855. In 1856 he moved back
to Pest, where he established a hydropathic institute, the first in the
country, and headed it until 1888, after which the government purchased it.

Very different was the career of his younger brother, Adolf Fischhof
(b. Óbuda, 1816; d. Emmersdorf, 1893), although he, too, studied medicine and earned his M.D. at the University of Vienna. For a while he
practiced medicine in Vienna, but he took active part in the 1848 Viennese revolution, organizing the university youth, and subsequently
became president of the Committee for Public Safety and the representative of a district of Vienna. In the liberal cabinet of Baron Anton
Doblhoff-Dier (1800–72) he was appointed counselor to the Minister of
the Interior, and after the defeat of the revolution he was arrested and
sentenced to nine months' imprisonment. Upon gaining freedom he
returned to medical practice but continued to be interested in the problems of Hungary and political issues, and devoted all his published writings to them. He wrote (jointly with F. Unger) the pamphlet "Lösung
der ungarischen Frage" (1861), in which he advocated dividing the
Habsburg Empire into two independent countries, Austria and Hungary. In another pamphlet, titled "Ein Blick auf Österreichs Lage"
(1866), he suggested that Austria ally itself with Germany. In his book
Österreich und die Bürgschaften seines Bestandes (1869), he proposed an
autonomous constitution for Austria. *Zur Reduktion der kontinentalen
Heere* (1875) tackled the problem posed by the existence of huge armies.

In 1882 he worked for the establishment of a German-Austrian People's Party for the purpose of securing concessions to the nationalities of the Habsburg Empire and uniting all its liberal elements. The last two works he published dealt with the language problem in the Austrian empire: *Die Sprachenrechte in den Staaten gemischter Nationalität* (1885) and *Der österreichische Sprachenzwist* (1888). Although Adolf Fischhof never achieved the renown of Max Nordau, their careers display remarkable similarities: both were born in Budapest (of which Óbuda was to become a district), and both studied medicine, went abroad, worked for a while as physicians, and then became absorbed in studying and writing in German about sociopolitical and cultural issues.

Only a few years younger than the Fischhof brothers was yet another son of Óbuda, the bibliographer Solomon Schiller-Szinessy (b. Óbuda, 1820; d. Cambridge, 1890), an early representtive of the type of Hungarian Jewish scholars who two and three generations later were to make names for themselves all over the Jewish scholarly world. Son of R. Mayer Schiller of Óbuda, he received a traditional Jewish education in the town of his birth and in Bátorkeszi and was awarded a rabbinical diploma. From 1840 to 1844 he attended the University of Pest, then went to Jena, where he earned his Ph.D. degree in 1845. His first position was as preacher of the newly founded Jewish community of Eperjes, and at the same time he was appointed assistant professor of Hebrew at the Eperjes Lutheran Theological College. Although a student of the religious reformer Aaron Chorin and other like-minded rabbis, in 1845 he sharply attacked the reform resolutions of the Frankfurt Rabbinical Conference in his *Tendenz und Geist der zweiten Rabbinerversammlung zu Frankfurt am Main*. In the same year he published two more works, *Die Befreiung durch unseren Glauben* and *Kanzelreden*. He became an enthusiastic advocate of the ideas of freedom and a fervent Hungarian patriot. He translated into Hebrew one of the two Hungarian national anthems, and published it, as well as his own poems, in Hebrew journals. When the 1848 War of Liberation broke out, he traveled all over the country, delivering patriotic speeches and calling for the enlistment of Jewish young men in the *honvéd* units. It was at this time that, conforming with the Magyarizing wave that swept the country, he added the Hungarian name Szinessy to his original German name Schiller. He himself enlisted as a sapper, in which capacity he carried out the dismantling of the bridge across the Tisza River, near Szöreg, that prevented the advance of the Austrian army. He was wounded and captured, imprisoned, and condemned to death, but managed to escape. He fled to Trieste, and from there went to England, where the Jewish congregation of Birmingham invited him to serve as its rabbi-preacher. In 1851 he became rabbi of the Manchester congregation of the United Synagogue, and while there was embroiled in a controversy with Chief Rabbi Nathan Adler, who tried to extend his rabbinical jurisdiction over northern England. When a Reform congregation was formed, he was persuaded to serve as its minister, even though his personal outlook and practice remained strongly traditional throughout his life. He resigned in 1860 and in 1863 moved to Cambridge to study Hebrew manuscripts. His bibliographical erudition brought him an appointment in 1866 as teacher, and later as reader, of talmudic and rabbinic literature at Cambridge University—the first professing Jew to be entrusted by the university with this subject. He taught and inspired a distinguished list of gentile scholars. His *Catalogue of Hebrew Manuscripts Preserved in the University Library, Cambridge*, published in 1876, established his reputation as a leading Jewish bibliographer. In 1878 the university awarded him the Master of Arts degree. When news of the blood libel of Tiszaeszlár reached him (1882, see chapter 31), he engaged in energetic propaganda against that travesty of justice, and in 1887 when a conflagration destroyed Eperjes, he organized a collection in England to help rebuild the Lutheran College and the Jewish community. He published several scholarly works, including David Kimchi's *Commentary on the Psalms* and Romanelli's *Massa' ba'Arav*. He wrote the entries on rabbinical literature for the *Encyclopaedia Britannica*, and his contributions were published in the *Expositor* and *Academy*.

Another Hungarian Jew who, like Schiller-Szinessy, was a *honvéd* in the War of Liberation and went on to distinguish himself abroad was Ferdinand Schlesinger (b. Pest, 1830; d. Vienna, 1889). After the Hungarian defeat he traveled to Mexico, and then to Nicaragua, where he became a colonel and commander of a fortress. He moved on to San Francisco, where he edited the German daily *San Francisco Journal* and became a contributor to the New York *Staatszeitung*. Returning to Europe, he settled in Vienna, where he edited the journals *Böse Zungen, Lasterschule,* and *Illustrierte Plaudereien* and published the books *Die letzten Tage des ungarischen Aufstandes* (1850) and *Sechs Monate in Vidise* (1850).

An actor, Adolf Sonnenthal (b. Pest, 1834; d. Prague, 1909), was the son of well-to-do parents yet worked as a tailor's apprentice until the age of sixteen, when he went to Vienna. There he attended a performance of Bogumil Dawison at the Burgtheater, and next day he sought out the celebrated actor, who, impressed by the youngster's daring, recommended him to the attention of Laube, the director of the theater. Laube enabled him to study at the Burgtheater, and soon Sonnenthal began performing in the German theaters of the provincial cities of Hungary.

In 1856 he was invited to the Viennese Burgtheater, where he had his first great success in *Don Carlos*, after which the theater offered him a life contract. His most impressive roles were Romeo, Hamlet, Macbeth, Othello, Egmont, Wallenstein, Nathan the Wise, and Uriel Acosta. In 1881 he was ennobled (with the title *Ritter*) by Emperor Francis Joseph I, and in 1884 he became manager, and in 1887 director, of the Burgtheater. In 1896 Vienna celebrated his forty years at the Burgtheater, but anti-Semitic agitation prevented Vienna from awarding him honorary citizenship. Sonnenthal was frequently the target of Christian persuasion to convert but remained all his life a practicing Jew.

The youngest one we wish to mention in this sampling is the astronomer Moritz Loew (b. Makó, 1841; d. Steglitcz, 1900), who studied at the universities of Leipzig and Vienna and earned his doctorate at the University of Pest in 1867. He became an assistant at the observatory of Leipzig and, in 1883, director of the Prussian Geodetic Institute of Berlin. He wrote an impressive series of studies on the elements of the planets and comets and other astronomical subjects.

Let us now return to general issues affecting Hungarian Jews in the mid-nineteenth century. One of the measures introduced by the Austrian government in 1850 for the purpose of gaining better control over them was to suspend the autonomy of the Jewish congregations and to place at their head government-appointed chief executives. This, of course, created resentment among the Jews, who felt they could not trust people whom the government considered reliable (that is, subservient to it). In the early 1850s S. W. Schossberger was appointed head of the Pest congregation, whose affairs he managed with the help of a similarly appointed council. This situation continued in Pest until 1861, when the board resigned and was replaced by a freely elected body, with ophthalmologist Dr. Ignác Hirschler as president of the congregation.

One consequence of the introduction of Austrian absolutist rule into Hungary was that the economic condition of the Jews improved in certain respects. Since the revolution had been accompanied by anti-Jewish outbreaks (see above, chapter 26), the Austrian measures taken after its defeat included punishing those who committed atrocities against the Jews. The government decreed that Jews whose businesses were destroyed during the revolution should be compensated. In 1850 it obliged the Slovak villages of Upper Hungary to indemnify the damages caused to the Jews. In the same year, in order to promote the economic unity of the empire, the government abolished the customs duties between Hungary and the other realms of Austria, a step that benefitted Jewish commercial activity.

In 1851 the government decreed that nobody could be excluded from engaging in commerce and industry because of religion, nationality, or birth. This stimulated Jewish investments in commercial and industrial enterprises. The Factory Act of 1859 removed all religious distinctions, and the last surviving restrictions were obliterated in 1860, when decrees permitted the Jews to engage in dispensing pharmaceuticals, distilling spirits, milling flour, and settling in the mining towns. As far as economic activities were concerned, all distinctions between Jews and Christians were thus definitely eliminated—that is, for a period of eighty years, until the introduction of anti-Jewish laws on the eve of World War II.

It was following these 1859–60 governmental measures that Jews began to establish large-scale industries in Hungary. The existing Jewish industrial enterprises continued to function and expand—the textile printing factory of the Goldbergers in Óbuda, for example, grew to employ 400 workers in the 1850s—and many more new enterprises were established by Jews in that decade. Only a few of them can be mentioned here.

It was due to the efforts of Jacob Kern that the Austrian National Bank opened a branch in Pest in 1852. Kern was also responsible for the establishment of warehouses that served the growth of commercial traffic and export. (By coincidence, at the same time there lived in Pest another Jew by the name Kern, the composer Leo Kern, whose opera *Benvenuto Cellini* was performed in Pest in 1855 with great success.)

An important contribution to Hungarian economic life was made by Henrik Lévay (1826–1907), who participated in his youth in the Hungarian revolution, became a lieutenant of the *honvéd* army, and after the defeat worked for the Riunione Adriatica insurance company, acquiring expertise in the insurance business. In 1857 he founded the Hungarian insurance industry by establishing the First Hungarian General Insurance Company. In 1868 he was awarded Hungarian nobility, in 1886 he became member of the Hungarian Upper House, and in 1897 the king created him a baron, with the full name of Baron Henrik Lévay de Kistelek. Like many other Hungarian Jews who became industrial leaders and were ennobled, he converted to Christianity.

On the lower end of the business scale, by the end of the 1850s there were so many Jewish tailors and tanners that they formed separate guilds of their own. In Pest, in 1861, the Jewish shoemakers wanted to form a guild, and the next year there were so many Jews among the sack carriers—not an occupation one usually associates with Jews—that they actually did form a society of their own.

Károly Lajos Posner (1823–87), who studied artistic bookbinding in Paris, established in Pest in 1854 a bindery institute that rapidly grew famous all over Europe, which he developed into a many-branched enterprise including the wholesale of paper, lithography, and all branches of bookbinding, from the simplest notebooks to the most artistic examples of the craft. Later (in 1884) he also founded a special institute for drawing and printing maps—again the first in Hungary. In recognition of his services he was knighted (created a *lovag*), made a royal counselor, awarded the Hungarian cross of the Order of Merit, and in 1873 ennobled. With all this, he continued to be active in the Jewish community, was an educational officer of the Israelite Congregation of Pest, and took part in the 1868 Hungarian Jewish Congress.

The brothers Falk, both of whom converted to Christianity, had important roles in Hungarian life in the 1850s and thereafter. Miksa (Max) Falk (1828–1908) was a journalist and politician who began his career as translator and later assistant editor of the journal *Ungar*. In 1847 he earned his Ph.D. at the University of Pest, then went to Vienna to study at the Polytechnic Institute while continuing to work as a journalist. He was a political leader and a writer for Viennese papers, and contributor to the *Pesti Hirlap*. In 1858 close friendship developed between him and István Széchenyi, who entrusted him with editing his anonymous writings. In 1861, at the recommendation of Ferenc Deák he was elected a member of the Hungarian Academy of Sciences, while coincidentally the Austrian authorities tried and sentenced him to six months' imprisonment for having urged the restoration of the Hungarian constitution. In 1866 he became the tutor in Magyar of the Empress Elisabeth, wife of Emperor Francis Joseph I, who found it desirable to learn Hungarian in view of the impending Austro-Hungarian Compromise (*Ausgleich*), which was to make her queen of Hungary. Falk himself played a role in preparing that all-important political agreement between Austria and Hungary, which could be realized only after many serious obstacles were overcome. After the Compromise he was appointed editor-in-chief of the Pest German-language daily *Pester Lloyd* and made it the leading daily of Hungary. From 1896 to 1905 he was a member of parliament, where he represented the liberal point of view. He wrote a large number of books, but it was his sparkling articles that made him known and liked all over the country. He translated into German the works of Dumas and Hungarian authors, wrote textbooks in history and geography, and edited his own political speeches.

His younger brother, Zsigmond Falk (1831–1913), served as a *honvéd* in the War of Liberation, started out as a printer's apprentice, and worked himself up to the position of director of a printing press. In 1868 he became director of the Pest Book Printing Company and played a large part in developing high-quality printing in Hungary. He was also active in philanthropy, became vice-president of the National Industrial Association, and received many distinctions, including nobility and court councillorship.

Móric Jellinek (b. Ungarisch-Brod, 1823; d. Budapest, 1883), economist and public activist, was a brother of Adolf Jellinek, the chief rabbi of Vienna. He studied law and economy at the universities of Leipzig and Vienna, and during the revolution edited a liberal paper in Brünn (Brno). Moving to Pest, he established a grain business, participated in the foundation of the Pest Stock Exchange, and became president of the grain exchange. In 1864 he founded the Street Tramway Company of Pest, whose president he remained to his death. He did much for the development of Hungarian commerce, and wrote much about it. Upon his death, his son Henrik Jellinek (1853–1919) took over the Budapest tramway as its managing director, and developed suburban lines around the city. He was awarded nobility and court councillorship. He converted to Christianity.

Having mentioned in the foregoing paragraphs the nobility and distinctions awarded to several Hungarian Jews, let me add that in the 1850s alone a dozen more Hungarian Jews were so honored by Emperor Francis Joseph, and this at a time when the Jews had not yet achieved civic equality with the Christian Hungarians.

The Viennese government recognized that the commercial and industrial abilities of the Jews could be an important asset in the development of Hungry's backward economy. A negative measure intended to channel Jewish talent and capital into commerce and industry was the barring of Jews from owning land. Although the 1849 constitution of Olmütz gave them in principle the right to acquire landed property, an imperial patent was issued on October 2, 1853, that deprived them of that right. The motivation for this law was clearly the government's desire to prevent Jewish capital from being tied down in investment in landed property and real estate. However, the Jewish communities smarted under this remaining restriction and protested against it. The Israelite Congregation of Pest submitted a petition to Archduke Albrecht, in which it requested its lifting, and supported the argument by enumerating the seventeen counties in which the Jews were engaged in agriculture. In 1857 the Chamber of Commerce and Industry of Pest and Buda submitted an application to the Ministry of Commerce, requesting the restoration to the Jews of the right to acquire landed property. They argued that excluding Jews from buying such property depressed the real estate market, which in turn contributed to the slump of the building trade. A year later, the municipality of Szeged was in fact forced to permit Jews to build anywhere within the city so as to put a stop to the decline in the value of building lots. Finally, on February 18, 1860, the emperor issued a decree granting the Jews the right to acquire and own landed property, and abolishing all obstacles to the acquisition of such property in Lower Austria, Bohemia, Hungary, Silesia, the Serb Voivodship, the Banat of Temes, Croatia and Slavonia, Transylvania, the seashore, and Dalmatia.

While the decade of the 1850s thus ended with considerable gains in the economic position of the Jews, their civic and political rights remained unchanged and unsatisfactory. A manifestation of the continued problems of the Jews in these areas was the reintroduction in 1852 of the ancient Jewish oath, which meant that Jews could appear before a court of law—whether as principals or as witnesses—only after having rendered an oath according to an approved Jewish religious rite.

In 1854 the emperor entrusted a committee with the task of preparing a new bill about the Jews. However, the committee did no more than obtain opinions from the governors of the lands of the crown. Thus, no clarification of the Jewish legal position took place until the 1867 Compromise between Austria and Hungary.

During the decade of the 1850s many Hungarian Jews became intoxicated by the first whiffs of freedom, that is, by the signs of impending equality with their Christian compatriots, manifested in such achievements as their penetration into commerce and industry, their successes in medicine, education, literature, and journalism, and their elevation by imperial grace into the ranks of knights, nobles, and court councillors in recognition of individuals' services in various areas of economic and public activity. To this were added the conspicuous careers of individual Hungarian Jews who went abroad and achieved renown in fields never before explored by their more tradition-bound coreligionists (see below). All this showed them that once they chose to break out of traditional orthodoxy, new worlds were waiting to open up to them, which in the past they had been barred from as much by their voluntary isolation as by the reluctance of Christian society to admit them. Many were also worried by the apostasy spreading precisely among the top layers of the Jewish community, which indicated that some Jews, having no alternative to extreme Orthodox Judaism, which they could not abide and which formed an impenetrable barrier to entering many secular fields of activity, were induced to leave the Jewish fold altogether. The conclusion they reached from all this was that the Jewish religion *had* to be modernized, so that Hungarian Israelites could remain Jewish without thereby being prevented from forging ahead in the new fields from which laws no longer excluded them.

The modernization they endeavored to achieve was moderate compared to what the German Jewish religious reformers put into practice, and what the latters' few Hungarian followers envisaged. However, even the modest reforms they proposed were considered sinful aberrations by the Orthodox wing, which adhered steadfastly to the position summed up by the great Moses Sofer of Pressburg half a century earlier in his pithy aphorism, "*Ḥadash asur min haTorah,*" by which he meant, "Innovation is forbidden by the Torah."

The conflict between the conservative and progressive wings of Hungarian Jewry worsened when the Viennese government tried to set up a unified religious and educational organization for the Hungarian Jews. In 1850 the civilian commissioner of Hungary, Dr. Karl Geringer, called upon the Jews of the country, through the district commissioners, to submit recommendations for the organization of the Jewish community and its educational system. Among the responses of the progressives was that of the Nagyvárad community, which proposed establishing a teachers' institute and a rabbinical seminary and setting up district committees consisting of rabbis and laymen, entrusted with the leadership of individual congregations. The district committees were to be responsible to a central organization, with its seat in Pest.

An opposite position was submitted by the conservative R. Meir Eisenstadt of Ungvár, who was against the establishment of denominational schools and the employment of Jewish teachers. He considered the teaching of religion to be outside the scope of public education and a matter for private instruction. He recommended that only conservative rabbis head the congregations, and he wanted them to be empowered with the right of jurisdiction over those who transgressed the rules of religion. His submission was supported by several congregations of northeastern Hungary, the district neighboring on Galicia and dominated by the religious element. Several of these communities took the opportunity to attack the Pest congregation, which, they declared, was guilty of violating Jewish traditional law. They claimed (incorrectly) that seven-eighths of Hungary's Jewry was conservative in its orientation, thus trying to demonstrate that the position and activities of the Pest Jews were unwarranted.

Once the opinions were in, the Viennese government convened a conference in Buda to discuss the contested issues. The Jewish representatives invited by the government belonged to the progressive camp, and included rabbis and personalities of renown whom the court considered suitable and capable of working out an understanding between the government and the Jews of Hungary. Among the rabbis were R. Lőb Schwab of Pest, R. Leopold Löw of Szeged, R. Jacob S. Freyer of Győr, and R. Mayer Zipser of Székesfehérvár. The meetings took place on September 23 and 24, 1851, and R. Löw was assigned to prepare the statutes of the planned organization of the Jewish communities. Löw went to work with his usual thoroughness and energy, and he produced a detailed draft consisting of 285 paragraphs, which covered all aspects of congregational life; discussed the civil status of the Jews, the practice of keeping birth and marriage registers, and the rights of the members and employees of the congregations and their duties; and prescribed the order of the synagogue services and educational practices.

It was the government's plan to effect the draft through an imperial patent, but this step was not carried out. What did happen was that within several communities sharp clashes took place between the progressives and the conservatives. In the heat of disagreement, minor issues loomed large and created unbridgeable antagonisms between the two sides. Typical was the conflict that broke out in Székesfehérvár in connection with a *get*, a Jewish letter of divorce. That city had a Hungarian, a German, and a Latin name, all of which were in use, and the local Jewish custom was not to issue letters of divorce in the city lest confusion arise in connection with its names (a similar problem arose centuries earlier in Buda, which was also designated by several names). Now, R. Mayer Zipser nevertheless wrote a *get* in the city, and this was considered a flagrant violation of tradition by the conservative members of the community. Led by the president of the congregation, Gottlieb Fischer, they attacked the rabbi and invalidated the *get*, which had been delivered, that is, executed, in the meantime, R. Zipser justified his act in a Hebrew pamphlet, whereupon Fischer responded with a counterstatement declaring the rabbi a dangerous reformer. The incident destroyed the peace of the community, and played a role in the resignation in 1858 of R. Zipser, who accepted an invitation of the community of Rohonc. He was replaced in Székesfehérvár by the conservative R. Joseph Guggenheimer.

A worse congregational fight took place in Pápa in 1853. It went so far that the intervention of the secular authorities was required. The conservative leaders of the community disallowed the addition of a German text to the Hebrew inscription on a tombstone. They based their objection on adherence to traditions, and argued that by giving the vital data of the deceased according to the civil calendar, the names of pagan deities would appear on the tombstone (January, Janus; March, Mars). The affair was brought before the county authorities, who supported the use of the German inscription, against the leaders of the congregation.

The peace of the Nagyvárad congregation was disturbed in 1861 by the question of the order of the synagogue services. The conservatives, led by R. Aaron Landesberg, objected to changes in the services, where-upon the progressives, who wanted an organ and a choir, seceded and founded a separate congregation, which they called the Hungarian Jew-ish Community. The mother congregation appealed to the council of the governor-general, which in October 1863 ordered the secessionists to return. However, to safeguard the freedom of conscience, it also ordred the mother congregation to maintain an additional synagogue for the use of its progressive members.

Sharp controversies were occasioned by the placement of the *bimah* (or *almemar*), the platform used for reading the Torah in the synagogue. The traditional place of the *bimah* had been for centuries, following the opinion of Maimonides, in the center of the synagogue, which, inciden-tally, allowed a festive procession between the pews of the congregants each time the Torah scroll was brought out of the Holy Ark (located on the eastern wall of the synagogue) for reading. The progressives, under the influence of Catholic church architecture, wanted to move the *bimah* to the front, immediately before the Holy Ark, and their learned rabbis referred to the ruling of R. Joseph Caro, who wrote in his com-mentary to Maimonides, "It is not essential to place the *bimah* in the center." Despite this halakhic permission, the Orthodox, led by R. Moses Sofer of Pressburg and R. Ezekiel Landau, vehemently opposed the innovation. Their stand led one hundred rabbis to issue a proclama-tion prohibiting worship in any synagogue that did not have the *bimah* in the center.

In Miskolc the congregation built a new synagogue in 1863, in which, with the consent of R. Ezekiel Moses Lipsitz Fischmann, who was its rabbi from 1836 until his death in 1874, the *bimah* was placed in the front. For the High Holy Days they had a choir to accompany the ser-vices, and R. Mór Klein, a Ph.D. from the University of Prague, was invited to preach. In order not to offend the sensibilities of their conser-vative members, they voluntarily followed the same arrangement imposed upon the Jews of Nagyvárad by the civil authorities, and they maintained the old synagogue for those who wished to attend more tra-ditional services. Consequently, no controversy developed within the congregation, but the new synagogue aroused the ire of R. Hillel Lich-tenstein of Margitta (later of Szikszó) and R. Joachim Schreiber of Sajószentpéter, who jointly put it under a ban (*herem*) and applied to its rabbi the traditional reprobatory term "rebellious old man" (*zaqen mored*).

In several congregations controversies arose about the gallery for women. Tradition required that the women's balcony in the synagogue be hidden behind wooden latticework with openings through which the women could just see, if they pressed their eyes to it, what was going on below in the men's section, but which made it impossible for the men to see the women sitting behind it. Acrimonious debates developed between the progressives, who wished to reduce the height and density of the latticework, and the conservatives, who warned, as did R. Jacob Singer of Losonc in 1865, that instead of a *Frauengallerie* (women's gallery) they were about to build a *Bildergallerie* (picture gallery), in which the faces of the women would be exhibited. The controversy over the same issue between R. Feivel Flaut of Surány and the congregation of Érsekujvár, which belonged to his circuit, dragged out for years.

Similar intracongregational wars took place as early as 1850 in Kolozsvár, 1852 in Székesfehérvár, and 1858 in Makó. The sharpening positions of the two sides were sadly characterized in 1922 by historian Lajos Venetianer:

> Those who considered the slightest changes in the external appearance of the ceremonies and religious practices, introduced so as to harmonize with the educated worldview, to be far-reaching religious reforms that violated the essentials, followed with a suspicious eye everything connected with the question of religion and, ready for an embittered war, rejected everything apt to deflect the believers even as little as a hair's breadth from established custom. But the suspicion was justified, because those who led the fight for equal rights disregarded all the religious practices, and as for the religious ceremonies tried to create a mood in the congregations that served the interest of emancipation. Thus, strife arose in the congregations whose membership comprised the most heterogeneous elements.

Venetianer goes on to explain that religiously the city-dwelling Jews were more progressive while those of the villages were more conservative, and that after 1840, when the Jews were given the freedom of movement and settlement in Hungary, there was sizable village-to-town migration that resulted inevitably in clashes between the more educated, religiously progressive city Jews and the less educated, religiously more conservative newcomers from the villages. These clashes foreshadowed the split of Hungarian Jewry into two nationwide organizations, one progressive (Neolog), the other conservative (Orthodox), that occurred at the government-sponsored Hungarian Jewish Congress of 1868–89.

In 1859 the great synagogue of Pest, in the Dohány Street, was completed. The competition for the plans had been won by Viennese and Pest architects, and the construction took five years. Most of the costs were covered by the sale of seats in the synagogue, the rest by donations. The building, completed in the spring of 1859, consisted mainly of a huge oblong nave, with two women's balconies (with no lattice barriers), one on top of the other running along each of its two longitudinal sides.

The *bimah* was not in the middle; this traditional requirement also having been disregarded, it was moved to the front. About one-third down the length of the nave there were two high pulpits at the two sides, each attached to a column. The style was pseudo-Moorish, with two tall, onion-capped towers flanking the entrance.

The "temple" was dedicated, after some delay because of the Italian war, in the fall of that year. As described by Ede Vadász, historian of the synagogue: "On the day of the dedication, Tuesday, September 6, 1859, already in the early hours of the morning, the multitude of the swarming curious and of those who hurried in from the side streets filled the Dohány Street . . . most of them appearing in festive clothes." The huge nave of the temple was filled by the owners of the seats and by invited dignitaries, including leaders of the city's civil and military authorities. In the afternoon, and on the days following the inaugural celebration, many Christians came to have a look at the synagogue, which was one of the biggest places of worship any denomination could boast in the city.

In addition to being the central house of prayer for the Jews of Pest, the Dohány Temple was the scene of important social gatherings as well. In the very next year, after the so-called October Diploma was issued (see the next chapter), which mitigated the absolutist Austrian rule in Hungary, the city's aristocrats and intellectual elite held a social evening at the Europa Hotel to celebrate the new "fraternity" established between the Christians and the Jews. The gala was attended by leaders of the Christian churches, civil authorities, and high society, as well as the cream of the Jewish community. The participants wanted to endow the occasion with a religious significance as well, so they planned to gather in one of the houses of worship of the city. Because of the differences among the Christian denominations, it was decided to meet in the new Jewish temple, which they did on the very next day, December 20. Thus, the Dohány Temple became the scene of a festive gathering of all denominations, with much waving of huge national flags, impassioned speeches, and singing of the Hungarian national anthem, all in celebration of the brotherhood of Jews and Christians. In the years to come, all kinds of national occasions, such as the death of a leading statesman and the coronation of Francis Joseph as king of Hungary (1867) were celebrated in the Dohány Temple, often with the attendance of Hungarian statesmen.

The style of services in the big temple represented a compromise between the demands of the progressive and traditional camps. The ritual remained entirely conservative and all the prayers were recited in Hebrew, exactly as in any Orthodox synagogue, but they were not only

Elevation of the Dohány Street synagogue at the time it was built (1854–59). Contemporary etching. Visible to the left of the synagogue is part of the house in which Theodor Herzl was born. (Courtesy of the Műszaki Könyvkiadó [Technical Publishers], Budapest.)

The Dohány Street synagogue as it appeared in the 1990s. The house in which Herzl was born (to the left of the synagogue) has been replaced by the building of the Jewish Museum. (Courtesy of the Műszaki Könyvkiadó [Technical Publishers], Budapest.)

Interior of the Dohány Street synagogue. (Courtesy of the Műszaki Könyvkiadó [Technical Publishers], Budapest.)

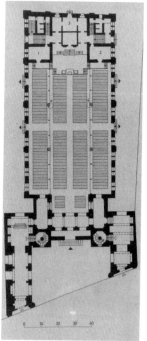

Ground plan of the Dohány Street synagogue (1857). Overall dimensions of the building: 38 by 84 meters, or 125 by 275 feet. Length of the central nave: 47 meters, or 154 feet. With its more than 3,000 seats (including the double-tiered women's galleries), it was (and still is) the largest synagogue in Europe. 1. Cantor's room. 2. Rabbi's room. 3. The Holy Ark. 4. Pulpits. 5. Main entrance from Dohány Street. (Courtesy of the Műszaki Könyvkiadó [Technical Publishers], Budapest.)

sung by a cantor but also accompanied by a male choir. And a magnificent organ was installed, which introduced an unmistakably Christian note into the services and made it impossible for Orthodox Jews even to set foot there. However, since the Halakha prohibits Jews from playing musical instruments on the Sabbath and holidays, a Christian was employed to serve as temple organist. While the pipes of the organ were built so as to add a beautiful, decorative feature to the architecture, the organist himself was hidden from the view of the public, as was the sizable choir.

The language of the sermon was German until 1866, when the new rabbi, Dr. Samuel Kohn, introduced preaching in Hungarian. From its dedication until the destruction of Hungarian Jewry at the end of World War II, the 3,000 seats of the Dohány temple always filled up for the Sabbath and holiday services.

28

Neoabsolutism II: The Moderate Years (1860–67)

In 1859 the anti-Habsburg French-Italian War ended with the defeat of Austria at Solferino, and the position of the Habsburg Empire as a major power in Europe was shaken. At home, the military defeat and chronic financial troubles forced the Austrian authorities to introduce constitutional reforms. In an effort to meet some of the demands of the various national groups of the empire, particularly the Magyars, Francis Joseph on October 20, 1850, issued the "October Diploma," which gave more power to the local diets controlled by the propertied classes and the nobility. In Hungary, it restored the legislature, albeit with limited powers, which did not satisfy the liberal nobility. Within four months the emperor replaced the Diploma with the February Patent of 1861, which again provided for a centralized government, to be based on an imperial parliament.

These hesitant steps toward replacing centralized monarchic absolutism with a limited constitutionalism did not leave the Jews of Hungary untouched. A few irritating incapacities were removed, to begin with. On November 29, 1859, an imperial decree canceled the requirement that Jews obtain permission from the authorities before they could marry. This new law was made retroactive, so that marriages entered into in the past without legal permission now were recognized as valid. On January 6, 1860, another imperial decree annulled the provision limiting the ability of the Jews to testify in court. These were relatively minor improvements, but they nurtured the hope of Hungarian Jewry that full emancipation was about to come.

Much of these hopes were attached to the Diet that was to convene in 1861. Although the Jews could not participate in the elections to it, more and more public voices were heard urging their emancipation. Gen. George Klapka, the leader of the 1848 revolution who was living in exile in Paris, published a letter in the French papers wholeheartedly supporting the granting of full civil rights to the Jews. He wrote: "We would have to blush for shame if at the Diet there were found even one Hungarian patriot who demanded the postponement of this act of justice."

The great majority of Hungarian political leaders went on record in favor of emancipation, and the argument all of them voiced was that the Jews deserved emancipation because of their patriotism and Magyarism. When the famous scholar-politician Ferenc Pulszky, an emigré living in Turin, was elected a representative, he declared that Hungarians must not forget those brothers who were not yet admitted by the laws of 1848 within the ramparts of the constitution. He referred to the political achievements of the Jews in other countries—in London a Jew was elected lord mayor and in England, France, the Netherlands, and the United States there were Jewish members of parliament, senators, and ministers of state—and asked why Hungarians excluded them from the country, which was anyway not strong, whereas they ought to welcome everybody who added to the strength of the nation. "It can only be in the interest of our enemies that we should exclude from enjoying liberty, solely because of their religion, our brothers who are Hungarians by birth, language, and feelings."

On April 2, 1861, Ferenc Deák, the leader of the Liberal Party, was asked by a delegation of the Pest Jews to be their spokesman at the Diet. He assured them of his full support. Similar declarations were made by Count Gyula Andrássy on the occasion of his election as representative of Sátoraljaujhely. Emancipation was urged by Count Kálmán Majláth in the *Pester Lloyd*, Móric Lukács in the *Pesti Napló*, and Kálmán Tisza in the *Magyarország*. In the last named paper on January 17, 1861, János Pompéry wrote, "Let us not forget that in 1848 the Jews also shed their blood for the fatherland." And the great Hungarian novelist Mór Jókai, when elected representative of a district of Pest, declared that nobody could be excluded, and "no nationality was more loyal to us than the Jews, and none did we treat more unfairly."

Aware of these favorable voices, the Israelite Congregation of Pest convened a conference of the Hungarian Jews to discuss "whether the Hungarian Israelites should appear as petitioners for political equality at the Diet, and in what form, or, relying on the magnanimity of the Hungarian Nation and on the liberal declarations of the great majority of the representatives, should take a passive position and leave the initiative in this matter to the legislative body about to convene." That not all of Hungarian Jewry was seized with the issue of emancipation at that juncture is eloquently attested by the meager response to his invitation. Of the 42 counties and 14 cities whose representatives were invited, only 19 counties and 9 cities responded, dispatching a total of 53 delegates, among them only two rabbis, R. Binyamin Zeev Meisel of Pest and R. Leopold Löw of Szeged—the rest were laymen. The conference, meeting on April 16–18, 1861, resolved not to submit a petition to the Diet but to issue only this statement:

> The delegates of the congregations gathered here leave the initiative with complete trust and great satisfaction to the noble representatives of the nation, being completely convinced that the Diet, with its noble endeavor, will not be tardy in satisfying as soon as possible the lawful desires of the Hungarians of Mosaic faith, and will admit them within the ramparts of the national equal rights, so that, fulfilling equal duties with the rest of the inhabitants, they should be able to grow enthusiastic for the benefit of the fatherland in equal measure. Therefore they avoid all steps that could lend themselves to obscuring the shining light of the magnanimous sentiments of the Hungarian nation.

This little masterpiece of diplomatic phrasing duly impressed the Diet, as we shall soon see. In the meantime, however, a disturbing event took place that indicated again how damaging it was to the interests of Hungarian Jews that they had no unified organization to speak in the name of all of them. While the aforementioned conference was taking place, Count Ede Károlyi invited a small number of Jewish delegates to discuss, contrary to the majority trend soon in evidence, what measures could be taken to effect the passing of a law of equal rights. The participants expressed readiness to introduce reforms into certain aspects of religious law, to curb Jewish immigration into Hungary, and to make the emancipation contingent on a preceding cultural improvement of the Jews; that is, they agreed to a division of Hungarian Jewry into classes on the basis of their cultural level. Needless to say, this plan of partial emancipation caused serious concern in the ranks of most Jewish leaders, who were committed to the emancipation of the entire Hungarian Jewish community.

The Diet opened on April 2, 1861, and when, after discussing many national problems, it finally took up the question of the emancipation of the Jews, both major parties supported the bill that read: "We want, with regard to the full enjoyment of civil rights, that neither religion nor nationality should make a difference among the citizens of the fatherland." On June 17 the House of Representatives appointed a committee to prepare the Law of Emancipation, but the committee, headed by Menyhért Lónyay, instead prepared a bill that only permitted free residence. The liberal press sharply criticized this whittling down of the emancipation, but before it could be reconsidered, the emperor, for whom the nationalist aspirations contained in the parliamentary address to the throne were unacceptable, dissolved the Diet on August 21.

While the issue of emancipation was thus postponed indefinitely, several religious differences arose to sow disharmony in the ranks of Hungarian Jewry. One was the question of the personal Messiah, which arose when the Jewish historian Heinrich Graetz published a paper in Wertheimer's *Jahrbuch für Israeliten* of 1863–64 (coedited by Leopold Kompert) in which he expressed the view that the suffering servant of Isaiah 53 represented not the personal Messiah but the People of Israel as a whole, and that the belief in the personal Messiah led to romantic infatuation. A Viennese Catholic journal attacked Graetz's views, since it saw in them a slur of not only Orthodox Jewish views but also Catholic dogma. The matter was litigated in court and, on the basis of testimony from two liberal Viennese rabbinical authorities, ended with Kompert's acquittal. This aroused the ire of the Hungarian Orthodox rabbis. One of their most articulate spokesmen, R. Azriel Hildesheimer of Kismarton, issued a declaration in which he presented the tenets of Orthodox Judaism. Among them, he stated, was the belief in the coming of the personal Messiah, a scion of the House of David. In the same paper R. Hildesheimer declared that an Orthodox Jew could find peace of mind only in a congregation that strictly observed the Jewish religious laws; Jewish religion comprised the written and the oral law revealed by God, and whoever denied even a single one of these laws denied the entire Sinaitic revelation. Hildesheimer's declaration was signed by 300 Hungarian rabbis and thirty-six rabbis from abroad.

Of long duration, and of more serious consequences, was the dispute over the rabbinical seminary. The 1856 decree, as we have seen, specified that one of the purposes of the education fund was to pay for the establishment of a rabbinical seminary. A year before, R. Hildesheimer tried to establish an Orthodox rabbinical school, but his plan was rejected by the government as a didactic fancy. In January 1859, twenty-two conservative rabbis submitted an application to the Viennese Ministry of Education, requesting that the plan for the seminary be dropped, and asking that instead the yeshiva of Pressburg, still glorying in the fame of Moses Sofer, be made a public institution.

An especially sore point with the Orthodox was that the students of the rabbinical seminary of Padua, the only public rabbinical school in the Habsburg Empire, enjoyed exemption from the duty of military service, and they found it prejudicial that the rabbinical candidates, in order to enjoy their military exemption, should have to enroll in a modern rabbinical school. The positive aspect of the petition was appreciated by the ministry, and the Pressburg yeshiva was given public status within the same year.

Nor was the progressive wing quiescent. In 1862, the new president of the Israelite Congregation of Pest, Dr. Ignác Hirschler, asked the court chancellery that a conference of Jewish delegates be convened to discuss establishing a modern rabbinical seminary. In response, on February 3, 1864, the government assigned a committee of three leading rabbis— Samuel Löb Brill, head of the Rabbinical Council of Pest, Mark Hirsch, rabbi of Óbuda, and Jacob Steinhardt, rabbi of Arad—to draft the statutes and regulations of the planned seminary. Their plan envisaged two departments: a lower one with a five-year study plan, corresponding to the upper forms of the *gimnázium*, in which, in addition to the usual secular subjects, also Bible, Talmud, and Jewish history were to be taught; and a higher college department with a curriculum of three years (later expanded to five), for only theological subjects. The languages of instruction were to be Hungarian and German. In drafting the curriculum of the college, the committee was influenced by that of the Jüdisch-Theologisches Seminar of Breslau, founded in 1854 with the basic aim of teaching "positive historical Judaism."

As soon as news of the seminary plan became known, the Orthodox rabbis sprang into action. On March 15, 1864, they called a meeting in Nyiregyháza, which, chaired by Yehuda Aszód, rabbi of Dunaszerdahely, prepared a petition, signed by ninety-two Orthodox rabbis, and published it on April 8. They also resolved to send deputations to the governor-general's council in Buda, and to the emperor in Vienna, to request that they reject the plan, which they considered a great danger to Judaism. They found no positive response at the council, but the petition to the emperor resulted in instructions from the court chancellery to the governor general's council to table the issue of the seminary.

This favorable outcome encouraged the Orthodox to undertake further steps. On November 28, 1865, under the leadership of Hillel Lichtenstein, rabbi of Szikszó (whom we have already met), a meeting convened in Nagymihály to deal with the growing danger of the Neolog movement. R. Lichtenstein was not only a strict traditionalist but also a man of Hasidic orientation (he was known as Reb Hillel). He traveled all over the country to arouse opposition to modernism, and disseminated his ideas in pamphlets as well. The Nagymihály meeting was attended by sixteen rabbis and eight substitute rabbis, all from the ultraconservative northeastern parts of Hungary. Nevertheless, they declared themselves the legislative body of all the Jews of Hungary, and they passed the following conciliar resolutions:

> 1. It is forbidden to listen to a synagogue sermon given in a foreign language. The true believer must leave such a synagogue. The rabbis should speak in Yiddish, which is used by the pious of the country.

2. It is forbidden to pray in a synagogue in which the *bimah* is not in the center.

3. It is forbidden to build a tower on the synagogue.

4. The cantor and the prayer leader are forbidden to wear a vestment for the services.

5. The women's gallery must be closed up with a dense lattice.

6. It is forbidden to listen to the singing of a choir, to pray together with it, or to say "Amen" after such prayer.

7. It is forbidden to enter a choir synagogue, because such synagogues are houses of heresy and are worse than the temples of the pagans.

8. Weddings can be celebrated only under the open sky.

9. It is forbidden to change any Jewish custom or rule inherited from the ancestors.

These decisions of the conference, accompanied by the threat of excommunication, were signed by seventy-one rabbis, printed in Buda in 1866, and sent out to all the congregations of Hungary.

A closer look at these resolutions reveals several interesting aspects of the position of the Orthodox and their differences with the progressives whom they so bitterly fought. First, all their prohibitions are directed against *external* forms of worship and of places of worship: no towers, no *bimah* except in the middle, no open women's galleries, no vestments, no choirs, no weddings inside the synagogue. The sixth resolution implies that if prayers—presumably the old, tradition-sanctioned prayers—are sung by a choir, they are thereby desecrated or invalidated so that it is forbidden to say "Amen" after them, and the seventh paragraph declares synagogues with choirs to be "houses of heresy, worse than the temples of pagans." In the whole declaration, not a word of criticism is directed against the progressives concerning the essential beliefs and tenets of Judaism. This can be interpreted as showing either that the attention of the Orthodox was focused on the external aspects of Jewish religious practice, to the neglect of its beliefs and ethical teachings, or that they had nothing to criticize in the conduct of the progressive congregations in the areas of creeds and moral tenets.

Even more peculiar is the last paragraph. One would have expected an Orthodox conclave to proclaim that it is forbidden, in the first place, to disobey any of the 613 traditional commandments (the *Taryag Mitzvot*) of the Jewish religion, or not to believe in the Thirteen Principles of Faith as formulated by Maimonides. Instead, what they execrate is only the nonobservance of "customs and rules," which in the total picture of the Jewish religious edifice were merely frills and which, moreover, varied from place to place.

The concrete content of the proclamation aside, what its issuance demonstrated was that a serious break in Hungarian Jewry was in the offing.

The reaction of the progressive wing to the Nagymihály decisions was, predictably, pained indignation. Within a week after they were passed, Leopold Löw wrote on December 7, 1865, to Dr. Ignác Hirschler: "Incredible as it will seem to you, it is nevertheless a fact that the Orthodox conferred in Nagymihály about the means by which the emancipation could be prevented." Although the Nagymihály decisions did not refer to emancipation, it was clear that the rabbis there were apprehensive lest the granting of equal rights to the Jews motivate them to leave the spiritual ghetto the Orthodox saw as the only guarantee for the survival of the Jews qua Jews. (There is no denying that their position was to some extent proven right by the assimilatory wave that engulfed the progressive elements of Hungarian Jewry before, and even more so after, emancipation and led many of its most talented children to the baptismal font.)

We must go back a few years to recount the activities of the progressive or Neolog Jews, as they came to be called, in the years preceding emancipation. On March 18, 1861, as heir to the Magyarizing Society of the prerevolutionary years, the Israelite Hungarian Society was founded, which soon had some 600 members. Its president was Dr. Joseph Rózsay and its secretary Mór Mezei. Its activities included weekly public lectures, which became a veritable folk academy and, over and above the propagation of the Hungarian language, served the aims of general education. The lectures dealt with subjects from the realms of pedagogy, anthropology, medical science, Jewish literature, Hungarian language, and so on. In 1862 it published the *First Hungarian Israelite Calendar and Yearbook*. It organized Hungarian language classes, headed by Pál Tenczer, and published the *First Hungarian-Hebrew-German Phonic and Elementary Reader*, which helped the teaching of the Hungarian language in the Jewish schools.

In 1863 the Viennese court removed the Jewish schools from the supervision of the Catholic clergy, as a result of which the former, unregulated conditions reemerged. This prompted leaders of the Pest Jews, headed by Pál Léderer, principal of the Pest Jewish model school, to renew the 1862 plan calling for the establishment of a national union of Jewish teachers. In October 1866 the National Israelite Teachers Union came into being, with Chief Rabbi Meisel of Pest as its president. The activities of the Union comprised the financial support of teachers and their widows and orphans and the publication of Jewish textbooks, especially in Hungarian. It published the Pentateuch in a Hungarian translation, later also prayerbooks, and by 1885 more than fourteen additional books.

The 1860s saw the emergence of a Jewish press in Hungary. Leopold Löw's *Ben Chananja*, which was launched in Szeged in 1858, continued to be published until 1867. In 1860 the *Allgemeine Illustrierte Zeitung* was founded, which merged right away with the *Carmel*. In 1861 the first Jewish journal in Hungarian appeared, the weekly *Magyar Izraelita* (Hungarian Israelite), published by the Israelite Hungarian Society, which became the foremost mouthpiece of Magyarization. It was founded by Lipót Rokonstein (or Rockonstein), rabbi of Zagreb (later of Szombathely), and was edited by him and Mór Mezei and Pál Tenczer. Through the initiative of Jewish medical students the weekly *Zsidó Magyar Közlöny* (Jewish Hungarian Gazette) was launched the same year, but it survived only three months. In 1864, Adolf Fenyvessy, who later became the head of the stenographic office of the Hungarian Parliament, launched the weekly *Izraelita Közlöny* (Israelite Gazette), whose editorship was taken over in 1868 by Henrik Deutsch, the future principal of the Jewish Teachers Institute. This journal, which appeared until 1871, was published half in Hungarian and half in German. The first journal of the Orthodox Jews in Hungary was the *Magyar Zsidó* (Hungarian Jew), launched in 1867 by the Orthodox group Hitőr Egylet (Society for Protecting the Faith, see next chapter).

Most impressive were the achievements of progressive Hungarian Jews in the fields of literature and scholarship in the 1860s. Prior to the 1867 emancipation, they published hundreds of books in Hungarian, German, Hebrew, French, and Italian, devoted to practically every existing field of literary activity. Their books discussed aspects of congregational life, the position of the Jews in Hungary, apologetics, biblical history and other biblical subjects, and the history of Jewish medicine. The included a talmudic Aramaic dictionary, studies on the Zohar, Jewish prayer books, and textbooks for the study of Jewish religion, Hebrew grammar, and the geography of Palestine. They printed the music of songs for synagogue services. They branched out into all fields of general scholarly literature, wrote on economics (including a book in French by Ede Horn on the economic progress of Egypt), history, Roman literature, mythology, general and religious philosophy, aesthetics, jurisprudence, Roman law, international law, political science, and linguistics. Jews produced textbooks on practical subjects such as the tailor's craft, algebra, stenography, commercial correspondence, German grammar for Hungarian speakers, geography, and nature studies. They wrote on oil drilling and mining, and authored an especially large number of medical treatises presenting the results of their experiments and research. And, of course, rabbis printed their sermons, while others made translations from and into Hungarian, German, and Hebrew. To these were added novels and collections of poems in Hungarian, German, and Hebrew, and plays (one of which, *Johanna of Naples* by Albert Farkas, was performed in 1862 in the Hungarian National Theater).

This list is interesting because it demonstrates the sudden irruption of Hungarian Jewish authors into all fields of literary and scholarly activity in the years immediately preceding 1867. The trend displayed in these publications intensified after the emancipation, as will be discussed in the next chapter.

Beginning in the late 1850s, the Jewish identification with the Hungarian nation was expressed in numerous communal celebrations. In 1859 Jews participated in the festivities commemorating the one-hundredth anniversary of the birth of Ferenc Kazinczy, the "father of Hungarian literary criticism," and contributed generously to the establishment of the Kazinczy Fund. In 1860 the Pest congregation collected a sizable sum for the Hungarian Academy of Sciences. In the same year, when István Széchenyi died, the Jewish congregations paid him homage with festive requiems, and the year thereafter they similarly honored Count László Teleki, leader of the radical magnates, upon his death.

While the progressive Hungarian Jews patiently labored to build up, brick by brick, the foundations of emancipation, Hungarian legislators were still not unanimous about the desirability of granting equal rights to the Jews. Thus, for instance, on December 1, 1862, Ágoston Trefort, the minister of education, gave a lecture at the Hungarian Academy of Sciences on the social conditions of Magyardom, in which he excoriated a layer of Jewry that, with its bad characteristics, had a harmful influence on the people, and he reproached Hungarian Jewry for still speaking German in its overwhelming majority. Although Leopold Löw energetically and effectively refuted Trefort's allegations—he pointed out, for example, that also many good Magyars, especially among the aristocracy, could not speak Hungarian—such an unwarranted attack caused apprehension among both the Jewish and non-Jewish supporters of emancipation.

At the next Diet, which convened on December 14, 1865, even Ferenc Deák, the greatest liberal leader of Hungary, indicated in a comprehensive address that he opposed a special law to emancipate the Jews, and suggested instead a general bill to declare equality without distinction of religion. Moreover, he added that he would have liked to see a parallel law to regulate the immigration "not only of those who follow the religion of Moses, but of all immigrants." Since most of the immigrants, however, were Jews, such a law would have in effect barred Jews from entering Hungary.

Before it could reach any conclusion, this Diet, too, was adjourned because of the outbreak of the Austro-Prussian war, which ended in June 1866 with the quick defeat of Austria at Königgrätz. As a consequence, Austria was excluded from the German Confederation, giving the emperor additional motivation to consolidate the situation within the empire, which meant, first of all, reaching an understanding with Hungary. In January 1867, negotiations were initiated in Vienna between the Austrians and the Hungarians with a view to working out a compromise between the imperial demands and those of the Hungarian legislature. The negotiations this time were brought to a positive conclusion, which became the basis of the Compromise (*Ausgleich*) of 1867. Its main provisions were the maintenance of certain "common affairs" in the form of a common army, common foreign relations, and the like, while granting Hungary complete internal independence. The Habsburg Empire was henceforward to be known as the Austro-Hungarian Empire. On this basis, on June 8, 1867, Emperor Francis Joseph of Austria was crowned king of Hungary.

29

Emancipation, Congress, and Schism (1867-69)

For several years before emancipation the Hungarian Jewish leadership had felt that a prime requirement of the community, in addition to securing equal rights, was to create a central denominational organization that would represent Hungarian Jewry in its relations with the government and the Christian churches. There can be little doubt that in feeling the need for such an organization, the Jews were influenced by the example of the Catholic Church, which enjoyed a powerful position in the country. As early as April 1860, R. Meisel of Pest submitted a plan to the executive board of his congregation urging the establishment of organizational links among the Jewish communities of the country. The same year, the Pápa congregation sent a memorandum to the Pest congregation, spelling out more concretely that the Jews of Hungary needed a central committee to represent their interests to the governmental authorities. In the following year, Leopold Löw raised his voice for the adoption of a constitution for the Jewish congregations, again emphasizing the need for a body that would enable the Jews to maintain official contact with the various governmental units. He coupled this demand with the suggestion that an institution be established for the training of rabbis with a thorough Jewish and secular education, able to preach in Hungarian, and a similar one for the training of Jewish teachers.

Dr. Ignác Hirschler, president of the Pest congregation, who was in close touch with Löw, reponded to these initiatives by submitting a memorandum to Chancellor Count Antal Forgách, asking him to convene a conference of representatives of Hungarian Jewry. R. Meisel, on his part, followed this up in 1863 with a memorandum of his own, suggesting that the governor's council form "a consistorial committee, to consist of several outstanding rabbis as well as educated and reliable laymen."

312

In April 1867, just a few months before the emancipation, the Pest congregation circulated a memorandum among the major Jewish communities in the country proposing the convocation of a national Jewish conference. Sixty-three of them responded positively, including several with a conservative majority. However, most conservatives felt they had to take action of their own and in the name of 124 Orthodox congregations prepared a countermemorandum, in which they accepted the need for a conference but requested equal representation in it for the Orthodox and advance assurance on a number of points that would have practically guaranteed the victory of their position.

To give more weight to their point of view, the Orthodox founded in 1867 a Society for Protecting the Faith, called Shomre haDat in Hebrew and Hitőr Egylet in Hungarian, with its seat in Pest, headed by a central committee consisting of twenty-one members. This committee elected a rabbinical college of five to guide them in religious and denominational questions. The stated aims of the Society were protecting Orthodox Jewry against unjust attacks, helping those congregations and individuals who suffered because of their faith, and propagating the Hungarian language. To demonstrate that this last item was to be taken seriously, Hitőr Egylet launched a bilingual German-Hungarian journal, the *Magyar Zsidó* (Hungarian Jew), which survived for almost three years (1867–1870), published thrice weekly the first two months and weekly thereafter, and this at a time when few Orthodox Jews in Hungary spoke Hungarian. (As mentioned in chapter 28, the Neolog Jews also had a bilingual publication, the *Izraelita Közlöny* [Israelite Gazette], which also existed from 1868 to 1871.) An even more remarkable testament to the penetration of Hungarian patriotism into Hungarian Orthodoxy was the appearance of a pamphlet titled *Entgegnung auf den Mahnruf an die Israeliten Ungarns . . .* (Pest, 1868), by an Orthodox author who used the pseudonym Veritas. Although Veritas wrote in German, he extolled the Hungarian language, because "Hungarian literature has not yet produced a single atheistic work," and went so far as to say that "one can boldly assert that the Hungarian language is, after Hebrew, the most holy tongue."

When finally the Emancipation Bill was voted into law, most Hungarian Jews (except the most Orthodox) considered it the well-deserved recognition of their devotion to the Hungarian fatherland, their self-sacrificing participation in the 1848 revolutionary war, and their unceasingly reiterated claim to be Hungarians like all other Hungarians, differing only in religion. The bill was submitted to the Lower House by Prime Minister Count Gyula Andrássy on November 25, 1867, and was passed unanimously, without any discussion, while in the Upper House sixty-four voted for it, and only four against it. The law, which became known as the Act of 1867:XVII, was as succinct as it was comprehensive. It read:

> 1. The Israelite inhabitants of the country are declared equally entitled to the practice of all civil and political rights as the Christian inhabitants.
> 2. All laws, customs, or decrees contrary to this are herewith invalidated.

The passing of the Emancipation Law by a near-unanimity of both houses of the National Assembly created tremendous elation, almost intoxication, among the Jews of Hungary. All over the country festive thanksgiving services were held in the synagogues, and on January 5, 1868, the Pest congregation issued a circular that stated:

> The memorial feast of the victory of the Maccabees [Hanukkah] became a double holiday for the Israelite inhabitants of the Hungarian fatherland through the legal emancipation. Our joy is the deeper, our enthusiasm the greater, since both legislative bodies passed the law of our emancipation— already sanctioned with the fatherly graciousness by His Majesty our King —with a dignity and cordiality that have not been evinced in any other country, without the expression of any offending antipathy or prejudice, and putting aside even the slightest limitation.

In February 1868, the minister of education, Baron Joseph Eötvös, invited to Buda thirty-six Jewish leaders whose names were submitted to him by Dr. Ignác Hirschler to discuss plans for a national Jewish congress. The invitees were all laymen, and Hirschler, in a letter to R. Löw, explained that he refrained from including rabbis so as to avoid, out of consideration for the feelings of the Orthodox, even the appearance of possibly dealing with religious matters. The agenda included preparing rules for the election of deputies to the planned congress, the organization of the congregations, and the establishment of schools.

Dissension on the part of the Orthodox surfaced on the very second day of the conference. Among the thirty-six men invited by Hirschler, only seven were Orthodox, and led by Zsigmond Krausz, they asked Eötvös to permit them to confer separately and to submit to him a separate propoasal. In fact, Krausz suggested that the government recognize that Hungarian Jewry consisted of two denominations, conduct a census to determine to which one each Jew belonged, and on that basis convene a congress in which the two groups would confer independently. On the last day of the conference, the seven Orthodox deputies submitted a separate opinion warning against centralization and demanding total autonomy for the congregations. Eötvös rejected their demand, saying that "the law knows only one Israelite religion."

The majority adopted three proposals, worked out by Mór Mezei, president of the National Israelite Hungarian Association. First, all adult Israelite men, irrespective of their economic status, should have the right to vote for deputies, but only those who knew one of the languages of the country should be eligible. Paid employees of the congregations including the rabbis, should be ineligible. Second, the manner of synagogue services should be determined by the majority of each congreation, but, upon the request of twenty dues-paying members, the mother congregation should be obliged to maintain a separate synagogue for them. Third, every congregation should maintain an elementary school, while those who wished to become rabbis or teachers should have the choice of studying either in Talmud Torah schools and yeshivas, or in the rabbinical seminary and teacher training school to be established.

In his closing address, Eötvös, by then fully aware of the serious dissension in the Jewish ranks, expressed the hope that the consciousness of common interests in the Jewish community would outweigh the differences of opinion within it, and cautioned the deputies to be patient and pliant.

Following the conference, in which the Orthodox did not achieve what they wanted, their efforts went into high gear. The Society for Protecting the Faith published a Hebrew pamphlet calling the exclusion of the rabbis from the congress a blasphemy. Zsigmond Krausz was joined in his fight by Dr. Azriel Hildesheimer, rabbi of Kismarton, by far the most articulate, capable, and scholarly spokesman of the Orthodox wing, who in his own person exemplified the compatibility of Orthodox traditionalism and modern education and scholarship.

Azriel Hildesheimer (b. Halberstadt, 1820; d. Berlin, 1899) received a traditional Jewish education and attended the University of Berlin studying Semitics, philosophy, history, and science, and earned his Ph.D. at the University of Halle. Married to the daughter of industrialist Aaron Hirsch, he was financially independent, but in 1851 he accepted the invitation of the Kismarton community to serve as its rabbi. There he organized the educational system and established a yeshiva whose curriculum included secular studies. He himself taught many subjects and within a short time attracted students from all over Europe. However, despite his great learning and emphatically conservative position, he was not sufficiently tradition-bound for the majority of the Orthodox Hungarian Jews, who opposed the measure of modernism he introduced into his school. When Dr. Hirschler failed to invite rabbis to the preliminary conference, Hildesheimer indignantly fought against their exclusion, asking rhetorically, "Who gave the right to the drafters of the majority proposal to deprive those who are neither thieves, nor robbers, nor involved in bankruptcy, of one of their most sacred human and civil rights?" When the exclusion of rabbis was eliminated, Hildesheimer was elected to the congress and took an active part in its deliberations, fighting against both the Neolog and the ultraorthodox factions. He submitted moderate proposals that could have saved the unity of Hungarian Jewry, but, as we shall see, it was not to be. Soon after the Congress, despairing of the developments in Hungarian Jewry, Hildesheimer accepted an invitation to the newly founded Adass Jisroel Orthodox congregation in Berlin, and in 1873 established there his second rabbinical seminary, which became the central institution for the training of Orthodox rabbis in Europe. It was due to Hildesheimer and his disciples that the idea of the compatibility of traditional Judaism with the scholarly investigation of Jewish sources and with modern culture gained acceptance in a major part of conservative Judaism. In contrast to Samson Raphael Hirsch, with whom he shared the leadership of Orthodox German Jewry and who advocated Orthodox separatism, Hildesheimer counseled cooperation among all segments of Jewry for the sake of the Jewish people as a whole. He was a devoted supporter of the Jews of the Land of Israel, and while still in Kismarton he collected large sums of money for them. In 1872 he founded the Palaestina Verein for raising the educational and vocational standards of Jerusalem Jews, and in 1879 he established an orphanage in Jerusalem, which brought down on his head the wrath of the ultraorthodox of the city, who put him under a ban (*herem*). Undaunted, he supported the *Hoveve Zion* (Lovers of Zion) and the Palestine colonization movement. His published writings secured for him a permanent place in the history of Jewish scholarship.

Upon Hildesheimer's clarion call in June 1868, thirty rabbis submitted an application to Eötvös, asking for the elimination of the exclusion of rabbis and congregational officials from the Congress, and in September the minister so ordered. The efforts of the Orthodox in connection with the planned congress were directed at achieving separate representation, even a separate organization, independent of the progressives. The latter, on the other hand, strove to preserve the unity of all the Jews in the country and to secure for them internal autonomy. For this purpose they issued another circular in August 1868, emphasizing that the congress could deal only with organizational and management issues and would not be able to take a position on religious and ritual questions, on either the Orthodox or Reform side.

Thereupon, as Venetianer writes with critical irony: "All over the country the electioneering movement began, which, with its canvasing, forests of flags, and bribery, could worthily compete with the parliamentary elections." On election day (November 18, 1868), 220 deputies were returned, 132 of them progressives and 88 conservatives. On December 14 the National Israelite Congress opened in the large hall of the County House in Pest, with the progressives seated on the right, the conservatives on the left. The opening address was given by Minister of Education Joseph Eötvös, who outlined the tasks awaiting the Congress and emphasized that they comprised only organizational issues, and that religious tenets and principles could not be discussed. Dr. Ignác Hirschler was elected president, and as the first step taken by the Congress a delegation was sent to the king-emperor, led by Mór Wahrmann —grandson of R. Israel Wahrmann of Pest and, despite his young age (thirty-seven at the time), already a power in the financial world of Hungary—to pay homage to the ruler, who expressed his hope that the Congress would work in brotherly harmony.

After two weeks of discussions of technical issues, on December 30 three committees were elected to prepare detailed proposals for consideration by the plenum: one committee was to deal with the rules of congregational organization and the disposition of the school fund, the second with the rules of the schools, and the third with the rules of elections to future congresses. Despite the avowed intention of the leadership to keep religious questions out of the agenda, this proved impossible. In deliberations on the most varied issues, the conservative minority emphasized again and again that when two religious views contradicted each other, the minority could not be forced to accede to principles represented by the majority—that is, to accept the views and decisions of the progressives. This position was opposed by the progressive majority, who argued that since they did not deviate from the ancestral faith, there was no justification in splitting Hungarian Jewry into two denominations.

On January 28, 1869, the Congress began to discuss the proposals of the organizational committee, presented by Joseph Popper. The intention of the committee was clearly to satisfy the demands of the Orthodox, and hence it did not include a single item that would have contradicted traditional religious teachings. Aware of the objections of the religious wing to centralization, the committee proposed a national presidium whose powers would be limited to carrying out the decisions of its autonomous member congregations and to serving relations between the Jews and the government.

These concessions did not satisfy the Orthodox. The recommendations of the conservative minority, presented by Zsigmond Krausz, argued that the Jews living in the Diaspora had never known any kind of centralization; the medium that kept Jewry together had always been the ancestral faith; the Jewish institutions were comprised in the teachings of the Bible, the Talmud, and the *Shulḥan 'Arukh*; and the seats of the rabbis were the only centers from which Jewish life had been directed. Hence, they roundly rejected the idea of a presidium. Contact with the government, they suggested, should be entrusted to committees to be elected by the congregations of the counties. They considered congregational administration a religious question and therefore protested against the decisions of the majority.

The presentation of the two proposals was followed by heated debates in which each side attacked the other. In a lengthy address, R. Azriel Hildesheimer presented the conservative position against the majority proposal, arguing that the sixteenth-century religious code *Shulḥan 'Arukh* must be the basis of Jewish life, since everything deduced by later sages from the laws of the Torah of Moses was in principle a part of the Torah. The eighty-eight deputies present, who were Guardians of the Faith (members of the Society for Protecting the Faith), submitted a motion urgently asking the Congress to declare that no draft of organizational and educational statutes would be discussed unless its provisions were expressly in agreement with the biblical and talmudic laws as codified in the *Shulḥan 'Arukh*. The president did not put the motion on the agenda, because it would have provoked a discussion of religious issues, but in the course of the general debate that followed, speaker after speaker referred to it with increasing sharpness. On February 5 forty-eight members of the Orthodox opposition marched out of the meeting hall, stating in writing that they would no longer participate in the deliberation and protesting in advance against the impending resolutions. As a result, when it finally came to voting, only 116 deputies were present out of the 220 elected. Of them, 103 voted for the proposals of the majority.

After additional modifications, the statutes adopted for the congregational organization included these points: The basis of the organization is the congregation, which is required to maintain the usual synagogal, ritual, educational, and charitable institutions. A congregation unable to do so will be attached to another one or, jointly with others, will form a district congregation. Every Israelite is required to become a member of the congregation existing in his place of residence. There can be only one congregation in one locality, and it is entitled to impose dues on its members for the maintenance of its activities. Each congregation will be managed by a representative body and an executive, elected by all the members. The executive and representative bodies jointly will form the general assembly, whose sphere of authority is to include the appointment of officials and the modification of statutes. The rabbi will be elected by all the members entitled to vote. The rights and duties of the rabbi are to supervise the synagogue services, to give sermons, to organize extraordinary services at the request of the executive, to help in talmudic study, to decide religious questions, to control synagogal and ritual institutions, to perform marriages and divorces, to keep the register of births, marriages, and deaths, and to direct the instruction of the youth. His sphere of authority extends only to his own congregation, which he can represent on the outside only with special authorization. He can participate in the deliberations of the executive and the general assembly only on the basis of special invitation. The congregations of the country will be grouped into twenty-six districts. The district council will consist of one deputy per every hundred members of each congregation. It will maintain a relationship with the government, through the national office, supervise the educational and charitable institutions, and supply members, to be selected by casting lots, to a judiciary committee, which will adjudicate differences that arise within the district. The presidents of the twenty-six districts will constitute a special body, which will meet once a year, to control the national school fund and decide on the convocation of a general congress. They will elect one of their rank as president of the national office, who will be the intermediary between the districts and the government.

As one can see from this summary, the intention of the majority actually was to carefully avoid any reference to the nature and style of religious observances. Nevertheless, the Orthodox minority was not appeased and, having mostly left the Congress, did not return even when the agenda moved on to the new subjects of election rules and educational issues. As a result, these subjects were dealt with much more expeditiously and with much less acrimony. The election rules, whose discussion began on February 17, 1869, envisaged the creation of eighty to ninety electoral districts in the country, and since in some parts of the country the dispersion of the Jews in very small groups made direct election impracticable, they proposed indirect elections: every Israelite inhabitant of Hungary would vote for an elector, and the electors, in turn, would elect the deputies to the congress.

The third subject of the agenda was the creation of rules for establishing Jewish schools. The school committee suggested the establishment of schools by each Jewish congregation, while the congregations that were too small to do so would be asked to organize Jewish religious instruction supplementary to the general schools. It made recommendations for the introduction of religious instruction into the general secondary schools and the foundation of Talmud Torah schools.

The discussion about the establishment of a rabbinical seminary was led by Samuel Kohn, chief rabbi of Pest, who was an enthusiastic supporter of the plan. His position was that the seminary would "stand strictly on Mosaic-rabbinic tenets, and would pay particular attention to teaching the Talmud and the ritual laws," while also not neglecting instruction in scholarship and modern knowledge. Despite objections raised by the few Orthodox deputies who continued to attend the meetings (led by Azriel Hildesheimer), the plan for the rabbinical seminary and Jewish schools was adopted by a vote of seventy for and only two against.

Before closing, the congress resolved to submit a petition to Baron Eötvös suggesting that the next session of Parliament take up the question of the equalization of the Jewish denomination. In the event, that endeavor was achieved only some thirty years later with the Law of Reception, which will be discussed later.

The Hungarian National Israelite Congress of 1868–69 had both positive and negative outcomes. Among its achievements was the creation of a central organization of the majority of Hungarian Jews, with a national office that represented the interests of the country's Jews vis-à-vis the government and could function as roughly an equivalent of the central organizations of the Christian churches. The Congress regulated the relationship between individual congregations and their rabbis and other employees, and resolved to establish a modern rabbinical seminary, a teachers' institute, and a Jewish school network. It became the expression of the desire and determination of most Hungarian Jews to be part of the cultural life of the country, and it effectively promoted the spread of Magyarization among the Jews. As Mór Wahrmann, the first Jewish representative in the Hungarian Lower House, put it in a spirited speech:

> What was the situation [of the Jews before the Congress] across the country? The congregations were in disorderly conditions, the schools neglected, everywhere friction, quarrels, among the congregations, among members of the same congregation, between the congregations and their priests [in Hungarian *pap*, "priest," is used to refer to rabbis as well], the congregations and the teachers. In these disturbances, in these quarrels, magistrates and subprefects disposed and decided administratively, arbitrarily. This could not continue. The functionaries of the Ministry of Education were overloaded with dealing with such issues; there were cases when, in quarrels arising out of ritual questions, magistrates had the decisive word.
> . . .
> True, the Congress had its opponents, in the ranks of those who like order nowhere and on no occasion, who do not wish to leave the crumbling walls of the ghetto, because they do not want to breathe fresh air; those who do not want to go out of the prison because their eyes are very

often unable to suffer the brightness of light, who in general are afraid lest their selfish interests be endangered by things being put in order. . . .

The Jewish Congress was based on the widest possible electoral basis, almost on a universal suffrage; each of its meetings, each of its conferences, was public; all parties, all shadings, all trends, were represented in it; all its deliberations and resolutions were given the widest publicity by the journals and public media.

Despite this glowing account of the Congress, it had its negative results as well. Above all, it was responsible for bringing out into the open, and thereby sharpening, the differences between the conservative and progressive elements in the Jewish population of Hungary. Without the Congress these differences would have remained confined, as they had been before, to small local squabbles and to the setting up in some places of a conservative and a progressive synagogue under the aegis of one and the same congregation. Now, in consequence of vehemently and often bitterly airing the differences between the two trends in a national forum, the disagreements assumed a countrywide dimension, and they soon led to a de facto national schism. This was recognized by non-Jewish observers as well, and one of them, the representative Kálmán Ghiczy, asked in Parliament on Feburary 16, 1870, "Was it necessary to convene the Israelite Congress, and thereby cause a split among our Israelite fellow citizens? Is it possible that in religious matters the majority should lay down the law for the minority?" (It was in response to this speech of Ghiczy that Wahrmann launched into his above-quoted panegyrics.)

After the conclusion of the Congress it became evident that it was only a question of a few weeks, or few months at the utmost, until the Orthodox opposition organized itself into a second, competing national body. The House was generally sympathetic to their endeavor, and several members (including Ferenc Deák) spoke up in support of the principle that in matters of religious conviction the will of the majority must not be imposed upon the minority. Hence, it came as no surprise when on March 18, 1870, after receiving an application from the Guardians of the Faith, the House passed a resolution stating: "Since it is contrary to the principle of religious liberty that the members of a religious group should be forced by the decision of the majority to become part of an organization that is contrary to their principles, it is desirable that the differences be straightened out, and therefore the minister of education is herewith instructed to suspend all decrees issued heretofore until the law is given thorough consideration." Consequently, on April 2, the minister of education ordered that nobody could be forced to accept the resolutions of the Congress.

This ruling enabled the Guardians of the Faith to convene (on August 9, 1870) their "countercongress" in Pest, where they resolved to organize the conservative congregations into a separate autonomous body, and adopted statutes that repeatedly emphasized that their organization was based in every respect on the *Shulḥan 'Arukh*. The entirety of their religious and ritual life, the rules of the employment of their officials, the congregational institutions, the customs to be observed—all this and much more was to be conducted in strict conformity with that sixteenth-century code of Judaism. Within the congregations they assigned much greater leadership roles to the rabbis, and resolved that rabbis should be appointed on the basis of letters of recommendation obtained from outstanding rabbinical authorities. To manage their affairs they elected a body of seven members, which they called the Orthodox Mediatory Committee, headed by Ignác Reich, president of the Guardians of the Faith.

Fate favored the Orthodox aspirations in that Baron Joseph Eötvös, the moving spirit behind the National Israelite Congress and devoted upholder of Hungarian Jewish organizational unity, died in February 1871, and with his death the major obstacle to Orthodox separatism was removed. His successor as minister of education, Tivadar (Theodor) Pauler, following a decree by the king-emperor, approved on October 22, 1871, the statutes of the Orthodox conference, and therewith with governmental sanction Hungarian Jewry became officially divided into two wings, almost two denominations: one that recognized the resolutions of the Congress, and one that followed the rulings of the Society for Protecting the Faith. The first came to be known as Congressional or Neolog congregations and the second as autonomous Orthodox congregations, or briefly, the Neolog and the Orthodox. To complicate things, a third group—smaller than either of the first two—also asserted its independence: it consisted of those congregations that refused to join either the Neolog or the Orthodox, but adhered to the status quo ante that existed prior to the split. They came to be called the Status Quo congregations.

For all practical purposes, Hungarian Jewry thus came to comprise three separate, autonomous national organizations, which in many respects behaved toward one another in the manner of competing denominations. Fights among them occurred not infrequently, and as we shall see in subsequent chapters, at times their narrowly denominational concerns prevailed over the basic need to unite for the sake of the common interest of Magyar Israel. In 1888 the government emphasized (in its bill 1888:MCXCI): "There can be no doubt that the Israelite congregations, which stand on the Congressional, as well as on the Orthodox and the Status Quo Ante basis, are to be considered, from the point of view of governmental policy as well as from the standpoint of Judaism, as belonging to one and the same religious denomination." It is clear that such a proclamation was felt to be necessary because there was a tendency in governmental circles, and also in the Jewish community itself, to consider Hungarian Jewry as comprising several independent and autonomous denominations, just as was the case with the Christian majority.

Serious religious differences existed in the Jewish communities of many other countries as well, yet in none of them did such a schism take place. Why precisely Hungary was the scene of such a split can be explained, I believe, with all due caution and reservations, by the marginal position Hungarian Jewry occupied between two Jewish worlds that can be termed eastern and western. Eastern European Jewry, to the northeast and east of Hungary, consisted of a solid majority of religious elements, whether Hasidim or Mitnagdim (Orthodox opponents of Hasidism), for whom it was a given that Jewish tradition—including both Halakha (law) and minhag (custom)—was the only imaginable basis of Jewish life, whether individual or communal. Whatever modernization the Jewish Enlightenment introduced into Eastern Europe, its proponents remained a small minority, and communal Jewish life continued to flow in the old channels. Such an environment was not conducive to the emergence of a progressive communal organization that would have competed with the existing conservative congregations.

In Western Europe, on the other hand, that is, to the northwest and west of Hungary, the Haskala made rapid headway, and by the time the Jews were emancipated there, most of them had adjusted, or were about to adjust, to the secular, primarily German culture of the gentile world in which they lived. To be sure, there were religious differences in the west as well, but even the Orthodox, while not abandoning the "four cubits of the Halakha," considered it permissible and even desirable to acquire a familiarity with German *Kultur*. No wonder a man like Azriel Hildesheimer, who had been denounced by the Hungarian Orthodox Jews, found a response in Germany and there became a great figure of German neo-orthodoxy. This atmosphere, and this demographic configuration, were again unfavorable to the emergence of two competing communal organizations, a conservative and a progressive.

Hungary was the borderland between these two types of Jewries. There were the Orthodox Jews, many of them still Yiddish-speaking, with their traditional religious worldview, not uniform by any means but ranging from the Orthodox to the ultraorthodox, with a sprinkling of Hasidim, all of whom were fervent enough and, what is equally important, numerous enough to feel that they could not bend to rules worked out by the progressives, even though the latter constituted by 1868 the majority. Many of these—precisely how many is not clear—were immigrants, or children of immigrants, from the east. Opposed to them were the progressives, of whom many were older inhabitants in the country, more advanced in Magyarization, more caught up in the patriotic fervor, more convinced that their religion could not and should not stand in the way of their becoming fully Magyars of the Mosaic faith. They tried their best to maintain the unity of Magyar Israel, but were not sufficiently preponderant numerically (as were the progressive Jews in, say, Germany) to dominate the large and vociferous minority of the Orthodox. Thus came about the presence in Hungary of both Eastern-type and Western-type Jews in a numerical relationship not duplicated in any other country, inevitably leading to the establishment of two, or rather three, independent countrywide Jewish religious organizations officially recognized by the Hungarian government.

The first issue with which Hungarian Jewry was seized after the Congress ended and once its aftershocks subsided, was the establishment of the Rabbinical Seminary. This, too, was an issue about which the government had to decide between the recommendations of the Neolog and the protests of the Orthodox. In 1873 the government allocated a building lot for the Seminary, and Minister of Education Ágoston Treffort appointed a committee of twenty-four to be responsible for the building and its equipment, the working out of the Seminary's statutes, and the appointment of its faculty. Soon thereafter, the Orthodox congregations submitted a petition to the House with over 200 signatures, protesting the establishment of the Seminary and arguing that this was an illegal use of the Jewish school fund. Reasoning that Hungarian Jewry comprised two independent denominations, they demanded the division into two of the school fund. Treffort opposed this view and held that the school fund was the common property of Hungarian Jewry, could not be divided, and had to be used equally for the expenses of the Rabbinical Seminary and the elementary schools of the Orthodox congregations.

The building of the Seminary, which housed the Jewish Teachers Institute as well, was completed in 1877. Its statutes, approved by the government in July of that year, provided the appointment by the minister of education of a board of twenty-four members, twelve from Budapest and twelve from the country. Márton Schweiger (1834–1905), president of the central Neolog National Office in Budapest, was appointed chairman of the board. The dedication festivities on October 4, 1877, were attended by Prime Minister Kálmán Tisza, Minister of Education Ágoston Treffort, President of the Upper House György Majláth, Chief Mayor of Budapest Károly Rath, several members of the House of Representatives, the rector and deans of the University of Budapest, representatives of Christian theological institutions, Hungarian Jewish leaders, and guests from abroad. In his dedication address, Chief Rabbi Samuel Kohn expressed his hope that

> the national rabbinical school will strengthen the millennial sacred covenant between Jewry and scholarship that the passing of times have loosened; that, as an intermediary between Jewish and Hungarian scholarship it will at long last open an access for the former to Hungarian literature; that pure religiosity, free of narrow-minded zealotry and dark fanaticism, will, together with the Hungarian word and the Hungarian spirit, spread its influence in all the congregations of this broad homeland; that it will educate for the future generations spiritual leaders, pastors, who will represent the sacred interests of their denomination in a dignified manner, will liberate their followers from the iron yoke of self-isolation and prejudice, will proclaim peace in our congregations, blessing instead of anathemas from their pulpits, and, standing on the cultural level of our age, will speak to our student youth in a language that it will understand and respect.

Six weeks after its dedication, King-Emperor Francis Joseph honored the Seminary with a visit.

The fact that a Jewish rabbinical school was established by the government and was to be financed by it, the festive dedication of the Seminary with the participation of the highest government officials and representatives of Christian theological schools, the distinction of the royal visit—all this created an atmosphere that greatly contributed to the feeling among the Hungarian Jews that they were, at long last, equal partners with the other denominations in the great national endeavor of advancing education, culture, and religious brotherhood in the beloved homeland.

To begin with, three full professors were appointed by the minister of education, in addition to several adjunct professors. Moses Bloch (b. Ronsperg, Moravia, 1815; d. Budapest, 1905) was appointed professor of Talmud and Codes and was elected chairman of the faculty. Educated and ordained by famous talmudic authorities, Bloch had served as rabbi of Wottiz, Hermann Mestetz, and Leipnik, and he was sixty-two when he received the appointment to the Seminary. After moving to Budapest he wrote several talmudic-historical studies, dealing mostly with talmudic law, which were published in Hebrew, Hungarian, and German.

Wilhelm Bacher (b. Liptószentmiklós, 1850; d. Budapest, 1913), the only Hungarian-born of the first three full professors of the Seminary, was the son of Simon Bacher (Bachrach, 1823–91), a Hebrew writer and poet. Wilhelm Bacher was a child prodigy who, after attending Hebrew schools, graduated at the age of seventeen from the Evangelical high-school of Pressburg, was admitted to the University of Pest (where he became a student of Ármin Vámbéry), and in 1870, at twenty, earned his Ph.D. at the University of Leipzig. In 1876 he got his rabbinical diploma at the Breslau Jüdisch-Theologisches Seminar and was appointed rabbi in Szeged as successor to Leopold Löw. He was twenty-seven when he was appointed full professor at the Budapest Seminary, where he taught Bible, Jewish history, Midrash, and Hebrew poetry and grammar. In 1884 he founded the Israelite Hungarian Literary Society (known from its Hungarian acronym as IMIT) and, jointly with Joseph Bánóczi, the *Magyar Zsidó Szemle* (Hungarian Jewish Review), which soon became one of the foremost periodicals devoted to Jewish scholarship. In 1907, upon Bloch's retirement at the age of ninety-two, Bacher was appointed by Francis Joseph director of the Seminary. His scholarly output was not only exceptionally rich (his bibliography published by Ludwig Blau lists forty-eight books and close to 700 articles) but also astoundingly many-sided. He was a master of Hebrew, Aramaic, Arabic, and Persian, made important contributions to the study of these languages and their literatures, was a leading historian of Hebrew grammar, and was the most outstanding researcher of the day of the talmudic Aggada. His multivolume work on the Aggada of the Tannaites and the Amorites (also translated into Hebrew) is to this day the indispensable introduction to the subject. The permanent value of Bacher's work is demonstrated by the fact that all his major books were reissued in reprints in the 1960s and 1970s by various German publishers.

David Kaufman (b. Kojetein, Moravia, 1852; d. Karlsbad, 1899), the third *ordinarius* (full professor) appointed to the Seminary faculty in 1877, earned his Ph.D. in Leipzig in 1874 and graduated from the Jüdisch-Theologisches Seminar of Breslau in 1877, by which time he was known for his publications on the history of Jewish philosophy. He taught Jewish philosophy and history, was for a time coeditor of the prestigious *Monatschrift für Geschicthe und Wissenschaft des Judentums* and, having married into a well-to-do family, was in a position to assemble a rich collection of rare Hebrew manuscripts, incunabula, and geniza fragments, which, after his premature death, became part of the library of the Hungarian Academy of Sciences. His multifaceted scholarly work included studies of medieval Jewish philosophy, a remarkable study titled *The Senses: A Contribution to the History of Medieval Physi-*

ology and Psychology Based on Hebrew and Arabic Sources (published in the Annual Report of the Rabbinical Seminary, Budapest, 1884), and a large number of historical and genealogical monographs, published either in German or in German and Hungarian. He was a pioneer in the investigation of Jewish art and co-founded the Viennese Society for the Collection and Conservation of Artistic and Historical Monuments of Judaism. In several of his writings he defended the Jewish community and Judaism against attacks by the gentile scholar Paul Lagarde and by the German preacher Adolf Stöcker, who in 1878 founded the German Anti-Semitic Party.

These three men set the tone and established the level of scholarship at the newly founded Budapest Rabbinical Seminary. As a result of their work, and of those who followed them on its faculty, the Seminary became one of the most important institutions for the training of Jewish scholars and rabbis. Before a student could graduate, he had first to earn his Ph.D. degree at the University of Budapest in either philosophy or Semitic studies. The teachers at the Seminary stimulated their students to pursue scholarly research, and a surprisingly high percentage of its graduates engaged in scholarly work in addition to filling positions as rabbis in congregations in Hungary and abroad. In the decades to come, many European Jewish institutions of learning drew on graduates of the Budapest Seminary to fill positions on their faculties and posts of leadership. Others of its graduates became professors at various universities and rabbis of many congregations in Europe and America. Part of the curriculum at the Seminary was training in homiletics, which enabled the students to acquire the impressive rabbinical oratorical style for which many Hungarian rabbis became famous. Until the Holocaust, the Budapest Seminary filled an essential role in the life of Hungarian Jewry.

30

Zionism: Precursors, Founders, Opponents (1839-97)

It is one of the paradoxes in the history of Hungarian Jewry that, on the one hand, the precursors and founders of the Zionist movement arose from its ranks, and, on the other, it produced the most fervent opponents of Zionism and provided the smallest contingents to rally around its flag. Individual Hungarian Jews had the lion's share not only in initiating political Zionism but also in launching, several decades earlier, the "return to the soil" movement and the establishment of Jewish agricultural settlements in Palestine; but at the same time, the Hungarian Jewish leadership, and under its influence the majority of Hungarian Jews, remained adamantly opposed to both. Further on we shall quote some of the pronouncements of Hungarian Jewish religious and secular leaders of the late nineteenth century who were faithful, convinced, capable, and enthusiastic fighters for the Jewish cause as they understood it and yet denounced Zionism and fought it tooth and nail.

Hungarian Jewish opposition to Zionism was motivated by two main factors: a conviction that the Jews, or at any rate the Hungarian Jews, were not a race, not a people, not an ethnic group, not a nationality, but purely and solely a religious denomination; an emotional reaction against Zionism, whose goals, in the eyes of the Hungarian Jews, from its very inception resembled those of the most virulent forms of nineteenth-century Hungarian anti-Semitism.

This, of course, did not mean there was no positive response at all to the Zionist initiative in Hungary, nor that absolutely no Hungarian Jews emigrated to Palestine. But the fact was that in the fifty years of its pre-state history, Zionism attracted only a small percentage of Hungarian Jews, and Hungarian 'aliya (immigration to Palestine) remained very small throughout that period.

Zionist historians distinguish between political Zionism, the creation of Theodor Herzl's genius, and what went before it among the Hoveve Zion (Lovers of Zion), considered romantic dreamers whose efforts resulted at most in establishing a few small, insignificant, and ineffectively run agricultural "colonies" in Palestine. Generally overlooked is the fact that Herzl's grand political design—the establishment for the Jews of a state of their own secured by public law—was prefigured by the ideas of several Hungarian Jewish proto-Zionists whose writings and practical efforts antedated him by several decades. This is not to diminish in any way Herzl's role in laying the foundations for the State of Israel, but to clarify that the differences between him and those who preceded him lay not in the originality of his idea but in his ability— never even approximated by his predecessors—to create a movement for its realization, organize a parliament for its members in the form of the Zionist Congress, and establish other Zionist public institutions. The movement Herzl created outlived him, continued to grow, and fifty years later achieved its goal in the State of Israel, making Herzl one of the greatest figures of Jewish history.

What his predecessors achieved was only to produce a few small ripples, which quickly disappeared in the crosscurrents that tossed and tore at European Jewish communities in the nineteenth century. Yet it was Herzl himself who said that a man should be judged not by what he achieved but by the goals he set for himself. What a man achieves depends on external circumstances over which he has no control; the goals a man sets for himself are his own free and autonomous creations and, as such, measures of his mind, his will, his grasp, his vision. If we measure Herzl's Hungarian predecessors with this Herzlian yardstick, we find that as far as the scope of their ideas was concerned, they were not only proto-Zionists but also proto-Herzlians, who wanted to achieve by and large what he succeeded in achieving, by the same methods he applied in the course of the eight short years of his Zionist work.

First a word about chronology. In the "prehistory of Zionism" (the term is that of the Zionist historian N. M. Gelber), the Ḥibbat Zion (Love of Zion) movement, a nonpolitical endeavor to promote Jewish settlement in Palestine on a philanthropic basis that began in the 1860s, is counted as the only forerunner of Zionism, with achievements so limited that when Herzl created his political Zionist movement most Hovevei Zion were ready to join it. However, we know of at least two rabbis, both of whom lived in southern Hungary, who some three decades before the inception of the Ḥibbat Zion movement put forward the idea of obtaining the Land of Israel (Eretz Israel) for the Jews by political means.

One of them was a student of R. Moses Sofer, R. Yequthiel Hirschenstein, who in 1812 became rabbi of Varazdin in the Slovenian area of southern Hungary and was a close friend and advisor of Moshe Sachs, another student of Moshe Sofer and an early proto-Zionist activist. In 1836 Hirschenstein wrote to Sachs: "In my view, the best strategy and the main thing is to win over the masters of the 'Holy Alliance' [the triple alliance of Austria, Germany, and Russia] to the cause of our country [Eretz Israel], and to show them the importance of this matter." He assumed that France and England would also be interested in supporting the plan of establishing a Jewish state in the Land of Israel, and was encouraged by the independence Greece gained from Turkey to work out a plan "that could be submitted to every government for approval." He believed that by diplomatic work for the establishment of a Jewish state, the words of the prophet would be fulfilled: "Not by an army and not by force, but by My spirit, saith the Lord of Hosts."

About the same time, a Sephardi Jew who filled a rabbinical post in the Croatian part of southern Hungary for fifty years conceived a political plan for obtaining Palestine for the Jews, and worked for its realization. Judah Alkalay (or Elkali; b. Sarajevo, 1798; d. Jerusalem, 1878) became teacher and preacher at the age of twenty-seven and later also rabbi, of the Sephardi community of Zemlin (Zemun, Zimony), near Belgrade, then in southern Hungary, which remained his home until 1874, when he settled in Jerusalem. His was a curious mixture of traditional Judaism—he was even a kabbalist—and modern worldliness. His superior in Zemlin was R. Samuel Masad, yet another former student of Moses Sofer. Zevi Zahavi, a historian of the Hungarian precursors of Zionism, suspects that Alkalay absorbed, through the intermediacy of R. Masad, the ideas of the great Pressburg halakhist concerning the religious duty of settling in the Land of Israel.

In any case, beginning in 1839 Alkalay published a number of books in which he called upon the Jews to return to the Land of Israel and—unusually for the age and for a man of his background—to engage in practical and political work for that purpose, instead of relying on and waiting for a miraculous return in the messianic days. In one of his early treatises, published in 1839, he wrote: "This great thing requires a petition to the kings of the land, for they are just kings, and the Holy One, blessed be He, will put it into their hearts that they should declare freedom for us to return to our estate, the inheritance of our fathers."

Alkalay argues that there was indeed hope that this would soon come about, and in support of this view he refers to the archbishop of Esztergom, Joseph Kopacsi, who declared to the emperor and the magnates, "We have never heard nor seen that anybody should be kept in prison for eighteen centuries as these miserable Jews who suffer under the hands of kings and princes, even though they comport themselves decently and properly."

Alkalay manages to produce a unique mixture of traditional Orthodoxy relying on divine intervention and modern confidence in statecraft when he asserts that the ingathering of the exiles of Israel will be not a miraculous but a natural process, "for the Holy One, blessed be He, will bring about the matter in a regular manner and with honor, and in the manner of *ḥokhmat hapolitiq* [the science of politics]."

In addition to publishing several treatises, Alkalay also traveled extensively to propagate his idea of Jewish return to Eretz Israel. In 1852, while he was on a visit to England, a booklet of his was published under the title "Harbinger of Good Tidings: An Address to the Jewish Nation by Rabbi Judah Elkali on the Propriety of Organizing an Association to Promote the Regaining of Their Fatherland." As the title shows, Alkalay's plan was not merely to settle Jews piecemeal in "their fatherland," but to "regain" it as a whole, which is precisely what Herzl wanted to achieve by obtaining a "charter" for all of Palestine from Turkey. Alkalay was also a true forerunner of Herzl in that he tried to organize an "association," prefiguring Herzl's Jewish agency. To realize his idea, Alkalay visited several countries, founding in each a Society for the Settlement of Eretz Israel, all of which, however, soon petered out. In 1871 he visited Palestine, and founded such a society there, too.

Although Alkalay's work did not leave behind concrete results, his is the undeniable merit of having been the first in modern times to conceive and put forward ideas that came astonishingly close to Herzl's political Zionism. It is tempting to speculate whether Herzl was in any way influenced by Alkalay's ideas and work. That he knew about him is more than likely, since Herzl's grandfather, Simon Leib Herzl, lived in Zemlin, was a member of the community of which Alkalay was the rabbi, and paid annual visits to his son Jacob, Herzl's father, in Budapest, and on those occasions may have told his son and teenage grandson of the activities of his rabbi.

Another student of R. Moses Sofer who became an early Hungarian forerunner of Zionism was Joseph Natonek (b. Komlód, 1813; d. Bátor, 1892). After studying in several yeshivas, he got his rabbinical qualification in Pressburg and became rabbi in Jászberény and then in Székesfehérvár. In 1861, Natonek published in Buda a pseudonymous book (signed Abir Amieli) titled *Messiás, avagy értekezés a zsidó emancipációról* (Messiah: or, A Treatise on Jewish Emancipation), in which he expressed the view that the Jews should oppose emancipation, because their true homeland was not in Hungary but in Jerusalem, and he argued that the Jews were a nation and not merely a religious community. One could no longer wait for miracles, he wrote, but had to undertake efforts, with the help of the nations, to realize Jewry's messianic destiny. Only after the Jews achieved independence in the Land of Israel would they be able to become "a light unto the nations." From the patriotism of the Hungarians the Jews should learn to be zealous for "Israelite nationalism":

> I can be a proud and worthy son of my ancient nation only if I shall succeed in awakening it from its apparent death, and in encouraging it to realize its national independence, of which our prophets prophesized. I want to devote my entire life to this single task, as long as my soul is in me. . . . Submit, therefore, to the will of the Master of the Universe, and let us devote our spiritual powers, our famous industriousness, and our eonomic abilities to the goal that the Master of the Universe set before us, that is to say, to reacquire our ancient inheritance, the Land of Israel, and to establish in it quickly our national independence. . . . The people of Israel, whom the generous hand of God has endowed with the most excellent intellectual traits, is forbidden to go begging at the doors of foreign peoples asking for little crumbs of equality, when it could enjoy fully its own national independence.

The Hungarian government considered *Messiás* so unpatriotic and so nearly treasonable that it ordered its confiscation. As a result the book was lost for almost a century, and a copy was rediscovered in the Hungarian National Library only in 1948.

A year after the appearance of Natonek's *Messiás*, Moses Hess's book *Rome and Jerusalem*, which later came to be considered a classic of Zionist literature, was published. When Natonek read it, he wrote a fan letter to Hess and expressed his indignation over the sharply critical review of Hess's book that reformer Leopold Löw had published in his journal *Ben Chananja*. This letter initiated a long friendship between Hess and Natonek. On the other hand, Natonek remained a foe of Leopold Löw, whom he attacked as "a hater of the Jewish nation, who endangers the safety of the Jewish people and has caused a split among the Jewish congregations."

In 1866 Natonek went to Paris, where he met Hess personally for the first time, and the two of them, together with Eliezer Levi Bing, prepared a memorandum addressed to the central committee of the Alliance Israélite Universelle (the important French Jewish organization founded in 1860) concerning the promotion of Jewish settlement in Palestine. In response, Isaac Adolphe Crémieux, president of the Alliance, wrote to Natonek that the Alliance was ready to support his plan but called his attention to the Turkish law that prohibited all non-Muslims from acquiring landed property anywhere in the Ottoman Empire. Therefore, he wrote, a way must first be found to have this prohibition abolished. Hess himself published a detailed report of Natonek's work in Paris in which he added that Crémieux had offered to intervene with the Turkish government for the purpose of getting the land-purchase ban lifted.

Before Natonek left Paris, he obtained letters of recommendation from Lazare Isidor, the newly appointed chief rabbi of France, and Albert Cohn, the French Jewish scholar and close associate of James de Rothschild in charge of his philanthropic works, and also received powers of attorney to act in their name in Constantinople.

Upon his return from France to Hungary, Natonek felt that he had to devote all his time to his grand design and hence resigned his rabbinical post in Székesfehérvár. Before setting out for Constantinople, he went to Vienna to obtain a letter of introduction to the Sublime Porte from the Turkish ambassador to the Habsburg court. The ambassador wrote to the Turkish foreign minister on March 10, 1867:

> An honored rabbi by the name of Natonek was introduced to the embassy, and he informed the humbly undersigned that among the Jews of Germany, Bohemia, and Hungary, with the participation of the community in Paris, a society was founded, based on joint funds, for the purpose of purchasing lands in the environs of Jerusalem and in Palestine in general, and establishing on them settlements for their brothers in Europe and in other parts of the world who desire emigration.The society also intends to act there to spread useful knowledge in commerce, handicraft, agriculture, and the arts, in order to encourage the Jews there also to make progress in this respect. It is self-evident that this society will be subject in every respect to the Turkish laws, and also these Israelite immigrants will enter the covenant of Turkish citizenship. Therefore, in order to learn first-hand about the laws that pertain to these matters, and also to discuss this significant issue personally with Your Excellency, Mr. Natonek himself is going to Constantinople, and therefore I permit myself to put the decision in this matter into the hands of Your Excellency alone.
>
> Asad Haidar
> Ambassador of the Sublime Porte in Vienna

As against the satisfaction Natonek must have derived from securing such a letter of introduction to the Sublime Porte, he suffered a setback from the Alliance Israélite Universelle, which informed him (in a letter dated April 24, 1867) that it did not agree with his grand plan of mass settlement of Jews in Palestine. They wrote to him, in a rather niggardly manner, that they did not have the means to cover the expenses of his planned trip, and that even though "the idea to lift up the intellectual and moral level of our neglected brothers in Jerusalem through education and agriculture [is a most worthy one], still, its realization, if it is at all possible, must be confined to those Jews who live there, and perhaps to a certain number of immigrants, without any political-social endeavor, and without resorting to commercial and industrial measures such as interest-bearing capital, shares, and the like."

Disappointed but not discouraged, Natonek obtained twenty florins from the Society for Settlement in Eretz Israel and with this paltry sum in his pocket set out for Constantinople. There he was well received by Chief Rabbi Yaqir Giron, head of the Austro-Hungarian community Hermann Klarfeld, and others, who advised him about his contact with the Sublime Porte. Upon Natonek's suggestion R. Giron wrote to the House of Rothschild and to Sir Moses Montefiore, the famous Anglo-Jewish philanthropist, requesting their help for Natonek's plan "to make *colonizasion* and to purchase fields and vineyards . . . and to establish workshops and schools." Natonek was received by the grand vizier several times, and most courteously (as was Herzl twenty-five years later). He reported of his experiences in a letter to his friend Judah Alkalay, who published this account in the Hebrew Journal *HaMaggid*:

Zemlin, New Moon of Tammuz, 5627 [1867]
Last week I received a letter from R. Joseph Natonek from Constanti-nople, dated the tenth of Sivan, in which he writes: "I spoke with Grand Vizier Fuad Pasha and with First Vizier Ali Pasha, and they assured me that they would help me with all their strength." This week I got the peri-odical *Journal Yisraelit*, in the language of Spain [Ladino], which is pub-lished in the city of Constantinople, no. 561, the sixteenth of Sivan, and this is its language: "R. Joseph Natonek came here with a mission from the holy society Yishuv Eretz Yisrael, to request permission from our lord the Sultan, may his majesty be exalted, to settle our Holy Land, to gather the dispersed, to work the soil, and to found workshops, so that the inhab-itants of the land and those who come to dwell in our land should be able to support themselves with the toil of their hands, and should no longer suffer the shame of famine among the gentiles. R. Natonek presented the certificates in his possession to the chief rabbi, Yaqir Giron, and the rabbi sent him, together with the leaders of the community, to Grand Vizier Fuad Pasha, who received him kindly. R. Natonek delivered into his hands the petitions and the letters he brought from the great ones of Israel and from the ambassadors of the kings. And when the grand vizier read the petition, he answered with a shining face: "I am sure that our lord the Sultan will fulfill your request, but the matter must be presented in the council, and the advisors of the kingdom will see how and what to do, and within a few days you will receive the answer that our lord the Sultan will command." May our God, King of the universe, bend the heart of the kingdom toward us in goodwill, so be His will!

R. Natonek adds that he has to stay here until our lord the Sultan returns from Paris. May the Lord watch over him, and preserve him, and make him happy in the land, so be his will!

The word of the slave Y'hudah ben Sh'lomoh Ḥay Alkalay,
S.T. [S'fardi Tahor, "pure Sephardi"]

This letter filled R. Alkalay with great hopes, and he appended to it a call to all Israel to come forward and donate generously to the Alliance toward the realization of the great plan.

It is almost uncanny to what extent each step in Theodor Herzl's strategy to establish a home for the Jews in Palestine had been prefigured by Joseph Natonek. Like Natonek, Herzl was convinced that Palestine must be obtained for the Jews by political and not philanthropic means; like Natonek, he began by first giving literary expression to his grand plan; both went to Constantinople to obtain a charter for Palestine from the sultan; both tried to convince the Rothschilds, other great "money Jews," and the existing large Jewish philanthropic organizations to support the plan with major donations; both came to the conclusion that a special society must be established for the purpose; and both founded a journal to serve the cause. Herzl's journal, *Die Welt*, became the central organ of the World Zionist Organization; Natonek's much more modest, and not very successful, attempt in this field was the weekly *Das Einige Israel*, which he launched in Budapest in 1872, and which was the first Zionist journal to appear. It is difficult to decide whether all this can be attributed to coincidence, or whether Herzl knew of Natonek's efforts and was determined to succeed where Natonek had failed by retracing his steps, or else whether the moves both of them made flowed logically from the idea of return to which they both devoted their lives.

Among the non-Zionist writings of Natonek are a translation and commentary of the Song of Songs (Budapest, 1871); a study in German titled *Science-Religion: A Pro and Con Investigation of Materialism, Darwin, Häckel, Büchner, etc.* (Budapest 1876); *Pentaglotte*, a Hebrew-Hungarian-Latin-German-French dictionary, written jointly with Bishop Joseph Pauer of Székesfehérvár, of which only the letter *A* was published (in 1861); and other books in German and Hebrew.

Hirschenstein, Alkalay, and Natonek were by no means the only Jewish leaders in Hungary who, in the half-century preceding Herzl's appearance, conceived of political Zionist ideas and tried to realize them. They only happen to be those of whose writings and activities most is known. It is tempting to speculate that there was something specific in the atmosphere in the Hungary of the middle of the nineteenth century that was conducive to directing those who were seized with the Jewish question toward political solution rather than charitable and philanthropic palliatives. Perhaps the fact that Hungary was a multinational country with large non-Magyar minorities—Germans, Slovaks, Rumanians, Croats, etc.—had something to do with it. While those national minorities chafed under the domination of the Magyars, who were the largest ethnic group in the country but still constituted less than half of its total population, among the Magyars themselves there took place in those years a nationalistic-patriotic awakening that led to the 1848 explosion, and also created great unrest among those minorities. In these circumstances the great majority of Hungarian Jews contracted the Magyar patriotic fever, but a few independent thinkers drew the opposite conclusion and became convinced that just as the Magyars fought for their national independence from the Habsburg realm, and just as the national minorities in Hungary demanded independence from Hungary or at least national autonomy within its borders, so for the Jews, too, there was no other way but to seek national autonomy, or better still, an independent national home—not in Hungary or anywhere else in Europe, where there was obviously no basis for it, but in their own ancient homeland, Eretz Israel. These proto-Zionists (one of whom lived in Slovenia and the other in Croatia, both in southern Hungary) felt political action was the only way to solve the problem of anti-Semitism, of Jewish separateness, of Jewish survival, for the communities of the European diaspora. This was the thinking that informed Herzl's precursors in Hungary and that, when his time came, also determined the direction of his work.

Both Alkalay and Natonek were still alive when emigrant Hungarian Jews of the Orthodox persuasion who had settled in Jerusalem conceived of the idea of founding an agricultural settlement in Palestine, and thus became the originators of the "return to the soil" movement that subsequently was to develop into the Hibbat Zion—Bilu movement (*Bilu* is the Hebrew acronym for "House of Jacob, come and let us go"), and later still into the crucial feature of *halutziyut* (pioneering) in the post-Herzlian development of political Zionism. The three men whose idea it was to establish an agricultural "colony"—as such a settlement was called at the time—were David Meir Gutmann, Akiva Joseph Schlesinger, and Joshua Stampfer.

David Meir Gutmann (b. Hungary 1827; d. Jaffa 1894) fought in the Hungarian War of Independence of 1848, but, disillusioned with the Hungarian attitude to the Jews, sold his property and in 1876 moved to Jerusalem. Akiva Joseph Schlesinger (b. Pressburg, 1837; d. Jerusalem, 1922), was a graduate of Moses Sofer's Pressburg yeshiva, and the author of several fervently Orthodox books, who became convinced that the sole hope for religious Jewry lay in the establishment of a religious community in the Land of Israel, and he himself settled there in 1870. Joshua Stampfer (1852–1908), studied at the yeshiva of Azriel Hildesheimer in Kismarton and, influenced by the attainment of Hungarian independence in 1867, was seized with the desire to go to Eretz Israel and work there for the survival of the Jewish people and their Torah. He left Hungary in 1869 and went by foot to Jerusalem.

In 1878 these three men acquired land next to the village of Mulabbis near the Yarkon River from a Greek owner, and proceeded to found the first Jewish agricultural settlement in Palestine, which they called Petaḥ Tiqvah, Gate of Hope. They established a local council, of which Stampfer became chairman. The problems encountered by Petaḥ Tiqvah before its existence became consolidated do not belong to the story of Hungarian Jews, but we might mention that today it is one of the biggest cities in Israel. What is noteworthy is that with the founding of Petaḥ Tiqvah, Hungarian Jews became the fathers of the Jewish agricultural settlement movement in Palestine, just as less than two decades later Herzl and Nordau became the founders of political Zionism.

When Herzl convened the First Zionist Congress in Basel (August 29–31, 1897), there were several factors on the Hungarian Jewish scene that impeded the proliferation of his movement in his erstwhile homeland. One of them was the spread of Hasidism in northeastern Hungary, where by the end of the nineteenth century local Hasidic rabbinical dynasties had become established in Sátoraljaujhely, Mármarossziget (Sighet), Munkács (Mukachevo), and Szatmár, and where also the *tzaddiqim* (Hasidic rabbis) of Belz, Zanz, and Vizhnitz had considerable influence. The classical position of Hasidism, especially pronounced in its Hungarian varieties, was that the return to the Land of Israel in the messianic days was a basic religious tenet of Judaism, and it was a grave sin to engage in any secular effort to regain the Holy Land prior to the coming of the Messiah. Although the non-Hasidic Orthodox Jews of Hungary had little sympathy for Hasidism, in their opposition to Zionism they saw eye to eye with it.

No less determined, as we shall soon see, was the opposition of the Neolog establishment of the Hungarian Israelites, who considered Zionism little short of treasonable activity—incompatible with the position of Hungarian Jews as patriotic Magyars of the Mosaic faith, totally and exclusively committed to their one and only Hungarian fatherland. They saw in Zionism a movement that endangered the historical attainments of Jewish emancipation, of Jewish Magyarization, and of the most recent Law of Reception, which assured the Jewish faith an equal position in Hungary alongside the other religious denominations (see chapter 32).

In view of this situation it is surprising that no fewer than seven Jews, from five Hungarian cities, participated in the First Zionist Congress. Of course, we have to keep in mind that the "delegates" to the First Zionist Congress were not elected by local Zionist bodies but were self-appointed volunteer participants. That is to say, the presence of seven Hungarian Jews at the Congress proves nothing more than the existence of seven individuals in Hungary who were sufficiently interested in it to attend. One of them was János Rónai (b. Gyulafehérvár, 1849; d. Budapest, 1919), an attorney from Transylvania, whose interest in Jewish politics antedated the Zionist Congress by more than two decades and found expression in his Hungarian book *Nationalism and Cosmopolitanism with Special Reference to the Present-Day Position of Jewry* (1875). In preparation for the Congress he published a pamphlet titled "Zion und Ungarn" (1897), in which he forcefully argues against both assimilationist and religious opponents of Zionism. An interesting point he makes is his reference to "the view of many of us [Hungarian Jews], who consider ourselves relatives of the Hungarian people, or at least think that at some time in the past the blood of the people of Arpad mixed with that of the Hungarian Jews." And, he continues,

> It is a fact that the many similarities of temperament, the peculiar custom of crying in merrymaking [in parentheses he adds here the saying "Sírva vigad a magyar," that is, "The Hungarian rejoices crying"], the related features of husbandry and of language structure, the generosity, the hospitality, the love of argument, the reverence for preserving tradition, as well as numerous parallels in the national history, etc., aroused the deep interest of the thoughtful Jews, and also their belief in a psychological-emotional relationship [between them and the Hungarians]. In what a wonderfully lively manner, with what a deep inwardness and how vigorously can the Bible and Jewish poetry be translated into Hungarian!

These observations, in a pamphlet whose purpose was to convince Hungarian Jews of the correctness and value of Zionism, shows how much thoughtful Hungarian Jews were imbued with a sense of the special affinity between Jewry and the Hungarian nation, which they recognized as a psychological obstacle to the spread of Zionism among them. At a speech in the Congress itself, Rónai emphasized the "normal," that is, favorable, conditions enjoyed by the Jews in Hungary, even though he also expressed his apprehension that the situation could deteriorate, and then Hungarian Jews would join the Zionist movement. After his return from the Congress, Rónai and a number of his friends established the first Hungarian Zionist Organization, of which he was elected first president.

Another Hungarian Jew who played a role at the First Zionist Congress was Samu Bettelheim (b. Pressburg, 1872; d. Budapest, 1942), a religious Zionist, who in 1897 founded the first Hungarian Zionist group, convened the first Hungarian Zionist Conference in Pressburg, and was president of the Hungarian Zionist Organization from 1904 to 1907. He was also one of the organizers of the first World Conference of the Mizrachi (religious Zionists) in Pressburg in 1904. He edited several Zionist periodicals and later in life became a supporter of the Orthodox

Jewish Agudat Israel organization, which opposed the Zionist Organization.

Soon after the First Zionist Congress, local Zionist societies were founded in several Hungarian cities, and at the Second Congress in 1898 it was reported that there were thirty-two Zionist groups in Hungary. In 1902 a provisional Hungarian national Zionist committee was established, and in the following year the first Hungarian Zionist Conference took place in Pressburg, chaired by Herzl. Also in 1903, twenty-four Jewish students at the University of Budapest founded the Hungarian Zionist students' organization Makkabea, whose first president was Samuel Krausz (b. Ukk, Hungary, 1868; d. Cambridge, 1948), who was later to become one of the most outstanding Jewish scholars and head of the Israelitische-Theologische Lehranstalt (rabbinical seminary) of Vienna. It was under the auspices of the Makkabea that in 1904 the first Hungarian Zionist periodical, the weekly *Zsidó Néplap* (Jewish Popular Paper), was launched. Members of the Makkabea also founded the Vivó és Atlétikai Club (Fencing and Athletic Club), which became the foremost Jewish sports club in the country. All the leaders of the Hungarian Zionist movement in the four decades that still remained until the Holocaust were to come from the ranks of the founding fathers of the Makkabea.

While these foundings, meetings, organizings, and launchings look like harbingers of a spreading popular Zionist movement in Hungary, in fact they were little more than scaffoldings that surrounded no solid structure: of the Hungarian Jewish population, which by the turn of the century approached the one million mark, only a few thousand were members of the various Zionist formations. The size of the Makkabea peaked in 1913, when it had one thousand members. During World War I some 300 local groups were nominally affiliated with the Hungarian Zionist Federation, but I could find no statistics as to the number of members.

However, the official Hungarian Jewish establishment was loath to put up with even these limited results of the Zionist efforts. The Jewish National Office (the official representative of Neolog Jewry) repeatedly expressed its opposition to Zionism, as a result of which the Ministry of the Interior withheld official approval of the statutes of the Zionist Federation. Fortunately, in the genteel legal conditions of pre-World War I Hungary, the Federation was able to function even without approved statutes.

Nevertheless, there were official obstacles. Thus, in 1908 the Hungarian authorities prohibited the collection of money for Zionist funds (collections for the Keren Kayemet, the Jewish National Fund, had begun in Hungary some five years earlier), whereupon the Hungarian Zionists asked the president of the World Zionist Organization, David Wolffsohn, to intervene. Wolffsohn came to Budapest and had a friendly discussion with Count Gyula Andrássy, the minister of the interior. Hungary's position was, as Andrássy explained to Wolffsohn, that the country was beset with the problems of minorities, and therefore had to oppose the emergence of an additional minority, that of the Jews. This view was obviously based on the well-known and ceaselessly reiterated position of the Jewish establishment, that the Jews were nothing but a Hungarian religious denomination. If, as the Jewish establishment alleged, the Zionists wished to transform the Jews into yet another national minority, their endeavor ran counter to the interests of the government.

Anti-Zionism thus became an important aspect of the official position of the Hungarian Jewish establishment. Although by the mid-1890s the anti-Semitic agitation that accompanied the Tiszaeszlár blood libel (see chapter 31), had subsided in Hungary, the very idea that the Jews should return to Palestine remained identified in the consciousness of Hungarian Jews with anti-Semitism. Consequently, when the First Zionist Congress convened in Basel in 1897 and the Zionist movement was joined by Jews from all the countries of the Western world, the Hungarian Jewish leadership found it necessary to register its sharp opposition to both the idea and the movement.

That the Basel Program of establishing a homeland for the Jews in Palestine differed greatly from the Hungarian anti-Semitic slogan calling for the forcible removal of the Jews to Palestine should have been quite clear to the political, intellectual, and religious leaders of Hungarian Israel, who were men of high political awareness and sensitivity. But conceptual grasp and emotional reaction are by no means one and the same. Conditioned as they were by many years of anti-Semitic agitation to associating the idea of Jews going to Palestine with crude prejudice, they could not help being instinctively opposed to the Zionist program, which, as they understood it, wanted to achieve basically the same goal: to take Jews from European countries (including Hungary) and settle them in Palestine to form there a new Jewish nation. And this was something they simply could not accept.

In this way a rare consensus developed between the Neolog and Orthodox leaders, expressed in their statements published on September 8, 1897, in the Budapest press. Dr. Samuel Kohn, a scholarly historian of Hungarian Jewry and chief rabbi of the Neolog Israelite Congregation of Pest, wrote: "I consider political Zionism, which wishes to create in Palestine a new Jew-state (*zsidóország*), sheer folly, a dangerous craze. . . . In Hungary, Zionism, which makes a nation out of a denomination, will never recruit adherents. In this everybody agrees, whether Neolog or Orthodox. The Hungarian clergymen of the Jewish religion have already energetically spoken up from the pulpits against the delusion of founding a new Jew-state."

Márton Schweiger, president of the Neolog National Office, proclaimed: "Every endeavor of Hungarian Jewry is diametrically opposed to the trends of Zionism. It does not dream of a Jewish kingdom, but wants to merge with Magyardom while maintaining intact its ancestral religion."

Lipót Lipschitz, president of the Orthodox Intermediary Office, stated:

> In judging Zionism, the Orthodox are unanimous with the Jews who belong to the progressives. They, too, condemn this rash movement, which sins against both patriotism and religion. The Magyars of the Jewish faith want to thrive here at home; they have not the slightest intention of founding a Jewish state in Palestine. On the occasion of the preliminary conference held in Karlsbad prior to the Basel Congress, one leader of the Hungarian Orthodox was asked whether the Zionist movement could find adherents in Hungary. His answer was that the half-idealistic, half-foolish fancy of the Zionists could have no attraction whatsoever for Hungarian Jews.

Some ten years later an even more virulent attack was launched against Zionism by Lipót Kecskeméti (1865–1936), chief rabbi of Nagyvárad, one of the most learned and influential Hungarian rabbis, who after the Trianon Treaty (by which Rumania acquired Transylvania following the First World War) fervently resisted the Rumanization of his city (renamed Oradea Mare) and of Transylvania as a whole. Writing in the 1908 *Year Book* of the Israelite Hungarian Literary Society (IMIT) Kecskeméti went even further than his Budapest colleagues in execrating Zionism. He not only rejected the doctrine of Jewish nationalism and declared that the Jews in Hungary were the sons of the Magyar, not Jewish, nation; he denounced Zionism for advocating the concept of the Jewish race at the expense of the religious and moral sublimity of Judaism, and condemned Zionism as disastrous to monotheism.

In this environment, which stigmatized Zionism as both unpatriotism and irreligiosity, even those few individuals whose sympathies lay with Zionism felt they had to tread very cautiously. Thus, when Max Nordau's pamphlet, *Zionism*, was published in a Hungarian translation by Gyula Gabel in 1902, the translator found it necessary to add a note explaining that while there were indeed Zionists in Hungary, they were "happy, emancipated citizens of a chivalrous nation," and the majority of Hungarian Jews "are not, and cannot be, in need of the good deeds of Zionism."

The rabbis' anti-Zionism was echoed by the Hungarian Jewish scholarly establishment. The highly respected central organ of Jewish studies, the *Magyar Zsidó Szemle* (Hungarian Jewish Review, founded in 1884), greeted the appearance of Theodor Herzl's *Der Judenstaat* (1896), which was the opening salvo of his grand strategy to create a World Zionist Organization, with a scathing review by Dr. Gábor Hajdu, in which he argued that the Jews, throughout their long history, even if they were expelled from a country, never tried to go back to Palestine. He concluded that "the establishment of a Jewish state is contrary to the past of Jewry, contradicts its exalted mission, and cannot be fitted into the patriotic thinking of Jewry that has been manifest in every period."

The weekly *Egyenlőség* (Equality) took the same position. By 1896 it was the most influential Jewish weekly in Hungary and represented the official position of the Neolog Jews. It was founded in 1881 by Mór Bogdányi, and in 1884 Miksa Szabolcsi (1856–1915) became its editor, and in 1886 also its publisher. Szabolcsi was a great champion of the rights of Hungarian Jews, a leader of the Jewish struggle for the Law of Reception, and a fearless fighter against anti-Semitism, especially during the difficult days of the Tiszaeszlár affair (see next chapter).

After the launching of political Zionism by Theodor Herzl, Szabolcsi's position became an ad hoc combination of execration of anti-Semitism, denial of the existence of anti-Semitism in Hungary, and condemnation of Zionism. He sharply criticized the Zionist political solution to the Jewish question, which he considered a faulty response to anti-Semitism. In a lead article in *Egyenlőség* (March 6, 1896) titled "We Don't Want a New Fatherland" he wrote: "Theodor Herzl left out of his calculation the patriotism of the Jews. . . . Never could such misery befall us here that we would not become infinitely more miserable if we had to exchange this fatherland for another one." A few weeks later Sándor Szabados, also writing in *Egyenlőség*, stated: "Patriotism is among the Jews an ethical and religious rule, and whoever tries to smuggle Jewish national aspirations into religion excludes himself from the community of honest men."

After the First Zionist Congress, Szabolcsi attacked Moritz Zobel, a young editor of *Die Welt* (the Viennese weekly of the World Zionist Organization) of Hungarian extraction, for having painted a dismal picture of anti-Semitism in Hungary:

> What does [Zobel] want? We know that it is one of the maneuvers of the Zionists to trumpet throughout the world about the greatest possible anti-Semitism, but as a Hungarian (?) how can Mr. Zobel reconcile with his patriotic honor the spreading of infamy about his fatherland in journals abroad? (Because even Mr. Zobel would not deny, I assume, that anti-

The editorial staff of *Egynlőség*. Photo taken on June 1, 1911. Left to right: Dr. Sándor Mezey, Dr. József Patai, Dr. Lajos Szabolcsi, Miksa Szabolcsi (editor-in-chief), Hugó Hazai, Ernő Mezei, Sándor Komáromi, Dr. Sándor Fleischman. (Courtesy Dr. Miklós Szabolcsi.)

Semitism is an infamy, however much he rejoices at it as a Zionist.) In any case, among the Hungarian Jews Mr. Zobel's party will achieve nothing, even if—God protect Hungary!—everything became true that is not true but which, according to Mr. Zobel, today already exists in this country. Even if anti-Semitism were to break out among us, even then Zionism would find no basis here. If our situation should worsen, we should wait until it became better. After all, the Magyar had already suffered bad situations, but that did not make him think of a new fatherland. The Jew has learned this from the Magyar, and he, too, has become sufficiently Magyar so that neither anti-Semitism, nor Zionism, nor any other calamity or plague, can uproot him from this soil. If the Zobels are searching for a new fatherland, so much the better; the real Hungarian Jew wants to live here and die here, because there is for him no room anywhere else in the great world.

In the last sentence we recognize a paraphrase of the well-known lines of the Hungarian *Szózat*, one of the two national anthems: "In the wide world outside this land / there is no room for you / Whether the hand of fate blesses or strikes you / here you must live and die."

Szabolcsi voiced the same ideas in a two-hour conversation with Herzl himself in the spring of 1903, which he described in the July 10,

1904, issue of *Egyenlőség*, a week after Herzl's death. (Interestingly, Herzl attached so little importance to Szabolcsi's visit that he made no mention at all of it in his *Diaries*, which otherwise are a meticulous and detailed record of all his meetings, encounters, and letters.) In his article, Szabolcsi reports mostly what he said to Herzl and gives only the gist of Herzl's counterarguments:

> Describing the position of the Hungarian Jews, I explained to [Herzl] what a folly it would be in Hungary, where the nationalities are the cause of so much trouble, to trot out with a new kind of nationality, the Jewish nationality, which is the basis of political Zionism. Nowhere is the idea of a new nationality as sensitive a matter as among us Hungarians. But quite apart from that, the Jew in Hungary is totally satisfied with being Jewish in terms of his religion (which, in fact, is totally sufficient). With regard to nationality he does not want to be anything else but Hungarian. And if he is of Hungarian nationality, he cannot be of Jewish nationality.

When Herzl argued that the Hungarians did not want to recognize the Jews as Hungarians, Szabolcsi retorted: "We are not Hungarian in order to be liked by others, but are Hungarians because our heart, our feeling, is Hungarian, because we cannot be anything else, because we do not want to be anything else. . . . The love of the fatherland often breaks through without our wanting it. Because it has become our blood, because it has struck its roots in our hearts. . . . How can you reconcile a new nationalist idea with this deeply deep love of the fatherland?"

Herzl replied that he did not wish this to happen in Hungary. "I want to spread the idea of the creation of a Jewish state," he said, "but I shall not insist on it in Hungary." And he went on to utter the prophetic words that have since often been quoted: "Before long you will have such an anti-Semitism in Hungary that compared to it our [Austrian anti-Semitism] will seem like nothing. If I were to force political Zionism there now, they would say that anti-Semitism was provoked by Zionism. I do not want that. In any case, you will become ours; anti-Semitism will drive you into our arms."

Szabolcsi's response to this dark prophecy was: "Even if anti-Semitism should rage as no pestilence has ever raged, it would never shake the patriotic sentiments of the Hungarian Jews. If it should break out, we shall suffer, but it will change nothing in our Magyar identity." He then described the Magyar character of the Hungarian Jews: "Don't forget that we have become Magyars not only in language and feelings but also in temperament. If somebody breaks our head, we break his head, and in addition throw him off his feet." In the rest of the conversation Szabolcsi offered several variations of his basic theme: the Hungarian Jews are Magyar patriots, and they will not tolerate anything coming between them and their Magyar brothers.

The importance of this discussion lies in the fact that Szabolcsi's anti-Zionist stand was shared by the Hungarian Jewish establishment, including the leadership of the Israelite Congregation of Pest and of the Neolog and Orthodox National Offices, all of whom joined in the fight against Zionism. The only group in which the Zionist movement made some headway in those early years, while Herzl still stood at its helm, was Jewish university students.

It was personal contacts such as this, added to his familiarity with the Hungarian Jewish situation in general, that forced Herzl to recognize that his movement had no immediate chance of winning a following in Hungary comparable in size to those in the other European countries. He resigned himself to this fact, and expressed his view of Hungarian Jewry as "a desiccated branch on the tree of Jewry."

A similarly critical view of Hungarian Jewry was voiced by Max Nordau (b. Pest, 1849; d. Paris, 1923), who became, after settling in Paris, a social critic of global fame, and was Herzl's lieutenant and successor at the head of the Zionist movement. Writing in *Die Welt* in 1904, Nordau commented on the opposition to Zionism expressed by Ernest Mezei (1851–1932), a Jewish deputy in the Hungarian Parliament, and at the same time recognized Mezei's consciously Jewish stand in the midst of the overwhelmingly assimilationist atmosphere of Hungarian Jewry. He stated:

> It is gratifying when such outstanding coreligionists as Mr. Ernest Mezei manfully and without reservation acknowledge their descent and draw the correct conclusions from their relationship to their tribe. The merit is all the greater here, since in the case of Mr. Mezei this acknowledgment was made under particularly difficult conditions. For Hungary is the land of assimilation that has its equal neither in France, which is familiar with the species of the "Gauls of the Jewish faith" and the freethinkers who "therefore" have nothing more in common with Judaism, nor in Germany, which has produced the peculiar phenomenon of Jewish anti-Semites. It may be sad but is nevertheless true that to say aloud and explicitly in such an environment, "I am a Jew, I am proud to be a Jew, and shall remain a Jew!" is an act of moral courage, a kind of *Shema* prayer before the whole world.

Frustrated in their attempts to win Hungarian Jewry for Zionism, Herzl, Nordau, and the Zionist leadership in general went on record characterizing Hungarian Jewry as a "desiccated branch" and an ultraassimilationist community. However, these critical views by no means told the whole story of Hungarian Israel, or gave a balanced picture of the great variety of its Jewish life. The fact is that well into the twentieth century, Hungarian Jewry comprised a wide spectrum ranging from religiously moderately reform and socially emphatically assimilatory congregations, whose ranks were constantly depleted by conversions and intermarriages, to extreme Orthodox communities whose numerical strength and uncompromising traditionalism were duplicated only in countries lying to the east of Hungary.

31

Istóczy and Tiszaeszlár

In addition to the powerful Hungarian patriotic sentiments vociferously and ceaselessly reiterated by the Hungarian Jewish leadership, whether Orthodox or Neolog, there was another development on the Magyar sociopolitical scene of the late nineteenth century that made the idea of a return to Palestine even more objectionable in the eyes of the Hungarian Jews. It so happened that in Hungary nasty suggestions that the Jews go to Palestine were raised by anti-Semites, who in this manner wanted to rid the country of Jews. The Hungarian anti-Semitic slogan "Jew, go to Palestine!" produced a revulsion in the minds of many Hungarian Jews to the Zionist program, which advocated that Jews build themselves a home in Palestine and those of them who wanted should have the right "to go to Palestine."

That anti-Semitic tendencies surfaced from time to time in the course of the millennial history of the Jews in Hungary we have amply seen in the preceding chapters. In the nineteenth century, emancipation enabled the Jews to consolidate their economic position, to become active in all kinds of intellectual and artistic endeavors, and to penetrate even the halls of politics. There was in the Christian population a sector that looked with a jaundiced eye at this ground gaining by the Jews, whom they considered, despite all oaths to the contrary by the Jews themselves, a foreign element in the body of the nation.

The rise of Hungarian anti-Semitism in the 1870s was undoubtedly influenced by developments in Germany, where Adolf Stöcker, preacher of the Prussian court, in 1878 founded the Christian Social Workers Party (renamed in 1881 the Christian Social Party) with an anti-Semitic program. In Hungary, the German example, added to the indigenous rise of anti-Jewish sentiment among the impoverished smallholders, facilitated the spread of the movement, whose main proponent was Győző Istóczy.

Istóczy (1842–1915) started his public career in County Vas, where he held various judiciary positions. An unpleasant experience with a Jewish litigant resulted in his losing his judgeship, and turned him into a rabid anti-Semite. In 1872 he was elected to the House as a member for a district of County Vas. In the House he specialized in questions to the ministers with a pronounced anti-Semitic tendency. The first of them, relating to the Jewish school fund, he introduced by proclaiming that "after the statements by the minister on the great influence of the Jews, and by Representative Ferenc Pulszky on the glorification of Jewry, it will be no news, in view of the dominant mood in the country, that this element threatens us not with outstripping but with suppressing us." Istóczy went on to ask the government "whether it has the intention to stem, as far as possible, the tide of naturalization of the Jews from abroad who inundate the country, and whether it would obstruct a self-defense movement that possibly will be initiated by non-Jewish elements against this aggressive caste." Béla Wenckheim, minister of the interior, energetically rejected the idea, but for several years thereafter Istóczy goaded the government with a series of interpellations and suggestions exhibiting a more and more virulent anti-Semitic position. On June 24, 1878, he actually advocated the establishment of a Jewish state (eighteen years before Herzl!), explaining that since the medieval method "by which the Christian nations solved the difficult problem of the Jews, which from time to time became burning, by the mass execution of the Jews," could today no longer be carried out, it would be much simpler if the government would do everything possible that Palestine should again become a Jewish state, into which the Jews would be transferred. On July 12 he submitted a motion to the House: the government should force Turkey to give up Palestine so that it would be possible to deport the Hungarian Jews there. Minister Trefort rejected the suggestion, and reprimanded Istóczy for discussing doctrines that were contrary to humanitarian principles and the noble spirit of the House. Istóczy withdrew his suggestion but called on the future as a witness to the verity of his words.

What is significant for the prehistory of Hungarian Zionism in Istóczy's anti-Semitically motivated plan to obtain Palestine as a Jewish state and to deport the Jews of Hungary is that his idea found a positive echo among some Hungarian and other Jews. Three men, of whom otherwise nothing is known, used Istóczy's "program" to lend weight to a petition to the Berlin Congress (June 13–July 13, 1878), which was dealing with problems of the Balkan peoples and the power position of Russia, Turkey, and the Austro-Hungarian Empire in the peninsula. They addressed a brief and naively worded memorandum to the Berlin Con-

gress, to the attention of Prince Otto von Bismarck and Benjamin Dis-
raeli (Lord Beaconsfield), and attached to it a copy of Istóczy's June 24
statement. They wrote:

Honored Congress
To Prince Bismarck and Lord Beaconsfield and the Delegates:
Like all the other eastern peoples, we Jews, poor and oppressed, also
request humbly that Your Excellencies make use of your power and goodwill to give us, through the intermediacy of our honored kings, a home in
the ancient land of our fathers, as a legal and independent kingdom,
according to the enclosed motion of Istóczy.
In the name of the many hundreds of thousands of Israelites,
M. Levy, T. Freund, C. Meir Reisler

The memorandum was not placed on the agenda of the Berlin Congress and thus passed into the dustbin of history. However, the strategy
it used—utilizing an anti-Semitic suggestion to bolster the Zionist
endeavor—was echoed a decade later by Herzl, who argued that even
the support of anti-Semites could and should be enlisted, for the establishment of a Jewish state would help solve their problems with Jews,
who were "unnecessary" in the host societies and whose very presence
disturbed social peace.

Istóczy's agitation prepared the ground for the blood libel of Tiszaeszlár, or at least helped create an atmosphere in which it could take
place. On April 1, 1882, Eszter Solymosi, a fourteen-year-old Catholic
girl of the village of Tiszaeszlár, for reasons unknown committed suicide by jumping into the Tisza River. When the girl could not be found,
the rumor arose in the village, and soon spread through the county and
then the whole country, that she had been killed by Jews for ritual purposes. Istóczy and his anti-Semitic colleagues took advantage of the
incident to move in the House that the Jews be expelled from Hungary.
Their countrywide agitation led in many places to attacks against the
Jews.

On May 4 Eszter's mother appeared before the village judge and
lodged a complaint against the Jews. Investigations began. Three Jewish
visitors, who happened to be in the village as candidates for the vacant
position of the *shohet* (ritual slaughterers), were arrested, and Simon,
the five-year-old son of József Scharf, an employee of the Jewish community, was interrogated. The child testified—as it later came to light,
persuaded to do so by threats and candy, and taught what to say—that
his father enticed Eszter to go into the synagogue and there cut her
throat. In the hearing Simon added that he and his thirteen-year-old
brother Móric helped by catching the blood of the girl.

349

On May 20 the boy Móric Scharf testified before the investigating judge that he did not know Eszter Solymosi, nor anything about her. The father, too, denied ever having seen her. Nevertheless, both were arrested. The same day, Móric Scharf was taken by gendarmes to the house of the notary Kálmán Péczely, a convicted murderer who had served twelve years in prison, and left the boy in his care. Péczely persuaded Móric, with threats and torture, to testify against his father and the other Jews, and to supply additional details of the alleged murder: his testimony was that the girl Eszter was taken into the synagogue by an itinerant beggar named Herman Wollner, who removed her clothes, whereupon the two ritual slaughterers, Abraham Buxbaum and Lajos Braun, took hold of her, while the third, Salomon Schwarz, cut her throat and caught her blood in a vessel. Then they dressed the girl again and covered up her neck. The whole procedure lasted forty-five minutes and occurred in the presence of four members of the Jewish community. Móric supposedly saw all this through the keyhole in the door of the synagogue, which he ran up to when he heard the girl's cries. Later it became established that it was impossible to see anything through the keyhole. On May 23 Móric repeated his testimony before the royal prosecutor of Nyiregyháza.

Inspection of the synagogue did not reveal any traces of the body nor any blood, whereupon the investigating magistrate, József Bary, had the whole area searched, as well as the Jewish cemetery, without finding anything. Nevertheless, he had several more Jews arrested, and the office of the public prosecutor formally charged four of them as suspects in murder, six as suspects of complicity in murder, and five for aiding and abetting and hiding the body. It later transpired that while they were in jail, Bary had them tortured in order to extract confessions. He had Móric Scharf jailed separately, presumably in order to subject him to further intimidation. József Bary himself, without any witnesses present, wrote out the confessions, including many details of the murder.

On June 18, near Tiszadada, raftsmen recovered from the Tisza River the body of a young woman that several witnesses recognized as that of Eszter Solymosi, although her mother and others denied that it was she. An autopsy performed on June 20 established without doubt that the body was that of a twenty-year-old woman who died not earlier than ten days before. The Catholic Church mercifully buried the unidentified girl in the cemetery of Tiszaeszlár. This mystification did not change anything in the treatment of the suspects, who were kept in jail for more than a year awaiting trial. The only one to be released, in September 1882, was Mrs. Scharf. At the requests of the defense, the body of the woman found in the river was exhumed, and the experts, three professors of the University of Budapest, found that her throat had not been cut.

The trial finally began on June 19, 1883. Anti-Semites had utilized the fourteen months that had passed since the arrest of the suspects to engage in vehement anti-Jewish propaganda, to flood the country with anti-Semitic pamphlets, and to instigate violent anti-Jewish incidents in several localities. In the course of those months, news of the case spread in the country and beyond and voices of protest were raised both in Hungary and abroad. The case aroused international attention, and several outstanding European theologians published condemnations of the blood libel, showing with scholarly thoroughness that the use of blood by the Jews for ritual purposes was a medieval superstition inherited from ancient times and lacked any basis in reality. Among the most important publications were those of Hermann Strack, founder-director of the Institutum Judaicum of the University of Berlin, an outstanding orientalist and theologian and the leading non-Jewish scholar of the Bible and Talmud, who in *Das Blut im Glauben und Aberglauben der Menschheit* and several other studies took a courageous stand against the growing German anti-Semitism in general, and the ritual blood libel in particular.

Nor did all Hungarian political and intellectual leaders succumb to the virus of anti-Semitism. Many of them condemned the proceedings and rose to the defense of the Jews. Lajos Kossuth, from his exile in Turin, protested and declared the whole blood libel issue a medieval prejudice, a shame for Hungary, and a blemish on civilization. Prime Minister Kálmán Tisza tried to stem the wave of anti-Jewish excesses. However, the mood in the House of Representatives was definitely anti-Jewish. The only one to speak up (in November 1882) protesting the anti-Semitic agitation was the Jewish representative Ernő Mezei, a well-known historian and journalist.

The trial itself, held in the court of Nyiregyháza, began with a long speech for the prosecution by State Attorney General Ede Szeyffert. He described in great detail the facts of the case as they had been ascertained up to that point and admitted that the ritual bloodletting was a superstitious belief with no basis in fact, but nevertheless concluded by asking for due punishment of those who would be found guilty.

The defense team was headed by Károly Eötvös, a leading liberal member of the House of Representatives and a highly respected attorney. His first move was to lodge a protest with Minister of Justice Tivadar Pauler against the torture to which Bary and two gendarmes subjected the accused, but this step had no practical consequences. The trial had many tense, dramatic moments, such as confrontations of the boy

Móric Scharf with his father and the other defendants, attempted violence in court, and unruly behavior of the audience. In the course of the
proceedings it became increasingly evident that the boy, the only eyewitness to the alleged crime, merely repeated what he was taught to say,
and that his testimony was full of contradictions. Several of the accused
were given opportunities to question Móric in open court, which led to
painful altercations and mutual recriminations. More than a dozen witnesses were called, and all the details of the case were again and again
aired, discussed, and rehashed. On July 23 prosecutor Szeyffert charac-
terzied Móric Scharf as having "here, before the Honorable Court, not
only insulted his father but also denied his religion, mocked the emblem
of prayer [the *tefillin*], calling it horses' straps, and thus having shown
unmistakable signs of a lack of religious and moral sentiments" and
having materially altered his testimony.

Eötvös's closing argument took several hours. It was not only a
defense of the accused but also a spirited vindication of the Jews and a
condemnation of anti-Semitism. He censured those who shout, "Out
with the Jews to Jerusalem!" and prided himself for having dared to
oppose the anti-Jewish "flood that swept away or trampled upon those
who dared to stand in its way." He ended by demanding acquittal. After
he finished his speech, prosecutor Szeyffert joined him in moving that
all the accused be found not guilty. On August 3, 1883, the not guilty
verdict was pronounced.

The data about the fifteen accused men given in the sentence permit a
glimpse into the cultural conditions among the Jews living in a country
where the majority of the population, and especially of the villages, was
still illiterate: of the fifteen, twelve are stated to be "able to read and
write." Of the three who were illiterate, one was a thirty-seven-year-old
unemployed day laborer, actually a beggar; the second, thirty-eight years
old, likewise a day laborer; and the third, a forty-eight-year-old river
raftsman. Of the twelve who were literate, three were ritual slaughterers,
two tenants, two day laborers, and one each an employee of the Jewish
congregation, a teacher, a merchant, a property owner, and a raftsman.
Only one of the fifteen accused, the tenant, had a prior conviction, for
embezzling.

After the release of József Scharf, a touching human drama took place
between him and his son Móric, who, under whatever pressure and
compulsion, had almost caused him to be unjustly condemned to death,
and now showed signs of emotional disturbance. The father wanted to
take Móric back to his home, but the boy, embarrassed, intimidated,
and confused, insisted that the county take charge of him and make
arrangements for his education. However, two days later he changed his

mind, and on August 6 he and his parents took the train to Budapest. For quite a while the boy was afraid that the Jews would take revenge on him, but gradually he gained some self-confidence. Sometime later Móric went to Amsterdam, where he became a diamond cutter. He supported his parents, got married, and died in 1924.

For several days following the not guilty verdict, violent anti-Jewish demonstrations raged in Budapest. Jewish stores were broken into and looted, Jews were attacked in the streets, the trains moving across the streets of the city stoned and damaged. Order was restored only on August 11, 1883, with the arrival in the capital of several army units. Similar demonstrations took place in several other cities as well, and in many places the streets reverberated with the cry, "Beat the Jew! Long live Istóczy!"

Istóczy, on his part, had continued this anti-Semitic agitation by trying to convene an anti-Jewish mass meeting (which the police prohibited) and by launching a periodical titled *Tizenkét Röpirat* (Twelve pamphlets) to serve as a forum for his anti-Semitic writings. In the July 15, 1882, issue of that periodical—while the Tiszaeszlár blood libel trial was nearing its conclusion—Istóczy published an article, signed "Titus Aemilius" and titled "The Judaized Hungary," that was a scurrilous attack against the Jews, more vulgar and brutal than anything he had said or written before, or anything that was to appear in the anti- Semitic press until *Der Stürmer* of Nazi fame. A few passages will demonstrate the style and tone of the article, unheard of until that time:

> We Hungarians cannot appear together with the Jews at the approaching millennial festivals [and] must first get rid of the Jews [because Jewry is] a foreign race, with corrupt morals, baleful character, that has sneaked into our nation with impudent cheek, gained control of our strength with its base devices, and now exploits our people with machinations stemming from filthy self-interest and directed at the final destruction of our homeland. . . . Against this, the newcomers' patriotism, which they vaunt so proudly, is of no avail. It is deception, treachery, an ugly lie, intended to blind the gullible and the shortsighted. . . .
>
> In our public life, misery and poverty is found everywhere among the autochthonous inhabitants; only the Jew prospers, advances, grows rich on our sweat, at the price of our well-being, our life. He ruined our whole public life, forced our progress into a new, slanted direction, brought into our midst crimes that had been unknown till then, and with his underhanded ways stole our material goods, our spiritual powers, polluted and deprived our people of its old strength and character, and made it a slave to his selfish interests. The lawyer, the physician, the magistrate, if he is not Jewish, is in the pockets of the Jews, and is a tool of the Jew exactly as is the peasant. . . . Intellectal activity has been almost totally monopolized by the Jew. . . .The public officers have been corrupted, bought by the Jewish entrepreneurs, suppliers. . . .

The Jews with their promissory notes have become masters of the members of parliament. Among the 450 representatives there are perhaps not even fifty who would not vote for the interests of the Jew, in support of the Jew, at the command of the Jew. The Jew has either bought them, or keeps them, or won them over for himself. . . . Parliament is the House of Representatives of Jewish interests. . . . Our society groans under the disgusting yoke of Jewish influence. . . . Usury and corruption ruin the people in the interest of the Jew. . . .

And as against all this the Jew cannot marshal anything as his merit—because the fact that he can, for fifty pennies, assume the names of our historical great men is not a merit, only a new and typical trait of Jewish impudence. That he stops wearing the caftan, the sidelocks, just as he ceases to speak German, is still not a merit but only externality, deception. . . . The Jew always remains a Jew in his soul and body, this does not change: the exterior he changes as many times as necessary, for, after all, there is the example of the Polish Jew, the Spanish Jew, and here are "our Jews"—the exterior has changed, but not the interior. . . .

The immoral doings of the Jews have poisoned our whole public life, led our development into a wrong direction. . . . The Jews are the sworn enemies of everything good, patriotic; they multiply like phyloxera [a vine disease], and nothing is done against them. . . . all this has taken place since the introduction of the Jewish emancipation, and with the multiplication of the Jews the trouble multiplies in direct relation. . . . We are not enthusiastic about the Magyarization of the Jews, their assimilation, because we do not want to nurture, to warm a viper in our bosom. . . .

For us it makes no difference whether the Jew is Orthodox, Neolog, or Status Quo, whether he is German or five-sixths Hungarian—we know that he is evil, and will be the ruin of our homeland as long as his accursed breath contaminates the air in this country. . . . Our principle is that the Jew is evil, and that he is unable to improve. Our program is: out with the Jews from Hungary! Out with them any way possible, out with them as one drives out an intruding burglar, a usurper, from the undeserved place.

This article was too much for the House of Representatives. By majority vote it resolved to permit the judiciary to bring a libel suit against Istóczy as editor of the journal in which it was published. The trial was held in Budapest on June 30, 1883. The public prosecutor charged Istóczy with the crime of inciting hatred against a religious denomination. The proceedings gave ample opportunity to his counsel and to Istóczy himself to elaborate on the anti-Jewish accusations contained in the article, and to argue that the statements contained in it attacked nowhere the Jewish faith but only the Jews as a people, a race, an ethnic group; hence,—Istóczy was not guilty of the crime with which he was charged.

The defender raised the spectre of the control exerted throughout the world by international Jewry, alleged that Baron Rothschild had a stranglehold on the Hungarian government, which "was writhing in the octopus arms of the Jewish money kings," and that the Parisian Alliance

Israélite Universelle had sent a memorandum to the Austrian and Hungarian governments demanding the most energetic steps against the spread of anti-Semitism. He quoted (in a very faulty manner) passages from the Talmud which, according to him, proved that the Jews hated the Christians, were engaged in constant efforts to harm them, and dreamed of a universal massacre of the gentile world.

Istóczy, speaking in his own defense, described in great detail how he had been damaged and persecuted by the Jews, and what a satisfaction it was for him that as a result of his activities, the majority of his compatriots had turned against the Jews—not against the Jewish religion, by any means, but against the evil Jewish race.

No witnesses were called. The presiding judge charged the jury, which within half an hour returned a not guilty verdict. Most of the people attending the trial sympathized with Istóczy and broke into loud jubilation, and when Istóczy left the court, the crowd in the street welcomed him as their hero.

Istóczy's acquittal was a signal victory for the anti-Semites, and in October 1883, following the Prussian example, together with three other like-minded representatives he founded the National Anti-Semitic Party. The electioneering efforts of the party had limited success, but seventeen of its candidates did win seats in the House in 1884. Added to this was the shock the House suffered from an unsuccessful assassination attempt against a member of the Independence Party, Ottó Herman, who was one of the sharpest critics of the anti-Semites.

These were disquieting developments, and Prime Minister Kálmán Tisza, who was opposed to the anti-Jewish agitation, made sure that the royal address from the throne to the opening session of the new Parliament that convened on September 29, 1883, contained a call for the cessation of agitation that led to friction among the races, denominations, and classes. This expression of royal concern was directed primarily at the Anti-Semitic Party, whose program threatened the established order in the country. That program demanded the elimination of the political, economic, and social power of the Jews, the introduction of a national agrarian policy, a revision of the industrial law, the restoration of the old Jewish oath, and the exclusion of Jews from the retailing of wine and spirits. The Anti-Semitic Party also demanded that Jews not be allowed to work as public officials or as employees of financial institutions and insurance companies, not be able to purchase or rent houses, lands, and mills, nor be able to to work as physicians, pharmacists, lawyers, engineers, or even bakers, grocers, and grain merchants. It called for a total boycott of the Jews, and prided itself on the acquittal of Istóczy, as well as of Károly Nendtwich, a university professor who was also tried for writing inciting articles. In vain did Ernő Mezei and others fight in the House against the anti-Semitic wave; in vain did Ignác Acsády, the prominent historian, publish an excellent pamphlet; the agitation increased to the point where the prime minister felt it necessary to state that the sanity of those who spread such ideas must be doubted.

An important contributing factor in the success of the anti-Semitic agitation of Istóczy and company was the near-catastrophic economic situation in which many Hungarians found themselves after the governmental reforms, which coincided with the emancipation of the Jews. The reforms liberated the serfs and granted them smallholdings, often insufficient to make a living, which they were unable to cultivate effectively. This legal step deprived the members of the lower nobility, the hereditary owners of middle-sized or small estates, of the free labor of the serfs on which their traditional livelihood was based, and forced many of them to sell their hereditary lands, thus creating a class of people who were unprepared or unwilling to engage in either commerce or industry, which they considered beneath their dignity. The newly impoverished lower nobles were forced to become public employees in governmental, county, and municipal offices, occupying low rungs in the official hierarchy and becoming dissatisfied with both their low salaries and the limited scope of the work available to them. This was the time when the adage started to be heard that "a government official has only one duty: to receive his salary every month." Little wonder that observing how the Jews forged ahead in commercial and industrial enterprises, this gentry transferred their resentment against the government—which they could not attack because they were dependent on it —to the Jews, whom they could, and whom it was emotionally satisfying to blame for their predicament.

In the early 1880s Parliament discussed, but was unable to agree on, the question of whether marriages between Jews and Christians should be made legal. On that issue, a political writer hiding behind the pseudonym "Demokritos" published a pamphlet in 1884 in which he unhesitatingly attributed the spread of anti-Semitism to the "national misery":

> Anti-Semitism here among us is merely a kind of coffee substitute. Political chicory. But it comprises the cry of pain of general dissatisfaction and embitterment over the national miseries, decline, impoverishment, the bad administration of justice, the clumsy public services. They cannot beat [Prime Minister Kálmán] Tisza, so they beat the Jew. It is a bad logic, but still it is a logic. Kálmán Tisza thinks that if he makes Jew-politics, he makes good politics, and so that we should no longer quarrel with the Jew, he marries the Evangel with the Talmud. Extinguishing fire with gunpowder! A certain explosion!

An anti-Semitic speech delivered in the House by Ignác Zimándy, a Catholic priest and member of parliament, prompted the rabbinate of Pest and the faculty of the Rabbinical Seminary to issue in October 1884 a joint declaration pointing out that the quotations from the Talmud and the Zohar with which Zimándy "proved" that the Jews were commanded by their religion to slaughter Christian girls were sheer falsifications, taken from the writings of the German anti-Semitic author August Rohling (who was discredited by Christian scholars of impeccable reputation), and that Zimándy himself was a complete ignoramus. They concluded by offering to testify before any competent scholarly forum.

Anti-Semitic agitation peaked in 1885, after which its decline set in. Under the influence of a powerful call from the great Turin exile Lajos Kossuth, who was still considered the oracle of Hungarian politics, and a pastoral letter by Haynau, the archbishop of Kalocsa, the hostile spirits began to calm down somewhat.

In the course of the parliamentary debates it became evident that, apart from its anti-Jewish program, there were no planks in the National Anti-Semitic Party's platform agreed to by all its members, who contradicted one another on questions of public law and on an economic-social program. Their lack of success prompted Istóczy to leave the party, which soon thereafter broke into two: the moderates left and founded the Moderate Anti-Semitic Parliamentary Party. Both parties participated in the 1887 elections but had very limited success, and in the 1892 elections they no longer took part.

Economics also played a role in changing the public mood. In 1885 there was a bumper crop of grains, a major source of income for most of the country's population. From 1887 on, the state budget showed steady improvement: while in that year there was still a deficit of 49.4 million forints, it was reduced in 1888 to 24.1 million and in 1889 to 3.3 million, and in 1890 there was a surplus of 28.5 million.

Within the next ten years the Anti-Semitic Party expired, and with it Hungarian political anti-Semitism practically vanished for the time being. By the time the "Reception" of the Jewish religion as an officially recognized religion became law (1895), the Jews would have grounds for feeling that they had weathered a difficult period, and that from now on it would be smooth sailing as far as their position in Hungary was concerned. Only a spate of anti-Semitic publications that continued to appear would remind them that anti-Semitic rivers were still running beneath the surface of politically sanctioned Christian-Jewish camaraderie.

32

The *Fin de Siècle* and Its Aftermath I: Economy and Society

In no period in their long history did Hungarian Jews feel as much at home in the *haza* (fatherland), as much at one with their Christian Magyar compatriots, as much part of the great national endeavor to modernize, to forge ahead, and to become an important cultural entity in Europe, as in the half-century between their emancipation and the end of World War I. They possessed complete equal rights, the Magyarization movement was in even fuller swing among them than among the Christian Magyars, and their Hungarian patriotism was welcomed by the nation as a factor that added weight to the Hungarian half of the Austro-Hungarian Empire and tipped the balance in favor of the Magyar half of the population within Hungary itself, as against the non-Magyar national minorities. They made great contributions to all aspects of the economic, social, and cultural ascent of the country. In many fields they soon came to play leading roles. Quite a few of them rose to high positions in the government on the national and local levels. The Jews were on their way to becoming the most educated, intellectual, and well-to-do element in the country, and were honored for their services by court councillorships, knighthood, and the baronial rank granted by the gracious king-emperor. They felt they were an integral part of the Magyar nation, as Magyar as any of the other confessional groups and that the only difference between them and the Christians was denominational, no greater than between, say, Catholic and Protestant Hungarians. To a remarkable extent, these same feelings even permeated the writings and utterances of many Hungarian Jews who had been born abroad, had immigrated as adults, and had had difficulty learning the Magyar tongue. As Lajos Venetianer put it in 1922, with his characteristic anti-Orthodox bias: "the Hungarian national strength gained much with the granting of citizenship to the Jews . . . for even the immigrants from the darkest districts of the [Austrian] hereditary provinces already became by the next generation totally Hungarian, the sympathetic sons of the fatherland." By "darkest districts" he meant, of course, the districts with the most tradition-bound Jewish communities, such as Galicia. In any case, the period was —as a friend of mine who barely escaped with his life and broken bones from the hell of the German-Magyar Holocaust remarked to me in the 1960s with nostalgic sadness—unquestionably the golden age of Magyar Jewry.

A golden age in Jewish history, of course, never could mean an Ovidian *aurea aetas,* a period of complete tranquility and happiness, without any problems or setbacks. Trials and tribulations were not absent even in the famous golden age of medieval Spanish Jewry; nor were they in the half-century of Hungarian Jewish history we are speaking about. However, in one very important respect, at least the second half of the period in question did deserve the designation "golden age." The twenty-five years between the 1895 Law of Reception granting equality to the Jewish religion and the Numerus Clausus Law of 1920 were the only period in the millennial history of the Hungarian Jews when *legally* no distinction whatsoever existed between the Jewish and non-Jewish population of the country. During that brief quarter of a century, *all* the laws of the state covered *all* the inhabitants, and there was not a single provision on the books that so much as mentioned the Jews as a special community. Thus, legally at least, the Jews of Hungary had a solid basis for the conviction that they were equal members of the Magyar nation, since the law of the land in no way discriminated among members of the various faiths nor among the denominations as organized religious bodies. These were the circumstances which created the feeling that all was well with the Magyars of the Mosaic faith, that theirs was a golden age in their beloved fatherland. From our present perspective a century later, comparing those twenty-five years not only with what went before but also with what was to follow, the designation "golden age" has added, tragic justification.

Within those memorable twenty-five years, the last decade of the nineteenth century was an especially heady time for the Jews of Hungary. The Law of Reception (see below) accorded the Israelite religion a status equal to that of the Christian denominations. The number of the Jews in the country was rapidly increasing. Their economic conditions were on the rise. Their successes in industry, commerce, and finance were remarkable. Their behavior patterns were well on the way to conforming to the *úri* (gentlemanly) attitudes of the Hungarian gentry and nobility, from whom many of them had learned to defend their honor by dueling (see below, chapter 32). Many believed—mistakenly, as it turned out—that by converting to Christianity they would be accepted by the Hungarian *urak* (gentlemen) as their equals. The intellectuals made conspicuous advances in the fields of Jewish scholarship, and increasingly also in the secular sciences, achieving recognition in the arts, literature, and the professions. The hold of Jewish religion on the masses, although no longer as strong as before emancipation, still made them fill their many synagogues on the Sabbath and the holy days, and observe Jewish traditions as required by the Orthodox, Status Quo, or Neolog varieties of the faith. To cap all this, anti-Semitism appeared to be held in check, and the entrenchment of Hungarian Israel as one religious community among equals seemed to have been accomplished.

A significant marker of the Jewish position in *fin de siècle* Hungary was the attitude of the leading layers of society to the Jews. Far from seeing the Jew as a ruthless competitor who deprived the Magyar of his livelihood—that view developed only after World War I as part of the new anti-Semitism—he was considered a necessary complementary element in the Hungarian social pyramid, one who performed the tasks the Christian Hungarians were unable, or rather unwilling, to shoulder. He was looked down upon, but needed. As Károly Eötvös, the noted liberal writer and politician, put it in those days, the Germans and the Jews were merchants, they were after riches, while the Hungarian gentleman was after landed estates. The former had only living quarters, the latter a home; the former judged things from a utilitarian point of view, the latter on the basis of ethical principles and hallowed traditions. The issue was formulated even more clearly and outspokenly by a *grand seigneur* of the Count Károlyi family who, when the German consul general asked him why nobody in his castle played music, answered, "Why should we play, when the gypsies serve that purpose?" and added, "Just as we keep the gypsies so that they play, we keep the Jews so that they work instead of us." These examples illustrate what we know from a plethora of other contemporary sources: that the *fin de siècle* was the time when in the leading sectors of Hungarian society the sympathetic image developed of the hard-working, resourceful, useful, Magyarizing Jew.

It was only during the years of World War I that this picture of the "good Jew" was replaced by another one that attributed to the Jew more and more negative traits. We shall discuss that development later, but let us mention here that in the 1917 survey of the influential sociological journal *Huszadik Század* (Twentieth Century), a considerable number of the non-Jewish respondents presented a dismal image of Hungarian Jewry that included such traits as selfishness, money grubbing, materialism, usuriousness, shrewd speculativeness, and a ruthless desire to succeed that was so powerful that it enabled the Jews to outsmart even the

Greek and Armenian "aboriginal merchant races." Most painful for the Jews was the accusation that beneath the mask of fervent Hungarian patriotism, they did not truly identify with the national interests of Hungary.

Let us now take a closer look at some of the major arenas in which the Hungarian Jewish history of the *fin de siècle* was played out.

The *Recepció*

In 1895 Hungarian Jewry achieved what it considered the acme of the slow and painful process of rising from rightlessness and grudging toleration to full legal equality with the other religious communities in the country: the *recepció* (the Magyarized form of Latin *receptio*, reception), that is, the admission of Judaism among the legally recognized religions of Hungary. Following the emancipation of 1867, an entire generation of Hungarian Jewish leaders fought for such a *recepció*, and its attainment in·1895 was considered by them, as well as by liberal-minded Christians, a signal victory not only for the Jews of the country but also for liberal principles.

The Jewish demand for the legal equalization of Jewish religion with the other religions in Hungary was first voiced by several leading figures at the 1868–69 Hungarian Jewish Congress. However, at that time even the most militant of them could not hope for much success, since the Protestant denominations themselves were still engaged in a fight for full legal equality. For more than a decade the matter lay dormant, until in 1883, right after the Tiszaeszlár affair, the district heads of the Jewish congregations submitted a petition to the minister of religions, requesting for the Jewish religion the same rights enjoyed by the legally accepted denominations in the country.

However, in the anti-Jewish atmosphere of the day, this step proved premature, and neither the government nor the legislature responded positively. The demand was kept alive by Jewish public opinion, and for ten years the foremost Jewish leaders of the country persisted in fighting for it in the Jewish press. Among the leaders in this fight were the politician Vilmos Vázsonyi; the editor of *Egyenlőség*, Miksa Szabolcsi; the publisher Ernő Mezei, member of parliament from Miskolc; the attorney and secretary of the Pest *Ḥevra Kadisha*, Ferenc Mezey; the attorney and later justice of the High Court (*Kuria*) Dezső Márkus; the rabbis Immanuel Löw, Ármin Perls, and Sándor Rosenberg; the poet Lajos Palágyi; his brother the philosopher Menyhért Palágyi (who later converted to Christianity); and the economist, philanthropist, and member of parliament Sándor Ullman de Erény (1850–97), who advocated the reception of the Jewish denomination in one of his many books, titled (in Hungarian) *The Putting in Order of Jewish Denominational Affairs* (1888). These Jewish voices were supported by the Protestant leader Árpád Zempléni, who saw in the Jewish demand a strengthening of the argument of the Reformed Churches in Hungary against Catholicism. The Protestants at the very same time became more and more vociferous in their complaints against the Catholic practice of registering as Catholics the children born to mixed Catholic-Protestant couples, in blatant disregard of the mutual reciprocity among the Christian denominations assured by the Law of 1868:LIII. This practice prompted the Protestant leadership to lodge protests with Parliament, which, in response, in 1891 and 1892 discussed a bill concerning the introduction of secular (nondenominational) registration of births. The more comprehensive issues of the free practice of religion, the equalization of the rights of denominations, and the introduction of civil marriages thus also came up for intensive parliamentary discussion.

These developments resulted in a governmental decision to introduce a comprehensive bill for the reform of ecclesiastical policy. At the same time, Vilmos Vázsonyi sent a memorandum to the Lower House to write the reception of Jewish religion into law. This memorandum was approved by a meeting of Hungarian Jewish leaders in Budapest, and on November 9, 1892, Prime Minister Count Gyula Szapáry informed the House that the government had "prepared bills on keeping general civil registries, the entering of the Israelite religion into the law, as well as the free practice of religion, and has obtained the consent of the crown for the introduction of these bills into Parliament."

It was Szapáry's successor as prime minister, Sándor Wekerle, who submitted the bill to the House on April 26, 1893. The bill provoked enormous excitement, the House split into sharply opposing parties, and everywhere there was unrestrained agitation pro and con. The minister of religions resigned, and his portfolio was entrusted to baron Lóránd Eötvös, son of József Eötvös, who had carried through the law emancipating the Jews. The younger Eötvös now wanted to complete his father's work by seeing the Bill of Reception through the House, and in fact managed to do so. All members of the House, with the exception of three Catholic priests, voted for it, while in the Upper House it was rejected with a slim margin. The bill was submitted to the Upper House twice more, and finally, on May 15, 1895, when the votes were split evenly, the chairman's yes vote secured its passage. On October 1 of the same year the king sanctioned the bill, which became Law 1895:XLII, the Law of Reception, with the following text:

1. The Israelite religion is declared an accepted religion.
2. The provisions of paragraphs 18, 19, 20, 21, and 22 are exended also to persons of the Israelite religion. [These paragraphs provide that foundlings follow the religion of those who bring them up; nobody can be forced to practice the ritual of another religion; everybody is obliged to be affiliated with a congregation; in military institutions and hospitals, services of clergy have to be maintained; and the cities must provide support for the congregational schools.]
3. Only such a member of the Jewish denomination can be a clergyman [rabbi] and congregational chief who is a Hungarian citizen and has obtained his qualifications in Hungary.
4. The ministry is entrusted with carrying out this law.

Among the most important practical effects of the new law were that non-Jewish Hungarian citizens were from now on able to convert to Judaism legally, and marriages between Jews and non-Jews could likewise be contracted legally. A corollary was that marriages, to be legally valid, had to be entered into a civil registry, which meant that rabbis (and priests) no longer had exclusive jurisdiction over this imporant step in people's lives. The Jews considered the law the final victory in their long fight for total equality, both individually and as a denomination, with non-Jewish Hungarians.

Within a few days after the promulgation of the long-sought *recepció* law, the Neolog rabbis convened a national conclave in Budapest to discuss their agenda in view of the new circumstances it created. In addition to expressing their gratification over the new law and their determination to carry out whatever was contained or implied in it, they resolved to establish a National Rabbinical Assembly, so that (in Venetianer's words in 1922) "a uniform spirit should guide and permeate the entire profession of Hungarian Jewish clergymen in its work for the amalgamation of Hungarian Jewry—now already a denomination enjoying equal rights—into Hungarian national culture."

A few weeks later, on January 5, 1896, the Hungarian Jewish leadership gathered in a nonrabbinical meeting in Budapest, where they dealt with administrative and cultural issues. Joseph Simon, secretary-general of the Israelite National Office, moved that "in commemoration of the reception of the Israelite religion into the ranks of legally accepted religions, the Hungarian Israelites should establish a public fund. The purpose of this fund should be to help in the attainment of those aims through which the development of Hungarian Jewry in the national spirit will be advanced." The motion was adopted with enthusiasm, and the fund was established and came to be headed by a committee consisting of the very elite of Hungarian Jewry, including several barons and nobles. It engaged in supporting congregations and individual needy persons and providing scholarships to young men preparing for artistic and scholarly professions.

As we see from this brief report of developments in the communal Jewish life of Hungary at the end of the nineteenth century, the achievement of total legal equality by the Jews was considered by their leaders an obligation to redouble their efforts at "amalgamating" the Jewish community into the Magyar national culture and national spirit. Improvement in the life of the Hungarian Jews was the equivalent of enabling them to be better Magyars.

Looking back, at the turn of the century, at what they had achieved within the preceding three decades, Hungarian Jewry had much reason for satisfaction. In public law it obtained individual emancipation and communal-denominational recognition, which not only made Jews and non-Jews equal before the law but also accorded equality to the Jewish religion. In the national economy they became one of the most active and successful segments of the population; they were leaders in industry, commerce, and finance; in education and the professions they forged ahead, represented in numbers exceeding several times their proportion in the total population; in politics they occupied influential seats in both houses of Parliament, and made their presence felt in the municipal governments as well; in science and scholarship they excelled, and at long last even the universities and the august Academy of Sciences began to open their doors to them; and last but not least, the proportion of those ennobled or awarded the coveted title of "court councillor" more than caught up with that of the Christian population. The optimists pointed with satisfaction to all these achievements and hoped for an even brighter future for Hungarian Israel in its beloved fatherland.

True, as everyone had to admit, some problem areas remained. The most painful among them was anti-Semitism, which, as the Tiszaeszlár blood libel and the subsequent anti-Jewish outbreaks of the 1880s showed, was very much alive and, even if quiescent in the 1890s, constituted a potential danger. A contributing factor was the upsurge of anti-Semitism in neighboring Austria, Hungary's senior partner in the dual monarchy, where, in the words of the modern Hungarian historian Géza Jeszenszky, the "peasants and petty bourgeois loyal to the Habsburgs adopted Christian Socialism, whose anticapitalist program had an openly anti-Semitic plank, turning it against Hungary, whose capital city they called 'Juda-Pest.'"

There remained also the painful internal problem of disunity, even antagonism, between the Neolog and Orthodox strands of Judaism, and the inability of the two to bridge the differences that separated them, even for the sake of presenting a united front toward the outside. In addition, there was the disquieting new development of Zionism, which, as the Hungarian Jews saw it, considered the Jews not merely a denomination but a people, whose basic problem was its dispersion among the nations, which made it the target of anti-Semitism and which could be solved only by reestablishing it as a nation in its own home-land—a concept that ran counter to everything the Magyar Jewish lead-ership believed in. There was social discrimination, expressed in such manifestations as the exclusion of Jews from the Nemzeti Kaszinó (Na-tional Club), and refusing to consider them "duelable" (see below). And there remained religious antagonism, especially on the part of the Cath-olic priesthood, which still considered Judaism anchored in the old reli-gious error of not recognizing Jesus and considered the Jewish people responsible for his crucifixion.

But despite these flaws, which the religious and secular leaders of the Hungarian Jews by no means overlooked, their overall evaluation of the position Hungarian Israel found itself in at the end of the century was emphatically positive—and justifiedly so. Hungarian Jewry had come a long way since the limitations and the legal deprivations of the pre-*Aus-gleich* days. It had every reason to believe that the future would con-tinue to demonstrate the correctness of its position, both official and emotional, that the Jews in Hungary were but one of the several legally equal religious denominations of the Hungarian nation. The first years of the twentieth century were actually to bear out these expectations.

Jews and Labor

Let us begin with a brief look at the Jews' share in the Hungarian labor movement, which began in 1868 with the foundation of the Com-prehensive Association of Workers. It followed the tenets of Ferdinand Lassalle (1825–64; incidentally, like Marx, a Jew), considered the father of the first German socialist movement, who worked for the recognition of the political and economic equality of the working class. In Hungary, the main sources of labor were the agrarian proletariat and the poor peasantry, unskilled people, who sought employment in construction, river regulation, railroad track laying, and the production of construc-tion materials. Most of the country's industrial labor force was concen-trated in Budapest, 80,000 of whose 500,000 inhabitants were workers. In 1871, after the fall of the Paris Commune, the Hungarian workers held a meeting and expressed enthusiastic support for the French com-rades' struggle. Their leaders were arrested and tried for disloyalty, and a series of ordinances were issued, which for a long time paralyzed the activities of the Hungarian socialists. The movement was revived only in the 1870s, owing mainly to the activities of Leo Frankel.

Leo Frankel (b. Óbuda, 1844; d. Paris, 1896), raised in a religious Jewish family, was a goldsmith in his youth, went at an early age to Austria and Germany, and in 1867 moved to Paris, where he became involved with the labor movement. He was imprisoned by the French government for his political activities but was released in 1870 at the outbreak of the revolution, and played a leading role in the Paris Commune. In 1871 he was made minister of labor of the Commune, organized an armed contingent, and participated in the fighting, for which he was sentenced to death. He managed to flee to London, where he became a member of the council of the Socialist International. In 1875 he returned to Austria and participated in the workers' conference at Wiener Neustadt. He was arrested, extradited to Hungary, and imprisoned. Upon his release, he began to develop a party press and to organize a workers' congress for 1878. In 1876–77 he edited the *Munkás Heti Krónika* (Workers' Weekly Chronicle) and thereafter the *Arbeiter Wochen-Kronik* until 1881. Frankel maintained a steady correspondence with Marx, Engels, and leaders of the French and German labor movements. In 1881 he was again arrested for having offended the press laws, and after his release he returned to Paris, where he became Engels's assistant in the Socialist International and a respected leader of the Socialist Labor Party. In June 1885 in Paris he met Theodor Herzl, and the two Hungarians did *not* hit it off—Herzl tried to win him over to his aristocratic ideas, while Frankel reciprocated by extolling collectivism. At the inaugural conference of the Second Socialist International in 1889, Frankel represented the Hungarian Social Democrats. Despite the short years he spent in Hungary, it was he who infused new life into the Hungarian labor movement. After Frankel died, the French socialists, together with the Hungarian Socialist Party, covered the expenses of erecting a monument on his grave. In 1951 he was portrayed on a Hungarian postal stamp, and in 1968 his remains were transferred to Budapest for reburial in the Workers' Pantheon.

By the turn of the century the share of the Jews among industrial workers rose to proportions much higher than would be expected from their numbers—5 percent—in the general population. Many of them were employed in small-sized workshops owned by other Jews or by Christians. Their highest percentage was found in printing, innkeeping, the butcher's trade, and tailoring. The statistics available are from 1910 but show a situation that had developed in the course of several preceding decades. In that year, of a total of 919 independent printers, 534, or 58.7 percent, were Jewish, and of 11,959 printers' helpers, 2,701, or 22.6

percent, were Jews. Of a total of 29,562 owners of inns, 12,343, or 41.6 percent, were Jewish; of a total of 28,145 persons employed in inns, 5,669, or 20.1 percent, were Jewish. Of 12,919 independent butchers, 3,110, or 24.1 percent, were Jews; of 17,839 butcher's helpers, 2,115, or 11.9 percent. Out of 25,596 independent tailors, 5,386, or 21 percent were Jews; and of 38,848 workers employed in tailoring, Jews accounted for 6,143, or 15.8 percent.

The Jews in Finance and Industry

While thus at least one Jew played an important role in creating the Hungarian socialist labor movement, and Jews were overrepresented in the labor force, the role of Jewish entrepreneurs in developing Hungarian industry was unquestionably even more decisive. We have already heard of the Jewish initiative in the industrialization of the country in the preemancipation years. After 1867, Jews' work in this field intensified greatly, and the Jewish bourgeoisie rapidly advanced to become an important factor in the newly developing capitalist economy. Among them were rich individuals who had earned their money in the grain, wood, and wool trade, and now could put it to use in the new credit institutions, or in the purchase of stocks. Within one generation, Jewish grain merchants became important members of the financial world. (Many of them sent their children to universities, thereby initiating the Jewish penetration of the professions that within a few years made the Jews a leading element among the country's physicians, lawyers, and journalists.) The richest of these Jewish entrepreneurs received or bought titles of nobility from the emperor.

This economic upsurge and professional advancement of the Jews did not take place without a reaction on the part of the landowning lower nobility, many of whom had been forced to sell their land and seek employment in the burgeoning government offices. They resented the growing importance of the Jews, whom they considered a "foreign" element. During the Tisza period—Kálmán Tisza was Hungary's prime minister from 1875 to 1890—this gentry appeared as a political formation with a neoconservative and anticapitalist program, and joining the "agrarians," its members became the first spokesmen of Hungarian anti-Semitism.

While these developments took place on the political scene, Jewish energy concentrated on economics. The results of Jewish enterprise were visible at the 1879 Paris Exposition, where products of Hungarian factories owned by Jews—such as an iron foundry, a distilling plant, factories of parquet, majolica, porcelain, and luggage, as well as two gold jewelers—received medals of distinction. In addition, Károly Lajos Posner was honored with the great gold medal of the Académie Nationale Agricole Manufacturière et Commerciale for organizing the whole Hungarian exhibit.

In the years between 1870 and 1890, dozens of Jewish factory owners and industrialists won gold and silver medals in Hungary itself from the National Industrial Association for their work in developing Hungarian industry. At the Millennial Exhibition of 1896, the number of Jews who received medals of distinction reached the hundreds, and there was practically no branch of industrial production in which the Jews were not among the leaders. Their list, given in the *Hungarian Jewish Lexicon*, takes up four tightly printed columns. At the same time, Jews took an active part in the management of the National Association of Manufacturers, the founding of the Budapest Stock Exchange, and the organization and management of the other financial institutions of the city.

This development continued through the first two decades of the twentieth century, as shown by the available statistical data, of which one of the most significant is this: in 1920 there were 2,739 industrial plants in the country, of which 1,109, or 40.5 percent, were owned by Jews. In the same year twelve of the ninety-seven mines, or 12.4 percent, were owned, directed, or rented by Jews.

A few words about the most outstanding Jewish (or ex-Jewish) leaders in Hungarian finance and industry will illustrate the crucial role Jews played in the economic modernization of Hungary around the turn of the century. One of the most important of them was Ferenc Chorin (b. Arad, 1842; d. Budapest, 1925), founder of the National Association of Manufacturers (Gyáriparosok Országos Szövetsége), which he developed into the most powerful factor controlling Hungarian industry. Chorin was two years old when his grandfather, the Arad reformist rabbi Aaron Chorin, died. He studied law in Budapest and abroad, and started to work as a lawyer in Arad, where he launched and edited an anti-Habsburg political daily, *Alföld* (The Plains). In 1867, at the young age of twenty-five, he was elected a member of the House as a representative of the left-center, participated actively in the deliberations on juridical issues, and was appointed to the parliamentary committees formed to develop laws for the regulation of industry and of criminal proceedings. He was a fervent Hungarian patriot, even questioning the need for the *Ausgleich* (Compromise) that established the Austro-Hungarian dual monarchy. After 1868 he sided with Kálmán Tisza in his moderate opposition to the new constitutional system. In 1875 he was elected to the Lower House as a liberal representing Arad, but a year later, unhappy with Tisza's failure to insist on the establishment of an independent Hungarian national bank, Chorin left the party and helped organize the parliamentary opposition.

From the 1870s on, Chorin took special interest in the struggling Hungarian industries, and grew involved in the Salgótarján Hard Coal Stock Corporation, one of the major Hungarian mining companies, becoming its president in 1890. By that time his company produced 40 percent of the total brown coal output of Hungary. Within ten years he had become Hungary's leading coal magnate, and a very rich man. In 1901 when he set about to organize the National Association of Industrialists, a conflict-of-interest law forced him to leave the House, and in this critical period of his life he found it expedient to convert to Christianity. His conversion close to the age of sixty, after a quarter of a century in parliament, and after attaining a leading position in the financial and industrial world of Hungary, shows to what extent the lure of assimilation to the aristocratic upper layer of society proved irresistible precisely to the high achievers among the Jews of Hungary around the turn of the century.

In 1903 Chorin was appointed a member of the Upper House (such an appointment did not carry with it the granting of nobility—the membership of commoners in the Hungarian Upper House was one of the basic differences between it and the British House of Lords), and in that position he continued to have great influence on the development of Hungarian industry.

The financial power behind Chorin, without whom he could not have achieved domination of the Hungarian coal industry, was Leó Lánczy (b. Pest, 1852; d. Budapest, 1921). The sons of a Jewish immigrant from Moravia by the name of Lazarsfeld, both he and his elder brother Gyula Lánczy (1850–1911), who became an outstanding historian, professor, and member of the Hungarian Academy of Sciences, Magyarized their name to Lánczy and converted to Christianity. Leó Lánczy made a fabulous career as a banker, developing the insignificant Pesti Magyar Kereskedelmi Bank (Pest Hungarian Commercial Bank) into a leading industrial bank. Lánczy was especially interested in two types of heavy industry: the production of pig iron, and coal mining. With his backing, these two essential industries underwent remarkable developments. Lánczy, in turn, became a member of the Lower House and then of the Upper House of Parliament, and a court councillor.

Another colorful and influential figure on the Hungarian economic scene of the late nineteenth century, who did more than anybody else to create a modern banking system in Hungary, was Zsigmond Kornfeld (b. Golcuv Jenikov, Bohemia, 1852; d. Budapest, 1909). Son of an impoverished distiller, from the age of eleven he had to support himself, which he did by becoming a clerk in a Prague bank. From then on his career was nothing short of phenomenal: by the age of twenty he was director in Vienna of the Böhmischer Bankverein and had close contact with the House of Rothschild. In 1878 the Rothschilds rescued the Hungarian General Credit Bank from insolvency, whereupon the twenty-six-year-old Kornfeld was invited to become general manager of that bank, which he completely reorganized.

The same year, Kornfeld, with the help of the Rothschilds, obtained a loan of 150 million crowns for the Hungarian state, which for years had hovered on the brink of insolvency. In 1881 he arranged the conversion of the entire state debt at a discount that was considered favorable—in 1888 and 1892 he was to arrange even more favorable debt conversions —and obtained for the Credit Bank the position of de facto Hungarian state bank. In these years Kornfeld transformed and rationalized the entire financial structure of the Hungarian state: he arranged the basing of the Hungarian state budget on the gold standard and the procuring of gold reserves, and introduced other financial reforms that benefited the state finances.

These transactions yielded enormous profits to the Credit Bank, which Kornfeld used to develop existing industries and to found new ones, thereby making the Credit Bank a major Hungarian industrial entrepreneur. Among the undertakings in which he involved the bank were the Budapest-Pécs railway and other rail lines, the Electrical and Transport Company, the Hungarian River and Maritime Navigation Company, and the Budapest Clearing and Cashier Society, as well as flour milling and sugar production. He developed the port city of Fiume on the Adriatic, Hungary's only outlet to the sea, where he established an oil refinery and a rice-processing plant, and expanded the Ganz Iron and Machinery Works, enabling it to become by the end of the century an internationally recognized producer of electrical equipment and loco-motive engines.

In 1891 Kornfeld became a member of the Budapest Stock Exchange, in which business was transacted in the German language, until Korn-feld, having himself learned Hungarian in the meantime, came forward with a plan to Magyarize it. Such a patriotic attitude was, as we have remarked, characteristic of the Jews of Hungary, including those of for-eign birth, for whom Magyardom was an acquired but all the more cher-ished trait. In 1899, Kornfeld was elected president of the Exchange.

In his financial strategies Kornfeld was not above engaging in manip-ulations that came perilously close to impropriety. In 1895, for example, he seems to have created an artificial panic by manipulating the divi-dends of the Credit Bank. This temporarily made him so unpopular that he saw fit to go on a vacation abroad. But he explained away his actions in terms of paternal concern for the welfare of the whole economy. His bank's industrial prominence was by then so great that the excuse sounded plausible. In any case, there can be no doubt that Kornfeld was the Hungarian financial and industrial giant of the age, who did more for the economic development of the country than any other individual. In recognition of his merits, in 1902 he was appointed member of the Upper House, and shortly before his death he was created a baron.

However, with all his involvement and leadership in the world of finance and industry, Kornfeld remained what was considered a good Jew, in the sense of observing a modicum of religious commandments, participating in the leadership of the Neolog Israelite Congregation of Pest (in 1893 he became its vice-president) and its philanthropic works, and staying a self-assured Jew all his life. When on the eve of the Russo-Japanese war of 1904–5, Kornfeld represented the Austro-Hungarian government in negotiating a sizable loan to the Russians, he refused a decoration offered by them. He told the czar's ambassador that he had conducted the negotiations as a banker, at the request of his government, but as a Jew he could not accept favors from a country in which Jews were persecuted and even massacred (in pogroms as recently as 1903). He also refused remuneration for his part in the transaction. Having been deprived in his youth of the advantages of higher education, he developed a respect for scholarship and learning, and sought out the friendship of such outstanding Hungarian Jewish scholars as Ignác Goldziher, Henrik Marczali, and Mór Kármán (of whom we shall hear more later).

That Zsigmond Kornfeld was a man of great talent cannot be doubted; whether he could have had such a splendid career and achieved such nationwide importance in any country other than Hungary is questionable.

His son, Baron Móric Kornfeld, was likewise an important industrial leader. He was general manager of the Ganz-Danubius Machine Factory, president of the National Association of Hungarian Iron Works and Machine Factories, an art collector, major donor to the Hungarian Academy of Sciences, member of the Upper House, and an author of conservative-nationalist sociological studies. He converted to Christianity.

Conversion and the *Úri* Class

This brings us to a consideration of the phenomenon of conversion, rampant especially among the talented, high-achieving, conspicuously successful Hungarian Jews of the period. The frequency of conversion can be seen, for instance, from the biographies of economists and industrialists contained in the *Hungarian Jewish Lexicon* (published in 1929). Fifty men were considered outstanding enough to be included: of them twenty-five remained Jewish and twenty-five converted to Christianity. Some of the latter converted in their youth, for whose explanation we need not look beyond the drive to achieve in a society in which it was much more difficult for a Jew to succeed than for a Christian. Conversion was the price young Jews had to pay to be able to secure an appointment at a university or to get ahead in a governmental, municipal, or private institution, and in practically any other field of activity. Hence, those who were ambitious, and less beholden to religion (for many possible reasons), converted—because forging ahead was more important for them than remaining faithful to a religion of which they knew less and less, of which they observed less and less, and which they valued less and less.

It is more difficult to understand the motivations for conversion of Jews who took the step *after* they had achieved whatever they could hope for, or were the sons of men who had managed to rise to top socioeconomic positions *without* converting, as was the case with Baron Móric Kornfeld. These men were rich, had all the educational advantages, and in some cases were titled nobles. (In the Hungarian as well as the Austrian system, in contrast to the British, if a man was knighted or created a baron, all his sons and daughters, and his sons' sons and daughters, etc., immediately became proud possessors of the title.) Hence, a man like Móric Kornfeld (and there were hundreds like him) already possessed everything others hoped to obtain by conversion—money, position, power, influence, recognition, even a title—and thus could have had no tangible, material reason to convert. If they nevertheless did convert, they must have had other incentives, which, though intangible, were no less compelling. To understand what these reasons could have been, we must examine the society the members of this elite group were, or wanted to be, part of.

The first thing we have to keep in mind is that the "Magyar nation" was considered, until the emancipation, to consist only of the nobility, which was a mere 5 percent of the total population of the country, while the rest had nothing to say in the management of the country's affairs. The nobles alone could be members of the Diet, officers in the army, participants in the government, representatives of Hungary to Austria, and owners of estates, and in many cases they filled the higher ranks of the priesthood as well. This privileged position created in the nobles that mentality of supreme self-assurance, self-importance, and haughtiness that was satirized by the great Hungarian poet of the revolutionary era, Sándor Petőfi, in his poem "The Magyar Noble," in which the Hungarian nobleman boasts of being entitled to doing nothing, to leading a life of indolence, to letting the bloody sword of his ancestors be eaten by rust, because—"I am a Magyar noble!" Historical studies on the role of the Hungarian nobility in the economic upsurge of nineteenth-century Hungary have convincingly shown how unable or unwilling members of that caste were, even after many of them had lost their estates and consequently their livelihood, to engage in any kind of economic, industrial, or commercial activity.

Yet the aura of Magyar nobility continued to surround them and to lend them a prestige, a mystique, that made them a group apart from, and also high above, all other inhabitants of Hungary. A Magyar noble was an *úriember,* or briefly an *úr,* an untranslatable term similar in meaning to the English "gentleman" but simultaneously both more restricted and more comprehensive, designating a person whose very demeanor proclaimed that he embodied such valued traits as scrupulous propriety, courtesy, decency, honor, helpfulness, and pride and was suffused by the inner conviction that, being an *úr,* he was greatly superior to everbody who did not have the same good fortune of birth. It went without saying that only a son of an *úr* could be an *úr,* and whatever a non-*úr* achieved in education, money, influence, power, fame, he still could never become an *úr.* In Hungarian there are, as with *tu* and *vous* in French, both familiar and formal forms of the second person pronoun; if an *úr* was introduced to another *úr,* they instantly addressed each other as *Te* (*tu*); it would never occur to an *úr* to address a non-*úr* in any other way but *maga* or *Ön* (*vous*). One essential characteristic of an *úr* was being the scion of either a Catholic or a Protestant family. A person outside these religions, even if born to a father who otherwise had acquired all the characteristics of the *urak* (plural of *úr*), and even if converted, could never become an *úr,* which, given the specific configuration of Hungarian society, was the most irresistible existential lure for the non-*urak.*

Herein, I believe, lies the explanation of the conversion to Christianity of men such as Móric Kornfeld, and hundreds like him, who were born into families that had risen to the top of the social ladder, except that they were still not *urak.* Since their fathers had done everything to get as close to the *úri* (gentlemanly) class as possible, the only additional step that remained for them, which they could not resist taking, was to convert. Needless to say, despite his money, his influence, his baronial title, and his conversion, Móric Kornfeld and his ilk never became *urak* in the eyes of the Magyar nobles. In general, Jews or ex-Jews, even the sons of the highest achievers among them, such as Móric Kornfeld, could approximate but never actually penetrate the real elite of the Christian *úri* class.

Despite these barriers, the Jews felt—or perhaps more precisely, felt the need to feel—at least as Hungarian as the Christian Hungarians. And since they frequently encountered subtle (or not so subtle) expressions of the seemingly unalterable circumstance that the Christian Hungarians considered them not quite their equals in terms of their belonging to the Hungarian nation, they also felt an unrelenting need to assert, to prove, their Magyardom. Hence their ceaseless harping on their Magyar patriotism and the great services they were rendering in all fields to the homeland. Hence also their vehement objection to being considered anything but "Magyars of the Mosaic faith," their insistence that they were not a race, not an ethnic group, not a people, nor—God forbid!—a nationality.

The Closed Door

By the end of the nineteenth century, the Jews as a group had achieved a power position in Hungary unmatched by their coreligionists in any other country. The average Jew was perhaps only a little better off than the average non-Jewish Hungarian, but at the top of the social scale the Jewish presence was conspicuous. Most of the members of the boards of directors of the banks, including the two biggest, the Credit Bank (established largely with Rothschild capital) and the Commercial Bank, were Jews or ex-Jews: some of them remained Jewish, but most were converted, and their sons and daughters often intermarried with the upper gentry. Some of them were elevated to the baronage or the ranks of the lower nobility. Their influence in the financing of Hungarian industrial enterprises was crucial. Manfred Weiss, who developed at Csepel the largest Hungarian manufacturing concern (arms, hardware, etc.), while he himself remained a professing Jew even after his elevation to the baronage, had in his family Catholic barons and Protestant nobles, and was supposed to be either the richest man in the country or one of the four richest—the other three being Habsburg Archduke Frederic, Hungarian Prince Eszterházy, and the head of the Count Károlyi family. Weiss was, incidentally, the only industrialist and the only Jew to be allowed an entailed estate.

Some Jewish capitalists were inevitably attracted to land ownership. They began as tenants of large estates (owned by Hungarian gentry or nobles) but by the end of the century were able to, and actually did, purchase estates. In the years prior to World War I, it was reckoned that almost 20 percent of the larger estates were owned by Jews, and more than half of the big rented estates were leased to them. Since for the Jews landed property was not a patrimony to be handled—managed or mismanaged—according to traditional rules handed down by generations of landowning ancestors, they considered an estate just another financial enterprise, and were able to make a go of it where the old Christian owners did not.

Money, financial leadership, industrial power, intermarriage, and conversion supplied the Jews with keys of many a door to the fortresses of entrenched Hungarian society, but not to all. One that remained stubbornly closed to them was the door leading to county positions, especially judicial appointments, including *szolgabíró* (magistrate or justice of the peace). These were poorly paid jobs, and if Jews aspired to them at all, it was not because of their financial attraction, but because of the *úri* association they carried. Another closed door barred the Jews from the National Casino of the gentry. Interestingly, in this respect the magnates (the higher nobility) were somewhat less exclusive than the gentry (the lower nobility). Their club, or casino, in very very exceptional cases, admitted some converted Jews, such as Professor Ármin Vámbéry, whom the prince of Wales (later Edward VII) wanted to meet there on the occasion of his visit to Budapest, and even two—only two, and no more—professing Jews; but the casino of the gentry remained absolutely closed to them.

What was the reaction to this situation of these otherwise greatly successful Jews whose upward mobility had to stop before the closed doors of gentry society? In many cases it created in them a confusing ambivalence, a feeling of being torn between their love of their Hungarian fatherland and the bitterness of rejection by those to whom they wanted to belong.

The emotional push-and-pull experienced by these Jewish or ex-Jewish Hungarians, who found their way to total Magyardom blocked by the unwillingness of Magyar society to admit them, is poignantly illustrated by Baron Lajos Hatvany (himself a converted Jew) in his semiautobiographical novel *Urak és Emberek* (Gentlemen and Men). Its protagonist, Hermann Bondy, employs a Christian tutor to teach his son Hungarian, and sees with misgivings that the tutor infuses the boy with a fiery sense of Magyardom. Before dismissing the tutor, he discusses the problem with him and tries to explain that young Bondy should not be filled with enthusiasm for Hungarian freedom, that he will have to remain, at least to some extent, a stranger in the country. When the tutor argues that the boy will live here, will be a Hungarian, and must love Magyardom, Hermann Bondy bursts out:

"What do you think? That I am blind and don't see this?" And Mr. Hermann points to the Chain Bridge, which, like the frozen slender bow across the violin of a dead virtuoso, lies over the shimmering scales of the river, and to the yellow, graceful palace, which the green-covered hill carries atop it like a wreath of tea roses. "Do you think that I don't love this? That I would not like to say, 'This is my home, this is my city, this is my country,' wouldn't I? . . . As you say, 'This is my homeland.' But look, what can I do when it is forbidden, it is impossible, because they talk to me as to a dog, and don't let me love it, even though . . . Look,"—and the voice of Mr. Hermann becomes quite thin in his great embarrassment— "I, too, would so very much love to love . . ."

Here you have in capsule the desire and the frustration of the upwardly mobile, assimilated Hungarian Jew of the late nineteenth century, very similar to the feelings of a rejected lover: he resents bitterly that his love rejects him, yet he cannot help continuing to love her, to desire her, to hope that he could ultimately win her.

A generation later, after the Law of Reception, the same feelings still reverberate in the bosom of Hermann's son Zsigmond: "*Recepció*—he murmured to himself—what does it mean that they received us? It means that they took us in. Their law takes us in, but their society throws us out. Even though I am a man just like them. I am even an *úr* like them."

Much of Hermann Bondy's feelings still haunted Lajos Hatvany himself yet another generation later. In January 1937, while he was working on the second volume of his *Urak és Emberek* trilogy, he invited me to visit him in his mansion atop the Buda Castle Hill. In the course of the evening I asked him why he returned from his self-imposed Viennese exile to face legal proceedings and imprisonment in Hungary. He took me to the window, drew aside the heavy velvet curtains and, pointing to the fairylandlike nocturnal view with its many strings of lights glittering far below on the Pest side of the Danube, said, "I just could not live without this!"

In the early 1970s the Hungarian literary critic Paul Ignotus returned to the same theme and painted a very similar picture of the ex-Jew who feels he must resign himself to being excluded from the society he so fervently wishes to be a part of:

You could be the richest, the best educated, even officially the highest-ranking man in the kingdom, but if you had Jewish blood you could not hope to play *chemin de fer* in the premises reserved for the upper-middle-class gentry in the center of Budapest. I knew a converted Jew, gentleman farmer, and ex-member of parliament, titled and dandified, who could outduel, outride, outserenade all the Hungarian gentry of his circles; and he married a dowerless, most attractive girl of the ancient lesser nobility, the "belle of the county hall" and of gentry parties in Budapest. After their wedding, she was still invited to the county balls, but they received a tactful warning that *he* had better plead public duties on that occasion. And he —and she—agreed; after all, she must not lose her old friends, and there was no way of getting round such limitations.

After presenting this "case history," Ignotus generalizes and observes that "the yearning for absorption by the gentry haunted even the [Jewish] baron millionaires. Patriotic nostalgia mingled in that yearning with snobbery."

Why should Jews who were successful in their fields of activity, who were among the prime movers and shakers of the country, who were richer, better educated, more cultured, and wider traveled than the Hungarian gentry, nevertheless have been subject to this essentially pathetic yearning to be accepted by them? The question is difficult to answer. Tentatively, I would venture to say that this yearning was nourished by the specifically Hungarian social atmosphere in which the members of the gentry were the unchallenged lords of creation, a very special race of human beings, enveloped in a mystique of their own and endowed with an assortment of traits that made the rest of the population willingly accept their superiority. The overwhelming majority of Hungarians, whether Christian or Jewish, were of course so poor and so involved in trying to make ends meet that the ambition to become gentrified even to the slightest degree was entirely beyond their horizon. It was, however, well within the purview of the rich and upwardly mobile Jews, who could achieve everything else life in Hungary had to offer, and for whom gentry society remained the last stronghold to be stormed. And the more stubbornly the gentry world remained closed to them, the more they desired that it would make an exception in their own personal instance. If there ever was an unrequited love, not in the personal realm but on the social level, this was it: a classical case of the persistent and irresistible attraction of an unattainable social embrace. In vain did sober critical observers remind them of the truth of the old proverb: "Don't run after a wagon that won't give you a lift." Run they did, and the carriage never stopped for them.

A few words are in place about the other side in the complex relationship between Jew and gentry. While social and industrial developments in Hungary did nothing to dull the glamor of the gentry, they did have the effect of undermining the economic position of its most numerous constituent, the *kisnemesség* (the small nobility), the heirs to great historical names and small feudal estates. As a result of the emancipation of their serfs, many of these gentry folk, who had never been burdened by such ungentrylike traits as thrift and providence, faced a precarious situation. Deprived of the free labor of their serfs, they could not afford to hire paid help to work their fields, and thus many of them were forced into selling their land, and the buyers were often Jews. Most of these newly landless gentry did not consider going into business—the very idea of becoming a businessman was, again, ungentrylike—but instead became employees of lower or middle rank in the burgeoning bureaucracy in the cities and the county seats, with modest salaries but secure positions. However, they could not help but observe that the life-style made possible for them by their offices was much more modest than that of the Jewish entrepreneurs. These circumstances, of course, only hardened their determination not to admit Jews into their social circles.

Not that the economically shaken lower nobility had only the increasing power of the bourgeoisie to contend with. Invoking their ancestral historical rights, they tried to protect their privileges vis-à-vis both the new upper middle class and the labor movement. Labor, however, was as undeniably Magyar as they themselves, so they could not oppose its demands by using the patriotic argument of "alien influence." The rising upper middle class, on the other hand, comprised a conspicuous Jewish component, which could be conveniently focused upon, and its progress labeled non-Hungarian Jewish encroachment. Even though by no means all the new capitalists were Jewish, plutocracy was identified with the Jews, just as they were singled out as inciting the socialists, termed "stateless," against the established order. The biggest and still rapidly growing city, Budapest, was declared to be writhing in the hands of rootless Jews. Thus, all critique of capitalism and the bourgeoisie had, or was perceived to have, anti-Semitic overtones, even in cases where those who made the criticism had no such intentions.

As for the Jewish haute bourgeoisie, since the doors to gentry society remained closed, they resorted to achieving what still was possible under the circumstances. Those of the topmost layer of the Jewish "plutocracy" strove to become ennobled, even though they knew that a Jewish or ex-Jewish noble or even baron could not expect admission into the magic circle of Hungarian gentry. Some sought out the company of those few Hungarian nobles who were willing to socialize with them. Many converted to Christianity, hoping to be accepted by or at least get nearer to the *úri* class with its inexplicable magnetic mystique. Many of the converted Jews married off their well-dowered daughters to those members of the Hungarian gentry whom economic necessity forced to accept such alliances in order to infuse much-needed money into impoverished families with great historical names. (Even Miklós Horthy de Nagybánya, who after World War I became regent of Hungary, married a Wodianer girl, a descendant of a converted rich Jewish family. This was the basis of the anti-Semites' demand appearing graffi-tilike on the walls of Budapest buildings, "Rebecca, get out of the royal palace!") Yet others of the Jewish industrialists, wholesalers, and bank-ers coopted Hungarian nobles with great names into their boards, thereby buying a respectability for their enterprises, and providing sine-cures for a few nobles with few duties and responsibilities, except when it came to utilizing their influence in dealings with governmental offices.

The result of all this was that despite the continuing social distance, certain areas of common interest developed between the Jewish haute bourgeoisie and the Hungarian nobility, which put a damper on Hungar-ian anti-Semitism, though it never succeeded in eliminating it.

Dueling and Sports

One of the most conspicuous manifestations of the irrepressible desire of the upper-middle-class Jews to be accepted as *urak* was their insistence on fighting duels with Christian Magyar *urak* whenever they were insulted, or thought they were insulted, by the latter. Dueling was a highly regarded act of courage in Hungary in which members of the *úri* class frequently engaged, and which served as a mark of distinction between insiders and outsiders. In the perception of the Hungarian *urak*, society was divided into two elements: those who were *párbaj-képes* (duelable, that is, qualified for dueling) and those who were not; the first were *urak*, the second common people. Although by the end of the nineteenth century dueling was outlawed (Law 1878:V) and was punishable—usually by a short-term confinement, with the jailers behaving like butlers—it was very frequent, and even members of par-liament and ministers of state were guilty of it. The judges usually took into account mitigating circumstances, of which in most cases "social compulsion" carried the greatest weight. If an *úr* insulted another *úr*, inevitably a duel ensued; if an *úr* was insulted by a person whom he did not know, or if he happened to insult such a person and the latter chal-lenged him to a duel, he had his seconds establish whether or not his opponent was qualified for dueling—if not, the only thing the insulted person could do was to beat up the other in public.

In this atmosphere, with the whole nobility constituting a large "dueling fraternity," it was nearly inevitable that Jews (as well as other individuals of the bourgeoisie) should try to achieve at least a partial approximation of the *úri* class by fighting duels with its members when-ever the occasion arose. In 1888, when the Jews constituted about 4.5 percent of Hungary's population, no less than 13 percent of those con-victed of dueling, nine out of seventy-one, were Jews. Since, as mentioned above, convictions for dueling were rare, the number of Jews (and others) who *engaged* in duels was, of course, many times higher. As for causes, or excuses, for dueling, they were many. A great variety of acts were considered insulting, and only a duel could restore the honor of the insulted party. Thus, many sqabbles, quarrels, verbal exchanges, and the like ended in duels.

Members of the Wahrmann family were involved in several. Mór Wahrmann (b. Pest, 1832; d. Budapest, 1892) was the grandson of Israel Wahrmann, chief rabbi of Pest, and son of a well-to-do merchant. He became an industrialist, played an important role in making Hungary economically independent of Austria, founded several industrial and commercial enterprises, and was elected president of the Budapest Chamber of Industry and Commerce. He fought for the emancipation of the Jews and was vice-president of the Hungarian Jewish Congress of 1868–69 and president of the Israelite Congregation of Pest. In 1869 he was the first Jew to be elected to the Hungarian Parliament, where he remained a lifelong representative of the Lipótváros (Leopold City) district of Budapest, and served for many years in the important position of chairman of the finance committee.

The incident that led to a duel between Wahrmann and the anti-Semitic deputy Győző Istóczy (of whom we heard above) took place in 1882, when Wahrmann was fifty, corpulent, and none too agile. Istóczy was ten years younger. After Istóczy delivered one of his anti-Semitic tirades in the House, Wahrmann took the floor in defense of the Jews and concluded by saying that the Hungarian people "does not let itself be easily misled, even though some try to fertilize the soil for it with all kinds of ordure." Istóczy thought that when Wahrmann said these words he looked at him, whereupon he sent his seconds to question Wahrmann. Wahrmann denied that he had had Istóczy in mind when he said "ordure," but Istóczy, encountering Wahrmann in the library of the House, slapped him and called him a scoundrel. Wahrmann challenged him to a duel, and Istóczy, since both he and Wahrmann were members of the House, had no choice but to meet his challenge. They exchanged pistol shots, but neither one was hit.

The two Wahrmann sons, Richard and Ernő, growing up in a rich home, without a mother, and pampered by their father, developed into young men with opposite character and demeanor of what their father would have liked. Both put on aristocratic airs, hobnobbed only with magnates, completely identified with their manners and customs, and exemplified total assimilation to the mores of the society they yearned to be members of. They incurred huge debts in card games and for years extorted money from their father by threatening suicide. In 1885 the two young Wahrmanns challenged a member of parliament, Géza Rácz, to a duel because of a speech he gave in the House, and when Rácz made his consent to a duel contingent on impossible conditions, their seconds sent insulting letters to Rácz, after which they considered the affair closed. However, Ernő Wahrmann did fight a duel with Count Andor Széchenyi, seriously wounding him, and also wanted to fight the pretender to the Spanish throne (later Alphonse XIII), whom he met at a Banat hunting party of Count Harancourt.

A duel with fatal outcome was fought in 1883 by the Jewish lawyer Dr. Gyula Rosenberg with Count István Batthyány over the hand of Ilona, the granddaughter of Simon Vilmos Schossberger, who had been the president of the Israelite Congregation of Pest, and whose son Henrik, the girl's father, had converted to Catholicism. Henrik Schossberger kept a great house in Budapest, and one of his daughters married Baron Bornemissza, a member of the Transylvanian aristocracy. The other daughter, Ilona, to the horror of her parents, fell in love with Gyula Rosenberg. When they rejected his suit, he eloped with Ilona to Marienbad, where a rabbi married them in a Jewish ceremony before two witnesses. When this became known to Baron Bornemissza, he declared that "he did not want to become connected in marriage with a Jewish pettifogger," whereupon Ilona's father forced her to go with him to Paris and then to Baden-Baden, where (not recognizing her first marriage) he engaged her to Count István Batthyány, an impoverished scion of a great Hungarian noble family. Rosenberg caught up with them in Wiesbaden and told the count that Ilona had agreed to marry him, Batthány, only under extreme paternal pressure. The count's answer was, "Fiddlesticks! Now she loves me." Rosenberg called his rival knavish and sent his seconds, two Prussian officers, to challenge him to a duel. The count refused the challenge, saying that he did not know Mr. Rosenberg and first wanted to inquire whether he was "duelable." Rosenberg issued several more public challenges, to which, however,the count gave no response. Both Schossberger and Batthyány considered the Jewish wedding null and void, and a proper Catholic wedding took place between Ilona and the count, which was duly announced in the press: "Mr. Henrik Schossberger de Tornya, big landowner, is happy to announce the marriage of his beloved daughter to Count István Batthány." Finally, the young couple returned to Budapest, and the count recognized that it was inevitable for him to face Rosenberg. The seconds of the two sides agreed that a duel would take place on October 22, 1883, in the woods of Temesvár, and that the weapons would be pistols. Shots were exchanged, and the count was hit in the head and died on the spot. The friends of the count heard Rosenberg say, "This I did not want." He was sentenced to nine months in state prison, but the sentence was reduced by royal clemency to three months. However, even after all this, Ilona did not become Mrs. Rosenberg: her father married her off to Baron Victor Offermann.

Of course, not all the duels involving Jews were fought between them and Christians. Having become influenced by the *úri* mentality, which considered dueling the noble way of rectifying wrongs, the Jews took to dueling among themselves as well. Even Vilmos Vázsonyi, a leading Jewish politician and outspoken opponent of dueling in his later years, in his youth fought a duel with the publisher and editor Miksa Márkus, likewise a Jew, in which both were wounded.

The attitude of Miksa Szabolcsi, whom we met above, changed in the opposite direction: from an opponent of dueling, he became its fervent advocate. Szabolcsi's fight against anti-Semitism and for Jewish rights was so courageous that it enraged the supporters of Istóczy, who tried to assassinate him. Szabolcsi was a great patriot and believer in Magyarization, and it was partly the result of his efforts that, on the occasion of the millennial festivities of Hungary in 1896, several thousands of Jews Magyarized their names. (Szabolcsi himself had done it earlier.) He had a major share, together with Vilmos Vázsonyi (originally Weiszfeld), in achieving the "reception" of Judaism in 1896. On the other hand, Szabolcsi was a fierce opponent of Zionism, which he fought as energetically as anti-Semitism, especially after the First Zionist Congress of 1897, which was convened by an emigré Hungarian Jew, Theodor Herzl, and chaired by another, Max Nordau.

In 1891 Szabolcsi had still been against dueling, and wrote in *Egyenlőség*: "Nowadays Jewish young men increasingly learn the wielding of the sword, and augment the number of duelers alarmingly." An example of this was what happened between two young Hungarian Jewish politicians, Vilmos Vázsonyi and Ferenc Mezey (1860–1927), who from 1880 to the end of his life served the Neolog National Office in various leading capacities. In 1892 a sharp disagreement developed between them over the struggle for the *recepció*. The quarrel led to a challenge to duel, causing the National Office to accuse Vázsonyi of having "an unsettled affair of honor," which was tantamount to calling him a coward. This, in turn, prompted Szabolcsi to try to settle the matter with a humorous article, in which he wrote:

> I beg the National Office to recover from its attack of heroism. If they continue with the affairs of honor, the Jewish congregation will become a battlefield, the synagogues dueling halls, the rabbinical schools courts of honor, . . . the cantor will fight a pistol duel with the rabbi, and even the funerary officials of the *Ḥevra Kadisha* will fight duels.

The Vázsonyi-Mezey conflict was in keeping with the fighting spirit of a certain segment of Hungarian Jewish youth who felt that by dueling they could prove they were as good as any Christian member of the *úri* class. One of the most notorious duelers was Pál Schlesinger, part owner of a big Budapest grain firm and a popular member of the Budapest grain exchange, who in the early 1890s fought more than a hundred duels, and was known to challenge anyone who dared so much as look askance at him because he was a Jew. At the same time, he was more than a wild Hungarian and an enthusiastic Jew: he collected huge amounts of money at the Exchange to aid the Jewish refugees who in 1899 arrived in Hungary by the hundreds fleeing cruel persecutions and pogroms in Rumania.

As for Szabolcsi, the anti-Semitic incidents that accompanied the Tiszaeszlár affair changed his mind about dueling, and he recognized it as a valuable means of defending Hungarian Jewry. In 1895 he wrote that patriotism and love of Magyardom were no convincing arguments in the eyes of anti-Semites, while a few well-directed sword strokes could alter their views.

> The epidemic of Jew-hatred has to be combatted by duels. Today our Jewish youth will convince the Jew-haters of our right only with the sword. By doing so, they will actually serve the cause of Magyar pride. The plague of Jew-hatred must be extirpated before the millennial exposition. Of the 4,000 university students, not more than 200 to 300 constitute the extremist element. The struggle is for the souls of the first-year students. The extremists among the anti-Semites come from the rural areas. They do not know yet that the Jews have learned well the wielding of the sword.

In the November 5, 1897, issue of the new Zionist weekly *Die Welt,* one of its editors, a young Hungarian student by the name of Moritz Zobel, described the duels that took place in the preceding year between Jewish and Christian students of Budapest University. (Duels between Jewish and Christian students of the University of Budapest took place as late as 1927. In that year, in connection with Prime Minister Bethlen's plan to modify the Numerus Clausus Law, Christian ultra-nationalist, anti-Semitic students, known as "race protectors," staged bloody attacks against the Jewish students at all the universities of the country. In Budapest, two Jewish students, Béla Glaser and István Király, challenged their attackers to satisfaction in duel, which the latter could not deny.)

Nor were members of the Jewish intelligentsia exempt from the attraction of dueling, or, if you wish, from the felt need of engaging in duels. In 1907, the literary and theatrical circles of Budapest were abuzz with the duel fought by Ferenc Molnár, the most celebrated Hungarian playwight, with Illés Szécsi, a wealthy manufacturer and husband of Irén Varsányi, Hungary's leading actress. Molnár, who only a few month earlier had married Margit Vészi (the talented daughter of the highly influential editor József Vészi—like Molnár, a Jew), was deeply involved with Irén Varsányi, and wrote for her his play *Az ördög* (The Devil), which brought him international fame. Although the challenger to the duel was the jealous Szécsi, Molnár drew a two-week jail sentence.

Because by "wielding the sword" a man outside the *úri* class could demonstrate his *úri* aspirations, fencing became a popular sport among Jewish students, who by 1894–95 constituted 31.33 percent of the total university enrollment (1,255 out of 4,006). As a master swordsman, a Jewish student could feel well equipped to defend his honor in case of insult. Before long, young Jews excelled among the Hungarian fencers.

The popularity of dueling had, of course, a commercial aspect as well. In 1852 a Jewish merchant, Bernát Spitz, opened a store selling, as stated in his ads, "dueling swords, daggers, pistols," and boasting of being "the largest fencing equipment store in Hungary." In 1906, the Zionist leader Lajos Dömény (1880–1914) founded in Budapest the Jewish Fencing and Athletic Club, and from that time on Hungarian Jewish fencers won many medals at Olympic Games and other international competitions. In 1908 in London, and again in 1912 in Stockholm, Jenő Fuchs won the Olympic gold medal in fencing. Also in the interwar years, Hungarian Jewish fencers won many medals in Hungarian and other international competitions.

The other sport in which Hungarian Jews were prominent was swimming: the first Olympic medal to be won by a Hungarian was awarded in 1896 to a Jew, Alfréd Hajós, who later converted to Christianity. The record of Hungarian Jews as swimmers, as individuals and as members of polo teams, was as outstanding as in fencing. Similar achievements were chalked up by Hungarian Jewish athletes in gymnastics, soccer, wrestling, bicycling, and athletics. All in all, between 1896 and 1964, Hungarian Jewish men and women athletes won no fewer than twenty-eight gold medals at the Olympic Games, in running, fencing, wrestling, jumping, gymnastics, and water polo.

Andrew Handler, the Hungarian-American Jewish historian of Hungarian Jewry, remarked that "to the Hungarian the love of sport is second only to the love of the nation, and preoccupation with the display of physical prowess and skill is proverbial. . . . Traditionally, participation in sports was not only a respected and popular fulfillment of patriotic duty, it was also believed to be as fundamentally Christian as it was unmistakably Hungarian." He added that the participation of Hungarian Jews in sports "was one of the most covincing signs of the success of emancipation of the Jews of Hungary and of the high degree of their assimilation." I might add that the disproportionate participation of Hungarian Jews in sports further corroborates the oft-quoted observation that Jews are like the gentiles, only more so. And just as the Jews had a disproportionately large share in purveying arts and literature (as editors of periodicals, organizers of salons and exhibits, and so on), so they had in organizing athletic activities in Hungary, establishing sports organizations, teams, clubs, and societies, and thus popularizing sports.

Ennoblement

A few words are in place here about ennoblement, considered the crowning achievement of a successful career by Jews and gentiles alike. As in many other arenas of equality, so in the ennoblement of outstanding Jews Hungary lagged chronologically behind most other European countries. Although as early as the thirteenth century Hungarian kings had given titles of nobility to their Jewish chamberlains, the practice lapsed, and it was only in 1874 that the first Hungarian Jewish family, the Wodianers, were made barons. Thereafter, between 1890 and 1899, five more were created barons; between 1900 and 1909, twelve; and between 1910 and 1918, eight; making, until the abolishment of the monarchy, a total of twenty-six Jewish families or about fifty individuals). None of them had the right to sit in the Upper House, and most of them converted to Christianity and intermarried with old Chrisitian Hungarian noble families. A few of them were also named Austrian barons, which was a separate honor. The recognition was given almost exclusively to men who chalked up extraordinary achievements in industry, commerce, or finances. Only one of them, Frigyes Korányi (originally Kronfeld) de Tolcsva, ennobled in 1884 and created a baron in 1908, was honored in recognition of his services as a professor of medicine. He also converted.

In the same period (1824–1918), 346 Jewish families (forming roughly 20 percent of the total ennoblements) were raised to the lower nobility, which meant that they were given a place name with which to preface their family name as an indication of their noble rank, e.g., budai Goldberger Samuel (Samuel Goldberger de Buda). Of them eight were ennobled before 1859, 118 between 1860 and 1899, and 220 between 1900 and 1918. About 20 percent of these converted to Christianity, and an unknown but certainly much higher percentage of the others' children followed the same path. Thus, the ennobling and the raising into baronial rank of the most outstanding Jewish industrial, commercial, and financial leaders as well as some notables in other fields, such as science and art, actually became a process of bloodletting for the Jewish community: many Jews thus distinguished left the fold, or if not them, their children. Many also intermarried with members of the old Hungarian nobility, and their children were brought up in the Christian faith.

Having examined the statistics of Hungarian Jewish ennoblement, we must say something about the mechanism through which it was accomplished. If a citizen felt he had accumulated enough merits to warrant ennoblement, he would draw up a petition to the emperor (after 1867 the king-emperor) describing in properly humble terms his achievements. This petition, together with documentation, he would submit to the *főispán* (lord lieutenant) of the county of his residence, and the latter, if he found it acceptable, forwarded it to the minister of the interior in Budapest, from whom it would be handed up to the prime minister, who in turn would consult with his cabinet and institute further investigations. Then the dossier, together with the accumulated documents and recommendations, would go to Vienna, to the king's personal minister, who would draw up the patent of nobility for his majesty to sign. The process was long, drawn out, full of pitfalls, and, in addition, very costly: each rank of nobility and aristocracy had its fixed price, payable to the crown, and payments were also due to the Viennese Office of Heraldry for drawing up a coat-of-arms for the new noble. Thus, a newly acquired title of nobility attested as much to the wealth of the man so "honored" as to his achievements and merits.

33

The *Fin de Siècle* and Its Aftermath II: Explorers and Scholars

Before we can conclude the story of the Jews in late nineteenth-century Hungary, we must first cover their achievements in the arts, the various genres of literature, and the main branches of scholarship. In general terms, in the course of the last one-third of that century, the Hungarian Jews moved from a negligible position to one of leadership in each of the three fields mentioned. But, of course, there is much more to this development than can be summarized in a brief, superficial statement. Since in most cases statistical data are available only from 1910, we shall have to base our picture of late-nineteenth-century developments on the assumption that the early-twentieth-century situation was the outcome of a process that had started some half-century earlier. The story we tell in this chapter also straddles the end of the nineteenth century and the beginning of the twentieth for the simple reason that most of the men who started to make a name for themselves in the last third of the nineteenth century lived well into the twentieth, and in many cases produced their major works and attained full recognition only in the early 1900s. From this perspective, the turn of the century itself was but a calendar date, without any specific significance; the landmark events were the emancipation of the Jews in 1867, which marked the beginning, and the end of World War I, which marked the end, of a period in the life of Hungarian Jews, which, as stated above, some of its chroniclers considered their golden age.

Having said this, we must also note that in the intellectual development of Hungary, the nineteenth century was a time of national expansion in every field, duplicating in many respects what had taken place in the countries of Western Europe in the preceding century. It was, first and foremost, the century in which the Hungarian language, up to that time little more than the colloquial of the illiterate peasantry, became the language of the nation as a whole, the medium of literary and scientific creativity, rapidly replacing German. We have repeatedly referred to the Magyarization movement as an expression of Hungarian patriotism; to that we must add that Magyarization, in the sense of switching to Hungarian, was also a dominant phenomenon in all fields of literary activity. In this atmosphere it was inevitable that the Hungarian Jews should adopt the Hungarian language as the medium of their literary expression, and should embark upon producing works of prose and poetry, belles lettres and scholarly writings, in Magyar. That they wrote in Hungarian to begin with was a manifestation of patriotic identification; that once they mastered the language they excelled in producing Hungarian literary works was a manifestation of talent.

As for the patriotic identity of Hungarian Jews, the attitude displayed by the Jewish historian Lajos Venetianer is instructive. Writing in the early 1920s, Venetianer, in his history of Hungarian Jewry, devotes some twenty pages to a listing of the names of hundreds of Hungarian Jews who in the half-century between emancipation and the end of World War I excelled in various branches of literature in the broadest sense—not only in belles lettres but also in scholarly, medical, juridical, historical, linguistic, philosophical, educational, and mathematical writing, and in Jewish studies. To this he adds a shorter but still very impressive list of Hungarian Jews who left their mark in music, the performing arts, architecture, legislation, politics, and journalism. He introduces these lists: "Let us list all the branches of intellectual life, so as to see whether the blessings of emancipation elicited from Hungarian Jews forces that can rightfully count on public recognition because they became a blessing for the Hungarian fatherland." That is, even after vicious anti-Semitic atrocities and the introduction of the anti-Jewish Numerus Clausus Law (see below), Venetianer still viewed the Jewish achievements of the foregoing decades through the criterion not of whether they were "good for the Jews," but whether they were "good for the Hungarian fatherland." In doing so, he represented the general Jewish position of the times, which, despite painful events, was still that of breast-thumping Magyarism. However, Venetianer was undoubtedly correct in his premise that it was in consequence of the emancipation (and, we should add, the loosening of the bonds of religion that accompanied it) that Hungarian Jews experienced an outburst of highly successful activity in every field into which Hungarian society as a whole branched out in that period of economic and intellectual ascent.

One of the factors that attracted proportionately so many more young Jews than Christians to the free professions was the inaccessibility of civil service positions for the Jews. To emancipate the Jews and give them equal rights before the law was one thing, to admit them into state, county, or municipal officialdom quite another. It was mentioned in the last chapter that members of the gentry, impoverished as a result of the emancipation of their serfs, flooded the civil service as the only profession compatible with their *úri* status. Although the civil service was not precisely a reserve of the *úri* class, the fact remained that for a Jew it was rather difficult to penetrate it.

This was, of course, but one of the factors that directed talented Hungarian Jews into the free professions. Others were the concentration of Jews in the capital, Budapest, and other cities; the age-old Jewish tradition of literacy and learning; the high proportion of Jews among high school graduates and university students; and the financial and social rewards offered by academic, professional, literary, and artistic careers. In any case, the fact is that about the turn of the century, the Jewish share in the professional, scholarly, literary, and artistic life of Hungary, most of which was concentrated in Budapest, increased phenomenally.

The Hungarian Academy of Sciences

The achievements of Hungarian Jews in the humanities and natural sciences, and the recognition they earned, can best be illustrated by a closer look at the Jewish membership in the Hungarian Academy of Sciences. The Academy, founded in 1830 by Count István Széchenyi, was the most exclusive scholarly society in the country, and was in fact even more exclusive than the French Académie with its forty *immortels*, who had to share the honors with several dozen members of other French academies. The Hungarian Academy had sixty-four members, and besides it there was no society even remotely comparable in prestige. It comprised three departments: linguistics and humanities; philosophy and social and historical sciences; and mathematics and natural sciences.

The first scholar of Jewish origin to become a member was the philologist Mór Ballagi (of whom we heard in chapter 24). A convert to Christianity, he was elected in 1840. For eighteen years after that, no Jew or ex-Jew was elected until, in 1858, Henrik Lajos Finályi de Kend, another philologist and converted Jew, was made a member. In 1860, two more converted Jews were elected: Lajos György Arányi, a professor of medicine and medical author, who was also ennobled, and the orientalist Ármin Vámbéry (see below). In 1861 yet another converted Jew, the political writer Miksa Falk, was elected. Finally, in 1864, the first unconverted Jew was elected: the physician Joseph Rózsay, who was also ennobled with the title "de Muraköz."

All in all, between 1840 and 1917 twenty Jews and twenty-one ex-Jews resident in Hungary were elected to the Academy of Sciences. In

The Jews of Hungary

addition, ten Jewish and three ex-Jewish foreigners were elected foreign members, seven of them (all Jewish) Hungarian emigrés. These figures indicate three interconnected phenomena: one, that by the second half of the nineteenth century Hungarian Jews had a disproportionately high share in the scholarly activities of the country; two, that the greater possibilities offered by other countries lured many of the best Hungarian Jewish minds into emigration; and three, that among those who remained at home, conversion to Christianity had made deep inroads. Even in the last decade of the period under review (1908–17)—by which time the election to the Academy of several unconverted Jewish scholars had amply shown that conversion was not a prerequisite of that coveted distinction—still there were five ex-Jews among the scientists elected, as against four Jews. Incidentally, of those nine elected, five were mathematicians, one a physicist, one a geographer, one a political economist, and one (my beloved teacher Ede Mahler) an orientalist.

Brief notes on the seven Jewish foreign members of the Academy who were of Hungarian origin illustrate diversity of remarkable careers Hungarian Jewish emigrés had in the countries where they settled. The earliest among them was Leopold Julius Klein (b. Miskolc, 1804; d. Berlin, 1875), the playwright and theater historian of whom we heard above. He was elected to the Academy in 1869. Louis Mandl (b. Pest, 1812; d. Paris, 1881), who got his medical education in Pest, went to Paris in 1836, where he taught physiology and anatomy at the Collège de France and published important studies in both fields. He was eight years younger than Klein but was elected to the Hungarian Academy in 1846, at the age of thirty-four, twenty-three years before Klein.

Next in chronological order of birth was Gottlieb William Leitner (b. Pest, 1840; d. Bonn, 1899), one in a series of Hungarian Jewish scholars motivated by the semilegendary traditions of the Central Asian origin of the Magyar tribes to explore that still largely unknown part of the world, as had Ármin Vámbéry only a few years earlier. Leitner was a child prodigy, who at the age of fourteen became an interpreter for the British army in the Crimean War of 1854–56 with the rank of colonel. He studied in Constantinople and London, and reorganized the Oriental Studies Department of King's College, London, where from 1859 he taught Arabic, Turkish, and Greek. He was entrusted by the British government with establishing and organizing the University of Punjab in Lahore, and while there he published journals in Arabic, Hindi, and English and organized public libraries. In 1868 the Lahore government commissioned him to lead an expedition to the unexplored territories between Kashmir and Afghanistan and to Tibet. Leitner was the first to discover the traces of Greek culture as far northeast as the Gobi Desert,

390

and published the results of his explorations in his *Graecobuddhist Discoveries* and several other important writings. Returning to England, Leitner established in Woking an institute for Indian teachers, founded and edited the *Asiatic Quarterly Review*, and participated actively in many congresses of orientalists. The Hungarian Academy of Sciences elected him a foreign member in 1869.

Next in line was Leopold Schulhof (b. Baja, 1847; d. Paris, 1921), who studied astronomy in Vienna and Paris, started to work at the Viennese observatory, and moved in 1877 to Paris, where he became an adjunct of the observatory and chief calculator of the Bureau des Longitudes. His main work concerned calculations of the orbits of planets and comets, which he published in various astronomical journals and publications. He was elected to the Hungarian Academy in 1878.

Yet another Hungarian Jew who was attracted to the East was Miksa Herz (1856–?), of whose youth little is known, except that he settled in Egypt. There he became the director and chief engineer of the Cairo State Architectural Office, with the title of bey. It was he who planned the Cairo Street for the Chicago World's Fair of 1893. He traveled all over the globe and was elected a member of many scholarly societies, including the Hungarian Academy of Sciences in 1896. His book on the museum treasures of the Arabs was published in Cairo in 1895, and his studies on Arab art and architecture appeared in many Egyptian and European journals. In 1895 he was awarded the knight's cross of the Order of Francis Joseph.

Next follows Ludwig Stein (1859–1930), who studied in Hungarian high schools, at the universities of Berlin and Halle, and at the Jewish Theological Seminary of Berlin. He served as rabbi in Berlin until 1883, from 1886 to 1891 taught philosophy at the University of Zurich, and from 1891 to 1911 taught at the University of Bern. In 1911 he resigned, moved back to Berlin, and became editor of the sociological journal *Nord und Süd, Archiv für systematische Philosophie*, and other philosophical periodicals. He published an impressive number of philosophical and sociological studies, in several of which he opposed the pessimism of Nietzsche and Spengler and developed a religiously tinged cultural and political optimism. During World War I he became involved with Gustav Stresemann, who later (1923–29) was to be Germany's foreign minister. He was elected to the Hungarian Academy in 1899.

The last of the Hungarian Jewish emigrés named to the Hungarian Academy of Sciences in this decade, Marc Aurel Stein (1862–1943), no relation to Ludwig, became by far the best known of the seven scholars discussed here. He studied Sanskrit philology in Vienna, Tübingen,

Oxford, and London, and was appointed in 1888 registrar of Punjab University, organized by Leitner a generation earlier. In 1889 he entered the Indian Education Service, and embarked on literary studies and voyages of archeological explorations in Central Asia, western China, the Gobi Desert, Persia, Iraq, and Transjordan, continuing the work initiated by Leitner. He published a series of pioneering works, including the *Catalogue of the Sanskrit Manuscripts in the Raghunatha Temple Library of His Highness the Maharaja of Jammu and Kashmir* (1884), *Zoroastrian Deities on Indo-Scythian Coins* (1888), *On Old Routes of Western Iran* (1940), and the posthumous *On Ancient Central Asian Tracks* (1964, with a biography by J. Mirsky). What Stein accomplished was to make Central Asia a subject of scholarly research, and to extend backward by several centuries the West's knowledge of the history of ancient Chinese art. In recognition of his achievements, Stein was knighted in 1912 and was awarded honorary degrees by Oxford and Cambridge. He was elected a member of the Hungarian Academy in 1895, after which he participated in the Hungarian Geological Survey of Tun-Huang (1897), which resulted in his greatest discovery, a Chinese cave shrine of the fourth century.

Having introduced seven Hungarian Jewish emigré scholars, it is only fair to complete the picture by brief sketches of four of the greatest world-class orientalists who remained at home despite many invitations they received to the most prestigious universities in the world. They were Ármin Vámbéry and his three students Ignác Goldziher, Ignác Kúnos, and Bernát Munkácsi.

Orientalists: Vámbéry, Goldziher, Kúnos, and Munkácsi

Ármin Vámbéry (b. Dunaszerdahely, 1832; d. Budapest, 1913; original name Vamberger), was congenitally lame, and another Hungarian Jewish child prodigy. In his childhood he studied only the Talmud, and from age twelve he supported himself as a tailor's apprentice. In 1846 he went to Pressburg and worked as a tutor while studying privately and passing the high school exam. He had a phenomenal memory and mastered numerous European languages, and then also Arabic, Turkish, and Persian, as well as the Turkic Tatar languages in which he was particularly interested because of the ancestral relationship between them and the Magyar tongue. He must have had something magically attractive in his personality, for at the age of twenty-two, after he was introduced to Baron Joseph Eötvös, the Hungarian minister of education, the baron gave him a scholarship to go to Constantinople. There young Vámbéry soon became the private secretary of Mehmet Fuad Pasha, the foreign minister of Turkey, and also won the sympathy and even esteem of Sultan Abdul Hamid II. In order to become fully accepted by the Sublime Porte, Vámbéry converted to Islam. During the six years he spent in Turkey he wrote and published a Turkish-German dictionary (1858) and several other works, which brought him membership in the Hungarian Academy in 1860. He also made use of his sojourn in Constantinople to perfect several Central Asian dialects, which he mastered to such an degree that soon he was able to pass as a native.

In 1861 he returned to Pest, received a stipend from the Academy, and instantly used the money to set out on a voyage of exploration of Central Asia. Disguised as a Sunni dervish and calling himself Rashid Effendi, he visited Asia Minor, Armenia, Persia, Afghanistan, Khiva, Bokhara, and Turkestan, joining caravans or going alone, and occasionally sojourning in one spot for several months. (When I was a student in Budapest in the 1920s I heard the story of a group of European travelers, of mixed nationality, who reached a village near Samarkand where the natives told them that there lived among them a dervish who by the grace of Allah knew all the languages of the world. The travelers were curious, asked to meet the dervish, and one after the other addressed him in English, French, Italian, Spanish, German. The dervish, who was of course none other than Vámbéry, answered them flawlessly in each tongue. There was a Hungarian in the group, and he said, "All right, those are world-famous languages which a man could have learned without divine help; but I will catch him—nobody in this place could even have heard of Hungarian." Imagine his astonishment when the dervish answered him in perfect, idiomatic Hungarian!)

Upon returning from his journey, Vámbéry published an account of his travels in English, *Travels and Adventures in Central Asia* (1864), which aroused great interest throughout Europe. This book was the first account by a trained European scholar of the life and culture of a major part of Central Asia, with special emphasis on its languages, dialects, religions, folk customs, and political systems. It is hard to imagine the difficulties Vámbéry had to overcome and the dangers he had to face in collecting material for this book (and others): he could take notes only at night, in secret, and had his identity been discovered he would have been put to death.

While still in Persia, Vámbéry made contact with the British legation, and his pro-British orientation, combined with his intimate knowledge of India and the lands to the north of it, earned him great appreciation and admiration in Britain. He was feted and lionized, awarded medals and distinctions, and he was repeatedly a guest in Windsor Castle, becoming a personal friend of the prince of Wales (later King Edward VII). In my student days, another rumor still circulating about Vámbéry was that while he was in Turkey and the East he worked as a spy for Britain, and that while he was in England he worked as a spy for Turkey. Be that as it may, the fact is that he served as adviser for the Indian and Asian policy of Britain, and was entrusted by Britain with various diplomatic missions in the East. It is likewise a fact that loyalty to a religion was not one of Vámbéry's characteristics. He viewed religious affiliation as a mere matter of utilitarian considerations; hence, in the East he was a Muslim, and in Western Europe he became a Christian.

Being officially a Christian, Vámbéry faced no religious obstacle in his appointment to the University of Pest, where he served from 1864 to his retirement in 1905 as professor of oriental languages. All the Hungarian scholars who from the late 1800s on made a name for themselves in the fields of oriental studies were his students. His scholarly output was phenomenal. He authored dozens of important books, including dictionaries and studies on the culture, linguistics, ethnography, folklore, history, politics, and archeology of the Asian countries he explored, all of which dealt with entirely new fields and subjects. He also wrote two autobiographies (in 1885 and 1904), both of them in English. He wrote with equal facility in English, German, French, and Hungarian, and his books were translated into several languages.

Despite his "practical" approach to religion, all his life Vámbéry remained committed to the cause of the Jews, supported Zionism, and willingly introduced Herzl to Sultan Abdul Hamid in 1901. After Herzl's death, his successor as president of the World Zionist Organization, David Wolffsohn, also sought out Vámbéry's advice. Vámbéry was a kind and helpful man, as can be seen from his friendly attitude to Ignác Goldziher, despite the hatred the latter conceived for his erstwhile master, whom he termed *der Schwindelderwisch* (the false dervish).

Ignác Goldziher (b. Székesfehérvár, 1850; d. Budapest, 1921), the world-famous founder of Islamology, was another child prodigy, who at the age of twelve published a study on the origin and composition of the Hebrew prayers (his father paid the printing costs) and at sixteen was admitted by Vámbéry as his student at the University of Pest. At nineteen he earned his doctorate in Leipzig and went on to study the oriental manuscripts in Oxford and Cambridge. At age twenty-two he became privat-docent (honorary lecturer) at the University of Pest, and a year later received from Baron Joseph Eötvös a stipend to enable him to go to the East to study Islam. He spent several months in Damascus and Cairo (passing rapidly through Jerusalem), and although he openly identified himself as a Jew (in this respect his behavior was the opposite of that of Vámbéry), he was admitted to el-Azhar, the highest institute of religious studies in the Muslim world, and astonished its *'ulamā* (scholars) with his mastery of the Arabic language and Islamic religious philosophy and jurisprudence. His diary of his oriental journey makes fascinating reading, revealing as it does both his impatience with Jewish religious formalism and his admiration for the forms of Muslim worship. By the time of his sojourn in Damascus and Cairo, he had also mastered the Turkish and Persian languages, and later, in order to be able to study the developments Islam underwent in India and Central Asia, he acquired Sanskrit and Russian as well.

Upon his return to Budapest, unable as a Jew to secure an appointment to the university (a privat-docent could give lectures but received no salary), Goldziher was forced to accept a position as secretary of the Israelite Congregation of Pest, in which job he remained until, finally, in 1905, at the age of fifty-five, he was appointed *ordinarius* (full professor) at the university, and could leave the congregation. (He was reputed to have said on that occasion, "Beni uven b'ne Yisroel aus hi l'olom," which is a famous biblical quotation (Exodus 31:17) meaning "Between me and the Children of Israel it is a sign forever," but of which he made a pun, giving the Hebrew word *aus* (sign) this is how it was pronounced by Hungarian Jews, the German meaning *aus* (out, finished), so that what he said was, "Between me and the Children of Israel it is finished forever.") During the thirty years of his service at the Israelite Congregation he conceived a consuming hatred of his bosses, the executives, whom he considered vulgar, ignorant, and contemptible. Yet, even though he received many invitations to the most coveted chairs of oriental studies at great universities, such as those of Vienna, Prague, Leiden, Berlin, Oxford, and Cambridge, he rejected all of them and preferred to continue his "slavery" in Budapest. One wonders how much this had to do with his Hungarian patriotism.

His genius, however, could not be denied by the mere fact of having to slave eight or ten hours a day as a clerk of ignorant bosses (as he viewed his position at the Pest congregation), and it was precisely during those thirty years that he wrote his great works, almost all in German, that secured for him the predominant position among orientalists in both the West and the East. He was elected a member of all the leading scholarly academies in Europe, including, of course, that of Hungary (corresponding member, 1875; regular member, 1892; later chairman of the Philological Department). His literary output was so huge that the mere listing of his major works would fill pages. His favorite disciple, Bernát Heller, compiled his bibliography in 1927 (published in Paris by the *Ecole Nationale des Langues Orientales Vivantes*): it lists 580 books and major studies.

Goldziher was the first to subject the traditions of Islam to stringent scholarly analysis, to interpret Islamic law and the millennial development of Muslim religion in its many sectarian manifestations, to demonstrate its internal intellectual and theological struggles—in short, to make Islamology a discipline commensurate with the scholarly study of Christianity and Judaism. Subjects to which he directed the searchlight of his attention he presented in such a definitive manner that a hundred years later many of his articles were reprinted in the new edition of the *Encyclopaedia of Islam* (still in progress at the time of this writing). And yet he was a man of jealous, unkind disposition, paranoid and deeply troubled, who fell in love with his own daughter-in-law, schemed against his relatives and colleagues, and confided to his diaries malicious, even venomous, judgments about his teacher and mentor Vámbéry and many of his contemporaries, such as Wilhelm Bacher, David Kaufmann, Samuel Kohn, Immanuel Löw, and Bernát Munkácsi, who were also great pioneers in Jewish and related scholarly fields. A gentile colleague of Goldziher at the university was supposed to have said about him, "I am known to be a bad person, but Náci [diminutive of Ignác] is a *roshe*," using the Yiddish term for an utterly evil person to characterize that man of undoubted genius.

If the two other Vámbéry students to whom we now turn briefly did not achieve an international renown similar to Goldziher's, the reason must be sought in the scholarly specialization they chose. Goldziher's was Islamology and Arabic studies, fields that by the nineteenth century scholars all over the world were deeply interested in, and in which the masterful, original contributions of Goldziher instantly reaped attention, recognition, and acclaim. Not so the fields of Turkish and Turkic studies, to which Ignác Kúnos devoted himself, or Ural-Altaic Central Asian studies, in which Bernát Munkácsi specialized. These were areas of great importance in Hungary because of the Central Asian origin of the Magyar tribes and their historic connections with the Turkic and other peoples of that part of the world, but for European scholarship in general they were of much less interest, since they dealt with peoples with whom Europe had no historical connection and who never achieved the high cultural development of Arab Islam. Another factor that resulted in the lesser renown of Kúnos and Munkácsi was that, in contrast to Goldziher, who wrote practically all his books and studies in German, Kúnos and Munkácsi wrote most of theirs in Hungarian, so that the language barrier kept them from becoming internationally celebrated scholars. Yet, as far as originality and lasting value are concerned, there can be no doubt that the work of Kúnos and Munkácsi stands right next to that of Vámbéry and Goldziher. In choosing their fields of specialization, both kept closer to their master, Vámbéry, whose major interest was in Turkic and Central Asian studies.

Ignác Kúnos (b. Sámson, near Debrecen, 1860; d. Budapest, 1945) learned English, French, and German in his childhood, studied under Vámbéry, and in 1885 set out on the first of his several voyages of exploration into Turkey, Syria, and Egypt, aided by the Hungarian Academy of Sciences and the Academy of St. Petersburg. In 1891 he became privat-docent at the University of Budapest and professor of Turkish at the Budapest Oriental Academy (an institute of higher learning), and later its director. In 1893 he was named to the Hungarian Academy. During World War I, he conducted intensive interviews of Tatar prisoners in various prisoner of war camps, and collected linguistic and ethnographic material that subsequently formed the basis of several of his books. In 1918 (at the age of fifty-eight!) he was finally appointed professor at the Budapest University, from which position, however, he retired two years later. In 1925–26, at the invitation of the Turkish government, he gave a series of lectures in Turkish at the universities of Ankara and Istanbul. The corpus of his publications includes dozens of volumes dealing with the Turkish and Turkic languages, folklore, folk poetry, folk plays (*Karagöz*), etc. His merits in incorporating the Turkish-Turkic language area into the compass of Western oriental studies must be judged as great as Goldziher's were in Islamology.

Bernát Munkácsi (originally Munk; b. Nagyvárad, 1860; d. Budapest, 1937) started to publish scholarly papers at the age of nineteen, at twenty set out to study the Tchangos, the Hungarian-speaking natives of Moldavia, and from then on devoted his entire scholarly life to the languages and cultures of the Asiatic relatives of the Hungarians. His work threw light upon the origins of the Magyar tribes, their movements in Central Asia, the influences the Hungarian language absorbed from other tongues, and related subjects. After earning his Ph.D., in the years 1885–1889 he made several trips to the Votyak and Chuwash peoples of the middle Volga and Kama rivers, the southern Ostyaks, and the Voguls of western Siberia, and reported the results of his explorations in a series of pioneering works on these peoples' languages, customs, and cultures. For several years he was editor of the Hungarian journal *Etnográfia*, and in 1900, he and Ignac Kúnos founded the *Keleti Szemle* (Oriental Review), which they made into an important international orientalist journal. In 1890 he was elected a corresponding member, and in 1910 a regular member, of the Hungarian Academy, and in 1915–18 he carried out linguistic and ethnological studies among Votyak and Ossete prisoners of war. Despite the generally recognized value of his contributions to Ural-Altaic scholarship, he was never appointed to a chair at the Budapest University, and from 1890 until his retirement forty years later he made a living as supervisor of education of the Israelite Congregation of Pest. However, in contrast to Goldziher, who, as we have seen, held a similar position until his appointment to the university, Munkácsi took much interest in his work for the congregation, reorganized and modernized the Jewish education in the city, and edited a series of textbooks for the Jewish religion courses in the elementary and high schools. While until the end of the nineteenth century he published his scholarly works in Hungarian, from 1900 on he wrote and published in German, making thus at least part of his research available to the international scholarly world. Still, it rankled him that he had not become a professor, and once, when I was a student at the university he told me that he regretted not having been able to educate students of his own who could have continued his work (his wife, née Paula Jacobi, was a cousin of my mother, and thus our families met occasionally, even after her death in 1925).

Jewish Studies

The picture I have tried to paint of the intellectual fermentation that propelled Hungarian Jews into the forefront of many fields in the second half of the nineteenth century would remain incomplete without at least a few words about a unique development that in the subsequent decades placed Hungarian Jewish scholars at the head of almost all the rabbinical seminaries in Europe and America. Prior to the outbreak of World War II, hundreds of rabbinical students and young aspirants to Jewish scholarly careers all over the world—probably the majority of them—studied in institutions established or headed by Hungarian rabbinical scholars and thus, in a sense, were indebted for their initiation into rabbinics to the phenomenal outburst of Jewish scholarly energy that occurred in Hungary in the late 1800s.

This global Hungarian influence was not, of course, confined to the work of those Hungarian rabbis who became heads of European and American seminaries. In the first half of the twentieth century many dozens, probably hundreds, of Hungarian-trained scholars in rabbinics, Hebrew, and Jewish studies, as well as Arabic and other Middle Eastern studies, made names for themselves in universities and rabbinical schools all over the world. To discuss them would, however, exceed the bounds of a general history of Hungarian Jewry. Even the stories of those most outstanding Hungarian rabbinical scholars who headed seminaries abroad belong here only inasmuch as their training in Hungary, in the second half of the nineteenth century, says something definite about the atmosphere they grew up in and the influences they were exposed to in their youth while acquiring the tools of their trade under the guidance of masters who taught and inspired them. I shall make just a few remarks about these men, in chronological order by birth, and with only the briefest of indications as to their achievements after emigrating from Hungary.

I shall pass over Azriel Hildesheimer, of whom we have heard in another context, because although he spent a major part of his life in Hungary and founded a rabbinical school in Kismarton before moving to Berlin, he himself was a product not of Hungarian but German universities and yeshivas.

Even the next-born notable, Sándor (Alexander) Kohut (b. Félegyháza, 1842; d. New York, 1894), was Hungarian educated only through his high school years, after which he studied oriental languages at the University of Leipzig and was ordained rabbi at the Breslau Jüdisch-Theologisches Seminar in 1867. In 1868 he became secretary of the National Israelite Congress (described in chapter 29), and Baron Joseph Eötvös appointed him supervisor of Jewish education in County Fejér. In 1872 he became chief rabbi of Pécs (Fünfkirchen), and then in 1880 of Nagyvárad in Transylvania. In 1884 the prime minister appointed him to the Parliament as representative of the Jews. By that time he had authored several important scholarly studies on Parsi religious influences on Judaism and other religious historical subjects, and was well advanced in the publication of his greatest scholarly venture, the *'Arukh haShalem* (8 vols., Vienna-Berlin, 1878–92), a ground-breaking contribution to talmudic philology. His fame spread abroad, bringing him an invitation to serve as rabbi of the Ahabath Chesed congregation of New York, where he moved in 1885. In New York he, together with Sabato Morais, took the initiative in establishing a rabbinical college, which led to the foundation in 1887 of the Jewish Theological Seminary of America, with Kohut as professor of Talmud.

Adolf Schwarz (b. near Pápa, 1846; d. Vienna, 1931) studied at the Pápa high school, the University and Bes Hamidrash (institute of Jewish studies) of Vienna, and the Breslau Seminary, and when the Viennese Israelitisch-Theologische Lehranstalt was founded (1893), he became its first head. In this capacity, during his long service, he educated several generations of rabbis and teachers. His own rich scholarly output concentrated mostly on talmudic studies.

Schwarz's successor as head of the Viennese seminary, Samuel Krausz (b. Ukk, County Zala, 1866; d. Cambridge, 1948), studied at the Pápa yeshiva and the Budapest Rabbinical Seminary and University, and earned his Ph.D. at the University of Giessen. From 1894 he taught at the Budapest Jewish Teachers Institute, and in 1905 he became professor at the Viennese Israelitisch-Theologische Lehranstalt. He became director upon the death of Adolf Schwarz (1932), and in 1937 rector, of that school. During the Kristallnacht (November 9, 1938) the Nazis destroyed his priceless library and papers, and he fled to Cambridge, where he remained to the end of his life. Krausz was an encyclopedic master of Jewish scholarship and a pioneer in many of its fields, although his main interest was in the talmudic period. Among his works of lasting value are *Griechische und lateinische Lehnwörter im Talmud, Midrasch und Targum* (2 vols., Berlin, 1898–99); *Das Leben Jesu nach jüdischen Quellen* (Berlin, 1902); and his magnum opus, *Talmudische Archaeologie* (3 vols., 1910–12). (I personally cherish his memory for the friendly manner in which he reviewed my 1936 Jerusalem dissertation *HaMayim*.)

Adolf Büchler (b. Prjekopa, County Túróc, 1867; d. London, 1939), earned his Ph.D. at the University of Leipzig and graduated as rabbi from the Budapest Seminary in 1891. After a short spell as rabbi in Budapest, he joined his uncle, Adolf Neubauer, librarian and professor at Oxford, and in 1893 became professor of Bible and history at the Viennese Lehranstalt, where he stayed until 1905. In that year he was invited to serve as chief assistant to Michael Friedlander, principal of Jews' College in London, and in 1907 he became its principal. Like several of his colleagues who were the products of the Budapest Rabbinical Seminary, Büchler, too, devoted most of his scholarly work to the talmudic period. Much of his work focused on the crucial overlap between the end of the second Temple period and the beginning of the talmudic era. Büchler was less successful in his public relations: he sharply criticized Chief Rabbi Herman Adler, and he even clashed with Adler's successor, Chief Rabbi Joseph Herman Hertz (a fellow Hungarian), who was chairman of the board of Jews' College and whose plan to introduce reforms in its curriculum Büchler strenuously opposed.

Joseph Herman Hertz (b. Rebrény, County Ung, 1872; d. London, 1946) was taken as a child by his father, a rabbi, to America, where he became the first graduate of the Jewish Theological Seminary of New York. From 1913 to his death he was chief rabbi of the United Hebrew Congregations of the British Commonwealth. Of his life and work we note only this: in contrast to his colleagues, the leading rabbis of Hungary in the first two decades of the twentieth century, who took a sharply anti-Zionist position, R. Hertz was a powerful advocate of Zionism in the name of religious Jewry, and was partly responsible for the successful outcome of the negotiations that led to Britain's Balfour Declaration of 1917. The contrasting positions of anti-Zionism in Hungary and the pro-Zionism of a major part of British Jewry can be attributed to a great extent to this difference between the attitudes embraced by their respective spiritual leaders.

Michael Guttmann (b. Félegyháza, County Bihar, 1872; d. Budapest, 1942) repaid the Breslau Rabbinical Seminary the debt the Budapest Seminary owed for having had it as a prototype, by leading the Breslau school during the period of its highest flourishing and reintroducing in it the tradition of talmudic study that developed in Budapest to a higher level than in any other rabbinical seminary of the time. Guttmann was a student at the Budapest Seminary from 1895 to 1903 and after graduation became rabbi in Csongrád. In 1907, following the retirement of Moses Bloch, he became professor of Talmud, and in 1921 he was appointed head of the Breslau Seminary with the official title of *Seminarrabbiner* (seminary rabbi). In 1925 he served for one year as professor of Talmud at the newly founded Hebrew University of Jerusalem. In 1933, after Hitler's rise to power, he returned from Breslau to Budapest as head of the seminary there. He authored important talmudic studies, and began to publish—many years before computers facilitated such work—an analytical index to the Talmud titled *Mafteah haTalmud* (letter *aleph*, 4 vols., 1910–30.)

The leadership of Hungarian Jewish scholars at the head of the rabbinical seminaries of Vienna, Berlin, Breslau, London, and New York is too distinct a pattern to be attributable to coincidence. The abilities these men developed during their apprenticeship in Hungary, in an atmosphere that also produced in Hungary itself scholars of the ilk of Vámbéry, Bacher, Goldziher, Kúnos, Munkácsi, and Blau could be a testimony to the powers contained in the Hungarian Jewish "race" and released by the emancipation and the Jewish economic upsurge that followed it. Perhaps what we see here is a manifestation of the hybrid vigor of a group that lived on the borderland between the Ashkenazi North and the Sephardi South, between the assimilationist West and the partly Hasidic, partly Mitnagdic Orthodox East. In any case, it certainly is a remarkable, unique phenomenon, which was significantly responsible for the transplantation of Jewish scholarship to the countries of the West before its centers in Eastern and Central Europe were destroyed by the Holocaust.

The contribution of Hungarian Jewry to Jewish scholarly and rabbinical leadership in the Western world was not confined to the few outstanding men discussed above. Quite to the contrary: in the late nineteenth century young Hungarian rabbis emigrated by the dozens to countries in Western Europe and overseas and came to occupy leading positions in important congregations, in addition to producing important scholarly works. To the United States alone some sixty Hungarian-born rabbis immigrated in those years, including Benjamin Szold (1829–1902), rabbi of Congregation Oheb Shalom in Baltimore from 1859, and father of Henrietta Szold; Adolph Huebsch (1830–84), who for many years was rabbi of the Ahabath Chesed Congregation in New York; Aaron (Albert Siegfried) Bettelheim (1830–90), rabbi in San Francisco and Baltimore, whose daughter Rebecca married Alexander Kohut; and Solomon H. Sonnenschein, Leopold Wintner, and Aaron Wise (father of R. Stephen S. Wise). These Hungarian-born rabbis played what Robert Perlman calls "a moderating and bridging role" between the Reform and Orthodox trends that dominated American Jewish life at the time, and their influence was such that in many congregations a pattern developed of transmitting a pulpit from one Hungarian rabbi to another. What is most remarkable, in light of Hungarian rabbis' strong opposition to Zionism in Hungary, is that the Hungarian rabbis who officiated in America had a very active role in introducing Zionism into American Jewish life.

34

The *Fin de Siècle* and Its Aftermath III: Literature, Criticism, and the Arts

In this chapter, we shall have to interpret the time frame indicated in its title especially loosely, for the simple reason that many of the Hungarian Jewish writers and artists discussed, although their talent unfolded around the *fin de siècle* and hence they unquestionably belong to that period, continued to live and work for many years thereafter, some of them even surviving, and continuing to produce after, the Holocaust, either in Hungary or abroad.

Writers and Poets

It is difficult to evaluate the significance of the Jewish contribution to Hungarian literature. The *Hungarian Jewish Lexicon*, published in 1929, contains biographies of, or references to, only forty-three Hungarian Jewish authors (novelists, dramatists, and poets). The *Encyclopaedia Judaica* (published in Jerusalem in 1972) lists or gives biographies of some hundred Hungarian Jewish writers, including quite a number of converts to Christianity. While these two sources provide information on authors who were considered important enough in 1929 and 1972 to deserve biographies or at least mentions in *Jewish* informative compilations, they give no idea of their significance from the perspective of *Hungarian* literary history. For that we have to go to general histories of Hungarian literature and see what place they assign Jewish writers.

The book-length article on Hungarian literature (some 100,000 words) contained in the 1,160-page volume *Information Hungary* seems to fill the bill. The book was published in 1968 under the aegis of the Hungarian Academy of Sciences through Pergamon Press in Oxford, and the article on literature is the work of Miklós Szabolcsi, himself an Academician and a foremost modern historian of Hungarian literature, whose father and grandfather were editors of the Hungarian Jewish weekly *Egyenlőség*. The article contains references to several hundreds of writers who lived in the nineteenth and twentieth centuries, among them thirty-two Jewish ones. However, observing the taboo imposed on all reference to Jews and Judaism by the Communist regime, not in one case is mention made of the fact that an author was Jewish, or that he treated Jewish themes in his writings. Only by checking their names against the list of Hungarian Jewish authors in the article in the *Encyclopaedia Judaica* does one discover that they were Jewish, and that several of them devoted most or some of their writings to Jewish subjects. Once one penetrates this wall of silence, one finds that many Jewish writers were important enough to be discussed in a general overview of the history of Hungarian literature.

More informative is *The Oxford History of Hungarian Literature* (1984) written by the Hungarian-English literary historian Lóránt Czigány, whose twenty-six-page chapter on "The Metropolitan Experience: The Cult of Illusion" outlines literary developments in Hungary (primarily in its undisputed cultural center, Budapest) in the late nineteenth and early twentieth centuries. In this chapter Czigány mentions the work of twenty-nine intellectual leaders, almost all writers, whom he evidently considered the most important of the many hundreds active in that period. The fact that nineteen of the twenty-nine, or two-thirds, were Jews (or ex-Jews) is a measure of the role Jews played at the time in the literary world of the Hungarian capital. And this given that Czigány is severely selective: such Jewish writers of note as Adolf Ágai, Lajos Hatvany, Emil Makai, and Béla Révész merit no mention at all in his literary history. More significant is the fact that all three of the men whom he discusses as having made Hungary's "special contribution" to psychoanalysis—Sándor Ferenczi, Géza Róheim, and Lipót Szondi—were Jews.

In summarizing his conclusions about Budapest of the early twentieth century, Czigány states that it was Hungarian Jewry that turned the city into an industrial and financial metropolis, and added a cosmopolitan flavor to an otherwise xenophobic city, while at the same time eagerly espousing the national cause, adopting Hungarian names, and championing social progress. He comes to the conclusion that "undoubtedly, urban Hungarian literature possessed a distinctly Jewish flavor," which manifested itself "in the wide variety of themes stressing a more general outlook than the traditionally self-centered Hungarian viewpoint. This outlook was eminently brought into focus by the 'export playwrights' and the subsequent theatrical revival. In the more traditional departments of literature, there also appeared a spirit of ferment, activated by ambition, talent, and a deep desire for changes in an otherwise static social structure, that were distinctly Jewish in origin."

After some hesitant and not too significant beginnings, Hungarian literature entered its modern phase in the middle of the nineteenth century, and almost instantly Hungarian Jews began to add their voices to it. The earliest of them to write in Hungarian were Károly Hugó and Gusztáv Zerffi.

Károly Hugó (originally Hugó Károly Bernstein; b. Pest, 1808; d. Milan, 1877) studied medicine, started to work as a physician, and wrote his first poems and plays in German. From 1846 on he published plays in Hungarian, some of which were translated from his German into Hungarian by Miksa Falk and were performed on the Hungarian stage until the early twentieth century. He lived for several years in Paris, Berlin, and Vienna, and died in Milan while giving a lecture on "Cantomimics," one of the eccentric ideologies he developed. He converted to Christianity.

Hugo's younger contemporary Gusztáv Zerffi (originally Hirsch; 1820–?) also began writing in German, edited several periodicals in that language, in 1848 became adjutant to Gen. Schweidel, and after the defeat of the revolution lived for years in Paris, London, and Bucharest. He started to publish studies and belles lettres in Hungarian in 1847. He, too, converted.

The first Jew to write poetry in Hungarian was Mihály (Michael) Heilprin (b. Piotrkov, Russian Poland, 1823; d. Summit, New Jersey, 1888). He received a thorough Hebrew education from his father, and at the age of twenty moved to Miskolc, Hungary, where he became a bookseller. He soon mastered Hungarian and in 1846 began to publish Hungarian volumes of poetry. After the defeat of the revolution he escaped to Cracow, then went to France, returned to Hungary in 1850, learned English, and in 1856 moved to England and on to America. There he became one of the editors of Appleton's *New American Cyclopedia* (1858–63) and was active on behalf of Russian Jewish refugees. He wrote, together with Ármin Vámbéry, a history of Hungary titled *Hungary in Ancient, Medieval, and Modern Times* (1887).

The first Hungarian-born Jewish author who wrote all his works in Hungarian was Bertalan Ormody (1836–1869). He was a poet and novelist who started out as a journalist, contributing poems and short stories to Hungarian popular journals. His collection *Magyar Romanzero* (Hungarian Romances) was published in Pest in 1859, followed by a volume of poems, *Magyar Hon Ébredése* (The Awakening of the Hungarian Homeland; Pest, 1860), and a novel in verse in seven cantos titled *Smüle Itzig* (Pest, 1861). The two central themes in his writings were Hungarian patriotism and his fellow Jews, whom he depicted in a realistic and sympathetic manner quite unusual for the age.

A contemporary of Ormody's was the journalist, satirist, feuilletonist, and juvenile author Adolf Ágai (originally Rosenzweig; b. Jánoshalma [Jankovac], 1836; d. Budapest, 1916). Son of a physician, he studied medicine and started working as a doctor but soon turned to literature and began to contribute to Hungarian dailies and periodicals. In the 1860s he edited, together with the Jewish journalist Zsigmond Bródy (1840–1906), the periodical *Látcső* (Telescope), and in 1867 he launched the weekly *Borsszem Jankó* (Johnny Peppercorn, the name of a mythical thumb-sized satirist), which remained well into the interwar years the only popular satirical paper in Hungary. In it he spoofed and castigated the awkward phenomena he observed in the social and political life of the country. One of the paper's popular columns, "The Selected Maledictions of Reb Menahem Tzitzesbeisser," made fun of the thinking and style of expression of the Jews (or rather some Jews) of Budapest. From 1870 to 1879 he also edited the journal *Magyarország és a Nagyvilág* (Hungary and the Great World).

Ágai's own writings comprised many genres: short stories, social sketches, family scenes, events of the day, travelogues from his trips in Europe, Asia, and Africa, and so forth. In addition, he was one of the creators of Hungarian juvenile literature. He launched in 1871 the children's paper *Kis Lap* (Little Journal), which appeared until 1904. The pen name "Uncle Forgó," which he used for his juvenile writings, became known and loved in the children's world. He translated several novels from German and French, and his racy Hungarian language won him wide recognition.

Expressions of his Jewish identity played a lesser role in the writings of Ágai than in his public activities. When the Magyarizing Society was resuscitated in 1860, he became one of its diligent workers. While the 1865 Diet was in sesssion, he was one of the most determined fighters for Jewish emancipation in the daily press. Although opposed to Zionism, Ágai did contribute to Herzl's German-language weekly *Die Welt*. In several of his essays he depicted provincial Jewish life based on memories of his childhood. Late in his life he became an enthusiastic supporter of the IMIT (Israelite Hungarian Literary Society).

The first Jewish writer to make a significant contribution to Hungarian literature both as a poet and as an editor was József Kiss (b. Mezőcsát, 1843; d. Budapest, 1921). The son of poor Orthodox parents, he received a traditional Jewish education and at the age of fourteen entered *gimnázium*. After several years of travel during which he imbibed lasting impressions of Hungarian peasant and Jewish life, he moved to Pest and published in 1868 his first book of poetry, in Hungarian, titled *Zsidó Dalok* (Jewish Poems). His poems were thoroughly

Jewish but also expressed the patriotism that permeated Hungarian Jewry of the times. In one of them he wrote: "Finally, O Jew, your day is dawning, now you, too, have a fatherland!" More important as an innovation in Hungarian literature were his Hungarian Jewish folk ballads (Songs About Poor Arye), which remained his hallmark throughout his career. From 1870 to 1873 he worked as editor of the magazine *Képes Világ* (Picture World) and started to write (under the pseudonym Rudolf Szentesi) a series of mystery stories titled *Budapesti rejtelmek* (Secrets of Budapest, 1874). In 1875–76 he co-edited *Zsidó Évkönyv* (Jewish Year Book).

Kiss's success and fame as a leading Hungarian poet date from 1875, when his ballad "Simon Judit" was presented by the critic Ferenc Toldy to the exclusive Kisfaludy Literary Society, and was acclaimed. (Still, Kiss had to wait until 1913, when he was seventy, to be elected a member.) In 1877 he was elected to the Petőfi Literary Society. For six years (1876–82) he earned a living as secretary of the Jewish community of Temesvár, producing at the same time several of the ballads that made him known and loved all over the country, and in which the sentiments, manners, and speech of the protagonists are those of Hungarian peasants who happen to be Jewish by faith. It was precisely this appearance of Jews in Hungarian guise that made his ballads popular among both Jews and non-Jews. At the same time the themes of anti-Semitism and the persecution of the Jews also appear in his poems, and it is these features that make him a *Jewish* poet par excellence. Most impressively Jewish is his poem "Jehova": its hero, Job, a tragic, majestic figure, unshakable in his rock-solid faith, rises against the spirit of the age, which sweeps away his children. The pain of the persecuted Jew—of living in dispersion, of being eternally alien—makes his poem "Uj Ahasvér" (New Ahasuerus) a gripping Jewish self-revelation. While singing of Jewish pain and suffering, Kiss had a profound love for and pride in his Jewish heritage: I remember how impressed I was in my youth by his sentimental-humorous poem "Legendák a nagyapámról" (Legends About My Grandfather, 1888) about his Lithuanian grandfather Reb Mayer Litvak who, as he writes, was "neither Von, nor Don, . . . but only Reb" ("Reb" is the familiar form of "Rabbi").

Kiss was asked by the Israelite Congregation of Pest to write poems to be sung in the synagogues, which he did, but the religious views he expressed in them were unacceptable to the leadership, so he had to publish them himself (*Ünnepnapok,* 1888). By that time Kiss was celebrated as a poet who introduced a new theme into Hungarian poetry: the urban scene in the new metropolis, its human problems, and the cruelty of economic life in the city (*De Profundis,* 1875; *Mese a varró-*

gépről [Tale of the Sewing Machine], 1884). In 1890 he founded the weekly *A Hét* (The Week), which soon became a focal point of new intellectual endeavors, and the forum for the literary reflection of city life that in those days rapidly gained importance. Inevitably, official criticism condemned the trend represented by Kiss's weekly as "cosmopolitan" and "urban," both derogatory terms. All in all, József Kiss achieved a rare synthesis between his Jewishness and his Magyardom, and captured the admiration of the country as a Hungarian *Jewish* poet.

The changing "guidelines" that literary historians had to follow in Communist Hungary in the 1960s can be illustrated by the characterizations given to József Kiss by one and the same critic in two largely identical sketches of the history of modern Hungarian literature. In 1962 the Corvina Press of Budapest published the book *History of Hungarian Literature*, written by Tibor Klaniczay, József Szauder, and Miklós Szabolcsi. It was also translated and published in French (1962), German (1963), and English (1964). In it Szabolcsi writes:

> József Kiss (1843–1921) was the first Hungarian man of letters to interpret Hungarian Jewish themes at a high artistic standard, though still using the equipment of the popular-nationalist school. The son of a village publican, he built up a long record of service as teacher and white-collar worker in the country before attracting attention by his ballads with a Jewish theme. Following his literary success, he went to live in Budapest, where he strove to create a new-type, big-city poetry; he interpreted the moods and feelings of the city dweller, loosening up and reshaping old verse and mixing the characteristic Magyar meter with Western forms. About the turn of the century (in *Fires*, and later in the poem *The Cruiser Potemkin*), he even voiced some revolutionary sympathies. Apart from that, Kiss moved in the world of Hungarian liberalism— a circumstance that made him sound irrevocably dated when, after 1905, new and more radical trends made their appearance in Hungarian literature.

Six years later (in 1968) the same studies of the three authors mentioned were included in the massive 1,144-page volume *Information Hungary*, edited by Ferenc Erdei. In it, the above capsule of József Kiss's work has been deleted and the following single sentence substituted: "József Kiss (1843–1921) interpreted the moods and feelings of the city dweller, loosening up and reshaping old verse and mixing the characteristic Magyar meter with Western forms." This is in keeping with the general tone of *Information Hungary*, which carefully says not a word about the life, work, or even existence of Jews in Hungary, except that the Gestapo "launched a campaign to exterminate the Hungarian Jews and the anti-Fascists," in which it was helped by the Sztójay government.

The first noted Hungarian dramatist of Jewish birth was Baron Lajos Dóczy (originally Dux; b. Sopron, 1845; d. Budapest, 1918), a convert to Christianity, who neither in his life nor in his writings had anything to do with Jews, Jewishness, or Judaism. Son of a Jewish leather merchant who became bankrupt during the Hungarian 1848 revolutionary war, Dóczy studied law at the University of Vienna, contributed to the Viennese *Neue Freie Presse*, the Hungarian satirical weekly *Borsszem Jankó*, and other Hungarian papers, and was an enthusiastic supporter of the politics of Ferenc Deák. His services earned him high recognition: he became ministerial department head, was made a court councillor, and was ennobled with the rank of baron. He wrote poems, novels, and literary studies, translated German classics into Hungarian, and Hungarian ones into German, but gained his greatest fame as a playwright whose dramas and comedies were performed in the Hungarian and Viennese theaters. His only writing with the slightest Jewish connection was his first drama, titled *The Last Prophet*, which dealt with the destruction of Jerusalem and was performed in Buda in 1869.

It is a remarkable fact that after József Kiss, Adolf Ágai, and Lajos Dóczy, no other important Hungarian Jewish (or Jewish-born) writers appeared until late in the nineteenth century. To this eventual younger generation belonged the novelist and dramatist Sándor Bródy (1863–1924), who, occasionally at least, took his topics from the Jewish environment. Miklós Szabolcsi characterizes Bródy as a "strikingly handsome hedonist, who squandered his talent, was idolized by women and generally admired by turn-of-the-century Budapest. . . . He captures themes of changing life, of love and poverty, of the merciless fate of the poor, and of the Budapest world of finance."

Of lesser importance were novelist, playwright, and sociologist Samu Fényes (1863–1937), who emigrated to Vienna and treated one or two Jewish subjects; poet Henrik Lenkei (1863–1943), many of whose poems have Jewish religious themes; and poet Lajos Palágyi (1866–1933), in whose poetry the Jewish themes often serve as symbols for Hungarian fate.

More significant was the novelist and journalist Tamás Kóbor (originally Adolf Berman, 1867–1942), who although an advocate of assimilation was also a spirited defender of Jewish rights in the daily *Ujság* (News), which he edited; as well as the novelist and dramatist Dezső Szomory (originally Weisz, 1869–1944), a master of the elegant and artificial style of the *fin de siècle* tradition, who devoted a few of his works to Jewish themes, especially provincial Jewish life.

Much more "Jewish" than these two was the novelist and journalist Péter Ujvári (originally Groszmann, 1869–1931). He, in fact, devoted most of his writings to Jewish subjects, such as the tragicomic story of the head of a small Jewish community who converts to Christianity (*Az uj keresztény* [The New Christian], 1907) and other pictures of provincial Jewish life. However, his one work that survived the test of time was the *Magyar Zsidó Lexikon* (Hungarian Jewish Lexicon), which he edited in 1929 and which was reprinted in Budapest in the 1980s.

Gyula Csermely (1869–1939) wrote novels and plays, and short stories many of which had a Jewish setting and dealt with subjects such as problems of Jewish assimilation. An important Jewish poet, heir to the mantle of József Kiss, was Emil Makai (originally Fischer, 1870–1901), who in the earlier years of his short life devoted himself exclusively to Jewish writings, including his 1892 volume *Zsidó Költők* (Jewish Poets), in which he presented, for the first time, Hungarian translations of medieval Spanish Hebrew poets. In his latter years he wrote on non-Jewish subjects, penned love stories and humorous plays, and translated some one-hundred operettas.

Jenő Heltai (originally Herzl, 1871–1957), a cousin of Theodor Herzl and a convert to Christianity, was one of those Hungarian Jewish authors in whose work their Jewish origin played no role whatsoever. He started to publish poems in József Kiss's *A Hét*, and a volume of his poems, *Modern Dalok* (Modern Songs), was published in 1892, when he was but twenty-one. He went on to become a highly successful novelist and playwright, and remained a leading figure on the Hungarian literary scene well into the interwar years. He was dramatic director of the Vigszinház (Light Theater) from 1914 to 1918, director of the Athenaeum publishing house, and from 1916 president of the Association of Hungarian Stage Writers. The protagonists of his novels and plays are young, jolly, slightly sentimental lovers, harmless adventurers, light-hearted bohemians, whom Heltai evidently liked most when they transgress the laws of bourgeois morality. His novels are a blend of sarcasm and cynicism, witty, imaginative, and full of surprise turns. The one "serious" novel Heltai wrote, *Álmokháza* (The House of Dreams, 1929), was, according to Czigány, "an ambitious attempt to portray postwar Budapest; it has an intricate plot, and is heavily influenced by Freudianism." Heltai's writings have been translated into English, French, German, Italian, Spanish, and Hebrew, while he himself translated many English and French plays for the Hungarian stage.

The number of Hungarian Jewish authors who were born in the last quarter of the nineteenth century, and began to make their impact on the Hungarian literary scene in the early twentieth, is so great that their enumeration and brief characterization would turn this chapter into a veritable *Who's Who* of Hungarian literature. We shall therefore have to be even more selective than hitherto and confine our comments to those few writers who, in the judgment of the critics of the 1980s, have stood the test of time and, after the passage of half a century or more, are considered important enough to figure prominently in their histories of Hungarian literature.

We are, however, faced with another problem. Among the prominent and successful Hungarian writers of the period there were many who were Jewish (at least by birth), but in whose works this fact played no role whatsoever. They did not write about Jewish themes, among their protagonists there were no Jews, and their own Jewishness or Jewish origin was kept stricly sub rosa. Shall we include them (or some of them) in our considerations? If yes, we shall be speaking not of Hungarian Jewish literature but of the contribution of Jewish (-born or -professing) writers to Hungarian literature. But if we omit them, we shall give only a very partial picture of the essential role that the Jews played in the development, modernization, and vitalization of Hungarian literature in the early twentieth century.

Moreover, even if we decide to confine ourselves to those authors in whose works Jewish themes do play a role, this is easier said than done, since it is difficult to settle on a criterion of "Jewishness" generally applicable to the variety of style, approach, interest, and theme represented by the works of the several dozens of Hungarian Jewish writers of note. Often the theme of a novel or a short story is not overtly Jewish at all, yet the problems or phenomena dealt with become Jewish, or can be considered Jewish, because of the explicit or implicit Jewishness of the protagonists. Other works reflect the specific attitude of "psychological Marranism" that has been characteristic of many Hungarian Jews: they show that the lifestyles of many Hungarian Jews were Hungarian in every respect, and only deep down in the inner recesses of the psyche was there a residual Jewishness, of which the individual either was unaware or did not want to be aware.

This psychological Marranism appeared in varying degrees. Some Hungarian Jewish authors would have been most embarrassed had anybody discovered "Jewish" traits in their writings. They chose to depict protagonists belonging to every kind of ethnic group and social class, some of them traveling to the four corners of the earth in their search for subject matter, but kept carefully away from Jewish themes, milieus, or characters.

Others, while they do have Jewish protagonists in their works, refer to their Jewishness only in an offhanded, incidental manner, as if it were a minor idiosyncrasy unimportant in the total picture of the personality. And then there were, of course, those authors who wrote about Jews because they knew them intimately, were concerned about their problems, and were themselves Jews and felt Jewish—even if they tried to solve their own Jewish problem by converting to Christianity.

This is not the place to pursue this particularly Jewish problem of Hungarian literary taxonomy. However, before we proceed to a few characteristic examples of each of these categories, one brief statistical aside seems appropriate to throw some light on the share of Jewish authors in the Hungarian literary scene in the decade preceeding World War I. In the popular but competent and judicious *History of Hungarian Literature* by Tibor Klaniczay, József Szauder, and Miklós Szabolcsi, already referred to, we find that the chapter on "The Rise of Modern Hungarian Literature (1905–1914)" discusses, mostly briefly, the work of twenty-eight authors born between 1869 and 1888. Evidently, these twenty-eight were considered by the authors of the *History* the most important writers in that decade, which witnessed significant intellectual ferment in Hungarian literature as a whole. We have to refer to the *Magyar Zsidó Lexikon* to find out who of these twenty-eight were Jewish. We learn that thirteen of them were born Jewish, of whom four converted to Christianity. The nine who remained Jewish were Ignotus (original name Hugo Veigelsberg, 1869–1949), Dezső Szomory (1869–1944), Béla Révész (1876–1944), Ernő Osvát (1877–1929), Ferenc Molnár (1878–1952), Lajos Biró (1880–1948), Menyhért Lengyel (1880–1974), Ernő Szép (1884–1953), and Milán Füst (1888–1967). Those who converted were Ervin Szabó (1877–1918), Lajos Barta (1878–1964), Baron Lajos Hatvany (1880–1961), and Oszkár Gellért (1882–1967). As this brief listing shows, in the period in question the Jews, who constituted some 5 percent of the population of Hungary, and many of whom had not yet acquired the Hungarian tongue, provided close to half (thirteen) of the total twenty-eight authors of note.

Let us now survey some of the most notable Jewish authors of the period, proceeding in chronological order. To begin with, a note on the novelist and literary historian Béla Révész (1876–1944), who, like most of the others to be considered here, started out as a journalist. He was on the staff of the Budapest social democratic daily *Népszava* (The People's Voice) and remained a lifelong socialist. He wrote an impressive number of novels, most of them dealing with problems of the working class but several devoted to Jewish subjects and displaying religious sentiment. He was a friend of the great modern Hungarian poet Endre Ady, about whom he wrote three volumes (1935). He also published a biography of the social critic and Zionist leader Max Nordau (1940). After the Nazi invasion of Hungary in 1944, he was arrested, together with other Jewish journalists, and is thought to have perished in Auschwitz.

The only woman among these writers of note was Renée Erdős (1879–1956), daughter of a Jewish small landowner, who started her career as a teacher in a school of the Israelite Congregation of Pest and published her first poems in József Kiss's *A Hét*. Her first book of poems, *Leányálmok* (A Girl's Dreams) appeared in 1899, and was followed by two more volumes, *Poems*, in 1906 and 1909. She moved to Florence and Rome, where she underwent a spectacular conversion. She translated several Catholic classics, including the Evangelical play *The Disciple John* and *Fioretti* (Little Flowers), the anonymous fourteenth-century collection of legends about St. Francis of Assisi. In her own poems, too, published in the volume *Aranyveder* (The Golden Bucket, 1910), her former sensuous note was replaced by a Catholic religious devotion. Before the war she switched from poetry to the novel, and in an autobiographical trilogy, *Ösök és ivadékok* (Ancestors and Descendants), which consists of the volumes *Az uj sarj* (The New Sprout, 1918), *Az élet királynője* (The Queen of Life, 1921), and *Berekesztett utak* (Barred Roads, 1923), she told the story of her own evolution. Her most successful—and most controversial—novel was *Santerra biboros* (Cardinal Santerra, 1922), which portrays in rich colors the pomp and splendor of the Vatican and the Roman milieu and, in lurid detail, the cardinal's wild erotic fantasies about a would-be mistress. Her rich output of novels, short stories, poems, travelogues, plays, letters, and diaries kept her in the forefront of the Budapest literary world.

A year younger than Renée Erdős was Ferenc Molnár (originally Neumann, 1878–1952), the most famous of the Hungarian Jewish authors, who became better known and more highly acclaimed outside Hungary than any other Hungarian author. Molnár belongs to that category of Hungarian Jewish authors in many of whose works there appear characters with a residual or vestigial Jewishness. After studying law at the universities of Budapest and Geneva, Molnár worked at the *Budapesti Napló* (Budapest Diary), edited by József Vészi, and contributed for years to other Hungarian dailies, as well as to *A Hét*. The characteristics of his later work were already evident in these early articles: they include sketches poking fun at the peculiarities of Budapest life, and reports wittily analyzing social problems, which made him one of the most popular young social commentators.

After two collections of short stories, Molnár's novel *Az éhes város* (The Hungry City, 1900) was a pronounced success. With powerful brushstrokes and somber colors it paints the life of the new metropolis, Budapest, at the end of the century, and dwells in particular on its Jewish quarter, without, however, containing any clue as to the Jewish identity of the author. This book was followed by a rich crop of novels, short stories, and humorous and satirical sketches, characterized by fresh and acute observation, psychological penetration, masterly structure, and an immediacy of narrative presentation. Outstanding among them was his juvenile novel *A Pál-utcai fiuk* (The Boys of Pál Street, 1907), the story of two competing gangs, told with an extraordinary understanding of the preadolescent mind and written with warmth and love. It was translated into all the major European languages (English: *The Paul Street Boys*, 1927), and spread its author's name internationally.

A novel of Molnár with a Jewish protagonist is *Andor* (1918). Although Andor is a young Jewish intellectual destroyed by the defects of his own character, he is clearly symbolic of the mental struggle of the average Budapest citizen. In summarizing Molnár's novels, the literary historian Baruch Yaron wrote: "In Molnár's books, which brilliantly expose contemporary Hungarian social problems, the central figure is always a weak-willed Jew who makes himself ridiculous by trying to imitate his surroundings." Although "always" should be corrected to "often," many of Molnár's novels do depict the Hungarian Jewish proclivity to assimilate to the gentile environment, which he consistently criticizes, despite the fact that he himself was also guilty of (or suffered from) assimilation. An external sign of this was that he wore a monocle, a Hungarian gentry affectation; an internal sign was his manner of writing about Jews, at times with sympathy, understanding, and psychological penetration, at others with sharp sarcasm and disdain, yet always with the same distance with which contemporary Jewish and non-Jewish authors wrote about Hungary's many ethnic groups and class segments that they did not belong to but whose problems, specificities, and peculiarities fascinated them. Molnár wrote about Jews just as the Jewish Béla Révész and the ex-Jewish Lajos Barta, both radical bourgeois and social democratic writers, depicted the workers' misery—with passion and compassion, but without conveying the feeling that they were one of them, which, of course, they were not. There is nothing in Molnár's portrayal of his Jewish characters to parallel the total immersion of the great Hungarian novelist Zsigmond Móritz (1879–1942) in the world of the Hungarian peasant, of which he clearly felt part. In fact, in several of Molnár's writings—including the *Pipes of Pan, The Pig Slaughter in the Leopold District, The Hungry City,* and even *Liliom*—either his protagonist, or he himself as narrator, utters negative opinions of the Jews. Also interesting is the fact that in some of his writings (*Miracle on the Mountain, The King's Maid*), a definite Christological hankering is evident. On the other hand, when Molnár was faced with the real-life news of Nazi persecution, he was shaken and his Jewishness reasserted himself.

Molnár achieved his greatest successes, both in Hungary and abroad, with his plays, which were performed in translation in many countries and to great acclaim. As Paul Ignotus puts it: "His comedies were a roaring success all over the world—more than anywhere else in German-speaking Europe (until Hitler intervened) and in the United States." To quote Baruch Yaron again, the characters in his plays are "almost without exception Jews fighting to improve their image, sometimes turning into caricatures in the process." One of his most popular plays, in which, incidentally, no Jews appear, is *Liliom* (1909), which became the basis of the story for the musical *Carousel* (1945) by Rodgers and Hammerstein. Its full title is *Liliom: The Life and Death of a Rascal*, and its story starts among the Hungarian tramps and hooligans, and then continues in heaven—a grotesque heaven, as imagined by the slumdwellers themselves. It combines picaresque drama with mystery play, in which cynicism alternates with sentimentality, satire with tearfulness.

Molnár's contemporary, the Jewish novelist and literary critic Géza Szilágyi (1875–1958), himself an outstanding figure of Hungarian letters, characterized Molnár's plays thus:

> Standing on the highest rung of self-knowledge, he is aware of his capabilities, is able to use them with a never-erring virtuosity, finds themes that captivate audiences of all nationalities equally, is master of the artfulness with which the writer can dazzle both the naive and sophisticated segments of the public, is the unsurpassed player on all the instruments of stage technique, but beyond technique and intoxicating ingenuity, beyond the determined striving for success, beyond the supreme mastery of stagecraft, he is a feeling man, a sensitive writer, a rare artist.

In the late 1930s, when the position of the Jews became increasingly difficult in Hungary, Molnár left the country, went first to France and Switzerland and then, in 1940, to the United States, where he wrote his last major work, the autobiography *Companion in Exile* (1950; its Hungarian original, *Utitárs a számüzetésben*, was published only in 1958, six years after his death).

Only slightly less successful on the international literary and theatrical scene than Molnár was his contemporary Menyhért Lengyel (1880–1974), in whose oeuvre Jews and Jewishness play no part whatsoever. He, too, started as a journalist in Budapest, then worked a while for an insurance company, and reaped early successes with his drama *The Great Prince* (1907) and *The Grateful Posterity*, which was performed at the Hungarian National Theater—the most prestigious stage in the country—and won the coveted Vojnich Prize of the Hungarian Academy of Sciences. Typical of the Jewish prevalence in the literary scene of

Budapest in the pre–World War I years is the fact that Lengyel settled on two other Jewish authors as collaborators for some of his dramas: one of his plays was written together with Baron Lajos Hatvany (a convert to Christianity) and another with Lajos Bíró (see below), an important Jewish novelist and playwright.

On the other hand, it was almost inevitable that a keen rivalry would develop between Ferenc Molnár and Menyhért Lengyel, the two most successful playwrights of the Hungarian stage, a rivalry that was the talk of Budapest for several years. After Irén Varsányi (1880–1932), one of the most acclaimed Hungarian actresses (and herself Jewish), terminated her affair with Molnár and he recovered from the trauma this caused him (he even attempted suicide), he had a ten-year-long stormy love affair with Sári Fedák, Hungary's tempestuous prima donna, married her in 1922, and immediately fell in love with another actress, the sixteen-year-old rising star of the stage, Lili Darvas. He wrote two plays for her, so incensing Fedák that she asked Menyhért Lengyel to write a play specifically for her. The play Lengyel wrote that allowed Fedák to triumph over Darvas was the comedy *Antonia* (1924). Molnár considered this a public humiliation, divorced Fedák, and within a year married Lili Darvas.

In several plays Lengyel castigated the conventional lies of society that hide under the guise of tradition and custom, tackled social issues, portrayed ardent passions, and attacked weaknesses with pitiless satire. He was one of those authors for whom the Hungarian ambience was too narrow and who roamed far afield in his search of human problems to dissect with the scalpel of his dramatist's skill. *Taifun* (Typhoon, 1907), the first of his plays to achieve international success, delves into the secrets of the Japanese psyche, while ostensibly dealing with the phenomenal progress of Japan and the danger it represented to the world. In *A próféta* (The Prophet, 1911), he presents the clash of a primitive, exotic culture with that of the European world. In yet another of his plays, *Sancho Pansa királyságában* (In the Kingdom of Sancho Panza) he used Cervantes's famous story to express his own ideas of social justice. The titles of several more of his plays indicate the international scope of Lengyel's subjects: *A cárnő* (The Czarina, 1913), *Charlotte kisasszony* (Mademoiselle Charlotte), *A waterlooi csata* (The Battle of Waterloo), *A csodálatos mandarin* (The Miraculous Mandarin, the text of Béla Bartók's pantomime).

One of Lengyel's last works in Hungary was the book for the film *The Blue Angel*, starring Marlene Dietrich (1930). A man with such international literary interest, he inevitably found the narrow world of Hungary too confining, and in 1931 he emigrated to London, and in 1937 to the

United States. In both places he was successful as a writer for the film industry. In 1934 he adapted, together with Lajos Biró, his own play *The Czarina* as the script for the film *Catherine the Great*, starring Elisabeth Bergner, and in 1940 he wrote the script for *Ninotchka*, starring Greta Garbo. However, from that time on he no longer wrote significant original work of his own. He spent the last years of his life in Rome.

Two more important Hungarian Jewish authors, both of whom wrote on Jewish themes, were born in 1880. One of them, Baron Lajos Hatvany, we heard of above. The other, novelist and playwright Lajos Biró (originally Blau, 1880–1948), had a career similar in many respects to that of Menyhért Lengyel, with one difference: Biró wrote one important Jewish novel. Biró spent his youth in Nagyvárad, where he edited a paper and was among the close friends of Endre Ady. Moving to Budapest, he continued his journalistic work, becoming editor-in-chief of *Világ* (The World). He was a prolific writer, turning out dozens of volumes of short stories, novels, and plays, which won him great praise. His style is rapid, ragged, and choppy, presenting the story line with dramatic density, and he arouses the curiosity and maintains the interest of the reader. His earlier writings were preoccupied with erotic issues, but later he increasingly turned to social problems.

Biró joined the political circle of the influential periodical *Huszadik Század* (Twentieth Century), and when several of his friends became members of the liberal government following the October revolution of 1918, he was appointed secretary of state for foreign affairs. Soon after that, however, he left Hungary for good, living at first in Vienna, then in Berlin, and finally settling in England, where, together with Sir Alexander Korda, another Hungarian Jewish emigré, he founded the London Film Production Company, whose director he remained until his death.

It was in 1921, while living in Vienna, that Biró published his historical novel *A bazini zsidók* (The Jews of Bazin), which tells the shattering story of the blood libel proceedings of 1529, in the course of which the entire Jewish community of a village near Pressburg was tortured and then burned at the stake (see above, chapter 15). While working on this novel, Biró was seized with an interest in the contemporary Jewish situation as well, and wrote a thoughtful essay titled "A zsidók útja" (The Way of the Jews, 1921), in which he took a negative position on both Jewish nationalism and assimilation, and considered the Jewish question unanswerable, but at the same time enthusiastically endorsed the historical inevitability of the survival of the Jewish people. These two works, the novel and the essay, make Biró an important *Jewish* writer. After settling abroad and getting involved with the film world, Biró wrote mostly film scripts, of which the most famous were *The Way of All Flesh* and *The Private Life of Henry VIII*.

The poet Oszkár Gellért (1882–1967), who converted to Christianity, remained largely unnoticed until 1920, when for a time he was editor of *Nyugat*. His early poetry revolved mostly around sexual fantasties, including incest and sadism, and was characterized by straightforward, unadorned language and startling revelations. In the Károlyi government of 1918–19 he became head of the prime minister's press office, and thereafter many of his poems dealt with the moral problems of the war years and the revolutionary era. In the mid- 1930s he stopped writing poetry altogether, and returned to it only in the post–World War II period, when the Communist establishment applauded him even for his lame efforts at socialist realism.

We shall hear later of the editorial, cultural, and Zionist work of József Patai (originally Klein, 1882–1953), my father. Here a few words are in place about his life and his own writings. Born into a Hasidic family in the village of Pata, near the city of Gyöngyös, he left the yeshiva, studied in a Piarist high school and at the University of Budapest, published a slight volume of Hebrew poetry at the age of twenty, earned his Ph.D., and started working as a high school teacher in Budapest. In 1911 he launched the monthly *Mult és Jövő* (Past and Future), a Jewish social, cultural, and artistic periodical, a unique journal of highest quality. He translated into Hungarian selections by Hebrew poets from the early Middle Ages to his own times (several multivolume editions), wrote Jewish religious poetry, Jewish lyrical love poems, Hasidic short stories, an autobiography of his childhood years, a biography of Theodor Herzl (published also in German, Hebrew, and English), a description of Jewish life in the new Palestine, and several volumes of polemical essays representing the Zionist point of view and upholding the value of Jewish culture as the only basis of a self-assured Jewish life in the Diaspora. He was a much sought-after lecturer, and also propagated the idea of Zionism and Jewish culture in cultural evenings and exhibitions of Palestinian Jewish artists that he organized. From 1924 on, he visited Palestine almost every year, leading groups of Hungarian tourists, lecturing at the Hebrew University, and constituting a living link between the Jewries of Palestine and Hungary. *Mult és Jövő*, which he continued to edit until 1939, developed into the center of a sizable group of Hungarian Jewish authors, whom Jenő Pintér, the foremost historian of Hungarian literature, termed "the literary circle of József Patai." In the fall of 1939, upon the outbreak of World War II, Patai and his wife, the author, poet, and art critic Edith Patai, went to Jerusalem to join their three children, who had moved there earlier (see chapter 40.) In Palestine, Patai returned to the language of his youth, and continued to write prose and poetry in Hebrew and to translate some of his own Hungarian writings into Hebrew. After his death, the Israeli literary critic Emil Feuerstein wrote: "Nobody did as much for Hungarian Jewish culture as József Patai."

The novelist and dramatist Béla Balázs (1884–1949) was, together with Georg Lukács, a mentor of the so-called Sunday Circle, an informal literary group that held animated discussions in private apartments, and most of whose members left Hungary after the revolution of 1919. Lukács hailed him at the time as the most profound young Hungarian poet and playwright. Between 1907 and 1919 Balázs produced twenty novels and plays, but today he is chiefly remembered as the author of the librettos for Bartók's *Bluebeard's Castle* (1912) and *The Wooden Prince* (1917). After leaving Hungary, Balázs became known as the first theoretician of what was then the new cinematic art form. His book *The Visible Man, or Film Culture* (1924) influenced the early great film directors. After years in exile in Vienna, Berlin, and Moscow, Balázs returned to Budapest in 1945, but was accused of sectarianism and was not allowed to participate fully in cultural life. His autobiography, *Dreaming Youth* (1946), is perhaps the best of his later works.

The poet, dramatist, and novelist Ernő Szép (1884–1953) was the foremost Hungarian exponent of the trend fashionable in the early twentieth century of presenting in artful poetry the mind of the child, the child's reaction to encountering the world of adults, at the same time revealing the child that lives on in the inner self of every adult. The child's psyche, as it appears in Szép's poems, is enveloped in constant sadness, because life itself is sad and is passing, but the world, with its countless animate objects—clouds, stars, flowers, falling leaves, even little dogs—is also a source of constant wonder and bafflement for the child. In view of the overall tone of Szép's writings, and especially their unquestionably artificial sensibility, it was an unexpected development that his autobiographical novel *Lila ákác* (*Wistaria*, published in 1919) became the most spectacular hit of the Hungarian cinema in its film version, made in 1934 by Steve Sekely (originally István Székely).

Critics

The scope of this book does not permit us to discuss the role of Jews in Hungarian literary criticism as extensively as it deserves. We must confine our comments to the three most outstanding modern Hungarian literary critics, two of whom were Jews, the third a converted Jew. They were Ignotus, Ernő Osvát, and Georg Lukács.

The progressive literary movement that from 1890 on centered on József Kiss's *A Hét* spawned several new progressive periodicals in the ensuing two decades, of which by far the most significant was *Nyugat* (West), published from 1908 to 1941. Of its first three editors, Ignotus (original name Hugo Veigelsberg, 1869–1949) and Ernő Osvát (1877–1929) were Jews, and Miksa Fenyő (1877–1972) was born Jewish. To say that *Nyugat* dominated the Hungarian literary scene until the outbreak of World War II tells only part of the role it played for about three decades. In fact, *Nyugat* functioned as a kind of informal literary academy: no self-respecting author considered himself established until he was published in *Nyugat*. Not that *Nyugat* lacked opponents or even enemies in both the literary and political worlds, but its prestige and the high standards it applied to the belles lettres, criticism, and translations it published made it the arbiter of what was considered serious literature. Its editors and critics did not demand literary conformity but were determined to wage war against conservative nationalism, responding to social changes, sympathizing with socialism, and advocating liberal views. It was with their writings in *Nyugat* that the careers of Endre Ady and practically all the other leading modern Hungarian poets and novelists were launched.

Ignotus, son of the journalist *Pester Lloyd* editor Leo Veigelsberg (1846–1907), was the most influential editor of *Nyugat*. He started out as a poet, short story writer, and translator, cut his teeth on József Kiss's *A Hét*, and then became a contributor to several important Budapest dailies. When he assumed the leadership of *Nyugat*, he was close to forty, a man of highly developed literary taste, an experienced critic, with definite ideas on the social role of the writer. During his tenure there he never ceased fighting for the freedom of the writer and his right to express unhindered whatever his convictions were. Under his stewardship the monthly became *the* representative in Hungary of liberalism, of the new Western, urban spirit, and of the fight for the individual's right to self-assertion. In 1919, during the short-lived Hungarian Communist Council Republic, Ignotus, although not prosecuted, was ostracized so ruthlessly for his liberal record that he chose voluntary exile. For the next twenty years he lived in Switzerland, Berlin, and Vienna, working as an editor or correspondent for democratic newspapers. In 1938 he returned to Budapest for a short time but left again for London, and then for the United States. After World War II he became reconciled to the new Communist regime of Hungary, and returned to Budapest shortly before his death.

Ernő Osvát (1877–1929), like Ignotus, came to *Nyugat* after apprenticeship at *A Hét*. He was one of those rare editors who resisted the temptation to write in the journal they edited, whose columns were at their disposal. As an editor of *Nyugat* he wrote only a very few pieces of literary criticism, but he nevertheless played an important role in guarding the high literary level of the monthly during the twenty years of his editorship, and even more so in discovering and publishing the writings of major Hungarian poets and writers. It seems appropriate to mention here that while the first three editors of *Nyugat* were Jews or converted Jews, the most important literary figures whose central forum *Nyugat* became under their stewardship were not Jewish but Christian Hungarians. The most outstanding Jewish writers who made their mark on the Hungarian literary scene of the period were not members of the *Nyugat* circle. But through their control of *Nyugat,* as through *A Hét* before it, Jewish editors were the chief purveyors of modern Hungarian literature. Jews played a similar role in the daily press, figuring prominently among the editors of the most influential papers. As Paul Ignotus (the son of Hugó Ignotus) put it, Ignotus and the co-founders of *Nyugat,* Miksa Fenyő and Ernő Osvát, "were determined to create a totally European Hungary, delivered from parochialism; but, at the same time, to assert the national character and to dig deep into the Magyar heritage of images, concepts, and melodies, and refurbish what had been debased by usage and foreign influences." Before long *Nyugat* achieved the same dominant position in Hungarian literature that *Huszadik Század* held in Hungarian sociology—and both were in the hands of Jewish (or ex-Jewish) editorial management.

What was remarkable about *Nyugat* was that while its protagonists and intellectual leaders were Jews, its most creative contributors were not only gentiles, but gentiles of the provincial gentry, such as Endre Ady, Mihály Babits, Margit Kaffka, Jenő Tersánszky, Dezső Kosztolányi, Béla Bartók, and Zoltán Kodály. To them were added Zsigmond Móricz, with his mixed peasant and lower-middle-class background, Dezső Szabó, and Lajos Nagy, who were exceptional in having neither Jews nor nobles in their family background. Of course, Jewish or ex-Jewish writers and intellectuals were also attracted to *Nyugat*—among the latter were the poet and playwright Jenő Heltai (whom we have already met), the poet Menyhért Szász, and two converted Jews whose fame spread beyond the border of Hungary, the social philosopher Georg Lukács and the psychoanalyst Sándor Ferenczi. However, the work of the Jewish contributors was definitely less important than that of the gentile writers, who, had the Hungarian language been at least as accessible to Europe as was Dutch, Swedish, or Norwegian, would have made *Nyugat* a literary journal of global significance.

One of the most remarkable minds on the Hungarian intellectual scene, whose active life spanned almost seven decades and who did significant work in aesthetics, literary theory, the history of philosopy, and the criticism of modern political thought, was Georg (György) Lukács (1885–1971). Son of a well-to-do Jewish banker, József Lukács, who became ennobled with the byname "de Szeged," György Lukács embodied the type of Magyar unable to tear himself away from the fatherland whom the poet Endre Ady apostrophized as the stone which, however often it is thrown up into the air, inevitably falls back unto the soil of "my sweet country." Lukács not only returned to Hungary after each sojourn abroad but, after winning international fame with his books written in German, he returned to Hungarian and wrote in that language from 1945 to his death. Circumstances forced Lukács to leave Hungary several times, but he was always drawn back (in a manner reminiscent not only of Ady's "up up hurled stone" but also of Baron Lajos Hatvany), and he spent the last twenty-six years of his life as the grand old man of letters of Communist Hungary.

His father had wanted him to become a banker, but he rebelled, and in demonstration placed on his desk a picture of his uncle who devoted himself to the study of the Talmud. Lukács himself studied law and philosophy at the University of Budapest, but before earning his Ph.D. he branched off in 1904 to found, together with two friends, the Thalia Theater in Budapest for the purpose of presenting modern plays. At the same time he joined the Sociological Society, which by that time was the focal point of the socially oriented liberal intelligentsia of Hungary. Under the influence of this environment Lukács converted to Christianity, and from then on, throughout his long career, he had nothing to do with and showed no interest in Judaism or the Jews, with the uncertain exception of his book on Moses Hess, the Jewish socialist whose humanitarian concept of socialism deeply influenced him (see below).

After earning his Ph.D. at the University of Budapest (1906), Lukács became a regular contributor to *Huszadik Század* and *Nyugat* and published a book on the development of the modern drama, which garnered him the coveted literary prize of the Kisfaludy Society at the age of twenty-three (1908). In 1909–10 he studied in Berlin under George Simmel, traveled in Germany, Italy, and France, and wrote his book of essays, *Die Seele und die Formen* (1911), which brought him international renown. From 1913 to 1918 he lived in Heidelberg, where under the influence of Max Weber he developed his method of "sociology of literature." During World War I, Lukács championed the cause of the proletariat and wrote his important *Theorie des Romans: Ein geschichtsphilosophischer Versuch über die Formen der grossen Epik*, which was published in Berlin in 1920. Back in Hungary, he joined the Communist Party in 1918, and in 1919 he became people's commissar for education and culture in the Hungarian Council Republic, and political commissar of the Hungarian Red Army on the Rumanian front. After the fall of Béla Kún's regime, Lukács had to flee to Vienna, where he was arrested but, upon the intervention of Thomas Mann and others, was soon freed and became a leader of the Viennese Hungarian Communist Party-in-exile. He stayed in Vienna until 1929, producing some of his most original works on socialist and Marxist theories and theoreticians. One of his books from this period was *Moses Hess und die Probleme der idealistischen Dialektik,* published in Leipzig in 1926.

Leaving Vienna, Lukács lived in 1930–31 in Moscow and from 1931 to 1933 in Berlin, where he devoted himself to ideological work in the German Communist Party. Upon Hitler's rise to power he returned to Russia, where he became a member of the Philosophical Institute of the USSR Academy of Science. However, his concept of "great realism" was found to be an impermissible deviation from the official "socialist realism," and in 1941 he was imprisoned for several months. He was set free only as a result of repeated and strenuous urgings by German and Austrian intellectual leaders. He stayed on in Moscow during World War II, working on studies that laid the foundation of Marxist criticism of German literature, and on other works, which were published in Germany soon after the war.

In March 1945, after the Russian occupation of Hungary, the sixty-year-old Lukács returned to Budapest, was appointed professor of aesthetics and cultural philosophy at the University of Budapest, and became a key figure, often highly controversial, on the Hungarian cultural and literary scene. He resumed writing in Hungarian, but all the books he wrote in the last twenty-six years of his life (he remained active and productive to the very end) were published simultaneously in German, and from 1950 on many were also translated into English. In addition to works on literary and aesthetic trends and political movements, in these years he wrote book-length studies of Marx and Engels, Mann, Balzac, Solzhenitsyn, Goethe, and Lenin. Today, almost a quarter-century after his death, no study of aesthetics and literature is possible that does not take into account what Georg Lukács had to say.

Sociologists

In 1901 the Társadalomtudományi Társaság (Society of Social Sciences, known as TT) was founded under the presidency of Ágoston Pulszky (son of Ferenc Pulszky), who died the same year. Among its leading members were three ex-Jews: Professor Gyula Pikler (1864–1934), a legal philosopher with a keen interest in natural sciences and psychology who stood for a rational and pragmatic interpretation of the law; Oszkár Jászi (1875–1957), at the time an official of the Ministry of Agriculture; and Ervin Szabó (1877–1918), the socialist theorist and historian who edited the Hungarian selection of Marx and Engels's works and achieved high scholarly renown.

Soon disagreements surfaced within the leadership of the Society. On one side stood Pikler, Szabó, and Jászi, who took a "soft" position on the nationalities question (recall that the non-Hungarian nationalities within the borders of Hungary constituted slightly more than half of the total population). Jászi emerged as the apostle of an "Eastern Switzerland" that he wished to establish on the banks of the Danube. This was unacceptable to those who took a "hard" position on the nationalities, including Count Gyula Andrássy, Jr. (1860–1929), speaker of the Parliament and president of the TT; Gusztáv Gratz, who was to become director-general of the Hungarian Industrialists' Association; and Lóránt Hegedűs, who later became a bank director and a liberal deputy in Parliament. Unable to come to an agreement with the radicals, these three men resigned and founded the Hungarian Society of Social Sciences, whereupon Pikler was elected president of the TT and Szabó its secretary-general, and Jászi took over the editorship of *Huszadik Század*, its influential periodical.

The interesting thing in this split was that the three gentile leaders who seceded were not only liberal but emphatically pro-Jewish, and vested great hopes in the progress of free enterprise as represented mainly by Jews, while the radical Jews (or rather, ex-Jews) who took control of the TT often took an anti-Jewish stance: Jászi, in his puritanical zeal, often attacked the Jews for their profit-mindedness and ultra-Magyarism, and Szabó, like many socialists who were products of the nineteenth century, stood for an austere and closed economic system that was unfavorable to Jewish interests. This being the case, it should have been evident that the liberal-conservatives who left the TT did not take the step because it was "too Jewish"—yet that is precisely how it seemed to the country, and the conventionally liberal gentry were left with the impression that no honest Hungarian could ever put up with the "Jewish" agnostic intellectuals whose sociological discourses dominated the TT.

A further interesting development indicating the degree to which Jewish intellectuals were the active element in Hungarian sociological endeavors and in grappling with the problems of contemporary society, was that the new "Hungarian" anti-TT faction petered out fairly soon. Despite the prestigious names of its leaders, the money at its disposal, and the sympathy of national opinion, no audience took an interest in its deliberations. It was, as Paul Ignotus put it, "killed by boredom."

Artists

Hungarian art had come into its own after the defeat of the 1848–49 revolution, when painting became almost the only medium for expressing the patriotic frustration in whose grip the nation found itself. It was the age when Hungarian national painting developed and branched out into several schools, including historical painting and critical realism against a Romantic background. And it was the age when Jewish painters appeared, making their mark in a field that up to that time had been largely alien to Jewish cultural endeavor. By the second half of the nineteenth century, dozens of Hungarian Jewish painters were at work, several of them taking their places next to the most significant non-Jewish Hungarian painters of the period.

To be sure, there had been at least one lonely precursor to this Hungarian Jewish artistic breakthrough. He was the painter Theodor Alconière (originally Hermann Cohn; b. Nagymarton, 1797; d. Vienna, 1865), who studied at the Viennese Academy and lived alternatingly in Vienna and several Hungarian cities. When he was in his thirties, following the example of the so-called Nazarenes (a group of painters founded in Vienna in 1809 and characterized by religious orthodoxy), Alconière converted to Catholicism, but he never ceased considering himself a Jew. In the 1840s one of his pupils in Vienna was Vilmos Beck (1824–62), who became a recognized Hungarian portrait and genre painter. Although Alconière acquired fame for his portraits of members of the nobility (he was court portraitist of the duke of Parma) and scenes from everyday life, his romantic and other misadventures attracted more attention than his art. For years he was enamored of a Hungarian lady, and painted some ten portraits of her, but he then married the daughter of a Viennese gardener. She lost her mind and died, whereupon he was seized with melancholy and totally withdrew from all social contact. Impoverished, he supported himself by producing humorous lithographs. He even used his artistic skill to counterfeit banknotes, but, troubled by his conscience, he turned himself in to the police. Two years later he died in a Viennese charity hospital.

Prior to the mid-nineteenth century only two other Hungarian Jewish artists made their appearance, both sculptors. One of them, Jakab Guttmann (1815–58 or –61) had a fate even worse than Alconière's: we heard about it and his artistic career above, in chapter 24). The other, József Engel (b. Sátoraljaujhely, 1815; d. Budapest, 1901), who lived in London and Rome, and settled in Budapest only in 1866, when he was fifty-one years old, has also been discussed (in the same chapter).

A younger contemporary of these two, the painter Mór Adler (b. Óbuda, 1826; d. Budapest, 1902), studied in Pest, Vienna, and Paris, settled in Pest in 1848, and remained there to the end of his life. He exhibited his work regularly, and it won him recognition and acceptance in the prestigious Budapest art museums.

The breakthrough of Jewish artists in Hungarian painting, which was itself in the throes of developmental upheavals at the time, came with the appearance of a dozen or more Jewish painters all born around or after the middle of the 1800s. Since the present book is not a history of Hungarian Jewish art (regrettably, no such study exists to date), I cannot speak of more than four or five of the most outstanding of them. First, however, let me remark in general that although Jewish artists made a significant contribution to Hungarian art beginning with the second half of the nineteenth century, their overall role was definitely less significant in the total field of Hungarian visual arts than in the development of Hungarian literature (novel, short story, poetry, and drama) in the same period.

The only one among this dozen who was Jewish not only by birth and religion but also in the focal interest of his art was Izidor Kaufmann (b. Arad, 1853; d. Vienna, 1921). His father, an army captain stationed in Arad, wanted his son to become a merchant, and young Izidor actually started working in stores, and then became a bank employee. However, his talent could not be denied, and his drawings caught the attention of the *főispán* of County Arad, with whose help he was able to study in the art schools of Budapest and Vienna. Before long he was attracted to the subject that was to become the hallmark of his entire artistic career: Jewish folk life, and in particular Jewish religious life. He spent several summers traveling through eastern Galicia, Poland, Moravia, the Ukraine, and northern Upper Hungary, where he made sketches and gathered material for his portrayal of poor Jewish families and communities. He did not strive to strike out in new directions with his art but rather worked as a faithful, almost photographic, recorder of Jewish life, which never ceased to fascinate him, and he did this at a time when most Jewish artists both in Hungary and in other countries of Europe shied away from Jewish subjects. The fact is that there were practically no other painters in the nineteenth century, even among those who remained Jewish all their lives, whose art was devoted to Jewish life with such a total commitment as that of Kaufmann.

It was a great satisfaction to Kaufmann that despite his self-restriction to Jewish subjects, his work won wide recognition. Emperor Francis Joseph bought one of his paintings, *The Rabbi's Visit*, and donated it to the Viennese Museum of Fine Art, and he was honored by the German kaiser and even by the Russian czar. If from today's perspective it appears that Kaufman did not accomplish anything new in approach and style, it must be recognized that his works of art have permanent value for their chronicling of traditional Jewish life with an obvious love for the people he painted.

We mention only in passing two Hungarian Jewish painters who made most successful careers abroad as portraitists of royalty and high society. One of them was Lajos Bruck (b. Pápa, 1846; d. Budapest, 1910), who during his decade in London was one of the most sought-after portrait painters of the court and the aristocracy but nevertheless returned to Budapest in 1885 and stayed and worked there until his death. Among the portraits he painted in this late period were those of Emperor Francis Joseph and Empress Elisabeth. The other was Fülöp László de Lombos (b. Pest, 1869; d. London, 1937), who started out as a genre painter but from 1894 on specialized in portraits, beginning with those of King Ferdinand and Queen Maria Luisa of Bulgaria. He painted portraits of Pope Leo XIII, Emperor Francis Joseph (1903), Kaiser Wilhelm II, and President Theodore Roosevelt (1908). In 1907 he settled in England, where he succeeded Lajos Bruck as the foremost portraitist of royalty and high society. In 1912 he was ennobled by Francis Joseph with the byname "de Lombos." He converted to Christianity.

One of the highly acclaimed Hungarian painters was Adolf Fényes (1867–1945), who studied art in Budapest, Weimar, and Paris, became in 1907 a founder of the Circle of Hungarian Impressionists and Naturalists, and was the most important figure of the Szolnok Colony, which represented a significant development in Hungarian art. Although Fényes never formally abandoned Judaism, neither did he identify himself in any way as a Jewish painter. In several of his works he gave a somewhat stylized presentation of the interiors of Christian churches, but the nearest he ever came to Jewish themes was in the small biblical scenes (*The Ark of Noah, The Jews Defeat the Amalekites, Abraham and the Angels, Moses Strikes the Rock*) he painted during and immediately after World War I.

Of the participation of Hungarian Jews in the third major branch of fine arts, architecture, all we can say here is that from the mid-nineteenth century on, several dozens of Jewish architects worked in Hungary, making plans for important public buildings as well as synagogues, many of which still adorn the great thoroughfares of Budapest. Some of these architects won recognition abroad as well. Common to many of them was that they spent some period of their working lives abroad and, returning to Hungary, utilized there the experiences they had gained and the individual styles they had developed in other countries.

In addition, as in several other fields of intellectual endeavor so in the fine arts as well, Hungarian Jewry produced an impressive number of painters, sculptors, and architects who left Hungary permanently at an early age and achieved recognition abroad. Although until the end of World War I Hungary was a medium-sized European country (afterwards it was reduced to one-third of its previous territory and population), that sector of society that enabled an artist to develop and prosper was small, so that many of the aspiring young artists recognized that the price they had to pay for the chance of success was emigration, to work in the *nagyvilág* (wide world) rather than in narrow Hungary. The Hungarian Jewish art critic Béla Fónagy, in his excellent article on fine arts in the *Hungarian Jewish Lexicon* of 1929, found it necessary to explain, with typical Hungarian Jewish patriotic commitment, why he also included artists who lived abroad: "We also meet [in this article] with names whom adverse circumstances or the chances of fate had already swept into foreign lands by their early youth, before opportunity and room opened up to them to develop their artistic activities here at home, and even though they were of Hungarian descent they maintained almost no connection, or none at all, with our indigenous art, nor exerted any influence on it. However, since they were of Hungarian Jewish origin, we did not pass them over in silence."

This is where we must leave our sampling of Jews' participation in the growth of Hungarian fine arts, which, in conclusion, is noteworthy for two reasons: one, that they branched out so rapidly into fields that prior to the early-nineteenth-century spread of the Haskala were entirely beyond the Jewish horizon; and two, that at a time when the Jewish community constituted some 5 percent of the total population of the country, by 1910 no less than 16.5 percent of Hungarian painters and 17.4 percent of the sculptors were Jewish. Interestingly, Jewish participation in the fine arts was slightly more intensive than in music, where only 15.4 percent were Jewish. In absolute figures, by that year 107 Jewish painters, 24 Jewish sculptors, and 78 Jewish musicians were active in Hungary, to which numbers must be added those who had left Hungary and made a name for themselves abroad.

35

Demography and Occupations (1890-1920)

As a sequel to our cursory presentation of Hungarian Jewish life around the *fin de siècle*, as exemplified by a few outstanding Jewish and ex-Jewish individuals who played leading roles in the cultural explosion of the country, a few demographic and statistical data will be useful to give us a concrete idea of the changes that occurred in the size and the occupational structure of the Hungarian Jewish community from about 1890. Fortunately, some basic data are available on both the numerical growth of the Jewish community of Hungary and the developments in its occupational structure in the thirty years from 1890 to 1920.

The data show that the Jewish population increase was especially marked in the cities. This was due primarily to the removal of the legal obstacles to Jews' settlement in the cities, which brought about a sizable internal Jewish village-to-town migration. Leading in this increase was the capital, Budapest. In 1850 only 17,618 Jews lived in the cities of Buda and Pest; by 1890 their number exceeded 100,000, or 20 percent of the total population of the capital, by then unified into Budapest. That year the proportion of Jews exceeded this figure only in Nagyvárad, where the Jews were 26.2 percent of the total population. In the other major cities their fraction was not that high but still considerable: in Szatmár-Németi it was 16.5 percent, in Komárom 14.7 percent, in Temesvár 12 percent, and in Arad, Baja, Győr, Kassa, Pressburg between 10 and 11 percent. By that time, as these figures show, the Jews were a definitely urban element in Hungary.

The total number of Jews in the country as a whole also grew rapidly. In 1840 their number (including those of Croatia and Slavonia, which formed part of Hungary) was around 240,000. Thereafter, according to the censuses, their numbers, and proportion in the population, developed as shown in Table 1.

This growth was the result of the greater natural increase of the Jewish than the non-Jewish population of Hungary, which more than counter-

Table 1. Jewish Population Increase in Hungary, 1869–1910

Year	General Increase	Jewish Increase	Jewish Increase as a Precentage of the Total
1869	13,579,326	542,279	4.0
1880	13,749,603	624,826	4.5
1890	15,162,988	707,961	4.7
1900	16,838,255	831,162	4.9
1910	18,264,533	911,227	5.0

Table 2. Annual Natural Population Increase of Hungary, 1871–1910

Period	General Annual Increase (%)	Jewish Annual Increase (%)
1871–80	0.72	1.64
1881–90	1.15	1.84
1891–1900	1.07	1.74
1901–10	1.14	1.43

Table 3. Emigrational Losses of Hungarians and Hungarian Jews, 1880–1910

Decade	Losses to the Total Population (%)	Losses to the Jewish Population (%)
1880–90	1.3	5.8
1890–1900	1.0	2.3
1900–10	3.4	5.8

balanced the demographic loss suffered by the Jews due to the larger number of Jews emigrating from Hungary than immigrating into the country. Table 2 shows the annual natural increase of the Jewish and general Hungarian population in the four decades from 1871 to 1910.

As we can see, the difference between the Jewish and general natural increase diminished in the course of the four decades in question, but even in 1901–10 was considerably higher among the Jews.

Interesting, and characteristic, is the difference between the emigrational losses of the Jewish and total populations of Hungary. Emigrational loss is the figure obtained by subtracting the number of immigrants from that of emigrants. Throughout 1880–1910 this figure was much higher among the Jews than in the country as a whole. See Table 3.

In interpreting these figures, one must take into account that the same decades saw a sizable immigration of Jews into Hungary from the neighboring lands to the north and northeast, not paralleled by a similar immigration of non-Jews. What the Jewish figures show is but the surplus of emigrants over immigrants. According to a 1992 study by László Varga, director of the Budapest Municipal Archives, in the four decades of 1871–1910 no fewer than 175,000 Jews emigrated from the northeastern counties of Hungary alone, while in the same period the total emigration from Hungary amounted to 2 million. This was the demographic reality, as against the patriotic declaration, "I stay at home!"

About Jewish immigration it should be noted that in the public opinion of both non-Jews and assimilated Neolog Jews (who were not in favor of the immigration of the "Galicians"), the Jewish immigration from the northeast was perceived as much larger than it actually was.

Most remarkable was the assimilatory force Hungarian language and culture exerted on the immigrant Jews. Practically all of them had brought along Yiddish as their mother tongue and home language, yet their linguistic Magyarization proceeded apace, and with it developed the feeling that they were Hungarians not only in speech but also in culture. A major factor in this process was the official position of the Hungarian government and the political leaders: they considered the Jews in Hungary—and hence also in the border areas where the majority population was Slovak, Rumanian, or southern Slav—not a nationality or an ethnic group like them, but a religious denomination, one of the officially recognized faiths, to which, since the *recepció*, the Hungarians could belong or convert. Added to this was the religious-cultural influence emanating from the Jewish community of the capital and propagating the doctrine of "Hungarians of the Mosaic faith." Thus, the Jews in the border provinces became, like their correligionists in the central part of the country, Hungarians of the "Mosaic persuasion," and fervent Magyar patriots. The effectiveness of the Jews' Magyarization in the border areas was especially to be proven after the end of World War I, when the Jews in the territories that were detached from Hungary and awarded to Czechoslovakia, Rumania, and Yugoslavia by the Trianon Peace Treaty remained stubbornly Hungarian in language and culture, often to a greater degree than the Christian Hungarians in the same areas.

By 1910, when the total number of the Jews in Hungary approached one million, most of the Yiddish-speaking immigrants who had entered Hungary by the turn of the century had become, or were well on the way to becoming, Hungarians in speech and culture, and Magyar patriots in mentality. In that year the mother tongue of 75.7 percent of the Jews in Hungary was reported as Hungarian, as against only 54.4 percent of the Roman Catholics, who constituted the dominant religious community in the country. Another result of the same movement was that the Jews

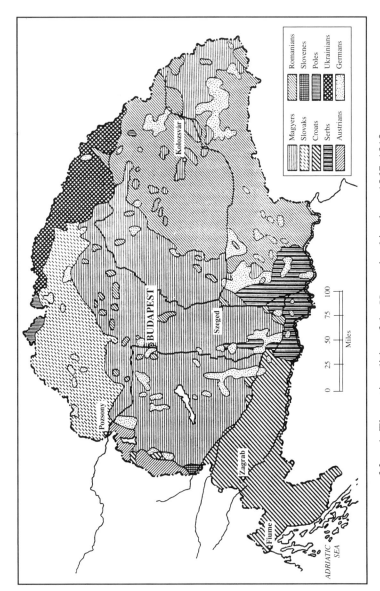

Magyers	Romanians
Slovaks	Slovenes
Croats	Poles
Serbs	Ukrainians
Austrians	Germans

Pozsony

BUDAPEST

Kolozsvár

Szeged

Zagrab

Fiume

ADRIATIC SEA

0   25   50   75   100
Miles

Map. 1. The nationalities of the Hungarian kingdom, 1867–1918.

became the most literate population element in Hungary: 74.9 percent of them could read and write, as against only 60.9 percent of the Roman Catholics.

The late nineteenth century was the time of the great transformation of Hungary as a whole from a traditional, feudal, agriculture-based economy to an urbanized, commercial-industrial economy, during which transition, as the Hungarian historian Géza Jeszenszky puts it, "the economy certainly needed [the Jews'] talent, entrepreneurial spirit, and cooperation, while their assimilation tilted the ethnic balance in favor of the Magyar." What the Jews received in exchange for their contribution to the modernization of Hungary was, as the same historian phrases it, "full legal and economic emancipation as well as a national identity and culture." There can be no doubt that the Jews' share in the economic and cultural development of *fin de siècle* Hungary was a powerful contributing factor to the feeling among them that they were as Magyar and as integral a part of the nation as their Christian compatriots.

A closer look at the changes that occurred in the Hungarian Jewish occupational structure from 1890 to 1920 shows that in a very few occupations the proportion of the Jews decreased in those thirty years, in some it remained practically unchanged, and in many it increased considerably. The most noteworthy overall phenomenon is that already by 1890, in most middle-class occupations the Jews were represented in proportions that far exceeded their proportion in the general population, which was about 5 percent. The exception to this rule was civil service: the proportion of Jews among judges and public prosecutors was 3.8 percent, among municipal officials 3.7 percent. Statistics available for the year 1910 show that of a total of 14,844 civil servants and clerks, only 810, or 5 percent, were Jews, and that even fewer Jews (2.6 percent) were found among the officials and clerks of the counties and municipalities. Although in practically each of these categories the Jewish fraction increased somewhat in the course of the decades, even in 1920 it was still far below the Jewish proportion in the population as a whole: evidently, government, state, county, and municipal officialdom remained unattractive or not easily accessible to Jews. Office holding was the domain of the gentry, and especially of the impoverished lower gentry, for whom it became a refuge after they lost their traditional income from their small estates based on serf labor.

The only other type of middle-class occupation in which the Jews had a relatively small share was academic teaching. Among the *gimnázium* (academic high school) teachers in 1890, only 2.2 percent were Jews, gradually increasing to 6.3 percent by 1920. The reason for the low representation of Jews in this profession was, at the outset, that in the late

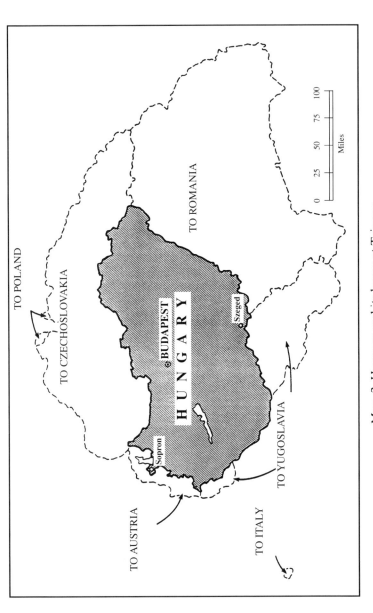

TO POLAND

TO CZECHOSLOVAKIA

TO AUSTRIA

Sopron

⊙ BUDAPEST

H U N G A R Y

Szeged

TO ROMANIA

TO ITALY

TO YUGOSLAVIA

0   25   50   75   100

Miles

Map. 2. Hungary and its losses at Trianon.

nineteenth century there were still relatively few academically trained Jewish teachers in Hungary. (To become a *gimnázium* teacher one had to go through four years of university studies and acquire a diploma.) Subsequently, since the academic high schools were controlled by municipal, religious, and other public bodies, which were disinclined to admit Jews into their faculties, the number of Jews in them remained small. Among the elementary and *polgári* ("civic," i.e., junior high school) teachers—much less prestigious than *gimnázium* teachers—the proportion of Jews remained somewhat higher than their percentage in the general population, while among those in other educational institutions (data available only for 1900, 1910, and 1920) marked changes were noticeable in both directions: the fraction of Jewish teachers in universities decreased from 10.0 percent in 1900 to 4 percent in 1910, then increased somewhat to 5.1 percent in 1920; in private schools the percentage of Jewish teachers decreased from 33.5 percent in 1900 to 13.6 percent in 1920, while in trade schools it increased from 10.4 percent in 1900 to 16.4 percent in 1920.

Only in the field of medicine were the Jews able to find public employment more easily: in 1910 not only were 1,295 out of 2,084 (or 62 percent) of the private physicians Jewish, but of the 3,481 doctors in public employment (government, hospitals, sick funds) no fewer than 1,406 (or 40 percent) were Jewish.

While the number of Jewish teachers in most branches of the Hungarian school system was limited, the percentage of Jewish students in the secondary schools and in higher education was disproportionately high, and was a clear advance indication of the increasing concentration of Jews in the professions. Once emancipation opened the doors of high schools to the Jews, they flocked to the *gimnázium*s and to the *reál* schools (eight-year high schools with emphasis on technical and practical subjects). In both types of schools, pupils were admitted at the age of ten, after completing four years of elementary schooling, and upon graduation eight years later with a *matura* certificate, they could go on to university studies. That is, these two types of schools were the gateway to academic and professional careers. Statistics available for the 1893–1913 period show that in those twenty years roughly 20 percent of all students in the Hungarian *gimnázium*s, and some 37 percent in the *reál* schools, were Jewish.

Equally instructive are the percentages of students within the Christian and Jewish populations of Hungary. In those two decades, out of every thousand Christians, 5 were students in *gimnázium*s; out of every thousand Jews, 22. The discrepancy was even more pronounced in the *reál* schools: among the Christians 6.3 per 10,000 of the population

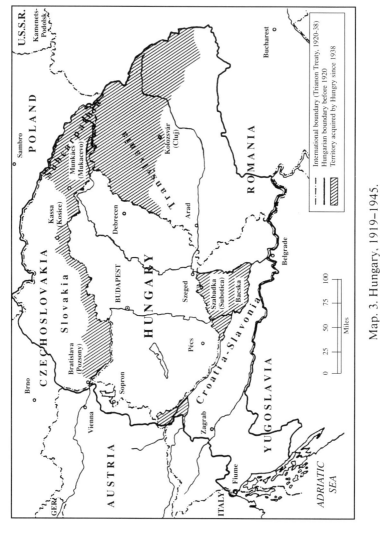

Map. 3. Hungary, 1919–1945.

studied in *reál* schools; among the Jews, 72.5, that is, almost twelve times as many.

The high proportion of Jewish students who attended and graduated from high school inevitably led to an increase of Jewish students at the universities. As early as 1867 at the University of Pest, 335 students, or 17.8 percent of the total, were Jewish; in 1895 the count was 1,304, or 29.6 percent; and in 1905 it was 2,049, or 36.3 percent. The highest Jewish proportion was found in the medical faculty, where 480 of 930 students, or 51.6 percent, were Jews in 1905. Next followed the faculty of law and political science, where in 1905 of a total of 3,313 students 1,175, or 35.5 percent, were Jews. These percentages remained roughly steady until the outbreak of World War I.

It is interesting that next to medicine and law, the highest percentage of Jewish students was found in technical higher education. At the Technical University (*Műegyetem*) of Budapest, which qualified students to become chemists, architects, and civil and mechanical engineers, the percentage of Jewish students between 1897 and 1913 ranged from 31.5 percent to 46.3 percent.

The proportion of Jews in the academic professions was in keeping with these high percentages of Jews in higher education. The greatest proportion of Jews in 1890 was among lawyers, 21.8 percent, and law clerks, 36.5 percent. These figures increased to 50.6 percent and 42.2 percent, respectively, by 1920. However, when it came to appointment as judges, the Jewish percentage was as low as in any other civil service position: in 1910 only 4.1 percent.

The number of Jewish journalists increased from 36.8 percent in 1890 to 39.1 percent in 1900 to 42.4 percent in 1910, and then decreased to 34.3 percent in 1920. Of the other professions, we have data only from 1900, 1910, and 1920: in those years the number of Jewish physicians moved from 48.3 percent to 48.5 percent to 46.8 percent. In 1910, when 48.5 percent of all Hungarian physicians were Jews, their percentage among private physicians was 62.1 percent, while among physicians employed by public institutions (government, hospitals, sick funds) it was 41 percent—an exceptionally high percentage for Jews in public employment. (The total number of physicians in the country in 1910 was still very low: there were 5,565 physicians in a population of 20 million, or one physician per every 3,594 persons.) From 1900 to 1910 to 1920 the number of Jewish pharmacists increased from 7.7 percent to 14.5 percent to 21.4 percent; of Jewish pharmacists' assistants from 15.8 percent to 24.2 percent to 25.5 percent; of Jewish veterinary surgeons from 24.8 percent to 40.0 percent to 41.3 percent; of Jewish writers and artists from 22.6 percent to 26.2 percent to 24.9 percent; and of Jewish chemical and other engineers from 23.9 percent to 37.6 percent to 39.2 percent.

Also remarkable was the increase in the number of rabbis: their proportion in the total number of clergy in Hungary increased from 4.2 percent in 1890 to 10.0 percent in 1920. That is, in 1920, relative to their numbers, the Jews employed twice as many clergymen as the other denominations. This is a development that indicates the gradual formalization of Jewish religious observance.

Most interesting is the high proportion of Jews among the owners and lessees of landed property, and among the owners and managers of business enterprises in 1910 (the earliest year from which statistical data exist). In that year 19.9 percent of all large estates (1,000 *hold*s, that is, around 1,400 acres, or larger) were owned by Jews, and 73.2 percent of those who rented and managed such estates were Jews. Of the middle-sized estates (200–1,000 *hold*s, or 280–1,400 acres) 19.0 percent were owned by, and 62 percent rented to, Jews. Of the small estates, the smaller their size, the smaller the percentage of Jews who owned or rented them, so that of estates under 5 *hold*s (about 7 acres), only 0.3 percent were owned by Jews, and the same proportion rented.

Equally noteworthy is the overrepresentation of Jews among the owners and managers of industrial enterprises, as shown by figures available for 1910. The only industry in which the Jews were disproportionately few was mining: only 3.1 percent of the owners, but 17.9 percent of the managers, were Jews, while among the workers and the low-ranking employes only 0.2 percent were Jews.

The highest percentage of Jewish ownership was in financial institutions, of which in 1910 no fewer than 85 percent were owned by Jews, though among the managers only 42 percent were Jewish. Of commercial firms 54 percent were owned by Jews, and 62.1 percent of the managerial personnel was Jewish, with 34 percent of the lower-ranking employees Jewish. Of the owners of transportation businesses 18.8 percent were Jews, and of their managers 12.9 percent, with only 2.4 percent Jews among the workers and low-ranking employees. Of industrial enterprises, 12.4 percent were owned by Jews, and 43.9 percent of their managers were Jewish, while of the workers and low-ranking employees 6.4 percent were Jewish. In the same year only 3 percent of those in the armed forces, 2.5 percent of day laborers, and 1.7 percent of domestic servants were Jewish.

As these figures show, Hungarian Jewry in the thirty years from 1890 to 1920 was a definitely middle- and upper-middle-class sector within Hungarian society, with strong overrepresentation in the higher-income occupations and low participation in manual labor and other low-

Table 4. The Jewish Share in the Occupational Structure of
Hungary, 1910—continued

Occupation	Total Number	Number of Jews	Number of Jews as a percentage of the Total
Agriculture, forestry, and mining			
Estate owners	2,237,207	13,131	0.6
Officials	9,611	2,553	26.6
Workers	938,998	2,270	0.2
Gardeners	11,837	12	0.1
Foresters	48,529	477	1.0
Miners	65,176	363	0.6
Commerce and credit			
Owners	98,150	59,832	61.0
Officials	37,312	20,475	54.9
Workers	89,426	29,637	33.1
Industry and trade			
Owners	351,824	41,992	11.9
Employees	738,615	42,505	5.9

income occupations. Very roughly, the three major occupational categories of the Hungarian Jews in 1910 were as follows: 38 percent of the economically active were craftsmen or merchants, 34 percent workers, and 20 percent clerks or professionals. Table 4 gives a more detailed picture of the proportion of the Jews in various occupations.

While the tendency of the Jews to concentrate in middle-class occupations is unmistakable, one general consideration must be kept in mind in evaluating the role the Jews played in the Hungarian economy in the late nineteenth century. At the time the middle class constituted a very small segment of the country's population, which was still largely agrarian. Of a population of close to 20 million, the middle class in 1890 is estimated to have been not more than 750,000 strong, or 3.8 percent of the total, consisting of public employees, owners of businesses, clerks in the private sector, and members of the free professions. This means that in the transition from a traditional argicultural economy to a modern commercial-industrial one, there was an urgent demand for middle-class activity, without which such a transition could not have been effected. The Christian population of Hungary, for a number of historical reasons, was able to meet this demand only partially. The Jews, a population more mobile than the Christians both economically and intellectually, were induced by the circumstances to fill this need. They were drawn into filling the occupational gap that opened up as the country's industrial-commercial economy developed. These were the circumstances that, within one or two decades, produced a middle class of which the Jews formed a disproportionately large segment: in the early twentieth century, about one out of every four members of the Hungarian middle class was Jewish. (Following the fall of the Hungarian Council Republic in 1919, this fact was repeatedly and heatedly pointed out by Hungary's anti-Semites, who considered the Jews an alien element in the body of the nation, and spoke of the Jewish "domination" and "exploitation" of the country.)

To conclude the foregoing survey of the Jewish condition in Hungary in the *fin de siècle* and the years immediately following it, a few words are in order about the Jewish community of Budapest, the European city with the largest concentration of Jews next to Warsaw. Budapest Jewry was organized into several Neolog, Orthodox, and Status Quo congregations, which, like all Jewish congregations in the country, had by law the right of collecting a congregational tax from Jews living within their territory. Only if a Jew officially notified the congregation that he seceded from Judaism was he freed from the onus of paying the congregational tax. It was this tax revenue that enabled the Jewish congregations of Hungary to maintain their religious, educational, cultural, medical, social, and charitable institutions.

By far the largest Jewish congregation in Budapest was the "Neolog" Israelite Congregation of Pest with a tax-paying membership in the 1920s of ca. 57,000, representing, according to the congregation's own estimate, 250,000 persons. It maintained no fewer than 42 synagogues, including the huge "Dohány Temple," a network of elementary, intermediate, and secondary schools, a library and archives, and published books of religious, cultural, and historical interest. It maintained several hospitals, institutes for the deaf-mute and for the blind, orphans' homes for boys and girls, an old people's home, a Ḥevra Kadisha charitable and burial society, a large cemetery, etc. In addition the congregation supported, and, in many cases in effect controlled, the National Hungarian Israelite Educational Union (OMIKE), the Israelite Woman's Organization of Pest, the National Union of Hungarian Israelite Women's Organizations, the Hungarian Israelite Crafts and Agricultural Organization (MIKÉFE), the Israelite Hungarian Literary Society (IMIT), the Hungarian Jewish Museum, the National Rabbinical Seminary, the National Israelite Teachers Institute, several Talmud Torah schools, the *Ahavasz Réim* charitable organization, the Patronage Society, a pension fund, the Bible Association of Jewish Women, the Jewish Youth Organization, the Central Jewish Students Aid Society, and subsidized several other smaller organizations, as well as a number of Jewish periodicals. The role the Pest congregation played in the Hungarian

Israelite National Office, the countrywide organization of Neolog Jewish congregations, was decisive.

The central office of the congregation employed a large staff, including lawyers and administrative experts. The rabbis who served the synagogues all over the city were also employees of the Israelite Congregation of Pest. The administration of the huge congregation was under the control of a president, an executive body of fourteen members, and a kind of a parliament in the form of a council of some seventy members (both bodies including several Jewish barons, noblemen, members of Parliament and the Upper House, lawyers, physicians, industrialists, financiers, etc.).

The Israelite Congregation of Pest consisted only of those Neolog Jews who lived in districts IV to IX of the city, on the Pest (left) bank of the Danube. The Jews of District X (Kőbánya) formed a separate congregation, which had in the 1920s 1,400 tax-paying members, representing an estimated 5,000 souls. The organization and institutions of the Israelite Congregation of Pest were duplicated, on a smaller scale, by those of the Israelite Congregation of Buda (the part of the capital that lay on the opposite, right bank of the Danube). The Buda congregation had in the 1920s 6,500 tax-paying members, representing an estimated 28,000 individuals. In Óbuda (Alt-Ofen), which forms part of the municipal area of Budapest, was yet another separate congregation with 1,400 tax-paying members, representing 5,500 souls. The entire administrative area of Budapest on both banks of the Danube were embraced by the Orthodox Congregation of Budapest, with 7,000 tax-paying members representing an estimated 50,000 individuals. There was also a Status Quo Israelite Congregation in Budapest (membership unavailable). Excluding the latter, the tax-paying members of the Jewish congregations of Budapest in 1920 totaled about 73,300, representing an estimated 338,500 persons. These figures from the 1929 *Hungarian Jewish Lexicon,* which based itself on data supplied by the congregations, seem to be exaggerated, since the official census reported only 215,512 Jews in 1920. Because it is likely that a certain number of Jews either avoided the census altogether or did not state their religion as Jewish, the actual number is probably somewhere between these two figures, say about 275,000.

All in all, the Jewish establishment in Budapest functioned almost like a state within the state—with the approval, of course, of the governmental and municipal authorities, whose attitude toward the Jews was, in the period in question, relatively free of the taint of anti-Semitism.

36

Zionism and Anti-Semitism in the Early Twentieth Century

To the great disappointment of the Jews, the legal equality they achieved with the 1895 Law of Reception did not mean the disappearance or even diminishing of anti-Semitism, which proved too deeply embedded in the Hungarian psyche to be eradicated by a stroke of the pen. What it did mean was strictly *legal* equality, which, however, proved a far cry from *social* acceptability, let alone acceptance, by the Magyars. This took many forms, but its common denominator everywhere was the sense of "otherness" the Christian Magyars felt toward the Jews. There were, to be sure, also differences between a Catholic and a Protestant Magyar, each of whom regretted and resented the religious incorrectness of the other, but neither of them ever cast doubt upon the total Hungarianness of the other. Not so in the case of the Jew: he may speak the finest idiomatic Hungarian, wear the best Hungarian gala dress, work most devotedly for the benefit of the fatherland, behave like the most sincere Hungarian patriot, and even convert to Christianity, and yet in the eyes of his Christian compatriot he remained the "other," not simply a Magyar but a Magyar Jew.

This was a gut reaction that could not easily be explained logically, and yet logical explanations for it were sought and found. One of those most frequently put forward by Christians was that the Jews themselves were, and wanted to be, different and separate from the non-Jewish Hungarians. This echoed the age-old allegation, effective because it contained more than a kernel of truth, with which even Haman tried to blacken the Jews in the eyes of King Ahasuerus, when he accused them of being "a people scattered and separated . . . and their laws are diverse from those of every people" (Esther 3:8). In trying to find proof of the Jews' separateness to justify their anti-Jewish feelings, the Magyars pointed, on the one hand, to the Orthodox, whose religious rigorism was an unquestionable barrier to assimilation, and, on the other, to the Zionists, who aspired to establish a Jewish state in Palestine.

The anti-Semitic Magyars were not the only ones the Zionists had to fight. Even more painful for them were the attacks launched against Zionism by the rabbinical and secular leaders of both the Neolog and Orthodox congregations (see above, chapter 30). It is noteworthy that the Hungarian Jewish objection to the settling of Jews in a country or territory of their own was confined to Zionism, whose program, adopted at Basel at the First Zionist Congress of 1897, called for the establishment of a "home for the Jewish people in Palestine secured under public law." When a similar program appeared *without* specifying that the eventual home would be located in Palestine, the spokesmen of Hungarian Jewry found it acceptable and gave it their support.

In 1905 the British Jewish novelist Israel Zangwill (1865–1926) took the initiative to create a new organization under the name of the Jewish Territorial Organization (ITO), whose aim was "to procure a territory on an autonomous basis for those Jews who cannot, or will not, remain in the lands in which at present they live." This formulation of aims was found inoffensive by many Jews who would not accept Herzl's political Zionism, and consequently ITO was able to secure Jewish support in many countries in circles that remained closed to Zionism. It was considered acceptable by those who objected to the political content of the Zionist program, and since it did not mention Palestine, with its historic-national connotation, but merely "a territory," and envisaged it as a refuge only for those Jews who were unable, or unwilling, to stay in their current countries, it had a purely philanthropic character that was unexceptionable even to the superpatriotic Hungarian Jews. After all, they felt that Hungarian Jews both could stay and wished to stay on in their beloved fatherland and hence could lend their disinterested support to a charitable philanthropic organization that aimed at simply helping unfortunate Jews elsewhere find a place of refuge.

Lajos Szabolcsi reports in his memoirs that in 1912 his father (who, we recall, edited the most influential Hungarian Jewish weekly, *Egyenlőség*) and a group of his friends conferred with Zangwill in Vienna, found themselves in agreement with his plans, and set out to organize ITO chapters in Hungary. "We explained to Hungarian Jewry," writes Szabolcsi, "what its duty was toward its brothers abroad." The Hungarian government approved the statutes of the movement, and by the eve of World War I there was a countrywide organization, with Mór Mezei and Gyula Winterberg as presidents, and no fewer than forty-two local groups counting 6,000 members. In the event, ITO achieved no practical results at all, and disbanded in 1926.

As against the unopposed, uneventful, and brief lifespan of ITO in Hungary, Hungarian Zionism was opposed sharply from its very inception (as we saw in chapter 30) and had to struggle ceaselessly with both Jewish and non-Jewish antagonists. The leader in the anti-Zionist efforts was the weekly *Egyenlőség*, which called Zionism "the perverse manifestation of religious fanaticism" and "the bastard of evil parents" and directed the attention of the Hungarian authorities to the possibility that the Hungarian Zionists were engaged in illegal activities.

Despite such formidable obstacles, Hungarian Zionism did make some modest headway in the years before World War I. The foundation of Makkabea, the Zionist student organization, in 1903 was followed in 1905 by the foundation of Judea, the Zionist association of clerical workers; Ivria, the Zionist association of high school students; and, in 1906, Deborah, the Zionist girls' association, and the Vivó és Atlétikai Club (VAC, Fencing and Athletics Club). In 1911 the Kadimah Zionist boy scouts society was created, and in 1913 the Bar Kochba Zionist association of technology students. Also founded in 1911 was the weekly *Zsidó Szemle* (Jewish Review), which was to remain for decades the central organ of the Hungarian Zionist movement. Likewise, from 1903 on, largely as a result of the work of Samu Bettelheim and local leaders, Zionist circles were founded in several country towns. That Magyarization was unfavorable to an interest in Zionism is demonstrated by the fact that in the outlying districts of Hungary, where the Jewish population was of more recent origin than in the center and its assimilation to Hungarian culture less advanced, Zionism found a greater echo than in the central areas, especially Budapest.

In 1904 the first Mizrahi World Conference took place in Pressburg, Hungary. Even though the Mizrahi was the organization of religious Zionists, its conference, and very existence, evoked strong apprehension on the part of Hungarian Orthodox rabbis, who considered the joining of the Zionist movement by Orthodox Jews a greater danger for Judaism than the Zionism of the nonreligious Neologs, who were already the lost sheep of the Jewish flock. No fewer than 129 Orthodox rabbis addressed an *issur* (ban) to all members of Orthodox congregations in Hungary, forbidding them to join the Mizrahi organization or attend its congress. Despite the ban, the congress took place in Pressburg in September 1904, and two leading Hungarian Orthodox rabbis, R. Moshe Arye Róth of Pápa and R. Moshe Glasner of Kolozsvár, attended it, and were elected to the presidium of the Mizrahi World Organization.

R. Róth was one of the few Orthodox exponents of Zionism in Hungary, who shortly before the Mizrahi congress published a pamphlet titled *Der Zionismus vom Standpunkt der jüdischen Orthodoxie* (Nagytapolcsány, 1904). After he visited Herzl's grave in Vienna's Doblinger Cemetery and recited a prayer for the soul of the recently departed

Zionist leader (in September 1904), R. Róth was attacked by other Hungarian rabbis for having offered prayers at the graveside of an "irreligious Jew." R. Róth himself died in 1906. His Orthodox Zionist colleague, R. Glasner, continued to work for Zionism, and published in 1920 a pamphlet titled *Der Zionismus und seine Nebenerscheinungen im Lichte der Religion* (Klausenburg [Kolozsvár]). His Zionist stance contributed materially to the strengthening of the Zionist movement in Transylvania, and that very year the Orthodox congregations of the entire province joined the Jewish National Council of Transylvania. R. Glasner died in Palestine in 1924.

These two men were exceptional among Hungarian Orthodox leaders in their embrace of Zionism. Hungarian Orthodoxy was generally as anti-Zionist as its Neolog brothers, with one difference: while the Neologs opposed Zionism in general, the ire of the Orthodox was directed specifically against the Mizrahi and the religious Zionists, whose position and collaboration with the World Zionist Organization they considered an acute danger for the survival of Hungarian Orthodox separatism. In consequence of Orthodox antagonism, it took almost a decade until a Hungarian Mizrahi Organization could be founded (in 1913).

Nor did the Hungarian Zionist Association have an easy time in its relationship with the government and its attempts at legitimation. Founded in 1903, it immediately submitted an application to the Ministry of the Interior for a legal charter, without which an association was not supposed to function. The Ministry, for whom the Neolog Israelite National Office was the legal representative of the majority of Jewry, requested its opinion, which was, predictably, uncompromisingly negative. It stated that "Zionism attempted to interfere in the affairs of a foreign nation"—meaning the Ottoman Empire, of which Palestine was part—and was therefore "a dangerous movement." On the basis of this expert opinion, the Ministry of the Interior rejected the requested charter.

In 1906 the Zionists submitted a second request for statutory legalization. The Ministry followed the same procedure, and this time the National Office—perhaps because it felt less secure in its position of rejection—delayed its response for a year. When it finally answered, it stated that the Zionist movement constituted a threat to the internal peace of the official Jewish religious communities. The Ministry denied the request.

A third attempt was made by the Zionists in 1910. Again the Israelite National Office objected, and the request was denied by the Ministry. The next petition was submitted in 1913, when the National Office simply did not respond to the Ministry's request of opinion. During the years of World War I, even though the number of local Zionist groups increased, no official action could be taken, and thus it was not until 1919, after the fall of the short-lived Hungarian Communist regime, that the Zionists submitted their sixth application for legitimation. The Ministry again asked for the opinion of the National Office, whose response came a year later. This time the National Office found it more expedient not to object outright to the legalization of Zionism, but to opine that granting a charter to the Zionist Association before the country's many foreign and domestic difficulties were alleviated might be detrimental to the interests of Hungary. Under the new governmental regulations, the Zionist Association became classified as an illegal organization and was compelled to suspend its activities, which up to that time it had been able to carry on even without official sanction.

The Zionists' response to this difficulty was to set up a new organization registered as a legal business firm under the name of the MCSz (Magyar Cionista Szövetség—that is, Hungarian Zionist Association) Corporation. The officially stated aim of this new body was "to promote Jewish culture through the publication of Jewish cultural, scientific, and scholarly books and periodicals." *Zsidó Szemle,* the official weekly of the Zionist Association, was thenceforward published as a business journal, carrying notices to "shareholders" about "business meetings" and prices of "corporation shares," and listing "profits on investments." For years thereafter the Hungarian Zionist Association was forced to confine its activities to collecting donations for the Keren Kayemet (Jewish National Fund) and the Keren Hayesod (Jewish Foundation Fund) and publishing books and periodicals. It was not until 1927, a year after the establishment of the Pro Palestine Federation of Hungarian Jews, in which leading personalities of Hungarian Jewry participated, that the Ministry of the Interior finally approved the statutes of the Hungarian Zionist Association.

While the Hungarian Zionist Association was thus engaged in an ongoing struggle for its political-organizational existence, another fight also went on to achieve recognition for Jewish culture as a life-sustaining force for Hungarian Jewry.

In 1913 *Alkotmány* (Constitution), the official daily of the parliamentary People's Party, which represented Catholic interests, published an attack on the Jewish monthly *Mult és Jövő"* (Past and Future), launched only a year earlier by József Patai, the young poet, writer, and Zionist cultural leader (introduced in chapter 34). It accused the monthly of fostering Jewish consciousness and separatism by presenting works of Jewish literature and art in an extremely attractive manner and by preaching, in its essays and articles, Jewish self-esteem and Zionism. In response Patai wrote a brief note in his column "Tollhegyről" ("From the Pen Point"), in the January 1914 issue of *Mult és Jövő*, stating that he welcomed the *Alkotmány* article, since it pointed out and brought to the attention of broader Christian circles precisely what he intended to do in his journal.

His self-assured Jewishness and pro-Zionist position—quite unusual in Hungary—attracted wide attention, and provoked attacks by both anti-Semitic Magyar and anti-Zionist Jewish writers. Responding to them in the March 1914 issue, Patai ridiculed some of the accusations directed against his journal. There are, he wrote, "concerned" people who pant,

> The armies of the Zionists are breathing down our necks, they are rushing to win Palestine! They are conspiring against the Hungarian kingdom, selling the poor fatherland for pennies, they want to exchange the Magyar tricolor for a kaftan with a *Mogen Dovid* [Star of David], and József Patai wants to be king of the Jews! He fights with fire and sword for the interests of the Jewish state, thus trying to acquire merits for the throne of Jerusalem, which is all the more dangerous in our midst, in fact, is outright high treason, since His Majesty bears also the title "king of Jerusalem."

At the same time the Christian Hungarian novelist Dezső Szabó (1879–1945) published an open letter to Patai in response to the latter's January note. Szabó was by that time one of the most celebrated Hungarian writers, acclaimed for his racy and spicy style and powerful characterizations. He was an intellectual anti-Semite, although it was only after the fall of the 1919 Hungarian Communist dictatorship that his anti-Semitism assumed a virulent form. Soon thereafter he attacked the Horthy regime, and from the late 1930s on, he also turned against the *Nyilaskeresztesek*, the Arrow Cross Party, as the Hungarian Nazis were called.

Dezső Szabó's "Open Letter to the editors of *Mult és Jövő*" was published in the March 1914 issue of *Huszadik Század* (Twentieth Century), the influential journal of the Hungarian Sociological Society, which was a political rather than scholarly group, largely responsible for the development of bourgeois radicalism in Hungary. *Huszadik Század* was founded in 1900, and, together with the Sociological Society established a year later, it educated the new generation of Hungarian intelligentsia. The Society, many of whose members were Jewish, became a political force in the early 1900s, when it rejected the dated liberalism of the previous generation, condemned the chauvinism and romantic bombast of the "national" ideal, and sought the answer to Hungary's internal problems in the modern social sciences. In 1907, its editor, the ex-Jew Oszkár Jászi, published an article, "Toward a New Hungary," in which he demanded a series of far-reaching reforms, such as an independent customs area, the dissolution of the large estates, a cooperative network for peasants, democratic local self-government, educational reform, graduated taxes, general health and social insurance, and the enforcement of the Nationalities Law. Jászi's article contributed greatly to making *Huszadik Század* a most influential factor on the Hungarian political scene.

It was this militant but highly respected forum that Szabó chose for his open letter to Patai. In it Szabó envisaged two possible roads for Hungarian Jewry: either to become a nation on the basis of preserved tradition, religion, and culture, or to break away from the binding force of centuries-old tradition, participate in the progress of Europe, and become the transformer of humankind. He wrote:

> Perhaps nowhere else in the whole world does Jewry have such a great mission as in Hungary. Let Jewry be the live cement that binds together the peoples of Hungary into a new, fertile community. Let Jewry respectfully place all its mental old stuff into a museum, let it be Jewish heroically, futuristically, humanly. . . . Let it kill Jehova, let it kill the Law, let it kill the Jew of the Old Testament and the Talmud, but let it again redeem man.

Szabó rejected the separatism of all nationalities and denominations. This position, in the context of early-twentieth-century relations among the nationalities and especially amidst the conflicts among the peoples in the Austro-Hungarian monarchy, counted as a progressive critique. But the role of "redeemer" he wished the Jews to assume was, not surprisingly, objected to by the Jews. R. Isaac Pfeiffer (1884–1945), a writer and poet, responded: "Should we deny ourselves, should we become, all of us, new Jesuses, profess the holiness of a world-redeeming self-crucifixion? . . . My God, how much naiveté, how much unconscious anti-Semitism! . . . We believe that the true criterion of the life of humanity is not monochromy—why should precisely the Jewish color be torn out of thousand-colored life?" In place of the alternative of national unification or the abandonment of traditions, Pfeiffer offers this solution: "Let us remain Jewish but remove the barrier that excludes us from life, let us live our own life, let us above all be ourselves to the tips of our nails, not the medicine of the world, not moonstruck nightwalkers panting for the redemption of the world, but human beings, able-bodied men of our own humanity."

József Patai, responding in *Mult és Jövő*, questioned the justification of Szabó's either-or proposition. He believed in the possibility of a dual Jewish-Magyar identity, in becoming Hungarian without giving up the Jewish past, Jewish culture. He rejected those views that "even today still judge Jewry as a separate complex" and assign it a special role. How can one generalize about the Jews and treat them as if they constituted an undifferentiated body of people, he asked, when, for instance, "among the Jews of Békéscsaba [a Hungarian city] there maybe some who have agrarian interests, and some who are led by mercantile points of view, they may be conservative and may be radical, may be partisans of Tisza and partisans of Justh?" And, in a spirited defense of Jewish tradition and Jewish values that he felt more than justified Jewry's historical determination to preserve its cultural specificity, he presented what was actually his journal's and his own consistent position:

> We lift out of the past everything that is future, that is cultural value, that is ethical purity, that is poetry, song, and beauty, and want to give it to life's Jewish wanderers as a provision for their journey, so that, in times of tired, gray twilights, they should be able to draw strength from it. . . .
>
> Modern Jewish literature and journalism proclaim no intransigent nationalism, no narrow backwardness, no monopoly on God, no miserly chauvinism, no aimless tradition. On the contrary, they want to present the eternal Jewish values that sparkle beyond ceremonies and partiality, want to implant into the consciousness Judaism as a cultural concept; and while they take up a position of defense against external attacks, they strengthen the internal fortifications, and supply them with nourishment, weapons, gunpowder. And precisely because, as you yourself [Dezső Szabó] have said, Jewry is more radically betrothed to advancement, humanity, culture, than Faust's soul to the devil, precisely because Jewry's worldview is itself progress, we must preserve, even for the sake of general culture, that idea content that, with its millennial innervation, has anointed the Jews fighters for human progress.

Szabó's response, published in the June 1914 issue of *Huszadik Század*, acknowledged the validity of Patai's argument without retreating from his own position:

> Dr. Patai's article moved me frankly, deeply. If any direction manifests itself in such humaneness, it becomes my own, and I feel that its representative is my brother. For the truth is not direction X or direction Y; it is every human trend. For opposing truths exclude each other only in logic; in life they presuppose each other. Let Dr. Patai's truth be effective inasmuch as it preserves the forces of the Jewish race, its deep human values, and can make them influential. But let my truth be effective each time Jewish racism and confessionalism intend to attack, imply hatred against other human forms. By saying this I surely do not preach the desirability of uniformity! The questions raised are deep problems. And I daresay that our debate was endowed with a noble tone precisely because both of us were able to raise ourselves from our Judaism and Magyarism up to humanism.

One cannot read this exchange in the 1990s without a feeling of nostalgia for those bygone days when anti-Semites and defenders of Judaism exchanged views in such a civilized manner!

After the outbreak of World War I, and especially from 1915 on, the economic situation in the country deteriorated, consumer goods were in short supply, and the hiding and hoarding of merchandise and black market operations increased, not without Jewish participation. The Jews were accused of chief responsibility for the abuses in connection with war contracts. These allegations were refuted energetically by Vilmos Vázsonyi in Parliament with the presentation of detailed data. One of the scandals was the supply of inferior cloth for army uniforms by a Jewish manufacturer. Patai commented on it bitterly in *Mult és Jövő* under the title "The Cloth Fraud":

> This human aberration, which deserves no pity at all, hurts, hurts us very much. . . . In vain shall we point out that the knees of the Jewish soldier will stick out of that torn cloth exactly as those of his Christian comrade in arms . . . that the indispensable prerequisite of the delivery of that false cloth was its acceptance, which was not done by Jews—all is in vain. It has been the tragic fate of Jewry for millennia that everywhere people generalized and still generalize to its detriment.

A blatant sign of the increasing utilization of the time-tested method of scapegoating Jewry for economic and social troubles, and of the growth of what could be termed intellectual anti-Semitism, was the appearance in 1917 of a book titled *A zsidók útja* (The Way of the Jews) by Péter Ágoston, a professor of law at Nagyvárad and a social democrat. Probing the bases of the disturbances in assimilation and the reasons for the growing anti-Semitism, Ágoston found the prime responsibility for these unwelcome phenomena to lie with the Jews themselves. The only way out of the quandary he could envisage was the abandonment of Jewish identity, the mass conversion of the Jews, and their national, religious, and economic assimilation. The interest aroused by the book and the timeliness of the problems it discussed prompted the editor of *Huszadik Század* to invite responses from some 150 people—members of the intelligentsia, politicians, artists, writers, teachers, church leaders, and other observers of the Hungarian social scene—to these three questions:

> 1. Is there a Jewish question in Hungary, and if yes, wherein do you see its substance?
> 2. What are the reasons for the Jewish question in Hungary? What phenomena of Hungarian society, what social relations, institutions, characteristics and customs of the Hungarian Jews, as opposed to non-Jews, play a role in giving rise to the Jewish question?
> 3. What do you see as the solution of the Hungarian Jewish question? What social or legislative reforms do you consider necessary?

The responses received were published in *Huszadik Század*. They showed a great variety of opinion. Of the sixty respondents (comprising many Jews), ten gave evasive answers; thirteen denied the existence of a Jewish question in Hungary; and thirty-seven considered it a real, serious problem. Among the deniers, especially interesting is the response of Professor Lajos Blau, one of the greatest Hungarian Jewish scholars of his age, rector of the Budapest Rabbinical Seminary, who considered the anti-Jewish sentiments a survival of medieval feeling and thinking. This was strictly in keeping with Blau's lifelong position that the Jews were a purely religious community, and that therefore the hatred of the Jews had only a religious basis. (I remember that some twelve years later, in one of his history classes in the Seminary, he mentioned Simon Dubnow's *World History of the Jewish People*, which was published at that time, and said with his characteristic sarcasm, "This book has only two errors in its title: the Jews don't have a world history, and they are not a people.")

Some of the respondents to *Huszadik Század*'s poll attributed the Jewish question to Christian clerical intrigue; an ethnographer viewed it as the reaction to features typical of commercial and merchant people and their interpretation as racial characteristics; a social democrat concurred, seeing in the Jewish question an ill-concealed economic antagonism. Yet another respondent interpreted Jew-hatred as a manifestation of the lack of purified culture. Several of the leading Hungarian intellectuals recognized a serious social, racial, or ethical problem in the Jewish question. Among the specific features some pointed out were the capitalistic origin of the problem, the survival of the ghetto situation in which a dividing line is drawn between Jew and non-Jew, and the contrasts between Hungarian and Jewish nationalism, between Christian and Jewish religion, and between Magyardom and world citizenship. Still others attributed the revival of anti-Semitism to the increasing Galician immigration, which prevented Hungarian Jewry from divesting itself of the alien features (more on this below); to basic differences in worldview between Jews and non-Jews; to a group antagonism that led to a conflict between Jewry and Magyardom; and even to a psychopathological development. Ignotus ascribed anti-Semitism to the specific Hungarian development of capitalism, which gave the contrast between gentry and bourgeois ideology a distinctly racial and religious character.

This profusion of analytical interpretations of the phenomenon of Hungarian anti-Semitism was paralleled by a similar variety of suggested solutions. Some felt that the solution lay in the democratization of Hungary; others (several of them Jews or ex-Jews) suggested the erection of legal barriers against new Jewish immigration and expected that the East European Jewish question would be solved by the Russian Revolution. One of them foresaw a gradual and voluntary fusion between the Jews and non-Jews in the country. Lajos Hatvany (whom we have encountered as the chronicler of the late-nineteenth-century rise of Jews into the haute bourgeoisie and its attendant problems) offered conversion to Christianity and intermarriage as the solution. József Patai expected that the deepening of Jewish racial self-assurance would bring about a change in the Jews' much-criticized comportment, a true inner liberation, a development of their self-esteem. The ex-Jewish poetess Anna Lesznai thought that education would put an end to the Jewish-Magyar separation. And finally, two Zionist leaders saw the solution in the development of a new Jewish state and Jewish national consciousness.

The multiplicity of observations on the nature of the Jewish question and of the suggested solutions indicates not only that Hungarian anti-Semitism was alive and well before and during World War I but also that it was enough of a *Hungarian* social problem that its public discussion was considered necessary by the intellectual leadership, which itself was of the most varied social orientations and political persuasions.

Mention was made above of the view that held the influx of Galician Jews responsible for reinforcing the "alien features" of Hungarian Jewry and thus hindering its assimilation to Magyardom. During the war many more Galacian Jews, fleeing before the Russian advance on the eastern front, actually managed to enter Hungary. We must not forget that until the Trianon Peace Treaty, Galicia was part of Austria and thus belonged to the same political entity (the Austro-Hungarian monarchy) as Hungary. Especially large was the number who came to Budapest, where they found better chances to eke out a living, and to obtain the support of their fellow Jews, many of whom were earlier immigrants from Galicia or the children or grandchildren of such immigrants. Responding to their obvious need, the Jewish community of the capital organized public support for them: the OMIKE (National Hungarian Israelite Educational Association) set up a soup kitchen where several hundreds of refugees received free meals, and the Hungarian Zionist Association provided them, as well as their fellow refugees from Bukovina (prewar Austria, postwar Rumania), with legal and moral assistance.

The appearance in the capital of a large number of Yiddish-speaking, kaftan-clad, bearded, sidelocked Jews—conspicuously foreign in appearance—fueled the argument of the anti-Semites that the rise in prices and the lack of consumer goods were due to the "inundation" of the country by Galician Jews. The Hungarian Jewish establishment extended to the Galician refugees all the help possible within the framework of organized charity, which, in turn, served as an excuse for the anti-Semites to lump together Hungarian and foreign Jews and to stamp all the Jews in the country with the onus of foreignness. It was rumored that as a reaction to this, some leaders of Budapest Jewry privately suggested to their contacts in the govenment not to allow Galicians refugees into the country. Not merely rumor but fact was that many Hungarian Jewish leaders stressed the distinction between Magyar and Galician Jews, took an emphatically negative attitude toward the Galicians, and used the term *Galizianer* as an epithet of contempt.

These signs of the desire to distance the assimilated Hungarian Jews from their unfortunate foreign kin—which was but an unwitting repetition of similar positions taken in earlier times by Sephardi Jews toward Ashkenazi newcomers in Western Europe—prompted József Patai in 1918 to denounce it in an article that historians consider the most detailed account of the development of anti-Semitism during the war in Hungary, and which is a scathing criticism of the way the Hungarian Jewish leadership reacted to it. "Here [in Hungary]," he wrote, "anti-Semitism was born as the twin brother of emancipation, and today, at the time of the fifty-year jubilee of emancipation, it too is fifty years old, is a Hungarian citizen, muscular, strong, and healthy." He pointed out that everywhere else in Europe, anti-Semitism also appeared together with the emancipation of the Jews:

As long as the Jews were only pariahs, there was rather contempt for them, which became among the noble-minded of the peoples a compassion, and ultimately led to the liberation of the Jews. As for the hatred of the Jews, they were hated, for example, in the Roman Empire while they were still powerful, and they were hated again after they were given political rights. . . . This is how anti-Semitism grew in Hungary, too, parallel with the growth of the territory the Hungarian Jews occupied in agriculture, commerce, industry, art, and politics, with their toilsome work and their steadfast application.

And how did the Jews among us "fight" this anti-Semitism? Not by organizing themselves, strengthening Jewish self-esteem, enriching internal Jewish content and values, but mainly by outshouting others and by joking. They simply declared the Jew-haters to be mad scoundrels and traitors since they wanted to annihilate a part of the body of the nation (that is, the Jews). They demonstrated with great perspicacity that the anti-Semites were at war not only with the Talmud but also with logic. But the number of falsifiers of the Talmud and logic grew day by day, and today we see among them some of the great ones of the nation. But many stuck their heads in the sand, saying "We see nothing!" The social boycott of the Jews could be felt in practically all social strata; if a Jew entered an office in the morning, conversation among his Christian colleagues suddenly came to a stop, because they were talking precisely about the Jews. Nevertheless, they beat their breasts proudly and with satisfaction, for, thank God, in Hungary there was no Jewish question, here everything was in order. And whoever dared to speak of the Jewish question was stigmatized either as an anti-Semite or as a Zionist, both of whom, according to the above theory, were, as is well known, equally "traitors" to the fatherland.

In some circles the assimilatory rage increased to the point of being nauseating. And the forwardness and flattery only swelled the flood of anti-Semitism that was rising anyway. In vain did they shore up defenses against anti-Semitism by claiming, "How much did we, Magyars of the Israelite faith, do for the nation. . . . The first national poet, the first linguist, the first factory owner, etc., etc., were all Jews!" This constant self-praise and big talk not only did not heal, it created resentment. For the "second" national poet, the "second" linguist, and the "second" factory owner were not at all happy about the national treasure contained in Jewry; they rather thought, "If that Jew were not here, I would be the first."

Then came the war, Patai writes, and with it times when it was irritating and annoying that the Jewish merchant was able (because he was forced) to pay high prices for food and other merchandise, which the officials of the state and the counties, many of them bankrupt members of the gentry who lived on fixed salaries, could not afford. Added to this was the fact that the Jews, who mostly knew German, were more often employed in the German-language offices of the Austro-Hungarian army than their gentile comrades who had no German. As against this feeling of frustration,

we shall in vain gather statistical data showing that the Jews exhibited befitting heroism also on the battlefield. It belongs to the natural history of hatred and envy that they want to know nothing of statistics, of logic, of sobriety, of truth. This, alas, cannot be helped.

Hungarian "scientific anti-Semitism" also owes its origin to public sentiment. It is not the private passion of one or two bishops or "radicals," not a motive but a result. Those Hungarian officers who, already by the beginning of the war, even in Russian or Italian captivity, refused to sit at one table with Jewish fellow officers, had not yet read the new Ágoston, nor the new Prohászka [two anti-Semitic authors], nor the Jewish issue of *Huszadik Század.*

And now some try to dump the great and general crisis on the heads of the Galicians. Teutons and Czechs can come and establish businesses and factories, can engage in wholesale or retail trade, can smuggle out foodstuffs and run up the prices, but the reason for all this is nevertheless that Galician into whose kaftan they found sewn two spools of yarn and a half a kilo of flour. The authorities can think what they want, the Jew-haters can thunder against the "Galicians," and should the people understand thereby all the Jews, and should there be pogroms here like those in Russia, the leaders can innocently wash their hands: they fulminated only against the "Polish" [Galicia was part of Poland before Austria acquired it in the late 1700s]. But it is disgraceful if there are also Jews who by crying shame upon their Galician brethren want to demonstrate that not they themselves are meant, and preach about a "different morality" as if the ancient law according to which "one justice shall be to him that is home-born and unto the stranger that sojourneth among you" [Exodus 12:49] were not the morality of all Jewry.

There have always been enough of those who indignantly condemned, long before the war, jeering songs strummed in certain Jewish circles against the kaftan, making the "Galicians" objects of derision even in peacetime, as if under the kaftan there could not beat just as noble a heart as under the best-cut dinner jacket, and as if under the *shtrayml* [traditional Jewish fur hat] there could not vibrate just as fine a brain as under the well-polished top hat. Today, there are already enough persons also here in Hungary who can distinguish between the external and the internal, who look with open eyes at the world, who expect and hope for the redemption of Jewry to come not from the outside but from the inside, from the deepening of the Jewish ego, from its becoming filled with Jewish content, who do not discriminate between Jew and Jew, and are con-vinced that it is folly to believe that the smaller the beard of the Jew, the bigger his morality.

Patai summed up his understanding of the target of Hungarian anti-Semitism by emphasizing that it had nothing to do with the arrival of the so-called Galician refugees:

> The truth is simply that a part of the Hungarian Jews either does not notice, or closes its eyes and does not want to notice, that when the Jew-haters speak of Galicians in Parliament or in the press, they do not mean those few hundred "Galician" refugees who got stuck here, but rather the children and grandchildren of the "Galicians" of yesterday, that is, the whole of Hungarian Jewry, as it is, including both fathers and sons.

In both his monthly and his weekly (also called *Mult és Jövő*) Patai devoted much space to the question of anti-Semitism in Hungary, and its alleged connection with the immigration of Galician Jews, which he, and the contributors whose articles he published, unanimously denied. Their position was that anti-Semitism was a quasi-natural phenome-non, fed by the resentment of Christian Hungarians at Jewish successes in all areas of Hungarian economy and culture, and by the incessant Jewish harping on the great value of their contribution. They could offer no ready-made recipe for healing the disease, but the palliatives they agreed upon—all directed at the Jewish community itself—included a greater emphasis on Jewish cultural values, an open embrace of the Zionist endeavor, and a muting of the incessant broadcasting of the Jews' invaluable contributions to and identification with Hungarian life. (In one unsigned note, a contributor quotes with sarcasm a statement of Pál Sándor, a leading Hungarian Jewish politician, that "if we [Jews] have to march out of this country, we shall march out with the Hungar-ian national anthem on our lips.")

Despite the various stratagems Hungarian Jews adopted in their fight against it, anti-Semitism increased toward the end of World War I (and was to intensify greatly in the years immediately following it). One of its leaders, the publicist Gyula Altenburger, went so far as to declare that the fountainhead of all the troubles of the country had been the emancipation of the Jews. A Catholic priest, Pater Bangha, raised 10 million crowns for a Christian press fund, and established the anti-Semitic Christian Press Company, headed by several university professors, for the purpose of "crushing the Jewish rule" in the country. István Dobai, commissioner of spas, refused to rent rooms to Jews in the Tatra Mountains. In 1918 the People's Party and the Christian Socialist Party merged into the Christian Socialist People's Party and intensified its anti-Jewish agitation. Anti-Semitic books and articles proliferated, and the thickening of the anti-Jewish atmosphere was unmistakable.

Not all the Christian critics of Hungarian Jewry agreed that the foreign influences brought into the midst of Hungarian Jewry by the Galician immigrants had nothing to do with the burgeoning of anti-Semitism in the country. Jenő Cholnoky, a Catholic author, for example, was of the opinion that the repeatedly renewed Galician immigration, which hindered the Hungarian Jews in sloughing off their foreign traits, was an important factor in the revival of anti-Semitism. Hence, he and several other critics (such as Barna Buday and Béla Túri) suggested that laws be passed against further Jewish immigration. Ádám Persián, a former government commissioner for Catholic affairs, published a pamphlet in 1920 on the Jewish question, in which he wrote:

> In the past, when immigrant elements had not yet infiltrated its ranks, Hungarian Jewry could in no way be criticized in matters of Hungarian feeling but, on the contrary, rendered services deserving all recognition to the Hungarian idea. This is valid regarding the assimilated Jewish intelligentsia of the provinces (the lawyer, physician, merchant), which, even in opposition to the dualistic [Austro-Hungarian] politics of the governments in power, was the protagonist of the idea of independence; and it is valid especially with regard to the native Jews living in the areas of the nationalities, who have always faithfully held on to the Hungarian state idea.

The praise, carefully limited to the past and to the "native" Jews, clearly implies that in the present, after being "infiltrated" by "immigrant elements," the Hungarian Jews no longer deserve praise for their patriotism but rather criticism for their lack of it.

Statements such as this, when read together with Pál Sándor's superpatriotic declaration above, illustrate the quandary in which the Hungarian Jewish leadership found itself in face of persistent Hungarian anti-Semitism. In the words of Simon Hevesi, the leading chief rabbi of the

Israelite Congregation of Pest, it was the destiny of Hungarian Jews that "living in their faith, they should love the fatherland into which God planted them, and serve its welfare faithfully." And yet this same homeland from time to time produced movements whose activites ranged from planning and actually carrying out legal strictures against the Jews to attacking them physically and demanding their expulsion. Worse perhaps was the fact that Magyar society as a whole never allowed the Jews to forget for a moment that in its eyes they were indelibly marked as different, as foreign. Thus, for decades prior to the horrible tragedy of their physical annihilation, the Hungarian Jews lived the psychological tragedy of unrequited love, of being rejected, at times politely, at others brutally, by the people of whom they so desperately wanted to be part.

37

World War I and the Communist Interlude

While the Jews of Hungary were basking in the sun of the *recepció* and enjoying legal equality with their Christian compatriots (for which they showed their gratitude by fighting against "the Zionist danger" and being at least as "red-white-green" as the Christian Magyars), clouds were gathering over the southern borders of Hungary, where sizable Slovene and Croat minorities lived, and beyond which lay Serbia (after the outbreak of the war often referred to in popular parlance as "dog Serbia"), Bosnia, and Herzegovina. From 1903 on, after Peter I Kara-georgevich became its king, the political and economic reforms carried out in Serbia attracted not only those Serbs who were still under Turk-ish rule, but also the Slavic minorities in Austria-Hungary. To forestall Serbian expansionism, the dual monarchy in 1908 annexed Bosnia and Herzegovina and started an economic war with the Serbs. The response of Serbia was to establish closer ties with the other Balkan states, and in 1912 the Balkan League, consisting of Serbia, Montenegro, Bulgaria, and Greece, engaged in war against Turkey, defeating it and liberating almost all of the Balkans after 500 years of Ottoman rule. Once the major external enemy was thus dealt a decisive blow, the Balkan allies fell out among themselves, and encouraged by Austria-Hungary, the Bulgarians attacked the Serbs as well as the Greeks. The Serbs, however, emerged victorious and in the 1913 Treaty of Bucharest were awarded extensive additional territories. Austria-Hungary became even more apprehensive, and the reduction of Serbia seemed more and more an inevitable necessity. It was at this juncture that on June 28, 1914, a Serbian revolutionary assassinated Archduke Franz Ferdinand, the Habsburg crown prince, in the Bosnian city of Sarajevo. The stage was set for the outbreak of the Great War, which involved most European powers, as well as the United States, and which brought about a com-plete reshaping of Central Europe, with the disappearance of the Habs-burg dual monarchy and the emergence of new nation-states.

The war was greeted with an enormous outburst of patriotic enthusiasn among all the Magyars, less so among the Slavic minorities in the northern and southern parts of the country and the Rumanians in the east. As for the Hungarian Jews, they saw in service in the army an opportunity to demonstrate their patriotism, and took great pride in being Hungarian soldiers and fighting side by side with Christian Magyars. For the first time in their history, the presence of Jews in the army was officially acknowledged by the appointment of rabbis as *tábori lelkészek* (camp clergymen) to take care of the spiritual needs of the Jewish soldiers, just as Catholic and Protestant clergymen did for their denominations.

Upon the outbreak of the war, both the Neolog and the Orthodox countrywide organizations and the individual rabbis engaged in what today would be described as an energetic publicity campaign, calling upon the Jews to show heroism and perseverance in protecting king and country, and to help the armed effort of the fatherland with willingness to sacrifice. As the war wore on, King Charles IV (who succeeded Franz Joseph in 1916), two Habsburg archdukes, and several army commanders repeatedly went on record praising the heroism of Jewish soldiers and the sacrifices of the Jewish community. Since by the 1910s the majority of the physicians in Hungary was Jewish, also in the army medical corps, inevitably, most doctors were Jews. All in all some 300,000 Jews served in the Austro-Hungarian army during World War I, of them 25,000 officers. Many in all the ranks were decorated for bravery. No fewer than 25 Jews or ex-Jews were generals. The most prominent figure among them was Samu Hazay (b. Rimaszombat, 1851; d. Budapest, 1942). He converted to Christianity in his youth, at the age of twenty-two was admitted to the Ludovica Academy (Hungary's West Point), and after graduating quickly rose through the ranks, becoming a general in 1907, and minister of defense in 1910. He served in that capacity until 1917, when he was put in charge of recruitment for the entire Austro-Hungarian army. He was created a baron in 1912. Following the collapse of the Austro-Hungarian monarchy he retired, and in 1919 was arrested and made a hostage by the Hungarian Communist regime. After his release he no longer played an active role. In addition to being an outstanding military administrator, Hazay was the author of a series of important military laws, and for many years was the editor of the gazette of the Ludovica Academy. Throughout his long career and life he never showed any interests in Jewish matters.

Jews also played a leading role in financing the war. Their contributions to the war loans, organizationally and individually, amounted to 10 percent of the total, even though they formed under 5 percent of the population. In the industrial production of war materiel the Jews had the lion's share. The organization of war production was carried out primarily by Jews, who effectively put the entire industrial output of the country, most of which was under Jewish control, on a war footing. Two of the leading Jewish industrialists, Manfred Weiss and Tivadar Wolfner, were rewarded by being created barons.

Yet the war statistics were also used by the anti-Semites to support their claim that the Jews had a less than total patriotic commitment to the war. Those figures were compiled by the National Statistical Office in 1920–21 and were published in the *Magyar Statisztikai Szemle* (Hungarian Statistical Review) in 1922, at a time when anti-Semitism was rampant. As the *Hungarian Jewish Lexicon* of 1929 points out, the data it published were incomplete: whether purposely or not, Jewish casualties were grossly underreported, which was possible since the army itself did not categorize its casualties according to religion. The *Magyar Statisztikai Szemle* stated that of the total of 378,000 Hungarian soldiers who fought in the war, 155,799, or 41.1 percent, were killed, while of the 23,500 Hungarian Jewish soldiers who fought in the war only 5,116, or 21.8 percent, were killed. These figures, in turn, were interpreted by the anti-Semites as demonstrating that the cowardly Jewish soldiers somehow managed to expose themselves to enemy action only half as frequently as the Hungarian army as a whole. However, the figure of 5,116 is suspect. It has been established by actual count that of the Jewish soldiers domiciled in Budapest, 4,000 were killed. The 200,000 Jews of Budapest accounted for around 40 percent of the total Jewish population of post-Trianon Hungary (which served as the basis of the above calculations); hence it is unlikely that of the Jewish soldiers who came from among the roughly 300,000 Jews who lived outside the capital only 1,116 (5,116 minus 4,000) should have been killed. It also happens to be known that the Jewish war dead of the three cities of Szeged, Miskolc, and Pécs totaled 384, which would leave the impossibly small figure of 732 for the Jewish dead of all the hundreds of other Hungarian cities and localities. It can also be pointed out that the 23,500 Hungarian Jewish soldiers who fought in the war constituted 6.2 percent of the total Hungarian army of 378,000, while only about 5 percent of the total Hungarian population was Jewish.

Of all the Central Powers, defeated in World War I, Hungary fared worst. In the war itself its total number of casualties (killed and wounded) was 352,292, or an almost incredible 93 percent of her entire armed forces. After the defeat Hungary lost 71 percent of its historical territory, and with it 60 percent of its population, which before the war had stood at 20.9 million. As a result of the wholesale redrawing of borders by the victorious Allies, 3.3 million, or 30 percent of all Magyars, came under foreign (Czechoslovakian, Rumanian, Yugoslavian, and Austrian) rule. Especially rankling was the readjustment of the borderline between Hungary and Austria, her erstwhile partner in the dual monarchy, which took away the Burgenland, composed of three western counties, and gave it to Austria. Hungary thus became the only defeated country that lost territory not only to the victors but also to its former ally and sister state.

Of the 3.3 million Hungarians who thus came under foreign rule, 438,000 were Jews, representing 48 percent of the total prewar Hungarian Jewish population of 911,000. As it turned out, these Jews proved to be more attached to Hungarian language, culture, and identity than the Christian Magyars and in many places maintained the only schools whose language of instruction was Hungarian.

Before the war (according to the 1910 census), the 911,000 Jews of Hungary constituted about 5 percent of the total population of Hungary (excluding Croatia-Slavonia). The official statistics counted the Jews as Hungarians, so that the Hungarians were shown to constitute 54.4 percent of the total population. Without the Jews, the Magyars would have been reduced to a minority of 49.4 percent in their own country. After the Trianon Peace Treaty, the 473,000 Jews remaining within the reduced borders of the country represented 6.2 percent of the total population, which at that time stood at a mere 7.6 million. Of the Jews, 215,000, or more than 45 percent, lived in Budapest. This change in the ratio between the Jews of the capital and the country meant a corresponding shift in their social structure toward professions, and, in general, toward occupations characteristic of a big city.

In the fall of 1918, events followed events with disconcerting rapidity. On October 2, the Joint Council of Ministers decided to ask for an armistice; on October 25, Count Mihály Károlyi organized a new democratic alliance, the Hungarian National Council. Of the twenty members of the National Council, two were Jewish—the politician Pál Sándor and the writer Lajos Biró—and two were converted Jewish writers—Lajos Hatvany and József Diner-Dénes. Under the leadership Vilmos Vázsonyi, the Democratic Party, whose members were recruited mainly from the well-to-do, mostly Jewish middle class of Budapest, declared that it would not join the Council. The Christian urban middle class and the democratic wing of the Christian Socialists also refused to join the Council, which consequently never achieved significant popular support. The Social Democrats ruled the streets of Budapest, which gave them the crucial role in the development of the revolution to come.

Also on October 25, Count Gyula Andrássy was appointed Austro-Hungarian foreign minister, and two days later Count János Hadik became Hungarian prime minister. On the same day, Andrássy accepted all of President Woodrow Wilson's conditions, which meant the dissolution of the dualist system. Before the end of the month, the Czechs, Croats, Slovaks, and Ruthenians seceded. On October 30, revolutionary groups gained control over much of Budapest, and Hadik, unable to cope with the situation, asked Károlyi to take over the government. Next day King Charles IV appointed Károlyi prime minister. Károlyi's government, composed of the parties that belonged to the National Council, had three ex-Jewish members: Zsigmond Kunfi became minister of welfare and education; Pál Szende, state secretary for financial affairs; and Oszkár Jászi, minister for nationality affairs, in which capacity he played an important role in formulating the nationalities policies. Jászi's plan called for a constitutional-federal democratic Hungary, coupled with a general land reform, other social programs, and autonomy for the Ruthenian, Swabian, and Slovak minorities.

On November 1, Károlyi asked to be released from his oath of allegiance to the king and proclaimed Hungary's unconditional independence. On November 3 the armistice was signed at Padua. During November Jászi tried to persuade the leaders of the minorities (Rumanians, Slovaks, Ruthenians, the latter also known as Carpatho-Ukrainians) to keep their peoples within the borders of Hungary. He was not successful. Consequently, Hungary had no choice but to withdraw whatever forces it still had in those territories, and more than half of what was formerly Hungary came under foreign occupation.

Upon the outbreak of the revolution, the Israelite Congregation of Pest convened a meeting of Jewish representatives from all over the country to express their support of the arrangements declared by the National Council. A Council of Free Organizations of Hungarian Jews was formed and developed an independent program for Jewry. The plan aimed at the internal democratization of Jewish organizations. It demanded the liquidation of Jewish national offices, the introduction of general, secret, and equal elections in the congregations, and the creation of a unified national Jewish council. It asked for the reform of Jewish education in a Jewish spirit and the introduction of the teaching of Hebrew. The group wished to regulate the salaries of rabbis, expected the new government to extend general suffrage to the Jews, and hoped for a proper Jewish representation in Parliament. Their plan also envisaged the creation of autonomous Jewish cultural units in the areas inhabited by a dense Jewish population, with the central government covering the expenses of their educational and cultural needs. It offered the mobilization of Jews' international connections for the support of the Hungarian government and foresaw Hungarian Jewish material and moral aid to the Jewish settlement work and cultural life in Palestine.

Also in 1918, a National Rabbinical Council was organized with the participation of close to a hundred of the spiritual leaders of the largest congregations, and it began to work to obtain government subsidies for confessional activities.

The inception of the revolutionary transformation of the country brought a freer intellectual atmosphere, which also motivated the Hungarian Zionist Association to subscribe to the new order. The Zionist student society Makkabea organized self-defense units, which late in 1918 were taken under the wing of the Ministry of War and termed Volunteer Armed Detachments. Other formations, known as Zionist Guards, were active in the country towns with the support of the local Jewish congregations. Their work was subsidized by sizable contributions from the Neolog and Orthodox organizations of Budapest. From November 1918, all over the country Jewish readers' circles and cultural societies sprang up, Hebrew language classes were organized, and youth groups founded.

The government, on its part, supported the work of the Zionist organizations, motivated primarily by a practical consideration: it hoped to gain sympathy for its position in the forthcoming peace conference, where, it assumed, the international Zionist movement would have a certain influence. When a Hungarian Zionist delegation was preparing to leave for the Paris Peace Conference of 1919, Dezső Berinkey, prime minister of the newly reshaped Hungarian government, addressed to it the following declaration: "The Hungarian People's Government follows with sympathy the Zionist movement, which endeavors to create a national home for the Jews in Palestine, and considers it necessary that the Jewish question, which has become connected with world politics, should find its solution according to the demands of justice and culture." The response of the Hungarian Zionist Association was to "declare solemnly that it has never engaged in 'nationality' politics in Hungary before, and neither will it do so in the unified Hungarian state. Every member of the organization feels himself a faithful, devoted citizen of the Hungarian state, ready for any sacrifice."

However, the main problem facing Count Mihály Károlyi, who in January 1919 was elected provisional president of Hungary, was the emergence of the Hungarian Communist Party. The party was established on November 24, 1918, by Béla Kún, a converted Jew who had recently returned from Russian captivity, where Kún and his fellow prisoners had observed the Russian Revolution and come to believe that it was a model the Hungarian socialist movement had to follow. Faced by the growing Communist menace, the government decided to destroy the party and arrested Béla Kún and some hundred other Communists. But this move did not prove effective. Kún's place was taken by men like Nikolai Ivanovich Bukharin's experienced revolutionary friend Tibor Szamuely and the aesthetician and philosopher George Lukács, both, incidentally, converted Jews.

The political tension in the country was greatly aggravated by the note handed on March 20, 1919, to the government by Lt. Col. Fernand Vix, head of the French military mission in Budapest, which demanded that the Hungarian forces evacuate the whole region east of the Tisza River. Erroneously, but understandably, the Hungarians assumed that this meant a definite relinquishing of a large, purely Hungarian area, and the country was gripped by a hysteria the Károlyi government could not control. The next day Károlyi appointed Zsigmond Kunfi prime minister in the hope that he could handle the situation, but it was too late. The same day, the workers' and soldiers' councils of Budapest proclaimed the dictatorship of the proletariat, and the Hungarian Council Republic was established with the stonemason Sándor Garbai as its formal president but Béla Kún as its real head.

The Communist government comprised no practicing Jews, but was dominated by converted Jews. In addition to Béla Kún, who was commissar for foreign affairs, its commissars of socialization, education, war, justice, the interior, finances, and food supply were all converted Jews, as were five more members of the government. On March 22, 1919, Tibor Szamuely (1890–1919) was appointed commissar in control of those classes of the population that belonged neither to the proletariat nor to the Red Army. Ottó Korvin-Klein, another ex-Jew, became head of the political investigating authority. The activities of these two men ravaged the bourgeois Jewry of the country.

Apart from economic oppression, the government resorted to taking hostages from the civilian population, hoping thereby to suppress any counterrevolutionary attempt. Of the 715 hostages taken in Budapest and thirteen other cities, 164 were Jewish. Among the latter were such leading Jewish capitalists as Baron Tivadar Wolfner, the president of the Hungarian National Leather Manufacturers Union, the banker Leo Lánczy (a converted Jew), Pál Kornfeld, Salomon Freund, and Bernát Goldschmidt. Worse than the taking of hostages were the daily executions: the revolutionary law court, headed by yet another ex-Jew, condemned and executed 570 persons, including 44 Jews, for alleged antirevolutionary activities.

One of the main concerns of the communist government was to liquidate private property and eliminate capitalist institutions, banks, and
privately owned commercial and industrial esablishments. Since the
great majority of Hungarian Jews were engaged in precisely these types
of economic activity, they had to bear the brunt of the Communist anticapitalist wrath. The fact that so many commissars in the government
were ex-Jews, who either had actually lost all sympathy for the community of their origin or felt they had to demonstrate their "evenhanded-
ness" when it came to Jews, contributed to the severity of governmental
proceedings against the Jews in particular. Thus, a situation developed
in which the ex-Jews in power positions made the powerless Jewish
public pay for what they felt was the sin of their own Jewish descent.

Despite the anticapitalist, and hence anti-Jewish, measures introduced by the Communist government, some young Jewish intellectuals
sympathized with it, and a few derived benefits from the liberalization
that was also part of its policy. Among the former were the physicist
Tódor von Kármán, who later earned world renown as the father of
modern aerodynamics, and the film producer Sándor Korda, who subsequently was knighted for his services to the British film industry.
Among the latter were psychoanalyst Sándor Ferenczi and sociologist
Karl Mannheim, both of whom became university professors and later
emigrated and acquired international fame in their fields.

The short-lived monuments erected by the Communist government
in Budapest in hasty preparation for the May 1 Workers' Day celebrations are among my earliest memories. I was eight years old at the time.
Seventy-four years later, I still remember the changes Parliament Square
underwent: the beautiful old classical bronze statues of historic Hungarian heroes that decorated the square were covered by huge red canvas
globes in honor of the day. I also remember the equally large white plaster statues of the heroes of the Communist revolution, although not precisely whom they represented. A few short weeks later I saw the canvas
of the globes torn to shreds and fluttering in the wind, and the plaster
statues overturned and their broken pieces littering the green lawns. My
only other memory from those few weeks of Communist rule is of a
frightening visit to a classmate whose father was one of the commissars
later executed for his role in the Communist government.

While the workers celebrated May Day with mass demonstrations,
the government realized that its position was growing more and more
precarious. Enemy armies from all sides were advancing toward the
center of the country. However, indecisive struggles, both military and
political, continued for several weeks. The number of people who suffered deprivations grew, and they became increasingly vocal. Working

women standing in endless lines for supplies repeated the slogans of the "white" (anti-"red," anti-revolutionary) pamphlets and cursed the "Jewish commissars."

Still in May, in the city of Arad a counterrevolutionary government was founded with the Jewish notary public Lajos Pálmay as its minister of justice and Tibor Eckhardt as secretary of state. The budget for administration and agitation was raised by a collection carried out in the Lloyd Club of Arad by two Jewish citizens. Simultaneously in Szeged, an Anti-Bolshevik Committee was set up, with leading Jewish citizens providing the funds and working for its organization. Its army units, led by seventy-two officers of whom fifteen were Jewish, succeeded in occupying the city barracks and disarming the local Red Army contingents. On May 17 they issued a proclamation declaring a holy unity, which was signed among others by the head of the Jewish community of Szeged and two other Jewish leaders. On May 19, under French protection, a "white" countergovernment was established, headed by Count Gyula Károlyi, whereupon the Arad countergovernment moved to Szeged.

Some of the members of this counterrevolutionary movement already declared at that juncture that prior to the consolidation of a new government, accounts with the Jews would have to be settled. Hence, the Jewish community of Szeged felt it necessary to issue a proclamation (on June 26, 1919) stating, inter alia, "We decry and reject every excuse that serves the tendency to cast suspicion on us Jews because of our religious denomination with respect to our faithfulness to the Hungarian fatherland and the Hungarian nation. We served the idea of the Hungarian nation in the past, and we also serve it today as we have at all times, in unshakable fidelity."

When Rumanian army units had crossed the Tisza River and were approaching Budapest, the Communist government had no choice but to resign. Its members fled, Szamuely was recognized while in flight and shot himself, and Kún and several of his colleagues were given refuge in Austria. On August 2, a unionist government was established, and two days later the Rumanian army marched into Budapest. (From a window of our fourth-floor apartment I and my mother watched the Rumanian army march along broad Podmanicky Street. I was frightened.)

While the four months of the 1919 Council Republic were but a brief episode in the history of Hungary, they left a lasting impression on the Hungarian mind. The prominent role a few individual Jews and ex-Jews played in the Communist leadership was generalized and "the Jews" were associated with Communism. This resulted in a marked increase

in anti-Semitic sentiment and prepared the ground for the excesses of
the White Terror (see chapter 38). Also, nationalist Hungarians felt that
the Communist Council Republic—an aberration that ran counter to all
true Hungarian values—could not have been established without the
Russian example, Russian help, and the training in Russia of the men
who headed it. This, associated with the still lingering memories of the
unforgettable national catastrophe of 1849, when the Hungarians were
defeated by the armed help Russia rendered the Austrians, reinforced
the fear and hatred of the Russian bear in Hungarian consciousness.

38

The White Terror and the Numerus Clausus

"White" was the designation by which the Hungarian nationalist right-ist, anti-Communist forces identified themselves from 1919 on. The most significant faction was the National Army, headed by Vice-Admiral Miklós Horthy, which, although it consisted only of officers and noncommissioned officers, was the only Hungarian armed formation and had the backing of the Szeged countergovernment. The unionist government in Budapest had no armed might and was not supported by the delegates at the peace conference. Also, the first openly counterrevolutionary government, formed in August 1919 by István Friedrich, was totally impotent. The Rumanians were occupying Budapest and much of the country, and conditions everywhere were chaotic.

In the middle of August, the National Army transferred its headquarters from Szeged to Siófok, and within a short time became the deciding factor in the course of events. It was primarily the action of its officers that introduced the "White Terror" by organizing ruthless pogroms without regard for civil authorities. The government contributed its share by ordering numerous arrests and prosecutions. In the first three months of the counterrevolution about 5,000 perople were executed and more than 70,000 locked up in jail or internment camps. This was the period when dozens of outstanding Hungarian intellectuals, scholars, scientists, and artists, many of them Jews or ex-Jews, who were in one way or another associated with the Communist regime, even if only remotely (such as by having been appointed to university positions), were either forced to leave the country or left on their own in fear for their lives.

For the Jews, the time of the White Terror was a period of severe affliction. In the eyes of the National Army, Jews were identified with Communism, and cleansing the country of Communists meant liquidating the Jews. Army detachments swept through towns murdering or "executing" Jews. Col. Pál Prónay, the commander of one such unit, the

"Black Legion of Death," which passed through the town of Marcali east of the Tisza River, commented in his notes: "Marcali and its environs were truly polluted by Communism; no wonder, since many vagrant Jews live in it." To combat the contagion, Prónay resorted to the radical method of excising it: he had six Jews hanged. This happened in the town whose ninety Jewish families only two years earlier had lost fifteen of their members in the war.

Similar events took place in other towns as well. In nearby Csurgó, the sixty-five Jewish families had lost thirteen members in the war, and in September 1919 seven of them were killed by unidentified members of terrorist groups, referred to by the euphemism "irresponsible elements." Other Jewish citizens were hanged or otherwise put to death in several other country towns, from some of which all the Jews fled after suffering the atrocities. Especially tragic was the sequence of events for the Jews of Kecskemét: 270 of them had fought in the war, twenty-seven of them fell; under the Communists several of them were taken hostage, and then, in November 1919, a White Terrorist formation murdered eight of them—two teachers, two lawyers, a banker, a merchant, a student, and a printer's apprentice. In many other localities, too, the Jews were savagely attacked by the Prónay units.

Jews tried to counteract the wave of White Terror by the old method of declaring and calling the country's attention to their patriotic stance through all the trials and tribulations of recent history. The Israelite Congregation of Pest issued a proclamation saying:

> The Congregation, in its own name and in the name of the entire Hungarian Jewry, expresses its boundless joy over the collapse . . . of the senseless and violent governmental method of the so-called dictatorship of the proletariat, which threatened with final destruction every congregation and its wonderful institutions built up with the work and unselfish generosity of many generations. The Congregation wishes to state that the false doctrine called Communism is in the first place an anticommercial trend, which is not as damaging and dangerous for anybody as for Jewry, which is mainly engaged in commercial and industrial enterprises. Therefore the Congregation states with regret and at the same time with indignation that in the commanding staff and camp of the Communist rule there were a great number of people of Jewish descent, who, almost without exception, had previously become unfaithful to their religion, as they later became to their fatherland. Since the role they played is being used by unconscientious and evil people to identify the Jews with the Communists, the Congregation wishes to state that for every single Communist there are at least a thousand Hungarian citizens of the Jewish faith who in both peace and war faithfully served the Hungarian fatherland and nation, and in the mournful period of proletarian dictatorship suffered beyond endurance and stand just as far from the erroneous doctrines of Communist morality as anybody else.

By October, 1919, Miklós Horthy himself recognized that the atrocities committed against the Jews were unjustified and in addition, harmed the image the new Hungarian leadership wished to project to the Entente powers on whom much of Hungary's future depended. In the course of negotiations he conducted with Archduke Joseph, who still functioned as *homo regius* (the king's representative) in Hungary, Horthy stated: "I declare solemnly that in matters of the persecution of the Jews, which are the crimes of irresponsible elements, I have instituted the most rigorous investigations. I shall bring the guilty, both the perpetrators and the instigators, inasmuch as they belong to my army, before the military court, and shall exclude them for all times from the Hungarian National Army. Otherwise, I consider it self-evident that all kinds of pogroms, denominational persecutions, and individual actions must be suppressed with implacable severity."

Such intentions, however, were easier stated than carried out, and further reassurance of the Jews was deemed required. Consequently, a few days later one of the leaders of the political department of the Ministry of Defense, a certain Colonel U. (not further identified), called upon József Patai, as a Jewish leader not associated with any particular faction of the Jewish community, and suggested that, in order to dispel the unease of the Jews, a Jewish delegation should go to Siófok, to the temporary headquarters of the National Army, for reassurances from the mouth of the commander-in-chief himself. Patai took instant action, and within a short time the delegation was assembled, consisting of Jenő Polnay de Tiszasüly, a former minister of commerce; Baron Adolf Kohner, an industrialist and president of the Neolog Israelite National Office; Joseph Vészi, editor-in-chief of the influential daily *Pester Lloyd*; Adolf Frankl, president of the Orthodox Jewish National Office; and Patai himself. Béla Feleki, vice-president of the Israelite Congregation of Pest, also declared himself ready to join, but his wife considered the undertaking too dangerous, and he withdrew at the last minute.

Armed with passes from the Ministry of Defense, the five men drove from Budapest to Siófok early in November 1919. In the course of a two-hour meeting with Horthy, Polnay, as spokesman of the delegation, emphasized how much the Hungarian Jews had done for the economic development of the country, and how much they had endured under Communist rule. He said: "Just as throughout the war the Jewish Hungarian suffered and fought together with the Christian Hungarian in trouble and danger, so we believe and hope that in the rebuilding of Hungary we shall likewise work shoulder to shoulder together with our Christian fellow citizens." Horthy answered at length, and from the questions he posed it was clear that he had been fed many anti-Semitic lies and calumnies, which the delegation tried to refute.

On November 16, after the Rumanian troops left the capital, Horthy, at the head of the National Army, entered Budapest, and a few days later he again received the same Jewish delegation, this time augmented by Feleki. On that occasion Horthy promised to have each case of "individual action" carefully investigated and the culprits punished. But he refused to issue general orders for the protection of the Jews, because, he said, "that would only create the opposite effect. They would say that I sold myself to the Jews. The nation has not yet fully recovered from its illness. But that, too, will come in time."

Also in 1919, after the fall of the Council Republic, the Hungarian Jews recognized that the palpable tensions in the country necessitated a central representation of all the Jewish denominational organizations, and they formed the National Union of Hungarian Jews. Its president became Jenő Polnay de Tiszasüly, and members of its executive were Mór Mezei, former president of the Neolog Israelite National Office; Adolf Frankl, president of the Orthodox National Office; Pál Sándor, president of the National Hungarian Israelite Educational Organization; the politician Vilmos Vázsonyi; Joseph Vészi, editor of the *Pester Lloyd*; and the leading industrialists Baron Manfred Weiss and Baron Tivadar Wolfner.

The Jews received the entry of the National Army into the capital joyfully, and Ferenc Székely, president of the Pest congregation, greeted it with an enthusiastic article arguing that the National Army and its commander-in-chief could not be held responsible for atrocities committed by a few individuals, just as Hungarian Jewry could not be held responsible for the crimes of the Communist dictatorship. On March 1, 1920, with officers of the National Army occupying the building, the Assembly elected Horthy regent, by 131 votes out of 141.

Despite Horthy's reassurances, which, as events showed, were not too seriously meant, the entry of the National Army into Budapest signaled the beginning of anti-Jewish atrocities in the capital as well. Béla Somogyi, a socialist politician and publisher (a converted Jew), and Béla Bacsó, another journalist and socialist leader, both associated with the socialist paper *Népszava* (The People's Voice), were murdered in February 1920. The anti-Semitic Union of Awakening Hungarians took the lead in assaulting Jews in the city night after night. In July a group of them penetrated the Café Club on Leopold Boulevard, stabbed to death one of the patrons, wounded others, and beat up the rest. In October they occupied another Jewish club, the Leopold District Casino, and the buildings of several Jewish organizations, placing homeless refugees in them. At the universities, members of the Turul student organization attacked the Jewish students, who tried to defend themselves by organizing into the Ezra Society.

The news of the atrocities, which reached the Paris Peace Conference, created considerable resentment against Hungary, and the chief Hungarian negotiator, Count Albert Apponyi, warned the National Assembly of the harm these acts could do the Hungarian cause. In a letter to the Assembly he demanded the immediate restoration of law and order, execrated the anti-Jewish excesses, and stated that if they continued he could not be held responsible for the possible failure of the negotiations. Apponyi's letter created an uproar in Parliament, with the "race protectors" attributing the powers' criticism of Hungary to the machinations of the Jews and the Jewish press. Nevertheless, in July 1920, the newly elected Teleki government tried to curb the anti-Semitic excesses, and late that year it dissolved the Union of Awakening Hungarians and, with the help of armed forces, broke up the special commandos stationed in the city.

Despite these governmental efforts, the anti-Jewish excesses continued and even intensified, until finally, in May and June 1921, the leaders of the Catholic Church—the prince-primate (as the only Hungarian cardinal was styled) and several bishops—also felt it was their duty to speak up against them. In the wake of their declarations, on June 12, 1921, István Haller, the minister of religion and education, stated to a Jewish delegation: "The Christian spirit, the Christian political order, exclude Jew-hatred. I know that under the red rule there was Jewish cruelty and Christian cruelty, but a faithful Jew is not able to commit such foul acts, just as the faithful Christian will not become a murderer. To incite hatred, to persecute the innocent—especially in today's situation—is the equivalent of treason."

Faced with the rising tide of anti-Semitism, the Jewish leadership felt there was only one thing it could do: intensify its avowals of Jewish loyalty to Hungary. The Trianon Peace Treaty, forced upon Hungary by the victorious Allies, gave the Jews a new opportunity to demonstrate their total identification with Hungarian interests. Here was a situation in which the Hungarian Jewish establishment was able to utilize for the benefit of Hungary whatever connections it had with the major Jewish institutions and organizations of the Western world. The same Hungarian Jewish leadership that had adamantly refused to acknowledge the existence of any ties between it and the Jewries of the other countries (and especially of Hungary's victorious enemy countries), and had indignantly rejected, and was to reject, all help offered in connection with the Numerus Clausus Law (see below) by such influential Jewish bodies as the Alliance Israélite Universelle and the Anglo-Jewish Association, now discovered that it could raise its voice in international Jewish forums to create sympathy for Hungary.

After the armistice of October 1918, the Hungarian Jewish leadership was among the first to raise its voice against the injustices of the peace treaty while they were still in the making. They appealed to the Jews of Europe to use their influence with the leaders of their countries to prevent the dismemberment of Hungary. In February 1919, Adolf Frankl, leader of the Orthodox Jews of Hungary, addressed the Zurich congress of Agudat Israel, the international organization of Orthodox Jews (at the time still strongly anti-Zionist), with an impassioned appeal to world Jewry for help in reestablishing Hungary's territorial integrity. In January 1920, the leaders of Hungary's Neolog Jewry appealed to the Jewish leaders of Britain, France, the United States, Switzerland, and Australia to pull their weight with their respective governments in support of the Hungarian delegation to the peace conference, with whose position, they emphasized, the Hungarian Jews totally identified. They stated: "We, Hungarian Jews, want to remain Hungarian. Especially now, in this most difficult period of need, during the difficult years of reorganization, we do not want to leave our Motherland. We want to take part in the rebuilding of our most beloved Homeland, with all our strength, and with the enthusiasm and tenacity of our origin."

At the same time the Hungarian Jewish leaders also appealed to the Jews in the detached territories, exhorting them to remain "indomitably" and "unswervingly" Magyar in their attitude. That exhortations such as this did not remain without effect—because they expressed sentiments shared by most Jews in the lands taken away from Hungary by the Trianon Peace Treaty—was to be amply proven in the course of the ensuing two interwar decades. In 1938 Samu Stern, president of the Israelite Congregation of Pest, could truthfully and proudly state that "everywhere in the occupied territories, the Jews torn from Hungary remain the loyal supporters and protectors of the Hungarian national spirit and of Hungarian culture."

While Hungarian Jewry engaged in such efforts to express its complete identification with Hungary and to help by mitigating the tragic blow Trianon meant for the country, anti-Semitic activities and atrocities continued. In reacting to them, the Jewish leadership cooperated with the government, and readily acquiesced to the always available official excuse that whatever atrocities did take place were but "individual actions" committed by "irresponsible elements," for which the government could not be blamed or held accountable.

Then, however, came an official governmental act, in the form of the passage of the first anti-Jewish law in Hungary ever since the imposition on the Jews of the notorious *malke gelt* under Maria Theresa. It was Law 1920:XXV, which became known as the Numerus Clausus Law.

While the Jews could find comfort in ascribing the anti-Jewish atrocities to a few misled and ill-willed anti-Semitic individuals and groups, they could not thus reassure themselves when faced with the Numerus Clausus Law, the first legal restriction imposed on the Jews of Hungary for generations. The passing of a law in Parliament that discriminated against the Jews because of their religion was a blow that could not be explained away as the aberration of the few—it was the considered will of the majority of the country's legislators. The Jewish leadership had no choice but recognize that, at least as far as higher education was concerned, the country had spoken out against the Jews.

Ever since the 1867 emancipation of the Jews, they tended to concentrate in the professions. In that very year, of the 1,885 students at the University of Pest, 335, or 17.8 percent, were Jews. In 1895, of 4,407 total, 1,304, or 29.6 percent, were Jews. By 1913 (the last prewar year), of the total of 7,091 students, 2,392, or 34.1 percent, were Jews. In that year, the proportion of Jewish students reached an especially high level in the medical faculty, where of the 2,717 students, 1,335, or 49.1 percent, were Jews, and in law, where of the total of 2,905 students, 766, or 26.4 percent, were Jewish. At the Technical University of Budapest in 1913, of the total of 2,115 students, 675, or 31.9 percent, were Jewish. Even considering the fact that most of the students at the Budapest institutions of higher learning were recruited from the population of the city, which was about one-fifth Jewish, these percentages were extremely high.

In the anti-Semitic atmosphere of 1919–20, the government found it expedient to pass a law that would limit the admission of Jewish students to the universities, the Technical University, the Faculty of National Economy (a separate school), and the legal academies for the training of lawyers. The bill was prepared by István Haller, minister of religion and education, in July 1920, and in August, even before Parliament had a chance to discuss it, he issued a ministerial order that in student admissions for the 1920–21 academic year, the Israelites would be considered "a separate nationality." This order was a sharp departure from the 1867 Law of Emancipation, which gave equal rights to the Jews, and the 1895 Law of Reception, which declared Judaism one of the accepted religious denominations. In vain did Jewish spokesmen, arguing against this order, claim that Hungarian law did not recognize racial classification, or that the international legal concept of nationality could not be applied to Hungarian Jewry. The order stood, and was put into effect with the Numerus Clausus Law of 1920.

The bill was discussed in Parliament and passed in September. Its operative part is section 3, which states that in admitting applicants to the universities, "one must also take into account that the proportion of the youth belonging to an individual race or nationality should, as far as possible, approximate among the students the proportion of that race or nationality in the country, but should reach at least nine-tenths of it."

Even though the law does not mention the Jews, its purpose and effect, when combined with the ministerial order of August 1920, was to reduce the fraction of Jewish students at the Hungarian institutions of higher learning to 5 percent. Soon after the promulgation of the Numerus Clausus Law, the Hungarian *kuria* (supreme court) found that "the expressions 'Israelite' and 'Jew' are suitable in Hungary, in the sense of the Hungarian constitution, only for a religious-denominational designation," and that "the Hebrew language cannot be considered the kind of mother tongue of Jewry that would fuse them into a separate nationality; consequently one cannot speak in Hungary of a Jewish nationality." Whatever the opinion of legal and constitutional experts, even if the Jews were, as they so vociferously claimed, just a religious denomination, the purpose of the law remained to reduce the fraction of Jewish students to 5 percent.

The passing of the Numerus Clausus Law triggered countrywide anti-Semitic demonstrations and incidents, in which the Union of Awakening Hungarians, which continued to function despite its official liquidation in 1920, played a leading role. It organized attacks on Jewish students and on several occasions beat them bloody. These incidents went on through 1921, 1922, and 1923. Some of the right-wing papers made their own contributions to the anti-Jewish agitation. In October 1922, the journal *Nép* (People) published a provocative article alleging that the owner of the Goldberger factory in Buda, in retaliation for the Numerus Clausus, refused to employ non-Jewish engineers in his plant. This news sparked additional anti-Jewish outbreaks at the universities, which subsided temporarily only after a government-sponsored investigation proved the allegation unfounded. In March 1923, a series of Jew beatings took place at the Veterinary College, which forced the authorities to close it. The dean of the medical faculty, Dr. Károly Hoor, demanded that the Israelite Congregation of Pest put at the disposal of the school, for the purpose of dissection, the unclaimed bodies of Jewish patients who died in hospitals, or else he would deny instruction to Jewish medical students. The demand was supported also by the Szeged University, causing a sharp controversy with the Szeged Jewish congregation, which objected, invoking the Jewish tradition to bury bodies intact, and denied the competence of the university to rule in the question. Finally, the minister of religions intervened, reserving for himself the right of decision, but not before many additional attacks on Jewish students had been perpetrated.

As soon as the Numerus Clausus Law was passed, a debate about it raged in the press and in Parliament. The half-dozen Jewish representatives in the Assembly, as well as the members of the opposition, denounced the law. Count Albert Apponyi and even members of the ruling government party demanded its annulment. International Jewry also took an active interest. In the summer of 1920, at the very time the Numerus Clausus Bill was submitted for parliamentary consideration, Dr. Nahum Goldmann, the European representative of the American Jewish Joint Distribution Committee, came to Budapest with a program of considerable financial aid from the Joint (as the great aid organization was commonly referred to), and began setting up a Hungarian office for it, which actually began its work under the leadership of the physician Dr. Ernő Deutsch. It aimed in the first place at improving conditions in the hospitals and reopening the discontinued Mensa Academica (students' canteen) of the National Hungarian Israelite Educational Society (OMIKE).

In the wake of the promulgation of the numerus clausus, a sequence of events took place that revealed the complex interrelationship between the "moderately" anti-Semitic Hungarian government of the 1920s and the superpatriotic, deferential Hungarian Jewish leadership. They began in November 1921, when the British Jewish leader Lucien Wolf (1857–1930), in his capacity as secretary of the Joint Foreign Committee of the British Board of Jewish Deputies and the Anglo-Jewish Association, as well as spokesman for the French Alliance Israélite Universelle, lodged a complaint with the League of Nations in Geneva against the numerus clausus, pointing out that it contravened the protection of racial-national and religious minorities contained in articles 56, 57, and 58 of the Trianon Peace Treaty, one of whose signatories was Hungary.

When this was brought to the attention of the Hungarian prime minister, Count István Bethlen (1874–1947), he reacted with an angry outburst against the Jews, who he said did not fulfill abroad their Hungarian patriotic duty, which was to undertake efforts for the revision of the unjust Trianon Peace Treaty. In January 1922, the Hungarian government, in its response in Geneva, asserted that the law in question had but the twofold aim of reducing the size of the Hungarian intellectual proletariat and guaranteeing the rights of the minorities in the country. In support of this position Hungary submitted statistics to the League, in September 1922, and again in January 1923 and August 1924, that purported to show that the official university admission policies were in fact favorable to the Jews, because the percentage of Jewish students at the universities was actually double that in the general population.

Early in 1923, Bethlen himself went to Paris to argue before the League for the alleviation of the burdens the Trianon Peace Treaty had imposed on Hungary. On that occasion he met with a delegation of the Alliance, during which he portrayed the Hungarian Jews as hostages whose fate improved or worsened according to whether Jews abroad did or did not fight for the Treaty's revision. Lucien Wolf, who participated in that meeting, protested sharply against this position, and an altercation developed between him and Bethlen, for whom, used as he was to the obsequious demeanor of the Hungarian Jewish leaders, Wolf's self-assured advocacy of the Jewish cause came as an unpleasant surprise.

That Bethlen was at all willing to meet with representatives of Western Jewry was due to his concern lest a charge of Hungary's violation of the peace treaty, or worse yet an adverse decision by the League, obstruct Hungary's efforts to obtain financial help from Western banks and credit institutions. A negative outcome of the negotiations would have been a serious economic setback for Hungary, which found itself in dire financial straits. Upon returning to Hungary, Bethlen vented his resentment: "The Jews abroad find it proper to push this unhappy country deeper and deeper with their propaganda, for the only reason that there is anti-Semitism here . . . The numerus clausus is a matter of national interest, and an exclusively Hungarian affair."

It was characteristic of the atmosphere in Hungary at the time that, as this statement clearly reveals, even for a moderate politician such as Bethlen anti-Semitism was neither a social disgrace nor a shameful aberration but a legitimate position well within the acceptable political spectrum. Hence, the existence of anti-Semitism in Hungary was, in Bethlen's eyes, no justification for the Jews abroad to take an anti-Hungarian stand.

However, Bethlen's stance was found unacceptable by Vilmos Vázsonyi, foremost spokesman of Hungarian Jews and a leader of the anti-Bethlen opposition. When Bethlen made his first pronouncement on the subject, Vázsonyi reacted energetically and bitterly in an article in *Egyenlőség* (June 2, 1923):

We do not understand. Why does Bethlen expect help precisely from the Jews abroad? Why not from the Protestants or Catholics abroad? . . . Why does he not threaten the English Protestants that he will hold the Hungarian Protestants hostage if those Britishers do not help? Is it logical that the prime minister, after representing the affair of Hungary as a Jewish question, wants us to believe that the numerus clausus is not directed against the Jews? According to him it is "a matter of national interest, and strikes equally at all the intelligent elements." . . . In Érsekujvár [a city in historic Hungary that the treaty assigned to Czechoslovakia] the Czechs threw out of the high school two Jewish students, Károly Fodor and György Hecht, because they sang the Hungarian national anthem in the Catholic church. At the same time the Hungarian prime minister—according to his declaration—says to the members of the Alliance Israélite Universelle, "Those gentlemen who for a hundred years had experienced from Hungary the greatest liberalism and had enjoyed benefits, took not a single step in our interest when the country was in trouble. And they don't do it even today, when our neighbors persecute the Hungarian people and the Hungarian intelligentsia."

Mr. Prime Minister! Who are these "gentlemen"? What does this word "gentlemen" mean? The Jews from abroad neither experienced nor enjoyed anything in Hungary. And as for the Hungarian Jews, they fulfilled their duty honestly, worked, bled, and they stand up for Magyardom even in the detached territories. When the Hungarian Jews gathered prior to the revolution [of 1919] to discuss their grievances and we already knew that the war was lost, they resolved, following my motion, not to speak of their grievances but to call upon the Jewish citizens of the Entente countries to speak up for the Hungarian cause, because Magyardom has always honored equal rights more than the neighboring states, which were always on the lookout for Hungarian booty. The Hungarian Jews never confused the [anti-Semitic political] *kurzus* [regime] with the fatherland. They had been given equal rights by the Hungary of [Ferenc] Deák and [Lajos] Kossuth. *Rights and not benefits.* It is impossible to uproot our gratitude to the Hungarians whom we can thank for our rights, and who are now denied by the hate-filled epigones.

It takes little effort to imagine that being called a "hate-filled epigone" did not sit well with Bethlen, but he recognized that he could no longer postpone taking some action on the issue. In August 1923, he announced in Parliament, "I do not deny that the solution of the Jewish question is extremely important. I have come to the conclusion that one must deal with the Jewish question."

In the meantime the League of Nations asked Prof. Hugh H. L. Bellot, a leading British expert on international law, for his opinion on the Numerus Clausus Law. Bellot's opinion was that the law could have fateful consequences for all European minorities and should be rescinded. The League also dispatched a three-man delegation to Hungary to report on the situation of the Hungarian Jews, and upon its return this team, too, condemned the numerus clausus unequivocally.

Hungary's response, communicated to the League by its representative, was to repeat the old arguments. At the same time the Hungarian foreign minister, Lajos Walkó (1880–1954), officially requested that the League reject Lucien Wolf's complaint, for the numerus clausus, he argued, was but a consequence of the situation produced by the Trianon Peace Treaty, and as soon as the shackles of that treaty were removed, it, too, would cease to exist.

While refusing to budge on the numerus clausus, apart from making vague promises, Bethlen continued to be worried by Hungary's financial situation. A resolution by the League against Hungary could, he felt, result in the Western financial powers' withholding desperately needed loans. There was, however, a political formation in Hungary that was interested in frustrating Bethlen's financial plans: the extreme right wing, which was prepared to try anything to bring down the Bethlen government. Hence, when Bethlen traveled abroad on national business, the rightists organized brutal physical attacks against Jews at the universities and in the streets of cities, so that the European press would report these atrocities, making Bethlen's task more difficult or even impossible to accomplish. In August, on the very day before the League was to vote on the large loan applied for by Hungary, rightists threw a bomb into the ballroom in the city of Csongrád where the local Jewish Women's Association was holding its ball, killing a man and a woman and wounding several others.

Despite these brutal attempts of the "race protectors" to frustrate the Hungarian government's efforts in Geneva, the League did approve in August 1924 the Hungarian loan, which was a veritable lifesaver for the tattered Hungarian economy. No small part was played by Lucien Wolf, who as early as January 1924 arranged a meeting of the Anglo-Jewish Association, in preparation for which he made sure that its president would respond with requisite diplomacy to a question addressed to him concerning the Hungarian loan.

Also in January 1924, a Jewish member of the Hungarian Parliament, Pál Sándor (1860–1936), combined a motion for the repeal of the Numerus Clausus Law with a proposal to authorize the Hungarian Jews to establish a university of their own. Neither the motion nor the proposal received any consideration in the House, and even among the Jews only Gyula Gábor, secretary-general of the Israelite Congregation of Pest, took up the idea of a Hungarian Jewish university, and discussed it in a pamphlet he published that year.

It took more than a year after these events for the Bethlen government finally to come to the conclusion that the Numerus Clausus Law had to be mitigated, or at least modified so as to assuage the Hungarian Jews and satisfy the demands of Western Jewry, as well as to forestall any action by the League of Nations. However, Bethlen was faced with an extremely difficult task, for any step in this direction would certainly be decried by the rightist-racist opposition. Even the mere announcement of his intention to put the numerus clausus on the agenda of the House sufficed for the racist representative Gyula Gömbös (who was to become prime minister in 1932) to create an uproar in the House and to attack Hungarian Jewry with a spate of old and new accusations.

While these maneuverings for positions took place on the home front, the League finally moved and put the numerus clausus question on its own agenda, prompted by a renewed application submitted in January 1925 by British and French Jewry. When this became known to the Hungarian Jewish leadership, already apprehensive from governmental and oppositional allegations that it had not lived up to its patriotic duties, both the Neolog and Orthodox establishments dispatched (in November 1925) strongly worded communications to the League's secretary-general protesting the intervention of the British Joint Foreign Committee, the French Alliance, and, in fact, the League itself, in what was a purely internal Hungarian and Hungarian Jewish affair.

In order to adhere to our chronology we turn here to a brief account of other developments that seized Hungarian Jewry in 1925, before the numerus clausus issue was taken up by the League. In August 1925, the Fourteenth Zionist Congress took place in Vienna, and proved an occasion for Hungarian Jews to make vociferous pronouncements against Zionism. At a meeting of the Israelite Congregation of Pest, the same Vilmos Vázsonyi who had fought with such courage against the prime minister for Hungarian Jewish rights stated with equal force that it was possible to contribute to Palestine "without politics and Zionism." This position was instantly rejected by Nahum Sokolow (1859–1936), the venerable Zionist leader and chairman of the congress, who said, "I warn Jewry of the newfangled position of those who state that they recognize the Palestine work but at the same time reject Zionism. This concept is but a mean excuse. Without a Zionist organization it is not possible to support Palestine."

However, the Hungarian Jewish representatives were unanimous in again rejecting Zionism, as they had done repeatedly in years past. On this occasion, Dr. Simon Hevesi (1868–1943), chief rabbi of the Israelite Congregation of Pest, issued the Jewish equivalent of a papal encyclical, in which he stated: "The Prophet Jeremiah calls upon us to serve the welfare of our fatherland, to seek in it our welfare and happiness as well. Zionism is incompatible with the soul of Hungarian Jewry." Lajos Hartstein, vice president of the Orthodox National Office, stated categorically, "Religion forbids the Zionist movement."

The secular leaders of Hungarian Jewry added their own warnings. Pál Sándor said, "We can have only one kind of politics: we are Hungarians of the Jewish faith." Sándor Lederer (1852–1927), president of the Israelite Congregation of Pest, fulminated, "We shall prevent the rise of a Zionist movement among us!" Mór Mezei (1836–1925), a famous attorney and spokesman of Neolog Jewry, warned, "We cannot have two fatherlands!" Ferenc Mezey (1860–1927), head of the Neolog National Office, agreed, "We are a religious denomination; we have no political aims or nationalistic endeavors." Jenő Gál (1872–1940), a well-known lawyer, journalist, and Jewish politician, who was elected in 1926 an opposition member of Parliament, said, "Zionist political organization is mistaken, aimless, and harmful for us."

The unanimity of these statements condemning Zionism should not be surprising in view of the pressure the Hungarian Jewish establishment felt from the gradually but perceptibly increasing influence of the right wing on the Hungarian political scene. Rejecting Zionism was an effective way of demonstrating Hungarian Jewry's identification with Hungarian patriotism and nationalism, and its self-exclusion from international Jewish endeavors dominated by Jews from the Entente countries. Notably, the Hungarian Jewish leadership was also unanimous in refraining from saying anything about (that is, against) Zionism in general, or from condemning the support the Zionist movement enjoyed in other countries. What the Hungarian Jewish position amounted to was, in effect, a self-isolation from the Jewries of other countries, and a claim that the relationship of the Hungarian Jews to Hungary was more intimate and more closely knit than that of the other Jews to their homelands.

The Hungarian anti-Semites, of course, felt differently. For them the Viennese Zionist Congress was proof of the unity of the "Jewish race." The *Nemzeti Ujság* (National News) wrote: "Behold, Zionism is the concern of the totality of Jewry, a proof of Jewish raciality. The other races must see clearly what is to be done for the preservation and development of their own national character." Similarly, *Magyarság* (Magyardom) wrote: "One must permit each country to offer inhabitants to the new Jewish state according to its own talents."

The Viennese Zionist Congress also served as the occasion for "race protector" leaders Gyula Gömbös and Tibor Eckhardt to launch an attack in Parliament on Hungarian Jewry, and to demand the esablishment of an internatioal anti-Semitic front, jointly with the anti-Semites of Rumania and Austria. When the three Jewish deputies in Parliament, Vilmos Vázsonyi, Pál Sándor, and Béla Fábián, rose to the defense of their coreligionists, they were rudely insulted by Gömbös and Eckhardt.

The reaction of the Hungarian Jewish establishment to these anti-Semitic attacks was to redouble its efforts to demonstrate that its Hungarian patriotism took precedence over its indignation at the injustice of the Numerus Clausus Law. The League of Nations was scheduled to take up Western Jewry's complaint on December 5, 1925, and in anticipation of the deliberations the Hungarian Jewish leadership formed a committee in November composed of the foremost Neolog leaders for the purpose of preparing a resolution to be adopted by a national congress of Hungarian Jewry, to take place soon, and submitting it to Geneva. A few hours prior to the meeting, two of the committee members, József Vészi and Pál Sándor, found it politically expedient to inform Prime Minister Bethlen of the plan. Bethlen responded that he had already prepared a text for such a resolution and would send it over to Sándor in time for the Jewish meeting to vote on it. The text prepared by the prime minister, which was hand delivered to Sándor by special messenger at 2 P.M., read:

> Hungarian Jewry declares that it does not, and did not, apply to the League of Nations concerning the numerus clausus.
> Hungarian Jewry considers this question its internal affair, and rejects all foreign intervention.
> Hungarian Jewry declares that it has not authorized anybody to represent its interests in Geneva, and denies the legal validity of the petition submitted there.
> Hungarian Jewry hopes that the Hungarian government will modify its Numerus Clausus Law within a short time.

The meeting of the Jewish committee opened at 6 P.M. Pál Sándor announced that he and Vészi had met that morning with the prime minister, that Bethlen told them of his draft resolution, which he would like the meeting to adopt, and that the draft was right here in Sándor's hand. A stormy debate ensued, with Vázsonyi—who was in opposition to the government—protesting that he would not allow the prime minister to dictate the position the Jews should adopt in what was an internal affair of the Jewish confession. The upshot was that Vázsonyi prevailed, and he sat down then and there to write out an alternative draft resolution, which the committee—and subsequently, on November 23, 1925, the plenum of the Hungarian National Jewish Congress—adopted without emendation. Essentially, Vázsonyi's text differed from Bethlen's only in that it emphasized Hungarian Jewry's reliance on its constitutionally guaranteed equal rights. Its full text read:

> In the name of the Hungarians of Jewish faith, who gathered on the occasion of the thirtieth anniversary of the Reception, we declare:
> The equal rights of our denomination are part of the Hungarian constitution. Our civic and political rights were given by the freely expressed Hungarian legislation, which entered our religion into the ranks of the received religions.
> For this reason, in fighting against the numerus clausus, we rely only on the Hungarian constitution, and will not refer to that point of the Peace Treaty that demands denominational equality.
> We are Hungarians, we declare ourselves part of Magyardom, and the Peace Treaty, which is the great bereavement of our nation, cannot be the

source of our rights. We declare with confidence that in the fight conducted for the integrity of our legally secured equal rights, which we shall
not cease to pursue, we will not remain alone, but with us will be the followers of the patriotic traditions of the great Hungarian statesmen.

Standing on the basis of the Hungarian constitution, expecting the victory of our equality of rights from the resurrection of the noble Hungarian
traditions, we want to settle the matter of the numerus clausus here at
home, with our own government and our own legislation. Therefore, we
did not apply, and do not appeal, to any foreign factor, and ask no help;
such help, even if it stems from good intentions, we reject.

At the November 23 Hungarian Jewish National Congress, Vázsonyi
made a speech that turned out to be his swansong. In it he said:

We are part of the Hungarian constitution, part of the Hungarian
nation. . . . We are not Hungarian Jews, but Jewish Hungarians. . . . We
adhere to our ancestral religion, but this fatherland is also ours. We do not
give away our fatherland; we do not give away our Magyardom. . . . Not
hatred can advance the cause of Magyardom. . . . If we are hurt, we call the
graves as witness. . . . The fatherland is not a minute, the fatherland is not
an hour, not a day, not even the compass of years; the fatherland is eternity.

The text of the resolution was instantly cabled to Geneva, Paris, and
London. In the Upper House, the Congress proceeded to discuss the
question of Jewish representation, which the Bethlen government had
offered the Hungarian Jews shortly before (see below).

The Jewish resolution concerning the Numerus Clausus Law had
wide repercussions in Hungary. Members of the government and leading political figures welcomed it, and emphasized that it demonstrated
Hungarian Jewry's unwavering patriotic commitment and its full
awareness of its patriotic duty. This reaction, of course, only strengthened the Jewish conviction that in order to get along in the political
arena it must continue to prove and declare its overarching patriotic
Magyardom. On the other hand, the "race protector" right took the
opportunity to let loose a new avalanche of anti-Semitic attacks in its
press and in Parliament. Faced with this outburst, both Prime Minister
Bethlen and Count Kunó Klebelsberg (1875–1932), the minister of
"kultusz" (religious affairs), felt it expedient to deliver speeches in Parliament that were definitely less than friendly to the Jews.

When the League of Nations finally got around to discussing the
numerus clausus, it first of all reviewed the exchange of notes between
the League and the Hungarian government from the preceding three
years and the complaints submitted by British and French Jewish
organizations. It was duly noted that the Hungarian Jewish National

Office and the Israelite Congregation of Pest sent protests against the League's deliberations on the issue. Then came the turn of the Hungarian minister of *"kultusz,"* Count Klebelsberg, who, speaking in French, took a thoroughly negative position. He submitted the texts of the protests of the Hungarian Jews, from which, he said, it became clear that those foreign Jewish organizations that had submitted the complaints acted against the express wishes of Hungarian Jewry, and the Hungarian government also considered it totally unjustified that foreign Jewish organizations should intervene in Hungary's internal affairs. He further argued that the Numerus Clausus Law was not permanent but merely "a transitional measure deriving from our exceptional situation created by the Treaty of Trianon, and it will be possible to modify it as soon as our social and economic life returns to its old stability." He went on to describe the situation in Hungary, the hypertrophy of the middle class, and the overabundance of intellectuals, which situation forced the Hungarian government to reduce drastically the *total* number of students admitted to the universities for the 1925–26 academic year. In fact, the universities had to refuse admission to more Christian than Jewish applicants. Klebelsberg concluded by saying that "that part of Hungarian Jewry that has fully assimilated to the nation—behold!—protests against the Geneva discussion of the question. And it does this because it trusts that as soon as possible, at a not very distant date and after suitable preparation, the numerus clausus will end in the spirit of reconciliation." But he coupled this conditional promise with the warning that if the Numerus Clausus Law were to be rescinded immediately, without a gradual transition, "it would result in a grave disruption between the Christian and Jewish citizens of the country."

The threat implied in this statement was not lost on the conferees of Geneva. They understood that what Klebelsberg meant by "grave disruptions" was anti-Semitic attacks. In any case, the League concluded that in view of the declaration of the Hungarian government that the numerus clausus was an exceptional and temporary measure, to be modified as soon as social conditions changed, it removed the issue from its agenda. The British and French Jewish organizations considered this outcome a victory, while Klebelsberg, upon returning to Budapest, was able to make it appear that he had managed to get the better of Geneva. He announced to a delegation of extreme right-wing youth that "everything is fine, the League of Nations retreated and postponed decision *ad kalendas Graecas.*" In Parliament he delivered such an anti-Semitic speech that the Jewish leadership was left gasping. He said, among other statements:

Jewry cannot ask for privileges. . . . The loosening of the numerus clausus, that is, if more Jews go to the university than the national proportion, would mean the other denominations would suffer disadvantage. We consider the numerus clausus an extraordinary provision, of a transitional nature, whose causes are in our social situation, and we shall propose its modification—not abrogation—at such time as the present social situation changes. The League of Nations appreciated this, and did not wish to block the process of consolidation, because that could lead to an expulsion. But here, on the left, they forget the dictatorship of the proletariat; we shall not eat barley and pumpkins again! The respect we have for the old Jewry of the fatherland cannot keep us from stating that the first and second generation of Galician Jewry brought the dictatorship of the proletariat upon us. Look at the catastrophic situation of the Hungarian middle class. It would in no way be proper to allow well-to-do Jewry to have an advantage in educating its children. The Bethlen government follows a policy of reconciliation, but it cannot be pushed by force. If they continue to keep the question on the agenda aggressively, they will create a new anti-Semitic wave.

The right wing applauded; the Jews were shaken. The three Jewish deputies in Parliament, Vázsonyi, Sándor, and Fábián, took the floor in spirited defense of Hungarian Jewry, refuting the minister's allegations on Communism, the Galicians, the rich Jews. Bethlen, responding to them, tried to be reassuring but made a statement that both the Christians and Jews found rather peculiar. He said that Jewry, if it had already assimilated so as to become Hungarian, was a denomination; if not, it counted as a race.

In the meantime, in the summer of 1926, the London Rothschild Banking House issued a loan of £2 million to the Hungarian government, which in the straitened circumstances of the country had great economic significance.

Throughout the 1920's, anti-Semitism continued to simmer, and occasional to boil over, while the government did little to restrain it. However, in view of the rabid anti-Semitic acts and demands of the right-wing opposition, Hungarian Jewry had little choice but to support the Bethlen government despite its "moderately anti-Semitic" stand. A frightening reminder of the alternative was the attempt made in the spring of 1926 on the life of Vilmos Vázsonyi while he was walking in the capital's streets. He remained unhurt, but a few weeks later he succumbed to a heart attack. With his death, Hungarian Jewry lost one of the bravest and most intrepid fighters for its rights.

Finally, in November 1927, Prime Minister Bethlen introduced a bill modifying the 1920 Numerus Clausus Law. Although the bill provided for what were essentially nothing but cosmetic changes, its voting into law took place only after fierce opposition. The new law substituted for the operative section 3 of the 1920 Numerus Clausus Law the following wording:

> In addition to the requirements of national loyalty and moral character to be met by every candidate, there shall further be taken into consideration the previous scholastic career and the intellectual capacity, as well as circumstances such as the following: whether the applicant is an orphan, and whether he is the son of a veteran, a public servant, or a member of one of the professions of agriculture, industry, trade, etc., or the liberal professions. In the case of candidates belonging to these categories, admission shall further be determined in proportion to the numerical and social importance of the professions in question, and the total number of those admitted shall be adequately distributed among the various administrative districts of the country.

Since the new law made no reference to "race and nationality," it removed the former basis of the Jewish community's grievance, but in effect it limited the number of Jewish students admitted to higher education just as effectively as the previous formulation. Since children of industrialists and tradesmen ranked low on the scale of admission preferences, the new law, which came into force in October 1929, even made it legally possible to exclude more Jewish applicants than did the old one. That the new law did not satisfy the demands of the Hungarian Jews was evident, and the Joint Foreign Committee was informed of this, but it had to recognize that for Hungarian Jewry it was the lesser evil to be barred from the universities because of occupational structure than because of race and nationality. It should also be added that the law was applied far from consistently, and in several faculties of Hungarian universities the percentage of Jewish students remained throughout the years considerably higher than 5 percent. Still, the wound inflicted by István Haller's ministerial order of August 1920, declaring the Jews "a separate nationality," was not healed. Nor was the number of Jewish high school graduates excluded from the universities reduced.

Finally, a word about the effect of the numerus clausus on the Jewish students of Hungary, whom it concerned most directly. As could be expected, thousands of Jewish high school graduates who were not admitted to the Hungarian higher educational network sought university education in other countries. In the 1920–21 academic year, 500 of them studied in Brünn (Brno), Czechoslovakia, and a similar number attended the German Technical University in Prague. In 1922, more than 800 applied for admission to the University of Vienna. Many others went to study in Italy, where a law passed in 1923 exempted Hungarian students from tuition and examination fees. Still others went to Germany (liberal Weimar Germany at the time), Switzerland, France, and Belgium. In 1922 a Central Student Aid Committee was founded in

Budapest, which in 1924 estimated the number of Hungarian Jewish students studying abroad at 5,000.

At the time the Numerus Clausus Law was introduced, it was considered to have dealt two major blows to Hungarian Jews: it stamped them, all their patriotic protestations notwithstanding, a national minority, which went against decades of preachment by their leaders about Hungarian Jews' being simply a religious denomination; and it blocked the road to academic careers for thousands of young Hungarian Jews whose plan throughout their high school years was to become doctors, lawyers, engineers, or members of the other professions.

However, as years passed, it became increasingly evident that the numerus clausus was, in effect, almost a blessing in disguise, whose ultimate outcome was to save several thousands of Hungarian Jews from perishing in the Holocaust twenty-five years later. Because of the clear evidence the numerus clausus offered that the majority of Hungarian legislators considered the Jews a national (or worse, racial) minority, more Jews turned to the "Zionist solution" of the Jewish question, or to emigration in general, as in many other European countries in the interwar period. We have no data to measure the causal relationship between the nationality position ascribed by the numerus clausus and the growth of interest in Zionist activities in Palestine, but it seems likely that without it the modest growth of the Zionist movement in Hungary and of the emigration of Hungarian Jews to Palestine would have been even smaller. We know that in the Burgenland, the three western counties of Hungary that under the Trianon Peace Treaty were assigned to Austria, the Jewish population showed a dramatic decrease, from 4,837 in 1910 to 3,632 in 1934, a decline of 25 percent, which can only be attributed to emigration. It is also known that in the fifty years from 1880 to 1929, no fewer than 952,000 Jews emigrated from Austria and Hungary. We also have data showing that the number of the Jews embraced by the Israelite Congregation of Pest, which had steadily increased until 1920, decreased from 215,512 in that year to 207,563 in 1925; that is, it experienced a decrease of 7,949, or 3.7 percent, in five years, and this despite the internal migration of Jews from the rural towns to Budapest in the same period. From Hungary as a whole in the years 1901 to 1910, some 44,500 Jews emigrated, or 5.3 percent of the total Jewish population.

As for the Jewish students whom the introduction of the numerus clausus forced to go abroad to study, only a few of them returned to Hungary after their university studies. There were several reasons for this. One was that in order to practice in Hungary with a foreign degree, the graduate had to undergo a rigorous so-called "nostrification" examination to validate his diploma. This exam was not easy, and in many cases difficulties arose from examiners being less than friendly toward Jews trying to obtain a licence to practice their profession in Hungary, which was what the Numerus Clausus Law was designed to prevent. A second reason was that during their years abroad, many students established connections that enabled them to find professional placement in the country where they earned their diplomas. A third factor was that having broken out of the confines of a language useless beyond a few miles of Budapest, and having gotten a whiff of the freer, more liberal, more cosmopolitan West European atmosphere, most of them preferred to stay abroad. Thus, the ultimate outcome of the Numerus Clausus Law was that several thousand Hungarian Jews were beyond the reach of the combined German and Hungarian genocide that destroyed four-fifths of Hungarian Jewry in 1944.

39

The Interwar Years

Let us start this chapter by going back a bit and presenting a few observations about how the Jews figured in the Hungarian national consciousness in the century that ended with the outbreak of World War II.
This will help us better understand how, in the crucial interwar years,
the Jews were totally unable to grasp the fact that their position within
the body of the nation had undergone a veritable sea change as a result
of the Trianon Peace Treaty, which at the stroke of a pen transformed
Hungary from a large, multinational state into a small one in which the
Jews remained as the only population element viewed, in Hungarian
eyes, as significantly "other."

Prior to Trianon, not only was it in the Magyar interest to count Jews
as Hungarians to add their numbers to that of the Hungarian Christians,
who alone constituted less than half the total population, but the otherness of the Jews in fact appeared minor compared to the pronounced
non-Hungarianness—often amounting to anti-Hungarianness—of the
self-consciously non-Hungarian Slovak, Ukrainian, Rumanian, Croat,
and Serb national minorities. After Trianon, when practically the entire
population of what remained of Hungary was Magyar, the demographic,
sociological, and of course religious differences between the Christian
Magyars and Hungarian Jews suddenly loomed large, the otherness of
the Jews assumed a formerly unknown significance, and its perception
inevitably brought about dislike and even hatred, that is, anti-Semitism.
We shall return to this issue later in the chapter.

Poets View the Jews

It is in view of this change in Christian Hungarians' attitudes that it is
instructive to consider the extent to which the Jews were part and parcel
of Hungarian life and consciousness before Trianon, and remained so
even afterwards in certain literary and intellectual circles. This is most

eloquently manifested in a remarkable literary phenomenon: many non-Jewish Hungarian poets, including the greatest, wrote poems about the Jews and, in particular, about the harshness of the Jewish fate, evincing an empathy and sympathy not often found in other European literatures. These poems testify not only to the sensitivity of the poets themselves but also to the ubiquity of the problem represented for Hungary by the Jewish presence in its midst, and the poets' familiarity with the painful dimension life in Hungary had for the Jews. For the Hungarian poets, the Jews were not merely examples of what social scientists later came to identify as "marginal." They were strange, almost mysterious beings, whose identity could not easily be grasped. They were Hungarians, spoke Hungarian, felt Hungarian, and in most cases also looked Hungarian. And yet there lingered in them an otherness, very difficult to define but nonetheless powerful enough to render them, with all their Hungarianness, non-Hungarian.

János Arany (1817–82), next to Petőfi the greatest Hungarian poet, gave classic expression to this feeling in his poem "The Eternal Jew," in which the Jew speaks with deep pain of the compulsion to wander ceaselessly, to go on and on without being able to find rest. He says (in my humble, literal prose translation):

O, to rest at last!—But, no, it cannot be:
Storm and disaster drive me on and on,
I have no solid earth under my feet,
Over my head a double-edged axe.
    Onward! Onward!
The road on which my feet tread
Sinks, and cracks and narrows down;
The leaden weight of the colossal sky
Would crush me were I to stop . . .
    Onward! Onward!
The present moment fills me with despair,
And every future moment is a threat;
With each step I tread on a snake,
I hate this day and the morrow . . .
    Onward! Onward!
I hunger, but I dread to eat;
If I drink, the draught like fire burns;
My dreams are violent nightmares, and the curtains
Hide daggers ready to plunge into my heart.
    Onward! Onward!
. . . .
Even the comet reaches its return,
The flying arrow finds its aim,
The stone hurled up falls back to earth:
But I, without a goal, without surcease,
    Onward! Onward!

. . . .
Poor Jew . . . poor heart:
Sooner or later it will find its rest.
Mercy is great and eternal,
It will pity me, and my curse will cease to thunder:
Onward! Onward!

Endre Ady (1877–1919), the greatest modern Hungarian poet—whose muse, whom he immortalized under the name of Léda, was a married Jewish woman of Nagyvárad—made frequent references in his poems to Jews and Judaism. One of them, a truly great poem titled "The Branded Host" expresses Ady's inner identification with the persecuted, driven, hunted host, whom he nowhere terms Jews but describes as unmistakably Jewish. (As with all the remaining poems in this chapter, unless indicated otherwise the translation is mine.)

The sacred shade of Christ and Heine's Satan-face
Dance before us on the road,
Down pours the abuse, the sneer, the rays.
There run the branded host,
And a big star is on their brow.

The chosen race: in the distance far ahead
Stand gallows on mournful mountaintops,
And on they march, tattered, scattered, and branded.
Sad devils, holy troublemakers.
I am going with you.

Your blood, even if a hundred times foreign,
Yet it is mine, is mine,
The blood-red lips of your honeyed women
And the open hearts of faithful men-friends
Transfused it into me.

Proud host of condemners, you may cast me aside
A hundred times, still my soul scurries after you.
Eternal wanderers, eternal alarmers,
Leavens of time, I too go with you,
Branded, bestarred.

To us belongs this tearful, this great Life.
Even on sickbed and under the cross,
Forward, forward, toward the Better.
My ugly, yellow-badged host,
I run with you and bless you.

Many of Ady's poems have Jewish and biblical references, but none is as "Jewish" as his long yet fragmentary novel in verse, *Margita Wants to Live* (first published in *Nyugat* in 1912). Not only is the heroine, Margita, a Jewish woman, but the entire ambience conjured up by the poem is permeated by Jewish presence. It makes reference to many Jew-

491

ish political and literary figures (such as Vilmos Vázsonyi, Sándor Bródy, József Vészi, Renée Erdős, and the publishers Singer and Wolfner) and describes the *belle époque* of Budapest, where Margita and the three men who love her live:

> We even heard of daring acts,
> the Esthers of Pest began to dress up.
> among the Jews men and women arose
> whose courage, beauty, and numbers were the greatest.
> And down below, in the Pest-aping marches,
> restless youths waited for a secret sign
> and became good disciples of Sándor Bródy,
> and not because he was handsome and desired by the women.
>
> The three of us, then, passed our time in waiting,
> in waiting for the storm, for woman, for something new.
> We shared the woman, she was white and remote,
> and gaily held our soul-wedding with her.
> Jewish girl—we said—she is a symbol of the new,
> fine Hungarian times that hasten to come.
> Until then, even though we were not too diligent,
> we lived for the many gods of our dreams.

In one passage of this peculiar poem, Margita becomes for Ady a symbol of Hungary as a whole: "Hungaria and Margita are almost one." On the other hand, in many of his poems Ady identified Hungary with Zion, or, in its distorted Hungarian form, "Sion" (pronounced *Shee-on*).

Lajos Kassák (1887–1967), Ady's heir as Hungary's uncrowned poet laureate, speaks of the unjust treatment accorded to the Jews in his poem "The Tragedy of the Jews":

> In the morning, as they awoke, the earth shook under their feet,
> and as they rubbed the shreds of a peaceful dream out of their eyes,
> the walls of the house already were strange to them.
> In their pitchers the water dried out, and friends did not recognize them.
> They wanted to cry: O, we are always the sacrifice!
> They wanted to show themselves so as to be seen
> in their true reality, together with their memories and desires,
> the smile of their loves and the sorrow of their disappointments.
> Once, in the faraway past, they too had a homeland,
> their laws honored the virtuous and punished the evil,
> they had kings, heroic soldiers, merry dancers, learned princes, and
>   princesses
> who conquered the world with their gentle charm and their laughter's
>   fragrant roses.
> They would have liked to shout all this into the dawn,
> but well they knew: they were being ground between hard millstones,
> and the wind scatters them again alongside unknown roads.
> Behold, their eyes are full of tears, and their hands are empty
> Even the silent mountains and the shady woods turn away from them.

And they lament in despair under the cloud-covered sky:
Yes, there are among us work-shy rascals and pitiless
extortioners, but where is the garden whose fruits
are not gnawed by worms? Where is the haystack
whose stalks are not plucked by the storm?
But why do they punish us when we are innocent?
Who grabs us together with cockle and tare?
And why does he want, unconcerned, to throw us on the dunghill?

The third modern Hungarian poet of great fame was Attila József (1905–37), who despite his short life was surrounded by adulation not only in literary circles but also among the socialist politicians of Hungary. He wrote the poem "Shma Yisroel" (Hear, O Israel) in 1936, a year before he committed suicide.

I wandered restlessly
wrapped in the dirty rags of poverty.
My heart cried, like a child.
Among merry folk I alone mourned.
Where is the bed where this tired soul
can find some rest? I cried:
    Shma Yisroel!

A servant waited for my word,
a silken cushion, with a faithful woman.
I counted my treasures, my gold,
I grew in brains, in power,
And when I gave I said to myself
Happily, with head raised high:
    Shma Yisroel!

And now, come whatever may,
glory, great fortune, grave illness:
anybody can cast stones at me,
but even while they prepare my deathbed,
I cry out the word of infinite
love, whatever happens:
    Shma Yisroel!

Gyula Illyés (1902–83) became a celebrated poet in the interwar years, and after World War II was regarded by many as one of the major poets of the century. He was a populist poet and at the same time a truly "national poet" with a feeling of social responsibility for the fate of the nation. He tried actively to help the victims of the Holocaust. His feelings found expression in this poem:

I too am branded. The badge
you wear on your breast,
whenever I see it, burns a mark
into my forehead: it is my shame!
Everybody's, only not yours!

That piece of rag (or that badge of honor)
is quickly removed from the clothes.
I know, in its place a wound remains, and
it will hurt only then: its depth opens up!
But there will be healing and there will be rest.

Other Hungarian poets also expressed similar sentiments about the Jewish fate in Hungary. The compassion and pain palpitating in these poems bear witness to the presence in the Hungarian consciousness of an awareness of the Jewish predicament, the Jewish anomaly, the Jewish fate. No more eloquent testimony could be found for the fact that the "Jewish question" in the pre–World War II years was perceived by the entire nation as a *Hungarian* problem of national dimensions and that it remained a burning issue in the years of national reconstruction.

The Jewish Stereotype

In contrast to the empathy palpable in the portrayals of Jews by sensitive poets from Arany to Illyés, the Hungarian gentry, and the dominant elements of Hungarian society in general, saw in the Jews in the interwar years a strange, unlikable, and even repugnant ethnic group, whose character traits differed essentially from those they attributed to themselves and held to be the important features of the ideal Hungarian personality. Not that the image of the Jew reflected in the Hungarian mind had any inner consistency or was monochromatic. Quite the contrary: Hungarians attributed to the Jews a complement of traits that contradicted, or even canceled out, one another. This, however, did not seem to bother those who subscribed to one or the other variety of the Jewish stereotype.

Thus, for example, Sándor Kiss, in a study he published in 1918 under the title "Jewish Racial Character—Hungarian Racial Character," found that in the consciousness of the leading Hungarian social strata the Jew figured as primitive, uneducated, and dirty, but also as the most intelligent among all the "races" inhabiting Hungary, and on the average possessed of the highest schooling and culture. The Jew was also seen as withdrawn and unsociable, very conservative, even "invariable," but on the other hand, was also found compliant, tractable, flexible, susceptible to all innovation, and variable. One opinion even held that precisely the Jews were the devotees, and hence representatives, of a better, richer, more humane Magyardom. (A like variety of Jewish stereotypes emerged from the opinions of non-Jewish respondents in the 1917 survey on the Jewish question published in *Huszadik Század*, discussed above in chapter 36.)

There was, of course, a basis in reality for these variations in the perception of Jews in Hungarian eyes. As late as the interwar years, Hungarian Jewry actually comprised a great variety of "types," ranging from the most Orthodox Yiddish-speaking Hasidim, who lived a totally and exclusively Jewish life, to the wholly irreligious "un-Jewish" assimilants, who did everything to hide their Jewish origin and appear as true Magyars. It is noteworthy in this connection that Jewish assimilation itself evoked mixed responses in the Hungarian Christian community. Liberal Hungarians in general welcomed assimilation in principle, but many of them were apprehensive that indelible traces of Jewish peculiarities that were "alien to the Hungarian character" might remain in even the most assimilated Jews, and that even they retained their loyalty to their own old community, through ties stronger than their devotion to Magyardom. One of the experts of the nationality problem of those days, Elemér Radisics, asserted as a fact that only Jewry "constitutes the kind of population, distinguishable from the rest, that while speaking Hungarian and declaring itself Hungarian yet does not always identify itself with the interests of Magyardom." That is, Jewry was still seen as dominated by its "racial solidarity." In the same period, Protestant bishop László Ravasz even termed the assimilant Jews "agents of the Jewish community," who were dangerous precisely because they did not constitute a separate nationality and outwardly looked like good Hungarians.

A major part of Hungarian society treated assimilant Jews as a separate element, in which it could discover, and mock with a feeling of superiority, its own faults: conceit, snobbery, title mania, selfishness, the empty extroverted life, the bragging and bluster, the lack of manners— all features it either did not recognize in itself or, if they were conspicuous, it excused as úri virtues. Thus, underlying the local, social, and temporal variants, a general stereotype of the Jew became fixed in the Hungarian mind: selfish, money grubbing, greedy, mercenary, profit seeking, shrewdly profiteering, materialist. As Zoltán Bosnyák put it in his contribution to the *Huszadik Század* poll, the Jew represented "the incarnation of the capitalist worldview in Hungary."

The contributors to that survey studied not only the phenomenology of the Jewish question but also its motivations. Most of them felt that its roots were in the Jewish "race," using the term "race" in the pre-racist-eugenicist sense of "ethnic group." They assumed that the character of the Jewish people was formed in the remote biblical days, when the Jews were first the "chosen" and later the "accursed" people. Only after the Nazi takeover in Germany did Hungarian newfangled "racists" also attribute the Jewish character to biological factors, speaking of the presence in the Jews of a mixture of ancient oriental Semitic and Armenoid racial heritage, with some admixture of Negroid blood, which had not changed for millennia.

Others referred to Jewish history and derived the Jewish character from the fate of the Jews, especially their socioeconomic position as strangers amid strange nations. It was, they argued, the fate of a ghettoized people, lacking of rights, prohibited from acquiring property or holding public office, that forced the Jews in medieval and modern times into commerce and the money business. This centuries-long "situational determination" became the basis of inherited abilities and inclinations, which rendered the Jews more capable in money matters than members of the rigid agricultural societies. This forced situation produced a constant "state of preparedness" in the Jews, a high degree of readiness for mobility, a critical viewing of the existing order, values, and truths, and a talent for rational doubting, for relativizing. To quote historian Péter Hanák, "Reflective and speculative thinking, utilitarianism, a distrust toward the environment, insufficient respect for the legal order and authority, all were seen to be the consequences of ghetto fate."

Yet others, especially scholars, writers, and other intellectuals, considered this explanation too one-sided. Marcell Benedek, a highly regarded non-Jewish scholarly writer, opined, "It is futile to trot out economic causes, since among hate exploiters there are many more non-Jews than Jews, and among the exploited the number of Jewish workers and employees is growing by leaps and bounds." The decisive role in the negative image of the Jew was played by sociopsychological factors. For the fact was that in Central Europe the ghetto ceased to exist only legally, and not yet socially. According to Benedek, in all Hungary "there was not one single Christian who would be able to take a totally unprejudiced, purely human position with regard to the Jews."

Several participants of the 1917 discussion proceeded from presenting the stereotypes of Jews to scrutinizing the Jewish character as it developed in reaction to the situation the Jews were forced to exist in for many generations. The exclusion, though often concealed and surreptitious, hurt the sensitivity of the assimilant Jews and increased their insecurity, which, in turn, easily changed over into unmannerliness, aggressivity. All these features had their origin in nervousness; they were the symptoms of a particular social neurosis.

The renowned Hungarian writer Anna Lesznai, in her contribution to the discussion, anticipated Kurt Lewin's famous analysis of the psychological problems of minority groups and Jewish self-hatred by some thirty years when she explained that to be a Jew was a specific "morbidly excited nervous state"; the assimilated "culture Jew" had inherited from his ghettoized ancestors a frayed nervous system, which was further constantly irritated by "that lack of stability he was swept into by not having his social place." He had broken with Orthodoxy, with ghetto Jewry, not only in externals but also in spirit, but the surrounding society did not accept him. He belonged nowhere, was everywhere a renegade, an outsider, and this produced in him an enduring, painful break in self-respect. "He whose self-esteem has been disturbed relates to the concept of authority in a false manner." On the one hand, he respects authority, fears power, and considers it desirable to acquire it, as well as rank and security, but at the same time he looks down upon authority and criticizes it sarcastically. This "belonging to nowhere" becomes the key to understanding everything, for the Jewish intellect is less bound by tradition, self-identification, and is better in recognizing the wrong in any point of view. From the sociopsychological isolation, from the Jewish "state of nerves," one can therefore also deduce the Jewish talent for relativization and abstraction, that special ability of "transmuting ideas into life-moving factors." And Lesznai summarizes: "It is under such influences and circumstances that the Jew becomes that solitary, intimidated, hurt, neurotic person, who holds himself great and yet frankly denies himself, who is deprived of all forms of earthly and heavenly eternity."

The two decades that passed between the two world wars added nothing to resolve the contradictions in the Hungarian view of the Jews. On the one hand, the Jewish stereotype remained that of a ruthless, unruly people, who, fully conscious of its own superiority, looked down upon the Christians, while, on the other, it painted the Jews as humble and subservient, compromising, even cowardly, laboring under serious inferiority complexes and neuroses. Opinions were even divided over whether it was the Orthodox Jews, who scrupulously observed their religion and customs, that were unruly and haughty; or were they, to begin with, modest, humble, timid, and only later, once they got acclimatized, did they become insolent and brazen-faced; or rather was it precisely the assimilant Jews who became more and more unsure, cowardly, opportunistic. The Jew was seen as not becoming a full-fledged Hungarian patriot even after acquiring the Hungarian language, but at the same time, the assimilated Jew represented extreme chauvinism, "a major and valuable factor of cultural nationalism." In 1938, the year the first modern anti-Jewish law was promulgated in Hungary, the well-known Hungarian cultural historian Gula Szekfü went so far as to write:

Nobody ever proclaimed Hungarian glory with such conviction, nobody ever caressed Hungarian vanity with such sweet thrill as these [Jewish] "assimilants." It was they who elevated to a dogma the greatness and almightiness of our state ideal. . . . It was they who belittled the power of the nationalities, indiscriminately attacked our allies and our enemies alike. . . . Without the Jewish press of Budapest it would have been impossible for the fight over public law and for national illusions to dominate Magyardom unrestrictedly for decades on end.

Péter Hanák in 1985 tried to resolve the contradiction between these contrasting images of the Jews by attributing the negatively weighted stereotypes to the Hungarian reaction to the Orthodox Jewish immigrants who "poured into Hungary in the interwar years from Galicia and spoke Yiddish," while ascribing the opinions that emphasized the intelligence, mental superiority, adaptability, and patriotism of the Jews to the impression the assimilant Jews made on the Hungarians. As for the former, quite a number of Hungarian students of the social scene agreed in condemning the "Galicians." One author, quoted by Miklós Bartha in a 1939 book, wrote about the "Galician": "He does not learn, does not become educated, does not wash. He makes business and children. . . . He prays loudly, and cheats silently. He is resourceful and impudent like the sparrow." Another anti-Semitic "expert" of the later interwar years, looking back at the early nineteenth century, found that the Jews, most of whom were new immigrants in that period, were "an externally filthy, culturally terribly backward social stratum."

That the timid, humble, servile Jewish type was still in evidence in the early twentieth century was attributed by Magyar observers mainly to the recurrent waves of immigrants from Galicia. They were seen as constituting the bulk of the Orthodox communities, which, despite emancipation, maintained a self-segregating ghetto existence and adhered to their old religious rules. This kind of Jew was viewed through the veil of all kinds of superstitious beliefs and was surrounded by an aura of mystery. With their peculiar garb, foreign tongue, strange religion and customs, mobility and loquacity, gestures and demeanor, they were, to the eyes of many a Hungarian observer, the very incarnation of otherness, of alienness. One also senses that behind these perceptions lurked the image of the "wandering Jew," who, as we saw, evoked the pity of Hungarian poets, but who, to the less sympathetic eye of the average Hungarian, appeared as the one who denied the Son of God, who never stopped, never rested, knew all languages but none of them well, and had no purse but had money even under his skin.

A special added feature, produced by envy masquerading as contempt, was condemnation of the alien Jew for being engaged in commerce, constantly buying and selling, mongering, doing "*gesheft.*" In the conservative worldview of the Hungarian gentry, adopted to a large extent also by the *úri* and other non-gentry layers of society, trading was

the equivalent of cheating. Hence, the Jewish merchant, from the peddler up to the mightiest master of commercial enterprises, was a dishonest character, capable of any crime. Honesty and decency, if they existed
at all among the Jews, we confined to dealings among themselves. To
cheat the gentile was part of their commercial ethic. As anti-Semitic
prejudice saw it, even if the Jew left the ghetto, rose into the ranks of the
bourgeoisie, and appeared completely Magyarized, his becoming civilized and rich only proved that he had succeeded in acquiring a fortune
by cheating.

The Hungarian antipathy for the trader Jew—as Péter Hanák
observed—soon expanded into a condemnation of the alleged Jewish
lack of sense of justice, of Jews' disregard of the legal order, and ultimately of Jewish morality in general. Especially the Budapest Jews, with
the preponderance among them of well-to-do and intellectual elements,
were seen as destructive of ancient custom, respect, family life. Thus,
two contrasting stereotypes developed: that of the Jew, who was characterized by "an unruly desire for innovation and conspicuousness, impudence, success-orientedness, criticism of every existing value, immoral-
ity; and, opposed to it, that of the Hungarian, who was characterized by
ponderous progress, manly modesty, respect for tradition and authority,
deep religious morality—and impracticality."

It was in this atmosphere, in this society that largely considered them
alien and inferior and, from whatever motivation, attributed to them
traits diametrically opposed to what it claimed for itself as the ideal
Magyar character, that the Hungarian Jews lived for a whole generation
prior to their destruction in the Holocaust. Inevitably, these stereotypes,
which the Jews constantly encountered in their contact with the gentile
Hungarians, left a mark on their self-image, and also on the kind of
character traits that they not only attributed to themselves but actually
developed.

This psychological process was complex, and manifested itself to
varying degrees in multiple phenomena in the disparate social layers of
Jewry and in its groupings by religious observance, from ultra-Neolog
assimilant to ultra-Orthodox conservative. But by and large one could
observe in most of the Jews, in any sector of the Jewish community, the
traces of psychological reaction to the way gentile Hungarians related to
them. For example, since Hungarians condemned the Jews for being
mercantile and profit-oriented, they themselves developed an internalized scale of values in which being a merchant occupied a low rung.
Since their readiness to embrace innovations was frowned upon by the
Hungarians as flightiness, they became inclined toward conservatism in
their attitudes toward social and intellectual values. Since landed prop-

erty was the only form of asset valued by the Hungarians, the Jews developed an interest in acquiring estates, even though financially those were not very profitable investments. Since the Hungarians opined that Jews maintained a stronger loyalty to the Jewish people around the world than to the Hungarian nation, the Jews emphasized that, to the contrary, they constituted a purely religious community, which had as little to do with Jews in other countries as the Hungarian Catholics had with the Catholics of France or Poland, and that they were precisely as Hungarian as the Hungarian Catholics or Protestants. And since patriotism was upheld by the Hungarians as the noblest trait, they became fervent patriots, to the point of exposing themselves to the criticism of the Hungarians that the upstart Jews wanted to teach *them* what patriotism was!

One cynically inclined historian said that every country had the Jews it deserved. If so, Hungary is a prime example of how a host country's attitude toward the Jews can affect the formation of the latters' character, and contribute to the development of a Jewish community whose specificity arose largely in response to the way the gentile enviroment saw and treated it.

The New Anti-Semitism and National Politics

The attitudes to the Jews presented above were accompanied in the interwar years by a growth of anti-Semitism, which took place not so much spontaneously among the population at large as rather due to organizational work by political leaders who saw eye to eye on little except blaming the Jews for all the ills of the country. They founded anti-Semitic associations, recruited members by the thousands, and embraced largely the same anti-Jewish programs that had been made popular by the armed and other units of the White Terror formations. Much of the impetus for these anti-Semitic organizations was resentment over the Communist regime that controlled Hungary for a few weeks in 1919, though the oldest of them, the Union of Awakening Hungarians (*Ébredö Magyarok Egyesülete*, ÉME) had been founded two years earlier, in 1917, by soldiers discharged during the war. After the war the Hungarian National Defense Association (*Magyar Országos Véderő Egyesület*, MOVE) was founded, and on January 19, 1919, Gyula Gömbös (1886–1936) was elected its president. Gömbös expanded and intensified the activities of MOVE by organizing a civilian and a military arm, both of which functioned as secret societies, with fearsome initiation ceremonies and oaths of total subordination to the leader. Under the leadeship of Gömbös, MOVE became such an influential organization that Miklós Horthy, after his election as regent of Hungary, accepted Gömbös's invitation to become its honorary president. In 1919, Dr. Károly Wolff founded the Christian National League (*Keresztény Nemzeti Liga*), likewise with two secret core groups, among whose leaders were prominent political and Church figures, including István Bethlen, Pál Teleki, László Bárdossy, and the bishops Ottokár Prohászka, Sándor Raffay, and László Ravasz. During the early 1920s, the members of these secret and public patriotic associations increased phenomenally—their number was estimated at ten thousand—and they constituted a huge nationwide network, whose activities came to be coordinated at first by the Association for Territorial Defense (*Terület-védő Liga*), and subsequently by its successor, the Federation of Social Associations (*Társadalmi Egyesületek Szövetsége*, TESz). The most important planks in the platforms of these organizations were revisionism and irredentism—that is, agitation against the Trianon Peace Treaty and the dismemberment of Hungary—and above all, anti-Semitism.

The new Hungarian anti-Semitism, which first manifested itself in the White Terror of the early post–World War I years, differed essentially from what can be called the "traditional" Hungarian anti-Semitism of the prewar decades. In those earlier times, anti-Semitism was an ideology and doctrine embraced by various elements of society and advocated in Parliament by the right-wing opposition, which had always been a small minority. The position of the government since the 1895 Law of Reception, was that the Jews were one of the several confessional denominations, all of whom had equal rights. The consistent, unfaltering stance of the government and the majority in Parliament, was based, as we have seen, both on true liberalism and on the political interest in counting the Jews as Magyars. Faced with this official position, anti-Semitism, throughout the period of the dual monarchy, remained a modest opposition movement, unable to seriously disrupt the Magyar-Jewish symbiosis.

The defeat of Hungary in World War I, and the Trianon Peace Treaty imposed after it, brought about a basic change in both the internal and external political situations, part of which was the new, postwar configuration of anti-Semitism. As already mentioned, in post-Trianon "rump" Hungary with its almost entirely Magyar population, the Jews lost their former significance as a group tipping the balance in favor of a Magyar majority in the country. Reduced to one-third of its prewar size in geography and population and struggling with great economic hardships, the country was seized with despondency and bitterness. In this mood it looked for scapegoats to blame for the catastrophe of defeat and the injustice of dismemberment visited upon it by the victorious allies. In this situation, arguments of the anti-Semites found more credence and greater resonance. Anti-Semitic agitation managed to have censuses taken that allegedly showed that the Jews were underrepresented in the fighting forces on the front, while they were "war profiteers." They were accused of responsibility for the harsh and unjust peace treaty and for the 1919 "Judeo-Bolshevism," and all other problems of the country were attributed to its having come under Jewish influence in the dual monarchy age. Similar anti-Semitic agitation took place in Germany after the war, but there it ran up against the democratic government of the Weimar Republic. In Hungary, the anti-Semites, in opposition up to that time, succeeded in penetrating the national political organs and local administrations, so that the official policy became that of the "Christian-National *kurzus*" (governmental system), of which anti-Semitism was an essential part.

Although governmental anti-Semitism was of the "moderate" variety during the Bethlen years (1921–31), and even until the eve of World War II, in word and deed the official reaction to anti-Semitic attacks was hesitant, belated, and lukewarm. Moreover, the government itself took the position, for the first time since 1895, that the Jews were a separate element in the body of the nation, different from the non-Jewish majority. This was the burden of the 1920 Numerus Clausus Law—a very bitter pill indeed for the patriotic Hungarian Jews to swallow, who until that time sincerely believed that their equality was a solidly entrenched, inalterable, and untouchable principle of the Hungarian constitution and legal system. It was extremely difficult for them to recognize that their position in the nation had changed radically, and that their otherness was now official policy subscribed to by the executive and legislative branches of their country's government.

The virulent phase of post–World War I Hungarian anti-Semitism subsided within a year or two, but open anti-Jewish agitation remained a part of the social and political scene in the country to an extent unimaginable in the preceding period.

On December 15, 1923, Tibor Eckhardt (1888–1972) was elected head of the Union of Awakening Hungarians (ÉME), and under his leadership its power increased and its anti-Semitic activities intensified. In 1924 a court in the city of Szolnok acquitted members of ÉME who were involved in bombing a Jewish charity ball in Csongrád, which has already been mentioned in chapter 38. On October 8, 1924, the Jewish deputy Béla Fábián (1889–1967), in an address to the Lower House, declared that the ÉME was primarily responsible for the cover-up of the many murders and crimes committed in Hungary during the previous four years, and he revealed the great power and influence of the Union. I could find no record of the House taking any action after Fábián's impassioned speech. What is known is that Gömbös, in his capacity as leader of the Hungarian "race protectors," was in contact with the German National Socialists and had a share in developing the myth of the Jewish exploiters of the country, agents of both Bolshevik Communism and "Jewish capitalism." Unconcerned about the contradictions in these roles attributed to the Jews, Gömbös performed another ideological sleight-of-hand: he opposed "exploitative," that is, Jewish, capitalism, but at the same time he declared himself a supporter of "creative," or Christian, capitalism, which he termed "racially homogeneous capitalism," one free of Jewish involvement. This is but one example of the common phenomenon in Hungarian anti-Semitic ideology that if Jews engaged in a certain activity or occupied a certain position, that was considered exploitation, harmful to national interests. If Christians did the same thing, it was patriotic and constructive. We shall have to come back to the role Gömbös played, but must mention here that despite his popularity as a leader of the "race protectors" and his personal friendship with Regent Horthy, he had to wait until the end of 1932 before achieving the position he had aspired to for a decade, that of prime minister of Hungary.

From the end of World War I to the end of World War II, Hungary, officially a kingdom, was headed by Adm. Miklós Horthy as regent, and for ten of these years, from 1921 to 1931, the country was governed by Prime Minister Count István Bethlen (1874–1947), a liberal-conservative, under whose stewardship conditions in the country became gradually consolidated. Bethlen, although he had a strong personal dislike for Jews, recognized that without the cooperation of Jewish capitalists the national economy could not be placed on a secure footing, and Hungary's ability to negotiate foreign credits would be poor. Gyula Gömbös, as leader of the radical right wing of the Party of Unity, and his "race protector" comrades accused the prime minister of betraying "Christian ideology" and once again placing the country at the mercy of "domestic and international Jewish capital." Regent Horthy, who had to decide between competing political programs, took Bethlen's side, and as a consequence, Gömbös left the governmental party and founded the racist Party of Hungarian Independence. Bethlen's 1923 negotiations succeeded in obtaining from the great powers a loan of 250 million gold crowns to eliminate Hungary's budgetary deficits. After 1925, Hungarian society began to feel the effects of the influx of capital, in the form of additional large-scale loans, which also contributed to diminishing the country's isolation on the international scene and developing closer relations with a *a külföld* ("the abroad").

It was this easing up of the relations between Hungary and the ex-Entente powers that motivated Vilmos Vázsonyi, without modifying his rigidly anti-Zionist stand, to admit the necessity of Hungarian Jewry's maintaining relations with foreign Jews. Vázsonyi, together with the Neolog Jewish establishment, had opposed all formal links with the Jewries of other countries, and even in 1925 he retracted as soon as the Zionists claimed that his words essentially supported their position. However, he could no longer deny that the Hungarian Jews, like the Russian and Rumanian Jews in the past, were sufficiently in danger to require the assistance of international Jewish organizations.

One of the last acts of the 1922–26 Second National Assembly was to reestablish the Upper House for the purpose of functioning as a "safety brake." Its membership was also to include representatives of the "received" religious denominations, but it took the intervention of a Jewish member of parliament, Pál Sándor, to modify the original plan to read that the Israelite denomination should be represented in it in the person of two rabbis, one Orthodox and one Neolog. The election of the Orthodox member went smoothly: there was only one candidate, the venerable octogenarian chief rabbi of the Orthodox Congregation of Budapest, R. Koppel Reich (1838–1929), who was elected unanimously.

Not so the election of the Neolog representative. Here a controversy developed between the Israelite Congregation of Pest and the Neolog National Office that rapidly degenerated into an ugly brawl. The former and its supporters wanted to see Dr. Simon Hevesi, chief rabbi of Pest, seated in the Upper House, while the latter, supported by most of the Jewish congregations outside Pest, wanted the chief rabbi of Szeged, Dr. Immanuel Löw (1854–1944), to have the honor. The struggle between the two parties was protracted and offensive of good taste, but at the end the laurels went to Dr. Löw, who, incidentally, in no way participated in the campaign. (To compensate Dr. Hevesi for the defeat, the Israelite Congregation of Pest gave him the title "leading chief rabbi," which was considered a slight by his colleague Chief Rabbi Dr. Gyula Fischer [1861–1944], who was seven years his senior and had been appointed to the Dohány Street Synagogue simultaneously with Hevesi in 1905, when both of them were accorded the rank of chief rabbi. The raising Hevesi above Fischer was an injury that Fischer was unable to overcome to the end of his life.)

As for their role in the Upper House, neither R. Reich (who was too old to attend its deliberations) nor R. Löw (who disliked traveling from Szeged to Budapest) made any significant contribution. That remained the privilege of the other Jewish members, of whom no fewer than seven were elected in 1927, not as Jews but as representatives of various public bodies, economic and financial institutions, and press organs. They were the attorneys Dr. Samu Glücksthal and Dr. Lajos Láng, both members of the Budapest Municipal Council; Jenő Vida, general manager of the Hungarian General Mining Company, Leo Budai-Goldberger, and Rudolf Frommer de Fegyvernek, all three representing big industry; the banker Sándor Fleissig, president of the Budapest Stock Exchange; and József Vészi, editor-in-chief of the foremost Budapest paper, *Pester Lloyd*. None of these men felt that it was their task to function as representatives of Hungarian Jewry in the Upper House; their work concentrated on the interests of their specific constituencies.

Also in 1927 three new Jewish members were elected to the Lower House. All three were attorneys: Géza Dési was returned as a member of the government party and Marcell Baracs and Jenő Gálas members of the opposition. Of the older members, Pál Sándor, Ernő Bródy, and Béla Fábián were returned, so that the Lower House had six Jewish legislators. (Vilmos Vázsonyi, as we recall, died in 1926.) All these politicians took an active part in the leadership of the Hungarian Jewish establishment until the very days of the first anti-Jewish law (1938), and did it, as Lajos Szabolcsi remarks in his memoirs, "better or worse, with more or less adroitness, but with undoubted goodwill"—to which one is tempted to add, "and with regrettable shortsightedness as far as Germany's increasing influence on Hungary's anti-Jewish stance was concerned."

In 1926 the government introduced a currency reform, replacing the overinflated old monetary unit with a new one, called *pengő*, which had the value of 12,500 old crowns and proved to be stable, not least thanks to the sizable foreign loans that bolstered the Hungarian economy. However, neither the economic and social improvements achieved by the Bethlen government nor the seating of Jewish representatives qua Jews in the Upper House meant that anti-Jewish feelings disappeared or even abated. The virulent anti-Semitism that peaked after the fall of the 1919 Communist dictatorship was too strongly embedded in Magyar thinking and feeling (undoubtedly nurtured also by the centuries-long insistence of the Christian Church that the Jews were Christ-killers) to be wiped away as easily as a law could be replaced. Jew-beatings, although not as violent as in the first two years after the fall of the Communist Council Republic, became something of an established routine at the universities: within a few days after the annual fall registration, notes would appear on the doors of classrooms and auditoriums saying, "I'll come tomorrow. Simon Hirig," or "ÉME, the dread of the Jew-boys." (Simon Hirig was the mythical embodiment of the Jew-beater, whose last name was taken from the Yiddish originally Hebrew word *hereg*, meaning "killing," and ÉME, as we recall, stood for the Union of Awakening Hungarians.) Those Jewish students who did not heed these warnings, or perhaps did not notice them, and showed up next day, were mercilessly beaten or thrown down the stairs, whereupon classes would be suspended for a few days.

The immediate impetus (or excuse) for an especially violent series of beatings was the announcement by Prime Minister Bethlen on October 20, 1927, that he was about to introduce a bill to modify the numerus clausus. The miniser of *kultusz*, Count Kunó Klebelsberg, opined that "the revision of the numerus clausus was premature, and I fear that great demonstrations will ensue at the universities." If a minister "fears" something, that something usually does take place, and four days after Bethlen's announcement, and for a full week thereafter, violent anti-Jewish attacks occurred in Budapest and several other cities. In Budapest alone, 174 wounded Jewish students were taken by ambulance from the university to the Rókus Hospital. (At the same time, coincidentally, brutal pogroms broke out against Hungarian Jews in Transylvania, Rumania, where they were accused of Hungarian patriotism.)

While the leadership of the Hungarian right heaped accusations and defamations on the heads of the Jews, the Jewish spokesmen reacted by engaging in abject demonstrations of their unshaken Magyardom. Pál Sándor, one of the most stouthearted defenders of the Jews in the Lower House, published an article in *Egyenlőség* whose title speaks for itself: "Hail to you, O Israel, that you could again suffer for the Hungarian fatherland!"

The manifestations of anti-Semitism were paralleled by certain demographic trends within the Hungarian Jewish community. In the Israelite Congregation of Pest, in which 40 percent of Hungarian Jewry was concentrated after Trianon, the total number of Jews had consistently increased until 1920: it grew from 44,890 (or 16.6 percent of the city's total population) in 1869, to 168,985 (23 percent of the total) in 1900, to 203,687 (23.1 percent) in 1910, to a maximum of 215,512 (23.2 percent) in 1920. After that, however, as pointed out by historian György Haraszti, a decline set in, brought about by the combined effects of conversions, mixed marriages, low birthrate, and emigration, so that in 1930 there were only 204,371 (20.3 percent) Jews in the city; in 1935, only 201,069 (19.2 percent), and in 1941, just 184,453 (15.8 percent). That is to say, the demographic losses of Budapest Jewry in the two decades between 1920 and 1941 amounted to 31,059, or 14.5 percent. Within this general loss, especially notable was the share of Jewish outmarriages and conversions. As shown by the studies of Victor Karády, the outmarriages had increased dramatically during the years of World War I, reaching 29.5 percent of all Jewish marriages in the city in 1916–17, then hovering around 25–32 percent in the interwar years and peaking at 35.5 percent in the four months of July through October 1941, which figure was exceeded only in 1945 (the year of Budapest's liberation from Nazi occupation), when it reached 37.8 percent. As for conversions, Karády has observed direct correlation between anti-Semitic activity and the relinquishing of their religion by the Jews: the more intense the former, the higher the latter. Thus, during the years of World War I only about 500 Jews left Judaism annually; in 1919 their number jumped to 7,146. Thereafter the figure receded until 1938 (the year of the first anti-Jewish law), when 8,548 left Judaism, and remained very high in the subsequent years. As these figures indicate, Hungarian Jewry seemed to be embarked on a road of gradual self-liquidation.

Internal Jewish Life—Zionism

As far as internal Jewish life was concerned, the outbreak of anti-Semitism in 1919 and its occasionally equally virulent sequels in the 1920s created two contrary trends: an increase in conversions, and a strengthening of Jewish self-identification.

While in the two decades from 1890 to 1910 a total of 5,046 Hungarian Jews, or an average of 252 annually, converted to Christianity, in 1919 conversions reached a record high of 7,146; in 1920 it was 1,925; in 1921, 821; in 1922, 499; in 1923, 458; and in 1924, 433. The figures for 1919–24 indicate a definite positive correlation between the intensity of anti-Semitism and the number of conversions: the outbreak of violent anti-Semitism after the fall of the 1919 Communist dictatorship produced a very high number of conversions. Thereafter, as the anti-Semitic tide receded, the number of conversions diminished. In the same years there was also an increase in the number of converted Jews who returned to Judaism (in 1924 reconversions reached 75 percent of the number of conversions), which indicates that many of the earlier conversions were acts of panic that were later regretted and rectified.

As for the strengthening of Jewish self-assurance, it was evidenced by several phenomena. Only one them can be quantified: in those years 8,300 new members were admitted to the *Hevra Kadisha* of Pest, the traditional Jewish religious society whose original purposes were to support the poor, take care of the sick, and bury the dead, but which in the form it assumed in the Israelite Congregation of Pest included a wide range of philanthropic activities. Other developments were either of an educational and literary nature, or pro-Zionist in character.

One of the most important educational developments was the opening of Jewish *gimnáziums*: in 1919 two, one for boys and one for girls, were established by the Israelite Congregation of Pest, and in 1921 a Jewish high school was also opened in Debrecen. Toward the end of the 1920s a Jewish public library started functioning in the building of the great synagogue in the Dohány Street. About the same time the Pest congregation initiated a lecture series on the relationship between religion and society. In 1927, the two-volume *Universal History of the Jews from the Babylonian Captivity to Our Days* (in Hungarian) was published in Budapest by Ármin Kecskeméti. In 1929, after a hiatus of ten years, the Israelite Hungarian Literary Society (IMIT) resumed publishing its *Year Book*s.

These efforts at disseminating Jewish culture and strengthening Jewish education were paralleled by the resumption and broadening of pro-Zionist work, which was facilitated after the mandate for Palestine was awarded to Great Britain by the League of Nations in 1920. This international sanctioning of the Jewish settlement and building activities in Palestine could not fail to impress Hungarian Jewry. In 1925 influential Jewish voices began to be heard in Budapest in favor of Hungarian Jewish participation in what was referred to not as "Zionism" but as "the Palestine work." Since the Hungarian Jewish establishment remained opposed to "political Zionism," the Zionist leaders tried to win its support for the cultural activities and institutions of the *yishuv* (the Jewish community of Palestine). At the general assembly of the Israelite Congregation of Pest in June 1925, Dr. Lipót Osztern, president of the Hungarian Zionist Organization (dormant because it had no official authorization) and member of the Congregation's governing council, reported on the founding of the Hebrew University of Jerusalem, and moved that the Congregation participate in its support. In September 1925, even Ferenc Mezey (1860–1927), president of the Neolog National Office and a staunch anti-Zionist, declared, "We must take part in the Palestine work, which is the rescuing, building, helping action of universal Jewry, in which the Jewry of the whole world participates, and the time has come for us to dispel the erroneous views connected with it."

The next summer, Gyula Fischer, chief rabbi of the Pest Congregation, came out in favor of "Palestine work." Speaking from the pulpit of the Dohány Street Synagogue, he said:

> Zionist and non-Zionist must equally welcome with enthusiastic joy the miracle of the resurrection of the Holy Land and the renaissance of Hebrew culture that takes place there. . . . I am no Zionist, but to deny our historical Jewish past, to exclude ourselves from the Jewish building work is impossible. . . . The Hungarian love of the fatherland and the Jewish

love of Palestine do not exclude each other: they are two flowers from whose intertwining only light and scent can spread into the souls.

R. Fischer's pro-Zionist stance was exceptional. The official Jewish leadership found itself in a political and psychological quandary: the World Zionist Organization and the great international Jewish welfare bodies had their headquarters in ex-Entente countries. To make common cause with them, the superpatriotic Hungarian Jewish establishment feared, could create the impression in Hungary that Hungarian Jewry was affiliated with or cooperated with the homeland's enemies.

Nevertheless, in December 1926, the Pro Palestine Federation of Hungarian Jews was founded with the purpose of attracting non-Zionists to the work of rebuilding a Jewish Palestine. The initiative was taken by József Patai, who thereby anticipated by almost three years the establishment of the expanded Jewish Agency for Palestine in Zurich in 1929 as a body representing both Zionists and non-Zionists. Utilizing his ability to make friends and influence people, Patai persuaded several leading Hungarian Jewish personalities to lend their names to the Pro Palestine Federation, whose aims were to be establishing economic and cultural ties between Hungary and Jewish Palestine, and supporting the scholarly and scientific work of the Hebrew University of Jerusalem. The Federation began functioning in 1927 with Baron Adolf Kohner (1865–1937), Court Councillor Károly Baracs (1868–1929), and Court Councillor Ferenc Székely (1858–1936) as presidents. Its sections and their presidents included the Colonization Section (Professor Ignác Pfeiffer), the Rebuilding Section (Government High Councillor Ignác Freidmann), Cultural Affairs (József Patai), University Affairs (Gyula Donáth), Library Affairs (Bernát Heller), Social Affairs (Mrs. Vilmos Bacher), and Economic and Commercial Affairs (Ernő Makai). The activities of the Keren Kayemet (National Fund) and the Keren Hayesod (Foundation Fund) were conducted under the aegis of the Pro Palestine Federation. Its membership remained small throughout: in 1928 it counted one thousand members. But by having among its leaders and members individuals who belonged to the Jewish economic, social, and intellectual elite of Hungary, it achieved something very important on the Hungarian Jewish scene of the 1920s, especially vis-à-vis the still anti-Zionist leadership of the Pest congregation, and that was to make Zionism—or at least work for Jewish Palestine—*salonfähig*, that is, acceptable in good society. It was also largely due to the existence of the Pro Palestine Federation that in 1929, at the founding conference of the enlarged Jewish Agency for Palestine in Zurich, for the first time Jewish representatives participated who filled important rabbinical positions in Hungary: they were Chief Rabbi Gyula Fischer of the Israelite Congregation of Pest and Chief Rabbi Immanuel Löw of Szeged, who, as we stated above, was the official representative of Hungarian Neolog Jewry in the Upper House of Parliament. Löw and Ferenc Székely were elected as non-Zionists, and József Patai as a Zionist, to the Council of the Jewish Agency, while Chief Rabbi Gyula Fischer, Ignác Friedmann, Ernő Makai, and Prof. Lajos Török, all of Budapest, were elected deputy members.

This did not mean that the official leadership of Hungarian Jewry ceased its opposition to Zionism. On the contrary: leaders of both the Neolog and Orthodox communities continued to oppose even the granting of government authorization to the Hungarian Zionist Organization. In 1927, when authorization was finally granted, Lajos Hartstein, vice-president of the Orthodox National Office, asked the Ministry of the Interior to withdraw it, or else he would convene an Orthodox rabbinical assembly to pronounce a ban (*herem*) on the Zionist Organization. In the event, the authorization was not withdrawn, and no Orthodox ban on Zionism was pronounced, but the sequence of events shows how strong the official Hungarian Jewish anti-Zionist position was, and how hesitant the change of attitude about establishing closer contact with (and obtaining some sorely needed help from) the international Jewish community.

Two more developments concerning the Zionist movement in Hungary must be mentioned, however briefly. One was the proliferation of Zionist literature in the interwar years, which saw the publication in Hungarian translation of writings by Theodor Herzl, Max Nordau, Ahad Haam, Chaim Weizmann, Nahum Goldmann, Martin Buber, Osias Thon, Adolf Böhm, and others, as well as of original works by Hungarian Zionist authors. These releases by various Hungarian Jewish publishers, including several not affiliated with the Zionist movement, was a tangible indication of the slow but steady growth in the popular appeal of Zionism despite all the antagonisms and obstacles put in its way by the official Jewish establishment, first and foremost by the leaders of the Israelite Congregation of Pest.

The other development was less edifying: it was the struggle, which degenerated into mutual denunciations, between the Hungarian Zionist Association and the Hungarian chapter of the Zionist Revisionists. The Revisionist Organization, known by its Hebrew name *haTzohar* (acrostic of *haTziyonim haRevizionistim*), was founded in 1925 in Paris. In 1933 Zeev Jabotinsky assumed its personal leadership, and in 1935 his followers voted to secede from the World Zionist Organization (WZO) and found the New Zionist Organization (NZO). The major difference between the two revolved around general political principles: the WZO was for accommodation and cooperation with Great Britain, the mandatory power in control of Palestine, while the NZO advocated maximalist, energetic, and (if necessary) anti-British activities for the purpose of establishing a Jewish state on both banks of the Jordan.

In Hungary the first Revisionist group was founded in April 1935, and soon thereafter the struggle began between the Hungarian Zionist Association (HZA) and the Hungarian New Zionist Organization (HNZO). It found expression in mutual attacks in the periodicals of the two groups (the HNZO launched several papers of its own), physical disturbances and disruptions of each other's meetings and lectures, and by 1937 also mutual accusations and denunciations addressed to the Ministry of the Interior.

The sorry spectacle of two Zionist formations fighting each other is not important enough to be detailed in a general history of Hungarian Jews, but it should be mentioned that the muckraking degenerated to a level lower than that of the quarrel between the Zionists and the anti-Zionist leaders of the Israelite Congregation of Pest. It was only with the promulgation of the first two anti-Jewish laws (in 1938 and 1939) that the vindictive animosity between the two Zionist groups subsided, as did the hostility between the Zionists and the anti-Zionists.

The Jew as the New "Other"

The reluctance of the Hungarian Jewish establishment to come to terms with Zionism was but one manifestation of the generally hidebound, conservative attitude it embraced toward the position of the Jews in Hungary in general. Another was the unwillingness (or inability) to recognize that as a consequence of the Trianon dismemberment of Hungary, the significance of the Jewish population in Hungarian politics had undergone a profound change. Prior to Trianon, of the roughly 20 million inhabitants of Hungary fewer than half were Magyar Christians, and somewhat more than half were non-Magyar minorities, with their own languages and ethnicities. It was thus in the political interest of the Magyars to count the Jews as Magyars (of the Israelite persuasion). After all, the Jews had become or were becoming Hungarian speakers, and their sentiments were Magyar, in sharp contrast with the Slovak, Ruthenian, Rumanian, and other minorities, who were opposed to Magyarization and openly strove for national autonomy or even full independence. Counting the million Jews as Magyars made the difference between the Magyar population being a majority or a minority in its own country. This was crucial not only within the borders of Hungary itself, but also in its relations with Austria and its position within the multiethnic Austro-Hungarian Empire. Thus, from the emancipation of the Jews (1867) and even more from the *recepció* of the Jewish religion (1895) until Trianon, Hungarian national interests coincided with the Magyar nationalistic sentiments of the Jews. Successive Hungarian governments treated the Jews as a fully Hungarian religious community. It was this position that ingrained itself into the Jewish consciousness during those pre-Trianon decades and made the Jews believe they were equal members of the Magyar nation.

After Trianon the attitude of the government underwent a fundamental change. There was, first of all, the painful interlude of the Communist Council Republic, the majority of whose leaders were Jews or converted Jews (even though neither category had special sympathy for Jews and Judaism, and both considered their Jewish birth an unimportant coincidence). The Hungarian political leadership and the people at large were opposed to the Communist regime, and identified Communism with Jews. The anti-Semitic atrocities of the White Terror of 1919-21—only diffidently opposed by government forces—was a telling sign of the upsurge of the new anti-Jewish attitude that gripped the nation. Even the "moderate," that is, less extreme, political leadership that gained power in the country after 1921 took a new look at the Jews and found that their value for Magyar politics had in effect disappeared with Trianon. In the new *Csonkamagyarország* (Rump Hungary), practically the entire population was homogeneously Magyar in language and ethnicity, so that it no longer needed the remaining half-million Jews for any demographic purpose. On the other hand, the "otherness" of the Jews, which in pre-Trianon Hungary passed unnoticed or was overlooked in the overall political perspective, was now felt to be grating in a country with an almost all-Magyar, all-Christian population.

Once official sanction was given to the feeling that the Jews were not an integral part of the nation but an alien (or at least differing) element, the position they had gained in the preceding decades appeared as "domination" of Hungarian economy, society, and culture. An added factor was that in the country reduced to one third of its former size and population, the overall economic situation was precarious, and the Jews —now openly considered a separate, not fully Hungarian element— were seen as having preempted jobs and positions that by right should be held by Magyars. The strength of the Jewish economic position in the country, in industry, commerce, and banking, as well as cultural fields, was suddenly felt to be out of proportion and lacking social justification. The Jews' concentration in higher-income occupations was taken as economic exploitation of the Magyar population; that so many of them were writers, journalists, artists, publishers, and professionals was taken to mean that they had imposed their alien culture and harmful mores on Magyar society. This was a gut feeling, which did not need, and did not have, any real underpinning. As far as I know, there existed no factual sociological studies to show what the concrete differences were between the autochthonous Hungarian Christian culture and the Jewish Hungarian culture represented by the Jewish intelligentsia, let alone why the Jewish variety was inferior and harmful to the non-Jewish majority. All anti-Semitic argument needed was to point out that in some field or other the Jews were "dominant," and it followed from this that such a "domination" was harmful, constituted a nefarious alien influence, and had to be eliminated. Singling out the Jews as culprits had yet another psychological advantage: once the Jews were felt to be "others," all the unsatisfactory circumstances of life in Rump Hungary could be ascribed to Jewish presence, Jewish influence, Jewish domination, and Jewish exploitation of the country.

This is, of course, a highly schematized and generalized interpretation of the change that took place after World War I in the Hungarian attitude toward the Jews, but by and large it points to the major factors that brought it about. The phenomenon itself was unmistakable, and the leaders of the Jewish community—intelligent and perceptive men who unquestionably had the welfare of their flock at heart—could not have failed to become painfully aware of it. Where they did fail was in recognizing the underlying factors of the change, in particular the sober fact that the Hungarian political leaders turned against the Jews simply because they no longer needed them to strengthen the position of Magyardom in the country. They also failed to recognize that the post-Trianon Hungarian attitude to the Jews proved something they just did not want to admit: that the otherness of the Jews had remained a permanent fixture in the Magyar mind all along. In the pre-Trianon era, the awareness of the Jew as "the other" had been buried under overriding political considerations, but once those considerations disappeared, it surfaced again and took an even stronger form—adding a new racial aspect to the old religious one.

Since the Jewish leadership did not understand, or acknowledge, the root causes of the new post-Trianon anti-Semitism, it countered with the same old arguments that had seemed effective in the pre-Trianon decades: We Jews—they never tired of proclaiming—are Magyars of the Mosaic faith, we are as good and as patriotic Magyars as any of the Christian Hungarians; therefore, this new anti-Semitic aberration has no basis in fact; once you recognize this, you will clasp us to your bosom again as in the good old days.

That this was basically the position of the Jewish leaders in the 1920s and most of the 1930s is documented by their reaction, first to the 1920 Numerus Clausus Law, and then to the 1938 and 1939 anti-Jewish laws. They put up a valiant struggle against these laws, which infringed on Hungarian Jewry's basic rights as equal citizens of the country, but until 1939 they rejected any help the influential Jewish communities of the West (primarily England and France) could have provided by putting political pressure on Hungary, either directly or through the League of Nations. The considerations that motivated the Hungarian Jewish leadership were complex, but the fact remains that it explicitly asked the Jews of England and France and the representatives of those two countries in the League of Nations not to interfere in an issue which, they insisted, was purely internal (see preceding chapter). This position certainly strengthened the hand of those in Hungary who felt they could legislate the Jews out of their positions without having to fear any adverse reaction from abroad.

This position of the Hungarian Jewish leadership, as we shall see in the next chapter, was modified only reluctantly and belatedly under the impact of the anti-Jewish laws of 1938 and 1939. First, however, we must go back to developments that took place in Hungary from the early 1930s on, and had a profound impact on the position of the Hungarian Jews.

The economic crisis that gripped Hungary in 1929 worsened so much in summer of 1931 that Prime Minister István Bethlen felt unable to cope with it, and tendered his resignation. Regent Horthy thereupon asked Count Gyula Károlyi (1871–1947), who in 1919 had headed the short-lived government of Arad and Szeged until the Communist takeover, to form a new government. A wave of strikes and mass arrests followed, and soon Károlyi, too, had no choice but to resign. At that juncture Horthy turned to the rightist leader Gyula Gömbös, and after extracting from him a promise to maintain the existing governmental system and to refrain from propagating racist ideas, asked him in October 1932 to form a new government.

Two more aspects of Jewish otherness must be considered: one is the criminality pattern of the Jewish segment, which was radically different from that of the general population. The differences between the Catholics (the majority population) and the Jews were most conspicuous in two areas: violent crimes, and what the statistics termed "economic" or "symbolic" crimes. In 1930 no Jew and in 1942 one Jew was convicted of murder or manslaughter, while in the same two years, 190 and 164 Catholics were convicted for those crimes. In 1930 nine Jews and 261 Catholics, and in 1942 one Jew and 155 Catholics, were convicted for rape; the convictions in those two years for infanticide, abortion, and exposure of infants were three and five for Jews as against 271 and 392 for Catholics; for grievous bodily harm, 34 and 38 Jews as against 3,481 and 2,489 Catholics; for assault on persons, no Jews as against 58 and 70 Catholics. On the other hand, the Jewish rates of white-collar "economic" and "symbolic" crimes (libel and slander, false accusation, perjury, forgery of handwriting, blackmail, embezzlement, misappropriation, larceny, fraud, extortion, extortionate pricing) were much higher than the Catholics'. As a result, the overall total number of those convicted for both types of crimes in 1930 was 342 Jews per 100,000 of the Jewish population over fifteen years of age, and 178 Catholics per 100,000 of the Catholic population over fifteen years of age. Of these 178 Catholics convicted, 106 were for violent crimes, while of the 342 Jews convicted, 13 were for violent crimes.The rate of conviction of Calvinists in the same year for violent crimes was 74 per 100,000 people over fifteen years of age, and of Lutherans also 74.

Two general observations can be appended to these statistics of crimes. One is psychological: they show that the Jews were much less prone to violence than the non-Jewish Hungarians. To commit murder, manslaughter, rape, or infanticide was, with a very few exceptions, beyond the ken of the Hungarian Jews. This was in keeping with the historical record of Jewish criminality in Hungary in the sixteenth to eighteenth centuries, which we discussed in chapter 11. The second observation is economic. The higher rate of "economic or symbolic" crimes among the Jews must be attributed not to a greater inclination among the Jews to commit such crimes but rather to the much higher proportion of Jews engaged in the types of occupations within which such crimes do occur in every society. If statistics were available comparing the numbers of such crimes committed in relation to the numbers of Jews and non-Jews engaged in commercial occupations, they would, in all probability, show similar rates among the Jews and non-Jews. This leaves the statistics of violent crimes as undoubted indications of a psychological otherness, as far as criminal behavior is concerned.

The second differentiating factor between the Jews and non-Jews was the level of education. As late as in 1930, of the total male population of Hungary aged six years and older, 7.8 percent were illiterate. Of the same age group among the Jews in Budapest only 0.8 percent and in the countryside only 2.0 percent were illiterate—according to official Hungarian statistical publications. However, it is not at all clear whether Jews who could not read Hungarian but could read Hebrew (an elementary religious requirement) and Yiddish (written in Hebrew characters) were counted as illiterate. Of the total male population aged six and older, 10.8 percent had attended at least four years of primary and four years of secondary school (or a total of eight years of schooling); among the Budapest Jews this percentage was 56.5 percent, among Jews of the countryside, 36.6 percent. Of all the Hungarian males aged six or older, 5.8 percent completed eight years of high school (a total of twelve years of school attendance), while among the Budapest Jews the level was 31.7 percent, and among the rural Jews, 17.0 percent. Finally, among the total population 2.1 percent graduated from a university or some other institution of higher learning, while among the Jews of Budapest 8.1 percent did, and among those of the countryside, 5.0 percent did. These figures show that the Jews of Hungary represented a much more literate, better-educated segment of the population than the non-Jews. As the data presented in chapter 35 indicated, this Jewish tendency to literacy and concentration in professional occupations had a history in Hungary of several decades. By the interwar years it constituted an additional significant element in the Jewish otherness, which the right wing did not fail to point to and use as an argument in its anti-Semitic propaganda efforts.

The Gömbös and Darányi Years

In his October 11, 1932, inaugural speech in the Lower House, Gyula Gömbös expressed ideas and intentions that strengthened the determination of the Hungarian Jewish leadership to continue its traditional policy of declaring Hungarian Jewry's patriotism and identification with the country and its people. Gömbös said:

> To Jewry, in turn, I openly and sincerely declare: I have revised my position. That part of Jewry that throws in its lot with the Hungarian nation I wish to regard as brothers, as I do my Hungarian brothers. I saw Jewish heroes in the war; I know some who earned gold medals for heroism, and I know they fought bravely and heroically. I know leading Jewish figures who are praying with me for Hungary's future. I know that they will be the first to condemn that part of Jewry that does not want to or cannot assimilate itself into the nation's social order.

These words, the likes of which Gömbös often repeated, clearly indicated to the Hungarian Jewish leaders what was expected of them, and they responded accordingly. On the one hand, they made use of whatever connections they had with the leaders of world Jewry to solicit its political help for *Hungary*, and on the other, they rejected all attempts by the same leaders to help Hungarian *Jewry* to better its position. In April 1933, the Hungarian Jewish leaders approached Herbert Lehman, the Jewish governor of New York State, asking him to use his influence with the representatives of the Powers then meeting in New York City to rectify the injustices done to Hungary at Trianon, not omitting to add that such intervention would benefit Hungarian Jewry. Yet, soon thereafter (in January 1934), the Israelite Congregation of Pest found it necessary to adopt a resolution at its general assembly that it would not follow the example of foreign Jewries, was "not animated by any special Jewish national chimera," and would "resist the attempts . . . to transplant into [its] midst the currents and movements that have taken root among the Jews abroad." They coupled this protestation with the usual patriotic declaration: "We want to go forward in our own way, and our way is the inseparably intertwined route of Jewry and Magyardom. . . . We cling indomitably to our Magyardom, and we cannot allow this to be interfered with by foreign, international currents, even praiseworthy ones."

While Hungarian Jewry was thus willing to ask for the help of world Jewry for the benefit of Hungary as a whole, but refused all foreign Jewish help ("interference") for Hungarian Jewry specifically, the position of the Gömbös government on the "Jewish question" was no less ambiguous. It was understood that the Jews, as a separate and not quite Hungarian population, had to be kept down and their influence in all aspects of Hungarian life drastically curtailed; however, it was likewise clear that the country's shaky economy needed the Jews' business and financial activities. What Gömbös tried to do was to sail a middle course between the conflicting demands of the anti-Semites, whose influence increased under his stewardship, and of the harsh economic realities, which could not be ignored.

Hitler's rise to power in Germany in 1933 affected both the internal and external politics of Hungary. Internally, the taking over of Germany's government by the National Socialists strengthened the Hungarian right, which considered the events in Hungary's powerful neighbor an example to follow. Externally, Gömbös was able to reach understandings with the new Germany, which he chalked up as successes in foreign affairs. He entered into a supplementary economic agreement with Germany, and in March 1934 signed in Rome the Italian-Hungarian-Austrian tripartite Danubian Agreement. In January 1935, Gömbös forced Béla Imrédy and Miklós Kállay to resign from the government, and submitted a plan to transform Hungary into a corporate state on the Italian model. Sharp disagreements between Gömbös and Bethlen obliged Gömbös to resign in March 1934, but Horthy promptly asked him to form a new government, and he, in turn, demanded the dissolution of Parliament and new elections.

According to contemporary observers, the 1935 elections, in which the Party of National Unity gained 170 of the 245 seats in Parliament, was the most corrupt and violent in Hungary's history. Following it, Gömbös was unable to obtain support from Germany and Italy for his irredentist ambitions, and the internal opposition to him intensified both from the liberal side and from the unexpected formation of an ultrarightist block. Still, just before his final illness, Gömbös had a chance to at least initiate some anti-Jewish steps that were in keeping with his right-wing nationalistic outlook.

One of these steps was to establish, in 1935, a separate Ministry of Industry headed by Géza Bornemissza, the one-time founder of *Hungaria*, the radical-rightist union of engineers. To enable the ministry to assume effective control over various aspects of Jewish industrial enterprises, it instructed the Chamber of Engineers to prepare a survey of all the engineers in the country, including their religion, field of specialization, place of employment, and earnings.

It is an interesting testimony to the complexities and inconsistencies of Hungarian internal politics that while Gömbös was a self-proclaimed racist, a leader of the Hungarian Race Protector Party, who would have liked to carry out a totally fascist program, under his administration the Hungarian Jews nevertheless achieved some minor improvements in their situation. For one thing, in addition to the two chief rabbis, six more Jews became members of the Upper House of Parliament. For another with the approval of the Gömbös government a national congress of the Neolog Jews and a conference of the Orthodox Jews took place in 1935, at which important modernizations were introduced into the organizational statutes of Hungarian Jewry.

Gömbös died in 1936, and Horthy asked Kálmán Darányi (1886–1939) to form a new government. Under Darányi's leadership the fascist parties, organized after foreign models, multiplied and gained in strength. Foremost among them were the Party of National Will, established in 1935 by Ferenc Szálasi, and the Hungarian National Defense Association (MOVE). This did not bode well for the Jews. In a speech at Szeged in April 1937, Darányi came out openly for introducing legal measures against what he described as Jewish domination of certain occupations. He promised to alleviate unemployment among the educated by "constitutionally" limiting the number of Jews in the professions to their percentage in the population. This was the first time since the Numerus Clausus Law of 1920 that the government again declared itself in favor of discriminatory measures against the Jews. Within less than a year, in a programmatic address at Győr on March 5, 1938, Darányi said about the "Jewish question":

I see the essence of the question in that the Jews living within the borders of the country, due to their specific disposition and situation, but partly also because of their indifference toward the Hungarian race, play a disproportionately great role in certain branches of economic life. . . . The contrast that has developed out of this particular situation hinders the total pooling of forces, and is a constant irritant in the public life of the country. Hence, a basic condition of the legal and planned solution of the question is that we create a just situation—a just situation that will remedy or eliminate the mentioned social disproportion, and reduce the influence of Jewry in the cultural and other areas of national life to a proper scale. Such an arrangement, which will provide the proper preconditions for Christian society in the areas of industry, commerce, and credit, in the undertakings of economic life, will also redound to the benefit of Jewry itself, because it will be suitable to substantially mitigating anti-Semitism, and with it the spread of extreme intolerant movements.

One week later, Germany annexed Austria (the *Anschluss*, March 12–13, 1938), the first of Hitler's moves to expand his control to the south and east of Germany. The enthusiastic welcome Vienna gave to Hitler speeded up the Hungarian turn to the right, and within a few weeks the Hungarian Parliament passed the Law of 1938:XV, which became known as the First Hungarian Jewish Law (see chapter 40).

The Jews in Industry

The engineering survey referred to above was carried out in 1937, and its data reveal the share of Jews in the Hungarian industry of the time. It shows that the Jewish ownership of industrial enterprises by far exceeded the percentage of Jews among engineers employed by industrial firms. Thus, while 64 percent of medium to large chemical industrial firms were owned by Jews, only 15 percent of the engineers they employed were Jews. The figures are similar for the textile, paper, and machine industries. In some of these, the percentage of Jewish engineers employed was minuscule: only 1.2 percent of the engineers in metallurgy and 0.5 percent of those in mining were Jewish, and there were no Jews in forestry. Exceptions were architecture and mechanical engineering: of the architects engaged in building construction in 1937, 38 percent were Jewish, most of them working in private practice; in mechanical engineering 22 percent of the engineers were originally Jewish (of whom 30 percent were converts to Christianity), many of them employed by such large Jewish-owned firms as Ganz and Co. and the Manfred Weiss Works. All in all, however, in no other profession was the decline in Jewish participation as swift and massive as in engineering, where the overall percentage of Jews dropped from a prewar 40 percent to less than 16 percent by 1937.

The Jews of Hungary

The year 1937 was memorable in that it signaled the beginning of Hungarian governmental engagement in fostering anti-Jewish sentiment by publicizing information that showed the overrepresentation of Jews in landownership, industry, the press and publishing, and high-income groups in general. The data basis for this agitation was readily available in the *Magyar Statisztikai Évkönyv 1935* (Hungarian Statistical Year Book 1935), which was published in Budapest in 1936. If the Jews were an alien element, then Jewish overrepresentation at any but the lowest rungs of the socioeconomic scale could be considered Jewish "domination" and "exploitation" of the country. Thus, it was sufficient to point out that in 1935, according to the *Statistical Year Book*, 50.8 percent of the owners and lessees of industrial enterprises in Hungary were Jews, as were 41.7 percent of their managers, to arouse indignation and resentment against them. The same reaction could unfailingly be elicited by showing that in 1937 among the "multipositional" business leaders, those who held three or more high positions (corresponding roughly to the apex, or tenth decile) in the economic elite, 45 percent were Jews, and that among the similarly defined banking elite 37 percent were Jews.

On January 23, 1937, the pro-German, government-subsidized paper *Uj Magyarság* (New Magyardom), which was read mostly by the Christian middle class, published an article that caused no little apprehension among the Jews. Basing itself on statistical publications made available in 1936, the article claimed that 13 percent of the owners of large estates (280–1,400 acres) and 37 percent of the lessees of very large estates (over 1,400 acres) were Jews, while only 0.9 percent of the agricultural workers were Jews. As for industrial ownership, the article claimed that of the country's industrial enterprises employing more than twenty workers, 46 percent (361 out of 783) were owned by Jews, and it enumerated the share of the Jews in iron and metal, machine and vehicle, stoneware, and pottery and glass industries, in spinning and weaving, and clothing, paper, and starch manufacturing. These figures showed, the article stated, that all of these basic industries were dominated by Jews.

The claim of Jewish domination was bolstered by figures published in the *Stock Exchange Year Book*, according to which in the twenty largest industrial enterprises of Hungary, 70 percent of the board members (235 out of 336) were Jews, and all except one had a majority of Jewish directors. As for privately owned medium-sized enterprises, 78 percent of them were owned by Jews. The tax returns disclosed further details about the economic primacy of the Jews in Hungary: 83.2 percent of those who declared fortunes in excess of one million pengős (not including land owners) were Jews, and 84.3 percent of those who declared an annual income above 100,000 pengős, and 85.5 percent of those who declared an income between 30,000 and 100,000 pengős, were Jews. Looking at the average per capita income of the Jews versus the gentiles of Hungary, it was found that the Jews' was 2,506 pengős, as against a gentile average of 426 pengős.

One of the intermediary enterprises between industry and intellectual endeavor whose Jewish domination was a long-standing complaint of the anti-Semites was the press. The 1936 *Press Year Book* published data according to which 306 out of 418 (or 73 percent) of the professional journalists were Jews, and in the nine largest newspapers of Hungary 77 percent to 97.5 percent of the journalists were Jewish. The situation was shown to be similar in the Hungarian theater, film, radio, sports, and other activities in the public eye. While the *Press Year Book* presented these data factually, they were utilized by the *Uj Magyarság* in a scurrilous article as grist for its anti-Semitic propaganda mill.

One of the foremost spokesmen to rise to the defense of Hungarian Jewry against these anti-Semitic attacks was Leó Budai-Goldberger (1878–1945), a Jewish member of the Upper House and a leading industrialist (whom we met above). His rejoinder, published in 1936 in the daily *Pesti Napló* (Diary of Pest), the majority of whose staff was Jewish, was consistent with the familiar old position of the Jewish establishment: he appealed to the Jews to resist Zionist propaganda, which tended to separate Hungarian Jews from other Hungarians, and called upon them to remain loyal to Hungary, and to provide poor relief in Hungary before helping the Jewish cause in other countries. In other words, Budai-Goldberger, and the Jewish establishment he represented, still believed that by demonstrating that Hungarian Jews had little in common with other Jewries of other countries and identified completely with Hungary, it was possible to stem the anti-Semitic tide and convince the leadership of Hungary that the Jews were devoted Magyars who must not be singled out in any respect. The futility of these arguments was to be demonstrated by the introduction of the First Jewish Law in 1938.

The Performing Arts

Beginning with the late nineteenth century, Jews played a seminal role in making Budapest a great center of theatrical life, boasting some two dozen legitimate theaters that offered outstanding performances, and at least as many cabarets and little theaters where skits and sketches were performed, seasoned with sharp satirical and political commentary and skillfully delivered by popular masters of ceremonies. Within the

---

next few years, many of the plays written by Hungarian Jewish playwrights and first performed in Budapest were translated into the major European languages and acclaimed in the leading theaters of Europe and America. Jews also filled important functions as founders and directors of theaters and were among the leading actors and actresses. The *Hungarian Jewish Lexicon* does not exaggerate when it says that in the pre–World War I years it was "the young guard of Hungarian Jewish playwrights" who "led the fight for the world success of the Hungarian drama" and "raised Hungarian drama to the level of global culture, and aroused interest abroad in the Hungarian stage."

In the prewar and interwar years, the Budapest playhouses owned or managed by Jews were filled night after night with thousands of theatergoers, most or many of them Jewish, who enjoyed sparkling plays written by Jewish playwrights, staged by Jewish directors, played by Jewish actors, and reviewed by Jewish critics in Jewish-owned papers. In addition, public interest in the world of the theater was kept alive by newspapers dishing up titillating tidbits about rivalries between leading Jewish playwrights and their love affairs with Jewish prima donnas, their intrigues, duels, and divorces. Katherine Anne Porter's *Ship of Fools* reminded me of the Budapest of those years. The whole city resembled a huge ship with a lighthearted crowd aboard, amusing and enjoying itself, while the currents drove it imperceptibly but inexorably toward its doom.

Of the Jewish playwrights who made Hungarian drama famous all over the Western world we have heard above (in chapter 34). Here we shall speak of the Jewish theater founders and directors, whose initiative provided the first stages for the initial successes of those playwrights.

Chronologically, the first was Gábor Faludi (1846–1932), who founded the Budapest Vigszinház (Comic Theater) in 1896, became its director, then its joint renter together with Count István Keglevich and Ferenc Szécsi, and finally was its sole owner until 1921, when he retired. Two of his sons, Miklós (1870–1942) and Jenő (1873–1933), followed in his footsteps: Miklós joined his father as co-director of Vigszinház, and Jenő became in 1925 the artistic director of the Magyar Szinház (Hungarian Theater). Under the Faludis' direction the Vigszinház became, next to the National Theater, the most important theater of Budapest. A contemporary of Gábor Faludi was Zsigmond Feld (1849–1939), an actor, and later director, of the Summer Theater (popularly known as the Feld Theater) of the City Park, who in 1890 was responsible for its switch from German to Hungarian as the language of performances.

Of greatest importance for the development of the Hungarian classical theater was the work of Sándor Hevesi (1873–1939). The son of Mór
Hoffmann (1843–1916), a Jewish teacher and pedagogical writer, Hevesi
converted to Christianity, earned his Ph.D. at Budapest University, and
started out as a teacher. In 1902 he became stage manager of the Nemzeti Szinház (National Theater), the most important theater in the country, and after shorter stints at the Vigopera (Comic Opera) and the Hungarian Royal Opera in the same capacity, he returned to the National
Theater in 1922 as its director. Under his leadership the National Theater became the undisputed center of serious Hungarian theatrical
endeavor with its performances of Hungarian and foreign classics, many
of the latter in Hevesi's own Hungarian translation. Hevesi also wrote
many plays that were performed there, as well as aesthetic and drama-
turgic studies. It was upon his initiative that the Chamber Theater of the
National Theater was established. In the judgment of Lóránt Czigány,
historian of Hungarian literature, Hevesi's "overall contribution to theatrical life . . . does not fall short of the achievement of Reinhardt in
Germany or Stanislavski in Russia: his reinterpretation of the classics,
his theoretical and directorial work certainly broke fresh ground."

The person who introduced and popularized the French-style satirical
comment as part of cabaret performance in Hungary was Endre Nagy
(1877–1938), a man of many talents, who, although he also converted,
wrote several short stories on Jewish themes and even authored a Jewish juvenile novel. He achieved considerable success with his humorous
writings, as well as his plays, which were performed by the Comic Theater, the Hungarian Theater, the Dunaparti Szinház (Danube Bank
Theater), and the Inner City Theater. He recorded in two volumes his
experiences in the 1914–18 war and wrote more than a dozen successful
novels. However, he achieved his greatest popularity as a witty, satirical
commentator, akin to the American stand-up comic, with sharp critical
footnotes, in which he mercilessly held up to ridicule the Hungarian
political and social phenomena of the age. His appearances proved to be
the main attraction of his playhouse: he was lionized, and many others
followed, or tried to follow, in his footsteps. In France such performers
were known as *chansonniers*, the most popular of whom was Aristide
Bruant (immortalized by the magnificent poster of Toulouse-Lautrec);
in Budapest, for some reason, such a stand-up satirist and cabaret master of ceremonies was called *konferanszié* (from the French *conférencier*,
"lecturer").

One of Endre Nagy's followers was László Békeffy (1891–1962), who
had his own cabaret of high artistic quality, with political overtones, in
which he functioned as *konferanszié*. In both Nagy's and Békeffy's cabarets, the works of the best authors were performed by fine actors.

Another multitalented man whose career included the ownership of a cabaret was Imre Roboz (1892–1944). He started as secretary of the Projectograph Film Company, then became editor of the first Hungarian motion picture magazine, *Mozgófénykép Hiradó* (Motion Picture News), and went on to direct the Phoenix Film Company and the Apollo Cabaret. In 1921 he also became director of the Vigszinház.

Two of the most popular Hungarian composers of musicals, or operettas, were Jews. Both started out in Budapest but achieved international acclaim after emigrating. The first was Imre Kálmán (1882–1953), who became world famous when his operetta *Tatárjárás* (The Tartar Invasion) was performed in Vienna and in New York, where it was given the title *The Gay Hussars* (1909). He lived for several years in Vienna, Switzerland, and France, and in 1940 moved to New York, returning to Europe in 1949. His most famous operettas were the *Gypsy Princess* (1915) and *Countess Maritza* (1924). The other composer was Victor Jacobi (1883–1921), whose operettas met with great success in various Budapest theaters in the prewar years. He emigrated to America and died in New York.

Another prolific composer and musical director of the Budapest Operetta Theater was Pál Ábrahám (1898–1960). Finally, Leo Weiner (1885–1960) was a professor at the Hungarian Academy of Music and a composer whose romantic music brought him great popularity in Hungary.

Writers at Home and Abroad

We return here once more to the Hungarian literary scene of the interwar years, in which Jewish authors played as important a role as in the early part of the twentieth century, despite the anti-Semitic atmosphere that prompted many of them to emigrate.

One who did emigrate was Illés Kaczér (1887–1980), who was also one of the few Hungarian Jewish writers of the period to devote almost all of his work to Jewish themes. Born in Szatmár (later Satu Mare, Rumania), to rigorously Orthodox parents, Kaczér lived first in Pressburg, Kolozsvár, Budapest, Vienna, and Berlin, then in 1938 moved to London, where he stayed for twenty years, and finally spent the last two decades of his life in Israel, where he died in 1980 at the age of ninety-three. However, while he was thus thoroughly cosmopolitan in terms of his places of residence and spoke Hungarian, German, Rumanian, English, and Hebrew, the language in which he wrote throughout his long life remained Hungarian. Several of his early works, published in József Patai's *Mult és Jövő* and the IMIT's 1916 *Year Book*, are set in the ancient Near East. They include the novel *Khafrit, az egyptomi asszony* (Khafrit the Egyptian Woman, published in installments in *Mult és Jövő* in 1914) and the short stories "The Killer Came Up Against Babylon" and "The King Wants to Sleep." His major work, a historical novel in four parts titled *The Jewish Legend*, was written in London but published, in Hungarian, in Tel Aviv (*Fear Not, My Servant Jacob*, 1953; *The Siege of Jericho*, 1954; *Three Are the Stars*, 1955; and *The Jew of Lajos Kossuth*, 1956). It is set first in the northeastern corner of Hungary, close to the Carpathian Mountains, then in Budapest, and its main protagonists are Jews of conflicting religious persuasions, ranging from the very pious, learned taverner Shulem and the old peddler "Rabbitskin" Abba to the modern, assimilated Jews of early-nineteenth-century Hungary who took an increasingly significant part in the creation of modern industries and the foundation of entire suburbs centered on an industrial plant (Ujpest). Early in his literary career Kaczér also wrote successful plays (such as *Siamese Twins*, Pressburg, 1925) and a visionary novel about the first Jewish settlers in Palestine, *Az álomtelepes* (The Dream Settler, Vienna, 1923). Because he lived most of his life abroad and his major works were published in Israel, Kaczér has been largely ignored by modern historians of Hungarian literature, and has only recently been rehabilitated, to some extent, by Sándor Scheiber and Ivan Sanders.

Milán Füst (original name Fürst, 1888–1967), a poet, novelist and dramatist of the *Nyugat* circle, started to experiment with free verse and remained throughout his life a poet of darkness, despair, loneliness, the fear of persecution, and after 1919 also of horror and aversion at the sight of brutal barbarity, and later still of the experience of old age and the fear of death. As Miklós Szabolcsi puts it, "All these themes are expressed against a peculiar mythological background created by him, in an entirely imaginary geographical or historical setting, in the pathetic-plaintive tone of the psalms or dirges." Likewise, Lóránt Czigány writes that "laments, dirges, or the psalms of an esoteric religion come to mind as possible parallels to or inspiration for Füst's poetry, particularly for the poems of his old age." Füst also wrote prose works: his novel *Advent* (1923) is a protest against the White Terror, and *A feleségem története* (The Story of My Wife, 1942) is a visionary psychological narrative about the all-consuming passion of jealousy.

While Füst never wrote anything devoted explicitly to a Jewish theme, his younger contemporary, Mihály Földi (1894–1943), did in at least one of his novels. Földi's early writings show Dostoevskian influences, with a pessimistic worldview, and the subject to which he returns again and again is the problem the fruitless search for redemption. His

"Jewish" novel *A Halasi-Hirsch fiu* (The Halasi-Hirsch Boy, 1926), whose hero breaks away from his Jewish background only to find himself vulnerable and rootless, addresses the painful problems of Jewish existence in contemporary Hungary: the clash between the fathers, who are faithful to their Jewish tradition, and the sons, who, influenced by the modern spirit of the times, turn their backs on it and convert to Christianity without thereby being able to solve the problem of their existence. Földi himself turned to metaphysics in an attempt to reconcile the conflicting pulls of ethics, intellect, and his psychological impulses but was unable to forge artistically plausible novels out of his inner uncertainty, doubts, and pessimism.

The last one of the impressive group of Hungarian Jewish authors to be born just before the end of the nineteenth century was Károly Pap (1897–1945), son of Miksa Pollák, the scholarly rabbi of Sopron. As a very young man he served as an officer in the Austro-Hungarian army and was decorated for bravery in World War I. After his discharge he joined the Communist revolution led by Béla Kun and became an officer in the Hungarian Red Army. Upon the collapse of the Council Republic, he was arrested and sentenced to eighteen months' imprisonment. Following his release he left Hugary but returned in 1925, settled in Budapest, and began writing short stories, which revealed a profound consciousness of his Jewish identity. His stories were published in *Nyugat* and *Mult és Jövő* and made his name known in literary circles. His literary output differed from that of his older Jewish contemporaries in that all his writings had Jewish or biblical themes, and his outlook on life, as expressed in his novels, was Jewish through and through.

In 1935 he published an eighty-seven-page essay titled "Zsidó sebek és bűnök" (Jewish Wounds and Sins) and subtitled *A Polemical Essay with Special Reference to Hungary.* In it he reviewed, from a highly individual point of view, biblical history and the role of major biblical figures such as Moses and Ezra in the foundation of Judaism, and went on to devote quite some space to Jesus. He made highly critical observations on both Hungarians and Jews, exposing and castigating the self-deception practiced by the Hungarian Jews, as manifested in their constant assertions that they differed from Christian Hungarians in nothing but religion. He defined the role of the Jews in Hungary in terms that endeared him to neither the Jews nor the Hungarians. He wrote:

> The role of Jews in the history of Magyardom is the faithful reflection of the deficiencies of Magyardom.
> That is to say:
> The leading role of Jewry in Hungarian economic life is the reflection of the economic impotence of Magyardom.

The leading role of Jewry in the organization of Hungarian culture of the most recent times is the reflection of the impotence of Magyardom in cultural organization.
Finally:
The leading role of Jewry in the Hungarian revolutions of the modern period is naturally a consequence of the preceding two:
A nation that is impotent in economic and cultural organization is incapable of rebirth.

As for Zionism, Károly Pap envisaged the new Zion that the Jews should establish in Palestine as a miniature precursor of the utopian ideal world. What he had to say on this subject he considered so basic that he italicized it: *"I cannot imagine the new Zion in any other manner but as a country that, on a small scale, will first bring into being the United World States, where the Hungarian Jew together with the Rumanian and Czech Jew, the German Jew with the French Jew, will, in a small country, first attempt world harmony."*
The only solution for the Jewish problem in Hungary envisaged by Pap was to accept the fate of a national minority, as in the countries to the east of Hungary. Needless to say, such views were anathema to the Hungarian Jewish leadership, which rejected and condemned them with profound indignation.

By the time Pap published this essay he was well known for his historical novel *Megszabadítottál a haláltól* (You Have Delivered Me From Death, 1932), which has a strange poetic quality, and tells the story of a Jewish Messiah in the days of Jesus. It was acclaimed by Hungarian critics and won him the friendship and encouragement of Zsigmond Móricz, the celebrated Hungarian writer. This was followed by the novel *The Eighth Station of the Cross* (1933), Pap's allegorical story of a painter's struggle to create a portrait of Christ.

I met Pap in Budapest in 1936 and clearly remember at least one heated discussion with him in my parents' house, where he was a frequent visitor. I had read a short story he had brought my father for publication in *Múlt és Jövő*, and our exchange revolved around the image of God he depicted in that story. For Pap God was "the Thunderer" and "the Avenger," a sinister, wrathful, merciless, in fact, cruel deity, against whom the chief protagonist of the story battles in vain. I tried to convince him—unsuccessfully—that this God lived only in his imagination and had no basis in the Bible, in which the basis of the relationship between God and Israel is mutual love.

Soon thereafter Pap's autobiographical novel *Azarel* (1937) was published, telling of the child Gyuri Azarel's struggle to find his way between his grandfather's Orthodox piety and his father's "neophyte hypocrisy" (the expression is Lóránt Czigány's). This time it was the cruel frankness of the description that aroused great indignation among his Jewish readers. In the increasingly intolerant atmosphere of World War II, Pap turned to biblical themes: two of his plays, *Bathsheba* (1940) and *Moses* (1942), were performed by the Budapest Jewish Theater, organized under the aegis of OMIKE (see chapter 41). *Moses* conveys the message that the prophet must represent his people even if their wish contradicts his own belief.

In May 1944, Pap was taken to a labor camp, where he refused the opportunity to escape. He was deported to Buchenwald and is presumed to have died in Bergen-Belsen in 1945. His father, R. Miksa Pollák, perished a year earlier in Auschwitz. Posthumously, several more of Pap's works were published in Hungary.

Two expatriate Hungarian Jewish novelists belong in this period, for although both survived the war, one in London, the other in Paris, both won recognition in the interwar period, and their later works added little to their reputation. One of them, Ferenc Körmendi (1900–1972), was born and educated in Budapest and became a music critic and journalist. He remained a struggling author until his novel *Budapesti Kaland* (English title *Escape to Life*, 1932) won an international competition organized by leading London publishers. It tells the story of a South African millionaire of Hungarian origin, whom his former classmates invite to a class reunion in Budapest in the hope of getting money out of him. In the same year Körmendi published another adventurous, action-packed novel, *Ind. 7:17 Via Bodenbach* (English title *Via Bodenbach*, 1932). This was followed by several other novels, none of which had the success of the first, though they were also published in English translation. In 1938 Körmendi fled to London, where he worked for the Hungarian section of the BBC, and later moved to the United States. He wrote only one "Jewish" novel, *Júniusi hétköznap* (1943; English title *Weekday in June*, 1946), which tells the tragic story of an assimilated Hungarian Jew who is killed on the very eve of his emigration, when a Nazi throws a bomb in front of a local synagogue.

Even greater was the international success of the novel written in the early 1930s by Jolán Földes (1903–1963) titled *A halászó macska utcája* (1936; English translation *The Street of the Fishing Cat*, 1937), which not only won an international fiction contest but was translated into twelve languages and sold over a million copies in the first six months. It is a bittersweet story of a simple, poor, Hungarian emigrant family, who has to struggle as hard in the squalor of their dingy lodging in the narrow Paris alley next to the Seine, called *rue du chat qui peche*, as they did in Hungary, until finally they decide to return home. Földes herself was more successful than the protagonists of her novel: she emigrated in the 1920s, settled in Paris, and after some years of struggle during which she had to sustain herself with menial work, the success of her *Fishing Cat* changed her life radically, and, writing in English, she produced a series of well-received novels.

In Hungary, the novels of these two emigré writers owed their popularity to two factors. One was the prestige of having won international prizes and having been translated into the great European languages and acclaimed by the readership in those languages. Hungary has always been impressed by what happens in the cultural life of the *külföld* (abroad), as amply shown by the life and work of many authors and artists. For a Hungarian writer or artists, to be successful abroad was the shortest and simplest way to achieve recognition in Hungary. Another aspect of the same attitude was the frequency and rapidity with which writings of newly emerging German, French, and English authors were translated into Hungarian and snapped up by readers. I remember vividly how as a teenager I gobbled up the novels of foreign authors that became available in Hungarian translation within a few months of their original publication.

The other factor that made for the popularity of these two and other similar authors was that they dealt with the life of Hungarian emigrants abroad. Emigration has always been a great lure for Hungarians—notwithstanding all the avowals of "I stay at home!"—and therefore stories of how Hungarian emigrants fared abroad, what work they engaged in, what their successes and failures were, why and how some of them became millionaires, what relationship they maintained with Hungary, etc., were of consuming interest to Hungarian readers. Both Körmendi's *Budapesti Kaland* and Jolán Földes's *Fishing Cat* belong to this category of novels.

These novels appealed to the Hungarian reader on several levels. Their protagonists were Hungarians, and therefore familiar figures with whom the reader could readily identify; the books told about adventures and happenings in the great world abroad; and their descriptions of the hardships of emigré life in other countries reaffirmed the reader's choice in eschewing emigration. Thus the "average intelligent readers," whose numbers grew in the interwar years as a result of the growth of the school network, found these novels attractive and appealing, and their success was assured.

The Brain Drain

When the racist and anti-Semitic tide engulfed Hungary, many Jewish musicians, composers, conductors, and performers left Hungary and enriched the musical life of other countries, particularly the United States. Let me mention only the names of six famous emigré conductors, all of them Hungarian Jews; Leo Weiner (1885–1960), Fritz Reiner (1888–1963), Dezső Szenkar (1891–1962), George Széll (1897–1970), Eugene Ormandy (1899–1985), and Sir George Solti (b. 1912).

The Hungarian Jewish actors were no less talented than their musical compatriots, but their careers abroad were blocked by a handicap it was almost impossible to overcome: their Hungarian accent, which came through no matter how well they mastered one or another major European language. This limited their chances, whether in film or theater, and restricted them to character roles of Hungarians or other foreigners. This was the fate of Szőke Szakáll, Paul Lukas, Oscar Beregi, the Gábor sisters, Peter Lorre, and many others. Only those who were taken abroad by their parents in early childhood, before the Hungarian accent indelibly impressed itself upon their speech pattern, or were born abroad after their parents emigrated from Hungary, escaped this limitation—for example, Leslie Howard (originally Stainer) and Tony Curtis (originally Bernard Schwartz). And having mentioned film actors, I might add that Hungarian Jewish directors had a seminal role in developing the film industry in England (Sir Alexander Korda) and the United States (Adolph Zukor, Joseph Pasternak).

The record of Hungarian Jewry as supplier of musical and acting talent to the world is matched only by its contribution to the natural sciences, and especially to atomic research. As has often been pointed out, most of the men who developed the atomic bomb (Leo Szilárd, Jenő Wigner, Edward Teller) were Hungarian Jewish emigrés, as was János (John) von Neumann, one of the greatest mathematicians of his time, Tódor (Theodor) von Kármán, the physicist, and Georg von Hevesy, the physical chemist. (This reminds me of the story about the atomic scientist who returns to New York after an international atomic conference in Buenos Aires. A friend of his asks him how all those scientists from so many countries could communicate. "Simple," he answers, "we all spoke Hungarian.")

It was unquestionably the anti-Semitic wave that swept Hungary after the fall of the Communist Republic and the introduction of the Numerus Clausus Law that tipped the balance in favor of emigration in the case of hundreds of young Jewish intellectuals, including many of the most talented and enterprising. To round out the picture, let us add a few more names to those mentioned above. To start with another technical man, it was in 1919 that József Breuer, a graduate of the Budapest Technical University, left for Palestine, where he carried out the draining of the Jezreel Valley, a swampy, malaria-infested area—the greatest ecological accomplishment in the country. The same year, Károly (Karl) Mannheim, the famous sociologist, left Hungary. Károly Polányi, the well-known economic historian, also left in 1919, while his brother, Mihály Polányi, the famous physical chemist, left in 1923. Sándor Ferenczi, Freud's pupil and friend, lost his university position and left after 1919. Among others who left Hungary in 1919 or soon thereafter were Pál Szende, the economist and sociologist; Franz Alexander, the psychoanalyst; the two converts Georg Lukács, the aesthetician and philosopher, who near the end of his life returned to Hungary, and Oszkár Jászi, the editor of *Huszadik Század*; and many other Hungarian Jewish scientists, scholars, writers, artists, musicians, intellectuals. Once it started, this brain drain may have varied in intensity, but it never let up.

The Question of Hungarian Jewish Literature

Before saying good-bye to the two decades of the interwar years, which in retrospect, and compared to what followed them, must appear as a happy period in the life of Hungarian Jewry, a brief reference seems in place to a major literary debate that had implications reaching far beyond the issue of literature alone. Ostensibly the discussion revolved around the question of who among the hundreds of Jewish-born Hungarian writers was and who was not a *Jewish* writer, and consequently how to define "Hungarian Jewish" literature. But the issue could not be confined to literature alone; it inevitably spread and involved the all-encompassing vexing general question of who was a Jew in Hungary.

The issue came to the fore in the 1920s when Péter Ujvári undertook the ambitious task of editing a Hungarian Jewish encyclopedia, which eventually was published in 1929 under the title of *Magyar Zsidó Lexikon* (Hungarian Jewish Lexicon). It was a hefty, thousand-page volume; its thirty-four contributors were among the foremost Hungarian Jewish writers and scholars, and yet by modern standards it left much to be desired. One of the major difficulties the editor was not able to overcome was caused by his initial decision to include not only items pertaining to Hungarian Jewry, but also general Jewish subjects (such as, to take a few examples from the very first pages, Abaryanim, Abel, Abraham, Achare moth, Acher, etc.), which, of course, could be dealt with only in rudimentary brevity. In fact, some of the Hungarian Jewish literary and scholarly critics dismissed the whole venture as *"gyarló"* (third-rate; Aladár Komlós's expression).

An important category of articles in this *Lexikon* were the biographical entries, which provided information on many hundreds of Hungarian Jews whose work, in the judgment of the editor and the contributors qualified them for inclusion. Undoubtedly there were many who tried some string-pulling to be included and thus given a place among the *immortels* of Hungarian Jewry. In that there was nothing surprising, given the well-known Hungarian (and Hungarian-Jewish) attitude epitomized in the adage "hand washes hand," which was the Hungarian equivalent of "You scratch my back, I scratch your back." What was surprising for those not familiar with the Hungarian Jewish scene was the opposite effort. As Aladár Komlós put it caustically in 1936, "He who had an opportunity to caste a glance behind the scenes of the preparation of the . . . *Hungarian Jewish Lexicon* will remember what a frightened buzzing was aroused, and what backstairs-influences were utilized by some so that the *Lexicon* should *not* mention them. Nor can we be astonished that in a place where the law-courts found the editors guilty of slander for mentioning that a Christian university professor was a converted Jew, not every Jewish writer rejoiced when he learned that his descent was being made public. . . ."

In that same *Lexicon* the Jewish historical scholar Mór Fényes defined Jewish literature within the Hungarian context as comprised of "those works that were written by Jews in a Jewish spirit (not necessarily for Jews)." In his a. m. essay Aladár Komlós referred to the view of Wilhelm Bacher and József Patai, according to whom "a writer belongs to Jewish literature only if what he has to say has an open bearing on Judaism," which excludes those, who, according to Patai "out of opportunism or caution or indifference avoid the mental areas of their Jewishness, as this is done among us by most of the writers" (as quoted by Aladár Komlós).

Komlós himself, in his essay, first of all bemoans the existing situation. "However sad it is, we must admit that today in most cases only those Jewish writers deal with Jewish issues who feel that in the general Hungarian literary life they could not succeed. . . . A terrible situation: we do have splendid writers, but they 'do not condescend' to Jewish problems, and there are those who do condescend but they are mostly not sufficiently writers." Following more of this type of critical rumination, Komlós reaches the conclusion that Hungarian Jewish literature comprises "even all those Hungarian writers of Jewish origin who perhaps in all their lives most tenaciously avoided the problems of their people [i.e., the Jews]. . . . If a writer was born a Jew, it no longer depends on his decision whether he becomes a Jewish writer, and whether or not he will give expression to the Jewish soul and the Jewish history of ideas. . . . Even with his convulsive averting the eyes, his hiding silences and the indifference he forced upon himself, he remains a characteristic phenomenon of Jewish life. It does not matter that he does not even suspect the Jewishness of his characters and their problems! Thereby he only gives vent more fully and more courageously to his Jewish instincts."

Hence, Komlós continues, "we must include every writer of Jewish origin into Jewish literature, irrespective of how he preferred to settle the problems arising out of his origin." He recognizes that the Jews, having lived for two thousand years in social situations differing from those of the gentiles, have a specific manner of feelings, attitudes, and outlook, and hence "we [Jewish writers in Hungary] can believe in being needed, and we can perform tasks for which the other layers of Magyardom are less suited. . . . The Jewish soul is not like a circle that has one center, but rather like the ellipse that has two focal points," that is, Hungarianness and Jewishness. In his conclusion Komlós argues that a history of Hungarian Jewish literature must not be confined to the role played by Jews as creators of literature; it must incude also their role as the supporters of non-Jewish Hungarian literary creativity, as sympathetic critics, as generous Maecenases, as enthusiastic readers. It should also comprise a study of the passive role of the *model* played by the Jews, and the image of the Jew as reflected in the mirror of Hungarian literature.

While other literary critics, including Antal Ijjas Jankovits, László Ujvári, and Imre Keszi, continued to discuss the subject, behind the façade of the Hungarian-Jewish literary issue lay, of course, the greater question of who of the one million individuals born of Hungarian Jewish parents should be regarded as Jewish. In the interwar years, more than ever before, the blurring of the boundaries between Jew and non-Jew affected larger and larger segments of the Jewish-born population. The question encompassed not only those who took the decisive step of converting to one of the Christian faiths in the country, but also the ever-growing element of those Jews who, while not taking the trouble of officially seceding from the Jewish community, had nothing to do with it or with Judaism, and whom nothing made happier than not being recognized as persons of Jewish birth. The contradictory opinions on who was a Jewish writer could without any change of wording be equally applied to the question of who was a Jew, but even for the Komlós-like inclusivists it had to be clear that the demographic mass of Hungarian Jewry was rapidly shrinking, and that within a generation or two the children of the Jewishly indifferent Jews, and of those who consciously and effortfully distanced themselves from their Jewish roots, would have to be recognized as being no longer Jewish.

Had the traditional, "mild" Hungarian social anti-Semitism continued its wonted course of the preceding two or three generations, the gradual shrinkage of Hungarian Jewry would undoubtedly have gone on without any appreciable change in extent or intensity. But that was not to be. The catastrophic upheavals that started with the first Jewish law of 1938 introduced an entirely new, and never before experienced dimension into the issue of Hungarian Jewish identification, and within six years brought this talented, proud, and fervently patriotic community, composed of both devoutly religious and extremely assimilant elements, to the brink of total extinction.

40

The First and Second Jewish Laws (1938–39)

The 1938 Jewish Law was a total break with the official position Hungary had embraced for more than forty years toward the Jews: that the Jews formed one of the legally accepted religious denominations, so no special legal provisions could single them out. Now Law 1938:XV did precisely this. First of all, it provided that the Ministry of the Interior should set up a chamber of the press and a chamber of theatrical and film arts, and only individuals accepted as members of these "chambers" should be allowed to work in those fields. After some technical and administrative preliminaries the anti-Jewish essence of the provisions then read:

> 4. Jews can be admitted as members of the press chamber as well as of the theatrical and film arts chamber only in such a proportion that their number does not exceed 20 percent of the total chambers' members. Not included in this 20 percent will be:
> a. Disabled veterans, soldiers who participated in combat, the children of a parent who died a hero's death, and war widows;
> b. Those who had converted prior to August 1, 1919, to another accepted denomination, and have been members of that denomination without interruption;
> c. The children of a parent covered under point b who are not members of the Israelite denomination.
>
> 7. Persons included in section 4a can be admitted as members of chambers of lawyers, engineers, and physicians only to the extent that their number does not exceed 20 percent of all the members. Until the number of the other chamber members reaches 80 pecent of the total membership, persons included in section 4, section 1, can constitute only 5 percent of the newly admitted members.

Subsequent paragraphs of the law limit Jews to 20 percent of the number engaged in various capacities in all kinds of commercial and other firms, and limit the total salaries paid to Jewish white-collar workers to 20 percent of the salaries paid to all white-collar workers. In its concluding paragraph the law indicates that its purpose is "to overcome the unemployment of white-collar workers."

This law was a much more serious blow to the Jewish community of Hungary than the Numerus Clausus Law of 1920 had been. That earlier law, although its intention was anti-Jewish, was camouflaged as a regulation of the percentages among students of *all* nationalities in the country, and did not mention the Jews by name; this one spoke explicitly and exclusively of the Jews. That one affected only the planned careers of Jewish high school graduates; this one deprived tens of thousands of Jews long established in the professions of their jobs and livelihood. Its avowed purpose was to alleviate unemployment among Christian Magyar professionals, and the method it adopted was to create unemployment among Jewish Magyar professionals. No more blatant measure could have been imagined to stamp the Jews second-class citizens.

The Jews could derive some small and temporary measure of comfort from the reaction of Christian Hungarian writers and artists. It was precisely the latter, whose benefit the law was supposed to serve, who protested most vehemently against it. In March 1938, while the bill was under consideration, most respected and cultural leaders declared it a violation of the historical Magyar-Jewish community of fate, and the exclusion of 400,000 Jewish citizens from the ranks of the nation a shame of Magyardom. Among the signatories of this statement were such famous men as composers Béla Bartók and Zoltán Kodály, writers Lajos Zilahy and Zoltán Szabó, painter Aurél Bernáth, and literary scholar László Bóka.

The government disregarded this protest just as it did the outcry of the Jewish community, and the parliamentary arguments of the Jewish deputies János Vázsonyi and Béla Fábián and their Christian Social Democratic colleagues in both Houses. Before the end of 1938, now headed by a new prime minister, Béla Imrédy (1891–1946), it prepared an additional bill aiming at further limiting Jewish participation in the country's economic and social life.

Psychologically most devastating for the Jewish community of Hungary was the approval of the bill by representatives of the Christian Churches while it was being debated in Parliament. Cardinal Jusztinian Serédy, prince-primate of Hungary and head of the dominant Catholic Church of the country, Evangelical (Lutheran) bishop Sándor Raffay, and László Ravasz, bishop of the Reformed (Calvinist) Church, were unanimous in approving of the bill's essential provisions and blaming Jewish faults for their necessity. They spoke of the "undesirable" traits of the Jews and of Jewish shortsightedness in not mending their ways while there was still time, and they suggested either total assimilation or emigration as the only possible solutions of the Jewish question. The only amendment the Christian leaders suggested was in the treatment of converted Jews, for whom they wanted to secure additional benefits. (The Christian support also prepared the ground for Hungarian public opinion to consider the anti-Jewish measures just and necessary.)

The initial reaction of the leaders of the Jewish community was a pathetic and cringing emulation of the governmental position in support of the anti-Jewish law. They echoed the spurious argument that the law's "reasonable" restrictions on the Jews would "take the wind out of the sails of the extremists" and prevent the adoption of the much more stringent laws the Arrow Cross movement clamored for (after the pattern established in Germany and Rumania) and the degeneration of anti-Semitic agitation into outright persecution. In fact, some Jewish leaders seem to have so accepted the inevitability of the situation that they actually *advocated* the introduction of "mildly restrictive" measures as a kind of vaccine to prevent the outbreak of a virulent anti-Semitic epidemic. And, of course, the Jewish leadership again rejected —as it had in connection with the Numerus Clausus Law—all "interference" on the part of Western Jewish organizations.

In the meantime, Hungary became more and more attached (and subordinated) to the expanionist policies of Hitlerian Germany. After the dismemberment of Czechoslovakia and the "return" to Hungary of the border districts of Slovakia and Ruthenia (in November 1938), the government was both politically and economically dependent on Germany. It permitted the Volksbund to organize in Hungary among the German minority, thereby legalizing the dissemination of Nazi ideology. The preparation of the Second Jewish Law was one of the steps Hungary took as a concession to German pressure.

The return of border areas from Czechoslovakia to Hungary brought some 163,000 Jews (almost 10 percent of the total population annexed) under Hungarian rule. For two decades these Jews had lived under Czechoslovak rule and had routinely been accused of supporting Magyardom, which in many cases they undoubtedly did. Now, after the reannexation, they were faced with the opposite allegation: that they had Slovak sympathies, betrayed Hungarian interests, cooperated with the Czechoslovak army, had secret radio transmitters, and the like. In the course of the reoccupation of the area by the Hungarian army, Jews were attacked in some places.

An openly inimical attitude toward the newly acquired Slovak Jews was expressed by Prime Minister Béla Imrédy. In a speech he explained why the government found it necessary to clamp down on them: "As a result of the reannexation of part of northern Upper Hungary, very strong Jewish centers returned to us, especially in areas in which the validation of Magyardom, of the Magyar spirit, is of special significance, so that in those areas the role of Jewry also had to be forced back into the formation of local politics."

The racial laws introduced in Hungary in 1938 had one tragicomic effect. When Prime Miniser Béla Imrédy (1891–1946), known as a devout Catholic, introduced the bill that several months later became the Second Jewish Law, he emphasized its importance by stating that "one drop of Jewish blood" was enough to infect a man's character and patriotism. No sooner had he made this statement than the liberal leader Károly Rassay and his legitimist friend Count Antal Sigray dug out a document that showed that Imrédy had a great-grandmother in his German-Bohemian ancestry who was Jewish. They presented the document to former prime minister Count István Bethlen, who in turn passed it on to Regent Horthy. When the regent, at a dramatic moment, showed the document to Imrédy, he fainted. This incident, it was rumored, was one of the factors that led to Imrédy's forced resignation in February 1939.

In addition to the homegrown and old established anti-Semitic tendencies, there were two other factors motivating the Hungarian government to prepare more stringent anti-Jewish laws. One was the wish—or the recognition of the need—to adjust the legal situation of the Jews in Hungary to match that in Germany, which by 1939 the Germans had also imposed in the countries they had annexed or occupied. The second was the apprehension that, unless such legal equalization was carried out, there would be a mass influx of Jews, not only from the German-controlled countries but also from Rumania, where the wave of panic that swept the country during the 1938 rule of terror of the Goga government had prompted Jews to seek refuge in Hungary.

The government's intentions to regulate the Jewish question in emulation of the German Nazi laws met with strong objections from the bourgeois-liberal opposition, led by Károly Rassay, and the Social Democrats. In fact, the opposition was so strong that the bill remained on the agenda of the House for four months (January–May 1939) before it could be voted into law. While it was being discussed, an assault took place (on February 3) in front of the big Dohány Street Synagogue: Arrow Cross guards lobbed hand grenades into the Jewish crowd coming out of services. Twenty-two Jews were wounded, several of them mortally. One of the organizers of the attack, Emil Kovárcz, was a leader of the Hungarian radical right, and a member of Parliament. He was brought to trial, but was able to escape to Germany. (He was again apprehended after the liberation of Hungary, tried by the People's Tribunal [Népbíróság], and executed in 1946.) The atrocity created sympathy for the Jews, and seemed to strengthen the hand of the bill's opponents. In the Upper House, Count Gyula Károlyi led a group fighting to mitigate the provisions of the bill, and 101 general officers who had fought in World War I submitted a memorandum demanding the preservation of equal rights for their Jewish comrades. However, Count Pál Teleki, who succeeded Imrédy as prime minister in February 1939, was able to have the bill approved, and with stiffened provisions to boot.

The bill, as it became law on May 5, 1939—Law 1939:IV, popularly known as the Second Jewish Law—is a very long document (comprising some 7,000 words) and evinces a definite affinity with the German racial laws. While the First Jewish Law (of 1938) was titled "About the More Effective Protection of the Equilibrium of Social and Economic Life," this one had the more explicit title "About the Restriction of Public and Economic Encroachment by the Jews." It defines as a Jew every person born to at least one Jewish parent or two Jewish grandparents, except those who were wounded or decorated in World War I or belonged to some other specified categories. It excluded Jews from public office (state, municipal, etc.). It dismissed Jewish teachers from all schools except those maintained by Jewish congregations. It limited the teaching of Hebrew and Jewish religion. It reintroduced the 1920 Numerus Clausus Law, stating explicitly that only 6 percent of students at the universities, and only 12 percent of the students at the economic and commercial departments of the Technical and Economic University could be Jews. It limited the Jewish membership in the chambers of lawyers, engineers, physicians, the press, theater, and film to 6 percent of the total, and similarly in the executive bodies of these chambers. Jews were altogether prohibited from being periodical editors and publishers, or their policy-making contributors, and from serving as directors, artistic secretaries, and dramatists of theaters. Jews were barred from acquiring plots of land for the erection of private residences larger than 600 square cubits. They were prohibited from serving on the executive or board or council of all labor unions. In like manner, the law specified in many more paragraphs the exclusion of Jews from all imaginable occupational specializations, and provided severe penalties for those who transgressed its provisions.

One subsection of the law, to forestall the possibility that the dismissal of Jews from some positions might cause disruptions in the national economy, stated that "if it is unavoidably necessary in the interest of the undisturbed functioning or the order of production that . . . a Jew should be retained in a position that requires special expertise —inasmuch as no non-Jewish Hungarian citizen suitable for the job is available—the ministry can exceptionally permit a Jew to remain in the job above the stated proportion and for a definite period." This provision opened a loophole for many Jews to remain in managerial positions or in jobs requiring professional expertise. Often a Christian figurehead officially became the head of, say, an industrial enterprise, while the Jewish manager continued to function as its de facto head. Thus, quite rapidly a so-called *stróman* system (from the German *Strohmann*, dummy) developed, with a Christian in front and a Jew in actual control. Ways were also found for many in the academic professions (lawyers, engineers, physicians, etc.) to continue working with certain shifts in the external arrangements of their jobs.

In areas where the execution of the laws did not cause economic problems, they were carried out much more stringently. One such area was voting rights. In Budapest alone 73,000 persons who could not prove with documents that they and their ancestors had lived in the city since 1867 were removed from the lists of those entitled to vote.

The 1938 and 1939 Jewish Laws were devastating blows to Hungarian Jews both economically and psychologically: economically, because tens of thousands were thrown out of work; psychologically, because these laws suddenly deprived them of a mainstay of their identity. For several generations their leaders had dinned into their ears that they were Hungarians just like Christian Hungarians; and now, suddenly and traumatically, they were excluded by law from the community of the nation they had so long felt integral parts of, and were treated as outcasts. The trauma these two laws caused to Hungarian Jewry was extremely severe, much worse than anything they had lived through in prior centuries. In the pre-emancipation past, Hungarian Jews (like the Jews in other countries) grew up with the knowledge that they were tolerated foreigners, or at best, guests, different from the Christian majority in every respect that counted. They lived in a society that had subscribed from time immemorial to anti-Jewish tenets, and treated them accordingly. In that situation, again from earliest childhood, every Jew developed effective psychological defense mechanisms, comprising such traits as the conviction of their own internal, moral and religious superiority vis-à-vis the *goyim*, their reliance on divine protection and belief in their reward in the World to Come, and an emotional preparedness to adjust to any adverse decree, such as special high taxation, limitations of residence and occupation, or even expulsion. The same psychological defenses came into play when attacks, looting, pogroms, murder, and rapine occurred, and helped reduce the pain and heal the wounds that such events inevitably left behind.

The anti-Jewish laws of 1938 and 1939 rained down on the heads of a Jewish community that had been deprived of such effective psychological defense mechanisms. For several decades prior to 1938 the Jews of Hungary had been assured of total legal equality; they had achieved a highly flattering share in the ranks of the Hungarian nobility; and had attained leading positions in the economic, intellectual, and artistic life of the country. Over and above all this, their religious and secular leaders had insisted that they were Hungarian patriots, that outside Hungary they had no other fatherland, and that they had nothing or very little in common with the Jews in other countries—certainly less than the Catholic Hungarians had with their coreligionists in other countries, since all Catholics recognized the pope as their spiritual head, while the Jews of Hungary had no spiritual leaders besides their own rabbis.

It was on Jews whose mentality was formed and informed by such convictions that the blows of the Jewish Laws fell, and the effects were devastating. Even if the laws did not immediately endanger their lives (that came only later, in 1944), the psychological unpreparedness for being legally cast on the dustheap rendered these laws more hurtful than the attacks on life and limb that had been perpetrated, say, in the 1880s after Tiszaeszlár. For one thing, the new situation demanded a total rethinking of their own position in Hungary, something of which most Hungarian Jews were simply incapable. As a result, in the months between the promulgation of the First Jewish Law and the closing of the frontiers of Hungary because of the war, fewer Jews left the country to seek safety abroad than could have done so had they energetically pursued all (admittedly not too many) emigration possibilities. In fact, the 1939 Jewish Law had a provision that not only foresaw but intended to facilitate the emigration of Jews. Section 22 read: "The ministry is empowered to issue by decree dispositions for the promotion of the emigration of Jews and the exportation of the property of Jews connected with it. . . . The ministry can determine by decree those customs and other regulations that are needed for the protection of the national assets in connection with the promotion of Jewish emigration." This law clearly envisaged that one result of the virtual exclusion of Jews from the Hungarian economy would be Jewish emigration, and even spoke of its "promotion" under certain financial restrictions. Regrettably, tragically, very few Jews were willing or able to use the escape route.

It was partly at least the official leadership of Hungarian Jewry that was responsible for the absence of effective attempts to escape while it was still at all possible. The leadership reacted to the Jewish Laws in the accustomed manner, by reemphasizing the Jews' patriotic attachment to Hungary. It believed, and led its flock to believe, that these laws were manifestations of what was merely a fleeting phenomenon, and that the anti-Jewish current would soon run its course, as had its predecessors in the early 1920s and earlier periods. Simon Hevesi, the leading chief rabbi of the Israelite Congregation of Pest, exhorted the community to show endurance and to bear the trials with patience. Even Immanuel Löw, chief rabbi of Szeged, who in 1929 had become a member of the council of the Jewish Agency for Palestine, predicted that the law would be short-lived. What none of the Jewish leaders took into account was that this time it was the Hungarian Parliament, representing the will of the nation, that acted against the Jews, and that it did so under the pressure of Germany, where institutionalized and legalized anti-Semitism had by that time been established for several years.

When the Hungarian Jewish leadership found itself faced with the Second Jewish Law, it engaged in two types of action it felt about to undertake: protestations and charity work. The protestations were two-pronged: they continued the traditional line of harping on the patriotism of Hungarian Jews, but added, for the first time on this occasion, a new, somewhat more outspoken note of critical objection to the law's anti-Semitism and unconstitutionality. On January 12, 1939, the central offices of the three nationwide Jewish communal organizations (of the Neolog, Orthodox, and Status Quo Jews) jointly appealed to the government and pointed out that the bill violated the Hungarian constitution, in whose basic principles were embedded the unitary character of the Hungarian nation, equality before the law, and the protection of acquired rights. Their appeal further emphasized that the bill conflicted with human justice and the divine commandment of the law and, moreover, was harming the eminent interests of the Hungarian nation. In its impassioned conclusion, the petition returned to the old theme of patriotism, tinged this time with bitterness:

> Is this what Hungarian Jewry deserved? The mutilation of our civil rights, the limitation of our private rights, the restrictions on our livelihood, the ostracism of our youth? Is this what was deserved by the Hungarian Jewish community, whose only wish in the course of its centuries-old history was to keep its religion and remain Hungarian and only Hungarian? Let the battlefields of the War of Independence, the marshes of Volhynia, and the Karst rocks speak out on behalf of justice for us; in the trenches no one asked who was of which religion.

And when, naively, they cited the possibility that the new law could compel the Jews to emigrate, disregarding the fact that the law itself considered emigration desirable from the point of view of Hungary, they instantly added that they would remain Hungarian patriots even in foreign countries:

Should we be disappointed, and this bill become law, one of the results would be that hundreds of thousands of us and our children would be compelled to change residence. Residence, but not homeland. Because no human law can deprive us of our Hungarian homeland, any more than we can be deprived of the worship of one God. Just as in the course of the millennial blows of fate, neither fire nor water, scaffolds nor stakes, galleon benches nor handcuffs could deter us, with the same determination we will cling to our Hungarian homeland, whose language is our language, whose history is our life.

Concurrently, the Jewish leadership commissioned or encouraged the publication of pamphlets and articles, and the distribution of fliers, posters, propaganda leaflets, and postcards, to enlighten the Hungarian public about the falsity of the accusations leveled against the Jews. Typically, the tone of these writings was likewise apologetic, defensive, and patriotic.

The Jewish Laws forced a change of attitude in the Hungarian Jewish leadership toward its relationship to the influential Jewish organizations of the West. The same men who formerly rejected all intervention by foreign Jewish bodies on behalf of Hungarian Jewry now found they had no choice but appeal to them. The initiative was taken by Sándor Eppler (1890–1942), secretary-general of the Israelite Congregation of Pest, a highly intelligent pragmatist in managing the affairs of the community, who suggested in September 1938 that the Joint Foreign Committee of the Anglo-Jewish Association and the Board of Deputies of British Jews send one of its members to Budapest to gather information on the situation of the Hungarian Jews. Several months later this contact was followed up, and in May 1939, Eppler and Samu Stern, president of the Pest congregation, during a visit to Paris and London pleaded with British Jewish leaders for help in enabling able-bodied Hungarian Jews to emigrate, and for monetary aid for the aged and infirm.

The latter plea became part of the charity work mentioned above, in which the Hungarian Jewish organizations engaged as a response to the tightening restrictions of the Jewish Laws. In December 1939, they established the Patronage Office of Hungarian Israelites (Magyar Izraeliták Pártfogó Irodája, MIPI) to support those whom the First Jewish Law deprived of livelihood. In this office, for the first time, the Neolog, Orthodox, and Status Quo National Offices cooperated with the Hungarian Zionist Organization. Its activities included aid both to individuals in need and to Jewish congregations. Much of its work was directed to alleviating the plight of the Jews in Sub-Carpathian Ruthenia. The Patronage Office also cooperated with the Jewish National Committee for Continuing Education in helping the unemployed find new jobs and retraining them. For this purpose it set up small farms that employed manual laborers, and placed several hundred young men who arrived from the northern territories in apprentices' hostels.

By this time the Hungarian Jewish leadeship welcomed, in fact solicited, aid from international Jewish organizations, primarily from the American Jewish Joint Distribution Committee. Early in 1939 the Joint undertook to contribute $25,000 monthly to the Patronage Office, provided the Hungarian Jews matched it with a like amount. In the fall of 1939, the Joint transferred $400,000 to Hungary as its first large-scale allocation of aid. At the same time, the National Hungarian Jewish Aid Action (Országos Magyar Zsidó Segitő Akció, OMZSA) was established, under the leadership of Géza Ribáry, the vice president of the Israelite Congregation of Pest. Authorized by Ferenc Keresztes-Fischer, the benevolent minister of the interior, it was able to raise substantial amounts. Indicative of the steady deterioration of the Jewish economic position in consequence of the Jewish Laws was the rapid annual increase of the budget the Patronage Office required for aiding the indigent: in 1939 it was 1.5 million pengős; in 1940, 2.4 million; in 1941, 3.5 million; and in 1942, 4.4 million. The money was raised by OMZSA, whose major single contributor (covering more than half of its budget) was the Israelite Congregation of Pest.

Especially hurtful for the Hungarian Jews was their treatment by the army. At the time of the promulgation of the Second Jewish Law a considerable number of Jews were on active duty in the Hungarian army. Their position was now given special attention in view of the law's provisions. In September 1939, the Ministry of Defense issued a decree that left the professional Jewish officers and noncommissioned officers as members of the armed forces but annulled the ranks they held and barred Jews from attaining any rank in the future.

As for the Jewish reservists, whose employment was suitable only for nonarmed service, their position was regulated in May 1940, when the army command ordered the establishment of "special labor companies" of Jews who were not required by the army for military service. At first this decree pertained only to Jewish ex-servicemen, and by July no fewer than sixty such labor companies were set up. However, from August it was gradually extended to Jews who were not ex-servicemen, and the 25- to 42-year-olds, then the 43–48 bracket, and finally the 49–60 age group were successively mobilized. By the fall of 1940, the Jewish members of the armed units that took part in the occupation of northern Transylvania were demobilized and placed into such labor companies. With that, the exclusion of Jews from the Hungarian armed forces was effectively accomplished, and the Jews were reduced to the inferior position of membership in labor companies only.

Finally, in the spring of 1941, the Ministry of Defense ordered that the Jews "will satisfy their liability to military service by fulfilling auxiliary services within the framework of the army. . . . They will carry out this service without any rank, even if earlier they had earned ranks of officers or noncommissioned officers. Accordingly, those obliged to fulfill auxiliary services must be registered and treated as persons without rank." The issuance of this order deprived close to 16,000 Jewish officers of their ranks right away, and made several tens of thousands subject to labor service.

Although Teleki had stiffened the provisions of the Second Jewish Law and promulgated it before the elections, even that law proved insufficient to quiet the anti-Semitic agitation. The Hungarian extreme right and its German sponsors continued to demand that the Jews not only be recognized as an "ethnic group," similar to the Germans and the Slovaks, but be deprived of all legal rights. The Jewish leadership protested the legal discrimination inherent in the "ethnic group" concept and, totally unrealistically in the actual circumstances, continued to demand governmental adherence to the principle of equal rights of all citizens. Even though he knew well that the Jews were loyal to the idea of Hungarian national unity, and that his action would have serious economic and other consequences, Teleki moved to identify the Jews legally as an alien race.

In the Second Vienna Decision (August 1940) the Germans awarded to Hungary certain areas of Rumania (that prior to Trianon had been part of Hungary), and in exchange Hungary accepted an "ethnic group" arrangement, under which Hungary's Germans could openly proclaim that their Volksbund organization was a National Socialist ethnic association. Teleki also agreed to begin preparations for a third anti-Jewish law, and for constitutional reforms in accordance with the Nazis' demands. Moreover, he was forced to make concessions to the Hungarian Nazis, whose leader, Ferenc Szálasi, was given amnesty, and Szálasi's Arrow Cross Party emerged as the strongest opposition party.

On the Jewish question, Hungarian politics was divided between two major trends: that of the government, which was "moderately" anti-Semitic, and that of the Arrow Cross Party, which was rabidly anti-Semitic. The two sides were mutually antagonistic, and even hated each other. The most important difference between them was that the moderates recognized the Jews' essential role in Hungary's cultural and economic life and advocated their gradual replacement by Christians, while the radical right clamored for the immediate and total elimination of the Jews from the Hungarian scene. In a letter Regent Horthy wrote to Prime Minister Teleki on October 14, 1940, he expressed his position on both the Jews and the Arrow Cross in no uncertain terms:

As regards the Jewish problem, I have been an anti-Semite throughout my life. I have never had contact with Jews. I have considered it intolerable that here in Hungary eveything, every factory, bank, large fortune, business, theater, press, commerce, etc., should be in Jewish hands, and that the Jew should be the image reflected of Hungary, especially abroad. Since, however, one of the most important tasks of the government is to raise the standard of living, i.e., we have to acquire wealth, it is impossible, in a year or two, to eliminate the Jews, who have everything in their hands, and to replace them with incompetent, mostly unworthy, bigmouthed elements, for we should become bankrupt. This requires a generation at least. I have perhaps been the first to loudly profess anti-Semitism, yet I cannot look with indifference at inhumanity, senseless humilation, when we still need them. In addition, I consider, for example, the Arrow Cross to be far more dangerous and worthless for my country than I do the Jew. The latter is tied to this country by interest, and is more faithful to his adopted country than the Arrow Cross, who, like the Iron Guard, with their muddled brain, want to swing the country into the hands of the Germans.

The sentiments expressed by Horthy were largely shared by Teleki. This, however, did not keep him from concluding that Hungary's national interests were best served by demonstrating its loyalty to Germany. Accordingly, on November 20, 1940, Teleki went to Vienna and joined the tripartite pact concluded by Germany, Italy, and Japan on September 27. With this step Hungary's fate became formally linked to that of the Axis.

The powerful—almost unbreakable—emotional hold the Hungarian fatherland had on its Jews even after the promulgation of successively more restrictive and inimical Jewish Laws can best be illustrated by a brief reference to the stubborn reluctance exhibited by József Patai to leaving Budapest in the late summer of 1939, when the Second Jewish Law had been in force for several months, and when, in addition, the war had started and the cutting off of all exit routes from Hungary to the West was imminent. Patai (as we have seen in earlier contexts) was a foremost Hungarian Zionist leader, who had devoted his life to creating interest in and sympathy for the *yishuv* among the Jews of Hungary, and to fighting the anti-Zionist Hungarian Jewish establishment, who for many years had been an annual visitor to "the Holy Land," and who brought up his own three children so that from adolescence they wanted nothing more than to go to live in Palestine, and in 1933 and 1938 had actually made their *'aliyah*. And yet, in that fateful summer of 1939, this same József Patai had to be practically coerced by repeated desperate demands of his elder son and almost hysterical outbursts of his daughter, made over a series of nightly long-distance phone calls, into leaving Budapest and taking what in the event turned out to be the last ship to sail from Trieste to Haifa. If this was the position of a József Patai, one need not be surprised at the attitude of the rank and file of Hungarian Jews, who, influenced and indoctrinated by their official leadership, continued to adhere to the traditional ideal embodied in the words of the Hungarian anthem, "Whether the hand of fate blesses or strike you, here you must live and die." Of course, no sane person could have imagined in 1939 that the poetic admonition of "here you must . . . die" would so horribly be turned into reality for the Hungarian Jews within a few years thereafter.

41

World War II (1939–45)

In the course of 1941 Hungary was gradually and irresistibly drawn into the war by Germany. Already in the 1939–40 Soviet-Finnish war Hungary had sent volunteer units to the front, and in the spring of 1941 the government (headed since April by László Bárdossy) ordered the army into action to occupy and recover former Hungarian territories from Rumania and Yugoslavia. In June, when Germany attacked the Soviet Union, the Bárdossy government broke diplomatic relations with Moscow, and under pressure from military circles, it decided to send regular troops to the eastern front. The Hungarian units achieved some initial success, reaching the Dniester River in July, the Dnieper by October, and the Donetz by November, after which they were withdrawn.

While Hungary was thus drawn into the war—very much against its will—it was also pressured by the Germans to conform its own treatment of the Jews to that of Germany, where, in the summer of 1941, Reinhard Heydrich, head of the German Sicherheitsdienst (Security Service of the SS), was entrusted with working out a program for the "final solution" of the "Jewish question." By that time the Jews had been deprived of all rights in Germany, and were, to all practical purposes, considered a subhuman pest of which the country (and Europe as a whole) had to be rid as soon as possible.

In Hungary, the Third Jewish Law was promulgated on August 2, 1941 (Law 1941:XV). Its official title was "About the Completion and Modification of the 1894:XXXI Law Dealing with Marriage Rights, As Well As About Race-Protecting Dispositions Necessary in Connection Therewith." Its central provision is stated in the very first sentence of section 9: "A non-Jew is forbidden to enter into marriage with a Jew." Next the law discusses in detail such questions as who is considered a Jew, the situation of a Hungarian Jewish woman who marries a non-Jewish foreigner, children born to unmarried mothers, Christians converting to Judaism, etc., and it then goes on to specify the punishments for violations. It also punishes with three years' imprisonment any Jewish man who has extramarital sexual relations with a "decent non-Jewish woman resident in Hungary."

The difference between the first two Jewish Laws and this one is that while the former two were directed against the economic positions of the Jews in the country, the 1941 law intended to prevent social relations between Jews and Christians, and took it for granted that the Jews were an alien and inferior race, interbreeding with whom was harmful for the Hungarian "national soul." It stated: "Mixed marriages had a definitely detrimental effect upon the evolution of our national soul; they brought into a position of influence that Jewish spirit whose harmful effect we have seen."

Simultaneously with the issuance of the third Jewish Law began the deportations of Jews from Hungary. The first to be affected were foreign Jews (variously estimated from 15,000 to 35,000), who had fled in 1938 from the territories occupied by Germany and found refuge in Hungary. They had been able to enter Hungary as a result of an order issued by Ferenc Keresztes-Fischer, the minister of the interior, in response to the urging of the Hungarian Jewish Palestine Office, which argued that the refugees would stay in Hungary only temporarily and within a short time would emigrate to Palestine. However, in 1941, the Hungarian National Office in Control of Aliens arrested the Austrian, Czechoslovak, Rumanian, Croatian, and Serbian Jewish refugees, who did not possess Hungarian citizenship certificates, and concentrated them in Kőrösmező, where they were handed over to the military authorities. They were transported to eastern Galicia, most of them to Kamenetz-Podolsk, others to Trans-Dnistria.

In those places there still existed a few Jewish communities, which, although they themselves were in a deplorable situation, tried to help the deportees, whose position was even more desperate. Some of the refugees were placed in the synagogues, others were sent to labor camps. Even though they endured inhuman sufferings, many of them continued to observe the religious precepts, including fasting on the Ninth of Av and the Day of Atonement, up until the very time they were massacred by the Nazis, beginning in May, 1944. It is estimated that the number of victims reached 15–16,000 before Keresztes-Fischer ordered a halt to the massacre. Only about 2,000 of the deportees escaped with their lives. However, within a few months, the Germans massacred a total of some 35,000 Jews deported from Hungary to hastily established camps in Galicia and the Ukraine.

In contrast to the foreign Jews, the Jews who were Hungarian citizens had a respite of three more years. They were degraded, treated like scum, deprived of their jobs and livelihood, and made miserable in every respect—but they were neither killed outright nor deported to death camps. However, the able-bodied Jewish men were forced to serve in labor battalions. That summer, eleven such battalions were sent to northern Hungary to work on the roads leading across the Carpathian Mountains; others were put to work to help out with the harvesting. They had to wear a yellow arm band, and their papers were stamped with a red "ZS," for *Zsidó* (Jew). They were treated in a most cruel manner, designed to kill them.

In December 1941, the Bárdossy government declared that Hungary was at war with Great Britain and the United States. He was able to prevent the expulsion of the Ukrainians from Ruthenia but could not, or in any case did not, prevent the shipping out of the Jews to death camps. Nor was Bárdossy able to prevent Hungarian military and gendarmerie units from carrying out mass slaughters in the south, especially around Novi Sad (Hungarian Ujvidék), where thousands of Serbs and Jews were put to death as supposed "partisans." The military perpetrated the bloodbath because it wanted to prove it was strong enough to break Serb resistance and control Jewish "subversion," and thus to convince Germany to hand over the Banat to Hungary. Between January 21 and 23, 1942, two Hungarian high army officers, claiming that Serbs had made attacks against the Hungarian army, carried out identity checks of all the inhabitants of the city. They went from house to house, and ordered many Serbs and Jews (Hungarian Jews, who had remained loyal to Hungary throughout the years when Ujvidék/Novi Sad was part of Yugoslavia) to gather on the banks of the Danube. There they forced them to undress, lined them up, let them wait in the great cold for hours, and then shot them into the river. According to German documents "several thousands" fell victim to this massacre, and a statement by the Hungarian minister of the exterior reported 3,755. Finally, the civilian authorities of Ujvidék contacted Budapest, and an order was issued to end the killing.

The Ujvidék deeds of horror created great indignation among those of the politicians and public who still harbored humane feelings toward the "aliens." The official Hungarian News Service sharply condemned the atrocities as unparalleled in Hungarian military history. The government, too, dissociated itself from the massacres, condemned them, and stated that those responsible would be punished. Legal proceedings were actually initiated, but the chief culprits were soon freed and managed to escape to Austria. Subsequently the *Pester Lloyd* condemned those (i.e., the Austrian Nazi authorities) who gave shelter to the escaped officers. Late in 1943 the proceedings were reopened, possibly (as the Germans interpreted it), "for reasons of external politics."

In March 1942, Miklós Kállay became prime minister of Hungary. He is credited by the historians of the period with saving Hungarian Jewry until the German occupation of March 1944, when he himself had to seek asylum in the Turkish Embassy. However, at first he continued the anti-Jewish policies of his predecessors, and in May 1942, his government prepared a bill that aimed at depriving the Jews of practically the last of their remaining rights: owning real estate. The bill, which was passed in September 1942, (Law 1942:XV) ruled that a Jew could own not more than 100 *hold*s (equaling 57 hectares or 142 acres) of land. This law resulted in the expropriation of 700,000 *hold*s of agricultural land and 500,000 *hold*s of forestry land from Jewish owners. In July 1942, the government officially invalidated the 1895 Law of Reception, thereby annulling the equality before the law of the Jewish religion and prohibiting conversion to Judaism.

In the spring of 1942, when Germany suffered its defeat at Moscow and needed all available manpower, it demanded of Hungary to supply, in addition to the combatant troops, also labor battalions to support the armed units on the front. In response, several thousands of Hungarian Jews were recruited, without consideration for their civilian occupation, including, for example, physicians who had not been admitted to membership in the physicians' chamber. By the summer of 1942, some 50,000 Hungarian Jews had been pressed into service in the labor battalions on the eastern front. Some worked in the military supply services, in road repair, and in unloading trains that brought arms, ammunition, and food to the front; others were employed in all kinds of technical tasks, in earthwork, in fortifications, and in clearing areas of mines.

They were forced to do all this in inhuman circumstances, without proper clothing or adequate food, amid constant harassment and cruelties by their commanders, who treated them like members of a prison gang. In the fall of 1942, when reports of this situation reached the newly appointed minister of defense, Vilmos Nagy de Nagybaczon, he demanded of the Council of Ministers that the Jewish labor battalions be supplied with adequate food and clothing, so as to be able to continue working without a breakdown. Consequently, the Ministry of the Interior issued a permit allowing the Jews to launch a collection of clothes for the Jewish labor battalions. Within a short time, the Jewish organizations of Budapest collected clothes that filled twenty-eight railway cars, which were duly dispatched to the eastern front. However, only part of the clothes reached their intended recipients, since the better-quality clothes were appropriated by the Wehrmacht.

The German defeats on the eastern front made Kállay doubt the ultimate German victory, and he began to sound out the Allies about the possibility of getting out of the war. Part of the policy he adopted within that context was to accord the Jews somewhat more humane treatment. In October 1942, in a note addressed to the Hungarian government, the Germans demanded that Hungary remove its Jews from the economic and cultural life of Hungary, force them to wear the yellow Star of David, and begin their deportation forthwith, as was already in progress in the neighboring countries. In its response of December 1942, the Hungarian government refused to comply, pointing to the severe legal restrictions already imposed upon the Jews, arguing that their treatment was an internal Hungarian affair, and that their "resettlement" would disrupt the Hungarian economy, 80 percent of which was now in the service of Germany. Kállay also maintained that the solution of the Jewish question in Hungary would be extremely difficult, because the fraction of Jews was much larger there than in other European countries. He emphasized that as far as their international influence was concerned, the Hungarian Jews were much less dangerous than the Jews of France, and that "the solution of the question would be difficult also because, for example, the Hungarian peasant was absolutely not anti-Semitic." At this time the Hungarian government adopted a less harsh attitude toward the Jews, recognizing the right of the family members of those who perished on the front to receive compensation. Nevertheless, in the winter of 1942–43, of the nearly 50,000 Jews in labor service on the eastern front, some 43–44,000 perished, and only 6–7,000 returned to Hungary.

In the spring of 1943 Germany intensified the pressure on Hungary with reference to the Hungarian Jews. At the demand of the Germans, the Hungarian government forced another 10,000 Jews into labor battalions and sent them to Serbia to work in the copper mines. By that time, the series of defeats suffered by the Germans on the eastern front left the total extermination of European Jewry as Hitler's one achievable aim. In his April meeting with Regent Horthy, Hitler sharply attacked Hungary for refusing to deport the Jews, and demanded Kállay's removal. In a secret report dated April 30, 1943, Edmund Veesenmayer, brigadier-general in the SS, informed the German government that the Hungarian Jews were primarily responsible for the defeatist attitude prevailing in the country, and that the Hungarians believed that by sheltering the Jews they would escape serious air raids and would be able to prove, after the war, that they had fought on the side of the Axis Powers only because they had been forced to. Veesenmayer portrayed Regent Horthy as surrounded by Jews and aristocrats with Jewish family connections, and he listed the Jews and aristocrats with such relations as the most important enemies of Germany.

552

It is a fact, and a highly paradoxical one, that while the noose was rapidly tightening around the neck of Hungarian Jewry, and more and more of them were dying under the inhuman conditions of forced labor service on the eastern front, a few wealthy Jews or ex-Jews remained members of the Hungarian Upper House and continued to serve on its Finance Committee. They were the converted financial and industrial leaders Ferenc Chorin, Aurél Egry, and Móric Kornfeld, as well as Leó Budai-Goldberger and Jenő Vida, both of whom played important roles in the life of the Jewish community. Even more remarkable is the fact that two of these men, Chorin and Egry, on April 13, 1943, were also elected members of the Foreign Affairs Committee of the Upper House, despite the increasing German pressure on Hungary to resolve the Jewish question.

Not only did the Hungarian resistance to these German demands continue but, as Germany's fortunes of war declined, voices were increasingly raised for Hungary to dissociate itself from Germany in general and its anti-Jewish policy in particular. After the Allies' landing in Sicily (July 1943) and the fall of the Italian Fascist government, Endre Bajcsy-Zsilinszky, leader of the minuscule Independent Smallholders Party, submitted to Kállay a memorandum demanding the reestablishment of equality before the law, which had been violated by the anti-Jewish laws, and daringly suggested that even a temporary German occupation of the country would be an acceptable price for leaving the war. The Social Democratic party accepted these demands and arguments, but neither Kállay nor Regent Horthy had the courage to turn against the Germans.

In December 1943, Veesenmayer sent a second secret report to his government in which he reiterated that in Hungary "the Jews are enemy number one, and the 1.1 million Jews amount to as many saboteurs . . . and they will have to be looked upon as Bolshevik vanguards." He also reported on the prime minister's contact with the Allies (which he was informed of by Minister of Supplies Béla Jurcsek) and suggested that Germany engage in "continuing and sharpening criticism with regard to the Jewish question" and in "maneuverlike concentration of troops—even if only to a modest extent—at several important points along the German-Hungarian border." In order to persuade Horthy to agree to a change of government, Veesenmayer suggested dangling before him several favors, the last of which was "the promise that the so-called court Jews would be spared." At the end of his forty-two-page typed report, Veesenmayer suggested that Germany notify the Allies that if Budapest were subjected to air raids, "for every Hungarian killed by bombs, one hundred rich Jews would be shot to death, and their property would be used to compensate for the damages."

As this document shows, by the end of 1943 the Germans recognized that the mood in Hungary was turning against them, and concluded that, in order to prevent its secession, they had to occupy it.

It is almost incredible that while the *Endlösung* was in full swing in the neighboring countries, and in Hungary herself the Jewish condition was precipitously deteriorating, with brutal physical attacks on the Jews increasing, the Jewish educational and cultural institutions continued to function relatively undisturbed. Several of the cultural activities were organized as part of the response of the Jewish community to the anti-Jewish laws which resulted in the summary dismissal of the Jewish artists, musicians, and actors from their jobs.

In November, 1939, the Hungarian government permitted the establishment of a Jewish theater, under the auspices of the *Országos Magyar Izraelita Közművelődési Egyesület* (National Hungarian Israelite Educational Association, in brief: OMIKE), which was founded as long ago as in 1910. OMIKE had at its disposal a sizable lecture hall, called the Goldmark Hall (named after the famed Hungarian-Jewish composer Károly Goldmark), and was able to adapt it to theatrical performances. Under the general title "OMIKE Art Evenings" OMIKE organized performances of serious plays, comedies, operas, musicals, and concerts, in which Jewish actors, singers, and musicians, who had become unemployed as a result of the Jewish laws, appeared. Some of these performers had been the greatest stars of the Hungarian theater and concert stage, and their appearances in the Jewish hall attracted even non-Jewish critics, who subsequently reviewed them in the general press. In addition to performing such classics as Hebbel's *Judith*, Racine's *Esther*, plays by Shakespeare, Moliere, Ibsen, Ferenc Molnár, OMIKE called upon some forty Hungarian Jewish playwrights to write plays especially for its theater. In its concert series the OMIKE orchestra performed more than three hundred musical compositions by about a hundred composers. OMIKE also organized exhibitions of paintings, graphic art and sculptures, in which the works of almost a hundred Jewish painters and sculptors could be viewed, many of whom were by that time in compulsory labor service from which they never returned. These exhibitions, concerts, and other performances continued until the very day of the German occupation of Hungary. In the years 1941–43 the Cultural Council of OMIKE was also instrumental in the publication of several books of Jewish contents.

While the Jewish writers, artists, musicians and actors tried in this manner to find a compensatory outlet within the Jewish congregational framework for their talents which the Jewish laws banished from their accustomed general Hungarian environment, these developments did nothing to diminish the Hungarian patriotic enthusiasm that burned in the bosom of Hungarian Israel. Typical was the review published in the *Magyar Zsidók Lapja* (Journal of Hungarian Jews) on the occasion of the opening on December 21, 1939, of an exhibition of Hungarian Jewish painters and sculptors in the halls of the Hungarian Jewish Museum. After enumerating the foremost artists whose works were exhibited, the reviewer asks rhetorically: "Were not all these artists the interpreters of the peculiarly Hungarian artistic vision, of the Hungarian colors, of the Hungarian forms, of the Hungarian life, and did they not understand that particular Hungarian spirit, specificity and special beauty which led the art of this age to such great triumphs?" And he goes on to explain that the artists exhibited were essentially Hungarian, and to deny that there was anything specifically Jewish in their art:

> Now, also in this exhibition of the mostly Hungarian Jewish new artistic generation, which has been forced into isolation, we get the overall impression that the Hungarian Jewish artists are forced to become separated only with respect to the place of the exhibition, but as far as their subject-matter, perception, vision are concerned they have remained Hungarian artists, and thus, even in the midst of the difficult throes of seeking new forms, they serve only one endeavor: to continue to build and develop that specific Hungarian art with which the generation of the early twentieth century achieved such great successes. . . . The Hungarian Jewish painters did not create a separate Jewish art of painting, did not take over the feature that has been most characteristic until now, and which finds expression mainly in the Jewish representational painting.

As a result of these congregational efforts in the fields of literature, art, music and the theater a paradox developed: while the Jewish Laws brought rapid and relentless economic ruin to the Jews, more cultural activities took place under Jewish auspices afterwards than while the Hungarian Jews were still a prosperous, well-established, socially and economically secure community.

It would, of course, be erroneous to interpret this phenomenon as indicating that Hungarian Jewry was oblivious to the catastrophe that had overtaken the Jews in the adjacent countries. It seems rather to reflect two interconnected reactions. One was defiance: the Jews, who for decades had been leaders in every field of Hungarian culture, felt impelled to show that despite everything done to them by the anti-Semitic government they were determined to continue in the same role. The other was naive belief in the special relationship between the Hungarian Jews and the Hungarian people: however much the Hungarians hurt the Jews—and goodness knows they had done that periodically for generations—it was simply impossible to them that the genocide undertaken by Germany in the neighboring countries should spread into Hungary.

It couldn't happen here, they thought, and until the wrath passed they felt they had to retain the greatest possible semblance of normal Jewish life, of which artistic and cultural activities were even in the existing circumstances an integral part, and more than that, a psychologically sustaining one.

It was largely due to Kállay's and Horthy's refusal to go along with the German policy of the "final solution" that Hungarian Jewry as a whole was able to survive with "only" incidental and occasional losses of life until the beginning of the German-organized deportations on May 15, 1944. According to the 1941 Hungarian statistics, in that year the total population of the country was 14,683,323, of whom 725,000 were Jews. In addition there were another 100,000 or so persons whom Law 1939: IV considered Jews, so that around 5.6 percent of the total population consisted of persons legally declared Jews. Of these, until May 1944 "only" some 50,000 lost their lives in consequence of various legally sanctioned or else unauthorized actions.

Of the roughly 775,000 Jews in Hungary on the eve of the German occupation of March 19, 1944, around 175,000 were concentrated in Budapest and 600,000 lived in the country towns. The number of communities outside Budapest was about 360, of which data covering 138 are available. They show that 58 were Neolog congregations, 68 Orthodox, and 12 Status Quo Ante. Their memberships ranged from a few hundred to several thousand. Despite the extremely trying circumstances, deprivations, and cruel treatment, these communities managed to maintain their institutions. They had eighty-two elementary schools, forty-one yeshivas, and five *gimnáziums*, in two of which (those of Ungvár and Munkács) the language of instruction was Hebrew. There was also one teacher training institute, in Miskolc. There functioned also heders and junior high (*polgári*) schools, number unknown. Four communities maintained hospitals. There were *Ḥevra Kadisha* (burial and charity) societies, women's and girls' societies, soup kitchens, old peoples' homes, social aid organizations, libraries, choirs and orchestras, youth circles, literary and educational societies, and charitable foundations. All in all, in even the smallest communities, Jewish life went on despite the gathering storm.

One of the most important questions, and one of the most difficult to answer, is how the Hungarian Jews reacted to the series of blows dealt them by the government, which successively deprived them of rights they had long considered inalienably theirs. There seem to have been three distinct reactions. The clearest was that of the official Jewish leadership. Its position was that "this, too, shall pass." Pronouncements of the leading rabbis and heads of communities were unanimous in counseling patience, endurance, biding one's time. They simultaneously tried to influence the government by reiterating their patriotism and by arguing that excluding Jews from economic and professional activities could only hurt the national economy and harm national interests.

The second reaction, that of the simple members of the Jewish communities, was diametrically opposed to that of the official Jewish establishment. It consisted of haphazard and unorganized individual attempts to escape from the rapidly closing trap that Hungary became for the Jews. However, in the absence of official directives, the realization that only emigration held out the hope of survival came too late for most. It was only shortly before the German occupation that some Orthodox Jews voiced this conclusion, as seen in a Hebrew writing published in Budapest in 1944 under the title *Em haBanim S'meḥa* (The Mother of the Sons Rejoices) by Rabbi Y. S. Teichthal, which advocated readiness for emigration and even reproached the Orthodox leadership for having been tardy in recognizing this necessity. The sad fact is that because of the unpreparedness to try to find a way out of the country, because of the increasing disabilities imposed upon the Jews inside Hungary, because of the tensions between Hungary and its neighbors, and finally, because of the British Mandatory Government's restrictions on immigration into Palestine, only 6,000 Jews were able to escape from Hungary between 1939 and 1944 and find refuge in Palestine.

The third reaction was that of those Jews who tried to keep informed of events on the fronts and the progress of the war. As the German positions weakened, these Jews came to the conclusion that time was on the Allied side and hoped that Germany would be defeated before long. True, they heard horrible things from the Polish and Slovak Jews who fled as refugees to Hungary, but still too many Hungarian Jews believed that "it can't happen here," because "Horthy would not tolerate it." What they left out of consideration, or rather, what they could not envisage, was that only a few weeks before the Nazi power itself was destroyed by the Allies it would still have time to carry out the last phase of its diabolic plan by destroying Hungarian Jewry.

I cannot conclude this account of the preamble to the Hungarian Jewish Holocaust without touching on a relatively unknown chapter of the history of the Jews in Hungary during World War II—relatively unknown because the existing scanty literature about it is in either Hungarian or Polish. It is the story of the Polish Jews who were given refuge in Hungary, and thereby got a brief lease on life until the Nazi fury overtook them.

The story began in the fall of 1939, after the Germans crushed the Polish army, sending many refuges to seek safety across the Hungarian border. Among them were soldiers and civilians, Jews and gentiles. Even though by that time the Second Jewish Law was in force, neither the military nor civilian authorities of Hungary paid much attention to it when faced with the refugees. The German Embassy demanded that the Polish Jews be intercepted at the border and sent back to German-occupied Poland, but the Hungarian border guards were instructed by József Antall, head of the General Aid Department of the Hungarian Ministry of the Interior, to register all Polish refugees as Christians, with the exception of those who insisted on registering their non-Christian religious affiliation. At Antall's request, the newly formed Polish Clergy Office issued Christian papers to everybody, so that only a very few refugees were identified as Jews. Cardinal Jusztinián Serédy, prince-primate of Hungary, also instructed his clergy to give Christian papers to all Jews applying for them. The Hungarian-Polish Committee of Refugee Affairs distributed printed copies of the basic Catholic prayers among the Polish Jews, so that in case they were tested by Germans they could pass as Christians.

The Polish refugees, gentiles and Jews together, were placed into transit camps, then into permanent camps. Those Jews who had insisted on being identified as Jews were placed in the care of the Jewish congregations of Budapest and the countryside, but received aid like all the others. Church institutions also opened their doors to the Polish Jews, many of whom were thus saved after the German occupation of Hungary. The intellectual leaders of the Polish Jews were sheltered in Esztergom, near the cardinal's palace, in houses that had two entrances, so that in case of searches they should have a better chance of escaping.

No exact figures are available for the number of Polish Jewish refugees, many of whom had already left Hungary in the fall of 1939 and tried to reach France, but it is estimated as probably between 3,000 and 5,000. During the winter of 1939–40 several educational institutions were set up near Budapest and elsewhere for Polish Jewish children, who were supplied with false Christian identification papers. Orphanages were established for those of them whom their parents managed to throw out of the death trains, or who escaped in some other way, and were saved by the Hungarian Red Cross.

After the beginning of the German-Soviet war a new wave of Polish refugees reached Hungary, many with the help of Hungarian army officers who enabled them to travel on Red Cross trains and military trains and trucks. After the promulgation of the Third Jewish Law (Law 1941:XV), bowing to renewed German pressure, the Hungarian government set up special camps in Fajsz, Vámosmikola, and Kadárkut for those Polish Jewish refugees (both ex-soldiers and civilians) who insisted on being identified as Jews.

All these efforts came to naught with the German occupation of Hungary, after which only a few of the Jews under Christian protection were saved.

42

The Hungarian Holocaust: The Beginnings

Geography is destiny. In the European context, no other nation supplies clearer proof of the truth of this observation than Hungary. It was Hungary's proximity to the Turkish-dominated Balkans that brought about the occupation of its heartland in 1526 by the Ottoman forces. It was its proximity to Austria that made it a province, and later the junior partner, of the Habsburg Empire, never enjoying full independence until the collapse of the dual monarchy after World War I. It was the proximity to Germany, especially after the Austrian *Anschluss* and the Nazi occupation of Czechoslovakia, that made Hungary a dependent of the Third Reich. And it was its proximity to Soviet Russia that made it, after the German defeat, a Russian satellite.

Within this serial subordination to its more powerful neighbors, even the internal policies of Hungary reflected the changes that occurred inside those neighboring powers. This is especially evident in this century. Within a short time after Russia became Communist, the Communists also managed to establish a government in Hungary (in 1919), though it was very short lived. In the late 1930s, when Germany introduced anti-Jewish laws, the long endemic anti-Semitism evinced an upsurge in Hungary too. As the Nazis tightened their grip on Germany, their Hungarian equivalent, the Arrow Cross Party, gained in strength and public support. When Germany embarked upon the systematic extermination of the Jews, the same policy received increasing support in Hungary. Following the Russian occupation in 1945, Hungarian leaders discovered that they were at heart Communists, and instituted economic and other reforms paralleling those of the Soviet Union. After the death of Stalin in 1953, when changes were introduced in the Soviet system, Hungarian Communists felt that very similar changes were necessary in Hungary. When Gorbachev shook up the Soviet Union in the 1980s with his glasnost and perestroika, corresponding Hungarian moves inevitably followed. And when the Communist Party was removed from power and reduced to an opposition party in Russia, the same step was also taken in Hungary. It is in the light of this "follower mentality" that we must understand the Hungarian support of the Holocaust after the German occupation of Hungary on March 19, 1944.

In this chapter and the next, we can present but the briefest recapitulation of the events of the most horrible year in the millennial history of Hungary's Jews, events about which a huge amount of information is available, and about which much has been written in the course of the decades that have passed since the liberation. The most detailed, complete, and judicious presentation of what led up to the German occupation of Hungary and what happened during it is found in Randolph L. Braham's two-volume work *The Politics of Genocide: The Holocaust in Hungary*, which the interested reader will undoubtedly wish to consult.

To say that March 19, 1944, was the beginning of the most catastrophic year in the eighteen centuries of Jewish history in Hungary does not even begin to convey the fact that the Holocaust perpetrated by the Germans and Hungarians that year was not only on an entirely different order of magnitude from any persecutions Hungarian Jews had experienced before, but was also of a totally different kind: never before had they been singled out for total extermination by the government of the country of which they were citizens or legal inhabitants.

The immediate prelude to the German occupation of Hungary was the invitation, amounting to a command, the Germans extended to Regent Horthy to come to Schloss Klessheim to discuss the terms under which Hungary would remain in the war. Horthy arrived on March 18, 1944, and that same afternoon Germany set in motion what it codenamed "Operation Margarete"—the military occupation of Hungary. During his short stay as Hitler's "guest," the will of the seventy-six-year-old Horthy seems to have been broken, and he acceded to all the German demands, including the dispatch to Germany of several thousand Hungarian Jews to work for the German war effort. The next day, March 19, by the time Horthy and his entourage returned to Hungary in the company of Edmund Veesenmayer, the newly appointed German minister and Reich plenipotentiary, the German occupation of Hungary had been accomplished. Veesenmayer's tasks included assisting in the formation of a new national government in Hungary and taking care of "police duties in connection with the Jewish problem."

On March 19, the very day of the German occupation of Hungary (which took place without any opposition by Hungarian forces), Hermann A. Krumey, SS *Obersturmbannführer*, and Dieter Wisliceny, SS *Hauptsturmführer*, asked the leaders of the Israelite Congregation of Pest to meet with them the following day. At the meeting they stated that the right of dealing with the Jews rested exclusively with the Germans, but reassured the Jews that no harm would befall Hungarian Jewry if they obeyed orders, and that there would be no arbitrary arrests or deportations. The Germans were interested only in increasing the output of the Hungarian war industries, for which purpose they might ask for Jewish "volunteers." Deceived by these indications of goodwill, the Jewish leaders left the meeting with a feeling of optimism.

The German moves to take control of all areas of economic and political life in Hungary were rapid, thorough, and all-encompassing. Within a short time the entire industry and agriculture of the country was put at the disposal of the German military effort. As for "the Jewish problem," the first step in its "solution" was to detain many members of the upper echelons of Hungarian Jewish society. Before the end of March no less than 3,364 of them were arrested in so-called "individual actions," and a month later their number had risen to 8,225.

Even before the occupation, Adolf Eichmann, head of a section in the German Reich Head Security Office (Reichssicherheitshauptamt) had met with the staff of his Sonderkommando and discussed in detail the agenda of the "final solution" that was to be put into effect upon occupation. Eichmann's units received the support of the newly formed, strongly pro-German Hungarian government, headed by Döme Sztójay, whom, at German insistence, Horthy had appointed prime minister. Also at German insistence, two pronouncedly anti-Semitic politicians, László Endre and László Baky, were appointed state secretaries in charge of the Jewish question. Both collaborated closely with Eichmann in effecting the "final solution" in Hungary.

On March 29, the Council of Ministers began issuing a series of anti-Jewish decrees aimed at depriving the Jews of the last remnants of their positions. The Jews were ordered to register their telephones, and soon thereafter to surrender them. On March 31 the wearing of the yellow star was made obligatory for all Jews and converted Jews (the Catholic Church protested the latter). Jews were forbidden to employ non-Jewish household help, were made to register automobiles in their possession, were summarily dismissed from state and public offices, and were excluded from the law, press, motion picture, and theater chambers. On April 7 Jews were prohibited from using cars, motorcycles, taxis, trains, buses, and ships—all forms of transportation except streetcars. All radios owned by Jews had to be delivered to the authorities. Before the end of April, a law excluded Jews from employment in any intellectual capacity and barred Jewish writers from publishing their works, with a view to "protecting Hungarian intellectual life."

In mid-April the government instituted the systematic expropriation of all property owned by Jews. The Jews were ordered to register all their assets, their current and savings accounts were closed, and the contents of their safe deposit boxes had to be registered and were frozen. A Jew could draw only 1,000 pengős from whatever accounts he had, and could not have in his possession more than 3,000 pengős at any time. On April 21 the Ministry of Commerce closed all Jewish businesses, which order affected 18,000 Jewish stores in Budapest alone. The effect of these decrees was to reduce Hungarian Jewry within a few days to the merest and barest level of subsistence, in which people's only concern became how to remain alive from one day to the next.

Simultaneously with this systematic destruction of Jewish existence began the planning of the concentration of Jews in special localities in preparation for their deportation. In early April a secret meeting took place at the Ministry of the Interior, chaired by László Baky, the political state secretary, with the participation of representatives of the Wehrmacht (the German army), leading officers of Eichmann's Sonderkommando, and representatives of the royal Hungarian gendarmerie. At that meeting László Endre presented his detailed plan for the concentration of Jews in ghettos and their removal by deportation. A highly confidential order was issued to all prefects, mayors, gendarmerie commanders, and other officials, informing them that the government had decided to clear the country of Jews "within a short period of time." The Jews were to be rounded up without regard to sex or age and would be allowed to take along only a minimum of supplies, such as the clothes they wore, two sets of underwear and shirts, food for fourteen days, and other baggage not exceeding fifty kilograms. They were not to be permitted to take along money, jewelry, gold, or other valuables. Since the German occupation forces were limited in number, the execution of the plan was to be the task of the local police and the Hungarian gendarmerie, which would be supported by Eichmann's Sonderkommando in a supervisory and advisory capacity.

While these preparations for the systematic genocide of Hungarian Jewry were underway, many of the assimilant Hungarian Jews and ex-Jews were still caught in the grip of the Magyarism they had inherited from several generations of Hungarian Jewish patriots. They felt so *Hungarian,* and were so sure that they were considered Hungarian by the Hungarian Christians, that they just could not imagine that Hungarian forces, or for that matter any kind of Hungarian formation, could become willing partners of the German Nazis in their extermination. A tragic illustration of this attitude was the case of György Sárközi (1899–1945), a Jew by descent though not by religion, a delicate poet, accomplished author, and efficient business organizer, who served the populist cause devotedly and was the last editor of *Válasz* (Response), the highbrow monthly of the March Front, which claimed kinship to the March Youth of 1848 and had a clear-cut program of democratic reforms. Sárközi fell totally under the spell of the nationalist mystique of the populist cause, and felt at least as Hungarian as his gentile colleagues. But nothing could exempt him from being forced, toward the end of the war, into a Jewish labor battalion. When some of his friends urged him to try to escape before being dispatched to an extermination camp, he merely shook his head and said, "We are in the hands of *Hungarian* Nazis, and however blinkered they may be, they won't do *that!*" The *Hungarian* Nazis then took his batallion to the Austrian border, whence he never returned.

Eichmann's plan called for the rounding up of Jews first in the northern border areas of Hungary, then in the east, the south and the west, and finally in Budapest. On April 13, Carpatho-Ruthenia and Transylvania in the northeastern part of the country were declared "operational zones" so as to justify the "removal of possible collaborators with the enemy." The evacuation of the Jews was carried out with great brutality by the police and gendarmerie. The Jews were aroused at dawn, given a few minutes to dress and pack, and driven to the local synagogues. There they were deprived of all the valuables they had brought along, and were shipped—in most cases forced to walk—to the major ghettos and assembly centers established in preselected cities such as Munkács, Ungvár, Beregszász, and Nagykanizsa. The conditions in the ghettos were appalling, purposely made as inhuman as possible. In many places the ghettos were situated in brickyards, or even under the open sky. Tens of thousands of Jews were crowded into small areas, maltreated, savagely beaten "in search of hidden valuables," subjected to starvation, and deprived of the most elementary sanitary facilities, so that many fell victim to epidemics.

Within a few days of occupying Hungary, the Germans set up—as they did in other countries they occupied—a *Judenrat* (Jewish council), and imposed on it the task of serving as the link between the Jews of the country and the German occupying forces. Samu Stern (seventy years old at the time), president of both the Israelite Congregation of Pest and the Neolog National Office, was made chairman, and its members were: Dr. Ernő Boda, Dr. Ernő Pető, and Dr. Károly Wilhelm, representing the Neolog Congregation of Pest; Dr. Samu Csobádi, representing the Neolog Congregation of Buda; Samu Kahan-Frankl and Fülöp Freudiger, representing the Orthodox community; and Dr. Nison Kahan, representing the Zionists. A short time thereafter, several of these members were replaced by Dr. Béla Berend, former chief rabbi of Szigetvár; Sándor Török, journalist; Dr. József Nagy, chief physician of the Budapest Jewish hospital; and Dr. János Gábor, secretary of the Pest congregation.

To begin with, the duties imposed by the Nazis on the Jewish Council seemed simple and innocuous. It had to supply information to the Germans to enable them to carry out the measures decided upon by their high command, and it had to carry out the instructions the Germans issued that were of an administrative nature. To enable the *Judenrat* to function efficiently, the Germans permitted it to publish a paper, titled *Magyar Zsidók Lapja* (Journal of Hungarian Jews), the only Jewish paper in existence during the occupation. As time passed, the Germans imposed harsher and harsher demands on the Council, until their true intentions—the extermination of the Hungarian Jews—became evident. Thus, unwittingly, and certainly against its own will, the Jewish Council became one of the instruments used by the German and Hungarian authorities to carry out their anti-Jewish measures.

No activity engaged in by Hungarian Jews in the course of their millennial history is more difficult to judge than the work of the Budapest Jewish Council. None gave rise to greater controversy or more contradictory opinions. Some historians of the period come to the conclusion that the members of the Jewish Council were ruthlessly selfish men who worked for the Germans and kept the Jewish masses in ignorance of the fate that awaited them in order to save their own lives and the lives of their relatives. Others find that they were honorable men, who fulfilled the thankless and dangerous function forced upon them by the Germans because they were ignorant of the Nazis' true intentions, or because they hoped that by cooperating they could mitigate or delay the German genocidal plans. In any case, it is a fact that membership in the *Judenrat* brought with it definite personal advantages, and several members made use of the their connections with Nazi high officials to save their own relatives or, when the occasion arose, to escape from Hungary. On the other hand, it is also a documented fact that members of the Jewish Council, sometimes at considerable personal risk, intervened and succeeded in saving the lives of thousands of Hungarian Jews. Much more research will be required before a definite judgment can be reached on the role of the Budapest Jewish Council in the tragedy of the Hungarian Jews.

In the case of two individuals, views on their actions during the Nazi occupation of Hungary were so sharply contradictory that they led to sensational lawsuits. One of them was Dr. Béla Berend (1911–87), a member of the Budapest Jewish Council, a quixotic personality, who made no secret of his disdain for the bouregois members of the Council. After the liberation he was tried and, on November 23, 1946, convicted for collaborating with the Nazis, extracting money and valuables from Jews, and other crimes, and he was sentenced to ten years' imprisonment. Berend's own defense was that the aim of everything he did was to save as many Jews as possible, and that he acted in the service of his concept of "Zionization of anti-Semitism," which called for convincing the Nazis that instead of killing off the Jews they could achieve their aim of a *Judenrein* (Jew-clean) Europe by enabling the Jews to emigrate and establish a homeland of their own. Upon appeal, and after listening to witnesses who described in glowing terms how Berend had saved their lives, how heroically he had behaved, and how he had risked his own life, the People's Tribunal reversed the verdict on April 11, 1947.

The other case was Dr. Rezső Kasztner (1906–57), a former Zionist leader from Cluj, Transylvania, who moved to Budapest in December 1940 and became executive officer of the Budapest Relief and Rescue Committee (Va'adat 'Ezra v'Hatzala, in brief Va'adah). After his immigration to Israel, he too was accused of having collaborated with the Nazis and was tried and found guilty in June 1955, despite the proven fact that he was instrumental in negotiating and purchasing the freedom (and thus the lives) of 1,686 Hungarian Jews. As in the case of Berend in Budapest, the higher court in Jerusalem reversed the verdict in January 1958 and found that Kasztner had actually tried to save the lives of as many Jews as possible, and in doing so had risked his own life. Kasztner did not live to enjoy his exoneration: he was shot dead by an assassin in March 1957. Without going into the merits of the cases here, we can see from the reversals of both verdicts how difficult it was to evaluate the activities of Jewish leaders who got involved with the Nazi authorities, in Hungary as elsewhere.

The extent to which Jewish intellectuals were part of Hungarian cultural life until their increasing exclusion by the Jewish Laws became fully apparent only after the German occupation. The press, increasingly controlled and centrally directed, became little more than a mouthpiece for German Nazi ideology. Many papers were suspended, and since only members of the press chamber could contribute articles, and the Jews were excluded from it, the quality of journalism dramatically declined. The same change could be observed in the programs offered by radio, the plays performed in theaters, and the films shown in the cinemas. The fine arts fared little better. The literary life of the country came under the control of the military leadership; writers' conferences were organized by the chief of staff, which meant that military patriotism—a new form of patriotism even for the traditionally superpatriotic Hungarians—had to be emphasized again and again, and the characteristic Hungarian satirical self-criticism and other typical manifestations of the national spirit had to go underground, or could be expressed only in a muted form. In scientific activity, the loss of contact with the outside world except the Fascist states was crippling. The elimination of the Jewish salt from the Hungarian intellectual diet rendered it bland. After the occupation began, those who opposed the Nazi trend and worked for a "spiritual national defense" were effectively silenced. What was left in Hungarian intellectual and artistic life was the Nazi–Arrow Cross counterpart of Russian socialist realism.

Not satisfied with the elimination of Jewish writers from the contemporary literary scene, in April and June 1944 the government published lists of several hundred Hungarian and foreign Jewish authors whose works were now banned. The foreign authors banned included Sigmund Freud, Ferdinand Lassalle, Karl Marx, André Maurois, Marcel Proust, Heinrich Heine, Hayyim Nahman Bialik, and Theodor Herzl; the Hungarians included Lajos Biró, Sándor Bródy, Renée Erdős, Jolán Földes, Lajos Hatvany, Lili Hatvany, Jenő Heltai, Ede Horn, József Kiss, Tamás Kóbor, Menyhért Lengyel, Georg Lukács, Ferenc Molnár, Károly Pap, József Patai, Rusztem Vámbéry, and Zoltán Zelk. To make sure that these decrees received nationwide attention, public book burnings were staged in several cities. On June 16, 1944, in Budapest, 447,627 books representing the works of 120 Hungarian and 130 foreign authors of Jewish background were burnt, and the ceremony was filmed for propaganda purposes.

About a month before these events, in emulation of the German example, a Hungarian Institute for the Research of the Jewish Question was set up, in order "to study the Jewish question in Hungary in a systematic and scientific manner, to collect and scientifically process the related data, and to inform Hungarian public opinion about the Hungarian and general Jewish question." The Institute, housed in the premises of the Jewish-owned Union Club in the Inner City of Budapest, collected books and ritual objects confiscated from various Jewish institutions. It published its own organ, *Harc* (Battle), modeled after the German *Der Stürmer*.

Simultaneously with these initiatives, the people of Hungary were frequently reminded that it was their patriotic duty to denounce any Jews who violated the measures adopted against them. A general atmosphere was thus created in which, as Braham puts it, the Jews had little choice but to "abide by the decrees enacted against them with the fatalism and submissiveness to which they had been accustomed through the ages."

43

The Destruction of Provincial Jewry

The diabolic cleverness with which the Germans managed to carry out the extermination of practically the entire Jewish community of the Hungarian provinces defies imagination. In order to prevent any overt resistance that the Jews could have been driven to had they found out what fate awaited them, the Germans worked out a master plan of deception. With this plan they were able not only to mislead the Jews but also to reassure those Hungarian authorities who would not have been willing to go along with the German plans of mass murder.

As early as April 24, 1944, Eichmann and Dieter Wisliceny (a member of his Sonderkommando), accompanied by four of their leading Hungarian henchmen, began a tour of the ghettos in northeastern Hungary. Upon their return they reported to Andor Jaross, minister of the interior in the Sztójay government, and to Regent Horthy that everything was in perfect order: "The provincial ghettos have the character of sanitoriums. At last the Jews have taken up an open-air life and exchanged their former mode of living for a healthier one." Jaross was a sworn Nazi (after the war he was executed for his crimes), but it is difficult to believe that such cynicism actually deceived Horthy.

A few days later the Jewish Council, which in the meantime had obtained information on the horrors that were taking place in northeastern Hungary, sent a detailed memorandum to Interior Minister Jaross describing the events county by county and asking him "to take measures so that the evacuated persons should receive suitable accommodations and food." On May 3 the Council sent a similar appeal to Eichmann. Neither Jaross nor Eichmann was moved by the Council's appeal, and the extermination of the Jews of the northeast proceeded according to plan.

Eichmann and his henchmen wished to maintain at least the external appearance of acting in accord with, or at the suggestion of, the Hungarian government. The deportation of the Jews was effected under the pretense that it was at the request of the local authorities, "because of the health and feeding difficulties prevailing in the ghettos." When László Ferenczy, liaison officer between Eichmann and the Hungarian gendarmerie, wanted the Jews either returned to their homes or removed to other areas, Eichmann responded that he "would be ready to take over the Jews if the Hungarian government made a special request." That same day, László Baky, secretary of state for Jewish affairs in the Ministry of the Interior, fulfilled the demanded request in the name of the Hungarian government.

After informing the Auschwitz authorities of the impending arrival of a large number of Jews from Hungary, on May 15, 1944, Eichmann began to organize and carry out the actual deportation. Within eight weeks, first 320,000 Jews were deported from northeastern Hungary, then 42,000 from northern Hungary, then 56,000 from southern Hungary including the Bácska (Batchka) territory, and finally 40,000 from western Hungary. That is to say, within those eight weeks a total of around 458,000 were sent to their death. These are the figures given by Dieter Wisliceny in his sworn affidavit before his execution in 1948; according to other sources the number was between 380,000 and 427,000.

The deportations and what happened to the Jews en route and after their arrival in Auschwitz are described by Braham as follows:

The deportations, personally supervised by Eichmann, took place under the most horrible and inhuman conditions. The day before the deportations began, hospital patients, newborn babies, the blind and deaf, the mentally disturbed, and prison inmates of Jewish origin were all brought into the ghettos. From there, together with the rest of the ghetto population, they were driven to the railway station, where they were loaded into freight cars. About eighty to one hundred people were crammed into each car, which was supplied with one bucket of water and one waste bucket. The trains were sealed off and escorted by units of the Hungarian gendarmerie to Kassa, where they were taken over by the SS. Hundreds of the deportees committed suicide, and many more died along the way. Many suffocated, as the deportation took place during the height of the summer heat, with the freight-car doors padlocked and windows and ventilators boarded up.

Some of the most brutal atrocities were committed en route, especially when the trains had to stop for traffic control. On May 24, for example, many Jews were killed and robbed by the escorting Germans at the Slovak railroad station of Kysak, evoking great consternation among the Slovak people who witnessed the incident.

Upon arrival at Auschwitz, the already weakened Jews were "processed" in accordance with the following preestablished rules: children up to the age of twelve or fourteen, older people above fifty, the sick, and people with criminal records (who were transported in specially marked wagons) were taken immediately on their arrival to the gas chambers. The others passed before an SS doctor who, on sight, indicated who was fit for work and who was not. Those unfit were sent to the gas chambers, while the others were sent to 386 different camps, most of them to Auschwitz, Bergen-Belsen, Mauthausen, Dachau, Buchenwald, and Ravensbruck. Relatively few of them managed to survive the hardships, cruelties, and degradations of camp life.

Despite the efforts of the Germans and the Hungarian Nazis to keep the Jews of Budapest unaware of the deportation of provincial Jewry, such a large-scale transportation of people out of the country could not be kept a secret for long. Late in May 1944, Fülöp Freudiger received a Hebrew letter from Pressburg informing him of the concentration of a large number of railroad cars in Slovakia, evidently in preparation for the deportation. At the same time the first reports from Auschwitz, telling about the fate of the deportees, also reached Hungary. The Jewish Council repeatedly appealed to the Hungarian government, but all it received in reponse were denials of the deportation. On May 25, the Jewish Council published in its official journal an article about the happenings in the provinces, which required considerable courage under the circumstances.

The Jewish Council, however, was willing to act only within the existing legal framework, which created dissatisfaction and, in fact, bitterness among the Budapest Jews in general. Most outspoken in their criticism of the Council's activities were the Zionists, who, early in June, without the Council's approval, published a broadside titled *To Christian Hungarian Society*. In it they gave a detailed account of the deportations and, emphasizing the Hungarian-Jewish community of fate, appealed to the Hungarian Christians for help. It also requested that, as the last resort, the Jews should be given the possibility to emigrate.

In mid-May 1944, independently of all organized Jewish effort at alleviating the situation of the Jews, a group of the wealthiest Jewish industrialists of Hungary, consisting mostly of the related baronial families of Weiss and Chorin, began negotiations with the German occupation authorities toward concluding a deal whereby the Manfred Weiss Works of Csepel, near Budapest, the largest industrial complex in Hungary, would be "leased" to the SS for a period of twenty-five years, in exchange for the negotiating families' being enabled to leave Hungary for the safety of neutral countries.

The Manfred Weiss Works were founded by two brothers, Berthold and Manfred Weiss (both of whom were ennobled by Francis Joseph), in about 1876. By 1896 the factory complex at Csepel was the largest in the country, and it continued to develop to the point that before the outbreak of World War I it dominated Hungarian ammunition production, employed 30,000 workers, and exported war materiel to England, Spain, Italy, Turkey, Mexico, and China. It was estimated that Manfred Weiss's wealth had reached 400–500 million crowns by 1917. (In that year alone he paid 34 million crowns in taxes!) Through his daughters' marriages he created alliances with the Chorin, Kornfeld, and Hatvany families, each an industrial and banking giant in its own right. (The Chorin family, incidentally, was descended from R. Aaron Chorin of Arad through his grandson, Ferenc Chorin, Sr., who converted to Christianity.) After the First World War the Weiss Works quickly recovered and before long was again at the head of the Hungarian production of agricultural machinery, iron and other metal products, and household appliances, as well as cloth and canned products and motor vehicles, employing by 1922 some ten thousand workers.

The German interest in obtaining a "lease" of the Manfred Weiss Works from their owners was due to the fact that under the Jewish Laws issued by Hungary, the Works were about to be expropriated by the Hungarian state, and the Germans wanted instead to have direct control over the plant, whose output was significant for their war effort. In any case, the plan was to vest control over the Manfred Weiss Works in the hands of Heinrich Himmler, *Reichsführer* SS, and the negotiations between Veesenmayer and the owners of the Works began in secret, without the knowledge of the Hungarian authorities. However, within a few days they became public knowledge and created a near scandal, especially since it was rumored that the Germans planned to rename the plant Hermann Göring Werk.

The negotiations were concluded with a compromise between the Hungarians and Germans, and it was agreed that the 55 percent of the shares that were in the hands of the "Aryan" members of the Chorin and Weiss families would be taken over in trust for twenty-five years by the Germans, who would pay Chorin 10 percent of the net profits, after deducting the damages caused or to be caused by Allied bombing. In exchange, the members of the families would be provided with ample funds and transported by air to Switzerland or Portugal. On June 24 nine members of the Weiss group were flown to Zurich, and on June 25 two German planes delivered the other Hungarian Jewish "millionaires" (as they were referred to in the official German correspondence) to Lisbon. The group of Jews thus saved also included members of the Kornfeld, Mauthner, and Billitz families, who bought their lives by handing over their own industrial enterprises to the Germans.

What these few ultrarich Jews and ex-Jews obtained for themselves, the Zionists tried to secure for as many Hungarian Jews as possible. Even before the outbreak of the war, but more emphatically after it, they understood, and tried to make Hungarian Jewry in general understand, that emigration was the only way of solving the Hungarian "Jewish question." In January 1943, the Zionists established the Hungarian Rescue Committee, headed by Ottó Komoly, president of the Hungarian Zionist Association, and Rezső Kasztner. Until the German occupation of Hungary, this committee worked primarily to help and protect the Jewish refugees who entered Hungary from the north and the east; afterwards, it tried to do whatever it could to save the Hungarian Jews.

In April, 1944, in the course of the contact the Rescue Committee established with the Germans, the idea developed that the Germans would agree to spare the lives of one million Jews and transport them to neutral countries in exchange for ten thousand trucks supplied them by the Allies. According to a sworn affidavit of Dieter Wisliceny, it was early in April that Kasztner, in his capacity as representative in Hungary of the American Jewish Joint Distribution Committee, gave Wisliceny 3 million pengős for Eichmann, to induce him to grant an interview to Kasztner and Jenő (Joel) Brand (1907–64), a member of the Rescue Committee. That month a series of talks followed during which the Jewish representatives offered to pay any amount if further actions against the Jews were discontinued. Eichmann reported to Himmler, who dispatched SS Standartenführer Kurt Becher to Budapest to continue negotiations. Becher was ready in principle to enter into a deal, and suggested that the payment for the Jews be made in trucks and raw materials, with the condition that they would not be used against England or America, that is, on the western front. According to Kasztner's 1945 affidavit, Eichmann said to him on April 3, 1944: "I can only sell the Hungarian Jews as if from Germany. Brand should leave at once for Istanbul and inform the Jews there and the Allies that I am repared to sell one million Hungarian Jews for goods, primarily vehicles. I will transport them to Oswiecim [Auschwitz] and 'put them on ice.' If my generous offer is accepted, I will release all of them. If not, they will all be gassed."

With this understanding, Brand went to Istanbul to present the suggested deal to the representatives of the Jewish Agency there. However, the British authorities prevented the representative of the Jewish Agency, Moshe Shertok (later Sharett), from going to Turkey to meet Brand. Brand thereupon continued to Palestine, but was arrested in Aleppo, Syria, by the British, who suspected (or claimed to suspect) that he was a German agent. What precise considerations motivated them to prevent

Brand from presenting Eichmann's *Blut für Ware* (blood for goods) deal is still not clear; it is likely that the saving of Jewish lives was not considered a sufficient price for strengthening the enemy army with a supply of trucks and materiel. In any case, Brand was arrested and interned in Cairo, and released only in October 1944, by which time the extermination of the Jews of the Hungarian provinces was a fait accompli. After the war, Brand remained in Palestine and devoted himself to tracking down Nazi war criminals. Both he and his wife testified at the 1961 Eichmann trial in Jerusalem.

Another initiative of the Rescue Committee achieved some limited results. It succeeded in concluding arrangements with the Nazis that a number of Jews who were able to pay what amounted to an exorbitant ransom should be allowed to depart for Switzerland. The negotiations were protracted. They referred at the beginning to only 300 Jews, but in the end two groups, one of 318, the other of 1,368, left Hungary and after a sojourn of several weeks in Bergen-Belsen were allowed (on August 18 and December 6) to depart for Switzerland. The Rescue Committee was also able to reach an understanding with the Germans that 20,000 Jews from the Hungarian provinces would be sent not to Auschwitz but to camps in the vicinity of Vienna, which meant that they would remain alive. However, all these arrangements saved no more than a very small percentage of the provincial Hungarian Jews, the great bulk of whom were destroyed by the Nazis.

As indicated earlier, the role played by the Jewish Council during the genocidal months from March 1944 to January 1945 was to become the subject of a bitter controversy that has not yet subsided at the time of this writing. Especially in the years immediately following the war, some scholars, historians, and social scientists accused the Jewish Councils—not only that of Hungary, but also those of other Nazi-occupied countries—of having collaborated with the Nazi authorities and having facilitated the effective implementation of mass murder. It is a fact that under the threat of brutal retaliation, the Hungarian Jewish Council supplied the Germans with lists of Jews and other information used to round up and deport Jews to labor and extermination camps. After the war, several members of the Jewish Councils were tried, and some were actually convicted.

From the late 1960s on, students of the Holocaust began to acquire a deeper understanding of what had actually happened during those days of horror. Their research uncovered the conditions in which the members of the Jewish Councils functioned, the compulsion to which they were exposed, the threat of death that hung over their heads—several members of *Judenrats* in various countries were actually murdered by the Nazis—and the belief (or delusion) that by obeying the Nazi orders they could mitigate, alleviate, or at least postpone what the Nazis planned for the Jews. With diabolic psychological maneuvering, the Nazis gradually increased the harshness of the demands they imposed upon the Jewish Councils. As Rezső Kasztner, who was closely involved in negotiations with the German authorities in Hungary for the purpose of rescuing Jews, put it, the members of the Jewish Council "were made step by step tractable. In the beginning relatively unimportant things were asked of them, replaceable things of material value, like personal possessions, money, and apartments. Later, however, the personal freedom of human beings was demanded. Finally, the Nazis asked for life itself."

Under the circumstances it was inevitable that the instinct of self-preservation should also play a role in the way the members of Jewish Councils carried the burden heaped upon their shoulders by the Nazis. The Council members were aware that as long as they fulfilled a useful function for the Nazis, their lives were spared. But this does not mean that they did not do their best to help their fellow Jews within the extremely limited scope of activities available to them.

The worst of which one can accuse the Hungarian Jewish leadership during the German occupation was a lack of courage to initiate, or even to encourage, any positive action for the rescue of the Jews. The risks of such action, were, of course, enormous, and the chances of success minimal. Still, many students of the period feel that *any* attempts would have resulted in the survival of more persons than did the policy of obedience followed by the Jewish Council. In support of this argument, they can point to the fact that a small number of Jews managed to escape from the Hungarian countryside by eluding deportation. Some paid off the Hungarian and German soldiers and thus were able to slip across the border into Rumania or Slovakia; others hid out on farms or in cellars with the help of compassionate or enterprising neighbors; and yet others succeeded in traveling to Budapest, where, at the time of the deportations from the countryside, the Jews could still feel relatively safe. Of the rescue efforts of a few Zionist leaders we have spoken above.

The policy followed by the Jewish Council was the direct continuation of the "hope for the best and do nothing" position taken by the Hungarian Jewish leadership even after it knew that in every occupied country, the Germans proceeded with the systematic extermination of the Jews. That had become common knowledge by 1942 at the latest, and yet the Hungarian Jewish leadership simply could not envisage something similar happening in Hungary. Hungary was, after all, an ally of Germany, and therefore neither the Hungarian political leaders nor the Jewish leadership could imagine that Hungary would be occupied by the Germans as though it were an enemy country. In addition, the Hungarian Jewish leaders had an implicit trust in the "chivalrous" Hungarians and their conservative-aristocratic government that they would not do what was done to the Jews in Germany, Austria, Poland, and other countries. When the Germans nevertheless occupied Hungary, and Eichmann found many willing helpers among the Hungarian Arrow Cross formations, the very basis of the Hungarian Jews' existence, of their century-old self-identification as Israelite Magyars, was shattered —but the policy of doing nothing, of obeying and cooperating with the authorities, was too deeply ingrained to allow for any radical change. True, by the time the Germans set up the Jewish Council, it could do pitifully little for the Jews for whom the Nazis made it responsible. Thus, the attitude of hoping for the best and doing nothing persisted. As Braham puts it, the Jewish leaders "lived and acted in the psychologically understandable illusion that their community would somehow weather the catastrophe that befell them."

At the same time, the position into which the Nazis forced the Jewish Council was calculated to deprive it of all initiative, of the energy to engage in any effective action, and to make it concentrate on issues of day to day survival.

In the spring and early summer of 1944, a tragic interlude took place that cost several ex-Hungarian Palestinian *halutzim* (pioneers) their lives. Becoming aware of the absence of any organized resistance among the Jews of Hungary, in January 1944 the Jewish Agency for Palestine began to consider the idea of sending to Hungary a small mission to advise the Hungarian Jewish leaders on organizing some kind of clandestine resistance. After protracted negotiations, the British authorities consented to the sending of a few Hungarian-speaking young Palestinian Jews to Hungary, on condition that they would act as individuals, and not under Palestinian Jewish direction but under a Special Operations Executive Command. Among the volunteers, three young persons, Peretz (Ferenc) Goldstein, Joel (Emil) Nussbacher (later Palgi), and Hannah Szenes, were selected for the mission. Szenes, the twenty-three-year-old daughter of the well-known Hungarian author and plawright Béla Szenes, was a member of the kibbutz S'dot Yam near Caesarea. The three parachuted into Yugoslavia, spent some three months with Yugoslav partisans, and then on June 9 Hannah Szenes, in the company of Reuben Dafni, a Yugoslav Jew, crossed the border into Hungary. She seems to have been betrayed, for she was promptly arrested, imprisoned in Budapest, tried, and executed on November 7. Goldstein and Nussbacher, who followed a few days later, managed to reach Budapest, where Nussbacher was arrested and the nineteen-year-old Goldstein gave himself up. Both were loaded onto a train, together with many prisoners of war, to be sent to Komárom. Nussbacher managed to escape and survived the war; Goldstein reportedly died in a German concentration camp. Although the entire parachutist mission was a failure, and even endangered the position of the Hungarian Jewish Rescue Committee, whose members were suspected of complicity with the parachutists, it had, in the judgment of Holocaust historian Randolph Braham, "a positive influence on many of the Zionist pioneers and unaffiliated younger Jewish intellectuals, who had become disillusioned with the leadership and politics of both the Vaada [Rescue Committee] and the Jewish Council." It might be added that the parachutists' mission cemented the relationship between the Hungarian Jews and the *yishuv* in Palestine.

As is bound to happen between partners in crime, there was a falling out between the Hungarian government and the German occupying forces over the property left behind by Jews who were deported or who managed to emigrate. The Germans claimed that since it was they who "solved" the Jewish question in Hungary, those possessions should belong to them. In fact, during the early phase of the deportation of the Jews from rural Hungary, the Germans took them to Germany together with their valuables, of which they were robbed once they arrived. We heard above of the arrangements concerning the "leasing" of the big munitions and other factories owned by the richest Jewish families (the Chorins, Kornfelds, Mauthners, and Weisses). In addition, the Germans demanded that the food rations of the nearly half-million deported Jews should be put at their disposal, and they extorted 2 billion pengős from the Sztójay government for removing the Jews from Hungary.

The Hungarian government, on its part, considered all Jewish property part of the national wealth, and tried to block its removal from the country by issuing a series of decrees. It set up a special ministry, headed by Béla Imrédy with the title minister without portfolio in charge of economic affairs, to handle the problems of Jewish property, and froze all Jewish safe deposits, savings accounts, and commercial assets, thus not only effectively preventing the Jews from access to their own property but also stopping the Germans from laying their hands on it. The Hungarian government also opposed the arrangements the Zionists negotiated with the Germans to enable well-to-do Jewish families to leave for neutral countries against the payment of sizable ransoms. It thus came about that because of the quarrel over whether the Hungarians or Germans would gain control of Jewish property, many more Jews who were able and willing to pay whatever the going rate was for Jewish lives remained caught in the death trap that Hungary had become for them.

44

How Half of Budapest Jewry Was Saved

While the deportation of the Jews from the Hungarian provinces proceeded more or less according to the German plan and schedule, Eichmann began preparations for liquidating the Budapest Jews as well. As we recall, the number of Jews in the Hungarian capital before the war was around 200,000; during the war this number was augmented by refugees who gathered in Budapest from the areas contested between the two opposing armies, and from other places where the danger, as it could be evaluated by those caught in the vise, was serious enough to motivate them to leave. After the German occupation began, even though Jews were forbidden to travel, many risked what they thought would be imprisonment, and took the train to Budapest. Consequently, the number of Jews concentrated in the capital by the summer of 1944 is estimated to have been between 250,000 and 280,000.

After some preparatory moves, on May 3, László Endre, secretary of state in charge of the administrative department, ordered the identification and registration of apartments and buildings in which Jews lived. This was completed within a few days, and was followed by the designation of 2,681 apartment houses (out of a total of 36,000) as "yellow star houses," identified by a big yellow Star of David over the entrance, to be inhabited exclusively by Jews. In response to complaints by Christian tenants who lived in those houses, some 700–800 houses were removed from the list, and in June the Jews of Budapest were ordered to move into the remaining 1,900 or so houses. It is estimated that early in August 170,000 Jews were concentrated in these yellow star houses, in which the overcrowding was appalling. Another 110,000 Jews continued to stay illegally in Christian buildings. In addition to the Jews, some 12,000 Christians also remained living in the Jewish houses.

Jewish life was constrained by a number of additional decrees. On June 23 the Jewish authorities were ordered to deliver their registers of births, marriages, and deaths, and before the end of that month the metropolitan police was reinforced by the arrival of several thousand gendarmes. On June 25, regulations were posted all over the city listing what the Jews were allowed and forbidden to do. They were allowed to leave their houses only between 2 P.M. and 5 P.M. A few days later this permission was extended to the hours from 11 A.M. to 5 P.M. They were allowed to travel only in the last car of trolleys consisting of several cars; they were forbidden to enter parks and promenades, to entertain guests in their apartments, or to carry on conversations from their windows with persons across the street.

In July 1944, in response to appeals of the Christian Churches and the Association of Hungarian Christian Jews (i.e., converted Jews), the Ministry of the Interior ordered the relocation of Jews who had converted prior to August 1, 1941, to separate houses, which were to be marked with both a yellow star and a cross. It was anticipated that this would cause the relocation of some 40–50,000 people, which was the estimated number of converted Jews. In the event, this order did not result in a mass relocation.

Although these decrees, coming as they did on top of the terrible news from the provinces, were unmistakable indications for the Jews of what the Germans and their Hungarian henchmen intended to do, the authorities tried to counterbalance them by assurances shrewdly and cynically designed for the consumption of the local Jews as well as the world at large. On July 17, Veesenmayer proposed that a communiqué be issued by the Hungarian government "revealing" the humane treatment accorded to the Jews during their trip to Germany, where they were being sent as Hungarian surplus labor. The suggestion was vetoed, however, by Joachim von Ribbentrop, Reich minister for foreign affairs, who did not want any statement issued in connection with the solution of the Jewish question. On July 29, 1944, Veesenmayer sent a cable to the German Foreign Office transmitting the Hungarian Press Agency's rebuttal of a report published by British newspapers on the Brand mission to Istanbul, and he stated that "it is emphasized here [meaning, by the Hungarian authorities] that the Hungarian government is willing and determined to solve definitively the Jewish question, whereby, however, the Anglo-Saxon circles can assuredly count on its being done in a humanitarian spirit."

Despite these continuing deceptive declarations, aimed at lulling the Jews of Budapest into a false sense of safety and reassuring the world of the "humanitarian" attitude of the Hungarians and their German overlords, the true state of affairs became known in the outside world. As early as June 1944, the Swiss press, and following it the press of other neutral and Allied countries, began to publish accounts of the fate of

The Jews of Hungary

Hungarian Jewry. On June 25, the pope was finally induced to act, and sent a personal plea to Horthy. On June 26 President Roosevelt sent a sharply worded note to Hungary demanding the cessation of the deportations, and the next day Secretary of State Cordell Hull and British Foreign Secretary Anthony Eden threatened the Hungarians with retaliation. On June 30, King Gustaf of Sweden sent a telegram to Horthy asking him to intervene to save the Hungarian Jews. One demand in a different direction was also received: it came from Ḥajj Amin al-Ḥusaini, the exiled mufti of Jerusalem, who on June 22 requested that the Hungarian government prevent the emigration of Jews to Palestine.

These pleas, warnings, and threats, coupled with the military successes of the Allies in both the eastern and western fronts and the heavy Allied air raid of Budapest on July 2, induced Horthy to demand the cessation of the deportations and the dismissal of Endre and Baky, the two chief helpers of the Germans in connection with the Jewish question. On June 27, Prime Minister Döme Sztójay asked the German government to permit the emigration of a part of the Hungarian Jews. Within a few days Endre and Baky were dismissed. Early in July, under the leadership of Baky, the Arrow Cross Party planned an anti-Horthy coup, which, however, misfired. On July 6 Horthy ordered the preparations for deporting the Budapest Jews stopped, and emphasized his order by bringing into the capital loyal armored military units from Esztergom. In the meantime, the Christian Churches demanded that the "Christian Jews" be saved. These developments prevented the Germans from beginning the deportation of the Budapest Jews, which they had planned for early July.

During these months, while the fate of Budapest Jewry hung in the balance, foreign diplomatic missions in Hungary, too, became active in its behalf. As early as April 26, 1944, the Swiss consul, Carl Lutz, requested emigration permits for 7,000 Jews from the Hungarian government. On July 24, the Swiss consulate opened its emigration department in Budapest, in which several hundred young Zionists helped draw up lists of Jews wishing to emigrate, thus preparing the emigration of 8,000 families.

Also in July, Raoul Wallenberg, an attaché to the Swedish Embassy, arrived in Budapest and began distributing Swedish certificates of protection (*Schutzpasse*) to Jews. His department employed 300 Jews for this work. When the Arrow Cross Party seized power (in October 1944; see below), Wallenberg initiated the establishment of an "international ghetto," in which about 33,000 Jews, 7,000 of them with Swedish papers, found protection in houses flying the flags of neutral countries. In November 1944, when thousands of Budapest Jews, including women and children, were forced on a death march toward the Austrian border, Wallenberg and Per Anger, secretary of the Swedish Embassy, followed them with a convoy of trucks carrying medicine, food, and clothing, and distributed these life-saving items among the marchers. By superhuman efforts Wallenberg managed to free 500 persons and return them to Budapest. He also saved several hundred Jews pressed into labor detachments who had been put on deportation trains. In Budapest he organized "international labor detachments," and even a "Jewish Guard," consisting of Aryan-looking Jews disguised in SS and Arrow Cross uniforms, and established two hospitals and soup kitchens. Eichmann threatened to kill him, and referred to him as "the Jew-dog Wallenberg." During the liberation, Wallenberg presented himself to Soviet army guards, and was last seen on January 17, 1945, traveling toward Debrecen in the company of a Russian officer.

But to return to July 1944, in that month the Spaniards prepared the transportation of 500 children to Tangier, and Portugal and the Vatican also participated in efforts to rescue Jews. The embassies and the Red Cross Societies of neutral countries issued safe-conduct passes that protected (or were supposed to protect) their owners and, in theory at least, exempted them from some regulations, such as the wearing of the yellow star. During July and August thousands of Jews waited in line daily before the office of the Swiss Embassy, where Palestinian immigration certificates were issued—those certificates provided the embassy's protection until departure.

Another way to safety was sought in conversion to a Christian denomination. In July 1944, as we have seen, the Christian Churches of Hungary intervened energetically with the Hungarian government in the interests of Jews who had converted, and the Association of Hungarian Christian Jews was also mentioned above. In these months thousands of Jews crowded the offices of vicarages and parsonages, and in July alone 4,770 conversions were registered. However, the number of forged certificates of baptism was several times higher.

Despite the limitations to which his deportation plans were subjected, Eichmann continued with his *Entjudung* ("dejewification") activities. Since he could no longer count on the help of the Hungarian gendarmerie, he used his own detachments to liquidate the Kistarcsa prison camp in the vicinity of Budapest. That camp had been established in the very first days of the German occupation of Hungary, and by the end of March 1944, 280 of those leaders of Hungarian Jewry who were arrested as hostages were placed into it. The story of the Kistarcsa hostages was recounted almost fifty years later by one of them, László (later Ladislas) Beck, who, however, remembered only 240 Jewish leaders in Kistarcsa:

When the idea of Jewish lives for trucks began to be mooted [see chapter 43], on April 10, 1944, the Germans arrested 240 leading Jewish personalities and relatives of such individuals, and transported them to Kistarcsa to keep them there "on ice," as they said—that is, as hostages, to be released if and when the truck deal went through. If it did not go through, they knew they would be dealt with as were the others who were held in Kistarcsa pending their deportation, hundreds of whom were put on trains every few days or weeks. Among the hostages was László Beck himself, twenty-one years old at the time, taken because he was a member of an important Jewish family. The others included Baron Marcel Madarasy-Beck; Frigyes Abelesz, who had a scrap-iron business at 8 Váci Street, út, Budapest, and whose nephew, Sir Peter Abel of Sydney, Australia, was the owner of TNT [Thomas International Transport Company], one of the largest transport companies in the world; Dr. Antal Goldberger [son of Leo Budai-Goldberger] and his son Berthold, who was seventeen years old at the time; Jakob Aschner, cousin of Lipót Aschner, who was the owner of the United Incandescent Bulbs and Electricity Co.; another Aschner, Izsó, owner of the Leipziger Spirits Factory of Óbuda; Baron Dirsztay; the Minkusz brothers; Henrik Kálmán, general manager of the English-Hungarian Bank; József Bun, general manager of the Hungarian Discount Bank; Ottó Konrád, general manager of the Hungarian Commercial Bank; Mihály Földi, author and journalist, who committed suicide in Kistarcsa; and so on.

All these men were placed into Pavilion B, which was a three-story building containing several large halls, in each of which there were about thirty bunks, each consisting of two beds, one on top of the other. Twice a day the hostages were allowed to go out into the courtyard to walk about; the rest of the day they spent reading, or chatting with each other. Food was sent in for them by the Jewish Council from Budapest, and occasionally one or another member of the Council would come to visit them. All in all, their situation in Kistarcsa was not bad, owing primarily to the attitude of Capt. István Vasdényei, a Hungarian Christian professional army man, who treated them decently. [After the war he was decorated by the Israeli government.] Of course, no words can describe what they felt, knowing that the inmates of the other pavilions were destined to die, and that their own fate was a toss-up between life and death. On September 6, 1944, all of them were released by an order of Regent Horthy, executed by Prime Minister Géza Lakatos. They went to Budapest, to the "protected house" at 2 Bethlen Place. Beck obtained false papers that identified him as a Christian, and went with seventeen other Jews to Eger, where he was when the city was taken by the Russians. The Russian contingent that liberated Eger was headed by a Russian Jewish officer who knew Yiddish, and Beck, who also knew some Yiddish, was able to talk to him, and to obtain from him a permit to move about freely.

Ladislas Beck did not have much information on the fate of the other prisoners of Kistarcsa, but from various sources it is known that the camp was used by the Germans as a place to collect and hold Jews whom they planned to deport to their death. Thus, they sent there the entire personnel of the X-ray department of the Jewish Hospital of Szabolcs Street, all the Jewish engineers and officials of the Hungarian General Anthracite Company, and any Jews who were caught transgressing one or another of the anti-Jewish regulations. On April 28, 1944, they deported 1,500 of the inmates, but soon thereafter the camp was again filled with newly arrested Jews. Early in July, Eichmann's commando began a second evacuation of the camp, and on July 14 the first deportation train, with 1,500 Jews aboard, actually left Kistarcsa. However, the commander of the camp (perhaps the same Capt. István Vasdényei?) revealed the plan to Sándor Bródy, the representative of the Jewish Patronage Office in Kistarcsa, who alerted the Jewish Council, at whose urgent plea Horthy instructed Minister of the Interior Jaross to stop all deportation, "even if he had to use force." The train was intercepted at Hatvan and the deportees returned to the camp.

Enraged over Horthy's "audacity" to countermand his orders, Eichmann now proceeded more circumspectly. On the morning of July 19, he summoned the members of the administrative committee of the Jewish Council to his suburban office to discuss "urgent matters" affecting Hungarian Jewry. There the men were kept incommunicado (even the telephones were disconnected) and busy all day with small talk by Eichmann's assistant, while an SS detachment occupied Kistarcsa and loaded 1,220 deportees into trains. By the time the Council members were released (at 7:30 in the evening) the deportation train was already beyond the borders of Hungary, on its way to Auschwitz.

Not satisfied with this, the Germans—for whom at that juncture the *Entjudung* of Hungary seemed the only still attainable war aim, to which they clung with a monomaniacal intensity—continued to press Horthy and the Hungarian government to continue deporting Jews. They set August 27 as the new date for the resumption of deportations from Budapest. However, by that time the German military and political situation had deteriorated to such an extent that they were unable to give military backing to their demand. On August 23 Rumania asked the Allies for a ceasefire, declared war on Germany, and began to fight the Germans on the side of Russians. In Slovakia an anti-Fascist revolt broke out. Eichmann was forced to leave Hungary on August 24. These developments enabled Horthy to dismiss the pro-German Sztójay government, and in September he appointed Col.-Gen. Géza Lakatos prime minister. Lakatos tried to stop the advance of the Soviet and Rumanian troops by sending the second and third Hungarian armies into southern Transylvania. The attempt failed, and Soviet-Rumanian forces soon appeared on the eastern rim of the Hungarian Plain.

In their weakened position, the Germans agreed that the responsibility for the Jews of Budapest should be taken over by the Hungarians.

On August 30, the Lakatos government entered into a new agreement with the Germans that the Budapest Jews would be removed from the city and concentrated in rural localities, where they would be held to performing necessary work, but their deportation would cease. At the same time some internment camps were liquidated and their inmates set free, including the hostages who had been kept at Kistarcsa for six months. The position of the Lakatos government vis-à-vis the remaining Jewish community of Hungary was that it should be enabled to live, but that it was a guilty and harmful element, and hence its isolation from the Hungarians should continue, including the wearing of the yellow star and the concentration in separate parts of the city.

In the meantime Horthy sent a secret mission to Moscow to negotiate an armistice with the Russians. A preliminary armistice agreement was actually signed on October 11, obligating Hungary to give up the territories it had annexed since 1937, and to declare war on Germany. Horthy's armistice proclamation was broadcast over the radio on October 15, but on the very next day his opponents succeeded in forcing his resignation in favor of Ferenc Szálasi, leader of the Arrow Cross Party. On October 17 Horthy was sent to Germany under "protective custody," and Szálasi became prime minister and head of state, with the title "nation leader."

The few months that remained before the total occupation of Hungary by the Soviet forces were a period of the starkest horror for the Jews who had survived in Budapest and the countryside. Pogroms, robbery, mayhem, and murder were the order of the day. On the night of October 15–16, Arrow Cross gangs slaughtered several hundred Jews who were concentrated in yellow star houses or in labor service units. Many were herded onto the Danube bridges and there shot into the river. Similar slaughters took place in the countryside as well.

On October 16 the Germans again took into their hands the responsibility for the Jews, and started by locking the gates of the Jewish houses so that their inhabitants could not leave the premises for ten full days. Still in October, they made the synagogues of Dohány and Rombach Streets provincial prisons, into which they crowded some 6,000 persons from the starred Jewish houses, and then put them on deportation trains headed toward the north.

On October 17 Eichmann returned to Budapest and demanded that as a matter of highest priority 50,000 able-bodied Jews be marched on foot to Germany to work there, and that the other able-bodied Jews be immediately employed in the construction of defense fortifications around Budapest. The remaining Jews were to be concentrated in ghettolike camps near the capital. The next day, Eichmann met with Gábor

Vajna, the new interior minister in the Szálasi government, and the two reached an agreement on all points Eichmann raised.

On October 20 the systematic drive against the Jews began. As the first step, the police and the Arrow Cross rounded up about 50,000 men between the ages of sixteen and sixty and put them to work on fortification lines. On October 22, they took all those who happened to have been left out, and all women aged eighteen to forty. By October 26, an estimated 25,000 Jewish men and 10,000 Jewish women were taken. They intended to send the men to the east to dig trenches, but because of the Soviet advance the approximately 15,000 remaining members of the labor battalions were instead sent, on November 2, to the west, to Transdanubia. At the Hegyeshalom border station they were taken over by the Gestapo. On November 8, together with around 25,000 Budapest Jews who were seized regardless of age or sex, they were forced to march 120 miles to the infamous Strasshof Camp in Austria. Thousands of them died on the way.

After the removal of the Jewish men and women of working age, the systematic looting of the remaining Jewish property began. On November 3 the Szálasi government declared all valuable objects owned by Jews—with the exception of the most personal items—part of the national wealth, and justified their expropriation by arguing that they would be used to compensate the nation for the cost of the war, to pay war damages, and—to cover the country's expenses for carrying out the regulations pertaining to the Jews! What this in effect meant was that the Arrow Cross bands used their raids to take possession of everything they could remove from the Jewish houses, and subsequently from the ghetto.

In November began the concentration into a big Jewish ghetto of the capital's Jews, who up to that time were living in starred Jewish houses scattered all over the city. As the first step, a ghetto was designated for Jews who had acquired the protection of neutral countries. Though in October 1944, Gábor Vajna had rejected the exceptional status of these Jews, when this created an international protest, he reconsidered, and declared himself ready to negotiate concerning the protected Jews. Early in November the papal nuncio and representatives of the Swiss and the International Red Cross and of neutral states came to Budapest and conducted negotiations with Count Gábor Kemény, the foreign minister, which led to an agreement that the protected Jews would be collected in a special part of the city pending their transportation out of the country. The agreement called for placing into this "international ghetto" some 7,800 Jews protected by Switzerland, 4,500 protected by Sweden, 690 by Portugal, 100 by Spain, and 2,500 by the Vatican, the regent, or the ministry of the interior. Most of the Jews who had been concentrated in this "international ghetto" were now evacuated to make room for the protected Jews, and were first transported to the brick factory of Ujlak, and then deported to the north.

In response to the protest of the foreign representatives, the protected Jews were taken out of the labor battalions and "protected battalions" were formed by them and directed not toward Austria but toward Budapest. The total number of all the international safe-conduct passes was supposed to be 15,600. In reality, however, the foreign representatives issued several times that number. The Swiss issued some 40–70,000, the Swedes 7–10,000, and the Spaniards around 3,000. In addition, there were a very large number of forged documents in the hands of the Jews. This served as the pretext for the Arrow Cross contingents to organize raids on the international ghetto, in the course of which they carried off all the inhabitants, shooting many of them into the Danube or, once the big Budapest ghetto was established, taking them there.

While this was taking place in Budapest, the Soviet army was closing in from the east, and the German and Hungarian forces began to withdraw, that is, to flee westward toward Transdanubia. Despite the approaching end of the Hungarian armed resistance, most of the surviving Jewish trench diggers were taken on a death march toward the west. After being kept for several days in inhuman conditions in various camps, they were marched, beginning November 8, toward the border point of Hegyeshalom, under conditions calculated to make all but the strongest perish. They were forced to cover the distance of 200–220 kilometers in seven to eight days. Those who became sick on the way, or too weak to continue marching, were shot to death, or were simply left behind on the roadside without any provisions. Those who managed to reach the border town were taken over by the Germans and sent on to build the "East Wall" for the defense of Vienna.

On November 29, the Hungarian Ministry of the Interior entered into an agreement with the Gestapo to deliver new labor battalions. This led to the beginning of the deportation of the so-called protected battalions. Raoul Wallenberg succeeded in liberating those who had Swedish passports, but the others were packed into railroad cars and deported to Fertőrákos, Balf, and Kőszeg. Their further fate is attested by mass graves.

Also on November 29, 1944, a small area in the vicinity of the Dohány Street Synagogue, containing a total of about 166 apartment houses, was designated as the ghetto for all the remaining Jews of Budapest. Since the men and women of working age had been removed from the city earlier, only children, the elderly, and the sick remained to be herded into the ghetto, totaling around 63,000. The concentration of these individuals into the ghetto was carried out with calculated brutality. More than ten persons were crowded into each room. The sanitary conditions were appalling. The danger of epidemics was ever present. On December 10 the gates of the ghetto were locked, and from that time on the provision of food and heating material was extremely difficult.

The Jewish Council tried everything it could to prevent the sending into the ghetto of the 6,000 Jewish children who had earlier been placed into a number of Red Cross institutions. But since the Szálasi government was not recognized by the neutral countries, the Arrow Cross did not honor the neutral or international protection extended to the children. They tried several times to remove them from the protection of the Red Cross and put them into the ghetto. The energetic action of the Jewish Council, however, succeeded in preventing this step, and thus a number of the Jewish children survived the Nazi terror in the children's homes of the International Red Cross.

It is a most shocking testimony to the quasi-psychotic obsession of the Hungarian and German authorities with the Jews, who after all constituted but a minuscule fraction of Hungary's population, that at a time when Hungary was faced with imminent defeat at the hand of its feared and hated traditional enemy, Russia, its political leaders still devoted inordinate attention to "the Jewish problem." On November 17, 1944, Szálasi issued his "final plan" for the solution of the Jewish question in Hungary, and communicated it to all interested parties, including the Germans and the Jewish Council of Budapest. In it he divided the remaining Jews of Hungary into six categories:

1. Jews holding foreign protective passes. They were to be relocated in a special building, and their departure from Hungary was to be subject to the development of diplomatic relations between Hungary and the neutral states.
2. Jews to be "lent" to the German government. These "loan Jews" (*kölcsönzsidók*) were to be employed by the German government for the advancement of the common war effort.
3. Jews awaiting departure from Hungary. These Jews, who were to be placed in ghettos, included the "loan Jews" whose departure was delayed, pregnant women, old people, the sick, children under the protection of the International Red Cross, and Christian (ex-) Jews.
4. Jews holding exemption certificates issued by Regent Horthy or by the previous minister of the interior, and some highly decorated or war-wounded Jews. They were subject to many restrictive measures.
5. Clerics, including priests and nuns, of Jewish origin.
6. Jews in possession of foreign citizenship, and Hungarian Jewish nationals with valid exit papers. These were expected to leave the country by December 1, 1944.

The dispositions concerning each of these groups were carefully spelled out. The whole document was clearly intended to counteract the protests of the neutral states, and to provide a political framework for the actions that were being implemented or planned against the remaining Jews of Budapest, including their concentration in a ghetto.

Perhaps even more characteristic of the obsessive preoccupation with the Jewish question was that in December, just a few days before he fled Budapest, Interior Minister Gábor Vajna devoted his attention to the "problem" of streets, roads, and squares in Hungary named after meritorious Jews, and issued detailed instructions ordering that they all be instantly renamed. On December 23 he decreed that all Jews in hiding must report within twenty-four hours to the Jewish Council for transfer into the ghetto. His order specified that Jewish patients receiving care in hospitals must be transferred to temporary hospitals established in the ghetto. This decree intensified the manhunt for Jews in hiding. While the Red Army commenced its siege of Budapest, inside the city Arrow Cross gangs intensified their looting and killing of defenseless Jews, most of them women and the elderly. The flags of neutral countries flying over buildings and identifying them as protected by those countries counted for nothing. Their inhabitants fell victim to indiscriminate Arrow Cross attacks. Even members of the Jewish Council were killed, and patients from the Jewish Hospital on Bethlen Square were dragged away. On January 11, 1945, the Arrow Cross massacred the patients, doctors, and nurses of the Jewish Hospital of Maros Street in Buda; they did the same on January 14 in the Orthodox Jewish Hospital in Városmajor Street; and again on January 19 in the almshouse maintained by the Orthodox Congregation at 2 Alma Road. These atrocities and group murders continued until the Red Army penetrated Budapest.

The Russian siege of Budapest began late in December. From that time on the Hungarian state machinery ground to a halt, some members of the government fled, and the Arrow Cross contingents had a free hand to loot, rob, and kill. Raids on the protected houses became practically daily events, and many Jews were murdered with inhuman cruelty. (The frequency of wanton murders is attested by the fact that within the first few months after the liberation, the People's Court adjudicated 6,200 cases of Arrow Cross murders.)

In those last few weeks of horror, the conduct of a few men stands out as a beacon of humanity and courage. Three of them were Raoul Wallenberg, Swiss Consul Carl Lutz, and the head of the Spanish legation, Jorge (Giorgio) Perlasca, who succeeded in persuading Gábor Vajna, Szálasi's accredited deputy, to stop the removal of Jews from the protected houses. Two more were Lajos Stöckler and Miksa Domonkos, leaders of the ghetto, who were able to prevail on Vajna to disregard the express prohibition of the Ministry of the Interior and detail a contingent of one hundred policemen to protect the ghetto. They also succeeded in establishing contact with Pál Szalai, liaison officer between the Arrow Cross Party and the police, with whose help they were able to prevent the annihilation of the ghetto shortly before the conquest of Budapest by the Russians.

On Christmas, 1944, when Budapest was totally surrounded by the Russian forces, the Arrow Cross organized a senseless "persistence" (as they called it), which brought another month of suffering and destruction to the city, and especially to its remaining Jews. The ghetto, defenseless and impotent, was the scene of mass murder, pillage, and brutality. But even that did not quench the bloodthirstiness of the SS and the Arrow Cross. Early in January 1945, Stöckler and Domonkos learned that the Arrow Cross, together with the Germans, was planning to liquidate the ghetto totally by killing all its surviving inmates. The plan was worked out between the SS command, headquartered in the Hotel Royal, and the party leaders of the Seventh District of Budapest. By January 15, there were 1,500 SS men, 200 policemen, and twenty-two armed Arrow Cross officers ready for action. Szálasi contacted the SS command and, based on information he had received from Wallenberg, warned Gen. Schmidthuber that the annihilation of the ghetto would mean his being tried and condemned not as a soldier but as a mass murderer after the war. The general heeded the warning and put a stop to the planned action. A few days later, the last units of the German occupying forces evacuated the Pest side of the city and moved over to the Buda side, which they were also forced to leave very shortly.

Szálasi himself escaped from Budapest and transferred his capital to the western borders of Hungary, from where he ruled the few northern and western Transdanubian counties that remained of his "Hungarist Empire." However, neither his demagoguery nor his terror could prevent the dissolution of his regime. He left Hungary on April 4, 1945, a few days before the total liberation of the country, taking with him the royal crown, the most venerated emblem of the Hungarian state. After the war he was tried, condemned as a war criminal, and hanged in Hungary.

As for the German position, some time between the middle of October and November 1944, Reichsführer SS Heinrich Himmler became convinced of the inevitable collapse of the Reich and, to establish an alibi for himself, issued an order forbidding the further liquidation of Jews. Kurt Becher, Himmler's economic representative in Hungary, showed a copy of this order to Eichmann, but Eichmann felt that it rendered impossible the execution of the task he was engaged in, and disregarded it. He continued, together with the Arrow Cross, the drive against the Jews. Consequently, in those last two months before the Russian occupation of Budapest, some 10–15,000 Jews were shot into the icy waters of the Danube or in the streets of the city. During the last battle for Budapest, the Nazis set up a human chain of Jews to pass shells from an ammunition depot to the German front line some six to eight kilometers away.

Despite the desperate situation in which Budapest's German and Hungarian Nazi defenders found themselves early in January 1945—or perhaps precisely because of it—they persisted in pursuing the only goal that still seemed attainable to them: annihilating the remaining Jews of the city. Unable to act against the inexorably advancing enemy, they vented their frustration and wrath by brutalizing and killing those who were in their power and whom they could treat as they wished, the Jews of Budapest.

On January 18, 1945, when Soviet units liberated the Budapest ghetto, some 70,000 persons were found alive in it. In addition, between 10,000 and 25,000 Jews were saved in the protected houses, and an unknown number survived in hiding in various parts of the city. All in all, it can be estimated that about 119,000 Jews survived the Nazi Holocaust in Budapest, about half the number who lived in the city before the outbreak of the war.

In 1994 the final numerical balance of the German-Hungarian genocide still remains in question. However, the following figures seem to be most likely: according to the 1941 census, the number of Jews in Hungary (including the territories regained by the grace of the Germans) was 725,000. Another 100,000 Jews who had converted, or were the children of converted Jews, were considered Jews by the Hungarian Jewish Laws. This gives a grand total of 825,000 persons. Prior to the German occupation of Hungary (March 19, 1944), 63,000 lost their lives under inhuman conditions in the labor service, deportations, and the Ujvidék (Novi Sad) massacre. During the German occupation 618,000 died after being deported or were otherwise killed. Another 5,000 managed to flee abroad. Thus, the total losses of Hungarian Jewry in the period 1941–45 were 686,000, leaving 139,000 who survived in Hungary (119,000 in Budapest and 20,000 in labor service in Hungarian territory). By the end of 1945, another 116,500 returned from deportation. The total number of Jews on December 31, 1945, in all Hungary, including the territories that were to be again detached in the late 1946 peace treaty, was thus 255,500. Of them, roughly two-thirds were women and one-third men.

590

In concluding this chapter of horrors, I wish to remember in particular the Hungarian Jewish writers who fell victim to the Nazi and Arrow Cross rampage, and whose death was an irreplaceable loss not only to Hungarian Jewry but also to the culture of Hungary as a whole. In age they ranged from the septuagenarian novelist and playwright Dezső Szomory to the poet Hannah Szenes, who was twenty-three when she was executed. Only two dozen of them are mentioned in brief notices in the 1972 *Encyclopaedia Judaica*, and some memory of another two dozen has survived. Many others, especially young writers, must have died without leaving any record of their short lives and the first fruits of their works. We shall never know what talents were nipped in the bud with their murder.

The extermination of a whole generation of Jewish writers meant that Hungarian Jewish literary activity was brought to an abrupt halt. Of course, in the midst of the chaotic circumstances that preceded and followed the 1945 liberation of Hungary by the Red Army, the presence or absence of literary activity was not an issue of consequence. And even though in the three years of the so-called Coalition Period that followed liberation, Hungarian literature (in Miklós Szabolcsi's words) "scrambled to its feet and began to live again," all that was again stifled in 1948, when the Communist dictatorship imposed strict control on all aspects of life, including literary expression, especially about Jewish subjects. It was only with the "thaw" that followed Stalin's death in 1953 that Hungarian literature recovered to a considerable extent, and Jewish writers again made their appearance in it and began to resume the role as the yeast in the dough of Hungarian literature, which they had unquestionably fulfilled in the pre-Holocaust period. We leave our further comments on that somewhat peripheral subject to the Appendix of the present book.

The following partial list of the Hungarian Jewish writers who perished in the Hungarian Holocaust gives some idea, not of what literature lost with their death—that will remain forever unknown—but of the extent of Jewish participation in Hungarian literature until that time of horror.

György Bálint, (1906–44), author
László Bánóczi (1881–1945), author, playwright
Oszkár Bárd (1893–1944), poet, writer, physician
László Berend (?–1944), author, poet
Sándor Berkó (1918–44), poet
Béla Bernstein (1868–1944), rabbi, historian
Moshe Bolgár (1882–1944), Hebrew poet, lawyer
Hugó Csergő (1877–1944), poet, playwright, journalist
Arthur Elek (1876–1944), author, art historian

László Fenyő (1902–45), poet
Ferenc Földes (1910–44), sociologist, author
Endre Friss (1896–1945), poet
Ignác Gábor (1868–1944), translator, editor, philologist
Andor Endre Gelléri (1907–45), novelist
Oszkár György (1882–1944), poet, writer
Gábor Halasz (1900–45), literary critic
Géza Havas (1905–45), journalist, essayist
András Hevesi (1900–42), author (half-Jewish)
János Honti (1910–45), folklorist, literary historian
Benő Karácsony (1888–1944), author, essayist, satirist
Albert Kardos (1861–1945), literary scholar, historian
György Kecskeméti (1901–44), playwright, editor of *Pester Lloyd*
Simon Kemény (1882–1945), poet and editor (converted to Christianity)
András Komor (1898–1944), poet and novelist
László Lakatos (1882–1944), author, journalist, playwright
Ernő Lengyel (1887–1944), poet, journalist
Ernő Ligeti (1891–1944), journalist, editor
Jenő Mohácsi (1886–1944), author, translator
Ákos Molnár (1895–1945), author, short story writer, biographer
Ernő Molnár (1890–1944), editor of the Jewish youth monthly *Remény* (Hope)
András Nagy (1906–43), poet, translator
Károly Pap (1897–1945), author, novelist
Béla Pásztor (1908–45), poet
Pál Péter (1906–44), literary critic, lawyer
Izsák Pfeiffer (Pap), rabbi, poet
Miklos Radnóti (1909–44), poet (converted to Christianity)
Antal Radó (1862–1944), journalist, translator
Béla Révész (1876–1944), author, journalist
Márta Sági (1902–45), poet
Ernő Salamon (1907–43), poet
György Sárközi (1899–1945), poet
Ernő Sebesi (1896–1944), author, physician
Károly Sebestyén (1872–1943), literary historian, critic
Miksa Strausz (?–1944), author, physician
Tibor Székely (1908–45), novelist
Hannah Szenes, (1921–44), poet
Antal Szerb (1901–44), literary historian
Dezső Szomory (1869–1944), novelist
Emil Szomory (1874–1944), writer, journalist
György Tamási (1910–44), poet, sociologist, lawyer
Ferenc Vághidi (1905–45), poet
Miklós Vető (1916–44), poet
Ede Zsigmond (1916–44), poet

Most of these writers were murdered by the Nazis in various death camps, some committed suicide, a few died of deprivations. No monument has been erected in their memory; they are remembered only from the books and writings they left behind. It is noteworthy that only two of them were converts, and only two were women.

Among the victims of the Hungarian Holocaust there were 409 rabbis whose names and communal affiliations are known. There is reason to assume that there were others of whose martyr death no records were left behind. In 1946, two years after the Holocaust, the *Ḥevrat Shas* (Talmud Study Society), a religious organization which in that year celebrated its fiftieth anniversary, published in Budapest a memorial volume titled *Y'rushat P'letah* (The Legacy of the Remnant), which listed the names and congregations of 320 Orthodox rabbis killed in the Holocaust. At the end of the list it states (in Hebrew), "This list is not complete, and certainly there are those whose names are not mentioned, and may their honor be preserved." While reading this list, I was again and again shaken by the realization that each of the rabbis listed was killed together with his congregation, so that the 320 names enumerated were symbolic of the destruction of Hungarian Orthodox Jewry as whole, which numbered several hundreds of thousands of souls.

What this list did for the Orthodox rabbis, Dr. Ernő Roth did for the Neolog rabbis in an article titled *"Mártirokká lettek a papok"* ("The Priests Became Martyrs"), employing the term *pap* (priest), which was commonly used in Hungary for Catholic priests, Protestant ministers, and Neolog rabbis. In this article, published in the 1943–46 Year Book of the Budapest Rabbinical Seminary, their *alma mater*, Dr. Roth lists the names, congregations, and major literary works of 89 Neolog rabbis killed in the Holocaust. The first of the rabbis who fell victim to the Nazi killing machine were those who went to the Ukraine as chaplains of the forced labor battalions. They were followed by the rabbis who were deported together with their congregations from all over the Hungarian countryside. The third group consisted of Budapest rabbis who were taken on foot in October–December 1944, to camps in Germany, mostly to Mauthausen. For me, to read this list was an even more shattering experience, since among them there were no fewer than seventeen who were either my relatives, or teachers, or classmates, or friends, or personal acquaintances.

Before proceding to the next chapter in the life of the Hungarian Jewish remnant, which began with the liberation of Budapest by the Russian army, I feel that we cannot pass in silence over the question of who was responsible for the genocide of more than half a million Hungarian Jews in the very last months and weeks before the defeat of Germany. This issue is of crucial importance, and has been repeatedly discussed by historians of World War II, and especially by Randolph Braham, the historian of the Hungarian Holocaust, with whose views I find myself in general agreement.

There can be, of course, no question that the primary initial responsibility rests with the Germans. But it seems that the Final Solution of the Jewish question in Hungary was only a wish, not an absolute demand, of the Germans. Moreover, the *Sonderkommando*, that was at the disposal of Eichmann, consisted only of a small contingent of two-hundred men, who on their own could have done little without the active help of various Hungarian armed formations that were put at his disposal. The examples of Bulgaria, Finland, and Rumania, and the July 1944 action of Regent Horthy himself, putting an end to the deportations, show that had they wished to do so, the Regent and his men could have saved most of the Hungarian Jews. However, the Horthy clique was interested only in saving the members of the Jewish financial elite with whom they had advantageous relations, and welcomed the opportunity to rid the country of the "Galician" Jews and the *Ostjuden*. That is to say, the rulers of Hungary were as much responsible for the Jewish genocide as were Eichmann and his SS.

Added to this was the active dislike of the Jews that characterized large segments of the Hungarian people and that enabled the Hungarian commanders to rely on many in the ranks of the gendarmerie, the police, and the army to carry out the deportation and mass murder of Jews with unrestrained brutality, while the public at large stood by with indifference and helped the Jews only in a few exceptional cases.

While the Germans and the Hungarians thus bear the main responsibility for actively orchestrating and carrying out the Holocaust, secondary passive responsibility must be assigned to the Allies and the Catholic Church. Their interest in saving the Hungarian Jews was, to say the least, lukewarm. To mention only one instance, the Allies were asked to bomb Auschwitz and the rail lines leading to it and thus make it impossible for the Germans to proceed with their organized transportation of Jews to the death factories. The Allied response was that they could not spare planes for bombing "secondary targets," but they were able to send large numbers of bombers to destroy Dresden, a target of no military value at all.

And finally, and most painfully, some responsibility must be assigned to the leadership of the Hungarian Jews themselves. The official leaders of the Hungarian Jews, and especially those in the capital Budapest, remained convinced to the very last moment that "it can't happen here." Their traditional ingrained patriotism blinded them to the inexorable progression in Hungary of deadly anti-Semitism *à la* Nazi Germany, and by serving in the Jewish Council and obeying the instructions issued by the German and Hungarian authorities, they became willy-nilly cogs in the Nazi–Arrow Cross killing machine. What were the innermost ultimate motivations, beliefs, intentions, hopes and fears of the Hungarian Jewish leaders, and especially of the members of the Jewish Council, will perhaps never be known for certain. But even if we assume that they all acted with the best of intentions, and were totally committed to doing what they believed was best for the community they represented, what is tragically patent is that their function contributed to the orderly procedure of first depriving the Jews of more and more of their rights, and in the end of sending them to their death without any appreciable resistance. This, within the general tragedy of Hungarian Jewry, was the special tragedy of its leadership in the days of the war and the Holocaust.

45

Liberation

The Red Army liberated Pest on January 17–18 and Buda on February 13, 1945. The liberation of the rest of Hungary was completed on April 4. The war ended officially on May 9.

The adjustment to the new order, which began piecemeal in the liberated parts of the country, had a basically different character and meaning for the Hungarian Christians and the Hungarian Jews. For the Christians it meant getting used to being a defeated country, occupied and controlled by a feared and hated enemy, to being despoiled, looted, and raped by a rough and ruthless army in almost the same manner in which it and its German comrades-in-arms had treated the Hungarian Jews up to the very end of resistance to the Russians. The only significant difference between the treatment meted out to the Jews by the Hungarians and Nazis and what the Hungarians themselves now experienced at the hands of the Russians was that mass murder was not part of the Russian agenda. This difference was, of course, enormous; but so was the trauma of being at the mercy of the Red Army.

For the surviving Jews, the taking of Budapest (and the rest of Hungary) by the Red Army was literally a last-minute reprieve from the death sentence that had been hanging over their heads for a year or longer. Not as if the Hungarian Jews had more reason to love the Russians than had the Hungarian Christians; Russia was, after all, the classical country of murderous pogroms, persecutions of Jews, and the denial of civil rights, whether by czarist or Communist governments. Yet the memories of past injuries done by the Russians to their own Jews, whom the Hungarian Jews disliked as much as the "Galizianers," paled into insignificance when the Red Army appeared at the gates of Budapest as liberators. The change in the situation of the Hungarian Jews brought about by the Russian occupation was immeasurable; it was the gift of life to those who for months had been the defenseless, hunted prey of Nazi and Arrow Cross inhumanity.

Occasionally it even happened that Jewish soldiers in the Red Army recognized as Jews individuals whom they encountered in the streets of Budapest and "fraternized" with them. Rabbi Ferenc Raj remembered such an incident from 1945, right after the liberation of Budapest, when as a child he was walking in the streets with his grandfather. A Russian officer, who evidently recognized the old man as Jewish, suddenly approached them and said "*Sh'ma Yisroel*," to which his grandfather automatically responded with the rest of the famous Jewish confession of faith, "*Adonai elohenu Adonai ehod!*" The Russian Jewish officer then brought food to the home of the family and saved them from starvation in those difficult days. As we may remember, some 260 years earlier, the same *Sh'ma Yisrael* served as the password of recognition and identification, when Sender Tausk rescued the Jews of Buda from being massacred by the victorious Austrian imperial army after the fall of the city. (See chapter 14.)

The task of reconstruction to which both the Hungarian Christians and Jews had to apply themselves after the liberation of Hungary from the German occupation was colossal. Much of Budapest and the countryside lay in ruins; the economy was in shambles; the services in the cities—water, gas, electricity, telephone—were barely functioning. Similarly disrupted was the food supply, which had to reach the capital from the provinces.

In addition to all this, a horrible distrust was now embedded in the hearts of the Jews; for years any Hungarian Christian could have been an anti-Semite, a Jew-hater, ready to kill and perhaps guilty of having killed Jews; how could one now, suddenly, merely because the Germans had been put to flight, trust the Christians, work together with them, and assume that they had changed their anti-Jewish position?

Nor was it easy for the Hungarian Christians to change their attitude to the Jews: for years they had been indoctrinated by the Nazi–Arrow Cross teachings that the Jews were subhuman beings, parasites on the body of the nation, whom exterminating was a praiseworthy patriotic act, commanded by the supreme leadership of the country. Could it be that now, simply because the Germans and their Hungarian followers had been defeated by the Russians, those same Jews had become good Hungarian citizens with rights equal to Christian Hungarians'? It had taken years for the traditional, historical Hungarian anti-Semitism to intensify into the Nazi–Arrow Cross genocidal mania that dominated Hungary during the months preceding the Russian occupation; how could those same Hungarians be expected to become virtually overnight if not exactly Jew-lovers, at least people who considered the Jews their fellow people, their coequal Hungarians?

These were some of the institutional, economic, and psychological problems that had to be faced and overcome after the liberation. Added to them was the hatred of the Russians most Hungarians had ever since 1849 and their aversion since the short-lived Communist dictatorship of 1919 to Communism as a governmental system. And yet, Hungary now found itself under the heel of the powerful Soviet army, intent on introducing its own Communist system into Hungary. Hungary had to learn not only to live with a Communist overlord but to adjust its own political system to Communism. Beside Russian domination, this was the most bitter pill Hungary had to swallow.

For a number of complex political considerations, Stalin decided not to insist on the immediate establishment of Communist rule in Hungary but instead to let the Hungarians set up a coalition government. Accordingly, in December 1944, the first postwar Hungarian Provisional Government came into being, headed by Gen. Béla Miklós, with headquarters in the east Hungarian city of Debrecen, one of the first to be conquered by the Red Army. It consisted of representatives of the Smallholders, Social Democratic, and National Peasant parties, as well as the newly formed Hungarian Communist Party. Of course, this government had to share power with the Soviet occupying forces and the Communist-controlled political police.

During the tenure of this first postwar government—which expired in November 1945—the reconstruction of the country began. Work on rebuilding the destroyed bridges spanning the Danube started, and transportation, education, and health care were improved. By the summer of 1945 there was an almost adequate food supply in the cities. Private enterprise was encouraged. A Land Reform Act was introduced, legislating the expropriation of estates larger than one thousand *holds* (1,420 acres). Confident of their power, the Communists called for general elections, which took place in November 1945 and were almost completely free. They resulted in a stunning defeat of the Communists who received only 17 percent of the votes, against 57 percent for the Smallholders Party (the Social Democrats got 17 percent and the National Peasant Party 7 percent). A new coalition government was formed, within which the Communists were nevertheless able to rapidly consolidate their power, using the so-called salami technique, which consisted of removing step by step (slice by slice, as it were) those they deemed undesirable from the coalition. In the winter of 1947–48, partly at Stalin's initiative, the Hungarian Communists took over the government under the leadership of Mátyás Rákosi, officially proclaimed and adulated as "the great Stalin's wise Hungarian pupil."

This was the first of several radical changes that characterized the Hungarian government in the ensuing decades. From the 1947–48 take-over to the death of Stalin in 1953 there were five years of Stalinist ter-ror; they were followed until 1956 by three years of gradual decompres-sion called "the New Course"; and after the anti-Soviet Hungarian uprising of October 1956, a strict, harsh Communist rule was reestab-lished, and remained in full force until 1957, though the collectivization of Hungarian agriculture continued and was completed only in 1959–60.

In 1948 was created under the Rákosi regime the armed formation for internal security called *Államvédelmi hatóság* (State Defense Authority), whose units, called *Államvédelmi Osztályok* (State Defense Sections, generally referred to by the acrostic ÁVO), apprehended, imprisoned, and tortured thousands of people, so that in effect they functioned as state-controlled terrorist bodies, with the knowledge or concurrence of the Ministry of Justice. The ÁVO kept the country in trepidation for several years until finally, in October, 1956, Prime Minister Imre Nagy abolished it.

In the 1960s, economic problems prompted the government to under-take far-reaching reforms, including the introduction of a new price sys-tem and the abolishment of obligatory directives in economic plans, both of which became effective on January 1, 1968. This meant a rapid moving away from classical Communist ideology and practice, as was demonstrated by the marked increase of the discrepancy between the highest and the lowest salaries: until 1968 the ratio was 3 to 1; after 1968 it quickly increased to 9 to 1. The growing social differentiation result-ing from this change was also indicated by the increasing segment of the population that could afford to own a car. By 1980 one out of every three families did own a car.

Historically, it has always been the case in Hungary that whenever the general economic situation improves the Jews manage to obtain a greater share of it than would be expected merely on the basis of their proportion in the population. This historical law came into play after the 1945 liberation was well. Statistical data from the new Hungary are rather scanty, but the impression definitely gained is that by the 1970s, and certainly by the 1980s, the Jews of Hungary were again, as they had been in the interwar years, better educated, more affluent, more concen-trated in the professions and other high-income occupations, more involved in political activity, and so on, than the population as a whole.

Nor does it come as a surprise that despite everything that had befal-len the Jews during the Nazi–Arrow Cross era, and despite the powerful assimilatory bent characterizing the surviving Jewish remnant in Hun-gary (see next chapter), the Christian Hungarians still considered the

Jews a population group tinged with unmistakable markers of "otherness." Not even the most rabidly chauvinistic, dyed-in-the-wool member of the Catholic majority would have ever conceived of a Calvinist or Lutheran Hungarian as being therefore in any manner less Hungarian. But the run-of-the-mill Christian Hungarian, whether Catholic, Calvinist, or Lutheran, again (or still) had the feeling that the Hungarian Jew, however strong the assertions to the contrary, was not as fully Hungarian as the Christian Hungarians. As the historian of modern Hungary George Barany observed: "Although no one questioned that any democracy, the emerging new Hungary included, must guarantee freedom of religion, debates about the role of churches and church-state relations raised serious problems and brought the reemergence of anti-Semitic statements and actions. Unemployment and austerity made it easy to blame minorities, including the Jews. Hungary's new government would have to combat this tendency, whatever the combination of parties forming the coalition turned out to be."

Barany views the problem from the point of view of religion. That religious differences are not the whole story has been amply shown in the course of this book; we have seen that conversion to Christianity, in the eyes of Christians, did make a Jew a fully Magyar person; from being a Jew, the convert would become a "converted Jew," and only one or even two generations later, once the Jewish origin of the descendants was forgotten, would they count as truly Magyar. This pattern has been completely repeated in the last several decades in Hungary.

As for the practical, economic and social aspects of reconstruction, they were energetically taken in hand even before the whole country was liberated. The death toll did not freeze instantly upon liberation: many of the liberated deportees suffered from severe disabilities, especially typhoid, malnutrition and depression, and thousands of them were beyond help. The international Jewish welfare institutions had to shoulder the task of supporting thousands who were left totally destitute. In the early weeks after liberation, the American Jewish Joint Distribution Committee and the Ezra (Relief) organization were the main agencies of support. Their work was organized primarily by Ernő Marton, former publisher of the Kolozsvár Jewish journal *Uj Kelet* (New East), and the distinguished lawyer and respected community leader Dr. Frigyes Görög, both of whom were also associated with the International Red Cross and its Southeast and Central European Section for Aiding the Victims. Within a few weeks of the liberation, the various welfare and relief organizations were united to form, under the chairmanship of Görög, the National Jewish Aid Committee (Országos Zsidó Segitő Bizottság or OZsSB), one of whose agencies, the National Committee for the Care of

Deportees (Deportáltakat Gondozó Országos Bizottság, or DEGOB), organized no fewer than twenty-six visits to concentration camps to locate and return to Hungary thousands of survivors. The size of the operations conducted by the Joint can be gauged from the fact that by October 1945, its staff in Hungary had grown close to one thousand, it had distributed 9 million Swiss francs in Budapest alone, it maintained thirty-eight children's hostels, and it provided food, medicine, and money to 210 communities.

The Armistice Agreement signed by Hungary on January 20, 1945, restored legal equality to the Jews with all other citizens of the country, and on March 17 the Provisional Government repealed all anti-Jewish laws and decrees that had been enacted during the Horthy and Arrow Cross eras.

Almost immediately after the end of the hostilities, the Neolog and Orthodox Jewish congregations of Budapest resumed their activities. The head of the Neolog congregation and of the National Office of Hungarian Jews was now Lajos Stöckler, while Samu Kahan-Frankl became the head of the Orthodox congregation and of the Central Bureau of Orthodox Communities. One of the grave problems of reactivating the congregations was the lack of rabbis: almost all of the provincial rabbis had been deported and killed together with their congregants, so that the few congregations that were reconstituted had to find new rabbis, in many cases from Rumania, to take their places. In Budapest, the National Rabbinical Seminary resumed functioning as the only rabbinical school in the Soviet sphere of influence, but its enrollment was minimal and it could graduate barely one rabbi a year.

Shortly after the signing of the armistice agreement, the Jewish leaders asked the government for restitution and indemnification of the deportees and other survivors. Because of its depleted finances, and because restitution would often have meant depriving Christian Hungarians of property they had held for several years, the government was able or willing to meet the Jewish demands in only a limited number of cases. Appropriate laws were adopted to restore to the Jews, under certain conditions, commercial, business, and industrial enterprises, as well as apartments, offices, shops, and personal property that had been forcibly taken from them. However, nothing remotely similar to the large-scale indemnification program of West Germany was ever introduced in Hungary. In carrying out whatever laws were passed, difficulties arose because the new owners of formerly Jewish property were unwilling to give it up; often litigation ensued, producing long delays; and the willingness of the new Communist-dominated government that came into power in 1948 to restore private property to Jews was minimal. The confrontations between the Jewish ex-owners of properties and their new Christian possessors were not conducive to inspiring sympathy for the Jews among the latter, or among the Christian population in general. Added to this was the prominent role Jews played from 1947–48 in the Hungarian Communist government, of which more will be said in chapter 47.

The upshot of these developments was that, mere weeks after the liberation, voices began to be heard, and actions taken, that overtly signaled a resurgence, or perhaps more correctly a survival, of anti-Semitism in Hungary. It was expressed in anti-Jewish statements by political leaders and in brutal attacks on Jews by various elements. In addition to the physical injury and damage these attacks caused, they had a devastating psychological effect on the Jewish survivors, most of whom had not yet begun to recover from the horrors they had experienced.

One of the worst pronouncements was that of Péter Veres, who was put in charge of agrarian reform. He was reputed to have stated that Hungary would rid itself of all foreigners, Jews as well as Germans. In 1946, serious anti-Semitic outbursts, some amounting to veritable pogroms, took place in several country towns. (See chapter 47). Moreover, some Hungarian sociologists, subjecting the events of the postwar era to ostensibly objective scholarly analysis, concluded that the Jews bore varying degrees of responsibility for the inimical attitude that developed toward them in Hungary after the liberation. In a word, things were back where they used to be in the pre-Hitler era; a considerable segment of the public returned to the traditional Hungarian anti-Semitism that had been part of the Hungarian mentality for many generations.

What was characteristic of the pregenocide period and remained so after it was a general overall, quasi-instinctive perception in the population as a whole of the separate group-identity of the Jews. There were, of course, enormous differences in reactions to the Jews, ranging from the most liberal to the most rabidly anti-Semitic. There were also differences of a similar magnitude as to what was to be done with the Jews: the plans ranged from those of the liberals, who thought that the Jews should ultimately be fully assimilated into the Magyar people, to those of the Arrow Cross, who demanded that they be exterminated or at least summarily expelled.

Yet beneath these greatly contrasting intentions, demands, and plans there was always a common denominator: the basic conviction that the Jews were a population group essentially other than, and separate from, the Christian Hungarians. This was the underlying premise of everything thought about the Jews, said about the Jews, planned for the Jews, and done to the Jews. The otherness of the Jews was so self-evident to the Hungarian mind that it never had to be explicitly mentioned or even hinted at: it was a fact of life, a natural phenomenon perceived almost on a subconscious level. All the plans, speeches, and acts concerning the Jews always dealt with single or multiple specific manifestations of that fundamental, all-pervasive, inalterable otherness. Laws concerning the Jews could be enacted or canceled; social contact with them could or could not be considered acceptable; their participation in the country's economic and cultural life could be appreciated and furthered, or deprecated and hindered; personally they could be liked, disliked, or even hated—none of this touched the fact of the Jew being perceived as *the other.*

As for the Jews themselves, although in some years conversion assumed epidemic proportions (see chapter 46), all in all only a small part of them sought that way of bettering their position. Most of the Jews, once assimilation and modernization had become widespread among them, either truly believed, or made believe, in sharp contrast to the general Christian position, that they were but a denominational subvariety of the Magyar nation. That is to say, they rejected, on both the emotional and cerebral levels, the notion that the Jews were different in any manner, except for their religious beliefs, from the other Hungarians. There was thus a basic incompatibility between the way the Jews saw themselves in relation to the Magyars, and the way the Magyars saw the Jews in relation to themselves.

As for the Jewish reaction to the postliberation neo-anti-Semitism (as some students of the contemporary Hungarian scene called it) and, more generally, to the new position in which they found themselves in Communist-dominated Hungary, it hewed close to the paths they had traditionally followed, right down to the German invasion. Those paths had been widely divergent in the century that preceded World War II, and now, after the liberation, they remained almost unchanged; this became increasingly evident as Hungarian life, and within it Jewish life, underwent the painful process of reconstruction. It is to a discussion of these old Jewish trends as they survived and resurfaced in the new, Soviet-dominated Hungary that we now turn.

46

Old Trends and the Post-Holocaust Stance

Community Character

In order to understand better the readiness of the post-Holocaust remnant of Hungarian Jewry to accommodate to Communism, which became after 1948 the form of government and the only tolerated ideology in Hungary for some forty years, we must go back two generations or more and look at the trends that had been most influential in shaping the Hungarian Jewish personality and psychology to which the post-Holocaust generation was heir. Our survey will show that the characteristic stance of the Hungarian Jews for two or three generations prior to World War II was that of assimilating to Magyardom, and going along willingly with whatever were the dominant cultural and political trends of the country. It was this inherited tendency that made the Hungarian Jews jump readily on the political bandwagon, no matter what melody the band was playing.

A second factor we must take into consideration was the specific nature of the Hungarian Jewish community as compared to that of the nation as a whole. By the interwar years, the Jews were—again as a result of developments that had taken place after their emancipation in 1867—a much more urbanized element than the non-Jews. The national census of 1920 showed that of the total of 473,310 Jews in post-Trianon Hungary, 264,508 (or 55.9 percent) lived in cities, and 208,802 (or 44.1 percent) in rural areas. In Budapest that year the census counted 215,512 Jews (accounting for 45.5 percent of all the Jews in the country, and for 23.2 percent of the total population of Budapest).

And even within the urban population, as shown by the various demographic surveys, the Jews were the best-educated element, concentrated in the professional, intellectual, and commercial occupations. A corollary of this not shown by the census was that as a population they were more open to new ideas, trends, and attitudes than the non-Jews who constituted the overwhelming majority of urban and rural workers.

604

Hence, there were relatively more Social Democrats, Socialists, and Communists among the Jews than in the rest of the population.

A third factor was that the Hungarian people comprised a sizable gentry and nobility class, traditionally dominant in the country, who had an entrenched interest in maintaining the status quo, and thus constituted a conservative counterweight to any innovative tendency that arose among the rest of the population. The Jews, on the other hand, lacked such an element with vested interest in the status quo; they constituted a socially upwardly mobile group whose basic interest lay in bettering their situation both individually and collectively. This meant that Jews were more receptive to ideas and movements that aimed at the introduction of changes in the social order, because any change facilitated upward mobility.

These three factors reinforced one another. Their net effect was to endow the Jews of Hungary with a community character that subtly, or often not so subtly, set them apart from the non-Jewish majority. However, neither the Jewish leadership, nor the general Jewish community was very clearly aware of this type of distinction between Jews and non-Jews, perhaps because their attention was focused on differences of quite another nature: residual differences that survived from preemancipation times, when the Jews differed from the majority not only in religion but also in manners and customs, language, culture, occupation, and garb and, of course, in the overarching fact of possessing no civil rights.

It was this complex of residual differences whose elimination had become a main concern of the Jews of Hungary in the decades following their emancipation. Their basic aspiration to be like the other Hungarians from time to time received new impetus from two opposite expressions of the Hungarian attitude toward them: anti-Semitic activity on the one hand and liberal pronouncements on the other. The Jewish reaction to both was to emphasize their Magyardom and their loyalty to the Hungarian fatherland. The patriotism and the quasi-instinctive aspiration of the Jews to be like the non-Jewish Hungarians are, I believe, sufficiently clear from the details of the foregoing chapters, but it took three specific forms that I want to consider here, because their generational impact left its mark on the Hungarian Jewish character, and thus bears much of the responsibility for the assimilatory tendency of the Jews in post-Holocaust Communist Hungary. These historically developed patterns of behavior, through which Jews had expressed their desire to become fully Magyars ever since the 1867 emancipation, and which greatly intensified after 1948, were first, the Magyarization of names; second, outmarriage; and third, conversion to Christianity. To them must be added the emigratory movement, which signaled the Jews' ultimate despair at finding their place in Hungary but was surprisingly limited in the decades after World War II. And finally, to this context also belongs the pathetic self-abnegation, the distancing oneself from the Jewish past, and the very denial of being Jewish, that developed among the Jews of Hungary after 1948 and amounted to a new Marranism, Hungarian-style.

A discussion of these patterns of communal behavior will help us to see more clearly where Hungarian Jewry stood just before the entirely unexpected Jewish revival and reconstruction that began in the 1980s.

Magyarizing German Names

We have spoken of this movement in earlier contexts, and pointed out that the Magyarizing of names was practiced and advocated by many Jews who were fervently Jewish in their outlook, who devoted their lives to the Jewish cause, and who considered the name change simply an expression of their patriotic identification with the cause of Magyar Hungary. These name changes were most frequent among the Jewish writers, artists, editors, scholars, and members of the intelligentsia in general, whose work brought them in daily contact with non-Jewish Hungarians, and for whom it was important to be able to appear as Hungarian, and not Hungarian-Jewish, writers and artists. Our discussion of the Jewish writers and artists in the late nineteenth and early twentieth centuries dealt in effect with individuals who almost all Magyarized their names. Among the painters and sculptors the fashion was to retain their original German names also, and to use double Hungarian-German family names, for example, Gusztáv Magyar–Mannheimer, Miklós Szines–Sternberg, Vilmos Perlrott-Csaba.

We have no data at our disposal to show what percentage of those who Magyarized their names did so with the intention of hiding their Jewish origin or identity. However, one can guess that many of them had this in mind, and the name change represented their desire not to be easily identifiable as Jews, even though they shied away from the final step of formally denouncing Judaism and entering another denomination. What we do have is the total number of people who Magyarized their names, and the percentage of Jews among them. These available figures show that in most of the years in question more than half of all those who Magyarized their names were Jews, and their numbers peaked in the years between the Reception and the end of World War I (1896–1918); see Table 5.

Table 5. Jews Magyarizing Their Names 1891–1918

Year	Annual Average	Percentage of Total Magyarizations
1891–93	532	53–62
1894	611	70.5
1895	660	67.8
1896	931	56.7
1897	1,450	81.5
1898	2,426	37.7
1899	1,628	54.9
1900–1904	1,887	69.6
1905–09	1,853	66.1
1910–13	1,570	62.1
1914–18	968	64.9
Total 1891–1918	39,122	62.3

These figures show that in the twenty-eight years from 1891 to 1918, that is, in roughly one generation, almost 40,000 Hungarian Jews, or some 4 percent of the total of about one million, changed their German names for Hungarian names, emphatically expressing their determination to be counted not as members of a minority group by any definition but as "Hungarians of the Mosaic persuasion." We have no data as to the percentages of men and women among those who changed their names, but we can assume that in the traditional socio-economic situation of that period most of them were men. If so, when a man changed his name, it meant that the names of his existing or future wife and children were also changed, so that within one generation every individual name change resulted in, say, four persons with a Hungarian name. We can thus figure that by the end of World War I there were in Hungary some 160,000 Jews (or 16 percent of the total) with newly acquired Hungarian names. The Hungarian names selected were almost always translations of the German names (thus Klein became Kiss, Gross became Nagy, Braun became Barna, Schwarz became Fekete) or else were similar in sound or initial letter (Schlesinger became Szilágyi, Handler or Hoffman became Hevesi, Bloch became Ballagi).

Although I am not aware of any relevant statistical study, my impression is that Orthodox Jews, whose life and outlook were circumscribed by more rigorous adherence to Jewish tradition than the Neologs', had no share or only a very slight one, in this Magyarizing movement. What was the motivation underlying this Orthodox objection to, or disapproval of, replacing German family names with Hungarian ones? The German family names themselves were, after all, imposed upon the Jews under Joseph II (1780–90) less than a century before the Magyarizing movement began. One factor certainly was the general Orthodox Jewish reluctance to change any feature at all, of whatever origin, that had become part and parcel of Jewish tradition. There are numerous examples in Jewish life illustrating this tendency. The wearing of various types of fur hats (*shtrayml, spodek*), for example, was adopted by the Jews in the late Middle Ages from the fashions of the Polish nobility, but once adopted, it acquired an aura of religious value, and its abandonment became the equivalent of rejecting part of a religiously sanctioned traditional Jewish custom. More striking examples are the acquisition of the German language among the Ashkenazi Jews, and of Spanish among the Sephardim, both from the gentile environment, their subsequent development into Yiddish and Ladino, respectively, and their endowment with a religious quasi-sanctity, to the extent that giving them up came to be considered an areligious, even antireligious, move. Similarly, the German names borne by the Hungarian Jews for two or three generations came to be considered by the tradition-directed element a part of Jewishness, divesting oneself of which was seen as distancing oneself from the Jewish community.

Another element in the Orthodox objection to name Magyarization seems to have been the well-founded suspicion that by adopting a Hungarian name a Jew displayed the desire not to be readily recognized as a Jew in his contact or dealings with the gentile Hungarian world. For the Orthodox this smacked of an assimilatory tendency, all signs of which they frowned upon. Orthodoxy, of course, came in many degrees, and in general the stricter it was, the more the appearance of its adherents revealed their Jewishness: the shape of the beard and sidelocks, the style of the hat and garb, all evinced the intensity of Orthodoxy. To them was added the name: to change one's traditional German (or German-Yiddish) name for a Hungarian one was similar to discarding any other external sign of Jewish identity.

Needless to say, the other two, much more blatant, manifestations of the assimilatory tendency—outmarriage and apostasy—also made little headway among the Orthodox Hungarian Jews, and remained largely confined to the Neologs, who, however, constituted the majority of Hungarian Jewry by the latter part of the nineteenth century.

Outmarriages, Conversions, Emigration

Precise data on the marriages between Hungarian Jews and Christians are available for the fifty one years from 1896 to 1946. They are given in the Hungarian statistical publications separately for the Jews of Budapest and those of the country outside the capital. They show that while

Table 6. Jewish Outmarriages in Budapest 1896–1946

Years	Jewish Bridegrooms (Annual Average)			Jewish Brides (Annual Average)		
	Total Number	Number of Them Outmarried	Percentage of Those Outmarried	Total Number	Number of Them Outmarried	Percentage of Those Outmarried
1896–1900	1,290	94	7.3	1,282	86	6.7
1901–1905	1,400	111	7.9	1,392	99	7.1
1906–10	1,706	171	10.0	1,686	148	8.8
1911–13	1,881	220	11.7	1,860	195	10.5
1914	1,867	316	16.9	1,754	196	11.2
1915–18	1,504	310	20.6	1,359	191	14.1
1919	2,219	357	16.1	2,105	240	11.4
1920	2,778	414	14.9	2,621	259	9.9
1921–25	2,292	360	15.7	2,240	307	13.7
1926–30	2,047	356	17.4	2,008	317	15.8
1931–35	2,078	401	19.3	2,011	363	16.5
1936–37	2,202	404	20.2	2,088	330	15.8
1938	2,071	385	18.6	1,982	291	14.7
1939	1,937	294	15.2	1,844	199	10.8
1940	1,555	227	14.6	1,444	117	8.1
1941	2,041	386	18.9	1,796	135	7.5
1942	1,420	47	3.3	1,424	51	3.6
1943	915	46	5.0	918	45	4.9
1944	?	?	?	?	?	?
1945	1,742	481	27.6	1,546	284	18.4
1946	2,734	429	15.7	2,533	228	9.0
Total 1896–1946	91,407	13,555	14.9	88,253	10,654	12.1

in Budapest the percentage of Jewish men who married non-Jewish women was almost without exception higher, and in some years much higher, than the percentage of Jewish women marrying non-Jewish men, in the countryside the two percentages were throughout very similar, with that of the outmarrying men somewhat higher in certain years, and that of the outmarrying women in others. The one preliminary conclusion one can draw from these numbers is that in the capital the Jewish men had a greater opportunity for social contact with non-Jewish women than vice versa, while in the country such opportunities were about equal for Jewish men and women. Tables 6 and 7 give the figures for both sexes.

The data in the tables include only those mixed marriages in which the bridegroom and bride belonged to different religions at the time of the marriage. They do not include marriages that were contracted

Table 7. Jewish Outmarriages in Hungary Outside Budapest 1901–46

Years	Total Number	Jewish Bridegrooms (Annual Average)		Jewish Brides (Annual Average)		
		Number of Them Outmarried	Percentage of Those Outmarried	Total Number	Number of Them Outmarried	Percentage of Those Outmarried
1901–1905	5,111	118	2.3	5,424	130	2.4
1906–10	5,578	156	2.8	5,638	175	3.1
1911–13	5,429	206	3.8	5,434	217	4.0
1914	4,422	234	5.3	4,383	202	4.6
1915–18	2,393	232	9.7	1,870	183	9.8
1919	3,573	343	9.6	3,523	299	8.5
1920	3,098	198	6.4	3,070	169	5.5
1921–25	2,305	148	6.4	2,324	167	7.2
1926–30	1,971	152	7.7	1,985	177	8.9
1931–35	1,755	163	9.3	1,756	169	9.6
1936–37	1,820	175	9.6	1,810	165	9.1
1938	1,685	182	10.8	1,641	143	8.7
1939	1,849	124	6.7	1,847	124	6.7
1940	2,214	97	4.4	2,198	81	3.7
1941	4,172	271	6.5	3,982	92	2.3
1942	2,640	13	0.5	2,647	21	0.8
1943–45	?	?	?	?	?	?
1946	2,735	410	15.0	2,420	97	4.0
Total 1901–1946	139,487	7,453	5.3	138,748	7,031	5.1

between a man and a woman originally belonging to two different religions, one of whom had converted to the religion of the other prior to the marriage. Since such cases must have been numerous, we can take it for granted that the number of Jewish outmarriages was considerably higher than shown in the tables.

No data are available as to the religion observed in households established by mixed couples, or the religion in which their children were being brought up. However, taking into account the general assimilationist atmosphere among the Neolog Jews in Hungary, to whom most if not all of the outmarrying Jewish men and women belonged, one must assume that in the great majority of cases the children of mixed marriages were brought up as Christians. That is to say, mixed marriages in most cases meant a demographic loss to the Hungarian Jewish community.

The motivations for conversion are a complex issue. In the absence of sociological-statistical studies, impressionistic estimates will have to serve as the basis for the following comments. Until the 1919 reaction to the short-lived Communist regime, Hungarian Jews could, at the price of conversion, achieve practically any position that was effectively closed to unconverted Jews. A Jewish scholar, if converted, could become a university professor, as at least a dozen thus did; a Jew who wanted to become part of gentile society could, if converted, join if not all, at least some gentile *kaszinós* (social clubs). Those aspiring to political careers could, once converted, rise to the highest ranks in the government—as shown, for example, by Baron Samu Hazay (1851–1942), a converted Jew who became minister of war, serving in that capacity from 1910 to 1917. This was the case in every field. Conversion was not only, as Heine said, the entry pass into gentile society but, in Hungary at least, the ladder on which a Jew could climb up to the top of it. At the same time, a Jew who converted did not, by the mere act of conversion, become a Catholic Hungarian or a Protestant Hungarian. As indicated above, he still remained stigmatized as a "converted Jew," but he was a step closer to being considered fully Hungarian than the unconverted Jews.

Until 1944, conversion was a movement confined to the assimilant sectors of Hungarian Jewry, that is to those who belonged, however tenuously and remotely, to the Neolog congregations, or were unaffiliated. Most conversions took place in response to the social pressure exercised by the Hungarian environment on the Jews, and their volume evinced a direct correlation. That is to say, when the prevailing attitude towards the Jews was liberal, the number of conversions was small; when it grew anti-Semitic, their number increased. This could be observed most clearly after the end of World War I. From 1896 to 1917 the annual number of Jews who converted to Christianity grew slowly, from 291 to 1896 to 527 in 1917. This gradual increase evidently reflected the growing assimilatory trend, which made conversion to Christianity a preferred option for only a relatively small number of Jews. A sudden and dramatic increase in conversions took place in 1919, especially after the fall of the Hungarian Council Republic, when the anti-Semitic White Terror brought with it a wave of anti-Jewish excesses, including many murders, and Jew-hatred became a fashionable expression of political convictions. In that year, the number of conversions jumped fifteenfold, reaching 7,146, demonstrating Jewish panic at the persecutions and their hopes of escaping them by the simple expedient of officially seceding from the Jewish community and joining one of the Christian Churches. Once the cruder forms of anti-Semitism were brought under control, the conversion movement abated, and many converts even returned to Judaism. In the nine years from 1922 to 1930 the number of conversions was again at the same level as in the 1900–1917 period, ranging between 449 and 587 annually.

Still, even this reduced number was a source of acute embarrassment for the Hungarian Jewish establishment and the observers and chroniclers of its Jewish life, as can be seen from the way the 1929 *Hungarian Jewish Lexicon* treats the subject of conversion. It has a seven-column survey article on "Apostasy and Conversion from Judaism." Five columns summarize the history of Jewish apostasy since the days of the Maccabees, followed by a two-column list of famous nineteenth-century converts in the Western world, mostly in Germany. However, all the article has to say about conversions in Hungary is contained in its concluding sentence, which reads: "Converts born in the territory of old [pre-Trianon] Hungary who played significant roles in public life, science, and art are dealt with under their respective entries." Their conversion is indicated in those biographical entries by an asterisk placed after their names in the heading, with no reference at all to their conversion in the article itself. The overall significance of the phenomenon—as one of the varieties of Jewish responses to anti-Semitic pressure and a damaging brain drain for Hungarian Jewry—is nowhere even alluded to.

After the Nazi takeover in Germany, conversion among the Hungarian Jews again picked up rapidly, reaching an annual average of 924 in 1931–35, rising to about 1,500 in 1936 and 1937, and hitting an all-time high of 8,548 in 1938, evidently in response to the First Jewish Law introduced in that year. It then decreased to 6,070 in 1939, and to an annual average of 3,326 in 1940–42. These statistics of conversions offer an interesting sidelight on the differences between the Jews of Budapest and the countryside. Throughout the period for which data are available (1919–42), the Jews of Budapest constituted between 25 percent and 40 percent of the total Jewish population of Hungary. Yet, as the demographer Victor Karády's studies have shown, in most of those years the Jews of the capital supplied between 60 and 70 percent of all Hungarian Jewish converts. The conclusion is inevitable that the Jewish loyalty of the provincial Jews was twice to three times as strong as that of the Budapest Jews. Or to put it differently, the hold Jewish religion had was one-half to one-third as strong on the Jews of Budapest as in the provinces. This finding, read together with the related fact that the ratio of Neolog to Orthodox Jews in Budapest was much higher than in the countryside, leads to the conclusion that the Neolog variety of Hungarian Judaism was much less effective than the Orthodox variety in constituting a bond that tied the individual Jew to Judaism.

From 1943 on no complete data are available, though indications are that conversions continued to remain high. In response to the German occupation of Hungary in March 1944, in the ensuing months conversions peaked, reaching 1,644 in July alone, and then again subsided somewhat. It has been estimated that in 1944 the number of conversions was at least 21,370, a figure other analysts consider much too low. In any case, conversion did not bring safety, for recent converts were considered Jews by the Third Jewish Law (of 1941) and treated as such, and it has been estimated that the Hungarian victims of the Holocaust included some hundred thousand converts to Christianity. Well known also is the fact that the leaders of the Christian Churches in Hungary made attempts to save the "Christian Jews," whom they considered Christians, while the new state laws regarded them as Jews. That the Churches largely confined their efforts to saving these "Christian Jews," raising only a few feeble voices against the extermination of the "Jewish Jews," is the greatest disgrace of Hungarian Christianity.

Yet another peak in the conversion movement was registered after the 1956 revolution, which triggered a considerable emigration (see below). Among those Jews who for various reasons would not or could not emigrate, a high percentage (exact figures unknown) chose to convert.

A paradoxical yet poignant indicator of the post-Holocaust attitudes of the Jewish remnant toward Hungary is that, despite the 1956 wave, the number of Hungarian Jewish emigrants remained throughout relatively small compared to the Jewish emigration from the neighboring countries. True, in absolute numbers the Jewish emigration from Hungary was several times greater after 1945 than in the early war years. In 1940–41, when war conditions made emigration very difficult, only 1,097 Jews (and 429 non-Jews) managed to leave Hungary. As against this, in 1945–57, between one-third and one-quarter of the Hungarian Jews who survived the Holocaust emigrated, of them about 28,000 to Israel and about the same number to West Europe and overseas countries, giving a total of around 56,000 emigrants (or 4,700 annually) out of a total Hungarian Jewish population estimated at between 150,000 and 200,000 in 1945. However, this emigration appears high only in comparison to the Jewish emigration of 1940–41. If one compares it with that of the neighboring countries in the same twelve-year period, which was estimated at 47 percent and 50 percent from Rumania, 58 percent from Czechoslovakia, 65 percent from Poland, and 90 percent from Bulgaria, it is seen to be relatively low. That is to say, two-thirds to three-quarters of the Hungarian Jews who escaped the *Shoah* (the Holocaust that singled out the Jews) chose to remain in Hungary despite the horrors they had lived through at the hands of the Nazis' Hungarian henchmen and the discrimination and occasional persecution visited upon them after 1945 by the Hungarian Communist regimes. To put it in different terms, they still felt sufficiently at home in Hungary not to undertake the effort required for emigration, and for facing the uncertainties that a new life in a foreign country inevitably entailed.

As Mária Schmidt, a gentile Hungarian student of contemporary Hungarian Jewish history, phrases it in her postscript to the 1991 reprint of Béla Dénes's 1957 memoir *ÁVÓs Világ Magyarországon: Egy cionista orvos emlékiratai* (The World of the Political Police in Hungary: Memoirs of a Zionist Physician):

> In contrast to the bulk of European Jewry, which, in consequence of the persecutions it survived and the anti-Semitic excesses that followed World War II, left its homelands and went to Palestine/Israel—the overwhelming majority of the Hungarian Jewish remnant chose to remain at home. They did not leave between 1945 and 1948, when it was still possible to go. . . . Between the spring of 1945 and December 1946 Hungary was one of the important transit stations of Palestine-bound emigration. More than 50,000 Polish, Sub-Carpathian, and Rumanian Jews passed through the country. But during the same time only 5–6,000 Hungarian Jews left, primarily children and young people. After January 1949, when the borders were closed, a few hundred members of the Zionist youth movements who had remained in the country crossed the border illegally. Thereafter, emigration was confined to those roughly 3,000 persons concerning whom on November 3, 1949, an understanding was reached between the Hungarian and the Israeli governments, and who were allowed to leave under a family reunion program, against a payment of $1 million by the Joint. From 1950 on some forty Zionist leaders with their families were also allowed to leave, but imprisoned Zionists were not included.

For several years after 1950 emigration was forcibly halted by the Communist dictatorship that held sway over Hungary. Only in October 1956, during the Hungarian anti-Soviet revolution, did some 200,000 Hungarians take the opportunity offered by the unsettled conditions and the temporary relaxation of the border control to escape, mostly to Austria. Among those who left Hungary in those days were some 20,000 Jews, that is some ten times more than their percentage of the total population of the country.

Silence Imposed

As for those Jews who chose to remain in Hungary, they found themselves faced with a socio-political environment that had radically changed the attitude to them in 1948–49. Between 1945 and 1948 the problems of the Jewish question and the Jewish genocide were in the very center of public debate. The representatives of practically every political trend participated in the discussion about the causes of the

Jewish question, the responsibility for the persecution of the Jews, and related issues. They included spokesmen of the Communists, the Social Democrats, the Peasant Party, the Bourgeois Radicals, and so on. Their analyses were published in both the daily press and sociological periodicals. By 1948 hundreds of books, pamphlets and articles were published, and plays and films performed, touching upon the Holocaust. Among the last of these writings were the study of István Bibó, titled "A zsidókérdés Magyarországon" ("The Jewish Question in Hungary"), published in the October-November 1948 issue of *Válasz* (Response); and Jenő Lévai's book *Zsidósors Magyarországon: Az üldözések kora* (Jewish Fate in Hungary: The Age of Persecutions). A list of the titles published in those three years on the Jewish question in Hungary is given in a detailed bibliography compiled by Arthur Geyer, *Bibliography of the Jewish Persecution of Hungarian Fascism* (in Hungarian), published in 1958 by the MIOK (Magyar Izraelitak Országos Képriselete—National Representation of Hungarian Israelites). The profusion of titles appearing between 1945 and 1948 and the dearth of items thereafter eloquently testify to the sudden change concerning the Jewish question that occurred in Hungarian politics in 1948.

For ten years thereafter (1948–58) the Hungarian government effectively prevented the publication of books, studies, and articles on the Jewish question and the persecution of the Jews in Hungary that culminated in the 1944 genocide. Practically no explicit mention could be made even of historical anti-Semitism. The official line was that what had happened prior to the Russian liberation of Hungary was that the Facists persecuted the anti-Fascists. The Communist leadership rejected the idea of the special Jewish suffering, saying that "in the old system the entire working people suffered." The suffering of the Jews, even though it was of an entirely different order of magnitude than that of the Christian Hungarians, was lumped together with the general troubles that befell the Hungarian nation as a whole. State-controlled media and textbooks alike treated the anti-Fascist resistance as a popular movement, without reference to the role played by the Jews or Zionists, or to the Nazi–Arrow Cross genocide directed at the Jews alone. This taboo applied equally to fiction, political discourse, and the social sciences (historiography, demography, folklore, ethnology). The fact that two-thirds or more of the Hungarian Jews were exterminated, and not because they were anti-Nazis or because of anything they did but merely because they were Jews (including those who had long before removed themselves from the Jewish community by conversion) was considered unmentionable, was passed over in silence, and its historicity was in effect erased. As Victor Karády puts it, "In a way both the *Shoah* and the Jewish past in Hungary were purged from collective memory." It is noteworthy that the bibliography of the Jewish persecution during the war years mentioned above could not be published before 1958, and that monographs dealing with the first deportations of 1941, the massacres of Ujvidék, the antecedents and history of the labor service, the Arrow Cross rule, the role of the Churches in connection with the persecution of Jews, and the period from the German occupation until the Russian liberation were all published only after 1960.

The fact that for ten years or more after 1948 the Jewish question was a taboo subject affected the identity-consciousness of the surviving Hungarian Jews in several ways. For one thing, it deprived them of the psychological consolation they could have derived from being recognized as the remnant of a community singled out for destruction by the German Nazis and their Hungarian counterparts, and from the expectation that from now on they would be treated with special consideration as the modern-day heirs of the ancient "brand saved from the fire." For another, it made them feel that any reference to the *Shoah* carried a connotation of reproach, of accusation, that would inevitably create resentment among the gentile Hungarians; thus, while for the first two or three years after the Holocaust its memory may have intensified the Jewish consciousness of otherness in relation to the gentile Hungarians, the subsequent governmental taboo on all public reference to Jews, Judaism, Jewish history, or Jewish fate inclined and induced the surviving Jews not to appear outwardly different from the surrounding society. A further consequence of this situation was an internalization of the official taboo on discussing Judaism: many Jews accepted the party line, and observed a voluntary silence about Jewishness, even inside the family.

The beginnings of this initially state-imposed and subsequently self-imposed silence happened to coincide with the establishment of the State of Israel (1948). The Communist policy was to ignore the very existence of the new Jewish state, just as it ignored the Jewish presence and Jewish life in the Western world. An anti-Zionist campaign was launched not only in Hungary but in the entire Soviet orbit, Zionism (dubbed "the hellhound of imperialism") suppressed, and the borderline between anti-Zionism and anti-Semitism blurred. The 1949 Rajk trial, in which László Rajk, former minister of internal affairs, was condemned and executed, had several Jewish victims as well, and was accompanied by persecution of Zionist leaders. All official contact between Hungarian Jewry and the Jews of Israel and the Western world was forbidden, and even family or friendship ties between Hungarian and foreign Jews could not be maintained. Hungarian Jewry was effectively isolated, its very Jewishness driven underground, and its existence reduced to Marranism.

Marranism Hungarian–Style

One need not be an expert in Jewish history to know about the many of thousands of Jews in late medieval Spain and Portugal, who, when forced to choose between expulsion and conversion, chose the latter, adopted Christianity, to be able to stay on in the places where their ancestors had lived for many centuries, but in secret remained faithful to their old Jewish faith, that is, became crypto-Jews, Marranos. Marranism thus resulted from the clash of two opposite wills: that of the Christian Iberians, who wanted the Jews to convert and would not tolerate Jews in the land, and that of the Jews, who wanted to remain Jews and yet could not bring themselves to leave the country they loved.

The imposition of Communist rule on Hungary in 1948 saw the emergence of a new type of Marranism. The Communist rulers, opposed to religion in general, wanted the surviving Jews to cease being Jewish, to give up whatever religious or cultural traditions they possessed, and to merge into the majority population of the country. They did not try to achieve this goal by brute force, as had the Catholic kings of Spain and Portugal five centuries earlier, but by creating conditions in the country that were enough of an inducement for most Jews to hide, or give up, their Jewishness. However, beyond that, the Hungarian Jews in the late 1940s reacted very differently from the Iberian Jews who chose Marranism: the great majority of Hungarian Jewry bent to the explicit or implicit demands of the ruling establishment, and went along with the politically correct position of abandoning its religious and cultural specificity and identification. That is to say, in contrast to the Iberian Marranos, who outwardly gave in to the demand of adopting Christianity but internally remained true to their Judaism, these new Hungarian Marranos denied their Judaism not only outwardly but inwardly as well. Had this situation continued only two or three decades longer than it actually did, it would have definitely spelled the end of the last remnant of Hungarian Jewry. As it happened, this prohibition lasted long enough for a generation of young Jews to grow up without knowing anything about Judaism. Many of them did not even know that they were Jewish. To quote Victor Karády again, Jewish children "were regularly brought up in ignorance of their own ancestry, of the martyrdom of their parents and kinfolk, of the historical fate of Jewry, of the *Shoah*. Many learned about their being Jewish only when facing demonstrations of everyday anti-Semitism at school, in sports associations, or at private parties." As we shall see in chapter 48, this situation was to present the Jewish schools that began to function in the late 1980s with serious educational and psychological problems.

In contrast to the Nazi genocide, the Hungarian Communists' approach to solving the "Jewish question" was mild and nonviolent. It did not aim at killing the Jews but at killing the Jewishness in them— but in the long run it would have proved no less effective. Its methods included ignoring the existence of any specific problem faced by the Jews (or faced by the country owing to the presence of Jews), denying that Jews were different from other Hungarians, decrying anti-Semitism, and subordinating special group interests to the struggle for what was hoped would become a just, classless, socialist society. If, in doing so, it dealt somewhat more harshly with the Jews than the non-Jews, this could always be justified by pointing out that the Jews constituted a more bourgeois element than the rest of the population, so therefore it was inevitable that they would suffer more from the inevitable hardships entailed by the building of new, egalitarian society.

Hand in hand with the efforts to erase all distinctions between Jews and non-Jews went the elimination of all traces of Jewish presence in the Hungarian past, in Hungary's history, economy, culture, art, music, and literature. Typical of this was the 1,200-page, lavishly illustrated oversized album titled *Information Hungary* that was published in 1968, after twenty years of Communist effort to reshape Hungary after the Russian model, by the publishing house of the Hungarian Academy of Sciences in cooperation with Pergamon Press of Oxford. Its editor-in-chief was Ferenc Erdei, vice-president of the Academy, and most of its sixty or so contributors were academicians and Hungarian university professors. If Hungary ever produced a monumental, official, literary self-portrait, sponsored and controlled by the government-approved scholarly establishment, this was it. Its eleven major sections give a comprehensive and impressive picture of practically everything the establishment wanted the world at large to know about the country, including (as indicated in the section headings) land and people, history, state and society, economy, health, education, scientific life, literature, theatre, cinema and music, arts, and international relations. In many of these fields, the Jews actually played an important, often seminal role, but of all that no trace is found in *Information Hungary*. Altogether, references to Jews appear in the 1,200 pages of the book only three times, on pages 287 and 288, each time in connection with their destruction. They state that in March 1944 "the Gestapo marched into Hungary with the German troops and launched a campaign to exterminate the Hungarian Jews and the anti-Facists"; that "the puppet government of Sztójay considered its most important task to place the whole country in the service of Germany, in economic and military matters, in the final solution of the 'Jewish question,' and in the complete liquidation of the anti-Fascists"; and that "from Budapest alone nearly 100,000 Hungarian Jews were driven on foot to concentration camps in Germany to join the 300,000 Jews of the country who had already been sent to Auschwitz."

Especially conspicuous is the absence of any mention of Jews in the 164-page section "Land and People," in which we are told of all the ethnic groups found in Hungary, their origins, patterns of immigration, and so on without so much as a single mention of the Jews. It appears as if the intention of the book—reflecting that of the regime that sponsored it —was to obliterate the Jews retroactively by the nonviolent but nonetheless deadly method of a conspiracy of silence.

The imperative of silence was imposed not only on the authors who contributed to this particular volume but, for about a decade, on the very existence of Jews in Hungary in general. After the liberation of 1945, literary life in Hungary revived somewhat, and the authors who were active in the ensuing years included, as discussed in the Appendix, quite a number of Jews, some of whom unquestionably would have written about what they had experienced, observed, or learned about Jewish fate before, during, and after the Holocaust—would have, but could not, because the literary dictatorship of Communist Hungary forbade writing on Jewish subjects.

We have spoken thus far of the Marranism imposed on the Hungarian Jews by the Communist regime, which made it almost impossible, or at least very difficult, to maintain Jewish life in a society that officially frowned upon or even suppressed all religious life and was especially hard on Jewish religious observance. We must now consider the back of the coin, the attitudes and behavioral patterns that developed within the Jewish community itself as a result of this official position of the Hungarian Communist establishment.

Those attitudes and behaviors presented a stark contrast to those of the Marranos of Spain and Portugal in the fifteenth and subsequent centuries. Many of the Iberian Jews who had chosen to remain in Spain and Portugal were determined to adhere in secret to Judaism. Those who made this choice were called officially Neuvos Christianos, New Christians, and those among them who were found observing Judaism in secret were contemptuously referred to as Marranos (which term probably derives from the Spanish word meaning "pigs," but was adopted by historians as a neutral term for crypto-Jews.) The ties that bound the Hungarian Jews to Judaism in the mid-twentieth century were much less strong. The hold of religion had been considerably weakened for one or two generations prior to the Holocaust. The Communist doctrine of nondifferentiation between Jew and non-Jew, coming as it did upon the heels of the unspeakable horrors of genocide, appeared to many survivors to be the way out of the lingering fear, the psychological devastation, the physical suffering, whose traces marked their body and soul. Thus, instead of becoming Marranos in the old Iberian sense of crypto-Jews, they internalized the alienation from Judaism imposed upon them from the oustide. To the governmental taboo that prevented them from openly identifying with their ancestral religion and traditions, they added a self-imposed abnegation of their Judaism. They became desirous of forgetting the past and thus erasing their Jewish identity. Out of concern for the future well-being of their children, they hid their Jewish origin from them. What they did not anticipate was that for many of their children, this ignorance of their Jewish origin would result in a spate of new, unforeseen, and peculiar problems.

In a conversation (in October 1993) with a group of Hungarian Jewish intellectuals and communal workers in the home of R. Tamás Raj, member of parliament, I was given a number of examples of these problems. One case was that of an eleven-year-old boy whose parents never told him that they were Jewish. One day the boy came home from school, extremely distraught, went to the bathroom, and started to scrub his hands with a nailbrush until they were rubbed raw and red. For several days he spent hours daily scrubbing and scraping himself, but would not tell his parents why he did it. Finally, they took him to a psychologist, who managed to learn from the boy that at school other children called him "dirty Jew," and therefore he felt that he had to cleanse himself.

In some cases, individuals actually reached adulthood without knowing that they were of Jewish birth, even though the people around them knew it. R. Raj himself, as a young clergyman, in 1964 visited Békéscsaba, a Hungarian country town, where a handful of Jews wanted to invite him to be their rabbi. He took the train, wearing his rabbinical cassock for the occasion, but upon his arrival nobody met him at the station—there seemed to have been a mixup. He took his valise, started to walk down the main street, and asked the first elderly person he met where the Jewish temple was. "There is no Jewish temple here," the man said. "Years ago it was converted into a storehouse."

"Do you know where the Jews live?" asked Dr. Raj.

"Yes," said the man and pointed to a house across the street. "Right there, on the second floor, lives one of them," and mentioned his name.

Raj thanked him, and walked toward the house, but just as he was about to enter its street door, the man came hurriedly after him and said, "On second thought, you'd better not go to see him. It is only we who know that he is Jewish; he himself does not know it."

In some Jewish circles, Jewishness came to be felt such a social embarrassment, added R. Raj to me, that when they wished to identify someone as Jewish, they did not simply say, "He is also a Jew," but used the code words "Szintén zenész," meaning literally, "He is also a musician." When referring to a Jew being buried in the Jewish cemetery, they would say, or print in the announcement, that the internment took place at "6 Kozma Street," and everybody knew that it referred to the Budapest Jewish cemetery located at that address. The Hungarian poet Ágnes Gergely even wrote a beautiful poem titled "Number 6 Kozma Street." That this indeed remained the usage even in 1993, I had occasion to observe myself when in the course of an interview with Prof. László Karsai he mentioned that a person who never in his entire life set foot in a synagogue was nevertheless buried at "6 Kozma Street."

Concluding Comments

For half a century—from the First Jewish Law of 1938 to the demise of Communism in 1988—the fate of the Jews in Hungary was marked by a series of events that ranged from such "mild" forms of persecution as discrimination, deportation, prohibition of emigration, and suppression of religious and communal life to brutal treatment including individual and group murders, and peaking in the unimaginable and unparalleled state-run extermination of half a million.

The way the Hungarian Jewish leadership behaved and acted in reaction to these manifestations of Hungarian animosity, persecution, and massacre has been criticized on many counts including ineptitude, shortsightedness, indecision, folly, and even selfishness. But one must recognize that there was a basic common goal to everything the leaders of Hungarian Jewry did in those decades, however different the roads they followed in order to achieve it: in a word, survival. In final balance, however, all the efforts of the Jewish leadership, and of the Jewish community as a whole, fell woefully short of achieving or even approximating that goal. The Jews of Hungary—like the Jewries of other countries under German rule—were powerless to save themselves.

As a result of the Holocaust, conversions, and emigration, the number of Hungarian-speaking Jews, which had approached a million at the end of World War I, was reduced to about a hundred thousand, after World War II. And even of this number only a fraction was affiliated with Jewish congregations or organizations, or at least was aware of its Jewishness, of having some kind of commitment to Jewry or Judaism, to the Jewish people or religion. It appeared as if Hungarian Jewry was doomed to disappear as a community, even though relatively more of them had survived than of the Jews in neighboring countries. This was the conclusion reached by Julius Fisher as early as 1955 in the survey he prepared for the World Jewish Congress. He found that while the remnants of Orthodox Jewry still clung tenaciously to their heritage,

> the majority of the rest of the Jews display utter indifference toward their religious organizations. There is no opportunity to educate a child in the spirit of Judaism; there are no Jewish youth movements, no Jewish lectures, no Jewish literature, not even an opportunity for an occasional get-together. Jewish youth, as well as the entire Jewish population of Hungary, is being cut off from any type of Jewish cultural activity. Thus, all ties between these Jews and their brethren in faith in other lands are bound to be severed. The overall picture is one of rapidly declining Jewish communities in the countryside, the desperate material plight of even the central congregation in Budapest, the absence of Jewish cultural activities, indifference on the part of the majority of the Jewish population, and a young generation estranged from the Jewish heritage.

For several decades after the publication of this report, the conditions it described did not change. As we have seen, even the public discussion of the Jewish past, and especially of the Jewish problem and the Holocaust, was under a strict taboo. The combined effect of these factors was that Jewish self-consciousness, self-knowledge, and familiarity with Judaism and Jewish values came close to zero. The future seemed to hold for the remaining Hungarian Jews nothing but full assimilation into the Magyar majority of the country.

But then something quite unexpected happened, which for those who still knew their Bible appeared as an almost miraculous realization of the prophetic vision of Isaiah, who 2,800 years ago spoke of the survival of a tithe that was to be saved from destruction and carry in it the seed of future growth. We shall consider this unforeseen revival of Jewishness and reconstruction of Jewish life in Hungary in chapter 48, but first we must look at the new relationships that developed between Hungary and its Jewish community after the country had become politically, and to a considerable extent also socially and culturally, a Soviet Satellite.

47

Under Communist Rule

Having discussed in the preceding chapter some of the sociological aspects of Jewish life in Communist Hungary (which, as we have seen, partly continued trends that went back to the interwar years or earlier), it is time now for a brief look at the impact of political developments in postwar Hungary on its surviving Jewish community.

Fifty years is a long period, not only in the life of a person but also in that of a people. In about fifty years from the late 1840s to 1896, the Jews of Hungary advanced from a status of second-class human beings with severely limited rights to complete legal equality with the rest of the inhabitants of the country. The subsequent fifty years, from 1896 to 1945, saw their position alternate between short-term improvements and deteriorations but ultimately end up with total rightlessness and culminate in their near-total physical destruction. The history of the surviving hundred thousand Hungarian Jews in the third fifty-year period, which drew to a close in the early 1990s, can best be described as a series of floundering and haphazard attempts to find a place for themselves in Communist Hungary.

One development that took place upon the German withdrawal from Budapest under the impact of the Russian onslaught was that many in the Hungarian nation became painfully aware of the genocide, of the unspeakable inhumanity perpetrated by some Hungarians on the Jews, whom the Hungarian laws for decades had held to be an equal Hungarian denominational group. But this awareness in no way translated into the elimination, or even diminution, of the feeling of "otherness" that had characterized the relationship between the Christian and the Jewish Hungarians in the pre-Holocaust days, and that was a contributing factor to the occasional occurrence of anti-Semitic incidents and the promulgation of increasingly severe anti-Jewish laws ever since the Numerus Clausus Law of 1920.

As a matter of fact, the nonidentity of the Christian and Jewish Hungarians remained as pronounced after the Russian takeover as it had been under the German occupation. Of course, while the Germans were in control, the distinction between Jew and Christian meant the difference between life and death. Christian Hungarians, whether they sympathized with the German effort to make Hungary *Judenrein* or loathed the Germans for it and all the rest of their highhanded control of the fatherland, were never in danger of life and limb from the SS or the other German forces. For the Jews, on the other hand, the very fact of their Jewish birth or descent meant that they were legally designated targets of the German killing machine, aided and abetted by the Germans' like-minded Arrow Cross followers. The barrier this distinction created between Christian and Jewish Hungarians was rarely breached. In any case, we know of no Hungarian counterpart of the act of the Swedish king, who appeared in public with a yellow star on his chest.

When the Soviets conquered Budapest, the Jews inevitably welcomed them as liberators and saviors. Had the Soviets not come, had they not driven out the Germans and Hungarians who defended Budapest, all the Jews of the capital would have been killed, as had been the Jews of the countryside. Hence, in the consciousness of the Hungarian Jews, the defeat of Hungary by the Soviets was the crucial event that snatched them from the jaws of death, whereas for the Hungarian Christians, the Soviet conquest meant ignominious defeat by the enemy. Ever since World War I, and from even earlier times, Hungary had considered the Germans its friends and the Russians its enemies. In World War II, whatever the antecedents and the circumstances, the Hungarians were allies of the Germans, and they jointly faced the Russian enemy. This enemy now defeated them. It occupied their capital, and behaved as conquering armies always behave. For the Hungarian nation the Russian victory was not merely a military defeat; it was a traumatic humiliation. There were, of course, some Hungarians whom the disintegration of the oppressive state machinery of the gentlemanly *úri* orders filled with a feeling of liberation and confidence in the possibility of building a new, free society. Still, the traditional image of the Russian bear as the enemy could not be mitigated by the mere fact that the Russian occupation of Hungary was an improvement over the Nazi rule it replaced. Thus, the unquestionably more positive reaction the Russian conquest and presence evoked among the Jews than the Christians reinforced the sense of otherness that had long shaped the latter's view of the former.

In a conversation I had a few years ago with a Hungarian Christian who had lived through those days in Budapest (and who insisted on not being identified), he recalled the Russians' entry into the city as an event that evoked mixed feelings in many. Hungarians in general were happy to be rid of the Germans but unhappy about coming under Russian occupation. What was most painful was that Hungary was again defeated, as in World War I, and people fantasized about what would have happened had Germany won the war; how wonderful it would have been to be, for once, a victorious nation! That in case of a German victory the remaining Jews of Budapest would have been exterminated was not given more than a passing thought.

As for the Jews themselves, the attention paid in the three years of 1945–48 to the Jewish question and Jewish fate (see chapter 46) had the overall effect of intensifying their awareness of difference from the majority population. They felt that the whole discussion—whatever the participants' perspectives—amounted to one thing: the Jews continued to constitute a separate element in the body of the nation.

However, this persistent feeling of otherness did not mean, at least not in those first few years after the Holocaust, that the Jews rejected assimilationism and consciously turned inward, toward a more intensive Jewish self-identification. On the contrary: many of the survivors turned to Communism as the new savior of humankind in general and the Jews in particular.

During the Nazi–Arrow Cross horrors, those Hungarian Jews who escaped death were shaken to the foundation of their existence by the devastating trauma of their community's having been destroyed by Hungary, by the nation with which they had so completely and enthusiastically identified. They had to accept something that only shortly before was totally unimaginable: that Hungary as a whole stood by with indifference while four-fifths of its Jewish citizens were murdered, and that many "good" Christian Hungarians even actively participated in their slaughter. Some survivors simply could not come to terms with the memory of what amounted to the exclusion of the Jewish community from the Hungarian body politic, and its quasi-surgical excision as though it were a malignant growth on that body. Judit Márványi describes this in her memoirs: "I was unequal to the task, I was not strong enough to look in the face of the bare facts. It was better for me to understand that the affront [Hungarian *bántalom*, a very mild term] was merely part of the millennial injustice to which the *entire* nation was subject." From this position of self-delusion to a belief in Communism as the panacea for the woes of the world, Hungary, and the Jews, it took only one step: "It was better to believe that with the elimination of social injustices, with the liquidation of class oppression, anti-Semitism too would cease. It was not questionable for me that I had to become a Communist."

As early as in 1946, within a year of the Russian liberation of Hungary, many Hungarian Jews gratefully and hopefully embraced the Communist ideology, which taught that the Jewish question and anti-Semitism were simply parts of the crumbling edifice of a world in decline. As the Communist Hungarian sociologist Erik Molnár expressed it that very year, for a believing Communist the Jewish question was but a by-product of the capitalist mode of production, and anti-Semitism an ideology serving as a manipulable outlet for the class antagonisms that created tensions in capitalism. Jewry was offered a new perspective: "Put an end to capitalism, and you have put an end to the Jewish question." Or, in the words the ex-Jewish Communist protagonist of a novel by Ervin Gyertyán published in 1975: "Marx says if we put an end to the promissory note, we put an end to the Jew as well." And he explains that everyone, both Jews and non-Jews, "all of us are children of an unjust and deformed society, whether this way or that, we carry its stamp on us. Hence we all must equally assimilate, if you wish, to a new human ideal. We all must transform ourselves into socialist man."

The trouble with this attitude was that reality not only fell short of the ideal, as it always does, but presented a sharp contrast to it. The Communist reality that the surviving Jews had to face in Hungary was that even if they were not specifically singled out for maltreatment, the social niches most of them had occupied made them, more than the Christians, targets of the Communist efforts to eliminate the bourgeois social order and transform Hungary into a people's republic. The dispositions of the Communist government were directed not against Jews but against business enterprises and "class-alien" (*osztályidegen*) elements and the like—but it so happened that most of the Jews fell into precisely these categories, and thus it was they who suffered most from these reshufflings. One example was the high proportion of Jews among those whom the government, in a futile effort to alleviate the dire economic slump in the cities, ordered to leave and settled in the provinces. The people forcibly removed from Budapest included 20–25,000 Jews (or ex-Jews), or some 30 percent of the total, even though they made up not more than 5 or 6 percent of the capital's population.

Thus the remnant of Hungarian Jewry, who hoped that with the Russian liberation not only would their survival be assured but their situation would turn from bad to good, experienced a bitter disappointment. Yes, the change of government from German-controlled Hungarian to Russian-installed Hungarian meant that Jews escaped death, that the danger of deportation to death camps and the murderous raids on defenseless Jewish men, women, and children packed into the ghetto ceased. But within an astoundingly short time the new Russian-sponsored Hungarian government revealed its anti-Semitic nature in a manner not essentially different from its prewar predecessors'.

At the same time, the traditional Hungarian anti-Semitism, officially augmented and intensified during the war, found new opportunities for expression in word and deed. It began in the very days of the return of Jewish survivors. No sooner had those miserable people, weakened by maltreatment, disease, and starvation, many of them barely alive, arrived in Budapest than the organ of the Communist Party, *Szabad Nép* (Free People) in its March 25, 1945, issue called upon them to have "understanding" for the Christians whom they found living in their-former apartments, even if many of them were enabled to occupy those premises thanks to their connections with the extreme right during the Nazi regime. Shortly after the liberation of the capital, the Budapest National Committee suggested that the Jews get their apartments back only if they reached an agreement with the present occupants—an almost impossible condition to meet. In the early summer of 1945, the well-known popular writer and leader of the National Peasants Party, József Darvas, who became minister of reconstruction, attacked the Jews in an article in which he asked, "Why do [the Jews] always want to grab the easier end of the work?" and declared that "nobody can shirk the shouldering of work and sacrifices . . . even by claiming past sufferings." Darvas's fellow writer, Péter Veres, who was responsible for the land reform carried out under the slogan "The land belongs to the one who works it," was reputed to have declared that Hungary must be liberated of all foreigners, Germans as well as Jews. Also, the friction among the political parties, aggravated by the difficult economic situation, often led to anti-Semitic outbreaks. In December 1945, the workers in a factory in Kispest (a suburb of Budapest) demanded the dismissal of all Jewish employees. These anti-Semitic manifestations had a psychologically devastating effect on the survivors, many of whom had barely recovered from the inhuman treatment they suffered and the wounds inflicted upon them.

Early in 1946, faced with a serious economic crisis, the Communist leadership engaged in a energetic campaign against the "black marketeers," which was often just a cover name for the Jews. In February, anti-Semitic attacks took place in a number of country towns with a predominantly worker population. In some places the attacks killed several Jews. In May 1946, in Kúnmadaras, anti-Semites angered by the survivors' demands for compensation spread the calumny that the returning Jews were engaged in killing Christian children—an appalling post-Holocaust resurrection of the ancient blood libel. Two Jews were killed and eighteen wounded in the attacks thus instigated. In the first six months of 1946 attacks on Jews occurred in more than a dozen cities, and in several localities the blood libel was resuscitated. In the city of Miskolc, Mátyás Rákosi, himself an ex-Jew, gave a speech demanding death for the black marketeers, with the result that a few days later in the neighboring town of Diósgyőr the Communists led the miners in an anti-black-market demonstration, which degenerated into anti-Semitic attacks. In several other cities, the local people, incited by those who had profited from the expropriation of Jewish property, forced the Jews to leave. The local authorities in some places not only rejected the lawful demands of the returning deportees but passed resolutions against employing Jews.

The new anti-Semitism that surfaced in Hungary after World War II was aggravated—paradoxically, but psychologically almost inevitably—by a development at the top of the Communist command structure: as had been the case twenty-five years earlier, during the short-lived 1919 Hungarian Council Republic, so after World War II, when Hungary became part of Russia's East European empire, Jews (and ex-Jews) rose to the leadership of the Communist government in control of the country.

In the fall of 1944, several months before the German evacuation of Hungary, Hungarian Communist exiles who later became known in Hungary as the Muscovites gathered in Moscow to hammer out their program and define their role in postwar Hungary. The group consisted of some two dozen men, and the most influential among them were Jews (or ex-Jews), including Mátyás Rákosi, Ernő Gerő, Mihály Farkas, József Révai, Zoltán Vas, Gábor Péter, and György Lukács. These men were soon to become the rulers, under Moscow, of the new, Communist Hungary.

After a brief transitional period, Zoltán Tildy became on February 1, 1946, the first president of the Hungarian Republic. The next two years witnessed the increase in Communists' power by the gradual removal from the coalition (by the so-called salami tactics) of elements they considered undesirable. In the winter of 1947–48 political pluralism was liquidated, the Communist Party achieved a monopoly of power, and its leader, Mátyás Rákosi, became prime minister of Hungary.

Mátyás Rákosi (1892–1971), son of a well-to-do Jewish country grocer, worked in his youth as a bank clerk in London and got involved with radical movements. Under the Béla Kún regime of 1919 he served in a junior ministerial post, and after its fall he escaped to Russia. In 1924 he was sent by the Soviets to Hungary, under a false identity, to reorganize the underground Communist Party. He was arrested, tried, maltreated, and sentenced to eight years of imprisonment, after which he was tried again, this time drawing a life sentence. However, after the German-Russian partition of Poland, when Hungary found itself with a stretch of common border with Russia, it was interested in establishing better relations with the USSR, and in 1940 when the Russians expressed their interest in a few political prisoners including Rákosi and Zoltán Vas, Hungary extradited them. Five years later Rákosi triumphantly returned to Hungary as the Workers' Leader and assumed the role of prophet of the country's resonstruction and the building of a "democracy rooted in the Hungarian soil." Within another four years (by the summer of 1949), Hungary was totally in the power of the imitators of "the great Stalin," and the personality cult of Rákosi as "Stalin's wise Hungarian pupil" was in full swing.

An important instrument of Rákosi's control over Hungary was the newly established State Security Department (Állam Védelmi Osztály, ÁVO), the most formidable body of armed terror. It was headed by Gen. Gábor Péter, a Jew, who had been a tailor in his early years and hence was known as "the little Jewish tailor." Many of the ÁVO officers were recruited from among the survivors of Auschwitz, whose memories of gassed parents and children motivated them to seek revenge. The activities of ÁVO created much revulsion; the poet, novelist, and journalist Béla Zsolt (1895–1949), himself a converted Jew, was acclaimed for commenting, "The pandour's jackboot ill becomes a Jew."

One of the top Communists who helped Rákosi most in applying his "salami slicing technique" (a metaphor supplied by Rákosi himself) was Ernő Gerő (1898–1980), a Jew of middle-class background, a former functionary of the Communist International, fluent in Russian, who headed the Ministry of Transport, and was in charge of building bridges and railways. Gen. Mihály Farkas was minister of defense, and József Révai minister of culture. These four Jewish (or ex-Jewish) "Muscovites," Rákosi, Gerő, Farkas, and Révai, were the "foursome" who ran the country until the summer of 1953. Rákosi and his henchmen were ruthless in their efforts to eliminate the bourgeois elements, and, in addition, felt that they could counterbalance the "Jewishness" of the government by persecuting, trying, and jailing as many Jews as possible, among them rabbis and Jewish community representatives, and while doing so pointing out their Jewishness and dubbing them Zionists (Zionism having been declared a grave anti-Communist crime in the USSR). It was not difficult to find many Jewish scapegoats, since the middle-class Communists who spent the war years as refugees in the West were overwhelmingly of Jewish extraction, and upon their return to Hungary some of them were put in key positions; Tibor Szőnyi, for instance, became head of the Cadre Department of the Communist Party, and as such decided about the allocation of jobs. It was common knowledge that these men, following the Kremlin's instructions, had made contact with Western agents in a joint effort to fight Hitlerism, but now this was leveled against them, and they figured prominently in the many fake trials staged to expose the sinister plots of Titoist-Zionist-Fascist-racist-nationalist-cosmopolitan-imperialist-capitalist scoundrels who had been in the pay of American, British, French, Yugoslav, and (before 1945) German and Hungarian secret agencies. To fall into the hands of the ÁVO meant torture and death, and quite a few of those arrested preferred to commit suicide.

The fate of the surviving remnant of Hungarian Jewry under the Communist regime was especially harsh, not to say tragic. On the one hand, there was a handful of Jews who ran the country (with the blessing of Moscow); on the other, there was the Jewish community, again disproportionately active in literature and other intellectual pursuits, whose very life was uncertain and even hazardous, since its undeniable sympathies with the West rendered it suspicious in the eyes of the hard-boiled Communist followers of the Moscow line. What made the Jews' position even more difficult was the compulsion in whose grip the Jewish leaders felt constrained to demonstrate that their own Jewish background (which, of course was common knowledge) did not at all predispose them favorably toward the Jews, that they were Communists and Hungarians first and last and had no ties whatsoever with the Jews. This was the psychological mechanism motivating the treatment, often exceptionally stringent but only superficially puzzling, accorded the survivors of the Holocaust by the Jewish or ex-Jewish Communist leaders of Hungary.

In 1948 the nationalization of the manufacturing industries and bigger companies was carried out, by decree, with brutal suddenness, without compensation, by barring the owners and directors from setting foot again in the premises. Similar procedures were instituted against the owners of small stores and businesses as well. These operations were headed by Gerő, who accompanied them by unleashing a hate campaign against the owners so as to prevent the emergence of any pity or sympathy for them. Since many if not most of these businesses were owned by Jews, it was again they who suffered most from these nationalizations. At the same time, the workers were also deprived of their right to participate in the control of the workshops through their councils. As Ferenc Biró, another Jew, and Mátyás Rákosi's brother, who was appointed general manager of the huge Manfred Weiss factory complex in Csepel, put it, "The factory is theirs anyway."

Yet another Hungarian Jewish Communist refugee who had spent sixteen years in Horthy's prison, was extradited to Moscow in 1948, and now returned in the wake of the Red Army, was Zoltán Vas (1903–83). His grandparents were Orthodox Jews, his maternal grandfather was J. H. Rosenberg, rabbi of the Nagyfuvaros Street synagogue in Budapest, where he continued to function as associate rabbi even during the tenure of Dr. Lajos Scheiber, and was styled by the congregants "*Shalesűdes Rabbi*," a Hungarian Jewish popular term literally meaning "rabbi of the third Shabbat meal." Vas was given the task of infusing new life into the moribund Hungarian market, in the course of performing which he became quite a popular figure, thanks primarily in his ability to improve the food supply and his jocular nature. When Ernő Gerő rose to power, Vas was demoted, and during the 1956 revolution, together with Imre Nagy and more than a dozen other Communist leaders involved in de-Stalinization, obtained asylum in the Yugoslav Embassy in Budapest. Nevertheless, the Russians managed to capture them, and deported them to Rumania. After his release, Vas divorced his Jewish wife, and married his Christian lover of many years.

In 1948 transformation of Hungary into a people's republic had dire consequences not only for the livelihood of the Jews but also for their social and cultural status. The new regime was definitely hostile to the Jewish national movement (which was considered anti-Communist). Zionist activities were severely curtailed, and eventually outlawed. In March 1949, the Zionist Organization was disbanded, and its leaders were sentenced to prison terms. The surviving Jewish schools were absorbed into the general school system, which meant that Jewish children and youth were no longer able to get a Jewish education. Contacts between the Hungarian Jews and world Jewry were restricted. The work of the American Jewish Joint Distribution Committee, whose financial support was essential for Hungarian Jewry in its straitened circumstances, was first curtailed and then, in 1953, brought to a complete stop.

Stalin's death in 1953 brought major changes in Moscow, and with them also in Hungary. Rákosi and his colleagues were summoned to Moscow and told in no uncertain terms that they had mismanaged the economy, that the personality cult must cease, and that they should use persuasion rather than terror in achieving Communism's aims in Hungary. Rákosi was allowed to keep his position as the Communist Party's secretary-general (or, rather, first secretary) but was instructed to resign the post of prime minister, which was then and there given to Imre Nagy. One of the steps Rákosi had to take was to order the melting down of the many copies of his bronze bust still awaiting sale.

A tug-of-war now ensued between the new premier, Imre Nagy, and the party boss, Mátyás Rákosi, in the course of which, on March 13, 1954, the former ÁVO chief. Gen. Gábor Péter, was sentenced to life imprisonment for "crimes against the State and the people." The Stalinist defense chief, Gen. Mihály Farkas, found it expeditious to change sides several times. The fall of Malenkov in early 1955 enabled Rákosi to get rid of Nagy, in whose place he had András Hegedűs appointed prime minister. But the reforms introduced by Nagy could not be reversed. Several political leaders were set free, and their harrowing accounts of the ÁVO torture chambers stirred up widespread indignation. They were joined by disillusioned Communist writers, whose key figure was the Jewish novelist Tibor Déry (for more on his literary work, see the Appendix).

While the whiff of freedom under Nagy was a great relief for Déry and his type of ideological Communists, what they learned from the released ÁVO prisoners was a shock they were totally unprepared for, which forced them to reevaluate the system whose lifelong adherents they had been. Déry played an important role in preparing the mood for the 1956 Hungarian revolution. On June 27, 1956, the newly founded Petőfi Circle, a literary society, in which two young intellectuals of Jewish origin, Gábor Tánczos and B. András Hegedűs (not identical with Prime Minister András Hegedűs) held a public debate about the press with Déry as the main speaker. He captivated the audience, which overflowed into neighboring courtyards and parks, where they could hear his voice amplified by loudspeakers. He recalled the 1848 revolution led by Petőfi and the "márciusi ifjak" (the Youths of March), a group of young revolutionaries who had since achieved mythological stature, and concluded with a rousing "I should like to see a 1956 youth equally worthy of being remembered by posterity." Within three days Déry was expelled from the Communist Party and the Petőfi Circle itself was condemned, but the drive for liberalization could not be stopped. Rákosi tried to compromise by releasing Smallholder and Social Democratic leaders, but he was more and more openly opposed, until, in July 1956, he was roundly ordered by Kruschchev to resign. Mihály Farkas fared worse: he, like Déry, was expelled from the party. As for Déry, his part in the 1956 revolution led to his arrest together with many other writers and journalists. He was sentenced to nine years' imprisonment, but was released in 1961.

After the fall of Nagy—whose execution was announced on June 17, 1958—Déry, poet Zoltán Zelk, and several like-minded friends in the Communist Hungarian Writers' Union drafted resolutions urging the extension of intellectual freedom. The Stalinists responded by publicly denouncing the activities of "Déry, Zelk, and Co." and accusing them of counterrevolutionary plots and incitement. Had this happened while Rákosi was still in full control, they would certainly have been arrested. However, after 1955 Rákosi was no longer the all-powerful dictator, and, fortunately for the protesters, the weekly of the Writer's Union, the *Irodalmi Ujság* (Literary Gazette) sided with them. Issues of the *Irodalmi Ujság* were confiscated from time to time, but this only increased its popularity.

Rákosi's attempts at personal intervention did little to ease the tension. He had heart-to-heart talks with Péter Veres, president of the Writers' Union, whose sympathies lay with the general trend toward freedom, even though he was not free of a certain leftish anti-Semitism, which Rákosi tried to utilize. "Don't you see," he said to Veres on one occasion, "that you are being duped by a pack of Jew-boys?" Then he talked to the "Jew-boys," castigating them in a fatherly tone: "Have you lost all sense of proportion, young comrades? The former pandour officers and county magistrates are applauding you; you are playing into the hands of the Jew-baiters! Once Péter Veres gets a bigger say, he won't allow Jews like yourselves to carry on in the limelight." As one can see, Rákosi managed, or at least tried, to keep his own Jewishness completely out of the picture, but at the same time his attempts at mediation showed that the attidues toward the Jews among people in high places and the Jewishness of the leaders in literary circles were very much at issue in Communist Hungary.

Rákosi's successor as first secretary of the party was Ernő Gerő (another of the Jewish "Muscovites"). He was, as Paul Ignotus put it, "a dry and lanky man, suggesting a cross between an inquisitor and a cashier." He was a hard worker, commanding respect rather than confidence. Rumor had it that he was "Moscow's eye" on the Hungarian Communist leadership, even on Rákosi, and years earlier he had acted in the Spanish civil war as an agent of the NKVD (predecessor of the KGB), responsible for the deaths of real or so-called deviators, including Hungarian fighters of the International Brigade. In his three months in power, Gerő could chalk up only one real success: the reestablishment of friendly relations with Tito's Yugoslavia. In September 1956, on the basis of free nomination and a secret ballot—in itself a giant step toward democratization—the Writers' Union elected a new presidium, which included mainly reform Communists, among them Déry, as well as a few nonparty socialists. With this development, the men of the Writers' Union became the leaders of the nation. At the October 6 commemoration of the 1849 hanging of Hungarian generals by the Austrians, some 200,000 people attended the solemn reburial of László Rajk, who had been tortured and executed in 1949 and then, in March 1956, post-humously rehabilitated by a shamefaced Rákosi.

After the October 6 memorial celebrations, at which for the first time the masses were able to express spontaneously their deeply burning anti-government feelings, the power base of the government rapidly contin-ued to shrink. This, in turn, led to the outbreak on October 23 of a truly popular uprising, the revolution, *The Thirteen Days That Shook the Kremlin*, as Tibor Méray termed them in the title of his 1959 bestseller. What happened during those thirteen days has been repeatedly described and analyzed; all we need say here is that after a few days in which it appeared as if Hungary were going to shake off the Soviet yoke, Ernő Gerő, recognizing that the Hungarian forces were unable to stem the tide of insurgency, called for Soviet armed assistance. On November 4, 1956, Soviet armed forces intervened and crushed the uprising—kill-ing in the process some 2,500–3,000 people, wounding some 13,000, and then orchestrating the trial and execution of 400–450 and the imprisonment of about 10–12,000. During or immediately after those thirteen days some 200,000 Hungarians escaped to the West, most of them through Austria, some through Yugoslavia. There were reports, seemingly well founded, of activity during the rebellion by anti-Semitic right-wing elements. Whether those were rumors or facts, the Jews had reason to fear that in case of the collapse of the Hungarian Communist government, there would be a repetition of the events that followed the fall of the 1919 Béla Kún regime: an upsurge of anti-Semitism, with pogromlike attacks against Jews, costing many lives. In any case, it is estimated that of he 200,000 who left Hungary at the time, around 20,000, or 10 percent were Jews, at a time when the total number of surviving Jews in the country was 100,000, less than 1 percent of the total population.

As the foregoing sketchy presentation of the political chessgame that went on in Communist Hungary shows, many of its major players were Jews or ex-Jews, who by and large displayed little interest in, let alone sympathy for, the specific problems the Jewish survivors of the Holo-caust faced within the generally very difficult struggle for national recon-struction.

The situation did not palpably change for the better after the 1956 revolution, when the general tendency to move away gradually from Communist dictatorship was all but lost in the alternate up-and-down movements between tightening and relaxation of government controls. To mention only a few of the important developments: on the one hand, in the three years of 1959–61 the collectivization of agriculture was completed, while on the other, in the early 1960s János Kádár, head of the Communist Party (now renamed the Socialist Workers Party) who professed to steer a middle course between Rákosi's "dogmatism" and Nagy's "revisionism," granted amnesty to political prisoners, and tried to appease the non-Communists with a policy of economic reforms and cultural tolerance. Under the Kádár regime Hungary gradually became less of a police state and tried to expand diplomatic and trade relations with the West, while at the same time it remained loyal and subservient to the Soviet Union, and participated in the Warsaw Pact invasion of Czechoslavokia in 1968.

An achievement of great symbolic significance for the country was the return by the United States of the ancient sacred royal crown in 1978. A sign of resurgent nationalism in the 1970s was the openly voiced concern of the Hungarian government about the fate and status of the Hungarian minorities in the neighboring countries, especially in Rumania. By the early 1980s, Hungary was arguably the most liberal country in the Soviet bloc, while her economy, despite sporadic reforms and Western credit, was faltering. Throughout this period, the life of the Hungarian Jews was characterized by an overall passivity, very few initiatives of their own, and a general preoccupation with individual survival and affairs of personal interest. As for leadership, there were no heirs to men of the stature of Vilmos Vázsonyi or Pál Sándor, who in the interwar years were Hungarian political leaders as well as leaders of the Jewish community.

True to its centuries-old tradition of imitating developments in its politically, militarily, economically, and culturally more powerful neighbors, in the mid-1980s Hungary emulated the new policies introduced by Mikhail Gorbachev in the Soviet Union. Groups demanding fundamental changes emerged, or became more vociferous. Taking advantage of the relative tolerance of the Kádár regime, political formations such as the Hungarian Democratic Forum and the Alliance of Free Democrats pressed for democratic government, market economics, freedom of the press and freedom of association, and environmental protection.

Within the Jewish community of Hungary these developments could not fail to have an effect. It would be exaggerated to speak of an awakening, but signs of stirring of Jewish life became visible. To a limited extent, changes in the general political atmosphere were anticipated within the Jewish community. Late in 1983, for the first time in several decades, the old Hungarian Jewish tradition of leadership by a staid establishment invariably beholden to the government of the country was shattered by the formation of a group calling itself Shalom: Independent Hungarian Jewish Peace Group. It stated modestly that it wished to be "nothing more than a political workshop." It took an emphatically pro-Zionist position, and its program included "the promotion of peace between Hungarian Jewry and the non-Jewish society, of understanding between Jews and Jews, and of peace in the Middle East." It published in 1987–88 three issues of a *samizdat* (underground) periodical titled *Magyar Zsidó* (Hungarian Jews), under the editorship of Dávid Vizsolyi-Wahrsager (pen name of György Gadó). The entire last issue was confiscated by the police as it came off the press, but two months later it was reprinted in secret.

The Shalom group took a position in opposition to the official Hungarian Jewish establishment, the National Representation of Hungarian Israelites (MIOK), in connection with one of the Kádár government's last attempts to shore up its influence in the various Hungarian religious communities. Late in 1983 the government established an Interdenominational Committee of the National Peace Council. Dr. László Salgó, chief rabbi of the Israelite Congregation of Budapest was appointed its vice-president, and Imre Héber, president of that congregation, joined its executive committee. In December of that year, the Council published a proclamation in which it totally identified itself with the Soviet position on the question of disarmament, and attacked the United States, accusing it of making huge profits from its arms sales: "We protest, with all our strength, against the aspiration to achieve global domination led by the government of the United States." This proclamation, and the official Jewish participation in it, were in turn protested by the Shalom society, which addressed an open letter to MIOK, and followed it up by a second, longer one dated May 1984, detailing its position, which was reprinted in *Hirmondó* (Messenger), the influential *samizdat* journal of the Hungarian political opposition. With these steps, the official Hungarian Jewish establishment was served notice that there existed an organized Jewish opposition to its policies.

The Shalom group disbanded in November 1989, since it felt that much of what it set out to achieve had been accomplished, and that the newly established Hungarian Jewish Cultural Society had undertaken, on a much broader basis, to work for similar aims.

As this series of incidents shows, in the early 1980s, while the power of the Hungarian Communist government was visibly ebbing, the official Jewish establishment was still a faithful and uncritical follower of its policies. This attitude had characterized Hungarian Jewry for several generations, even though in the interwar years there were also Jewish politicians who joined the opposition parties. The emergence in the early 1990s of pluralism in post-Communist Hungarian political life again created an environment in which Hungarian Jews felt free to make their own choice between supporting the government party (or parties) and siding with the political opposition. The total number of Jewish or ex-Jewish members of parliament is unknown (it was variously estimated from sixteen to thirty two), but it appeared that most of them belonged to the opposition parties. Only three known Jewish parliamentarians (including György Szabad, the president of Parliament) were members of the Hungarian Democratic Forum, the dominant government party, while at least thirteen (including Ivan Pető, president of the Alliance of Free Democrats) belonged to the opposition parties. However, of these Jewish and ex-Jewish members, only a few were sufficiently committed to the cause of Hungarian Jewry to make use of their position as legislators to speak up on behalf of Jewish interests. Thus, while Jewish participation in the political life of the country exceeded by far the fraction of Jews in the country (around 1 percent), the 1980s were a far cry from the interwar situation in which the same Jewish individuals were both Hungarian political leaders and Jewish communal leaders.

48

Reconstruction

Statistics: Data Known and Unknown

In chapter 46 we spoke of the new style of Marranism that developed in Hungary from 1948 on, and threatened with extinction the Hungarian Jewish "brand" snatched from the conflagration of the Holocaust. We also indicated that in the 1980s an entirely unforeseen revival set in, which seemed to those who still knew their Bible to be another fulfillment of the ancient Isaian prophecy.

As a matter of fact, some signs of a renewal could be discerned even amid the general disintegration of the early postwar years. Demographers consider increase in the marriage rates of a population a telling signal of its renewed vitality, since people who enter into marriages usually do so with the hope that a better future lies ahead. It is a remarkable fact that as early as one or two years after the Holocaust, the number of Jewish marriages showed a marked increase. We have considered Jewish outmarriages—whose numbers were considerable—but did not yet speak of intra-Jewish marriages (marriages in which both partners were Jewish), which are a more significant indicator of demographic vitality. Statistical data available from 1946 show that 2,305 (or according to another source, 2,209) intra-Jewish marriages took place in Budapest, and 2,325 (or 2,946) outside the capital.

These numbers indicate exceptionally, in fact, surprisingly high marriage rates in comparison with those of the general population. The Jewish marriage rate of Budapest—23 (or (22) marriages per thousand people—was more than twice as high as that of the Christian population of the city. In the countryside the Jewish marriage rates were three times (according to another source four times) as high as the general rate. They were also two to three times as high as the Jewish marriage rates in Hungary in the 1920s, when they were between 8 and 10 per thousand. Such exceptionally high marriage rates a year or two after the Holocaust are an eloquent testimony to the demographic resilience of the Jewish survivors.

The same conclusion can be reached on the basis of the Jewish birth statistics for the years 1945–47. As could be expected, in the 1945 year of horrors, the number of Jewish children born in Budapest was very small: 518. However, already by 1946, this number more than doubled, to 1,303, and it was expected to go even higher in 1947 (final figures were not available). These figures correspond to a birthrate of 5 in 1945, 13 in 1946, and 14 in 1947 (per thousand Jews). In the provinces the Jewish birthrates were double that of the Budapest Jews. Again, a comparison with the Jewish birthrates of the 1920s (between 9 and 10) shows these rates to be exceptionally high.

Demographic rates apart, the recuperative power of the Hungarian Jewish remnant was also illustrated by the reestablishment of congregations. By the spring of 1948 no fewer than 158 Jewish congregations (as well as numerous other Jewish institutions) had been reestablished. Undoubtedly, this was done in a sense as a demonstration of the Jewish determination to survive, to reconstruct a framework of Jewish life, for in many country towns the number of Jews who survived the Holocaust was so small that they could not even muster a *minyan*, the ten adult males traditionally required for communal synagogue services. In 1949, in fact, 153 of the congregations numbered fewer than one hundred souls, and they continued to shrink as a result of emigration (in 1948–51 around 14,300 Hungarian Jews emigrated to Israel alone) and relocation to the larger cities, so that by 1955 only some 180 congregations were still in existence. Even the largest of them, except those of Budapest, shrank drastically between 1949 and 1955—Debrecen's from 4,500 persons to 800, Miskolc's from 2,357 to 500, Szeged's from 1,800 to 500, and Pécs's from 928 to 600. As a result of these population movements, by 1955 some 80 percent of Hungary's Jews were concentrated in Budapest.

This 80 percent figure is a guesstimate. Censuses in Hungary do not state the religious affiliation of those enumerated, so the actual number of Jews in the country is unknown. The estimates differ widely. There is not even a consensus on who should be counted as Jewish. According to the sociologist László Karsai, who made a special study of the Jewish organizations in Hungary in March 1992, the number of Jews who regularly went to a synagogue (whether Neolog, Orthodox, or Status Quo) every Friday evening and observed the religious prescriptions was between 4,000 and 5,000. The number who considered themselves Jewish, and were so considered by others, was variously estimated from 60,000 to 200,000.

The numbers from another Hungarian sociologist who responded to my query, Prof. Péter Hanák (himself Jewish), were even more vague.

According to him there were in Hungary perhaps 10,000 Jews who considered themselves first of all Jewish, and only secondly Hungarian, and who wished to be considered a Jewish minority in the country. Then there were perhaps another 40,000, who confessed to the Jewish religion but felt more Hungarian than Jewish and observed none of the Jewish religious prescriptions. Finally, there were those who had nothing to do with Judaism, did not believe in anything Jewish, had no connection at all with the Jewish community, and preferred intermarriage and total assimilation. Their number could not even be estimated.

According to Dr. Tibor Englander, president of the Hungarian Zionist Union, the Jewish congregations claimed to have 8,000 dues-paying members, but in actuality they had much fewer. He estimated their number at 5,000, together with their families some 15,000 persons. Most of these were senior citizens. The Zionist Union, comprising all the Zionist adult and youth groups, had a membership of around 1,500.

According to yet others, those who were members of any Jewish organization, including dues-paying members of Jewish congregations, numbered between 7,000 and 10,000, or together with their families between 14,000 and 20,000. The total who were born Jewish was between 80,000 and 100,000. The overall number who counted as Jewish under the various Jewish laws that were in force until the end of World War II was estimated (together with their descendants) at 200,000 to 250,0000.

Cultural Revival

Demographic reconstruction was followed by a cultural revival of the Hungarian Jewish remnant. Its expressions were manifold. First of all, there was a rapid reemergence of the participation of Jews in the various aspects of Hungarian cultural life. What this meant in literature is a major subject with which we shall deal in the Appendix. In other areas of cultural activity, including the press, scholarship, fine arts, decorative arts, music, the performing arts, as well as in the occupations serving them (editing, publishing, production of motion pictures, directing of plays in the legitimate theaters and of films), the participation of Jews was at least as intense from the 1960s or 1970s on, as it had been in the interwar period, and this despite the fact that after the Nazi genocide only about one-fifth of their former numbers remained alive. The same was the situation in the fields of industry, commerce, the academic professions, the media, and politics.

As an example of the disproportionately high percentage of Jews in the performing arts in the period in question we may mention the situation in the governmental *Szinház és Film Művészeti Főiskola* (College of Theater and Film Arts) in Budapest. This most prestigious college, part of the governmental system of higher education, trained actors as well as theatrical and film directors, and had in the 1970s some 200 students. According to János Edelényi, who himself was a student in the film department of the college in those years, and subsequently became a well-known Israeli-American film director, at least 50 percent of the students, and 30 percent of the faculty were Jews—and this at a time when the Jews of Hungary, as already stated several times, were not more than 1 percent of the total population. Since the students of this college in the 1970s were the future actors and directors of the Hungarian stage and film, this high percentage was indicative of the foreseeable continued Jewish "domination" of Hungarian theatrical arts in the closing decades of the century.

This situation, the disproportionate presence of Jews in the most highly visible fields of Hungarian life, which happened to have also the most highly remunerated positions, contributed its share to the reemergence of anti-Semitism in more-or-less the same form in which it had been endemic in Hungary in the interwar years as well as the three or four decades preceding them. We shall have a closer look at this phenomenon later in this chapter, but first we want to refer briefly to the inner-Jewish cultural developments that took place in the second half of the twentieth century, and were undoubtedly facilitiated by an official government policy of rehabilitating the surviving Jewish community and recognizing it as a culturally different, but nevertheless integral, element in the demographic and socio-cultural configuration of Hungary.

One of the important developments in the fostering of Jewish cultural interests was the establishment of departments of Hebrew and Jewish studies at the Budapest University and the Hungarian Academy of Sciences—both innovations that could not have been envisaged in interwar Hungary or in any period preceding it. The official name of the department at the Budapest University is the Chair of Assyriology and Hebraistics (headed by Prof. Géza Komoróczy, a non-Jew), but it is the Hebrew and Jewish studies that constitutes its backbone. The Academy's department is called in Hungarian Judaisztikai Kutatócsoport (Judaistic Research Group), which it translates into English as the Center of Jewish Studies. There was close cooperation between the two institutions, which from 1992 on have jointly offered several Hebrew language courses: biblical Hebrew for beginners, and modern Hebrew for beginners and advanced students. The courses are open, free of charge, to students of the non-Jewish high schools, which do not offer Hebrew classes.

Another initiative of the Academy's Judaistic Research Group, with the help of the Soros Foundation, has been the preparation of a central catalog of the Hungarian Jewish registers of births, marriages, and deaths, which were dispersed in institutions all over the country. This work was concluded in January 1992. Other activities of the Judaistic Research Group included the publication of a bulletin, from 1988 on, containing Hungarian Jewish and general Jewish studies, and from 1991 of a book series titled *Hungaria Judaica* devoted to Hungarian Jewish historical subjects. The significance of these activities and publications was that they demonstrated that the Academy, the highest Hungarian scholarly institution, considered it one of its tasks to foster Jewish studies, and so established a separate department to serve this purpose. In the historical context of the Hungarian government's excluding attitude toward the Jewish denomination in the past, this appeared as an important gesture of reaching out to the Jewish community. The same change of attitude was revealed in the organization of public lectures on Jewish subjects by the Academy and the Budapest University.

Yet another sign of the integration of Hungarian Jewish culture into general Hungarian culture was the inclusion of Jewish music into the program of the Muzsikás Együttes (Musical Ensemble), the central organization for researching and performing Hungarian folk music, founded in 1973. The initiative came from János Kőbányai, who in 1989 revived József Patai's Jewish cultural quarterly *Mult és Jövő*. Since 1987 the Ensemble has collected, published, and performed in Hungary and other European countries a rich selection of Hungarian Jewish folk music. Part of its program was to investigate the relationship between Hungarian, Gypsy, and Jewish folk music.

Jewish cultural products have begun to find their way into general Hungarian cultural festivities—another development that could not have been imagined in earlier times. In March 1993, the Hungarian Spring Festival took place in Budapest, an important cultural event for the country as a whole. Among its offerings was a Day of Jewish Culture, organized by the Hungarian Jewish Cultural Society, which featured the children's choir of the Bethlen Square Synagogue, the children's karate class of the Maccabi Sports Club, the Menorah children's playhouse, hora dances, an art auction by the Jewish Ayin Art Group, the performance of a Jewish monodrama, a lecture by Dr. Péter Feldmajer, president of the Association of Hungarian Jewish Congregations, another lecture by Mihály Sipos on collecting Jewish folklore, and a literary evening at which several contributors to the monthly *Szombat* read from their works.

Jewish literary and cultural evenings have become part of the Budapest cultural scene in the last several years. The publishers of the quarterly *Mult és Jövő* organized a number of such evenings, which offered varied programs of music, readings, and group appearances. Exhibitions of Jewish photographs, artwork, crafts and costumes frequently took place in both Budapest and the provincial towns, as did lectures on Jewish subjects.

Equally important is the publication of Jewish books and periodicals, which have proliferated since the liberalization. There seems to be a new receptivity for books on through-and-through "Jewish" subjects of the kind that in the earlier post-Holocaust years lay outside of the Jewish readership's interest. Thus, for example, in 1991 a Hungarian translation of Isaac Bashevis Singer's novel *Love and Exile* was published. In this connection it is of interest to note that the Yiddish language, which formerly had been looked down upon and even despised by Hungarian Jews as *zsargón,* the jargon of the "Galicians," in recent years had undergone a veritable rehabilitation: books, stories, articles written in Yiddish by authors outside Hungary are being translated and printed by Hungarian Jewish and non-Jewish publishers and periodicals, lectures are given on the Yiddish language and its history, Yiddish folksongs with the lyrics in Hungarian translation are being released on tape, Yiddish musical ensembles make appearances, and old Yiddish films are being shown in cinemas.

An important index of the interest in things Jewish is the publication of Jewish periodicals. In 1989 the monthly of the Hungarian Jewish Cultural Association, *Szombat* (Sabbath), was launched, edited by Gábor T. Szántó. It deals mainly with Jewish affairs in Hungary and abroad, focusing on political and cultural developments. Also, in 1989 started the new series of *Mult és Jövő* (Past and Future), edited as a quarterly by János Kőbányai, and identified as a "Jewish cultural review." It publishes longer pieces on Jewish cultural and scholarly subjects. Both periodicals are supported by the Soros Foundation and other public institutions, and both devote much space to Israel, publish writings of non-Hungarian Jewish authors in translation, discuss developments in the Jewish world outside Hungary, and thus are important media for fostering contact between Jews in Hungary and other countries, and of Jewish culture in Hungary itself. Another Jewish magazine is *Uj Élet* (New Life), the official publication of the Jewish congregations. Much attention to Jews and Judaism was paid by the short-lived journal *Kommentár,* which, as its ads proclaimed, was fashioned after the example of the American Jewish periodical *Commentary,* and was "deeply concerned about the fate of the minorities, thus that of Jewry, which has an especially problematic character in Hungary."

Yet more evidence for the extent of interest in matters Jewish is supplied by the great number of conferences that have been organized, especially since 1987, on Jewish historical and scholarly subjects by such central Hungarian scholarly and educational institutions as the Ethnographic Department and the Judaistic Research Group of the Hungarian Academy of Sciences, the Teachers Training College of Szombathely, the Batthány Society, the Institute of Political History, the Chief Mayoral Institute of Budapest, and the Goethe Institute of Budapest, as well as by such Jewish organizations as the Hungarian Jewish Cultural Association, the Union of Hungarian Jewish Students, the Rabbinical Seminary, the B'nai B'rith of Budapest, and the Foundation for the Preservation of Hungarian Jewish Culture. To them must be added those conferences devoted to Hungarian Jewish cultural affairs organized by Hungarian Jewish scholars abroad (in Haifa, Jerusalem, Paris, New York, and Boston). Several Jewish youth camps enabled interested Jewish boys and girls to spend their summers in a positive Jewish educational atmosphere.

Hungarian Jewish cultural life was also given impetus by the intensifying contact between Hungary and Israel. Only a few examples can be mentioned. In the spring of 1992 the Hungarian PEN Club held an Israeli Cultural Week, part of which was a literary evening in which Itamar Jaoz-Keszt and Shlomo Tanni, Hungarian Jewish poets living in Israel, were interviewed and their poems read in Hungarian translaton, and the Budapest Klezmer Band (a Jewish musical ensemble) performed musical numbers. In the summer of 1992 the Hungarian Ethnographic Museum of Budapest mounted a photographic exhibit by László Müller titled "Jews, Christians, and Muslims in Israel." In each of their issues *Szombat* and *Mult és Jövő* publish articles about Israel, which create interest in and provide information on developments in the Jewish state, its problems, its economic, cultural, and political life and its relationship with its Arab neighbors and the world at large.

Jewish Education

One of the most important developments in the reconstruction of Jewish life in Hungary after the demise of the Communist regime was the reestablishment of Jewish schools, including three high schools. At the same time, it is characteristic of the dependence of Hungarian Jewry on American Jewish support that the two largest Jewish high schools in Budapest could come into being and function only thanks to the generosity of American Jewish donors of Hungarian descent.

In 1990, the Ronald S. Lauder Foundation (named after its founder, son of Estée Lauder, who herself was of Hungarian birth), established the Lauder Javne Jewish Community School and Kindergarten, a modern Jewish school in Budapest, and has continued to support the school in subsequent years as well, with $300,000 annually. In 1993 Dr. György Lippner served as the headmaster of a faculty of about eighty, and the school had an enrollment of about 500, aged from three to eighteen. The annual tuition fee ranged from 70,000 to 100,000 forints (approximately $800–1100). The curriculum included English, German, Spanish, and Hebrew languages, computer studies, and all the subjects taught in the general schools in Hungary. Its diploma, like the diploma of any other accredited high school, entitled the graduate to university admission. In addition to Hebrew language (three hours weekly), there were also courses in Jewish studies and Bible (two hours weekly), and in the general subjects Jewish themes and motivations were also emphasized. The school had a theater department, which staged Jewish plays and on Purim and Hanukkah performed in Goldmark Hall, the big meeting hall of the Jewish Congregation of Budapest. However, the atmosphere in the school was not religious, the observance of *mitzvot* (religious commandments) neither was taught nor played a role in school life. On the other hand, much emphasis was put on the participation of the pupils' parents in the life and activities of the school, which was considered of special importance since many of the parents were completely ignorant of Judaism and sent their children to the school only because of its excellent reputation as an educational institution.

The other of the two most important Jewish schools in Budapest was the American Endowment School, Mesorat Avot, also founded in 1990, by Albert Reichmann and David Moskovits. The Hungarian-Canadian Reichmann brothers, well known for their real estate empire and philantropy, undertook the financial backing of the school, and David Moskovits, a businessman from New York, known for his civic activities in Israel and Eastern Europe, served as the American chair of the school board.

Mesorat Avot has an elementary and a high school division, with an enrollment in 1993 of 425 boys and girls aged four to sixteen. It is hoped that in 1995 the school will have its first graduating class, and that those who wish to go on to university studies will have no difficulty in qualifying for admission. Among the plans of the school is the establishment of a business department. The school had in 1993 a faculty of sixty-four teachers, of whom fourteen were Israelis or Americans. Its principal was the historian Dr. György Haraszti.

At first tuition was free, but it soon became evident that in order to maintain the school a fee would have to be charged. By 1993 the annual tuition fee was 45,000 forints (about $500), but some 30 percent of the pupils, whose parents could not afford it, paid nothing. When the Reichmann brothers suffered financial setbacks, the school went through a critical period, but prominent American Jewish individuals and organizations, such as the Jewish Agency, the Jewish Memorial Foundation, the American Jewish Joint Distribution Committee, and Agudat Israel came to its rescue.

The school is officially designated as religious: the boys wear *kippot* (skullcaps), the girl skirts, and no food can be brought into the school from outside; the pupils are served kosher meals during the school day. Every morning at 7:45, classes open with communal prayers in the school synagogue, conducted by a rabbi who reads the prayers in the Sephardic (Israeli) pronunciation, and serves also as the religious director of the school. In addition to all the subjects taught in the public high schools of Hungary, the tuition plan includes ten hours weekly devoted to Hebrew and Jewish studies, and another ten to English subjects. This means that the school day is very long: from 7:45 A.M. to 4 P.M. An important part of the school's activities is the organization of three-month trips by the pupils of the upper classes to Israel and America. In the course of 1991–93, no fewer than 430 pupils visited one of those two countries, getting acquainted with Jewish life in them.

The school has had serious problems with both faculty and pupils. There were in Hungary simply not enough teachers qualified to teach Hebrew and Jewish studies. (In 1993 the Hungarian Rabbinical Seminary had only seven students and the Jewish Teacher Training Institute only twenty.) Mesorat Avot has had to resort to bringing teachers for these subjects from Israel and America. The problem with this was that they did not know Hungarian, and tried to teach the Bible and other Jewish subjects in English, which was but another foreign language for the pupils. Another problem for and with the students is that some 90 percent of them, when they entered the school, knew nothing at all of Judaism, not to mention Hebrew, and were barely aware or not at all aware that they were Jewish. A high percentage come from mixed marriages. The school has a very difficult task in trying to inculcate in them an interest in Judaism. The situation is well known to the American sponsors of the school, who felt they would be satisfied even if not more than 6 or 8 percent of the pupils "become Jewish" under the influence of what the school imparts to them, and retain, after graduation, a lasting consciousness of Jewish identity.

The third Jewish high school is the Anna Frank Gimnázium of the Jewish Congregation of Budapest, the successor to the boys' and girls' high schools founded by the Israelite Congregation of Pest in 1919. Those two schools had in the 1930s an enrollment of 500–600 boys and 600–700 girls. During the war the spacious Abonyi Street building housing the two schools was taken over by the Hungarian military, so the schools continued to function in various temporary quarters. Nevertheless, the number of students increased to 700 boys and 715 girls by 1943–44, owing primarily to the exclusion of Jewish students from the city's general high schools. In March 1944, a few days after the German occupation of Budapest, the schools closed down, but they opened again in the fall of 1945 in the building of the Rabbinical Seminary. The number of students decreased, reaching a low in 1955–56, when only twenty-five boys attended. In 1959–60 the two schools were united into one coeducational institution, still housed in the Seminary building, and in 1965 it was named the Anna Frank Gimnázium. In 1993 it had about a hundred students.

As becomes evident from these brief accounts of the state of Jewish education in Hungary in the early 1990s, the community is still suffering the consequences of the stifling of Jewish life for a whole generation. The post-Communist Jewish school system in Hungary was still too new—essentially not more than four years old in 1993—to serve as a basis for forecasting its likely significance for the survival of the Jewish community in Hungary. It is but a bare beginning, but even so it should be noted that relative to the total number of Jews, the number of Jewish pupils attending the three Jewish schools (about 1,200) in 1993 was far from negligible. It can be hoped that together with the revival of interest in Jewish culture, the Jewish schools will become a significant factor in the future of the Jews in Hungary.

In sum, since the late 1980s, despite the reduction of the number of Hungarian Jews to some one-tenth of their prewar contingent, there has come about a varitable resurrection of Jewish cultural life, with an abundance of Jewish cultural events and activities, and one can live as full a Jewish life, a least in the capital city with its 80,000 Jews, as in any of the Western countries in which the Jews had not been exposed to the trauma of genocide and persecution.

A New Self-Definition

Following the demise of Communism, an understanding was reached on a basic issue that had sharply divided Hungarian Jewry in the pre-Holocaust days: the issue of Jewish peoplehood versus Jewish religion.

As we recall, the overwhelming majority of the Hungarian Jews in those earlier days, led by the rabbis and the official representatives of both Neolog and Orthodox Jewry, insisted that Jewry, and especially Hungarian Jewry, was a purely religious denomination, and execrated the Zionist minority, which held that the Jews were a people with a cultural and historic tradition of their own, and that it was their duty to work to regain their ancestral homeland in Palestine. Once the post-Holocaust silence was broken and anti-Semitism reemerged, the new, democratic government of Hungary felt that within the general framework of a new nationalities law the identity of Hungarian Jewry should also be officially defined. At government initiative, the Union of Hungarian Jewish Congregations (MAZSIHISZ), on March 15, 1992, took up the question of how it wished to be legally identified. Its deliberations proceeded at a leisurely pace, until, on May 8, the president of Parliament, György Szabad (himself of Jewish birth), asked Dr. Gusztáv Zoltai, director of MAZSIHISZ, for a statement on the position of his organization on this question, so as to enable Parliament, in its forthcoming debate, to take the Jewish point of view into consideration. He wrote:

> In the course of its legislative activities, the National Assembly of the Hungarian Republic repeatedly encounters the opinion of both private persons and minor groups wishing to qualify Hungarian Jewry as an ethnic minority, and to liquidate the traditional view, asserted also in the emancipatory laws of 1849, 1867, and 1894–95, that recognized the citizens of our homeland professing the Jewish religion as members of the Hungarian nation enjoying equal rights.
>
> With due respect, I request the expression of the unambiguous position of the National Union of the Hungarian Jewish Congregations on this question, since I consider it absolutely necessary to avoid the Hungarian National Assembly by any chance producing a description that Hungarian Jewry, or the body representing its overwhelming majority, considers discriminatory, or considers a deprivation of the rights entered into the law in the nineteenth century, annulled in 1938–44, and subsequently restored.

On May 18, 1992, Dr. Péter Feldmajer, president of MAZSIHISZ, and Dr. Zoltai responded in a lengthy letter, in which they stated:

> Jewry living in Hungary from the end of the past century to the middle of this century professed in its overwhelming majority to belong to the Hungarian nation, and made no distinction between its Magyardom and Jewishness; it considered both conditions natural, and believed that its Judaism could not be in contradiction to its belonging to the Magyar nation....
>
> We believe that outside Israel, in the Diaspora, religious life can be the only active Jewish life. In our opinion Jewry is a people, an ethnic group, which is defined by its religion, which can be differentiated by its religion from other groups of the inhabitants of a given territory....

The Jewry of Hungary is a part of the Jewish people, a part which lives in Hungary and whose overwhelming majority wishes to live here—insofar as it will have the possibility to do so. Since the peoplehood of Hungarian Jewry is religiously determined, the majority of the religious Jews living in Hungary at the same time holds themselves a constituent element of the Hungarian nation, considering that belonging to the Hungarian nation is not based on religious or territorial definition, but its determinant is the link to Hungarian culture; thus, religious Hungarian Jewry is a part of the Jewish people, but simultaneously also a part of the Hungarian nation. . . .

The peoplehood of Jewry cannot be separated from its religion, and hence neither can the definition of ethnic group nor that of nationality be applied to the majority of the Jews living in Hungary. That is, they must be considered an ethnic group that is defined by its religion; thus, its members must be regarded as belonging to the Jewish people, on the one hand, and to the Hungarian nation, on the other. In harmony with this, this is how the majority of the Jews living in Hungary consider themselves, this is how they interpret their lives: identifying on the one hand with the Jewish people, and being tied to it, and, on the other identifying with the Hungarian nation, and being tied to it. . . .

As the reprsentatives of religious Hungarian Jewry, we believe that if the National Assembly makes a decision in the question of defining the identity of Jewry, it must take into consideration the principles and facts referred to above, and must take a position in such a manner as to consider Jewry a people, an ethnic group, defined by its religion, while the individuals belonging to this people are at the same time also members with equal rights of the Hungarian Nation.

With all its ambiguity and vacillation, this is a remarkable document. Gone are the denials of Jewish peoplehood that characterized the position of the Hungarian Jewish establishment in the pre-Holocaust period; no trace is left of the condemnation of those who considered the Jews a people. Logicians may find fault with the new formulation—the assertion that the Hungarian Jews are members of both the Hungarian nation and of the Jewish people, that their peoplehood is religiously defined—but the fact remains that for the first time in history, Hungarian Jewish leaders recognized and officially expressed the view that the Hungarian Jews were an ethnic group, even if they qualified this peoplehood with a religious definition.

The president of the Parliament, understandably, had difficulty interpreting the MAZSIHISZ letter, and on May 25 wrote to the group a second time, complimenting it for "the profound analytical disquisition," and yet asking for a more clear-cut statment: "Political practice is forced," he wrote, "to grasp the essence, as far as possible, in the course of preparatory work on a legislative measure. Hence I ask—calling again your kind attention to the contents of my May 8 letter—whether your Union (in harmony with the position of the series of former generations, which considered themselves an integral part of the Hungarian nation), sees the defining factor as the religious minority status of Hungarian Jewry."

After several hours of deliberations, MAZSIHISZ settled on the final text of its response, which read: "As representatives of the religious Jewry of Hungary we repeatedly assert that in our view Hungarian Jewry is part of Hungarian society. We consider the religious status of Hungarian Jewry the defining factor."

Since some members were dissatisfied with this formulation, it was not submitted to Szabad. Instead, it was decided to convene an extraordinary general meeting of MAZSIHISZ. On June 3, Minister without Portfolio Ferenc József Nagy requested the opinion of several Jewish leaders on the planned nationalities law, which was to contain a list of the national minorities. On June 9 some thirty Jewish leaders met, agreed on an amended text, and after some additional give-and-take the following text was submitted to Szabad and Nagy: "We, the representatives of the Hungarian Jewish congregations, repeatedly declare our attachment to the religion of our ancestors, and faithfuly adhere to universal Jewry and to the unity of the Jewish people, while at the same time we declare that Hungarian Jewry considers itself an integral part of Hungarian society. We proclaim that we do not wish that our present position in public law should be changed."

Some time prior to these events a group of Hungarian Jews, including Zionists and others more Jewish-national in their feelings than those represented by MAZSIHISZ, formed a group they called Magyar Zsidók Nemzeti Szövetsége (National Association of Hungarian Jews, MAZSI-NESZ), which defined itself as the organization of nationalist Jews. When MAZSIHISZ agreed upon a formulation of its position on the identity of Hungarian Jews, MAZSINESZ made public its concurring position, stating that it accepted the resolution of MAZSIHISZ, but adding, "At the same time—in our opinion—it will cause no harm to anybody if, with regard to the future, the possibility remains open that the minority law now in preparation will ensure also the possiblity of a modification of status for any *etnikum* [ethnic group] or, in our case, an ethnospecific religion." The reference to this "possibility" did not, of course, affect the basic agreement between MAZSINESZ and MAZSI-HISZ.

Late in July 1992, the government returned to its deliberation about the nationalities law, but taking into consideration the Jewish position, it did not include the Jews among the enumerated nationalities. That is, the official position of the Hungarian government of the 1990s again was that the Jews did not count as a national minority, while the Jews declared themselves, somewhat ambiguously a "religioethnic" community.

The Reemergence of Anti-Semitism

These developments were the bright side of the picture presented by Jewish life in Hungary in the early 1990s. The other, dark side was that despite the official governmental stance, which insisted that all Hungarians, irrespective of their religious affiliation, have equal rights and must be treated equally in every respect, the government and the dominant political parties did not unequivocally condemn past and present Hungarian anti-Semitism, nor did they take effective steps to combat its contemporary incarnations.

The liberal Jewish parliamentarian György Gadó, a member of the Alliance of Free Democrats, wrote to me on November 16, 1993:

> In principle, it is true, the prime minister repeatedly took a position against anti-Semitism. One of the ministers of state even went so far as to apologize to Hungarian Jewry for the persecution it suffered in the days of the Holocaust. The Jews were given indemnification, though only partial and rather symbolic, for the damages they sustained in that period. As against this, however, both the government and the governmental parties tried to excuse the Horthy era that led into the Holocaust, to justify its key politicians, and to minimize their responsibility for the Holocaust. [I might add that only recently Regent Horthy was reburied in his ancestral mausoleum with great governmental pomp and circumstance.] They kept silent, as far as possible, about the responsibility of Hungarian society for the Holocaust and, beyond condemning anti-Semitism in princple, did nothing to denounce the concrete manifestations of anti-Semitism, let alone prevent them, or punish the individually known anti-Semitic instigators and their accomplices, or even stigmatize them morally and politically.

Gadó repeatedly raised his voice against the extreme right, their presence in the Hungarian Democratic Forum (the largest governmental party), and the protection accorded them by members of that party. The dangers in this situation, according to Gadó, lay precisely in the fact that representatives of the anti-Semitic extreme right were present in the political establishment formed by the governmental majority. He pointed this out several times in his parliamentary speeches. On February 2, 1992, in an interpellation addressed to the minister of the interior, he referred to numerous anti-Semitic incidents and attacks that had taken place, both in Budapest and in the provincial towns, within the preceding year; to the open display and sale of officially banned anti-Semitic books at the national conference of the Hungarian Democratic Forum; to the abuse of Jews at popular soccer matches, with cries such as "Dirty Jews, go back to Auschwitz!" and "Jews contaminate the blood of the pure Hungarian people!" accompanied by brutal physical assaults; to the appearance of skinheads with swastika armbands in the streets of Budapest; to an attack on a seventeen-year-old Jewish girl that almost cost her her life; and more along these lines. In addition to György Gadó, Tamás Raj and Tamás Suchmann were most energetic in representing Jewish interests in Parliament. Raj was a member of the Alliance of Free Democrats and also an active rabbi, the spiritual leader of one of the important synagogues of Budapest. After the establishment of a free Hungarian Parliament, late in 1990 Raj organized a parliamentary group against anti-Semitism, among whose forty members all parties were represented. He was strongly critical of the old Jewish communal leadership, which he condered partly responsible for the atrophy of the community and its institutions.

Tamás Suchmann was a member of the Hungarian Socialist Party (the re-cycled Communist Party). Both of his parents were Jewish, and although he himself married a non-Jew, he gave his son a Jewish upbringing. Suchmann was much involved in Jewish communal life, and was a vice-president of the Jewish congregation of Keszthely, the city near which he resided (in Marcali). In 1993, when the issue of "protected languages" came up in Parliament, Suchmann suggested that Hebrew be one of them (next to German, Slovak, etc.), and that the government should subsidize its study as it did that of the other languages spoken by minorities in Hungary. On that occasion, and since his speech was delivered about the time of the Jewish New Year, Suchmann recited prayers from the Jewish liturgy and concluded with the traditional *"L'shanah tovah"* (Happy New Year!). By the way, his motion was narrowly defeated.

Another prominent member of Parliament was János Schiffer of the Hungarian Socialist Party. He considered himself Jewish, even though he had a non-Jewish grandmother, who was the daughter of Árpád Szakasits, president of Hungary from August 1948 to May 1950.

The picture of the Hungarian Jewish situation in the 1980s and early 1990s that emerges from these few details is comprised of contrary traits. On the one hand, anti-Semitism was officially condemned, the equality of the Jews with all other elements in the country officially upheld, and Jewish culture officially recognized and even fostered as a valuable constituent of the culture of Hungary. On the other, there was a marked presence of ani-Semitism, represented in Parliament, and expressive of an anti-Jewish sentiment in certain sectors of society.

As to the extent, intensity and importance of the anti-Semitic sentiments and incidents, the opinions of the Jewish leadership and of the observers of the Hungarian socio-political scene were sharply divided. There were those who were deeply disquieted by the phenomena mentioned above, and by the continued appearance of avowedly anti-Semi-

tic periodicals and books, produced by such extreme right leaders as István Csurka, Ferenc Kúnszabó and László Romhányi, and anti-Semitic
speeches by Emil Bogdán and Zoltán Szokolay. A typical example of
such utterances was the one published in Csurka's periodical *Magyar
Fórum* (Hungarian Forum), that stated that in the defensive warfare
engaged in by "Jewry which has separated itself on a racial basis,"
Magyardom was being destroyed, and that this Jewish minority was
engaged in a "satanic game."

On the other hand, there were others who considered all these to be
insignificant, peripheral phenomena, and adjudged the attitude of Hungary of its Jewish population as generally satisfactory. (They pointed
out, for instance, that the publications of the extreme right had but a
minuscule circulaton and most of their readers were Jews and observers
of the social scene who were curious to know what the anti-Semitic
fringe was writing about the Jews.) And there were yet others whose
views placed them at various points between these two extreme positions.

György Gadó's outspoken and militant denunciations of anti-Semitism have produced misgivings among certain Jews who felt that his
energetic demands of parliamentary and governmental action against
anti-Semitism had the opposite effect, by furnishing anti-Semites with
publicity, and even creating sympathy for them. Such criticism, however, was voiced only privately and unofficially, and nowhere (as far as I
could ascertain) did any Jewish religious or secular organization go on
record saying that Gadó's activities were too militant or that they augmented anti-Semitism. Gadó himself (in an interview) insisted that only
a courageous, determined fight against anti-Semitism stood a chance of
preventing the spread of this contagious disease in wider circles of Hungarian society.

Foremost among the liberal politicians who do not consider anti-
Semitism or the Jewish question important issues in Hungarian public
life is the historian György Szabad, president of the Parliament and
leader of the largest government party, himself of Jewish birth, who
stated (in an interview in the fall of 1993) that both issues were of insignificant dimensions, anti-Semitism existed only within a tiny minority
in the country, and there was no "Jewish question" to speak of in contemporary Hungary. As for the future of Hungarian Jewry, Szabad stated,

> The assimilatory process will continue, but Jewry will not become
> extinct. Emigration is, and will remain, very small, which says something
> to the historian. I am convinced that most practitioners of the Jewish reli-
> gion will remain here, even if their numbers diminish somewhat. At the

utmost, the intensity and character of religious ties will weaken, and there will be an increasing Neologization. As a historian I see the main problem of Jewry as whether it can develop what I would call a "Jewish Protestant-ism," which will make the language of the country the language of liturgy so that the prayers become intelligible. Vatican II did this for Catholicism. At the same time, I can foresee that Jewish culture, Jewish tradition, the enormous artistic, literary, and scientific production that Jewry contrib-uted to the elevation of Hungary, will continue and will receive increasing recognition. . . . In all this the influence of Israeli culture will surely play an important role, but I don't think that Jewry's search for identity can be approached merely from a national point of view.

This optimistic-assimilant outlook on the actual presence of the Jew-ish question is not borne out by the anti-Semitic incidents referred to above, nor by the continued interest of the Hungarian daily press and periodicals in anti-Semitism. Day after day, Hungarian papers and jour-nals analyze the problems represented by the Jews in the country, dis-cuss the relationships between Jews and Christians, and report events in Jewish life, making the small Jewish community "newsworthy" to an extent that far exceeds what one would expect of a religioethnic group constituting 1 percent of the country's population. That this indeed is the case has been shown by the continuing bibliographies published by Paula Volenszky in *Múlt és Jövő*: every three months they listed between 200 and 300 articles dealing with anti-Semitism and the Jewish question published in the preceding quarter in the Hungarian daily papers and periodicals. As for books, in the nine months from Novem-ber 1992 to July 1993, forty-four were published on Jewish themes, and eleven of them dealt with anti-Semitism.

This intensive preoccupation with anti-Semitism, however, does not mean that anti-Jewish sentiments in the Hungary of the early 1990s are stronger than they were under the Communist regime following World War II. It merely shows that in the 1990s there is a greater openness and frankness about it. But it also shows that while Hungary is struggling to find its way into the community of Western nations, of which in the past it has never been fully a part, its traditional anti-Semitism, as stated earlier, is still alive and thriving.

A more significant difference can be discerned between the pre–World War II period and that of the 1980s and 1990s with reference to Jewish self-definition and the Jewish relationship to Hungary. In that earlier period, the official Jewish position was that the Hungarian Jews were one of the religious denominations in the country, were not a "people," not a national minority, had nothing in common with the Jewish com-munities of other countries. Hence, it rejected the help of the influential Jewries of the Western world, and decried Zionism as unpatriotic. Now,

654

in the late 1980s and the 1990s, Hungarian Jewry has defined itself, as we have seen, as a religio-ethnic community, considers itself part of the Jewish people comprising Israel and the Diaspora, seeks out the cooperation and help of Western and in particular American Jewry, is deeply concerned about Israel, and welcomes the Hebrew-Jewish cultural influences emanating from it. Just as Hungary as a whole is well underway to becoming part of the global community of nations, so is Hungarian Jewry en route to becoming part of the global Jewish community.

While governmental and institutional anti-Semitism can be considered a thing of the past in the Hungary of the early 1990s, social and political anti-Semitism is still (or again) present to a not negligible degree. The Jews respond to it with either of two reactions. One is that of those who (as indicated in chapter 46) seek refuge in a new Marranism, a denial or hiding of their own Jewishness, and the assumption of the appearance of genuine Hungarianness, ranging from mere camouflage to full internalization. Those who react in this manner are solving their individual Jewish problem: having denied that they were Jews, they exclude themselves from the Jewish community and opt for Hungarianness, with the result that for them personally the Jewish problem no longer exists—except, of course, in those not infrequent cases when their Jewish origin becomes known to anti-Semitic Christian Hungarians, who thus relate to them as to Jews in general.

The other reaction contrasts sharply with the first. It is the reaction of Jews in whom encountering anti-Semitism creates or enhances interest in Judaism and the will to maintain their own Jewish identification. For them the problem that has plagued Hungarian Jews for generations continues to exist, often in a sharpened form; they want to find a way of reconciling their Jewishness with their Hungarianness *despite* the anti-Semitic exclusion of Jews from the Hungarian community. This was the problem, we recall, that Hermann, the protagonist of Lajos Hatvany's famous novel, struggled to solve for his son Zsiga about the turn of the century. Essentially the same problem has to be faced in the early 1990s, almost a century later, by those Jews whose reactions and attitudes place them into this category. The modern Transylvanian-Hungarian novelist and essayist Pál Bodor has poignantly expressed the turmoil and psychological trauma created by this situation:

> What should the person do who—even though he never denies that he is a Jew—adheres to Hungariandom despite all slaps, all spittings in the face, deaths, humiliations. Hungarian is his mother tongue, his culture, his historical conscience, Hungarian are his feelings. . . . I am the descendant of Székely soldier-noblemen, Reformed clergymen, Austrian alchemists, Saxon architects, Spanish-Jewish rabbis. I never denied any one of my ancestors. . . . But ever since I have been in Hungary [since 1983], I am

reminded of this every minute. . . . I confess with respect and remorse: if anti-Semitism did not exist, I would possibly consider it an insignificant biographical detail that there is also a Jew in me. I have devoted the whole series of my novels, of my volumes of essays and published writings, to the Hungarian minority's fate [in Transylvania]. One-sided love? In any case: love.

This entire passage is quoted by Béla Várdy, a well-known Hungarian-Jewish sociologist, who goes one step further and argues that anyone who carries also the blood of another nation or national group in his veins, but nevertheless, despite incessant "spittings in the face," adheres to Magyardom and his own Hungarianness, is a more Hungarian Hungarian than one who can trace back his descent to Árpád the conqueror but feels no community with the Hungarian nation, Hungarian life, or Hungarian mentality. Várdy demands that the still dominant, "excluding" (kirekesztő) Hungarian national consciousness should be combatted, so as to be replaced by "an up-to-date, tolerant national consciousness that is able to admit every Hungarian who declares himself Hungarian."

Discussions such as these have abounded in the Hungarian periodical press since the late 1980s, and constitute a certain counterbalance to the anti-Semitic publications that continue to follow the traditional line of the "excluders." The term itself was made popular in 1992 by László Karsai, a liberal, half-Jewish sociologist, whose book Kirekesztők: Antiszemita írások 1881–1992 (Excluders: Anti-Semitic Writings 1881– 1992) created considerable literary, sociological, and even political controversy. Some seventy of the 200 pages of this book contain excerpts from twenty-three anti-Semitic writings published in Hungary between 1938 and 1945, while its last fifty pages present similar excerpts from thirty-seven pieces of writing originally published between 1988 and 1992. The fact that Karsai found no Hungarian anti-Semitic writings dating from the years 1946 to 1987 to include in his book indicates— although he does not comment on it—that in those forty-two years of Communist rule in Hungary, public displays of anti-Semitism were effectively suppressed. This, of course, does not mean that the sociopolitical anti-Semitism that found its outlet after 1988 in a slew of anti-Jewish speeches and publications did not exist prior to that date, but merely that the Communist rulers of the country found it politically expedient not to allow its public expression.

The fall of the Communist dictatorship, which brought about the itroduction of a multiparty system into Hungarian politics, opened the floodgates of public anti-Semitic expression. Several papers and periodicals began to publish anti-Semitic articles and speeches. Among them were the *Szent Korona* (The Holy Crown), *Magyar Fórum* (Hungarian Forum), *Hunnia, Hunnia Füzetek* (Hunnia Noteboks), *Magyar Nemzet* (Hungarian Nation), *Hitel* (Credit), *Igen* (Yes), and *Uj Magyarország* (New Hungary), in which dozens of anti-Semitic politicians and writers aired their anti-Jewish feelings, accusations, and propositions.

The anti-Jewish arguments contain nothing new in view of the well-known arsenal of prewar Hungarian (or German) allegations of a global Jewish conspiracy wreaking havoc with the Hungarian (or German) state, life, economy, morals, etc. for the purpose of promoting the power, wealth, control, etc., of that mythical entity most often referred to as "international Jewry." What is most depressing about the excerpts from these speeches and writings assembled by László Karsai is that this attitude still exists, and these accusations are still being voiced, against Hungarian Jewry, which the Holocaust reduced to one-fifth of its prewar numbers and of which in the early 1990s less than a tenth are Jewishly committed individuals—less than ten thousand, or 0.1 percent of Hungary's total population of 10 million. It is a classical example of the survival of anti-Semitism without the survival of Jews, a phenomenon also seen in other European countries.

Yet withal, one must not exaggerate the significance of these anti-Semitic manifestations for the future of Hungarian Jewry. The fact remains that of all the Jewish communities in the central European countries that had been under Nazi rule during World War II, that of the Hungarian Jews emerged with the largest number of survivors. Next, the remnant that escaped the Hungarian Holocaust had to endure the bloodless but likewise pernicious threat of more than four decades of officially imposed Marranism under Communist dictatorship, and managed to live through it, even though its numbers were further reduced by attrition. Following the *"rendszerváltozás"* (change of regime) of the late 1980s from a Communist to a non-Communist multi-party form of government, hailed as a second liberation by the great majority of the Hungarians, signs of a cultural and religious renaissance, sketched in this chapter, became discernable in the Jewish community. The reemergence of a Jewish communal life, manifested in the fields of education, religion, the arts, literature, scholarship, contact with world Jewry, and interest in Israel, is a very important development in which may lie, if not a promise, at least a hope for the future. As for anti-Semitism, its legal and official forms that had prepared the ground for the 1944 genocide and had been abolished after the war by the Communist regime remained outlawed by the new multi-party government. Whatever anti-Semitism reemerged was again of the social, attitudinal, and emotional character it had had for two or three generations preceding the introduction of the Jewish Laws from 1938 on, an anti-Semitism against which the Hungarian Jews were inured by long historical experience. As one of my informants, who had visited Israel in the summer of 1993, told me in Budapest later that year: "We live with anti-Semitism in Hungary as the Jews of Tiberias live with the heat. It is unpleasant, often even hurtful, but we can live with it."

Appendix: Post-Holocaust Jewish Authors

If one looks into a history of French literature, one finds the authors of the post–World War II period grouped under headings that identify the major literary trends or schools to which the most important of them belonged. Among these trends or schools figure existentialism, surrealism, Christianism, nationalism, Communism, the new novel, structuralism, deconstructionism, etc. It is precisely the existence of these greatly differing schools that gives French literature its vibrancy, attraction, and fascination. The same holds true, to a somewhat lesser extent, for English and American literatures.

In the history of post–World War II Hungarian literature, one will look in vain for a similarly vigorous outcropping of literary trends. During the short period of 1945–48, before the imposition of monolithic Communism on the country, literary life in Hungary, just liberated from the Nazi–Arrow Cross reign of terror, displayed a certain vitality and variety, and the avant-garde, the "European School," flourished in both arts and literature. However, this effervescence was short lived, and once Communist control was firmly established, only the urbanist-populist split managed to persist, and the one major question that continued to agitate Hungarian authors was how and to what extent to conform to the imperative of "socialist realism" and the other Communist prescriptions for the correct approach to literature: that is, how far to go with the risky business of nonconformity and the expression of individual ideas and interests. Writers' overriding preoccupation with this single concern rendered the accident of their Christian or Jewish birth (and residual identification) of little or no consequence. In view of this situation, it is remarkable that, after the "thaw" that followed the 1956 revolution, several Jewish authors of the younger generation did turn to Jewish subjects, and gave expression in their writings to the internal turmoil produced in them by their awareness of their own Jewishness, their knowledge of the horrors of the Hungarian Holocaust, and the problem of continuing to live in society that had tolerated, and in many cases actively participated in, the slaughter of half a million Jewish Hungarians.

In the post–World War II period, Hungarian authors in general had to cope with the changes in governmental orientation that took place every few years and that brought about the demise of the Communist system in 1989. Each of these changes, especially in the earlier years, was accompanied by the imposition of new rules pertaining to literature and the arts, which meant disruptions in the continuity of literary developments before they could crystalize into anything like an established literary tradition. In the work of several individual writers, this was reflected in a switch from one political perspective to another—for instance, from condemning a certain line to embracing it, or vice versa. A salient example of such changeovers is supplied by the work of the (Jewish) poet Zoltán Zelk (see below).

Yet another factor that impinged on post–World War II Hungarian literature, and even more on the Jewish contribution to it, was emigration. Just as many Hungarian Jewish writers had left the country in the pre–World War II days, so did many of their successors after the war: they emigrated, settled abroad, and often switched to languages other than Hungarian. To what extent such writers can count as Hungarian authors, if their reputation is based primarily on works they wrote abroad and in other languages, is not easy to decide. It is these conditions of flux, change, and disruption that make it difficult to portray the writings of Jewish authors in the turbulent post–World War II years of Hungarian history.

Perhaps even more difficult is the task of evaluating the importance of Jewish (or ex-Jewish) writers in the postwar development of Hungarian literature. If one reads the detailed review of Hungarian literature in the postwar decades up to the mid-1960s, which is included in the massive government-sponsored volume *Information Hungary* (Budapest and Oxford, 1968), one gets the impression that there were no Jews at all among the writers of that period. It is not mentioned that a single one of the authors dealt with was of Jewish origin, nor do we learn of any Jewish theme figuring in the writings produced in that period. Quite a different picture emerges from the presentation of post–World War II Hungarian literature in Lóránt Czigány's *Oxford History of Hungarian Literature*, published sixteen years later. In it we find repeated statements that this or that writer came from a Jewish background and this or that work treats a Jewish theme. This *History* shows that Jewish authors played a role in the last few decades of Hungary's literary development not too dissimilar from the one they filled prior to World War II, and that many of them treat the new problem of Jewish life in a post-Holocaust society with greater empathy and psychological grasp than the authors of the interwar years displayed toward problems (admittedly of quite a different dimension) of an earlier generation. Czigány tells us that the "shameful memory of the deportation during the war, about which, like the annihilation of the Hungarian Second Army in Russia or the *Uividék* massacre, official silence has been kept for a long time," became the subject of novels by several young Jewish and non-Jewish Hungarian writers. We also learn from an informative paragraph in his book that among the Hungarian Jews who settled in Israel after World War II, there were several writers who produced fiction and poetry in Israel, and edited Hungarian periodicals.

A discussion in detail, with names and dates, of the writings produced by Hungarian Jewish authors since the 1960s and 1970s could serve as an excellent illustration of the surprising—because completely unexpected—revival of Jewish cultural life in the country in which, only a decade or two earier, the surviving remnant of the Jewish community seemed to be moribund, drifting irresistibly toward assimilation. However, the compass of this book, despite my admitted bias for the cultural aspects of history, does not allow full treatment of what was without doubt an amazing reawakening of cultural powers that had seemed to be dead. Thus, a few brief comments will have to do.

This reawakening was not unconnected to the breaking of the three decades of what the American-Hungarian Jewish literary historian Ivan Sanders called "a conspiracy of silence between those who did not dare to speak out on the subject, and those who did not care to." From the late 1960s and early 1970s, a number of autobiographical and semiauto-biographical works were published by authors who had been victims of persecution during the war. These writings have rendered the Holocaust, and the Hungarian national responsibility for it, openly discussed subjects, issues that have to be faced, and have made them part of the retrospective attitude that has come to dominate much of contemporary Hungarian culture. Several of these novels come to grips with the generation gap that separated the parents from their grandparents. Significantly, the sympathy of the young authors lies, almost without exception, with the old-fashioned, religious, Jewishly-anchored, often doddering and daydreaming grandparents rather than with their own parents. The fathers are often missing altogether, having been deported and never heard from again. Of those fathers who survived, several have joined the ruling powers, become members of the hated and feared ÁVO, and gotten involved in clashes with *their* fathers, who remained rooted in the world that is no more. The sympathy that the young authors display for their grandfathers is, *mutatis mutandis*, reminiscent of the "third generation return" already noted by students of the American Jewish scene.

Those writings that present a negative picture of their Jewish protagonists drew much adverse reaction from Jewish, and even non-Jewish, readers and critics. Evidently, the dominant feeling in post-Holocaust Hungary was that the remnant of a community that suffered such unspeakable horrors had earned the right to be shown only in a favorable light. It is noteworthy that this sensitivity to critical portrayal of Jews did not extend to the writings of *foreign* Jewish authors who likewise endow their Jewish characters with less than pleasant features—such as Philip Roth, Saul Bellow, Bernard Malamud and Joseph Heller, whose novels and stories have been translated and become popular in Hungary. Equally intriguing is Ivan Sander's observation that while many American novels with secularized, alienated Jewish heroes have been translated and are widely read in Hungary, Jewish writers for whom Judaism remains a compelling spiritual force, such as Elie Wiesel (who is even of Hungarian origin), Chaim Potok, and Cynthia Ozick, have not been published in Hungarian translation. These are, Sanders remarks caustically, "in all probablity 'too Jewish' for Hungarian taste." I might add, to make this explanation somewhat more explicit, that the Jewish readers in Hungary seem to be able to identify with, and take an interest in, assimilated American-Jewish protagonists of novels, and enjoy the portraiture of their foibles, but were too far removed from such thoroughly Jewish religious characters as, for example, Potok's hero in *The Chosen*, and are alienated by the warmly sympathetic picture of him. This may have something to do with the old Hungarian Jewish behavioral pattern that seems to have been inherited by the post-Holocaust generation, of trying to camouflage one's Jewishness: even those who were "good Jews" at home and regular attendees at synagogue services, did not cherish being recognized as Jews in the street. The phenomenon of Jewish youngsters and adults demonstratively advertising their Jewishness by walking about with *yarmulkes* on their head—an everyday sight in some American cities—had no counterpart in Hungary—at least not until around 1990. This negative attitude to a public display of one's Jewish identity rendered the fictional hero who engages in it less simpatico: one did not want to be like him, and did not want to read about him.

When the Jews became a "kosher" subject of literary discussion, interest was primarily focused on the prewar period and the Jewish past in Hungary. Only gradually did it extend to contemporary Jewish life. What, we must ask, was the reason for this initial concentration on the past, to the neglect of the present?

It would seem that when the study of the past finally became possible, after having been stifled for many years, this opening up itself endowed its discussion with a note of self-assertion. Also, so much was disquieting about the unknown events of the past, especially about the horrible chapter of Hungarian participation in the Holocaust, that it was almost inevitable that historiographical and literary attention should be drawn to it. To these factors was added the instability of the current situation, in which there was no permanent, established, and settled policy line—not only with reference to the Jews but with regard to the governance of the whole country. This meant there had not yet been time for the development of a definite, fixed governmental policy on the "Jewish question," nor could a Jewish consensus crystallize concerning the Jews' self-identification and their own relationship to the nation as a whole. Sociological observation of the contemporary scene requires time, and it is extremely difficult to discuss, in a social study, situations in flux that change during the very time that the scholar is writing about them.

In any case, it was only after the mid-1980s that the number of studies and other writings dealing with the contemporary Jewish condition in Hungary began to increase. As the years passed, and the situation of Hungarian Jewry became consolidated, settled into a routine, and assumed the character or at least appearance of permanence, more and more students of society turned their attention to the environment that surrounded them and its characteristics. They now could base their studies on an increasing number of years of observation, and they produced articles, as well as longer, more detailed studies, analyzing and interpreting the social conditions in which they themselves lived.

During the 1948–53 period, literary life was totally under the control of the government, or rather the Communist Party, which, as represented by József Révai (1898–1959), demanded social realism in general, and the adulation of Mátyás Rákosi, "Stalin's wise pupil," in particular. The party-sponsored Writers' Union monitored literary activity with the same rigor as other organs of the Party controlled political and economic life. After the death of Stalin in 1953, and even more so after the 1956 anti-Communist revolt in Hungary, the thaw in the government's control of Hungarian life extended to literature as well, which enabled writers to breathe more freely and to express their views—within certain limits. As a result, literature experienced a measure of renaissance, in which Jewish writers participated fully. An amnesty declared in 1956 set free several writers imprisoned for counterrevolutionary literary activity. It was followed in 1964 by a general amnesty for political prisoners. These developments brought about a gradual emergence of new literary trends and the publication in Hungarian translation of many works by formerly blacklisted well-known Western authors, so that both writers and readers had a chance to become acquainted with developments in the literature of the world at large. This was, at last, again an environment in which Jewish authors, whether dealing with Jewish or non-Jewish themes, could live and work.

There is a simple, direct way to get a general idea of the role of Jewish writers in modern Hungarian literature: just glance through the two articles titled "Hungarian Literature" in the *Encyclopedia of World Literature in the Twentieth Century*, by Ann Demaitre (2:412-16) and Ivan Sanders (5:295-99), which discuss or at least mention some hundred writers born between 1869 and 1949, whom the authors of the articles evidently considered the most important Hungarian literary figures of the period in question. If one takes the trouble to ascertain who of these writers were Jewish (that is, born to Jewish parents), one finds that about *half* of them belonged to this category—and this in a country in which after 1945 Jewish-born individuals constituted only 1 percent of the total population. Within this general picture, what is most remarkable is that the share of Jewish authors in Hungarian literature did not diminish after the Holocaust, which reduced the number of Jews in Hungary from about 500,000 (or 5 percent) to about 100,000 (or 1 percent).

A partial explanation of this notable phenomenon can be found in the observations of Victor Karády. He writes that in the period preceding the Holocaust the Jewish intelligentsia was largely concentrated in Budapest, a major part of whose Jewish population, in contrast to that of the countryside, escaped the genocide, and that even within Budapest Jewry the intellectuals belonged to the most assimilated layer, which stood a better chance of surviving than the rest. The statistical data assembled by Karády indeed show a surprising fact: while the total economically active Jewish population of Budapest was reduced from 100,000 in 1935 to about 46,000 in 1945, the only occupational group that nevertheless showed an increase during the same period (from 3,783, or 3.8 percent of the total, to 4,210, or 9.2 percent) was practitioners of the liberal professions and intellectuals.

That this statistical-demographic explanation does not tell the whole story is demonstrated by the list of the fifty Jewish writers who perished in the Holocaust (see chapter 44). The list shows that despite the intellectuals' more favorable chances of survival, a very large number (more than half?) of the Jewish writers alive at the start of World War II did perish in the Holocaust. The remarkable fact therefore remains that the elimination of a major part of a whole generation of Jewish writers in the 1944-45 year of horror was soon followed by a replenishment of their ranks by a new generation, with the result that in the Hungarian

literature of the post-Holocaust era, Jews' participation was as important as it had been prior to World War II, and this despite the fact that,
as mentioned, the Holocaust reduced their proportion in the total population of Hungary from 5 percent to 1 percent.

To illustrate these general observations with concrete examples, I
present in the following pages brief sketches of some of the representative Hungarian authors of Jewish birth whose literary activity either
peaked or began in the post–World War II years. I use the description
"Hungarian authors of Jewish birth" and not "Hungarian Jewish
authors" advisedly, because, in order to demonstrate the overall contribution Jews made to Hungarian literature in the post-Holocaust era, I
shall speak of Hungarian authors born to Jewish parents irrespective of
whether or not their Jewish origin found any expression in their works.

As far as their "Jewishness" is concerned, the modern Hungarian
writers of Jewish birth fall into two major categories. One comprises
those whose works, or at least some of them, portray Jewish characters
in either major or minor capacities, or describe or touch upon a Jewish
milieu, events that affect Jews, problems encountered by protagonists
because they are Jewish, or any variety of relationships between Jews
and the non-Jewish environment. For these authors, their Jewishness is
evidently a factor that endows their work with a specific nuance. Among
the post–World War II authors who belonged to this category were
Tibor Déry, Ágnes Gergely, Imre Kertész, Imre Keszi, György Konrád,
Mihály Kornis, József Lengyel, György Moldova, Péter Nádas, György
Spiró, and István Vas.

The second category consists of writers who, while of Jewish birth,
neither manifest in their writings any indication of this fact nor deal
with any Jewish theme. None of the protagonists of their works are
Jews, Jews do not appear even as secondary characters, and no reference
is made to the existence in the country of a Jewish population segment,
so that, as far as their writings are concerned, one would not suspect
that the presence of Jews in Hungary is a social issue of considerable
importance for the country. For these writers, their "Jewishness" is nothing more than a mere hereditary detail, forgotten or dismissed because it
is no more significant for them than the fact that they were born in this
or that street, house, or hospital. The question of whether writers of this
second group can in any meaningful sense be termed "Jewish writers" is
hard to answer, and in fact, as we have seen in chapter 39, Hungarian
Jewish literary critics grappled with it as early as in the 1930's.

The issue was further complicated by the fact that by the 1930s Hungarian literature could look back upon a period of more than a century

during which a number of the foremost Hungarian writers of Christian birth had taken up "Jewish" themes in several of their works, or had Jewish protagonists appear in them. Among these writers were the greatest names of Hungarian literature (József Eötvös, Mór Jókai, Kálmán Mikszáth, Zoltán Ambrus, Ferenc Herczeg, Dezső Szabó, Mihály Babits, Zsigmond Móricz), and the Jewish characters in their works are painted in the widest variety of colors, from the brightest to the darkest. References to these writers were used to bolster the position of those in the interwar years who argued that the appearance of Jewish themes in the work of a writer does not necessarily make that work part of Jewish literature.

The interest of non-Jewish Hungarian writers in Jewish themes continued and even intensified following World War II. Jewish protagonists appeared in the works of Gyula Illyés, Ferenc Karinthy, Péter Hajnóczy, Pál Bárdos, among others, and the problem of Jewish life in post-Holocaust Hungary was discussed by György Száraz in his important study *Egy előitélet nyomában* (Tracing a Prejudice, 1976).

Thus, Hungarian literary works that had somthing to do with Jews fell into not two but three overall categories: first, works written by non-Jews on Jewish themes; second, works written by Jews on Jewish themes; and third, works written by Jews on non-Jewish themes. The critical consensus in the interwar years was that the first did not belong to Jewish literature and the second did. As to the third category, critical opinon was (and still is) divided. The most inclusive position was that of the highly respected Hungarian Jewish poet and literary critic Aladár Komlós, who wrote in 1936 a thoughtful essay titled "Prologue to a Hungarian Jewish Literary History" (published in the Hungarian Jewish journal *Libanon*), in which his conclusion was: "I hold . . . that to it [Hungarian Jewish literature] belongs every Hungarian writer of Jewish origin, even those who perhaps throughout their lives avoided the problems of their people with the most persistent effort."

In selecting the authors to whom we now turn, I am aware that my choices reflect my individual tastes, judgments, and preferences, and that other reviewers would probably come up with a different assortment. I want to cite in particular the studies of Ivan Sanders (listed in the bibliography), in which the interested reader can find much more complete presentations and evaluations of post–World War II Hungarian Jewish literature.

One of the older writers who started to publish in the interwar years but whose work came to full fruition only after the war was Tibor Déry (originally Deutsch, 1894–1977), whose role in the political developments in Hungary under Mátyás Rákosi was described in chapter 47.

Here we wish to speak only of his work as a writer. Born into a Jewish upper-middle-class family, he published his early work, naturalistic and romantic, in *Nyugat*. His conversion to socialism took place during World War I, and under the 1919 Communist regime he became a member of the Writers' *Directoire*. When the Communist Council Republic nationalized private property, Déry's father lost the apartment houses that had provided him with his livelihood, and committed suicide. In 1920 Déry moved to Vienna, where he experimented with both poetry and fiction, and was influenced by the activist-surrealist school, flirting also with expressionism and dadaism. In 1933–38 he wrote an ambitious trilogy, *Befejezetlen mondat* (Unfinished Sentence, published in Budapest in 1947), in which he portrayed Hungarian society, depicting the problems of a young man of burgeois origin (much like Déry himself), seeking the road to Communism. As a result of his involvement with the workers' uprising, Déry was forced to leave Vienna, and he eventually returned to Budapest, where he survived World War II and the Holocaust by hiding. After the war he was forbidden to publish most of his work, but his wrestling with socialist realism matured his faculties, and his writing became more direct in both observation and style. He embarked on another trilogy, titled *Felelet* (Answer), setting the life of its "positive hero," Bálint Köpe, against the background of the changes in which Hungarian society was caught in the interwar years. However, when the first two parts were published (in 1950 and 1952), they incurred the personal wrath of cultural dictator József Révai, one of the "Muscovite" foursome who ran the country. Déry was severely rebuked for having violated the rules of socialist realism and was ordered to rewrite the book and corect his "mistakes."

Instead of doing as he was bidden, Déry turned to themes that enabled him to expose the "malpractices of socialist legality" (the contemporary euphemism for bare-knuckled party control). Especially in his long short story, *Niki, the Story of a Dog* (1956; English translation, New York, 1958, 1961), he gave symbolic expression, following an old Hungarian literary practice, to the woes of the nation under the guise of an animal's adventures. Déry was punished for his daring by being sentenced to nine years' imprisonment for "conspiracy against the state." In 1960 he was released, and recorded his commitment to Hungary in a likewise symbolic story, "Reckoning" (1962), in which a professor decides to escape after the 1956 revolution is crushed but, within sight of the Austrian border and freedom, changes his mind and returns. In the last twenty years of his life Déry produced a series of novels, each with a social message to convey, and also an autobiography, *No Verdict* (1968), in which he renounced his illusions about the possibility of artistic creativity in the service of the Party.

Were one acquainted only with Déry's political activities and his novels, one would conclude that his Jewishness consisted of nothing more than the accident of his birth, and that throughout his life it played no role whatsoever in his consciousness. However, from an auto-biographical sketch he wrote in jail in the late 1950s, which was published only in 1990, we know that this was not at all the case. In it he not only writes with what Ivan Sanders terms "stunning candor" about his Jewishness but reveals that his life was beset by a "tragic duality" and a compunction over not having written on Jewish themes:

> I must sooner or later ask the question: By what right do I call myself a Hungarian writer? My father came from a Jewish family in Szeged, my mother's people were Viennese Jews; all my relatives and friends and acquaintances are Jewish. My graduating class in the commercial college I attended had some sixty-odd students, of whom only two were non-Jews. . . . Naturally, I do not stand on racial ground, but shouldn't I have rather written about things Jewish? But in what language? With my mother I spoke German, with my father only Hungarian, though I used the latter much less. Ever since I became a writer, Hungarian has been my mother tongue. But even today, how can my knowledge of the language compare with that of [the Hungarian writers] Arany, Illyés, Attila József, Móricz, etc.? The tragic duality of my life: with my German-Jewish background I chose to become a Hungarian writer. I was a proper bourgeois who bolted from the middle class to become a Communist. What am I then? An accursed mixture with no firm grounding in either race or class.

Another Hungarian Jewish author who started out on the fringes of the *Nyugat* circle in World War I but had to wait four decades for recognition was József Lengyel (1896-1975). He was one of the founders of the Hungarian Communist Party in 1918, and was arrested shortly before the establishment of the Hungarian Council Republic. After its fall he fled to Vienna, then went on to Berlin, and ended up in Moscow, where he worked in the circle of the Hungarian emigré writers, perhaps the only significant author among them. However, he was arrested there, too, in 1938, and sent to a Soviet concentration camp. After World War II he was exiled to Siberia, released in 1953, and sent to work as a night watchman in a *kolkhoz* (collective farm). Finally, in 1955 he was allowed to return to Hungary, where, after another few years of party-imposed silence, he was able to start publishing his novels in 1958.

Much of what Lengyel wrote is based on his personal experiences. It was in Moscow that his first novel, *Visegrádi utca*, (Visegrad Street) was published in 1930 (or 1932), and where in 1937 he began writing his important novel *Prenn Ferenc hányotott élete*, which was published only in 1958 (English translation *Prenn Drifting*, 1966). In this novel, as well as in those that followed it (*Igéző*, 1961, and *Elejétől végig*, 1963, published together in English as *Spell* and *From Beginning to End*, 1966), the central subject is human suffering, human misery, and the loss of human dignity in the individual exposed to the cruelty and degradation of prison camps. The same theme preoccupied Lengyel when he wrote about the horrors of Auschwitz, which he did not experience personally (*Ujra a kezdet*, 1964; English title *The Judge's Chair*, 1968), but to which he brought the same empathy as to Siberia. His style in all his writings is intense, unrhetorical, and resounding of the authority of one who not only has full, detailed knowledge of his subject but also is imbued with the conviction that he has the right to say what he does. Lengyel never reached the point of confronting the Communist system, as several of the other writers discussed in this chapter did, but in one of his last novels, titled *Szembesítés* (1968. Available only in English, *Confrontation*, 1973), one protagonist expresses his (Lengyel's) serious doubts about the moral position of Communism, and faces new arrest.

Ten years younger than Lengyel was the poet Zoltán Zelk (1906–81), who, although he never formally renounced his Jewish affiliation, gave no evidence in his poetry of any Jewish identification or interest. He started out as a fringe member of the *Nyugat* circle, wrote expressionistic free verse, until his war experiences—forced labor in the Ukraine—turned him into a true believer in Communism and the Rákosi regime. He wrote what Czigány terms "sickening eulogies" (*A hűség és a hála éneke*—A Song of Loyalty and Gratitude, 1949), but soon recognized and renounced his gullibility, and became a spokesman of reform Communism. He joined the 1956 revolution, after which he served two years in prison. His books of poetry include *Mint égő lelkiismeret* (As a Burning Conscience, 1954) and *Zuzmara a rózsafán* (Hoarfrost on the Rosebush, 1964), as well as some fine poems for children.

Imre Keszi (1910–74) was my classmate for eight years in the *reálgimnázium* of the Israelite Congregation of Pest, and I remember him clearly, especially from the later years, when we were about fifteen and older. He was different from "the boys" and kept mostly to himself. Since I myself had a strong dislike for the raucous and rowdy gang of boys who dominated the classroom whenever no teacher was present—I myself was often a target of their verbal abuse for being a "Zionist"—I felt a sympathy for Kramer—his name at the time. After our graduation I had no more contact with him, so I do not know when he Magyarized his name to Keszi. He was a slightly built, timid boy, retiring, and had about him a kind of defenselessness that inevitably provoked the bullies in the class to poke fun at him, and not infrequently also to poke him in the ribs. I recall one or two occasions when I felt impelled to rise to the defense of the meek and mild Kramer. I had, of course, no inkling of the talents that inhabited his frail body.

What Kramer-Keszi achieved is part of the history of Hungarian literature. He became a student of the composer Zoltán Kodály, and came to be recognized as one of the foremost music critics in the country. As his aesthetic interests broadened, he entered the field of literary criticism as well, and before World War II branched out into writing the novels and short stories for which he is chiefly remembered today. The themes he returned to again and again were Jewish life and his World War II experiences. In 1944, just before the Hungarian Holocaust, his collection of stories and meditations on the Passover Seder was published, titled *A várakozók lakomája* (The Feast of Those Who Wait; 2d ed. Budapest, 1969). It was followed by two works on the Holocaust, *Elysium* (1958), and *Szőlőből bor* (Out of the Grape—Wine, 1961).

A Jewish author who exemplifies the trials and tribulations of writers in post–World War II Communist Hungary was the poet György Faludy. Born in Budapest in 1913 into a middle-class Jewish family, Faludy is considered the outstanding exception among the other, mediocre poets of the age, who wrote little that deserves mention. While still in his early twenties, Faludy published his Hungarian adaptation of François Villon's ballads (1937), in which, influenced by Bertolt Brecht's similar venture, he successfully recreated the image of the medieval vagabond. Czigány finds that the "effectively clattering rhymes, a pulsating beat, and harsh colors" characterizing Faludy's version of Villon are "never entirely absent" from Faludy's own poetry either. In 1939 Faludy fled to France, and then went to the United States, where he volunteered for service in the army. During the Nazi rule, Faludy's books were burned in Hungary. In 1946 he returned to Hungary, was imprisoned for alleged spying activities, and his books were confiscated. After his release from prison in 1953, he joined the editorial board of *Irodalmi Ujság* (Literary Journal), in which, in 1956, he published a poem about his experiences in prison. The publication of this poem was regarded at the time as a sign of the liberalization of the regime. After the 1956 revolution, Faludy fled to England, from where he moved to Canada. His prose work *Tragödie eines Volkes* (in German) was published in 1958. In 1962 he published his autobiography, *My Happy Days in Hell* (in English), and in 1980 his volume of *Collected Poetry* appeared in New York.

Another Hungarian Jewish poet, whose life and inner poetic development were no less adventurous than those of Zelk, was László Benjámin (b. 1915). He made his debut with a volume of poems titled *A csillag nem jött fel* (The Star Did Not Rise, 1939) permeated with the hopelessness of the pre–World War II years. As a promising "worker poet" (until the end of World War II he held various blue-collar jobs) his verse was included in the anthology *Tizenkét költő* (Twelve Poets, 1940). After the war he edited several literary magazines and after a long period of hesitation and doubts joined the Communist Party, becoming one of the chief literary spokesmen of the Communist government formed in 1948. This was the period when he published his collections *Betüöntők diadala* (Victory of the Typecasters, 1946) and *A teremtés után* (After Creation, 1948), in which much of his poetic wrath was directed at the servility, lack of courage, and political indifference of the Hungarians during the war. In 1953 his tone changed, and his writing evinced a disturbing inner crisis and was suffused with themes of self-criticism and a groping for personal values (*Éveink mulása*, The Passing of Our Years, 1954; *Egyetlen élet*, A Single Life, 1956).

After the defeat of the 1956 uprising, Benjámin withdrew into virtual seclusion, but eventually his inner development led to a recognition of past blunders, and in the mid-1960s he began writing and publishing again, reaffirming his commitment to the "community and the nation," and reaching a certain balance that entailed a loss of the "revolutionary *élan*, bitter self-accusations, and . . . defiance in upholding the tarnished image of socialism" (Czigány's words). He won recognition as one of the most significant masters of socialist poetry in Hungary, and was twice awarded the prestigious Kossuth Prize, while holding down the bourgeois job of librarian at the Municipal Library of Budapest.

A member of the young generation of Hungarian Jewish writers was György Konrád (b. Debrecen, 1933), who lived through the Holocaust as a child, studied at the University of Budapest, and worked for years as a social worker and town planner at the Budapest Institute of Urban Planning. Much of his early writing reflects the professional experiences he gathered in these jobs. His first novel, *A látogató* (1969; translated into English as *The Caseworker*, 1974), is "a sociologically precise and at the same time stunningly lyrical and provocatively nonpolitical examination of urban squalor and degradation" (as described by Ivan Sanders), which secured Konrád's place as a major modern Hungarian novelist. His second novel, *A városalapító* (1977; English translation *The City Builder*, 1977), is a sober portrait of a city whose rulers keep changing but remain intoxicated with power and within it of a city planner-builder who over time is reduced from a man of daring visions to a middle-echelon official content with his modest share of power. In his next novel, *A cinkos* (1978; in English *The Loser*, 1982), a grim political parable, the one solid anchor in the protagonist's vicissitudinous life is the image of this pious Jewish grandfather, with his long beard and black hat and coat, whom the hero considers a morally superior man, an ideal of steadfastness.

These novels were followed by a series of essays on dissidence and censorship and, in 1989, by an autobiographical novel *Kerti mulatság* (in English *Feast in the Garden*, 1992), chronicling much of Konrád's family history, childhood, miraculous survival of the Holocaust, and his tribulations as a barely tolerated dissident. Although during most of the 1970s and early 1980s Konrád was under a publication ban in Hungary —where his books began to appear only in the late 1980s—he nevertheless was able to publish even prior to that date several political and cultural-historical essays criticizing the contemporary environment.

Konrád's was one of the few modern Hungarian writers who became known outside Hungary as well. He received prestigious literary prizes in Austria, Switzerland, and Germany and was elected president of PEN International, the worldwide writers' organization, and much of his work is available in English translation.

A contemporary of Konrád, the prolific György Moldova (b. 1934), depicts in several of his novels Jewish life in Hungary in the years of World War II, the months of the Holocaust, and the years thereafter. In his semi-autobiographical novel *A Szent Imre-induló* (The St. Emeric March), written in the early 1970's, he tells the story of a twelve-year old Jewish boy, Miklós Kőhidai, who, although he lives through the horrors of the genocide, the ghetto, the senseless cruelty, physically unscathed, sustains deep emotional wounds. Those wounds remain with him in his adolescence and early manhood, and determine the relationships he is able to establish with either men or women. This is the subject of a second novel, *Elhúzódó szűzesség* (Receding Virginity), written in 1980. The two novels together, in their dry, matter-of-fact style, present a shattering picture, not only of the experiences and reactions of young Miklós, but also of the apparently inescapable hardships and humiliations inflicted upon the surviving Hungarian Jews by the relentlessly anti-Semitic Hungarian society, in which they pathetically try to find their places.

Yet another important modern Hungarian Jewish writer was Péter Nádas (b. 1942), who worked in Budapest as an editor, reader, and drama consultant, and then left the capital and settled in the small village of Gombosszeg in southwestern Hungary. The first two volumes he published, *A biblia* (The Bible, 1967) and *Kulcskereső játék* (The Game of Searching for the Key, 1969), contain autobiographically inspired stories of a child's world in the grim years of the early 1950s; his later writings are also often autobiographical, harking back to his own childhood. In *Egy családregény vége* (The End of a Family Novel, 1977) the main protagonist is the father, a fanatical state security officer, but the child, Péter Simon, is attracted and influenced by his grandfather, who tells him fascinating and often fantastic stories about their Jewish ancestors, going as far back as biblical times, so that the novel becomes a condensed history of the Jewish people as filtered through the imagination of the grandfather and understood by the spellbound child.

The memoirist mood persists in Nádas's second novel, *Emlékiratok könyve* (Book of Memoirs, 1986), whose hero, a young Hungarian writer, is passionately in love with another man, a German poet in East Berlin, while his consciousness is dominated by the imaginary memories of the life of a turn-of-the-century overrefined aesthete. Memories return in his *Évkönyv* (Yearbook, 1989), a book of autobiographical reminiscences. Nádas also wrote plays, essays, and meditations, which contributed to his stature as a major European literary figure.

The figure of the Jewish grandfather-mentor, which appears in the works of Konrád and Nádas, plays an important role in the writings of István Vas (1910–91): it was his grandfather, a rabbi, who taught him the Book of Genesis in Hebrew, and whose synagogue sermons remained etched in his memory. (See his memoirs titled *Miért vijjog a saskeselyű"* [Why Does the Vulture Scream? 2 vols., Budapest, 1981].) Also Géza Hegedüs paints a detailed picture of the Jewish world of his grandparents in his *Előjátékok egy önéletrajzhoz* (Preludes to an Autobiography, Budapest, 1981). The old Jewish grandfather, presented as the embodiment of precious traditional values, also figures prominently in the works of Pál Bárdos, Mihály Kornis (b. 1949), András Mezei, György Moldova (b. 1934), and others. The aged religious Jew—not necessarily the author's grandfather—presented with sympathy or even idealized, recurs in the work of several modern Hungarian Jewish writers among them G. György Kardos, György Láng, and György Dalos.

This, of course, does not mean that modern Hungarian Jewish writers' only Jewish theme of interest was the world of the grandfathers. Several of them dealt with the trials and tribulations experienced by members of the new Jewish generation in their contact with post-Holocaust and even post-Communist Hungarian society. One of the outstanding works of this genre is the novel *A tolmács* (The Interpreter, 1973), by Ágnes Gergely, whose Jewish hero, after having lived a totally assimilated non-Jewish life for many years in post–World War II Hungary, is brutally reminded in 1956 of his Jewishness and of Auschwitz.

However one interprets the prominent role of Jewish writers in recent Hungarian literature, and the likewise considerable interest of non-Jewish modern Hungarian writers in Jewish themes, these phenomena unquestionably demonstrate the extraordinary significance of the Jews' minuscule 1 percent (among the 10 million Hungarian Christians) for the country as a whole in the late twentieth century. There can be no doubt that the Jewish 1 percent of the country's population constitutes a culturally (as well as politically and economically) most active element and, equally important, is perceived as such by the non-Jewish majority.

Implied in this situation is the persistence of Jewish otherness in relation to the rest of the Hungarian nation. In fact, András Kovács, in a penetrating anlysis of "The Jewish Question in Today's Hungarian Society," reached the sobering conclusion that in the Hungary of the 1980s, Jewish consciousness no longer contained significant historical, religious or cultural elements, but was simply reduced to a sense of otherness.

While this conclusion may be an overstatement, there can be no doubt that conscious Jewish self-identification has become, as the century draws to its close, the exception rather than the rule among Hungary's surviving 100,000 Jews, while the sense of Jewish otherness has not diminished either among the Jews themselves or in general Hungarian society. Ivan Sanders in 1984 called attention to the fact that recent publications "dealing with [Hungarian] Christian-Jewish relations . . . emphasize that the two cultures do not live their own separate lives, but have become intertwined in the course of centuries, enriching each other, so that they can no longer be separated." I want to call attention to the expression "two cultures" in this significant observation, which shows that the sociologists referred to by Sanders, and he himself, consider the Christians and the Jews in Hungary carriers of two separate cultures. To be a carrier of a separate culture after a millennial sojourn in the midst of an unfriendly, occasionally inimical, and even lethal, non-Jewish environment must be interpreted as a sign of considerable vitality. This allows a more optimistic view of the chances of the survival of Hungarian Jewry. Global Jewish history, in its great richness, abounds with examples of Jewish communities that, whether owing to external or internal factors, were on the verge of extinction and nevertheless regained their vitality and recovered. In light of these historical examples, it does not seem farfetched to interpret the intensity of the interest in Jewish themes by both Jewish and non-Jewish writers in late-twentieth-century Hungary as a harbinger of such an impending recovery.

Bibliography

This compendium lists, first, the most important general works and bibliographies on the history of Hungarian Jewry, which were consulted for several chapters of the present book, and then the sources and studies consulted chapter by chapter. Hence, some titles appear more than once. English translations have been added in parentheses to titles in Hebrew, Hungarian, Latin, and Yiddish.

General Works and Bibliographies

Braham, Randolph L. *The Hungarian Jewish Catastrophe: A Selected and Annotated Bibliography.* New York, 1984.

Büchler, Sándor. *A zsidók története Budapesten a legrégibb időktől 1867-ig* (The History of the Jews in Budapest from Earliest Times to 1867). Budapest 1901.

Dalmat, Dan. *Bibliographia Hungarica Judaica 1945–1990* (Hungarian Jewish Bibliography 1945–1990). Budapest, 1991.

Encyclopaedia Judaica. 16 vols. and supplements. Jerusalem, 1972.

Geyer, Artur. *A magyarországi fasizmus zsidóüldözésének bibliográfiája 1945–1958.* (Bibliography of the Jewish Persecution of Hungarian Fascism 1945–1958). Budapest, 1958.

Gonda, László. *A zsidóság Magyarországon 1526–1945* (Jewry in Hungary 1526–1945). Budapest, 1992.

Greenwald, Leopold. *Toyznt Yor Yidish Lebn in Ungarn* (A Thousand Years of Jewish Life in Hungary). Columbus and New York, 1945.

Ki Kicsoda? Életrajzi Lexikon (Who's Who? Bibliographical Lexicon). Budapest, 1969, and later.

Kohn, Sámuel. *A zsidók története Magyarországon a legrégibb időktől a mohácsi vészig* (The History of the Jews in Hungary from Earliest Times to the Disaster of Mohács). Budapest, 1884.

Kolosváry-Borcsa, Mihály. *A zsidókérdés magyarországi irodalma* (The Hungarian Literature of the Jewish Question). Budapest, n.d. (ca. 1943).

Landeszman, György. *A magyarországi fasizmus zsidóüldözésének bibliográfiája 1959–1965* (The Bibliography of the Jewish Persecution of Hungarian Fascism 1959–1965). Unpublished manuscript.

Löw, Leopold. *Zur neueren Geschichte der Juden in Ungarn.* 2d ed. Budapest, 1874.

Magyar Életrajzi Lexikon (Hungarian Biographical Lexicon). 3 vols. Budapest, 1967–85.

Magyar Zsidó Levéltári Repertórium (Hungarian Jewish Archival Repertory). 2 vols. Edited by György Haraszti. Budapest, 1993.

Magyar Zsidó Lexikon (Hungarian Jewish Lexicon). Edited by Péter Ujvári. Budapest, 1929.

Magyar Zsidó Oklevéltár (Hungarian Jewish Archives; Latin title: *Monumenta Hungariae Judaica*). 18 vols. in 19. Budapest, 1903–80.

Sugar, Peter F. (ed.). *A History of Hungary*. Bloomington and Indianapolis, 1990.

Venetianer, Lajos. *A magyar zsidóság története* (The History of Hungarian Jewry). Budapest, 1992; repr. Budapest, 1986.

Yaron, Barukh and B. Pinkus. *5566 Hungary: A Bibliography*. Jerusalem, 1972.

1. The Jews in Roman Pannonia and Dacia

Baron, Salo W. *A Social and Religious History of the Jews*. Vol. 3. New York and Philadelphia, 1957.

Gerö László (ed.). *Magyarországi zsinagógák* (Hungarian Syngagogues). Budapest, 1989.

Makkai, László. "Hungary Before the Hungarian Conquest." In Sugar, *History of Hungary*.

Póczy, Klára. "A zsidók Pannoniában" (The Jews in Pannonia), in Gerö, *Magyarországi zsinagógák*.

Scheiber, Alexander. *Jewish Inscriptions in Hungary from the Third Century to 1686*. Budapest and Leiden, 1983.

Sugar, Peter F. (ed.). *A History of Hungary*. Bloomington and Indianapolis, 1990.

2. Medieval Origins and the Khazar Question

Baron, Salo W. *A Social and Religious History of the Jews*. Vol. 3. New York and Phildelphia, 1957.

Makkai, László. "The Hungarians' Prehistory." In Sugar, *A History of Hungary*.

——————. *"The Foundation of the Hungarian Christian State."* In Sugar, *History of Hungary*.

Scheiber, Alexander. *Jewish Inscriptions in Hungary from the Third Century to 1686*. Budapest and Leiden, 1983.

Sugar, Peter F. (ed.). *A History of Hungary*. Bloomington and Indianapolis, 1990.

3. After The Magyar Conquest

'Anav, Zedekiah ben Abraham haRofe. *Shibbolei haLeqet* (A Gathering of Sheaths). Edited by Solomon Buber, 1886.

Bak, János. "The Late Medieval Period," In Sugar, *A History of Hungary*.

Braham, Randolph L. (ed.). *Hungarian Jewish Studies*. 2 vols. New York, 1966–69.

Bibliography

Kohn, Samuel. "Das Land Hagar." *Monatschrift für Geschichte und Wissenschaft des Judentums* 30.

László, Ernő. "Hungarian Jewry: Settlement and Demography, 1753–38 to 1910." In Braham, *Hungarian Jewish Studies*. Vol. 1. New York, 1966.

——————. "Hungary's Jewry: A Demogrphic Overview, 1919–1945." In Braham, *Hungarian Jewish Studies*. Vol. 2. New York, 1969.

Mandl, Bernát. "Adalékok a magyar zsidók történetéhez" (Materials on the History of the Hungarian Jews). *Magyar Zsidó Szemle* (Hungarian Jewish Review) 25 (1908).

Meir ben Barukh of Rothenburg. *T'shuvot, P'saqim uMinhagim* (Responsa, Decisions, and Customs). Edited by Yitzḥaq Zeev Kahana. 4 vols. Jerusalem, 1957–77.

Neubauer, Adolph. "Memorbuch de Mayence." *Revue des Etudes Juives* 4 (1882): 1–30.

Rashi (R. Shlomo Yitzḥaqi). *Sefer haPardes* (Book of the Orchard). Constantinople, 1807; Warsaw, 1870.

Yitzḥaq ben Moshe. *Sefer Or Zaru'a* (Book of Light Sown). Parts 1–2. Zhitomir, 1862; part 3. Jerusalem, 1887.

Zunz, Leopold. *Die Synagogale Poesie des Mittelalters*. Berlin, 1855–59.

——————. *Literaturgeschichte der Synagogalen Poesie*. Berlin, 1865.

4. The Jews in Early Hungarian Law (Eleventh to Thirteenth Centuries)

Árpádkori uj okmánytár (New Archives from th Arpadian Age).

Bak, János. "The Late Medieval Period, 1382–1526. In Peter F. Sugar (ed.). *A History of Hungary*. Bloomington and Indianapolis, 1990.

Baron, Salo W. *A Social and Religious History of the Jews*. Vol. 10. New York and Phildelphia, 1965.

Büchler, Alexander. "Das Judenprivilegium Bélas IV vom Jahre 1251" In Alexander Scheiber (ed.), *Jubilee Volume in Honor of Bernhard Heller*. Budapest, 1941.

Csetényi, Imre. "Magyar Zsidók az Aranybulla Korában" (Hungarian Jews in the Period of the Golden Bull). *Magyar Zsidó Szemle* vol. 40 (1923).

Endlicher, S. F. L. (ed.). *Rerum Hungaricarum Monumenta Arpadiana* (Arpadian Monuments of Hungarian Matters). Sangalli, 1849.

Fejér, György. *Index codicis diplomatici Hungariae . . .* Buda. 1835.

Gerö, László (ed.). *Magyarországi zsinagógák* (Hungarian Synagogues). Budapest, 1989.

Gombos, Albinus Franciscus. *Catalogus fontium historiae Hungaricae aevo ducum et regum ex stirpe Arpad descendentium* (Catalog of Hungarian Historical Sources from the Age of Leaders and Kings of Arpadian Descent). Budapest, 1937.

Graetz, Heinrich. *Geschichte der Juden*. 11 vols. in 13. Leipzig, 1897–1911.

Hajnik, Imre. "A zsidók Magyarországon a vegyesházbeli királyok alatt" (The Jews in Hungary Under the Kings of the Mixed Houses). In *Magyar akadémiai értesitő* (Hungarian Academic Gazetteer). Budapest, 1941.

Helmar, Ágost. *A magyar zsidótörvények az Árpádkorszakban* (The Hungarian Jewish Law in the Arpadian Age). Pozsony, 1879.

Bibliography

Horváth, Mihály. *Magyarország történelme* (History of Hungary). Budapest, 1871.

Kohn, Sámuel. *Történelmi tár* (Historical Collection). Budapest, 1881.

Kubinyi, András. "A zsidóság története a középkori Magyarországon" (The History of Jewry in Medieval Hungary). In Gerö, *Magyarországi zsinagógák.*

Magyar Zsidó Oklevéltár (Hungarian Jewish Archives). Documents contained in vols. 1 and 5.

Stobbe, Otto. *Die Juden in Deutschland während des Mittelalters.* Braunschweig, 1886.

Theiner, Agost. *Vetera monumenta historica Hungariam sacram illustrantia* (Ancient Historical Monuments Illustrating Sacred Hungary). Rome, 1859.

5. Expulsion and Recall (Fourteenth Century)

Engel, Pál. "The Age of the Angevins (1301–1382). In Peter F. Sugar. *A History of Hungary.* Bloomington an Indianapolis, 1990.

Magyar Zsidó Oklevéltár (Hungarian Jewish Archives). Documents in vols. 1 (1903) and 5 (1959).

Scheiber, Alexander. *Jewish Inscriptions in Hungary.* Budapest and Leiden, 1983.

Theiner, Agost. *Vetera monumenta historica Hungariam sacram illustrantia* (Ancient Historical Monuments Illustrating Sacred Hungary). Rome, 1859.

Túróczi, Joannes. "Chronica Hungarorum" (Chronicles of the Hungarians). In Schwandtner, Johann Georg (ed.). *Scriptores rerum Hungaricarum* (Writers of Hungarian Affairs). Vol. 1. Vienna, 1766.

6. The Jew Judge and "the Perfidious Jews" (Thirteenth to Fifteenth Centuries)

Kohn, Sámuel. *A zsidók története Magyarországon* (The History of the Jews in Hungary). Budapest, 1884.

Magyar Zsidó Oklevéltár (Hungarian Jewish Archives). Vols. 1, 5, 13, and 18.

7. From Sigismund to Matthias (1385–1490)

Bak, János. "The Late Medieval Period." In Sugar, *History of Hungary.*

Dubnow, Simon. *History of the Jews in Russia and Poland.* 3 vols. Phildelphia, 1916–20.

Isserlein, Israel. *P'saqim uKhtavim* (Decisions and Writings). Venice, 1519.

Magyar Zsidó Oklevéltár (Hungarian Jewish Archives). Vol. 12.

Stobbe, Otto. *Die Juden in Deutschland während des Mittelalters.* Braunschweig, 1866.

Vogelstein, Hermann and Paul Rieger. *Geschichte der Juden in Rom.* 2 vols. Berlin, 1895–96.

8. The Jewish Prefects: The Mendels (1475–1531)

Magyar Zsidó Oklevéltár (Hungarian Jewish Archives). Vols. 1, 4, and 5.

678

Scheiber, Alexander. "Akiva ben Menahem." In *Encyclopaedia Judaica*. Jerusalem, 1972.

Szerémi, György, *Magyarország romlásáról*. Latin title: Georgius Sirimiensis, *De perditione regni Hungarorum* (On the Perdition of the Kingdom of the Hungarians), Budapest, 1961.

9. The First Scholars and the First Blood Libel (Fifteenth and Sixteenth Centuries)

Bonfinius, Antonius de. *Rerum Ungaricarum Decades* (Decades of Hungarian Matters). Edited by J. Fogel, B. Iványi, and L. Juhász. Budapest, 1941.

Bruna, R. Jacob. *P'saqim* (Decisions).

Cohen, J. J. in *HaMa'ayan* (The Source). 8:4 (1968): 4–12.

Eliyahu Halevi. *P'saqim* (Decisions).

Etzba Elohim o Ma'aseh she'Ira l'haRav Yitzḥaq Tyrnau (The Finger of God, or an Event that Happened to R. Isaac Tyrnau), Königsberg, 1857; in Yiddish, Frankfurt am Main, 1715.

Ghirondi, Mordekhai Samuel. *Toldot G'dole Yisrael* (History of Great Men of Israel). Trieste, 1853.

Isserlein, Israel. *P'saqim uKhtavim* (Decisions ad Writings). Venice, 1519.

Löw, Immanuel. *Aramäische Pflanzennamen*. Leipzig 1881.

Meir of Padua (Meir ben Isaac Katzenellenbogen). *P'saqim u Sh'elot uT'shuvot* (Decisions and Responses). Venice, 1553.

Michael, H. H. *Or haḤayyim: Ḥakhme Yisrael veSifrehem* (The Light of Life: The Sages of Israel and Their Books). Edited by S. Z. Halbertstam and N. Ben-Menaḥem. 2d. ed. Jerusalem, 1965, no. 328.

Moellin, R. Jacob (Maharil). *Sefer haMinhagim*. Sabionetta. Italy, 1556.

Tyrnau, Isaac. *Sefer haMinhagim* (Book of Customs). Venice, 1566; Amsterdam, 1723; German transl. by Simon Guenzburg, Mantua, 1590.

Weingarten, Shmuel Hakohen. "R. Eizik Tyrna v'toldotav" (R. Eizik Tyrna and His History). *HaMa'ayan* (The Source), 10:2 (1970): 48–56.

Yitzḥaq ben Moshe. *Sefer Or Zaru'a* (Book of Light Sown). Parts 1–2, Zhitomir, 1862; part 3, Jerusalem, 1887.

Yosef ben Mordekhai Gershon haKohen. *Sh'erit Yosef* (The Remnant of Joseph). Cracow, 1590.

Zacuto, Abraham ben Samuel. *Sefer Yuḥasin*. Cracow, 1580–81.

10. Jewish Physicians in the Fourteenth to Eighteenth Centuries

Bethlen, Count Miklós. *Mémoires historiques des derniers troubles de Transylvanie*. Amsterdam, 1736.

Efrayim haKohen. *Sha'ar Efrayim* (The Gate of Ephraim). Sulzbach, 1689.

Magyar Zsidó Oklevéltár (Hungarian Jewish Archives). Vols. 2, 3, 8, and 11.

Molnár, Béla. *Kassa orvosi története* (The Medical History of Kassa). Kassa, 1944.

Stella (Kokhav), Joseph. *Sefer Totzaot Ḥayyim* (The Book of the Sources of Life) Venice, 1714.

Bibliography

Wachstein, Bernhard, *Die Inschriften des alten Judenfriedhofes in Wien*, 2 vols., Vienna, 1912, 1917.

11. Jewish Criminals in the Sixteenth to Eighteenth Centuries

Magyar Zsidó Oklevéltár. Vols. 2, 3, 6, 9, 10, 11, 13, 14, and 15.

12. Emericus Fortunatus (Fifteenth and Sixteenth Centuries)

Elijah Halevi. *P'saqim* (Decisions). Constantinople, 1734.

Kohn, Sámuel. *Héber kútforrások és adatok Magyarország történetéhez* (Hebrew Sources and Data on the History of Hungary). Budapest, 1881; repr. Budapest, 1990.

Isserles, R. Moshe. *P'saqim* (Decisions). In *Otzar haPosqim.* Jerusalem, 1947.

Magyar Zsidó Oklevéltár (Hungarian Jewish Archives). Vols. 1, 2, 4, 5, 11, and 15.

Meir (Maharam) of Padua. *P'saqim* (Decisions). Several editions.

Verböczy (Werböczy), Stephan. *Codex tripartitum. Werböczy István hármaskönyve* (W.I.'s Triple Book). Budapest, 1897.

13. Transylvania and the Sabbatarians (Sixteenth and Seventeenth Centuries)

Bitskey, István. *Hitviták tűzében* (In the Fire of Religious Disputations). Budapest, 1978.

Dán, Róbert. *Az erdélyi szombatosok* (The Sabbatarians of Transylvania). Budapest, 1987.

Kohn, Sámuel. *A szombatosok: Történetük, dogmatikájuk és irodalmuk* (The Sabbatarians: Their History, Dogma, and Literature). Budapest, 1889.

Magyar Zsidó Oklevéltár (Hungarian Jewish Archives). Vols. 2, 17, and 18.

Marton, Ernö. *A magyar zsidóság családfája: Vázlatok a magyarországi zsidóság településtörténetéhez* (The Family Tree of Hungarian Jewry: Sketches on the History of Jewish Settlement in Hungary). Kolozsvár (Cluj), 1941. Also in English translation in Braham (ed.). *Hungarian Jewish Studies* I, New York, 1966.

Sugar, Peter F. "The Principality of Transylvania." In his edited *History of Hungary.* Bloomington and Indianapolis, 1990.

Szilágyi, Sándor (ed.). *Monumenta Comitalia Regni Transylvaniae: Erdélyi országgyülési emlékek* (Memorabilia of the Transylvanian Diet). Budapest, 1877.

14. The Jews in Turkish-Occupied Hungary (1526–1686)

Eliyahu ben Ḥayyim. *Sh'elot uT'shuvot* (Responsa). Constantinople, n.d.

Encyclopaedia of Islam. New edition, Leiden and London, 1960–s.v. Budin.

Bibliography

Encyclopaedia Judaica. Vol. 6, Jerusalem, 1972. s.v. Hakohen, Ephraim ben Jacob.

Evlia Cselebi török világutazó magyaroszági utazásai 1660–1664 (The Hungarian Travels of Evliya Chelebi, the Turkish World Traveler, 1660–64). 2nd ed. Budapest, 1985.

Ferdi Efendi. *Tarih-i-sahib kamun Sultan Suleyman* (The History of Sultan Suleiman the Lawgiver). In József Thúry (transl.). *Török történetirók* (Turkish Historians). Vol. 2. Budapest, 1896.

Fürst, Aladár. "Buda visszafoglalásának zsidó irodalmi emlékei" (The Jewish Historical Records of the Reconquest of Buda). In *IMIT Évkönyv* (IMIT Year Book). Budapest, 1936.

Gerevich, László and Domokos Kosáry (eds.). *Budapest története a későbbi középkorban ás a török hódoltság idején* (The History of Budapest in the Later Middle Ages and Under Turkish Rule). Vol. 2. Budapest, 1975.

Hakohen, Efrayim. *Sha'ar Efrayim* (The Gate of Ephraim). Sulzbach, 1689.

Hakohen, Joseph. *Divre haYamim l'Malkhe Tzarfat uMalkhe Bet Otoman haTogar* (History of the Kings of France and of the Ottoman Royal House). Venice and Sabionetta, Italy, 1554; Amsterdam, 1733.

——————————. *'Emeq haBakha* (Valley of Tears). Leipzig, 1858.

Ḥayyim ben Shabbetai. *Torat Ḥayyim* (The Teaching of Life). Vol. 2. Salonika, 1713.

Kohn, Sámuel. *Héber kútforrások és adatok Magyarország történetéhez.* Budapest, 1881.

Krausz, Samuel. "Magyar zsidók a Balkánon" (Hungarian Jews in the Balkans). In *IMIT Évkönyv* (IMIT Year Book). Budapest, 1932.

Magyar Zsidó Oklevéltár (Hungarian Jewish Archives). Vols. 2, 12, 16, 17, and 18.

Patai, Raphael. "The 'Control of Rain' in Ancient Palestine." *Hebrew Union College Annual.* Cincinnati, 1939.

Rodrigue, Aron (ed.), *Ottoman and Turkish Jewry: Community and Leadership,* Bloomington, Ind., 1992.

Schweiger, Salamon. *Eine neue Reisebeschreibung aus Deutschland nach Constantinople und Jerusalem.* Nürnberg, 1608.

Sender ben Yosef. Yiddish poem. Bodleian Library, Oxford. Repr. in *Múlt és Jövő,*" new series, no. 2 (1993).

Szakály, Ferenc. "The Early Ottoman Period, Including Royal Hungary, 1526–1606." In Peter F. Sugar (ed.). *A History of Hungary.* Bloomington and Indianapolis, 1990.

Takáts, Sándor, et al. (eds.). *A budai basák magyar nyelvü levelezése* (The Hungarian Correspondence of the Pashas of Buda). *I. 1553–1589. Budapest, 1915.*

15. The Jews in Royal Hungary (1526–1686)

Büchler, Sándor. "A Szentszék es a magyar zsidók a xvi. században" (The Holy See and the Hungarian Jews in the Sixteenth Century). In *Emlékkönyv Bloch Mózes tiszteletére* (Memorial Volume in Honor of Moses Bloch). Budapest, 1903.

Magyar Zsidó Oklevéltár (Hungarian Jewish Archives). Vols. 1, 2, and 10.

Pollák, Miksa. *A zsidók története Sopronban* (The History of the Jews in Sopron). Budapest, 1896.

16. The Jews in Reunited Hungary (1686–1740)

Magyar Zsidó Oklevéltár (Hungarian Jewish Archives). Vols. 2, 7, and 14.

Patai, Raphael. "Eisenstadt." In *'Arim v'Imahot b'Yisrael* (Major Jewish Cities in the World). Jerusalem, 1946.

Péter, Katalin. "The Later Ottoman Period and Royal Hungary, 1606–1711." In Peter F. Sugar (ed.). *A History of Hungary*. Bloomington ad Indianaplis, 1990.

Schulhof, Isaac. *Budai krónika* (Chronicle of Buda). Transl. from the Hebrew by László Jólesz. Budapest, 1979.

17. Jewish Women in the Sixteenth to Eighteenth Centuries

Magyar Zsidó Oklevéltár (Hungarian Jewish Archives). Vol. 3, 8, 9, 10, 11, 14, 18.

18. Conversions in the Seventeenth and Eighteenth Centuries

Magyar Zsidó Oklevéltár (Hungarian Jewish Archives). Vols. 3, 6, 9, 10, 11, 12, 14, 18.

19. The Jews Under Maria Theresa (1740–80)

Barbi, Maharam. *Ḥiddushe Maharam Barbi* (Novellae of Maharam Barbi). Dyrhenfurth, 1785; Prague, 1793.

Deutsch, Mordecai. *Mor D'ror* (Liquid Myrrh). Prague, 1738.

Eger, R. Akiba (the Elder). Novellae, responsa, etc. Various ed.

Eisenstadt, Moses. *Ein neu Klaglied*. Amsterdam, 1714.

——————. *Ḥokhmat haMispar* (The Science of Numbers). Dyrhenfurth, 1712.

Eisenstadt, Simon ben Efrayim Y'huda. *Gilgule N'shamot* (Transmigration of Souls). Prague, 1688.

Eliyahu ben Moshe Gershon. *M'lekhet Maḥshevet*. (Expert Works). Frankfurt, 1765.

——————. *Ḥeleq Shim'on* (Simon's Share). Prague. 1687.

——————. *Ḥiddushim* (Novellae). Prague, 1677.

Gál, Éva. "Adalékok az óbudai zsidók xviii. századi történetéhez" (Contributions to the History of the Jews of Altofen in the Eighteenth Century). *MIOK Évkönyv 1975–76* (MIOK Year Book) 1975–76. Budapest, 1976.

Haselsteiner, Horst. "Cooperation and Confrontation Between Rulers and the Noble Estates, 1711–1790." In Sugar, *A History of Hungary*.

Katzenelbogen, R. Meir. *Mishte Yayin* (A Banquet of Wine). Furth, 1697 (or 1695?).

——————. *Qinna* (Dirge). Prague, 1705.

Bibliography

_____. *Sefer haGilgulim* (The Book of Transmigrations). Frankfurt, 1684.

_____. *Sefer Ner laMaor* (The Book of a Candle to the Lamp). Wilmersdorf, 1675.

_____. *Zemer* (Song). Prague, 1703.

Magyar Zsidó Oklevéltár (Hungarian Jewish Archives). Vol. 7.

Marton, Ernő. *A magyar zsidóság családfája: Vázlat a magyarországi zsidóság településtörténetéhez* (The Family Tree of Hungarian Jewry: Sketches on the History of Jewish Settlement in Hungary). Kolozsvár (Cluj), 1941.

Sugar Peter F. (ed.). *A History of Hungary*. Bloomington and Indianapolis, 1990.

20. The Jews Under Joseph II (1780–90)

Büchler, Sándor. "De Judeis" (About the Jews). In *IMIT Évkönyv* (IMIT Year Book). Budapest, 1900.

_____. "A magyarországi zsidó iskolák multjából" (From the Past of the Hungarian Jewish Schools). *Magyar Zsidó Szemle* (Hungarian Jewish Review), 11, 1894.

Haselsteiner, Horst. "Cooperation and Confrontation Between Rulers and the Noble Estates, 1711–1790." In Peter F. Sugar, ed. *A History of Hungary*. Bloomington and Indianapolis, 1990.

Löw, Immanuel and Zsigmond Kulinyi. *A szegedi zsidók 1785–től 1885–ig* (The Jews of Szeged from 1785 to 1885). Szeged, 1885.

Mandl, Bernát. "A magyarhoni zsidók tanügye II. József korában" (The Education of Hungarian Jews in the Days of Joseph II). *IMIT Évkönyv* (IMIT Year Book). 1901.

Marczali, Henrik. "A magyarországi zsidók II. József korában" (The Hungarian Jews in the Days of Joseph II). *Magyar Zsidó Szemele* (Hungarian Jewish Review) I, 1884.

21. The Theben Story (Eighteenth and Nineteenth Centuries)

Löw, Leopold. *Gesammelte Schriften*. repr. Hildesheim and New York, 1979.

Patai, Erwin Georg (Raphael). "Der Judenrichter beim Kaiser." *Die Stimme*. September 8, 1932. Repr. *Der Israelit*. October 13, 1932; *Jewish World*, November 19, 1932.

Reich, Ignac. *Beth-El: Ehrentempel verdienter ungarischer Israeliten*. Pest, 1856–65; 2d ed. Pest, 1868.

22. Early Struggles for Emancipation, 1790–1848

Barany, George. "The Age of Royal Absolutism." In Peter F. Sugar (ed.). *A History of Hungary*. Bloomington and Indianapolis, 1990.

Fényes, Elek. *Magyar országnak 's a hozzá kapcsolt tartományoknak mostani állapota statisztikai és geographiai tekintetben* (The Present State of Hungary and the Attached Territories Statistically and Geographically). 6 vols. Pest, 1836–40.

Széchenyi, Count István. *Addresses.* Edited by Antal Zichy. Budapest, 1887.
───────. *Hitel* (Credit). Pest, 1830.
───────. *Világ* (The World). Pest, 1831.

23. Religious Reform (1798–1852)

Büchler, Sándor. "A zsidó reform uttörői Magyarországon" (Pathfinders of Jewish Reform in Hungary). *Magyar Zsidó Szemle* (Hungarian Jewish Review) (1900).

Gilon, Meir. "R. David Friesenhausen ben Qotve haHaskala v'haHasidut" (R. David Friesenhausen Between the Poles of Enlightenment and Hasidism). In Moshe Carmilly-Weinberger (ed.). *The Rabbinic Seminary of Budapest: 1877–1977.* New York, 1986.

Groszmann, Zsigmond. *A Magyar zsidók a xix, század közepén* (Hungarian Jews in the Mid-Nineteenth Century). Budapest, 1917.

───────. "A pesti kultusztemplom" (The Temple of Pest). *Magyar Zsidó Szemle* (Hungarian Jewish Review) 40, (1923).

Gruenwald, Y. Y. *Qorot haTorah vehaEmunah b'Hungaria* (History of Torah and Belief in Hungary). Budapest, 1921.

Loew, William N. *Leopold Loew: A Biography with a Translation of the . . . Tributes Paid to His Memory.* New York, 1912.

Löw, Leopold. *Der jüdische Kongress in Ungarn, historisch beleuchtet.* Pest, 1871.

Vadász, Ede. *A pesti zsidótemplom első ötven éve* (The First Fifty years of the Jewish Temple of Pest). Budapest, 1909.

24. New Horizons (1800–48)

This list does not include works written by Hungarian Jews in the nineteenth century and referred to in this chapter.

Csiky, Kálmán et al. *Corpus Juris Hungarici: Magyar Törvénytár, 1836–1868.* (Hungarian Code of Laws). Budapest, 1896.

Glatzel, Max Julius. *Leopold Klein als Dramatiker.* Stuttgart, 1914.

IMIT Évkönyv (IMIT Year Book). Budapest, 1910.

Loeb, Isidor. *Biographie d'Albert Cohn.* Paris, 1878.

Reich, Ignac. *Beth-El Ehrentempel verdienter ungarischer Israeliten.* Pest, 1856–65; 2d ed. Pest, 1868.

Robitsek, M. *Saphir Gottlieb Moric.* Budapest, 1938.

Roth, Cecil. *Jewish Art.* London and New York, 1961.

Tessedik, Ferenc. *Utazás Franciaország déli részeiben* (Travel in the Southern Parts of France). Pest, 1831.

25. The Patriotic Imperative (1800–48)

Barany, George. "The Age of Royal Absolutism 1790–1848." In Peter F. Sugar (ed.). *A History of Hungary.* Bloomington and Indianapolis, 1990.

Schmelzer, Menahem. "Löw Henrik Jakab, egy magyar *maszkil,* Lord Byron Kain-jának héber forditója (Henrik Jakab Löw, a Hungarian *Maskil,* the Hebrew Translator of Lord Byron's *Cain*). In György Landeszman and Robert Deutsch

Bibliography

(eds.), *Hetven Év: Emlékkönyv Dr. Schweitzer József születésnapjára* (Seventy Years: Memorial Volume for Dr. Joseph Schweitzer's Birthday). Budapest, 1992.

Venetianer, Lajos. *A zsidóság szervezete az európai államokban* (The Organization of Jewry in the European States). Budapest, 1901.

26. The 1848 Revolution

Horváth, Mihály. *Huszonöt év Magyarország történetéből* (Twenty-Five Years of Hungary's History). Quoted by Lajos Venetianer. *A magyar zsidóság története* (The History of Hungarian Jewry). Budapest, 1922; repr. Budapest, 1986; p. 167.

Stearns, Peter. *1848: The Revolutionary Tide in Europe.* New York, 1974.

27. Neoabsolutism I: The Harsh Years (1849–59)

Except for a few historical studies, works by the nineteenth-century authors mentioned in this chapter are not listed.

Bánóczi, József. *Az országos izraelita tanítóképző intézet története* (History of the National Israelite Teachers Institute). Budapest, 1897.

Bernstein, Béla. *A negyvennyolcas szabadságharc és a zsidók* (The 1848 War of Freedom and the Jews). Budapest, 1939.

Eisenberg, Ludwig Julius. *Adolf Sonnental: Eine Künstlerlaufbahn . . .* Dresden, 1896.

Groszmann, Zsigmond. *A magyar zsidók a xix, század közepén* (The Hungarian Jews in the Mid-Nineteenth Century). Budapest, 1917.

Löw, Leopold. *Der jüdische Kongress in Ungarn historisch beleuchtet.* Pest, 1871.

Magyar Irodalmi Lexikon (Hungarian Literary Lexicon). Budapest, 1963.

Somogyi, Éva. "The Age of Neoabsolutism, 1849–1867." In Peter F. Sugar (ed.). *A History of Hungary.* Bloomington and Indianapolis, 1990.

Steiner, R. *Gesammelte Aufsätze zur Dramaturgie 1889–1900.* 2d ed. 1960.

Vadász, Ede. *A Pesti zsidótemplom első ötven éve* (The First Fifty Years of the Jewish Temple of Pest). Budapest, 1909.

28. Neoabsolutism II: The Moderate Years (1860–67)

Except for a few historical studies, works by nineteenth-century authors mentioned in this chapter are not listed.

Bánóczi, József. *Az országos izraelita tanítóképző intézet története* (History of the National Israelite Teachers Institute). Budapest, 1897.

Carmilly-Weinberger, Moshe (ed.). *The Rabbinical Seminary of Budapest 1877–1977.* New York, 1986.

Groszmann, Zsigmond. *A Magyar zsidók a xix. század közepén* (The Hungarian Jews in the Mid-Nineteenth Century). Budapest, 1917.

Ignotus, Paul. *Hungary.* New York and Washington, 1972.

Katzburg, Nathaniel. *P'raqim b'Toldot haḤevra haY'hudit* (Chapters in the History of Jewish Society). Jerusalem, 1980.

Löw, Leopold (ed.). *Ben Chananja.* May 11, 1864.

Somogyi, Éva. "The Age of Neoabsolutism, 1849–1867." In Peter F. Sugar, ed. *A History of Hungary.* Bloomington an Indianapolis.

29. Emancipation, Congress, and Schism (1867–69)

A magyarországi és erdélyi israeliták 1868, december 10-iki egyetemes gyűlése által hozott szabályzatok és határozatok (The Statutes and Resolutions Adopted by the General Assembly of the Hungarian and Transylvanian Israelites on December 10, 1868, official record). Pest, 1869.

Bánóczi, József. *Die Geschichte des ersten Jahrzehnt der Landesrabbinerschule.* Budapest, 1888.

Groszmann, Zsigmond. *A magyar zsidók a xix. század közepén* (The Hungarian Jews in the Mid-Nineteenth Century). Budapest, 1917.

Löw, Leopold (ed.). *Ben Chananja.* July 19, 1861.

Patai, Joseph. *MiS'fune haShirah.* Tel Aviv, 1939.

Patai, Raphael. "Wilhelm Bacher." In Moshe Carmilly-Weinberger (ed.). *The Rabbinical Seminary of Budapest.* New York, 1986.

30. Zionism: Precursors, Founders, Opponents (1839–67)

Alkalay, Judah. *Harbinger of Good Tidings, an Address to the Jewish Nation by Rabbi Judah Elkali on the Propriety of Organizing an Association to Promote the Regaining of Their Fatherland.* London, 1852.

Les Archives Israélites de France. March 15, 1852.

Egyenlőség, March 6 and April 10, 1896; November 14, 1897.

Frankel, Dov. *Reshit haTziyonut haM'dinit haModernit* (The Beginning of Modern Political Zionism). Haifa, 1956.

Gelber, N. M. *Zur Vorgeshichte des Zionismus.* Vienna 1927.

HaMaggid. 1867.

IMIT Évkönyv (IMIT Year Book). Edited by József Bánóczi. Budapest, 1908.

Der Israelit. 4:4 (1967).

Kecseméti, Lipót. "A cionizmus" (Zionism). In *IMIT Évkönyv.* 1908, p. 237.

Kressel, G. *Leqsiqon haSifrut ha'Ivrit* (Lexicon of Hebrew Literature). 2 vols. Merhavia, Israel, 1965.

——————. *Moshe Hess uV'ne Doro* (Moses Hess and His Generation). Tel Aviv, 1947.

Magyar Zsidó Szemle (Hungarian Jewish Review), vol. 13, 1896.

Natonek, Joseph. *Messiás, avagy értekezés a zsidó emancipációról* (Messiah, or a Treatise on Jewish Emancipation). Buda, 1861.

——————. *R. Mosche Sofer und der Magier Ben Chananjah.* Prague, 1865.

——————. *Pentaglotte.* Pest, 1861.

——————. *Schir Haschirim, Das Hohelied. Mit Hollanders deutscher Übersetzung und Commentar.* Ofen (Buda), 1871.

——————. *Wissenschaft-Religion: Eine pro u. contra Beleuchtung des Materialismus. Darwin, Häckel. Büchner, etc.* Budapest, 1876.

Patai, Joseph. *Hezyon Herzl* (Herzl's Vision). Tel Aviv, 1943.

Rónai, János. *Zion und Ungarn.* Balázsfalva, 1897.

Univers Israélite. 1867.

Varga, László. "Zsidó bevándorlás Magyarországon" (Jewish Immigration in Hungary). *Századok* (Centuries) 126:1 (1992): 59–79.

Die Welt. 1897.

Bibliography

Werfel, Yitzhaq (ed.). *Kitve haRav Y'huda Alkalay* (The Writings of Yehuda Alkalay). Jerusalem, 1944.

Zehavi, Zevi. *MehaHatam Sofer v'ad Herzl* (From the Hatam Sofer [Moses Sofer] to Herzl). Jerusalem, 1966.

31. Istóczy and Tiszaeszlár

Egyenlőség. March 6 and April 10, 1896; November 14,1897.

Elek, Judit and Mihály Sükösd (eds.). *Tutajosok: A tiszaeszlári per dokumentumai.* Budapest, 1990.

Handler, Andrew. *Blood Libel at Tiszaeszlár* (East European Monographs, no. 68). Boulder and New York, 1980.

Hegedűs, Sándor. *A tiszaeszlári vérvád* (The Blood Libel of Tiszaeszlár). Budapest, 1966.

Istóczy Győző országgyűlési beszédei, indítványai és törvényjavaslatai (The Parliamentary Speeches, Motions, and Bills of Istóczy Győző. Budapest, 1904.

Istóczy, Győző. *Emlékiratfélék és egyebek* (Memoirs and Other Things). Budapest, 1911.

Katzburg, Nathaniel. *Antishemiyut b'Hungaria 1867–1914* (Anti-Semitism in Hungary 1867–1914). Tel Aviv, 1969.

Magyar Országgyülés Képviselőházának Naplói (Minutes of the House of Representatives of the Hungarian National Assembly). Vols. iii, vi, and xii. Budapest, 1881–84.

Merhavya, H. *HaTziyonut: Otzar haT'udot haPolitiyot* (Zionism: A Collection of Political Documents). Jerusalem, 1955.

Pulzer, Peter J. G. *The Rise of Political Anti-Semitism in Germany and Austria.* New York, 1964.

Strack, Hermann L. *Der Blutaberglaube in der Menschheit, Blutmorde und Blutritus.* Munich, 1892.

Szatmári, Mór. *Húsz esztendő parlamenti viharai* (The Parliamentary Storms of Twenty Years). Budapest, 1928.

32. The *Fin de Siècle* and Its Aftermath I: Economy and Society

Works of the scholars discussed in this chapter are not included in this list.

Aranyossi, Magda. *Leo Frankel.* Berlin, 1957.

Braham, Randolph L. (ed.). *Hungarian Jewish Studies.* Vol. 2. New York, 1969.

Egyenlőség. July 10, 1891; November 8, 1895; March 6 and April 10, 1896; November 14, 1897.

Frank, Tibor. "Hungary and the Dual Monarchy 1867–1890." In Peter F. Sugar (ed.). *A History of Hungary.* Bloomington and Indianapolis, 1990.

Györgyei, Clara. *Ferenc Molnár.* Boston, 1980.

Hanák, Péter. "A másokról alkotott kép" (The Picture Formed of Others). *Századok* (Centuries), nos. 5–6 (1985).

Handler, Andrew (ed.). *The Holocaust in Hungary: An Anthology of Jewish Response.* University, Alabama, 1982.

Bibliography

Hatvany, Lajos. *Urak és emberek: Zsiga az életben.* Budapest, 1963. Postscript by László Bóka.

Huszadik Század (Twentieth Century). 1917.

Jeszenszky, Géza. "Hungary Through World War I and the End of the Dual Monarchy." In Peter F. Sugar (ed.). *A History of Hungary.* Bloomington and Indianapolis, 1990.

Katzburg, Nathaniel. *Antishemiyut b'Hungaria 1867–1914* (Anti-Semitism in Hungary 1867–1914). Tel Aviv, 1969.

Kőrössy, Joseph and Gustav Thirring. "Budapest fővárosa az 1891. évben: A népleirás és népszámlálás eredményei" (The Capital City of Budapest in 1891: The Results of Its Demography and Census). *Budapest székesfőváros statisztikai hivatalának közleményei* (Publications of the Statistical Office of the Capital City of Budapest) XXV/1–3, (1894–98) 1:44.

Kovćs, Alajos. *A zsidóság térfoglalása Magyarországon* (Jewry's Expansion in Hungary). Budapest, 1922.

Löwenheim, Avigdor. "Zsidók és a párbaj" (Jews and Dueling). *Múlt és Jövő,* new series, no. 4, Fall 1992.

Magyar Statisztikai Közlemények (Hungarian Statistical Publications). Budapest 1893, 1915. (Census reports.)

Marton, Ernő. *A magyar zsidóság családfája: Vázlat a magyarországi zsidóság településtörténetéhez* (The Family Tree of Hungarian Jewry: An Outline of the History of the Settlement of the Jews in Hungary). Kolozsvár, 1941.

McCagg, William O., Jr. "Ennoblement in Dualistic Hungary." *East European Quarterly* 5:1 (March 1971): 13–26.

——————. *Jewish Nobles and Geniuses in Modern Hungary.* Boulder, 1972.

Patai, Raphael. *Apprentice in Budapest.* Salt Lake City, 1988.

—————— (ed.). *The Complete Diaries of Theodor Herzl.* 5 vols. New York, 1960.

Radnóti, József. *Kornfeld Zsigmond.* Budapest, 1931.

Silber, Michael K. "A zsidók társadalmi befogadása Magyarországon a reformkorban: A kaszinók" (The Social Acceptance of the Jews in Hungary in the Age of Reform: The Casinos). *Századok* (Centuries), 126:1 (1993). In English in Jonathan Frankel and Steven J. Zipperstein (eds.). *Assimilation and Community: The Jews in Nineteenth-Century Europe.* Cambridge and New York, 1992.

Ullmann, Sándor de Erény. *A zsidó felekezeti ügyek rendezése.* (Putting in Order the Jewish Denominational Affairs). Budapest, 1888.

Zobel, Moritz. "Ungarischer Antisemitismus." *Die Welt.* November 5, 1897.

33. The *Fin de Siècle* and Its Aftermath II: Explorers and Scholars

Patai, Raphael (ed.). *The Complete Diaries of Theodor Herzl.* New York, 1960.

——————. *Ignaz Goldziher and His Oriental Diary: A Translation and Psychological Portrait.* Detroit, 1987.

Perlman, Robert. *Bridging Three Worlds: Hungarian-Jewish Americans 1848–1914.* Amherst, Mass., 1991.

Scheiber, Alexander (ed.). *Ignaz Goldziher: Tagebuch.* Leiden, 1978.

34. The *Fin de Siècle* and Its Aftermath III: Literature, Criticism, and the Arts

Most works of the authors discussed in this chapter are not listed here.

Bahr, Ehrhard and Ruth Goldschmidt Kunzer. *Georg Lukacs.* New York, 1972.

Barany, George. "Magyar Jew or Jewish Magyar? To the Question of Jewish Assimilation in Hungary." *Canadian American Slavic Studies* 8 (1974).

Bródy, Sándor. *Művei* (Works). 20 vols. Budapest, 1888–1914.

Czigány, Lóránt. *The Oxford History of Hungarian Literature.* Oxford, 1984.

Erdős, Renée. *Összegyüjtött munkái* (Collected Works). 30 vols., Budapest, 1931.

Farkas, G. *Az asszimiláció kora a magyar irodalomban, 1867–1914* (The Age of Assimilation in Hungarian Literature, 1867–1914). Budapest, 1938.

Feuerstein, Emil. *Egy marék virág* (A Fistful of Flowers). Tel Aviv, 1986.

Gergely, E. J. *Hungarian Drama in New York.* New York, 1947.

Györgyei, Clara. *Ferenc Molnár.* Boston, 1980.

Halmi, B. *Kóbor Tamás az iró és az ember* (Tamás Kóbor, the Writer and the Man). Budapest, 1935.

Heltai, Jenő. *Munkái* (Works). 10 vols. Budapest, 1926–27.

Klaniczay, T., et. al. (eds.). *A Magyar irodalom története* (History of Hungarian Literature). Budapest, 1982.

Kóbor, Tamás. *Válogatott munkái* (Selected Works). Budapest, 1930.

————. "When They First Called Me a Jew," *Irodalmi Szemle* (Literary Review). Budapest, 1976.

Lengyel, Menyhért. *Szinművei* (Plays). 5 vols. Budapest, 1928.

Lichtheim, George. *Georg Lukacs.* New York, 1970.

Magyar Irodalmi Lexikon (Hungarian Literary Lexicon). Budapest, 1965.

Molnár, Ferenc. *All the Plays of Molnar.* New York, 1937.

————. *The Paul Street Boys.* New York, 1927.

————. *Companion in Exile.* New York, 1950.

Nagy, M. K. *Balázs Béla Világa* (The World of Béla Balazs). Budapest, 1973.

Pap, Károly. *B. városában történt* (It Happened in the City of B.). 2 vols. Budapest, 1964.

Patai, Raphael. *Apprentice in Budapest.* Salt Lake City, 1988.

Pintér, Jenő. *A Magyar irodalom története* (History of Hungarian Literature). 8 vols. Budapest, 1930–41.

Ránki György (ed.). *Hungary and European Civilization,* Budapest, 1989.

Reményi, J. "Ignotus, Man of Letters." *Slavonic and East European Review* (1949).

Rubinyi, M. *Kiss József élete és munkássága* (Life of Works of Joseph Kiss). Budapest, 1926.

Sanders, Ivan. "Ancient Legends, Modern History—Jewish Themes in the Works of Illés Kaczér. *Studia Judaica.* Cluj-Napoca (1993).

————. "Lukacs and Hungarian Literature." In György Ránki (ed.). *Hungary and European Civilization.* Budapest, 1989.

————. "Milán Füst, 1888–1967." *The New Hungarian Quarterly* XXVII: 106 (Spring 1987).

Schöpflin, Aladár. *A Magyar irodalom története a XX, században* (The History of Hungarian Literature in the Twentieth Century). Budapest, 1937.

35. Demography and Occupations (1890–1920)

K. k. Direction der administrativen Statistik, Wien, *Tafeln zur Statistik der Österreichischen Monarchie.* Vienna, 1823.

Magyar Statisztikai Közlemények (Hungarian Statistical Publications). New series. Vol. 1. *A magyar korona országaiban az 1891, év elején végrehajtott népszámlálás eredményei* (Results of the Census Carried Out in the Lands of the Hungarian Crown in the Beginning of the Year 1891). Budapest, 1893. New series. Vol. 1: Census of 1900, Budapest, 1902. Vol. 56: Census of 1910, 1915. Vol. 69: Census of 1920, Budapest, 1923.

Szabad, György. "A polgári jogegyenlőség felszámolására irányuló első kísérlet visszaverése Magyarországon" (The Repulsing of the First Attempt at Liquidating Civic Equality in Hungary). *Társadalmi Szemle* (Social Review) 1982.

Varga, László. "Zsidó bevándorlás Magyarországon" (Jewish Immigration into Hungary). *Századok* (Centuries) 126:1 (1992).

36. Zionism and Anti-Semitism in the Early Twentieth Century

Ágoston, Péter. *A zsidók útja* (The Way of the Jews). Budapest, 1917.

Bató, Y. T. "A Magyar cionizmus hőskora." *Uj Kelet,* April 9, 1954.

Bitton, Livia E. "Zionism in Hungary: The First Twenty-Five Years." In Raphael Patai (ed.). *Herzl Year Book.* Vol. 7, New York, 1971.

Braham, Randolph L. "Hungary, Zionism in." In Raphael Patai (ed.). *Encyclopaedia of Zionism and Israel.* New York, 1971.

Hanák, Péter (ed.), *Zsidóság, asszimiláció, antiszemitizmus* (Jewry, Assimilation, Anti-Semitism). Budapest, 1984.

Huszadik Század (Twentieth Century), a literary and sociological journal.

Jeszenszky, Géza. "Hungary Through World War I and the End of the Dual Monarchy." In Peter F. Sugar (ed.). *A History of Hungary.* Bloomington and Indianapolis, 1990.

Katzburg, Nathaniel. *Antishemiyut b'Hungaria 1867–1944* (Anti-Semitism in Hungary 1867–1944), Jerusalem, 1992.

McCagg, William O., Jr. *Jewish Nobles and Geniuses in Modern Hungary.* Boulder, 1972.

Patai, József. Articles in *Mult és Jövő,* monthly, 1914 and 1915.

————. "Antiszemitizmus Magyarországon, a galiciaiak, és a morál" (Anti-Semitism in Hungary, the Galicians, and Morality). *Mult és Jövő,* monthly, August 1918.

Patai, Raphael. *Apprentice in Budapest.* Salt Lake City, 1988.

Pfeiffer, Izsák "A zsidóság problémája" (The Problem of Jewry). *Huszadik Század* (1914).

Szabó, Dezső. "Nyilt levél a *Múlt és Jövő* szerkesztőinek" (Open Letter to the Editors of *Múlt és Jövő. Huszadik Század,* 1914.

37. World War I and the Communist Interlude

Hajdu, Tibor and Zsuzsa L. Nagy, "Revolution, Counterrevolution, Consolidation." In Peter F. Sugar (ed.). *A History of Hungary.* Bloomington and Indianapolis, 1990.

Bibliography

Jászi, Oscar. *The Dissolution of the Hapsburg Monarchy*. Chicago, 1929.
Magyar statisztikai szemle (Hungarian Statistical Review). Budapest, 1922.
Múlt és Jövő, monthly, 1918, 1919.
Patai, Raphael. *Apprentice in Budapest*. Salt Lake City, 1988.

38. The White Terror and Numerus Clausus

Bethlen, Pál (ed.). *Numerus Clausus: A Magyar zsidóság almanachja* (Numerus Clausus: Almanac of Hungarian Jewry). Budapest, 1926.
Guttman, Yisrael, Bela Vago, and Livia Rothkirchen (eds.), *Hanhagat Y'hude Hungaria b'Mivḥan haShoah* (The Leadership of the Hungarian Jews in the Test of the Holocaust), Jerusalem, 1976.
Jászi, Oscar. *Revolution and Counter-Revolution in Hungary*. London, 1924.
Karady, Victor and István Kemény. "Antisèmitisme universitaire et concurrence de classe: La loi du numerus clausus en Hongrie entre les deux guerres." *Actes de la recherche en sciences sociales* 34 (September 1980).
Katsburg, Nathaniel. *Hungary and the Jews: Policy and Legislation 1920–1943*. Ramat Gan, Israel, 1981.
Mult és Jövő, monthly, April 1930.
Mult és Jövő, weekly, October 3, November 1, December 6, 1919; January 2 and 9, March 12, October 15, December 3, 1920.
Patai, Raphael. *Apprentice in Budapest*. Salt Lake City, 1988.
Romsics, Ignác. *Ellenforradalom és konszolidáció: A Horthy-rendszer első tiz éve* (Counterrevolution and Consolidation: The First Ten Years of the Horthy Regime). Budapest, 1982.
Ruppin, Arthur. *Soziologie der Juden*. Berlin, 1930.
Szabó, Ágnes and Ervin Pamlényi (eds.). A határban a halál kaszál . . . Fejezetek Prónay Pál feljegyzéseiből (Death Reaps on the Border . . . Chapters from the Notes of Pál Prónay). Budapest, 1963.
Szegvári, Katalin. *Numerus clausus rendelkezések az elleforradalmi Magyarországon: A zsidók és nőhallgatók főiskolai felvételéről* (Numerus Clausus Dispositions in Counterrevolutionary Hungary: On the Academic Admission of Jewish and Women Students). Budapest, 1988.
Térfy, Gyula. *Corpus Juris Hungarici, Magyar Törvénytár 1920* (The Hungarian Body of Laws of 1920). Budapest, 1921.

39. The Interwar Years

Bartha, Miklós. *Kazár földön* (In Khazar Land). Budapest, 1939.
Benedek, Marcell, *Huszadik Század*, 1917.
Bosnyák, Zoltán. *Az idegen vér* (The Alien Blood). Budapest, 1938.
——————. *Huszadik Század*, 1917.
Braham, Randolph L. (ed.). *The Tragedy of Hungarian Jewry: Essays, Documents, Depositions*. Boulder and New York, 1966.
Egyenlőség (Equality [Jewish weekly]), (July 4 and August 29, 1925).
Fischer, Rolf. *Entwicklungstufen des Antisemitismus in Ungarn 1867–1939: Die Zerstörung der magyarisch-jüdischen Symbiose*. Munich, 1988.
Hanák, Péter. "A másokról alkotott kép" (The Picture Created of the Others). *Századok* (Centuries) 5–6 (1985): 1079–1104.

Bibliography

Karady, Victor. "Some Social Aspects of Jewish Assimilation in Socialist Hungary, 1945–1956." In Braham. *Tragedy of Hungarian Jewry*.

——————. "Szociológiai kisérlet a magyar zsidóság 1945 és 1956 közötti helyzetének elemzésére" (Sociological Attempt at the Analysis of the Situation of Hungarian Jewry Between 1945 and 1956). In Péter Kende (ed.). *A zsidóság az 1945 utáni Magyarországon* (Jewry in Hungary After 1945). Paris, 1984.

Karfunkel, Thomas. "The Impact of Trianon on the Jews of Hungary." In Béla K. Király, Peter Pastor, and Ivan Sanders (eds.). *War and Society in East-Central Europe*, Vol. VI. *Essays on World War I: Total War and Peacemaking: A Case Study on Trianon*. New York, 1982.

Katzburg, Nathaniel. *Hungary and the Jews: Policy and Legislation, 1920–43*. Ramat Gan, Israel, 1981.

Kiss, Sándor. "Zsidó fajiság—magyar fajiság" (Jewish Raciality—Hungarian Raciality), *A cél* (The Aim) 1–2 (1918).

Komlós, Aladár, "Egy megirandó magyar-zsidó irodalom-történet elé" (Prolegomena to a Still-to-be Written History of Hungarian Jewish Literature). *Libanon*, Jan.-Feb., 1936.

Kovács, Mária. "Interwar Antisemitism in the Professions: The Case of the Engineers." In Silber. *Jews in the Hungarian Economy*.

Lengyel, György. "Hungarian Banking and Business Leaders Between the Wars." In Silber. *Jews in the Hungarian Economy*.

Lesznai, Anna. *Huszadik Század*, 1917.

Lévai, Jenő. *Fekete könyv a magyar zsidóság szenvedéseiről* (Black Book of the Sufferings of Hungarian Jewry). Budapest, 1946.

——————. *Zsidósors Magyarországon* (Jewish Fate in Hungary). Budapest, 1948.

Lewin, Kurt. *Resolving Social Conflicts*. New York, Evanston and London, 1948.

Macartney, C. A. *October Fifteenth: A History of Modern Hungary, 1929–1945*. Edinburgh, 1957.

Magyar statisztikai évkönyv 1935 (Hungarian Statistical Yearbook 1935). Budapest, 1936.

Magyar Statisztikai Közlemények (Hungarian Statistical Publications) 96 (1936).

Mult és Jövő (Past and Future), monthly, April 1918; June and July–August 1926; February 1928; March and November 1930; November 1932; September 1935.

Novak, Attila. "Testvérharc" (Fraternal War). *Múlt és Jövő*: 4, (1993).

Opinion poll on the Jewish question in Hungary. *Huszadik Század* (1917).

Ormos, Mária. "The Early Interwar Years, 1921–1938. In Sugar, Peter F. (ed.). *A History of Hungary*. Bloomington and Indianapolis, 1990.

Patai, József. Personal communications. Jerusalem, 1940–47.

Patai, Raphael (ed.). *Encyclopedia of Zionism and Israel*. 2 vols., New York, 1971.

——————. Personal Reminiscences from 1928–36.

Radisics, Elemér. *Huszadik Század* (1917).

Ravasz, László. *Huszadik Század* (1917).

Silver, Michael S. (ed.). *Jews in the Hungarian Economy 1760–1945*. Jerusalem, 1992.

Statisztikai Szemle (Statistical Review) (1934).

Bibliography

Sulyok, Dezső. *A magyar tragédia* (The Hungarian Tragedy). Newark, N.J. 1954.

Szabolcsi, Lajos. *Két emberöltő: Az Egyenlőség évtizedei (1881–1931)*. *Emlékezések, dokumentumok* (Two Generations: The Decades of *Egyenlőség*. Memories, Documents). Budapest, 1993.

Szekfü, Gyula. *Három nemzedék és mi utána következik* (Three Generations and What Followed Them). Budapest, 1938.

Zsidó Szemle (Jewish Review). July 1 and September 17, 1925; December 1927.

40. The First and Second Jewish Laws (1938–39)

Bibó, István. "Zsidókérdés Magyarországon 1944 után" (The Jewish Question in Hungary After 1944). *Válasz* (Response) (1948).

————————. *Harmadik ut* (The Third Road). London, 1960.

Braham, Randolph L. *The Politics of Genocide: The Holocaust in Hungary.* 2 vols. New York, 1981.

Hanák, Péter (ed.). *Zsidókérdés, asszimiláció, antiszemitizmus* (The Jewish Question, Assimilation, Anti-Semitism). Budapest, 1984.

Ignotus, Paul. *Hungary.* New York and Washington, 1972.

Karády, Viktor. "A magyar zsidóság helyzete az antiszemita törvények idején" (The Position of Hungarian Jewry at the Time of the Anti-Semitic Laws), *Medvetánc* (Bear Dance) 1–2 (1985).

Karsai, Elek (ed.). *"Fegyvertelen álltak az aknamezőkön . . . " Dokumentumok a munkaszolgálat történetéhez Magyarországon* ("Unarmed They Stood in the Minefields . . ." Documents on the History of Labor Service in Hungary). 2 vols. Budapest, 1962.

Katzburg, Nathaniel. *Hungary and the Jews: Policy and Legislation, 1920–43.* Ramat Gan. Israel, 1981.

————————. "The Hungarian Jewish Situation in the Late 1930s." *Annual of Bar Ilan University Studies in Judaica and the Humanities.* Ramat Gan, Israel, 1977., pp. 73–99.

Kovács, András. "A zsidókérdés a mai magyar társadalomban" (The Jewish Question in Today's Hungarian Society). In Victor Karády et al. *Zsidóság az 1945 utáni Magyarországon* (Jewry in Post-1945 Hungary). Paris, 1984.

Lévai, Jenő. *Fekete könyv a magyar zsidóság szemvedéseiről* (Black Book of the Sufferings of Hungarian Jewry). Budapest, 1946.

————————. *Zsidósors Magyarországon* (Jewish Fate in Hungary). Budapest, 1948.

Magyar Statisztikai Közlemények (Hungarian Statistical Publications). New series. Vol. 114 (1941).

OMZSA Évkönyv 5704 (OMZSA Year Book 5704). Budapest, 1944.

Országos Törvénytár (National Legislative Records) (May 29, 1938).

Pásztor, József. "Négy éves a Magyar Izraeliták Pártfogó Irodája" (The Patronage Office of the Hungarian Israelites Is Four Years Old). *OMZSA Évkönyv.* (OMZSA Year Book). Budapest, 1942–43.

Tilkowsky, Lorand. "The Late Interwar Years and World War II." In Peter F. Sugar (ed.). *A History of Hungary.* Bloomington and Indianapolis, 1990.

41. World War II (1939–45)

Braham, Randolph L. *The Destruction of Hungarian Jewry: A Documentary Account.* 2 vols. New York, 1963.

Horák, Magda, "Kirekesztetten is előitélet nélkül: Az OMIKE művészakciója" (Excluded Without Prejudice: The Art Enterprise of OMIKE), *Múlt és Jövő,* new series, 5:2 (1994), pp. 105–13.

Kapronczy, Károly. "Lengyel zsidó menekültek Magyarországon a második világháboru idején" (Polish Jewish Refugees in Hungary During World War II). In Schweitzer, *Évkönyv 1985–1991.*

Karsai, Elek (ed.). *"Fegyvertelen álltak az aknamezőkön . . ."* Dokumentumok *a munkaszolgálat történetéhez Magyarországon* ("Unarmed They Stood in the Minefields . . ." Documents on the History of Labor Service in Hungary). 2 vols. Budapest, 1962.

Landeszman, György and József Schweitzer. "A magyar zsidóság a német megszállás és a deportáció közötti időszakban" (Hungarian Jewry in the Period Between the German Occupation and the Deportation). In Schweitzer, *Évkönyv 1985–1991.*

Lévai, Jenő. *Fekete könyv a magyar zsidóság szenvedéseiről* (Black Book of the Sufferings of Hungarian Jewry). Budapest, 1946.

Ránki, György (ed.). *Magyarország története 1918–1945* (The History of Hungary 1918–1945). Budapest, 1976.

Schindler, P. *T'guvat haHasidut laShoah* (The Reaction of Hasidism to the Holocaust). Jerusalem, 1980.

Schweitzer, József (ed.). *Évkönyv 1985–1991* (Year Book 1985–1991). Budapest, 1991.

Tilkowsky, Lorand. "The Late Interwar Years and World War II." In Sugar. *A History of Hungary.*

42. The Hungarian Holocaust: The Beginnings

Benoschofsky, Ilona and Elek Karsai (eds.). *Vádirat a nácizmus ellen* (Bill of Indictment Against Nazism). 3 vols. Budapest, 1958–67.

Braham, Randolph L. *The Destruction of Hungarian Jewry: A Documentary Account.* 2 vols. New York, 1963.

——————. "A Holocaust Madyarországon" (The Holocaust in Hungary). *Múlt és Jövő,* new series, 5:2 (1994), pp. 12–19.

——————. *The Politics of Genocide.* 2 vols. New York, 1981; 2d ed., New York, 1994.

——————. "'Legitimism,' Zionism, and the Jewish Catastrophe in Hungary." In Raphael Patai (ed.). *Herzl Year Book.* Vol. 6, New York, 1964–65.

Guttman, Yisrael, and Efrayim Zuroff (eds.). *Nisyonot uF'ulot Hatzalah biT'qufat haShoah* (Rescue Attempts and Actions in the Holocaust Era). Jerusalem, 1977.

Handler, Andrew (ed.). *The Holocaust in Hungary: An Anthology of Jewish Response.* University, Alabama, 1982.

Ignotus, Paul. *Hungary.* New York and Washington, 1972.

Lévai, Jenő. *Eichmann in Hungary.* Budapest, 1961.

Schmidt, Maria. *Kollaboráció vagy kooperáció?* (Collaboration or Cooperation?). Budapest, 1990.

————————. "Mentés vagy árulás? Magyar zsidó önmentési akciók a második világháboru alatt" (Rescue or Betrayal? Hungarian Jewish Attempts at Self-
Rescue During World War II). *Medvetánc* 2–3 (1985).

Varga, László. "Manfred Weiss: The Profile of a Munitions King." In Silber,
Jews in the Hungarian Economy.

43. The Destruction of Provincial Jewry

Benoschofsky, Ilona and Elek Karsai (eds.). *Vádirat a nácizmus ellen* (Bill of
Indictment Against Nazism). 3 vols. Budapest, 1958–67.

Braham, Randolph L. *The Destruction of Hungarian Jewry: A Documentary
Account.* 2 vols. New York, 1963.

————————. *The Politics of Genocide.* 2 vols. New York, 1981; 2d ed., New
York, 1994.

Lévai, Jenő. *Fekete Könyv a magyar zsidóság szenvedéseiről* (Black Book of
the Sufferings of Hungarian Jewry). Budapest, 1946.

Munkácsi, Ernő. *Hogyan történt? Adatok és okmányok a magyar zsidóság tragédiájához* (How Did It Happen? Data and Documents on the Tragedy of Hungarian Jewry). Budapest, 1947.

Schmidt, Maria. "Mentés vagy árulás? Magyar zsidó önmentési akciók a
második világháboru alatt" (Rescue or Betrayal? Hungarian Jewish Attempts at
Self-Rescue During World War II). *Medvetánc* 2–3 (1985).

Varga, László. "Manfréd Weiss: The Profile of a Munitions King." In Michael
K. Silber (ed.). *Jews in the Hungarian Economy, 1760–1945.* Jerusalem, 1992.

44. How Half of Budapest Jewry Was Saved

Balla, Erzsébet, "The Jews of Hungary: A Cultural Overview." In Braham.
Hungarian Jewish Studies.

Beck, Ladislas. Interview in New York, March 26, 1993.

Benoschofsky, Ilona and Elek Karsai (eds.). *Vádirat a nácizmus ellen* (Bill of
Indictment Against Nazism). 3 vols. Budapest, 1958–67.

Braham, Randolph L. *The Destruction of Hungarian Jewry: A Documentary
Account.* 2 vols. New York, 1963.

————————. *The Politics of Genocide: The Holocaust in Hungary.* 2 vols.
New York, 1981; 2d ed., New York, 1994.

Klaniczay, Tibor, József Szauder, and Miklós Szabolcsi. *History of Hungarian
Literature.* London, 1964.

Lévai, Jenő. *Fekete könyv a magyar zsidóság szenvedéseiről* (Black Book of the
Sufferings of Hungarian Jewry). Budapest, 1946.

————————. *A pesti gettó csodálatos megmenekülésének hiteles története*
(The Authentic History of the Miraculous Deliverance of the Pest Ghetto). Budapest, 1946.

Pach, Zsigmond Pál and Vilmos Sándor (eds.). *A Zsidó Világkongresszus
Magyarországi Képviselete statisztikai osztályának közleményei* (Publications of
the Statistical Department of the Hungarian Representation of the World Jewish
Congress) 1–4 (1947–49).

Roth, Ernő, "Mártirokká letter a papok" (The Priests Became Martyrs). In
Évkönyv 1943–46, Országos Rabbiképző Intézet (Year Book 1943–46 of the
National Rabbinical Seminary), Budapest, 1946.

Bibliography

Reitlinger, G. *The Final Solution*. New York, 1953.

Snyder (Schneider), Árpád. "Becslés Magyarországnak a második világháboru következtében elszenvedett emberveszteségeiről" (Estimate of Hungary's Human Losses in Consequence of World War II). *Magyar Statisztikai Szemle* (Hungarian Statistical Review) 1–6 (1946).

Tilkowsky, Lorand. "The Late Interwar Years and World War II." In Peter F. Sugar (ed.). *A History of Hungary*. Bloomington and Indianapolis, 1990.

Váradi, László. "Külföldi diplomáciai mentési kisérletek a budapesti zsidóságért" (Foreign Diplomatic Attempts to Rescue Budapest Jewry). *Medvetánc* 2–3 (1985).

Várdy, Péter. "A magyarországi zsidóüldözések a hazai történetirásban: Szemléleti problémák és a kérdés aktualitása" (The Persecutions of the Jews in Hungarian Historiography: Theoretical Problems and the Relevance of the Question). In Péter Kende (ed.). *Zsidóság az 1945 utáni Magyarországon* (Jewry in Post-1945 Hungary). Paris, 1984.

World Jewish Congrss, Hungarian Section. *Hungarian Jewry Before and After the Persecution*. Budapest, n.d.

Y'rushat Pletah (Legacy of the Remnant). An anonymous pamphlet. Budapest, 1946.

45. Liberation

Bán, Péter (ed.). *Magyar történelmi fogalomtár* (Thesaurus of Hungarian Historical Concepts). Vol. 1. Budapest, 1989.

Benoschofsky, Ilona and Elek Karsai (eds.). *Vádirat a nácizmus ellen* (Bill of Indictment Against Nazism). 3 vols. Budapest, 1958–67.

Bibó, István. "Zsidókérdés Magyarországon 1944 után" (The Jewish Question in Hungary After 1944), *Válasz* (Response) 8 (October–November 1948): 778–877. Repr. in Zoltán Szabó (ed.). *Harmadik út* (The Third Road), 227–354, London, 1960.

Braham, Randolph L. *The Politics of Genocide*. 2 vols. New York, 1981; 2d ed., New York, 1994.

Karsai, Elek. "Evian után tizenegy hónappal" (Eleven Months After Evian). *MIOK Évkönyv* (MIOK Year Book 1971). Budapest, 1972.

Lévai, Jenő. *Fekete könyv a magyar zsidóság szenvedéseiről* (Black Book of the Sufferings of Hungarian Jewry). Budapest, 1946.

—————. *Zsidósors Magyarországon* (Jewish Fate in Hungary). Budapest, 1948.

Munkácsi, Ernő. *Hogyan történt? Adatok és okmányok a magyar zsidóság tragédiájához* (How Did It Happen? Data and Documents on the Tragedy of Hungarian Jewry). Budapest, 1947.

46. Old Trends and the Post-Holocaust Stance

Bibó, István. "A zsidókérdés Magyarországon" (The Jewish Question in Hungary). *Válasz* (Response) (October–November 1948).

Dénes, Béla. *ÁVOs világ Magyarországon* (ÁVO World in Hungary). Budapest, 1957; reissued with a Postscript by Maria Schmidt, Budapest, 1991.

Don, Jehuda and George Magos. "A magyarországi zsidóság demográfiai fejlődése" (The Demographic Development of Hungarian Jewry), *Történelmi Szemle* (Historical Review) 28:3. Budapest, 1985.

Bibliography

Fisher, Julius. "Hungary." In Nehemia Robinson (ed.). *European Jewry Ten Years After the War.* New York, 1956.

Karády, Viktor. "Asszimiláció és társadalmi krizis" (Assimilation and Social Crisis). *Világosság* (Light) (March 1993).

——————. "A Shoah, a rendszerváltás és a zsidó azonosságtudat válsága Magyarországon," (The *Shoah*, the Change of Regime, and the Crisis of Jewish Identity-Consciousness in Hungary). In M. Mária Kovács, Yitzhak M. Kashi, and Ferenc Erdős (eds.). *Zsidóság, Identitás, Történelem* (Jewry, Identity, History). Budapest, 1992.

——————. "A zsidó vallásváltás szociológiai problémai 1945 után" (The Sociological Problems of Jewish Religious Conversion After 1945). Unpublished paper.

——————. "Szociológiai kisérlet a magyar zsidóság 1945 és 1956 közötti helyzetének elemzésére" (Sociological Attempt at Analyzing the Situation of Hungarian Jewry Between 1945 and 1956). In Péter Kende (ed.). *Zsidóság az 1945 utáni Magyarországon* (Jewry in Post-1945 Hungary). Paris, 1984.

——————. "The Transformation of Hungarian-Jewish Identity After the Shoah." Unpublished paper.

Lévai, Jenő. *Zsidósors Magyarországon* (Jewish Fate in Hungary). Budapest, 1948.

Magyar Statisztikai Évkönyv (Hungarian Statistical Year Book) 1940 and 1941. Budapest 1941 and 1942.

47. Under Communist Rule

Bibó István. "Zsidókérdés Magyarországon 1944 után" (The Jewish Question in Hungary After 1944), *Válasz* (Response) 8 (October–November): 778–877. Repr. in Zoltán Szabó (ed.). *Harmadik út* (The Third Road), 227–354 London, 1960.

Braham, Randolph L. *A Magyar holocaust* (The Hungarian Holocaust). Budapest, 1989.

Columbia University Research Project on Hungary (unpublished interviews).

Darvas, József. "Öszinte szót a zsidókérdésben! (A Frank Word About the Jewish Question). *Szabad Nép* (Free People) (March 25, 1945).

Déry, Tibor. *Itélet nincs* (There Is No Verdict). Budapest, 1969.

Duschinsky, Eugene. "Hungary," in Peter Meyer, Bernard D. Weinryb, Eugene Duschinsky, and Nicolas Silvain (eds.), *The Jews in the Soviet Satellites.* Syracuse, N.Y., 1953.

Erdélyi, Ágnes. "Eltorzult kozmopolita alkat" (Distorted Cosmopolitan Structure). In *Bibó Emlékkönyv* (Bibó Memorial Volume). Budapest, 1980.

Fejtő, Francois. *Judentum und Kommunismus.* Vienna, Frankfurt and Zurich, 1967.

Gyertyán, Ervin. *Szemüveg a porban* (Eyeglasses in the Dust). Budapest, 1975.

Horváth, Márton. "Zsidóság és asszimiláció" (Jewry and Assimilation). *Társadalmi Szemle* (Social Review) 7 (1946).

Horváth, Zoltán. *Hogy vizsgázott a magyarság?* (How Did Magyardom Stand the Test?). Budapest, 1945.

Ignotus, Paul. *Hungary.* New York and Washington, 1971.

Irving, David. *Uprising!* London, 1981.

Bibliography

Karady, Victor and István Kemény. "Les juifs dans la structure des classes en Hongrie: Essai sur les antécédents historiques des crises d'antisémitisms du XXe siècle." *Actes de la Rescherche en Sciences Sociales* 22 (June 1978).

Karády, Viktor, Péter Kende, András Kovács, Ivan Sanders and Péter Várdy. *Zsidóság az 1945 utáni Magyarországon* (Jewry in Post-1945 Hungary). Paris, 1984.

Marton, László. "Zsidó sors: Zsidókérdés a háború utáni Magyarországon" (Jewish Fate: The Jewish Question in Postwar Hungary), in Hollandiai Mikes Kelemen Kör (ed.) *Eszmék Nyomában* (Tracking Down Ideas). Munich, 1965.

Márványi, Judit. "Köszönet helyett" (Instead of Thanks). In *Bibó Emlékkönyv* (Bibó Memorial Volume). Budapest, 1980.

Moldova, György. "Elhúzódó szüzesség" (Receding Virginity). *Kortárs* (The Contemporary) 11 (1980).

Molnár, Erik. "Zsidókérdés Magyarországon" (The Jewish Question in Hungary). *Társadalmi Szemle* (Social Review) 5 (1946).

Sanders, Ivan. "Tétova vonzalmak: Zsidó témák a kortársi magyar irodalomban" (Hesitant Attractions: Jewish Themes in Contemporary Hungarian Literature). *Uj Látóhatár* (New Horizons) 5 (1975).

Száraz, György. *Egy előitélet nyomában* (Tracking Down a Prejudice). Budapest, 1976.

Várdy, Péter. "Befejezetlen mult—mai magyar zsidó valóság" (Unfinished Past—Today's Hungarian Jewish Reality). In *Belső tilalomfák* (Internal Prohibitory Signs), 81–146. Budapest, 1982.

Vincze, László. "Kisérletek megmentésemre . . ." (Attempts to Rescue Me . . ."). In József Schweitzer (ed.), *Évkönyv 1985–1991). (Year Book 1985–1991. Budapest, 1991).

48. Reconstruction

Interviews conducted in Budapest in September and October 1993

Ákos, Dr. Károly, physician

Bálint, Éva V., journalist, staff member of the Budapest daily *Magyar Hirlap*

Ember, Mária, author of books on the Holocaust

Englander, Dr. Tibor, president of the Hungarian Zionist Union and director of the research group in psychology at the Hungarian Academy of Sciences

Feldmajer, Dr. Péter, attorney and president of the Association of Hungarian Jewish Congregations

Fenyő, Ágnes, manager of the editorial office of *Múlt és Jövő*

Gábor, Dénes, teacher of dramatic arts at the Lauder-Yavne School, Budapest

Gadó, György, member of parliament (Union of Free Democrats)

Hanák, Dr. Péter, professor emeritus of history at the University of Budapest

Hanthy, Kinga, journalist on the staff of the Budapest daily *Magyar Nemzet*

Haraszti, Dr. György, principal of the high school of the Budapest Jewish Community

Herzog, László, secretary of the Budapest Orthodox Jewish Congregation

Hoffman, George, retired Hungarian-American technical photographer

Karsai, Dr. László, professor of history at the University of Szeged and author of *A kirekesztők* and other studies on the Jews of Hungary

Kőbányai, János, author, editor of the Jewish quarterly *Múlt és Jövő*

Lippner, Dr. György, principal of the Lauder-Yavne School, Budapest

698

Bibliography

Quittner, János, managing director of the Soros Foundation, Budapest
Raj, Rabbi Tamás, member of parliament
Szabad, György, president of the Hungarian Parliament and a historian
Szabolcsi, Dr. Miklós, professor emeritus of literature at the University of Budapest
Szántó, Gábor, book designer
Vidor, Mrs. Pál (née Zsuzsa Kálmán), retired teacher
Voigt, Dr. Vilmos, professor of folklore at the University of Budapest
Weber, Lajos, photojournalist on the stafff of the Budapest daily *Magyar Nemzet*

Literature

Benoschofsky, Ilona. "The Position of Hungarian Jewry after the Liberation." In Braham, Randolph L. (ed.), *Hungarian Jewish Studies*. Vol. 1. New York, 1966.

Bodor, Pál. "Irónikus kisérlet a zsidókérdés (ideiglenes) megoldására" (Ironic Attempt at the (Temporary) Solution of the Jewish Question). *Élet ás Irodalom* (Life and Literature), 35:20 (May 17, 1991).

Csorba, László. "Izraelita felekezeti élet Magyarországon a vészkorszaktól a nyolcvanas évekig" (Israelite Congregational Life in Hungary from the Years of the Disaster Until the 1980s). In Ferenc L. Lendvai, Anikó Sohár, and Pál Horváth (eds.). *Hét évtized a hazai zsidóság életében* (Seven Decades in the Life of Hungarian Jewry). 2 vols. Budapest, 1990. Vol. 2, pp. 61–190.

Hatvany, Lajos. *Urak és emberek* (Gentlemen and Men). New ed. Budapest, 1980.

Herzog Avigdor. "Hol van a zsidó zene? A Muzsikás Együttes zsidó népzenei kazettájáról" (Where Is Jewish Music? About the Jewish Folk Music Cassette of the Musical Ensemble). *Múlt és Jövő*, no. 1 (1993).

Karsai, László. *Kirekesztők: antiszemita irások 1881–1991* (The Excluders: Anti-Semitic Writings 1881–1991). Budapest, 1992.

Múlt és Jövő (Past and Future), a Jewish quarterly, new series, edited by János Kőbányai.

Raj, Ferenc, Belmont, Md. Personal communication, 1994.

Ruppin, Arthur. *Soziologie der Juden*. 2 vols. Berlin, 1930.

Sándor, Vilmos. "Házasság, születés, halálozás a felszabadulás óta" (Marriage, Birth, and Death since the Liberation). *Uj Élet* (New Life), official journal of the Union of Hungarian Jewish Congregations, December 24, 1947.

Szántó, Gábor T. "Ezek a dallamok csak együtt müködnek" (These Melodies Work Only Together). *Szombat* (March 1993).

Szombat (Sabbath), monthly, edited by Gábor T. Szántó.

Tamássy, Györgyi. "Zsidó szellemi élet Magyarországon 1945 után" (Jewish Intellectual Life in Hungary After 1945). In Ferenc L. Lendvai, Anikó Sohár, and Pál Horváth (eds.). *Hét évtized a hazai zsidóság életében* (Seven Decades in the Life of Hungarian Jewry). 2 vols., Budapest, 1990. Vol. 2, pp. 191–300.

Várdy, Béla. A kettős és tőbbes kőtődés" (The Double and Plural Linkage). *Valóság* (Reality) 35:12, (December 1994).

Volenszky, Paula. Quarterly bibliographies of publications of Jewish interest. *Múlt és Jövő*, new series, every issue.

World Jewish Congress. A Zsidó Világkongresszus magyarországi képviselete statisztikai osztályának közleményei (Publications of the Statistical Department of the Hungarian Representation of the World Jewish Congress) 8–9 (April 1948) and 11 (December 1948).

World Jewish Congress, Institute of Jewish Affairs. *European Jewry Ten Years After the War.* New York, 1956.

Appendix: Post-Holocaust Jewish Authors

This list does not include the works of the modern Hungarian Jewish writers discussed or mentioned in the Appendix.

Braham, Randolph L. and Bela Vago (eds.). *The Holocaust in Hungary Forty Years Later.* New York, 1985.

Czigány, Lóránt. *The Oxford History of Hungarian Literature.* Oxford, 1984.

Encyclopaedia of World Literature in the Twentieth Century. 5 vols. New York, 1981–93.

Fényes Mór. "Zsidó irodalom" (Jewish Literature). In *Magyar Zsidó Lexikon.*

Hanák, Péter (ed.). *Zsidókérdés, asszimiláció, antiszemitizmus* (The Jewish Question, Assimilation, Anti-Semitism). Budapest, 1984.

Ignotus, Pal. "The Return of József Lengyel." *Encounter* (1965).

Jaoz-Keszt, Itamar. *A csadaszarvas: Cvi-haplaot* (The Miraculous Deer). Part 3. Tel Aviv, 1989.

Karády, Viktor. "Szociologiai kísérlet a magyar zsidóság 1945 és 1956 közötti helyzetének elemzésére" (Sociological Attempt to Analyze the Situation of Hungarian Jewry Between 1945 and 1956). In Kende, *Zsidóság az 1945 utáni Magyarországon.*

Karátson, Endre and Ninon Neményi (eds.). *Belső tilalomfák: Tanulmányok a társadalmi öncenzuráról* (Inner Prohibitory Signs: Studies in Social Self-Censorship). Budapest, 1982.

Karsai, László, *Kirekesztők* (Excluders). Budapest, 1992.

Kende, Péter. *Röpirat a zsidókérdésről* (Pamphlet on the Jewish Question). Budapest, 1989.

——————— (ed.). *Zsidóság az 1945 utáni Magyarországon* (Jewry in Post-1945 Hungary). Paris, 1984.

Ki kicsoda: Eletrajzi Lexikon (Who's Who: Biographical Lexicon). Budapest, 1969 and later, eds.

Kovács, András. "A zsidókérdés a mai magyar társadalomban" (The Jewish Question in Today's Hungarian Society). In Kende, *Zsidóság az 1945 utáni Magyarországon.*

Magyar Életrajzi Lexikon (Hungarian Biographical Lexicon) 3 vols. Budapest, 1967–1985.

Magyar Irodalmi Lexikon (Hungarian Literary Lexicon). Budapest, 1963.

Magyar Zsidó Lexikon (Hungarian Jewish Lexicon). Ed. Péter Ujvári. Budapest, 1929.

Miller, Judith. "Out of Hiding." *The New York Times Magazine*, December 9, 1990.

Múlt és Jövő (Past and Future), original series, vol. 20 (1930).

Patai, Raphael. "The Cultural Losses of Hungarian Jewry." In Braham and Vago, *Holocaust in Hungary.*

Sanders, Ivan. "Jewish Revival in Central Europe: A Survey of Recent Hungarian Judaica." In *Jewish Book Annual 1991–92.*

Bibliography

—————————. "Sequels and Revisions: The Hungarian Jewish Experience in Recent Hungarian Literature." *Soviet Jewish Affairs*, vol. 14, no. 1 (1984). Also published in Hungarian in Kende, *Zsidóság*.

—————————. "Tétova vonzalmak: zsidó témák a kortársi magyar irodalomban" (Hesitant Attractions: Jewish Themes in Contemporary Hungarian Literature). *Uj Látóhatár* (New Horizons), vol. 26 (December 15, 1975).

Simon, Z. *Benjámin László*. Budapest, 1972.

Szabó, J. *Lengyel József alkotásai és vallomásai tükrében* (József Lengyel as Mirrored in His Works and Confessions). Budapest, 1966.

Száraz, György. *Egy előitélet nyomában* (Tracing a Prejudice). Budapest, 1976.

Várdy, Péter. "Befejezetlen mult: Mai Magyar zsidó valóság" (Unfinished Past: Today's Hungarian Jewish Reality). In Karátson and Neményi, *Belső tilalomfák*.

Index

Abbreviations: H. = Hungarian or Hungary; R. = Rabbi.

Index

Index

Index

Ephraim haKohen R., of Buda, 172, 177–78, 187
Eppler, Dr. Sándor, 543
Erdei, Ferenc, 618
Erdély, 153. *See also* Transylvania
Erdős, Renée, 413, 492
Eretz Israel, 329, 331, 336
Ernest, Archduke, 165, 170
Ernust, Sigismund, bishop of Pécs, 83
Érsekujvár, 477–78
Eszék, 172
Esztergom (Gran), 31, 32, 34, 46, 135, 558; Council of, 44
Eszterházy, 374; Prince Paul, 189; family, 190–91
Eucharist, 54
Europe, Central, 29, 33, 496; Eastern, 12, 33, 112; Western, 29, 387, 453
European Jews, 35, 54, 323
Evacuation of Jews from Europe, 564
Expropriation of Jewish property, 1944, 563
Explusion of Jews, 57, 184, 457; from Transylvania, 212
Eybeschütz, Mordecai, 228
Eybeschütz, R. Jonathan, 192, 228
Eysack, Jews of, 59
Ezra, relief organization, 600

Fábián, Béla, 481, 485, 502–3, 505, 536
Factory owners, Jewish, 368
Falk, Miksa, 291, 389, 405
Falk, Zsigmond, 291–92
Faludi, Gábor, Jenő, and Miklós, 522
Faludy, György, 670
Farkas, Albert, playwright, 310
Farkas, General Mihály, 628–29, 632
Farkas (Wolf), Count of Bazin. *See* Wolf, Count Ferenc
Farkas and Mayor (Mayer), 80
February Patent of Francis Joseph I, 1861, 302
Federaton of Social Associations, 501
Fehérvár, Jews of, 62
Fekete Mendel (Mendellus Niger), 93–94
Feld, Zsigmond, 522
Feldmajer, Dr. Péter, 642; quoted, 648–49
Feleki, Béla, 470
Fencing and Athletics Club (VAC), 339, 384, 444
Fényes, Adolf, painter, 427
Fényes, Mór, 532
Fényes, Samu, 409

Fenyő, Miksa, 420
Ferdi Efendi, historian, quoted, 163
Ferdinand, Archduke, 374
Ferdinand I, Holy Roman Emperor, King of H., 90, 103, 114, 118, 151, 163, 182–84
Ferdinand II, 185
Ferdinand III, 185
Ferdinand V, 266
Ferenczi, Sándor, 404, 421, 465, 531
Ferenczy, László, 569
Fertőrákos, 586
Feuerstein, Emil, quoted, 419
"Final Solution," 548, 556, 562, 587, 594, 619. *See also Endlösung*
Finályi, Henrik Lajos, 389
Financiers, Jewish, 266–67, 367–71. *See also* Bankers
First H.-Hebrew German Phonic and Elementary Reader, 308
First H. Israelite Calendar and Yearbook, 308
Fischer, Móric, industrialist, 624–25
Fischer, R. Gyula (Julius), 504, 509–10; quoted, 508–9, 622
Fischhof, Adolf, M.D., 286–87
Fischhof, Ignác Vilmos, M.D., 286
Flagellants, 54
Földes, Jolán, 528–29
Földi, Mihály, 525–26, 582
Fónagy, Béla, art critic, 428
Foundation for the Preservation of H. Jewish Culture, 644
France, 41, 45, 54; H. Jewish students in, 486; Jews of, 112, 210, 286, 333, 522
Francis I, Emperor, 227, 231
Francis (Franz) Joseph I, Emperor, 281, 289, 291–92, 298, 311, 325–26, 426–27, 459
Frankel, Leo, 366
Frankfurt, 188; Jews of, 71
Frankl, Adolf, 471, 473
Franz Ferdinand, Archduke, 458
Frederick II, "the Bellicose," 47, 61; Jewish law of, 47
Frederick IV, King of Germany (Frederick III, Holy Roman Emperor), 78
French Academy, 255
French Jews, 480, 483–84; in H., 72
Freudiger, Fülöp, 564, 570
Freund, Salomon, 464
Friedmann, Dr. Ignác, 509–10
Friedrich, István, 468
Friesenhausen, David, 242–44, 273

Index

711

Index

National Peasants Party, 598, 627
National Rabbinical Assembly, 363
National Rabbinical Council, 463
National Representation of H.
  Israelites (MIOK), 615
National Statistical Office, 460
"Native" Jews in H., 456
Natonek, Joseph, 331–36
Nazarenes, Viennese painters, 425
Nazis, in Germany, 560; in H., 412,
  414, 495, 507, 549, 573–74, 596
Nebuchadnezzar, 164
Németkeresztúr (Deutschkreuz), 190
Nemzeti Ujság, daily, 481
Neoabsolutism, Austrian, 282–85,
  302–11
Neo-anti-Semitism, 603
Neolog congregations, Jewry, 297, 308,
  445, 473, 480, 504, 519, 556, 601,
  607, 648; assimilation of, 610;
  National Office, 324–25, 341, 382,
  508, 543 (see also National H.
  Israelite Office); Rabbinical
  conclave, 363; rabbis, 593
"Neophyte" (convert), 82
Nép, daily, 475
Népszava, daily, 471
Neubauer, Adolf, 400
Neue Freie Presse, Viennese daily, 409
Neumann, John von, 530
Neuschloss brothers, industrialists,
  265
Neustadt, Adolf, 254–55
New York, 249, 524
New Zionist Organization, 511–12
Nicholas, Count of Nagymarton, 58
Nicholas I, Pope, 27
Nicholas III, Pope, 52
Nikolsburg, 137–38, 194
Nikopol, 172
Nobility, H., 372–73, 377–78, 605
Nobles, Jewish. See Ennoblement
Nodier, Charles, 260
Nordau, Max, 287, 341, 382, 412, 511;
  quoted, 345
Norimberg, 104; Jews of, 97
"Nostrification," 487–88
Novi Sad massacre. See Ujvidék
  massacre
Nuevos Christianos, 619
Numerus Clausus Law, 59, 383, 388,
  472–79, 482–88, 502, 506, 514,
  536–37, 539, 623
Nussbacher (Palgi), Joel, 575–76
Nyiregyháza, 350–51
Nyitra (Nitra), 34, 44, 123

Nykus, Jew of Pressburg, 59
Nyugat, circle, 525, 668; periodical,
  418, 420–21, 491, 526, 667

Oath, Jewish, 64, 293
Óbuda (Alt-Ofen), 135, 186, 207–24;
  Jews in, 189, 202, 223–24, 283, 440
Occupations, Jewish, 202–3, 366–67,
  433–40
"October Diploma" of Francis Joseph
  I, 302
Ödenburg. See Sopron
Offerman. Baron Victor, 382
Officialdom closed to Jews, 433
Olmütz, 1849 Constitution of, 292
Olympic Games, Jews in, 384
OMIKE, 528. See also National H.
  Israelite Educational Association
Oppenheimer, Samuel, of Vienna,
  178–80, 188–89
Oppenheimer, Samuel Bernard,
  physician, 123
Orenburg, 110
Organ music in synagogues, 241, 301
Orientalists, H. Jewish, 392–98
Orkuta blood libel, 203–4
Ormándy, Eugene, 530
Ormody, Bertalan, 405
Oroszlán (Lion), Jew, 101
Ország, Mihály, Jew judge, 62
Orthodox congregations, 297, 313,
  440, 444–45, 488, 556, 601
Orthodox Intermediary Office, 341
Orthodox Jews in H., 244–45, 293,
  307, 309, 313–14, 316, 337, 360,
  473, 497, 504, 518, 593, 607, 648;
  leadership, 557; National Office,
  470–71, 480, 510, 543; object to
  Magyarization, 608; oppose
  Zionism, 444–45; settle in
  Palestine, 336
Orthodox-Neolog schism, 225, 317–
  18, 321
Orthodox rabbis, 305–6, 593
Österreicher, Joseph Manes,
  physician, 123–24, 224
Ostjuden, 594
Ostrogoths, 21
Osvát, Ernő, 420–21
Oswiecim, 572. See also Auschwitz
Osztern, Dr. Lipót, 508
Otherness, Jewish, 105, 250, 442, 489,
  511–14, 600, 602–3
Otto I, King, 28
Ottoman army, 163

Index

Relief and Rescue Committee (*Va'adah*) of Budapest, 566, 573
Responsa literature, 12
Révai, József, 628–29, 663, 667
Révész, Béla, 412, 414
Revisionists in H., 511
Revolution of 1848, 238, 255, 280; of 1956, 634
Ribáry, Géza, 544
Ribbentrop, Joachim von, 579
Ritual bath, 34. *See also Miqveh*
Ritual murder libel, 39, 124. *See also* Blood libels
Roboz, Imre, 524
Róheim, Géza, 404
Roman(s), 21, 24, 27; Empire, 24
Rombach Street synagogue, 584
Rome, 83, 118
Romhányi, László, 653
Rónai, János, quoted, 338
Ronald S. Lauder Foundation, 645
Roosevelt, Theodore, 427
Rosenberg, Gyula, 381
Rosenberg, R. J. H., 631
Roth, Dr. Ernő, 593
Roth, Philip, 662
Roth, R. Moshe Arye, 444–45
Rothschild, House of, 257, 370, 485
Rothschild, James de, 261, 333
Rothschilds, 335
Royal cities in H., 62, 73
Royal Hungary, 153, 165; Jews in, 182–86
Rózsavölgyi, Mark, composer, 259
Rózsay, Dr. Joseph, 308, 389
Rudolf, Duke of Austria, 57
Rudolph II, Holy Roman Emperor, 165–66
Rumania, 383, 452, 548, 574, 635
Rumanian army in Budapest, 459, 466, 468, 471; Jews flee to H., 538; territory awarded to H., 545;—ns in H., 269
"Rump" H., 501, 512–13
Russia(ns), 11, 12, 28, 29, 31, 32, 276, 281, 348, 596; hated in H., 567, 598, 624; occupy Budapest, 560, 589–90, 593, 596–97, 616, 623–27; Revolution, 463; social realism, 567. *See also* Soviet
Ruthenia, 537;—ns in H., 269
Ryberius, physician, 120

Sabbatarians of Transylvania, 29, 157, 199
Sabbath, 27, 31, 32, 241, 248, 360

Sachs, Moshe, 329–30
Safed, 167
Saint George, town, 101
Salamon, physician of King Matthias, 117
Salgó, Chief R. László, 636
Salimun Yahudi, 172–73
Salomon, Sir David, 256
Salonika, 176; Jews of, 171; rabbis of, 177
Samuel, Chamber Count, 46
Sanders, Ivan, 525; cited, 662, 664, 668; quoted, 671, 674
Sándor, Pál, 455–56, 461, 471, 479, 481–82, 485, 504–6, 635
Sanhedrin, 234, 273; of Paris, 242
Saphir, Moritz Gottlieb, 251–52, 257
Saphir, Zsigmond, 254
Saracens, 42, 45, 53
Sarajevo, 458
Sárközi, György, 563–64
Sárospatak, 121, 198
Sarsa, Abraham, physician, 120
Sar Shalom, 108
Sárvár, 117
Sátoraljaujhely, 243, 337
Savaria, 22
Scechtinus, 44
Scharf, József, Móric, Simon. *See* Tiszaeszlár, blood libel of
Scheiber, R. Lajos, 631
Scheiber, Sándor, 525
Schickerlein, Nicholas, Jew judge, 47
Schiffer, János, 652
Schiller-Szinessy, Solomon, 287–88
Schlesinger, Akiba Joseph, 336–37
Schlesinger, Ferdinand, editor, 288
Schlesinger, Pál, 383
Schmidt, Mária, quoted, 614
Schmidthuber, General, 589
Scholarship, H. Jewish, 108–10, 309, 387–89
School fund of 1850, 284
Schools, 284–85
Schossberger, Simon Vilmos, 289, 381
Schulhof, Isaac, 187
Schulhof, Leopold, 391
Schutzgeld (protection money), 78
Schwab, R. Löb (Arszlán), 245, 250, 272–74, 294
Schwarz, Adolph, 399
Schwarzenberg, Prince Felix, 282
Schweiger, Márton, 324–25, 341
Sculptors, H. Jewish, 428
Sefer haGilgulim, 205
Segesvár, 121

721

Index

Suleiman, Sultan, 33, 119, 162, 171
Supreme Court of H., 475
Surány, 261
Swastika armband, 651
Sweden 585; embassy in Budapest, 581
Switzerland, 573, 585; embasssy in Budapest, 581; H. Jewish students in, 486; Jews of, 112
Synagogue(s), 22, 31, 50, 55, 57, 110; in Buda, 178. *See also* Dohány Street synagogue
Syria(ns), 21, 24
Szabad, György, 637; quoted, 648–50, 653–54
Szabad Nép, journal, 627
Szabó, Dezső, 447–49, 666; quoted, 448
Szabó, Ervin, 424
Szabó, Zoltán, 536
Szabolcs, Council of, 1092, 41
Szabolcsi, Lajos, 443; quoted, 505
Szabolcsi, Miklós, 412; cited, 403–4; quoted, 408–9, 525, 591
Szabolcsi, Miksa, 342–45, 361, 382–83, 443; quoted, 342–43
Szalai, Pál, 589
Szálasi, Ferenc, 518, 545, 584, 587–89; government, 585, 587
Szalkay, László, 97, 99, 144–46
Szamuely, Tibor, 464, 466
Szántó, Gábor T., 643
Szapáry, Count Gyula, 362
Szapolyai, György, 148–49
Szapolyai, István, Palatine, 112, 146
Szapolyai, János, Voivod of Transylvania (King John), 103, 145, 182
Szapolyais, 150
Száraz, György, 666
Szarvaskő, 169
Szász, Menyhért, 421
Szászsebes, 154
Szatmár, 337
Szeben, 154
Széchenyi, Count Andor, 381
Széchenyi, Count István, 231–32, 254, 261, 271, 291, 310, 389; memorial statue, 257
Szedikert. *See* Orkuta blood libel
Szeged, 245, 293, 466, 468; Jews of, 173, 460, 475; university of, 475
Székely, Ferenc, 471, 509–10
Székelys of Transylvania, 28, 158, 160
Székesfehérvár (Stuhlweissenburg), 70, 73, 76, 89, 91, 158, 173, 277

Szekfű, Gyula, quoted 497–98
Széll, George, 540
Szemere, Bertalan, quoted, 275
Szendrő, 172
Szenes, Hannah, 575–76, 591
Szenic, 135
Szenkar, Dezső, conductor, 530
Szentgyörgyi, Count, 60
Szép, Ernő, 419
Szerémség, Jews in, 173
Szerencsés, Imre. *See* Emericus Fortunatus
Szigetvár, 119
Szilágyi, Géza, quoted, 415
Szilárd, Leó, 530
Szokolyai, Zoltán, 653
Szold, Benjamin, 402
Szolnok, 502
Szombat, periodical, 642–44
Szombathely, 277
Szombatosok. See Sabbatarians of Transylvania
Szomory, Dezső, 409, 591
Szondi, Lipót, 404
Szőnyi, Tibor, 629
Sztójay, Döme, 562, 580; government, 408, 568, 576, 583, 618–19

Tallith, 90; *tallith qatan,* 160
Talmud, 240, 320, 356; burning of the, 45
Talmud Torah schools, 245, 319
Táncsics, Michael (Mihály), 279–80
Tata, 38, 129
Tausk, Sender, saves Buda Jews, 178–79, 597
Tax administrators, collectors, Jewish, 45, 53
Taxes paid by Jews, 62–64, 73, 74, 76, 78–81, 85, 87, 96, 97, 100–102, 106, 190–91
Teachers, Jewish, 433–34
Technical University, Budapest, Jews in, 474
Technology, Jews in, 437
Teha, Count, 36, 37
Teichthal, Rabbi Y. S., 557
Teitelbaum, R. Moshe, 244
Teleki, Count László, 310
Teleki, Count Pál, 501, 539, 545–46
Teller, Edward, 530
Temesvár, Jews of, 283
Temlinus, Count, Jew judge, 59, 62
Ten Commandments, 248
Textbooks for Jewish schools, 285
Thalmus (Talmács), 26

Index

Valmarin, Israel, physician, 123
Vámbéry, Armin, 326, 375, 389–90, 392–95, 405
Várad, Treaty of, 163
Várdy, Béla, 656
Varna, Battle of, 79
Varsányi, Irén, 384
Vas, Zoltán, 628–29, 631
Vasdényei, István, 582–83
Vasvár, 50
Vatican, 150, 581, 585
Vázsonyi, János, 536
Vázsonyi, Vilmos, 361–62, 382–83, 450, 461, 471, 477–78, 480–82, 485, 492, 504–5, 635; quoted, 477–78, 482–83
Veesenmayer, Edmund, 552–53, 561, 571, 579
Veigelsberg, Leo, 420
Venetian Republic, 119
Venetianer, R. Lajos, 13; cited, 388; quoted, 236, 271, 278–79, 297, 315–17, 358–59
Venice, 83, 94, 95
Ventur, Gaspar, Jew judge, 77
Veres, Péter, 602, 633; cited, 627
Vészi, József, 384, 470, 482, 505
Vészi, Margit, 384
Veszprém, 135
Veterinary College, Jews in, 475
Veterinary surgeons, Jewish, 437
Victoria, Queen, 256–57
Vida, Jenő, 505
Vienna, 34, 37, 60, 80, 97, 108, 116, 118–19, 164, 171, 177, 241, 269, 443, 480, 486, 586; court of, 186, 227; Decision of August 1940, 545; Jews in, 58, 75
Viennese Academy of Fine Arts, 256–57; Burgtheater, 288–89; Rabbinical Conference of 1851, 246
Világos, H. capitulation at, 281–82
Vilna, 177
Vix, Lt.-Col. Fernand, 464
Vizhnitz, 337
Viziváros (part of Buda), 196
Vizsolyi-Wahrsager, David (György Gadó), 636
Vladislav, King of Poland (Ulászló, King of H.), 77
Vlajka, Wallachian Voivod, 59
Volenszky, Paula, 654
Volga River, 28
Volksbund, 545
Vörösmarty, Mihály, quoted, 278

Wahrmann, Ernő, 380–81
Wahrmann, Israel, 244, 271, 317, 380
Wahrmann, Mór, 317, 320, 380
Wahrmann, Richard, 380
Walkó, Lajos, 478
Wallachia, 119
Wallenberg, Raoul, 580–81, 586, 588–89
"Wandering Jew," 498
War, casualties, Jewish, 460; indemnity, imposed on Jews in 1849, 283; loan, subscribed by Jews, 459–60; production organized by Jews, 460; service of Jews, 459
Warsaw, 126; Pact, 635
Wehrmacht, 551
Weimar Republic, 502
Weiner, Leó, 524, 530
Weiss, baronial family, 570, 576
Weiss, Baron Manfred, 374, 460, 471
Weiss, Bethold and Manfred, 570
Weisz, Marcus (Mordecai) Nissa, 242
Weizen. *See* Vác
Weizmann, Chaim, 511
Wekerle, Sándor, 362
Webőczy (Verbőczy), István, 145–46, 150–51
Wertheimer, Samson, banker, 188, 191
Western world, 616, 654
"White Terror," 468–69, 500–501, 512, 525
Wholesale merchants, Jewish, 189, 265–66
Wiener Neustadt, 56, 77, 108, 366; Jews in, 58, 191
Wiesel, Elie, 662
Wigner, Jenő, 530
Wilhelm, Dr. Károly, 564
Wilson, Woodrow, 462
Windischgrätz, Prince Alfred, 283
Winterberg, Gyula, 443
Wise, Aaron, 402
Wise, Stephen S., 402
Wisliceny, Dieter, 561, 568–69, 572
Wissenschaft des Judentums, 260
Wodianer family, 378–79, 385
Wolf, Count Ferenc, of Bazin, 183–84, 194
Wolf, Lucian, 476–79
Wolff, Dr. Károly, 501
Wolffsohn, David, 340, 394
Wolfner, Baron Tivadar, 460, 464, 471

Comments and Corrections

By Miklós Szabolcsi

[Proofs of this book were sent to Prof. Miklós Szabolcsi, the well-known Hungarian literary historian, for his comments. His response arrived too late to be taken into account in the text, but at my request Dr. Szabolcsi agreed that it should be added to the book as an appendix, under his name. I wish to thank him for his extremely useful comments and corrections, even though we don't see eye to eye on what he calls my "two main theses." What follows is my literal translation of his Hungarian letter and notes. R. P.]

Budapest, November 16, 1995

My Dear Friend!

As I already wrote to you earlier, *The Jews of Hungary* is a rich, interesting, and well-written book, with many new points-of-view and surprising discoveries. At the same time, I cannot always be in agreement with your two main theses, your two main points-of-view. What visibly agitates you most is why are the Hungarian Jews such faithful Magyars and patriots? You search for its reasons in history, somewhat angrily and shaking the head. Much could be said about this, but now only one thing: the German Jews of the modern age—the Finnish, Danish, Czech Jews, and above all the French Jews—were they not patriots? Is this not a natural consequence of the assimilatory process of the eighteenth-nineteenth centuries?

The other point: the relatively small support Zionism obtained in Hungary. I understand why—also for human and family reasons—this rouses you to such indignation. Still, here too I see the picture more shaded.

I enclose a few detailed comments.

Yours with a friendly hand-clasp,
Miklós Szabolcsi

Chapter 7, p. 83. Is it certain that Thuz and the Thuz family were converted Jews? Were they not German?

Chapter 8, p. 107. I find the final conclusion somewhat daring; the world of the fifteenth century was, after all, very different from that of the nineteenth.

Chapter 10 and chapter 17. There are repetitions that can easily be eliminated.

Chapter 14, p. 173. Attention! *Szerémség* is not a town but an area, a district, in Eastern Slavonia, the territory central to many events at the present time.

Chapter 20. Joseph II's general policies deserve a few sentences to indicate that his edicts discussed here were part of his overall modernizing, centralizing, and Germanizing program of enlightened absolutism.

Chapter 20, p. 224. The building of the Óbuda synagogue still stands, but does no longer serve as a synagogue.

Chapter 24, p. 252. About Karl Beck, together with other authors, there is a detailed monograph written by the Hungarian Germanist Antal Mádl, titled *Politische Dichtung in Österreich* (Political Poetry in Austria), Budapest, 1969.

Chapter 24, p. 266. "Financiers and Bankers." Following this subtitle not this subject is discussed.

Chapter 25, p. 276. There is a chronological jump here to 1849, and the chapter dealing with 1848 follows only thereafter. The raising of the question of Zionism here also constitutes a chronological jump.

Chapter 28, p. 310. Trefort became minister only later, after the death of Joseph Eötvös (1872).

Chapter 32, pp. 371ff. Apropos your striking characterization of the *"úri"* concept: don't you think that this is not only a Hungarian specificity? Was the German "Junker," or the Polish "Slachtic" not similar?

Chapter 32, p. 374. The desire to assimilate to the *"urak"* in itself does not explain the patriotism of the Hungarian Jews. Economic, other social, as well as national factors (the self-differentiation from the national minorities living in the territory of Hungary) also played a role in it.

Chapter 21, p. 378. As far as I know the wife of Regent Horthy was only a distant relation of the Wodianers, perhaps one of her grandparents was one. In any case, she was certainly not a "Wodianer-girl."

Chapter 33. I miss here such names as that of Zsigmond Simonyi, or the creator of the Hungarian penal code, Károly Csemegi.

Chapter 34, p. 403. Here (and in several other places) you refer to my sketch of literary history published by Pergamon Press, and you criticize that I do not mention the Jewishness of the Hungarian Jewish writers. Do not forget: That is a small-size Hungarian literary history—speaking of Ferenc Toldy, Ferenc Herczeg, or Sándor Márai I don't mention their German descent, nor Petőfi's Slavic, or Babits's Serbian ancestors.

P. 407. The missing part of the quote from Joseph Kiss is ". . . nor Pan . . ."

P. 409. Today we consider Szomory a much more significant and important writer.

P. 411. Perhaps it is here that I least agree with you. Is it "psychological Marranism" if a writer of Jewish descent writes about non-Jewish, that is, Hungarian or general, themes? This is an unthinkable narrowing-down. . .

P. 412. Today we reckon Milán Füst and Ernő Szép among the most important writers of *Nyugat*. Their reputation is constantly growing in today's literary life.

P. 437. Komoróczy and others have written much more about Jewish architects in *A Zsidó Budapest* (Jewish Budapest) [2 vols., Budapest, 1994].

Chapters 35 and 36. These chapters present a very detailed history of Hungarian Jewish inner life. Some things are nevertheless missing, such as e.g., the IMIT (Israelite Hungarian Literary Society).[1] And, permit me to remark that not a word is said about *Egyenlőség*, and the name of Miksa Szabolcsi is not even mentioned. (On the subject discussed in chapter 36, p. 456, *Egyenlőség* too has written several things . . .)[2]

Chapter 38, p. 468. A trifle: Prónay was only a major. This is important because 19 was a movement, not of colonels, but of captains and majors.

Chapter 39, p. 506. Repetition!

P. 507. Inner Jewish life. Here again several things are missing. Again only personally: the National Committee for Student Aid, etc. Nor is the name of Lajos Szabolcsi mentioned.[3]

P. 508. Nevertheless, Graetz was published in a Hungarian translation, and so was in the 1930s also a Hungarian Dubnow.

In general: it will be difficult to supplement it now, but I must note that the part dealing with the period between the two World Wars, and especially the presentation of intellectual life, is much more incomplete and sketchy than that of the preceding period.

P. 523. I am not sure that Békeffy was actually Jewish.

P. 524. Illés Kaczér was a very mediocre writer in relation to the space devoted to him. On the other hand, Milán Füst was most outstanding, and, as I already mentioned, is today more and more important. He belonged to *Nyugat*. Missing from this part are such names as András Komoly and Ákos Molnár, as well as Béla Pásztor, one of the best poets of the 1940s (*Méregkóstolók* [Poison Tasters], *Bábuk és halottak* [The Puppets and the Dead], etc.). Actually, also missing are such scholars as Sándor Ferenczi, József Túróczi-Trostler, Bence Szabolcsi.[4]

Chapter 40, p. 542. Emigration required also admitting countries, and at that time already very strict quotas were in effect (cf. Evian).

Chapter 47, p. 624. Not Swedish, but Danish king. Here too there are many repetitions.

P. 627. This saying of Péter Veres cannot be interpreted as either anti-German or anti-Jewish. For that matter, it was not his slogan, but that of the Hungarian Communist Party, and it referred to the conditions of property ownership.

P. 631. The divorce of Zoltán Vas was not an issue of Jewishness. His wife was simply insufferable. The Jewish *gimnázium* existed to the end.

P. 632. The arrest of Déry and company took place actually because of their activities after 1956—at least formally this was the case.

P. 633. To this Rákosi-Veres affair one should, at least, add "allegedly," or "they say."

P. 652. Subsequently Suchman became a minister without portfolio, supervising privatization.

P. 662. Appendix. I don't share these views on the reception of American Jewish writers. It is also factually debatable. After all, Potok, for instance, is not such a great writer.

P. 663. This section on Révai-Rákosi does not belong here.

P. 664. This statistical calculation is very debatable—a handbook as a statistical source?

P. 669. Zelk wrote many poems about Jewish themes; one of the most beautiful is his *Dorosici alkony* (The Twilight of Dorosic). He has many other [Jewish] poems as well. The statement must be corrected.

P. 670. Imre Keszi's *Elysium*—his most important and best writing on a Jewish subject—speaks of a thirteen-year old boy deported to Auschwitz (modelled, by the way, on my cousin, the son of Bence Szabolcsi).

On the appendix in general: the most significant, György G. Kardos, is not even mentioned![5] I would mention also the works of Örkény.

To the Bibliography: Bence Szabolcsi wrote a brief but complete Hungarian Jewish history as a postscript to the Hungarian edition of Dubnow.

[Notes

1. But see references to IMIT (Israelite Hungarian Literary Society) on pp. 326, 341, 406, 440, 508.
2. But see references to *Egyenlőség* on pp. 342, 361, 403, 444, 477, and to Miksa Szabolcsi on pp. 342–45, 361, 382–83, 443.
3. But see references to Lajos Szabolcsi on pp. 443, 505.
4. But see references to Sándor Ferenczi on pp. 404, 421, 465, 531.
5. But see reference to G. György Kardos on p. 673.

R. P.]

Principal publications by Raphael Patai

Shire Yisrael Berekhya Fontanella (In Hebrew: *The Poems of Y.B.F.)*
HaMayim (In Hebrew: *Water: A Study in Palestinology and
Palestinian Folklore)*
HaSappanut ha'Ivrith bIme Qedem (In Hebrew: *Ancient
Jewish Seafaring)*
Adam wa'Adama (In Hebrew: *Man and Earth in Hebrew Custom,
Belief, and Legend)*
Mada' ha'Adam (In Hebrew: *The Science of Man: An Introduction
to Anthropology)*
Man and Temple in Ancient Jewish Myth and Ritual
On Culture Contact and Its Working in Modern Palestine
Israel between East and West
Annotated Bibliography of Syria, Lebanon and Jordan
The Kingdom of Jordan
Current Jewish Social Research
Cultures in Conflict
Sex and Family in the Bible and the Middle East
*Golden River to Golden Road: Society, Culture and Change in the
Middle East*
Hebrew Myths (with Robert Graves)
Tents of Jacob: The Diaspora Yesterday and Today
The Hebrew Goddess
Myth and Modern Man
The Arab Mind
The Myth of the Jewish Race (with Jennifer Patai)
The Messiah Texts
Gates to the Old City
The Vanished Worlds of Jewry
The Seed of Abraham
Ignaz Goldziher and His Oriental Diary
Nahum Goldmann: His Missions to the Gentiles
Apprentice in Budapest
The Hebrew Goddess, third enlarged edition
Between Budapest and Jerusalem
Journeyman in Jerusalem
The Jewish Alchemists: A History and Source Book

Raphael Patai also edited these works:

Mivḥar haSippur haArtziYis'reli (with Zevi Wohlmut)
(In Hebrew: *Anthology of Palestinian Short Stories)*
EDOTH (Communities): A Quarterly for Folklore and Ethnology (with
Joseph J. Rivlin) (In Hebrew and English)
Sifriya l' Folqlor v'Etnologia (with Joseph J. Rivlin)
(In Hebrew: *Studies in Folklore and Ethnology)*
Meḥqarim Ḥevrutiyyim (with Roberto Bachi) (In Hebrew and
English: *Social Studies)*
Erich Brauer: Y'hude Kurdistan (In Hebrew; translated and edited
by R.P.)
The Hashemite Kingdom of Jordan
The Republic of Syria
The Republic of Lebanon
Herzl Year Book
The Complete Diaries of Theodor Herzl
Angelo S. Rappoport: Myth and Legend of Ancient Israel
Women in the Modern World
Encyclopaedia of Zionism and Israel
Erich Brauer, *The Jews of Kurdistan*
Thinkers and Teachers of Modern Judaism
(with Emanuel S. Goldsmith)
Events and Movements in Modern Judaism
(with Emanuel S. Goldsmith)